To Paula & Frank

from Victor R. Rolando

200 Years of Soot and Sweat

The History and Archeology of Vermont's Iron, Charcoal, and Lime Industries

Victor R. Rolando

Vermont Archaeological Society

Published by the Vermont Archaeological Society, with financial assistance from the author and the Vermont Statehood Bicentennial Commission.

Library of Congress Catalog Card Number: 91-65439

ISBN 0-9628944-0-0 (paper)

Design by
Debi Lynne
Boothbay Harbor, Maine

Production by
Post Scripts
Federalsburg, Maryland

Printed by
Dover Litho Printing Co.
Dover, Delaware

Cover and title page: Green Mountain Iron Company furnace ruin at Forest Dale in 1991.

Contents

Tables

Foreword _____

In 1978, Vic Rolando made me an offer that I couldn't refuse. In exchange for my enthusiasm and moral support, he would begin to inventory the ruins and other surviving remains of Vermont's iron industry. He hugely underestimated his task.

The more research he did, the more complex the puzzle became. After a few years, Vic decided he couldn't fully understand Vermont's iron industry unless he also understood about charcoal production. And one kiln leading to another kiln, he further complicated (and extended) his efforts by embarking on the study of lime manufacture. Each year since 1978 Vic drove and walked more miles, studied more documents, and provided the State of Vermont with ever more information.

Those of us who study Vermont's rich prehistoric and historic legacy well know that so much of our heritage is little known and, consequently, insufficiently appreciated. The complex stories of Vermont's once thriving iron, charcoal, and lime producing industries lay virtually forgotten in forest and field, in libraries and attics, until Vic's exhaustive effort brought this part of Vermont's heritage to light. Vic's research has revealed stories of new inventions and technologies; of land exploitation and family intrigues; of big business and famous men; of once thriving communities now long abandoned; of economic forces that affected many people and many places; and of hundreds of working people and their families over many decades whose lives centered on these industries but about whom so little was recorded.

There is no doubt that Vic's devoted and extraordinary efforts—all on a volunteer basis—have immeasurably enriched our knowledge about several of Vermont's most vital but, until now, little known industrial endeavors. There is no way to thank someone who has done so much for the people of Vermont, in general, and for the Division for Historic Preservation, in particular. I hope that this volume gives him some measure of reward for an immense job well done (and, he would say, still not finished). I also hope that all of us in Vermont who share responsibility for these parts of our heritage—as property owners, as custodians of public lands, as historians and archeologists, as users of the land, as citizens interested in our communities' history—will heed Vic's words when he reminds us that this is a fragile, irreplaceable heritage that needs to be protected and cared for and, in some cases, interpreted for the interested public. By learning about and better appreciating—through reading this volume—the important role of these archeological sites in the history of our state and our communities, I hope that we will be better armed in our efforts to preserve this forgotten legacy of our history for future generations of Vermonters.

Giovanna Peebles, State Archeologist
Vermont Division for Historic Preservation
Montpelier, Vermont

As I grew up in southern Vermont, I frequently wondered for what purpose the massive stone chimney-like structure on the west side of then U.S. Route 7 in the South Village of East Dorset had been constructed. With no knowledge of any similar structures, and aware that there was little manufacturing activity in the community, I would not be enlightened for many years. I did, however, become somewhat familiar over the years with other types of industrial sites: charcoal kilns observable at a number of places along the Long Trail, and lime kilns located in Manchester.

I was to learn much more about all of these, though, as a result of subsequently serving as program chairman of the Rutland Historical Society. Frequently wondering where I could find speakers to fill a schedule of monthly programs, I learned that there was a person from Pittsfield, Massachusetts, who was an authority on Vermont's early iron industry. Unaware, like many people, I suspect, that Vermont had ever had an iron industry, I invited Vic Rolando to give his slide-illustrated presentation. That evening I learned that the chimney-like structure in East Dorset was the stack of a blast furnace that had produced iron from about 1846 to 1854, and learned much more about the charcoal kilns along the Long Trail.

Just as I had unwittingly encountered my first Vermont iron blast furnace in the South Village of East Dorset in my youth, so had I encountered circular brick remains while hiking along the Long Trail. I had been told by older family members that these were "charcoal kilns," but no one had ever been able to tell me for what all this charcoal had been used. During the Rutland Historical Society presentation, Vic revealed that the fuel employed to heat the iron ore and separate the iron from the ore was charcoal and that blast furnaces had required great amounts of charcoal.

The importance of Vic Rolando's research and site documentation is to make evident to Vermonters that the state had industrial activity from earliest times and that in that activity lay the origins of our current manufacturing industries. Moreover, he makes clear to us the wide extent of that activity. He has found archival or field evidence of iron furnaces, forges, and foundries operating throughout the state in the 19th century and foundries that are still in operation.

It has been a privilege and pleasure to make Vic Rolando's acquaintance, to search Vermont for early industrial sites with him, and to critique this important book as he developed it. Vic has made a major contribution to the study of Vermont history and industrial archeology not only by documenting much of Vermont's early industrial activity in this thoroughly researched volume, but also by locating the sites of this activity at a time when natural deterioration or human development activities threaten them. Vic's research activities and preparation of site reports for the Vermont Division for Historic Preservation and the Green Mountain National Forest have already stimulated research in this area and interest in protecting these sites, and the most significant contribution of his book is that it will stimulate even more.

Robert Edward West
Manchester, Vermont

Preface

On April 28, 1978, I "discovered" Vermont through the attendance of a one-day seminar on historic preservation presented by Chester Liebs at the University of Vermont. I was at that time residing in New York State, commuting daily to Pittsfield, Massachusetts, where I was a technical publications editor at the General Electric Company Ordnance Systems Department. I was also very involved in my graduate thesis at The College of Saint Rose, the thesis being a study of 19th-century ironworks in New York State.

I knew of the existence of only three blast furnace sites in Vermont; but an invitation to present a paper to the Vermont Archaeological Society (VAS) later that year in Burlington motivated me to do some further research into the early iron-making history of that state. And it was at some obscure moment in the midst of my warmly received presentation to the VAS later that October that I decided to switch my area of thesis research from New York State to Vermont.

The decision did not seem all that momentous at the time, since Vermont is much smaller than New York and therefore had fewer ironworks sites. After receiving faculty permission to make the thesis switch, I figured I had traded into an easier project. But the easier project soon developed into a major effort that found me spending many lunch hours and evenings after work doing library research in Pittsfield, and holidays, weekends, and summer vacations from GE driving to Vermont's mountains and valleys, searching out clues to the whereabouts of blast furnaces, forges, and charcoal kilns. Secondary road touring gave way to fearful wilderness driving on many well-furrowed, narrow, and boulder-strewn back roads that seemed never to end but led ever upward, over relentless miles of curves and through pond-sized puddles (County Road from Pownal to Stamford, for example). Early on, I learned firsthand what "the mud season" meant. And since successful completion of both thesis and graduate studies in history in 1980 (including some transfer credits from UVM), my strong and continuing interest in the subject of this work is best reflected by my little green "I Love Vermont" bumper sticker.

This work is not meant to be a comprehensive history of the entire iron, charcoal, and lime industries of Vermont. It is hoped, however, that most of the published and unpublished data relating specifically to these industries in Vermont have been pulled together. All known blast furnace sites have been inspected. Most bloomery forge and foundry sites were inspected where something was expected to be found, plus others where it was expected that little, if anything, would be found. Hundreds of charcoal mounds, charcoal kilns, and lime kilns have been found. Almost all sites took hours of library research and often days of field work to find, resulting in the development of a research and field technique.

Although this work represents research accomplished during the 15-year period from 1978 through 1992, it was research restricted by time constraints that resulted from living and working full-time in Massachusetts. (On March 1, 1992 I retired from GE; in August my wife, Donna, and I moved to Manchester, Vermont.) This left weekends, holidays, and personal vacation time for Vermont that wasn't otherwise committed to house and auto maintenance, or limited by scary winter driving conditions. Time was made for one-day "quick runs" to the Vermont Historical Society Library, Montpelier, for instance, to check out some gnawing question, or to a mountaintop at Mount Tabor to recheck some charcoal kiln detail not found during the previous visit. Some one-day trips took me as far north as Highgate, Troy, and Richford. Many one-week trips were made for field and library work with nights spent at small motels, tourist homes, or camping. As such, it is obvious that the research was not continuous, but rather an on-again, off-again struggle, with keeping track of numbers of clues, notes, photo negatives, personal contacts, and subjects of interest all squeezed between days at work or weekends answering to the domestic needs of my life.

Thousands of miles were driven throughout the Northeast in search of materials relative to this project; hundreds of hours were spent in libraries and at home poring over books, maps, and photographs (and orthophotos); hundreds of miles were hiked from the crests of the beautiful Green Mountains to the sometimes fetid village streams. And no activity in pursuit of research materials was reimbursed through any grant or fellowship.

I have a sense of satisfaction from exploring Vermont and finding the remnants of so many industrial activities, the remaining artifacts of which are unknown to most Vermonters themselves. But most important, a small niche in the passing scene of Vermont history has been yanked back from certain oblivion for our mutual study and appreciation and, I hope, its preservation. The tottering old furnace stack at Forest Dale, a surviving, silent sentinel of an otherwise nearly forgotten era—will that interpretive park ever be built? Might there someday in fact be a "life after death" for the old stone soldier?

The quantity and quality of ruins studied in Vermont emphasize this state's significant position in the availability of physical IA research materials in the Northeast. The reporting of these sites to the State Archeological Inventory has provided the Vermont Division for Historic Preservation and the United States Forest Service a valuable basic tool with which to work. The results of this undertaking underscore the need to look beyond the better-known, more visible IA ruins (such as standing blast furnaces and factory structures) and to search out and study less well-known and less visible sites (such as charcoal kilns and lime kilns) in the more remote corners of the countryside.

Information collected thus far will not become static but will serve as a guide toward continuing IA research in Vermont. As time passes, new data regarding the early iron, charcoal, and lime industries in this state will become available, further contributing both to the understanding of the broader context of these early industries and to the significance of the parts that make up the whole.

One result of this study should be to dispel the popular myth that the early history of Vermont was strictly that of making maple syrup and milking cows. Most important, however, is the hope that this study will encourage residents, students, historians, tourists, developers, property owners, legislators, environmentalists, and archeologists—all stewards of the land—to become more aware of both the range of these early industries and the quality, quantity, and value of their surviving fragile remains; and that it will inspire further work toward a broad, intense, and in-depth research into the industrial archeology of Vermont so that our generation and future generations may be able to appreciate and understand the industrial heritage of this truly beautiful state.

Acknowledgements

My research in Vermont was made possible through the support of many friends with various levels of interest in investigating, recording, and preserving these nearly forgotten industries, and by the staff of the Vermont Division for Historic Preservation, Vermont State Papers Library, and Vermont Historical Society Library at Montpelier; the Vermont Statehood Bicentennial Commission, the Vermont Mapping Program at Waterbury, the Special Collections Library at UVM, the Shelburne Museum, the Bennington Museum, the Sheldon Museum at Middlebury, the Rokeby Museum at Ferrisburgh, the Russell Collection at Arlington, the Mark Skinner Library at Manchester, the Bixby Memorial Library at Vergennes, the Rutland Free Library, the little Tyson Library at Plymouth, the Berkshire Athenaeum Local History Room at Pittsfield, Mass., the State University of New York Library at Albany, the New York State Historical Association Library at Cooperstown, the Green Mountain National Forest District Offices at Manchester, Rutland, and Middlebury, and the Green Mountain Race Track at Pownal; the officers and members of the Vermont Archaeological Society, the New Hampshire Archaeological Society, and the Rutland Historical Society; historical societies at Barton, Danby-Mount Tabor, Manchester, Pittsford, Swanton, Tinmouth, and Woodstock; the Society for Industrial Archeology and its Northern and Southern New England Chapters, and the Council for Northeast Historical Archaeology; and also Parks Canada, the Vermont State Police, Vermont Castings, Inc., White Pigment Corp., the Connecticut Charcoal Company at Union, Conn., Dover Publications, Inc. for permission to copy Diderot illustrations, the Hagley Museum and Library, Wilmington, Del., the CTC Photographic Corp. at Bennington, and Master Darkroom at Pittsfield, Mass.

Each of the following assisted to ensure that various material in this book could be published:

Field and archival data informants: Collamar Abbott, Robert L. Allcott, the late Irene Allen, Danny Andrews, Bill Badger, Dan Baker, Dr. Louise A. Basa, T. D. Seymour Bassett, Bradley Bender, Mary Bort, the late Paul Brazier, Mrs. Leonard Breton, Gina Campoli Brodhead, Joan D. Bromley, Jesse Bugbee, Don Burns, Jacqueline Calder, Lilian Baker Carlisle, Robert Carpenter, Leon Carr, Adelaide Casey, Barbara Chiolino, Phyllis Cobb, Barbara and Edward Colvin, Charles Comstock, Cindy Cook, Martha Coons, R. John Corby, Polly C. Darnell, Gordon Delong, Maggie Dexter, Tom Dexter, Robert Douglas, the late Frederick Elwert, Edward Eno, Gail Fallar, Richard Fifield, Michelle Figliomeni, Robert Filler, Tom Fitzgerald, Eric Gilbertson, Bertha Gilman, Morris Glenn, Robert Gordon, William Gove, J. Kevin Graffagnino, John Griffith, Jr., Allie Hart, Dr. William A. Haviland, Shelley Hight, Charles D. Hockensmith, Welland Horn, Edith Fisher Hunter, the late Oliver Huntley, David Ingram, Tordis Isselhardt, William Jenney, Yvonne Keith, Mary Kennedy, Eugene Kosche, Ed Krause, Dave Lacy, Tom Lawrence, Rod Ledoux, Dr. Aulis Lind, Margaret MacDonough, Barbara Mahon, Mrs. Ray Martin, Mr. Maxfield (Waterville), Allan McBean, Loralee Moon, Mario Morselli, James A. Murphy, Pat Murtagh, Bert Muzzy, Amos Newton, Ken Nicholson, Nancy Otis, Christine Peleszak, John Peters, Karen Petersen, Mr. and Mrs. Karl Pfister, Art Phenning, Emilie Piper, David E. Potter, the late Henry Potter, Charles Prior, John Read, Tyler Resch, Daly Rizio, Pat Rondeau, Harry Rousch, Fred Royce, Nancy Rucker, D. Gregory Sanford, Eliot and Rosemary Sherman, Harley Smith, Larry Smith, Nadia Smith, Floyd Snow, James G. Stewart, Mrs. Stone (Cavendish), Peter Stott, Robin Tenny, Mary Lou Thomas, Dr. Peter Thomas, Breffny Walsh, Richard Ward, Trip Wescott, Anna Whitney, Robert J. Williams, Eben Wolcott, the late Allen S. Wood, Warren Wood, and Rob Woolmington.

Field guides: Deanna Bright Star, Nancy Bushika, Irving "Red" and the late Betty Call, Harold D. Campbell IV, Bob Carpenter, Polly C. Darnell, Dick DeBonis, Charles Dewey, Tom Dexter, Bob Dion, Noel Fritzinger, Steve Halford and Cathy Hepburn, Shelley Hight, Nelson Jaquay, Bill Jordan, Mr. Labbee (Troy), Dave Lacy, Edgar Lawrence, Ted Lylis, Robert Neville, Sandy Partridge, John Peters, Charles Prior, Wilma Rice, and Betty Vadnais.

Cooperating property owners: Mr. and Mrs. William Bauer, Mr. and Mrs. Robert Bemis, Lee Bills, Celia and Hank Bissel, Steve Bromley, George Butts, William Calkins, the late Ralph Carvage, Sylvia and the late Frank E. Casey, Sr., Cathy and Dennis Conroy, Bud Crossman, Ms. Dekuyper (Waitsfield), Gordon Delong, Mrs. and the late Mr. Paul Doran, Tom Fitzgerald, Mrs. Roland Fortin, Mrs. Robert Geise, Janet Greene, Rick and Mina Harootunian, Allen Hitchcock, Donald Holt, Howell's Campground (Arlington), Nelson and Betti Jaquay, Herbert John, Robert Kaufmann, Keewaydin Camps (Salisbury), Hank Kennedy, Robert Kennett, Arnold Kingsley, Charles and Keith Knapp, Mr. Laberge, Sr., Mr. LaVictorie (Chippenhook), Charles L'Herault, Maplebrook Farm (Tinmouth), Alson Martell, Mrs. Mulholland (Cavendish), Anna Rice, Caleb and Louise Scott, Leslie and Mark Shiff, Ken Smith, Dennis Sparling, Specialty Paperboard Co. (Sheldon), Walter Stugger, Mr. Taylor (Reading), Dianne and Kenneth Terminini, Sandra Thompson, Dr. Edwin Treat, the Vermont Division for Historic Preservation, Mr. Walker (Benson), and Harold Welch.

Helpers in many various ways: Nina and Bill Bonney, Nancy Boone, Judy Calkins, Art Cohn, Linda and Roger Cole, the late Dr. Warren Cook, the late Mary Davis, Candice Deininger, Warren Dexter, Bertha Dodge, John Dumville, Shirley Dunn, Lia and Roy Elk, Emily Feldman, the late Michael Folsom, Chester Gallup, Marjorie Galusha, Grover Grillio, Jean Harvie, Toni and Dennis Howe, Lois Feister and Paul Huey, Curtis Johnson, Patricia Krouson, Ed Lenik, Ron Lewis, Bill McDevitt, Carl Nordstrom, Joseph T. Popecki, Audrey Porsche, Dr. Marjory W. Power, Maj. John Rolando, USAF, Edward Rutsch, Gwen Schauer, Robert Sharp, Michael Sherman, David Skinas, Dr. David R. Starbuck, Prof. William Taylor, Megan Battey Todd, Robert M. Vogel, Diana Waite, the late Edmund Winslow, Bill Zimmerman, and many good friends at GE Aerospace in Pittsfield, Massachusetts and Burlington, Vermont.

Dian Post of Post Scripts, Federalsburg, Maryland supervised overall production of this book, and set into action the mechanics of getting it published. The phone company made lots of money on us. Joan Mentzer of Washington, D.C. was editor. Debi Lynne of Boothbay Harbor, Maine did publication design and layout. Norman McGlothlin of Mac's Composition, Riverdale, Maryland did composition. Thank you Dian, Joan,

Debi, and Norm for handling the production as if this book were your own.

Francine Dempsey CSJ, of The College of Saint Rose, my mentor and advisor during nontraditional graduate studies, approved and supported my research into the nontraditional aspect of industrial history.

David Lacy, Green Mountain Forest Archeologist, Richard Ackerman, Staff Officer for Resources, Billee Hoornbeek, former Forest Archeologist (now at Siuslaw National Forest, Oregon), and Steve Harper, former Forest Supervisor gave me much support and encouragement. They recognized my charcoal kiln survey efforts in the Green Mountain National Forest with Forest Service Volunteer Certificates of Appreciation in 1985 and 1992.

I met Nelson Jaquay at a Rutland Historical Society meeting one memorable cold night in February 1979, and he and his wife Betti and daughter Sarah are proof that the finest people live in some of Vermont's most remote places. Camping out back, painting the Tinmouth schoolhouse, and making friends with people who make the town function had to be a pinnacle of my Vermont experience (I wish I had a furnace ruin in my back yard).

Richard S. "Rick" Allen, fellow researcher in ironworks, was forever generous with data, books, photos, and new clues; to him goes much credit for encouraging me to investigate furnace ruins in New York State. Rick is one of those rare people who unselfishly share whatever they have with anyone who has a similar interest.

"Griffy," my field companion, part Labrador and part whatever, was born the runt of a litter of 10 on May 19, 1983, and accompanied me everywhere in Vermont, exploring all the streams and ruins along the way. She was coal black and so I named her for Silas Griffith, charcoal baron of Mount Tabor. She endured the long, boring drives to Vermont in the back of the pickup, coming alive when we started bouncing on rough back roads, and shot for the woods at the drop of the tailgate. We shared cool streams on hot days and a sleeping bag on cold nights. She patiently waited for me to return from the many offices and libraries to which this work took me, usually whiling away the hours by successfully begging handouts of ice cream and donuts from students passing through the parking lots, the grassy edges of which she roamed to the limit of her 20-foot chain. Griffy was instantly killed on February 25, 1988 in front of her house by a hit-and-run driver when she ran into the street instead of hopping into the pickup. I've never gotten over her absence in the woods.

Bill Murphy filled in the application forms while serving as President of the Vermont Archaeological Society in 1988–89 that resulted in a modest grant from the Vermont Statehood Bicentennial Commission for the production of this book.

Rudy Yondorf, fellow outdoorsman and a timely computer resource person at GE Aerospace, guided me through many near-violent confrontations with my PC.

Jack Trowill is a good friend, founder of Searchers for All Possible Solutions (SAPS), and GE associate since 1957; we have explored caves, furnace ruins, and battlefields. Jack encouraged me to buy quality photographic equipment, provided me with timely publishing advice, and tried (with only marginal success) to get me to always do things right the first time at GE Aerospace.

The late Philip Elwert, Deputy Director and Museum Curator of the Vermont Historical Society, died suddenly in 1988 as a result of a tragic accident. Phil had kept a steady stream of postcards coming to me, containing data and references to brickyards, ironworks, kilns, and various other important archival materials. He always greeted my VHS visits with happy chatter and was never at a loss for time to assist me. As well as being a valuable resource person, in time Phil came to be a good friend.

Giovanna Peebles, both a sincere friend and a professional advisor in her capacity as the Vermont State Archaeologist, generously included this non-Vermonter in the mainstream of historical and archeological research in her state. At a seminar on historic preservation at the University of Vermont in 1978, she was enthusiastically interested in my research into 19th-century stone-built blast furnaces of New England.

Christopher Rolando accompanied me on hiking expeditions to ironworks in New York and New England; twenty-three years ago at the age of nine, he had already stood in the shadows of more 19th-century blast furnace ruins than most historians knew existed. My son disassembled and repaired my Datsun engine on the kitchen floor and camped for a month on the roof of McDonald's in Pittsfield, Mass. (he comes from fine Rolando stock). Chris also provides me with valuable PC support; I don't know what I would do without him.

Robert Edward "Bob" West, of whom not enough can be said and I am at a loss for the right words, broke many trails in search of elusive charcoal and lime kilns and is responsible for many of the leads that resulted in successful finds (except that single-kiln ruin in Peru). He was an ever-dependable critic and supporter in helping me pull the original manuscript together and enthusiastically encouraging me to continue. It is a privilege to be counted among his friends. A native Vermonter, former state legislator, past Program Chairman of the Rutland Historical Society and President of the Manchester Historical Society, Bob gives his state's best interests a high personal priority, but I don't believe he has been fully appreciated for this by many of his contemporaries.

Donna Marie Rolando, lover of dolls, stray cats, and a good mystery, sometimes waited patiently for me at the edge of the forest but usually whiled away her time at home. When I finally arrived, tired, bug-bitten, muddy, scratched, and limping slightly, she wondered to herself "why?" Not a totally enthusiastic industrial archeologist, she supports my work, although we have our own theories about Nazca lines. Donna greets my homecomings with a chilled glass of burgundy, feeds me only low-sodium and low-fat meals, and keeps my body and soul in good mend.

And finally, special and affectionate thanks to my parents— Madeline and the late Renato Rolando—for always being there with love and support, and for patiently trying to understand the apparent aimless wanderings of their oldest son. I wish Dad were here to see what I accomplished.

Victor Renato Rolando
Manchester, Vermont

Introduction

For most people, the name Vermont is synonymous with a rolling landscape of cultivated fields and forests punctuated by small villages complete with town hall, church, general store, and white clapboard homes. Because of this popular image, we tend to overlook the fact that Vermont has been a national leader in the production of iron, copper, slate, marble, and granite, and the manufacture of farm machines and machine tools; and that in the 19th century, most towns had at least one mill or factory and often more.

Typical of the mills were those engaged in the manufacture of iron, either working the ore into wrought iron at small bloomery forges, or smelting ore into cast iron in tall blast furnaces. These early forges dotted banks of swift-running streams and rivers, answering to the needs of the first Vermont settlers.

Associated with the making of iron was the need for charcoal to fuel the forges and furnaces. Initially made in mounds, charcoal kilns evolved into circular stone structures and eventually into round, red-bricked kilns. By the 1880s, hundreds of these kilns were reducing the Green Mountain forests into black charcoal for ironworks inside and outside Vermont.

Not directly associated with iron and charcoal making, yet somewhat related, was lime burning. Lime kilns also dotted the early countryside, capitalizing on both the agricultural and industrial need for burnt lime and the availability of limestone. Less well-known, and the least understood of rural furnaces, lime kiln ruins continue to mystify those who happen upon them in obscure corners of the forest, sometimes prompting speculation of prehistoric or exotic origins.

Hundreds of these ruins lie in varying degrees of abandon up and down the spine and the eastern and western slopes of the Green Mountains. Some tower dozens of feet upward; others display mere foundation walls. They range in shape from square to rectangular to oval. They are near waterways in broad valleys or high up in the mountains. Some are single ruins; some are clusters of ruins. Most are made of native Vermont stone. Some are made partially or wholly of brick. They are seemingly unconnected with the traditional concept of Vermont history.

Industrial Archeology

A new interest in the archeology of industrial history from social, technological, and architectural perspectives has gained momentum since the early 1970s. Studies of 19th-century factory systems and disciplines have revealed the social consequences of the period. Early-19th-century America saw the emergence of pioneer entrepreneur-owners of factories, mills, and forges. The post-Civil War period witnessed a dramatic consolidation of these entrepreneurships into a revolution of industry, as larger, more efficient factories demanded more raw materials, larger and faster machines, and more cheap labor. Finally came the revolution of industrial labor itself, as the working class found its identity and demanded its share of the fruits of the Industrial Revolution.

Archeologists sift through the remains of that period, identifying and interpreting the architectural, technological, and social dimensions of the artifactual remains. They do not see history as powdered wigs, pitched battles, and treaties. Rather, from the refuse discarded a century ago at today's site of workers' housing, the archeologist learns whether there was such a thing as a quality of life for the 19th-century factory family. Through meager historical records and field inspection, we can determine how technologically advanced (or backward) a forge may have been compared to its contemporaries nearby, in the next state, or in Europe. When we find, for instance, that an underpowered mill was operating in a remote corner of Vermont with machinery that was then already years behind the latest state of the art, what questions of economics must be considered? How could such an ancient and inefficient mill compete? Yet economics seems far removed from finding bits of slag, buttons, creamware, nails, and glass in a caved-in and overgrown cellar hole at a mountaintop mill site, abandoned 150 years ago, and apparently forgotten by everyone.

Those who search out and study these industrial remains are part of a relatively new discipline called Industrial Archeology (IA). The industrial archeologist seeks out, identifies, and records industrial sites. The industrial archeologist, working alongside architectural historians, is also concerned with the preservation of industrial structures. Abandoned mill and factory buildings have new life breathed into them through adaptive reuse, that is, renovating the structure (into, for example, shopping malls or condominiums) while retaining its basic architectural fabric.

Since the excavation and reconstruction of the Saugus Ironworks in the 1940s, a strong, continuing interest has developed in industries associated with making and working iron. A 1974 publication by the Council for Northeast Historical Archaeology included articles about work undertaken at the forges of Charlotteburg, New Jersey, and the iron industries in the vicinity of Seaford, Delaware (Lenik 1974:9-17; Heite 1974:18-34). The founding of the Society for Industrial Archeology (SIA) in 1971 gave archeologists and historians of industry a focal organization, reflecting the continuing growth of this interest in industrial archeology.

An immense amount of effort has been expended throughout the country to research, excavate, record, preserve, stabilize, and reconstruct the various remains of the iron industry. These efforts have, in most cases, afforded new insights into the technological state of the industry in the 18th and 19th centuries. Unfortunately, however, the number of papers that have been published on the results of these archeological projects falls far short of the quantity of work accomplished in the field. The following are some examples of what has been published, by the SIA, about the ironworks industry.

In 1981, Bruce Seely wrote a study of mid-19th-century blast-furnace technology using remains of the Adirondack Iron and Steel Company in northern New York State as the model. This study was the product of a large recording project by the Historic American Engineering Record (HAER). Through inspection and interpretation of the remains of the blast furnace and machinery, Seely "fleshed out" the pattern by which this isolated charcoal iron furnace adapted its process rather than converting to coke for fuel, thereby demonstrating the complexity of technological innovation at the site. "The Adirondack Iron and Steel Company's history and site help to provide a more realistic picture of both the charcoal iron industry and the broader American iron industry as a whole by illustrating how some charcoal iron makers accommodated themselves to a period of changing technological possibilities in the late antebellum period" (Seely 1981:52).

Three years later Robert B. Gordon and Michael S. Raber conducted a study of an 1865 ironworks at Mine Hill, near Roxbury, Connecticut, in the west-central part of the state. The authors concluded that the physical and archival evidence illustrated the range of problems that such an enterprise faced in 19th-century America. Not all the obstacles were related to getting the machinery to work as it should; many times the best scientific opinions of the time were no match for the lack of practical experience needed to get the machinery to perform as expected in the first place.

> ... the most eminent applied scientists in America, had little practical experience with iron and steelmaking—to which, at that time, science indeed had little to contribute. The notion that siderite was a "steel ore," originally suggested by Benjamin Silliman after his visit to Mine Hill in 1817, seems to have had a strong influence on successive owners of the property.... Large and in some cases apparently unnecessary expenditures were made by the proprietors ... [who] ... committed themselves to a series of iron and steelmaking procedures that were costly ... the puddled steel process that they selected later was less labor-intensive but likewise required skills that were not easily found in the United States (Gordon and Raber 1984:33).

More recently, the SIA published a study by Nicholas Honerkamp of a pre-Civil War blast furnace that operated at Chattanooga, Tennessee. Honerkamp showed how a charcoal iron furnace that converted to coke was affected by "larger economic, political, technological, and ecological forces and conditions present in the South on the eve of the Civil War ... research at sites such as Bluff Furnace compel archeologists to examine past cultural dynamics in order to explain adequately specific features of industrial sites.... Bluff Furnace, and other industrial sites like it, offer more than elegant reconstructions of past events. They challenge archeologists to carry out anthropology in the past tense" (Honerkamp 1987:55, 67).

In the area of charcoal making, the Society for Historical Archaeology (SHA) published a paper by Charles D. Zeier that dealt with archeological excavations conducted northeast of Eureka in central Nevada, and resulted in the identification and evaluation of a wide variety of charcoal-making sites. The charcoal-fueled smelters reduced silver ore in the 1870–1890 period. Although well past the time that most charcoal makers in Vermont and the Northeast had abandoned making charcoal

in mounds in favor of structured kilns, mounds (called "ovens" in the paper) were still operating in Nevada up to the late 1880s.

These mounds were operated by Carbonari, that is, Italian charcoal burners, who emigrated to the west in the mid-19th century. Fuel for the mounds was pinyon and juniper wood, abundant in the vicinity. Production yield was in the range of 25 to 30 bushels of charcoal per cord of pinyon (compared with 30 to 35 bushels of charcoal per cord of wood generally realized by mounds in Vermont during an earlier period). The paper also addressed the chronology of charcoal production at Eureka, the ethnic affiliations of the charcoal burners, and the lifestyles of the Carbonari.

As in Vermont, historical accounts and technical literature provided scant information on charcoal making. "Evidence contained in historical documents provides only a limited picture of late nineteenth century charcoal production in the Eureka area. Much of the discussion is dominated by the ethnicity of the charcoal producers and their role in social and political events of the time. Limited information of a technical nature is presented. Earthen ovens were expected to be the predominant form of charcoal production, and few, if any, kilns were expected. Historical estimates of oven size and yield allowed the volume of archaeologically described pits to be estimated" (Zeier 1987:96-97).

Presentation of the Study

To simplify presentation of the furnace, forge, and kiln sites study, chapters 4, 6, and 8 are divided into northern, central, and southern districts, as follows:

District	Counties
Northern	Caledonia, Chittenden, Essex, Franklin, Grand Isle, Lamoille, Orleans, Washington
Central	Addison, Orange, Rutland, Windsor
Southern	Bennington, Windham

Physical disposition of the sites is indicated in maps accompanying each district presentation; photos and illustrations support the chapters.

All sites in the study are preceded by their site identification number, the principal (or assigned) site name, and town in which the site is located. Counties are presented in generally north-to-south order within districts; sites within counties in as close a north-to-south sequence as possible, regardless of their site number sequence. County abbreviations used in the site identification numbers are:

County	Abbr.	County	Abbr.	County	Abbr.
Addison	AD	Franklin	FR	Rutland	RU
Bennington	BE	Grand Isle	GI	Washington	WA
Caledonia	CA	Lamoille	LA	Windham	WD
Chittenden	CH	Orange	OR	Windsor	WN
Essex	ES	Orleans	OL		

The site identification numbers are a modification of those used by the Vermont Division for Historic Preservation for all recorded sites. Site number VT-BE-36, for example, assigned by the State Archeologist, identifies the site as being in Vermont (VT), in Bennington County (BE), and it is site number 36 (the 36th site recorded in that county). For the purposes of this work and since all sites are in Vermont, "VT-" is assumed and therefore deleted from the site identification number so that the site is identified as BE-36.

Sites formally reported to the state but considered inconclusive or of questionable archeological value are assigned field site (FS) numbers by the State Archeologist. AD-FS49, an example of a field site number used in this work, is the 49th field site recorded in Addison County. Note that FS49(AD) is the state's designation of this site. Identification of sites reported in this book but not yet formally reported to the state take a form dependent on whether the type of site is iron making, ironworking, or charcoal- or lime-burning related, as follows:

Type Site	Typical Ident. No.	Type Code
Blast Furnace	RU-IW03	IW = Ironworks
Bloomery Forge	AD-IW13	IW = Ironworks
Foundry	OL-IW03	IW = Ironworks
Charcoal Kiln	BE-CK02	CK = Charcoal Kiln
Lime Kiln	CH-LK01	LK = Lime Kiln

RU-IW03, for example, is the third unreported ironwork-related site in Rutland County; AD-IW13, although a bloomery forge, is likewise ironworks-related and also assigned the IW code. Unreported numbers repeat from "01" for each county; thus, it is not an error to have both AD-IW01 and RU-IW01. The county (AD versus RU) designation is the distinction.

All cities and towns mentioned are in Vermont unless identified by state. Repeated state identification is avoided in the sites chapters.

Results of the Study

The number of industrial sites that have been identified, inspected, and recorded in Vermont as a result of this study bears witness to the technological impact that the Industrial Revolution made on the iron-making, ironworking, and charcoal- and lime-burning industries in the state. This is a fact that has not been fully reflected in most of Vermont's history books. Some books give the state's iron industry a scant sentence of recognition; others none at all. Most ignore altogether the charcoal- and lime-burning industries. Probably because they are still active, the state's granite, marble, and slate industries receive more attention.

This study, including all archival and field work, resulted in the identification of 288 sites of blast furnaces, bloomery forges, foundries, charcoal mounds and kilns, and lime kilns (see table below). Of these, 162 sites yielded 319 ruins or remains, which are now part of the State Archeological Inventory. Almost all ruins were found to be extremely fragile. Of the remaining 126 sites, 96 have not yet been precisely located (work-in-progress) and no surface remains were found at 30 others. Many of the latter are disturbed beyond surface recognition, but after further study might be determined to have some potential archeological value. Sadly, there will remain a significant number of sites that probably will never be found in the field, either due to insufficient archival data or because the sites have been completely destroyed through commercial development of the land or natural deterioration.

In terms of significant IA materials, the study found the ruins or remains of 22 blast furnaces, 18 bloomery forges, 5 foundries, 130 charcoal kilns, 51 charcoal mounds, and 93 lime kilns. The majority of these were built in the 1790s–1860s, which is the generally accepted period of the Industrial Revolution in the United States. These valuable artifacts are, therefore, some of the last physical links between the end of Vermont's pre-Industrial Revolution era and the modern industrial period.

Summary of Results

County	Ironworks		Charcoal		Lime Kilns		Total	
	Sites	Remains	Sites	Remains	Sites	Remains	Sites	Remains
Addison	32	17	13	26	12	10	57	53
Bennington	13	7	38	83	15	4	66	94
Caledonia	2		1		1		4	
Chittenden	7	2	1	2	5	5	13	9
Franklin	7	2			9	16	16	18
Grand Isle	1				1		2	
Lamoille	1		2		5		8	
Orange	1				1		2	
Orleans	2	1					2	1
Rutland	27	14	13	69	19	19	59	102
Washington	2		1				3	
Windham	1	1	1	1	16	12	18	14
Windsor	3	1	1		34	27	38	28
Total:	99	45	71	181	118	93	288	319

A ca.-1900 painting of Tyson Furnace by Myron Dimmick, who is supposed to have worked at the furnace. The blast furnace is in the center building with three chimneys; blast-producing machinery is in the building to the left (courtesy Vermont Historical Society).

Chapter 1
Historical Overview of Iron Making

Pre-American Ironworks

The distinction of being the earliest person in recorded history to work iron goes to Tubal Cain, who was born in the seventh generation from Adam and is described as "Tubalcain, the ancestor of all who forge instruments of bronze and iron" (Genesis 4:22). The first evidence of iron implements actually transmitted to us from ancient times comes from Egypt, the joint between two stones revealing a tool that had been lost.

1-1. *Depiction of a small furnace (center) and foot-operated bellows (left and right) on the wall of an Egyptian tomb dating to about 1500 BC (Wilkinson 1883:312).*

This was perhaps 5,000 years ago (Moldenke 1930:2-4). Recent investigations in Africa have disclosed that prehistoric civilizations in what is today Tanzania practiced a method of smelting iron and making carbon steel that was technologically superior to any steelmaking process in Europe until the middle of the 19th century:

> At the request of the scientists and working entirely from memory, the Haya [of Tanzania] constructed a traditional furnace. It was 5 feet high, cone-shaped, made of slag and mud and built over a pit packed with partially burned swamp grass; these charred reeds provided the carbon that combined with the molten iron to produce steel. Eight ceramic blow-pipes extended into the furnace chamber near the base, each connected to a goat-skin bellows outside. Using these pipes to force air into the furnace, which was fueled by the charcoal, the Haya were able to achieve temperatures higher than 3275° F, high enough to produce their carbon steel.
>
> In excavations on the western shore of Lake Victoria, they discovered remnants of 13 furnaces nearly identical in design to the one the Haya had built. Using radioactive-dating process on the charcoal, they found that these furnaces were between 1500 and 2000 years old, which proved that the sophisticated steelmaking techniques demonstrated by the contemporary Haya were indeed practiced by their ancestors. This discovery, the scientists conclude, "will help to change scholarly and popular ideas that technological sophistication

developed in Europe but not in Africa" ("Africa's Ancient Steelmakers" *Time* Sept. 25, 1978:80).

True cast iron is a relatively recent achievement, but it was occasionally made in prehistoric bloomeries existing at the close of the Dark Ages. The process, conducted in an ancient form of hearth and blast furnace combined, was the prototype of our modern developments in these directions. The remains of some 400 of these prehistoric furnaces were discovered about a century ago in the Jura Mountains, which border France and Switzerland. The enormous amount of charcoal used as fuel compelled the selection of locations rich in wood, charcoal being made on the spot. Iron ore came from nearby, and the mining operations conducted by these primitive men, rediscovered by the German miners of the Middle Ages who found stone implements in the tunnels, gave rise to legends of dwarfs and gnomes, implicitly believed then, and current in those regions to the present day.

A careful study of the furnace ruins, which were found by tracing the paths of slag backward into the mountains, indicates that a hearth of fireclay from 6 to 8 inches thick was laid on the ground. Material of the same kind and thickness formed the furnace lining, which was reinforced by a heavy stone backing, the total thickness varying from 18 to 27 inches. About 2½ to 3 inches above the bottom of the hearth a door was provided for, a substantially arched entrance having the full width of the shaft of the furnace and carried outward through the earth covering of the furnace proper. This shaft, or chimney, was 8 to 12 feet high, and had on top of it a ring of stones to prevent damage while charging. The general shape of the furnace was that of a truncated cone leaning forward somewhat, so that in throwing in charcoal and iron ore on top, the door below would be kept free from spilled accumulations.

After drying out such a furnace, it was charged with alternate layers of charcoal and ore, ignited, and left to the action of the natural draft. The temperatures obtained were such that only the front of the furnace became red hot—the rear was merely glazed. The fire cracks thus produced necessitated repairs. One man would remain with such a furnace constantly. As slag appeared on the hearth, he would pull it out with a hook, slice up the fire, eventually draw out a red-hot cake of iron, and immediately forge it into bars. As everything was done by hand and only 30 to 60 pounds of iron were produced at a time, the metal was highly expensive. Hence, even some of the hammers used and found in these excavations were of stone. Furnaces of this kind were still in existence in the time of the early Romans. In fact, the Romans took the art with them into their colonies, and both Spain and Britain saw the making of arms from the iron of native ores.

While the furnace men, who were held in high respect for their indispensable knowledge, were only aiming at the production of wrought iron, unquestionably they noticed occasional molten metal. Indeed, this knowledge was old even though the use of cast iron in the arts is of very recent date. There is a record of a bridge with cast-iron chains being built in Japan in AD 70. The Greek geographer Pausanias spoke a century later of cast-iron statuary introduced by Theodorus (of Samnium, an ancient country in central Italy). Possibly the crucible figured considerably in these early developments, with wrought-iron scraps and charcoal being melted together. But the first recorded example of making pig iron harks back to AD 1311, in the Siegerland of Westphalia (a region of Germany bordering the Netherlands). Knowledge of the subject must have spread widely in spite of the secrecy then prevailing, most likely through the medium of journeymen operatives, because cast-iron castings were made about 40 years later in Sussex (south-eastern England). While molten iron was known by the Romans in Britain at a very early period, however, the actual first recorded English example of cast iron is a gravestone dated 1450 at Burwash Church.

A small forge operating in the mountains of Catalonia in northeastern Spain during the 8th century represented one of the early significant metallurgical advances in iron making. The Catalan forge was a stone-built cup, called a hearth, about 3 feet high and 2½ feet in diameter. A short distance above the front of the base was a small opening that allowed the tuyere (nozzle) of a leather bellows to supply air. The hearth was filled with charcoal to the level of the tuyere.

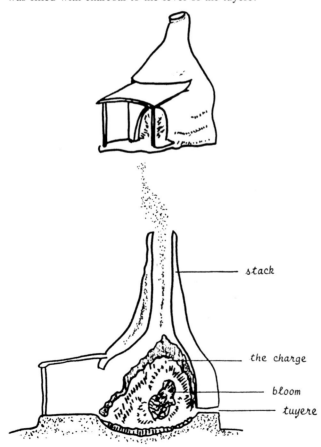

1-2. *A representation of an early Catalan forge.*

On top of this, more charcoal filled the front half and iron ore filled the back half (nearest the tuyere). Air from the bellows forced hot carbon monoxide from the burning charcoal to combine with the oxygen in the iron ore, reducing the ore to a hot, pasty (non-molten) mass of iron. The lump of iron was removed from the hearth with tongs and was alternately hammered and reheated, both to squeeze out pieces of stone and charcoal, and to fashion the iron into a manageably shaped bar called an ancony. The product was a relatively low-carbon iron capable of being hammered (wrought) into many useful shapes. It was also resistant to rust since the charcoal (unlike today's high-sulfur coal) did not introduce sulfur into the iron (Kauffman 1966:32). The Catalan forge could yield 350 pounds of iron in the same 5 hours it took predecessor forges to make only 50 pounds.

By the 9th century, variations of the Catalan forge were operating in central Europe. At forges along the Rhine River, a stone shaft (chimney) 10 to 16 feet high was built above the hearth to increase the capacity of the forge. It became known as a stuckofen (pronounced stook-ofen), which means stack-oven. It was also known as a wolf furnace, but it was basically still a Catalan forge. The Catalan forge, however, did not evolve into a furnace everywhere. In England it was called a bloomery forge (or bloomery). In France, the product of the forge was called a loupe (loop). As the size of the forge increased, so did the size of the bellows. Whereas the forge location formerly was determined primarily by accessibility of wood for charcoal, the switch from manual (or animal) to waterpower, to drive the larger bellows, forced the forges out of the deep forests into the valleys near swift-running streams and rivers.

The wolf furnace, meanwhile, which was a European attempt to utilize the waste heat of the old Catalan forge, did not replace the bloomery forge. Its larger bellows did succeed, however, in heating the charge to a temperature sufficient to melt the iron and allow it to trickle to the bottom of the hearth where it cooled and solidified. Having been subjected to higher temperatures, this iron chemically absorbed enough carbon (from the charcoal fuel) to transform it into a hard iron. However hard, it was too brittle to be worked at the hammer. Production of molten iron in the furnaces in use during these very early days was considered a serious detriment. It was looked on as a waste and an annoyance by many ironworkers; some threw it away and others recycled it back into the furnace. The operatives were heavily fined for the latter (Moldenke 1930:3).

The transition from bloomery to blast furnace was never a "great leap forward." Rather, it varied geographically with time, as the technology stimulated it or market conditions demanded it. And not all bloomeries evolved into blast furnaces. While the blast furnace concept of making cast iron branched away from the bloomery process, the bloomery process itself continued to thrive, advance, and evolve. In fact, during the medieval period, it was difficult to distinguish a blast furnace from a bloomery. "The blast furnace and the bloomery process are usually described as distinct, but [it was] pointed out that a nearly continuous transition between them can be found in the historical and archaeological record from the Austrian Alps between 1541 and 1775. This appears in the sequence, *renn-*

In the figure, the labels read: *stack*, *the charge*, *bloom*, *tuyere*.

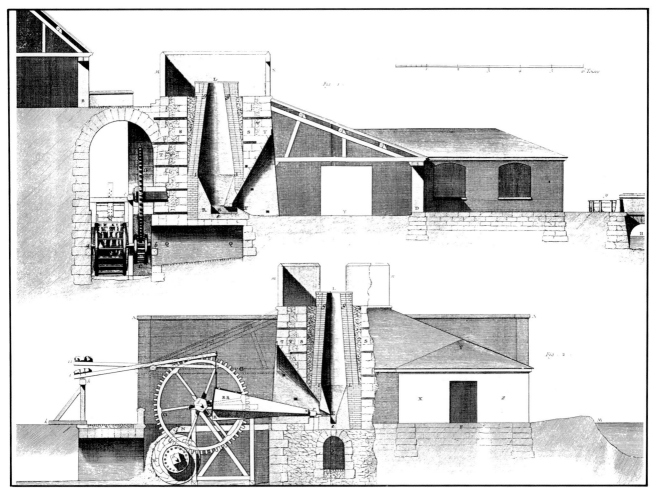

1-3. *A ca.-1760s blast furnace (Diderot 1763: plate 87).*

ofen-stuckofen-flossofen-hochofen, of furnace types. The proportion of pig iron to bloom iron produced by a *stuckofen* could be varied to meet the demands of the market" (Gordon and Reynolds Jan. 1986:113).

The stuckofen (wolf furnace), therefore, was an attempt to increase the output capacity of the old Catalan forge. Its distinctive tall chimney, to increase its draft, earned it the name of high bloomery; and it was this furnace that could, at the whim of the ironmaster, produce either cast iron or wrought iron. In an analysis of medieval and early modern processes in the manufacture of iron, it was noted that:

> The wolf furnace, or stuckofen, was a high bloomery, and as such was simply an enlargement of the primitive low bloomery or forges. The stuckofen was only a Catalan furnace extended upwards in the form of a quadrangular or circular shaft. The Germans call it a "stuck" or "wolf's ofen" because the large metallic mass which is extracted from the bottom is termed "stuck" or "wolf".... These furnaces, or bloomeries . . . are generally 10 to 16 feet high,

2 feet wide at the top and bottom and about 5 feet wide at the widest. . . .

The transition from the old bloomery to the modern blast furnace was very gradual, and the stuckofen is the final development of the furnaces in which iron in the malleable state was produced direct from the ore. By increasing the dimensions of the stuckofen, especially its height, the conditions favorable to the formation of cast iron are obtained; and, indeed, in the stuckofen cast iron was generally, if not always, produced in greater or less degree, to the annoyance of the smelter.

The stuckofen itself was gradually superseded by the blast furnace, the first furnace which replaced the stuckofen being the blauofen, or blow oven. Originally there was no essential difference between them, these names being applied according to the nature of the metal they yielded, and not in consequence of difference of construction; malleable iron being obtained with much less charcoal than was used when cast iron was desired. When the blauofen was used as a stuckofen it was only necessary to make an opening in the fore part of the hearth large enough for the extraction of the lump.

The blauofen, which is not entirely extinct on the Continent [in 1884], dates from about the beginning of the fourteenth century. The flussofen was substantially the same furnace as the blauofen. "Blast furnace" may be properly substituted for either term. Hochofen was another German name that was applied to the blast furnace, and it is still retained (Swank 1892:57-60).

Only when it was found that this metal could be successfully cast into cannonballs (1388, in Memmingen, Germany) was there the dawning of a new industry. Then for a while the furnaces were alternately used for production of cast and wrought iron by proper draft regulation and air blast. As experience was gained, higher temperatures were realized and low-manganese ores brought into use. Gray iron castings could be made, with cannon and stove plates being the almost-exclusive products. This change from a puddling process to the actual making of pig iron, called direct casting, took place in the 14th century.

Although early blast furnaces did some direct casting at the hearth, later techniques of remelting and casting at a cupola furnace designed specifically for this purpose allowed blast furnaces to specialize in smelting the ore and molding the iron into easily transportable ingots. Some iron-making communities contained a blast furnace plus one or more bloomery forges. These, plus the charcoal kilns for the reduction of wood into charcoal to fuel the furnace and forges, and the various associated ironworks-related buildings, made up these pioneer industrial complexes. Until the blast furnaces developed to a practical state of technical and economic efficiency, however, bloomeries supplied nearly all mankind's iron needs. The few exceptions to this rule were those iron objects hammered directly from high-grade ore outcroppings or from meteorites. Bloomery forges in Vermont evolved from a long metallurgical history dating back to antiquity and progressing with inconsistent speed for about a thousand years to the Catalan forge (Bining 1973:55-68; Fisher 1963:25-29; Harte 1935:31-69).

Early Euro-American Ironworks

The first known ironworking in the Western Hemisphere by European explorers/settlers took place at an inlet on the northern tip of Newfoundland about the year AD 1000. At L'Anse-aux-Meadows, a small, short-lived Norse settlement struggled with the harsh elements before retreating back across the ocean, probably to Iceland or Greenland. Archeology at the site in the 1960s uncovered slag, iron artifacts, and a charcoal kiln site, leading to the conclusion that the Norse had worked some iron from local bog ore (Ingstad 1977:93, 392-403).

Nearly 600 years after the Norse settlement, an expedition to North America by Sir Walter Raleigh in 1584 discovered iron ore at Roanoke, Virginia. Analysis of the ore showed that it was comparable to European quality, and in 1609 a boatload was shipped to England where it was reduced to about 25 tons of cast iron. A number of attempts to set up an ironworks in the James River area failed until James Berkeley succeeded in constructing a forge at Falling Creek, near today's Richmond (Fisher 1963:67-68). In the spring of 1622, however, just as the furnace was fired up, the settlement was attacked by Indians and the ironworks destroyed.

Farther north, the Pilgrims had discovered bog ore in many coastline marshes and inland ponds, mainly Monponsett, Sampson, and Assawompsett ponds in eastern Massachusetts (Bishop vol. 1 1868:479). Ore samples sent to England led to the formation of the Company of Undertakers of the Iron Works of New England. Their first venture at Braintree failed, but the second at Saugus succeeded (Hartley 1957:56-57). The blast furnace at Saugus was fired in the spring of 1648 and the works operated until 1675. Although it operated intermittently, it has been recognized as the birthplace of the American iron and steel industry. Saugus Ironworks is today a National Historical Park, containing the reconstructed blast furnace plus a forge, finery, rolling mill, and worker housing.

In 1700 the king of England was called on to mediate a border dispute between New York and Connecticut. Part of the settlement included a survey of the border, which ran along the top of the Taconic Mountains, separating the two colonies.

1-4. *Making cannonballs by hand-pumped draft in a small, late-18th-century blast furnace* (American Malleable Iron *1944:197*).

1-5. *Ira Allen, builder of some of Vermont's earlier ironworks, is immortalized by his statue at the college he founded (University of Vermont) at Burlington.*

In the process of the survey, some high grades of iron ore were discovered near the tri-state corner with Massachusetts. A bloomery was built in 1734 by Thomas Lamb nearby at Lime Rock, Connecticut. More forges soon followed at Canaan, Colebrook, Kent, Cornwall, and Salisbury. Ore for Lamb's forge came from Ore Hill in Salisbury. Business was profitable, and Lamb bought additional mining property and the water rights to Wononscopomuc Lake. Around 1760, he sold it all to the Owen brothers, who in turn sold it in 1762 to the partnership of Samuel and Elisha Forbes of Canaan, John Hazeltine of Uxbridge, and a 22-year-old adventurer from Cornwall named Ethan Allen. The partnership constructed a blast furnace at the outlet of Wononscopomuc Lake, which was the first blast furnace built in the Taconic Mountains of western New England. A small prosperous community called Furnace Village (today's Lakeville) developed around the furnace (Smith 1946:257-259). Allen soon tired of staying put, sold his share in the successful ironworks to Charles and George Cadwell in 1765, moved on to Northampton, Massachusetts, and went into the silver mining business.

Meanwhile, dozens of blast furnaces sprang up all over the Taconics of Massachusetts and Connecticut, many providing valuable ordnance during the Revolutionary War. One of these, the Lakeville furnace, provided iron that was cast into guns and cannon at the nearby Salisbury cannon foundry. At Ancram, New York, an ironworks cast parts of the huge chain that was· initially planned to block British access to Lake Champlain at the head of the Richelieu River near the Canadian border; it was finally strung across the Hudson River at West Point. Continuing his ever-northward migration, Ethan Allen followed the frontier into Vermont and kept himself (plus New York and the British) busy in other ventures.

Some of Ethan Allen's ironworks experience and abilities rubbed off on younger brother Ira Allen, who in turn became one of the progenitors of Vermont's iron industry. The Allens, maintaining their former contacts in Connecticut, ordered much iron hardware from the Salisbury forges for the construction of an anchor shop at Colchester and other forges in northern Vermont. Down at Lakeville, meanwhile, the furnace continued in operation until 1823. It had outlived not only Ethan and Ira Allen, but all its founding partners. (There are no visible remains of Ethan Allen's furnace at Lakeville, although his house still stands.)

Early Vermonters

Exhaustive research has not been made into the matter, but it does not appear that Indian inhabitants of Vermont ever worked iron. Chance finds of bits of meteoric iron might have been pounded into ornaments, but judging from published archeological work done in Vermont, the only prehistoric working of metal was that of copper. But the Indians did know of red ocher, an oxide of iron that takes the physical form of a reddish powder. They used it in burials, relating the red powder to blood. "When the first white men came to America, the natives had no knowledge of working iron. Now and then they picked up a bit of meteoric iron and fashioned it into some charm of iron. Copper and bronze were used, but no iron" (Perkins 1971:61). "The red stained soils [of the Indian burials at Swanton] are undoubtedly due to the liberal use of red ocher. Evidently all but two burials were accomplished by this 'red paint'" (Haviland and Power 1981:119). If the Indians noticed the outcrops of iron-bearing stone, they either could not learn how to extract and work it, or its lusterless appearance as compared to their bright copper beads did not encourage them to investigate it. It was left to the next wave of settlers, the Euro-Vermonters, to discover the iron resources of the land and to become the first Vermont iron makers.

The first non-Indian Vermont residents were the French. In the century-and-a-half following Samuel de Champlain's 1609 exploration of the lake that today bears his name, the French sent missionaries up the lake in attempts to enforce their claims to it and by the 1750s had granted patents for vast tracts of land, called seigniories, along lands bordering both sides of the lake. One seigniory, to Rene-Nicolas Levasseur, included what is today the falls of the Missisquoi at Swanton. At the

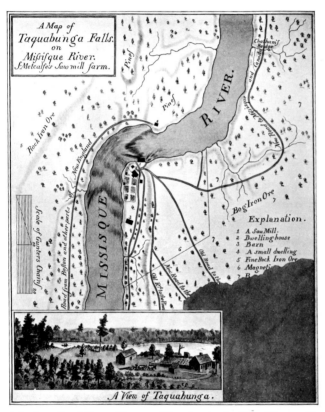

1-6. A pre-Revolutionary War map of Swanton showing Metcalfe's sawmill village on the inside curve of the river, with indications of iron ore in the vicinity (Tercentenary 1910:facing 24).

falls, a community of 50 French families developed around a sawmill (Graffagnino 1983:16). British victories in Canada forced the French to abandon the falls before 1760. Ten years later the old Levasseur mill site came into the hands of New York surveyor and land speculator Simeon Metcalfe, as part of a 25,000-acre grant from New York identified as Prattsburg.

Metcalfe's holdings in the vicinity of the falls at Swanton are depicted on a 1772 map that shows the Missisquoi River and the sawmill farm on the east side of the falls (*Tercentenary* 1910:24ff, 29). The falls were known as Taquahunga Falls at the time (Huden 1971:65). In addition to showing the falls at today's Swanton village, the map also shows roads north to

Canada, south to Boston, and eastward. Symbols indicate the sites of the sawmill, a house and barn, and a small house across the river. The map also indicates "fine rock iron ore" northwest of the falls, magnetic iron ore to the southeast, and bog iron ore to the east and northeast. With all the iron ore deposits around the falls, it is difficult to believe that no iron ore was worked here in the early 1770s, if not previously by the French in a small bloomery. When Metcalfe returned after the Revolutionary War, settlers holding leases issued by Ira Allen (from the New Hampshire charters) were already occupying the area of the falls (Graffagnino 1983:17). The stage was now set for the third wave of settlers.

Following the end of the Revolutionary War, settlers and land speculators by the thousands came into Vermont from all directions. Many were families of men whose introduction to Vermont had been military action at or near Hubbardton or Bennington. With the clearing of land and opening of farmlands, the natural resources of the countryside were immediately exploited by settler and speculator alike. The latter attempted, in some cases, to capitalize on these resources as inducement to sell tracts of land, and either leased already-built mills or advertised the proximity of potentially excellent mill sites to available acreage. Whatever the method, a Vermont population that was about 7,000 people in 1771 became 85,000 by 1791; 155,000 in 1800; and 218,000 by 1810 (Holbrook 1982:xii; U.S. Census).

As steady as the growth of population was, it was geographically irregular. The valleys containing good farmland and abundant resources were settled first; the balance went to late arrivals. Accordingly, the development of Vermont's pioneer industries reflected this irregular pattern that found sawmills and forges commencing operation in widely scattered locations. During the 1780s, for example, a forge operated at Colchester 3 years before one of similar size opened 125 miles to the south in Bennington.

Commercial Empire of the St. Lawrence _____

This pioneer period was affected by political as well as geographic and economic factors. At the end of the Revolution much of Vermont was still being claimed by both New York and New Hampshire, a situation that discouraged many from investing capital and effort there. Since Vermont was not a British colony before the Revolution, no colonial authority was displaced. Whereas patriot governors replaced colonial governors in bordering New York and New Hampshire, a political vacuum existed in Vermont. Into this vacuum came outside people with all their political, religious, and family prejudices, each jockeying with the other for position in the power struggle. Nowhere is this more obvious than in the antagonisms that existed between Ira Allen, Nathaniel Chipman, and Matthew Lyon. The state of political warfare that prevailed affected not only the lives of those concerned, but also their struggling attempts to develop the timber and iron resources of the emerging state.

Industrial production activity in New England in general, which for a time was given a boost by the Revolutionary War, dropped off following the war, and 10 years of unhindered international trade cut into markets of domestic products (Robertson 1955:183-185). Manufacturing output could do no more than keep pace with the population increase. National production fluctuations, however, did not fit the Vermont experience.

A number of factors unrelated to the national production and trade picture had a direct effect on early industrial expansion in Vermont. One was the character of the state itself. Vermont in 1780 was essentially still a wilderness with settlers just starting to trickle in, joining those who had settled before the Revolution. Pre-1800 mills generally supported the needs of these settlers, with sawmills to cut lumber, forges to make nails, horseshoes, and wagon hardware, and gristmills to grind grain. What production surplus remained (and in the area of grain and lumber, early Vermont had a significant surplus) found ready markets outside the state. The character of this market was the second factor.

The nature of Vermont's trading with the outside world was molded by its geography. Its external geographic characteristic was its land-locked situation. Vermont was the only such state in New England until the construction of the Champlain Canal. Internally, the Green Mountains essentially divided Vermont down the middle. The eastern towns identified with New Hampshire and the Connecticut River Valley, using the port of Boston. But the western towns were further fractured, north and south. The latter, mostly in Bennington County, were economically oriented over poor roads to the Hudson River Valley ports of Albany, Troy, and New York City. Central and northwestern towns on the Champlain plateau found their economic future gravitating more and more toward strong ties northward—with British Canada.

Ira Allen was not the first to take advantage of Lake Champlain and funnel lumber and bar iron northward to the natural markets at Québec. Philip Skene and William Gilliland, two prominent colonial New Yorkers who were developing respective estates at Skenesboro (Whitehall) and Willsboro, New York, were also buying supplies in Québec with shipments of lumber in the 1760s and 1770s. But Ira Allen's shipments of lumber and iron northward were needed so badly by Québec merchants that in 1787 they persuaded the Canadian government to no longer consider Vermont as being part of the United States (Williamson 1949:142). This exempted Vermont from Britain's Navigation Acts and drew it closer into the commercial empire of the St. Lawrence.

The Champlain Canal

The realization in Albany that Canadian markets were attracting an increased amount of Champlain Valley trade that might otherwise profit New York prompted action in 1792 to build a canal connecting the lake with the Hudson River. Vermont had been interested as early as 1790 in such a canal. A committee representing Rutland and communities bordering on the lake surveyed the region through which a canal could pass and reported that it was not only practical but the advantages of the canal would be "almost inconceivably great." It recommended the Vermont legislature and governor afford reasonable encouragement and aid to New York to build the canal. But

the recommendations were largely ignored by both (O'Hara 1984:30). A New York company went on alone with the canal, and actually succeeded in digging many miles of it before going bankrupt in 1796. Repeated appeals to Vermont failed at upper levels, although some help was afforded on a lesser scale. One such form of aid came from Matthew Lyon, who owned forges at Fair Haven, and who accepted a contract to construct one section of the canal (O'Hara 1984:31). But even this was too little effort to have any effect. Other leaders such as Ira Allen did much to discourage official support for the canal and instead supported the construction of a canal from the lake northward to the St. Lawrence River. Allen argued that the lake's flow northward showed that nature never intended New York as a seaport for Vermont (O'Hara 1984:322).

Not until after the War of 1812 was the canal to the Hudson River finally built. And as it turned out, the first boat to pass the entire length, in September 1823, was a Vermont boat named the *Gleaner,* out of St. Albans. On its return trip from New York City it carried lobster, oyster, crab, and other shellfish as witness that the vessel had found her way to the ocean (O'Hara 1984:114-115). That same month some 59 tons of nails, 78 tons of iron, 2 tons of iron castings, and 95 tons of ore were locked through (O'Hara 1984:268). The effect of the canal on trade with Canada was immediate and significant. The amount of lumber passing down the Richelieu River to Québec in 1821 from both New York and Vermont was 780,000 feet. The next year, after only a portion of the Champlain Canal had opened, only 22,000 feet went north to Canada. And soon after, lumber trade with Canada was reduced to practically nothing (O'Hara 1984:211).

The effect of the canal on Vermont's iron industry, however, was quite different from that on its logging industry. As early as 1792, the high-quality ore and smelting facilities of the Champlain Valley caused many to agree that this part of the country was to become the seat of the nation's iron and steel industry (O'Hara 1984:265). At that time, a few forges operated on the New York side of the lake, but more forges plus blast furnaces and rolling mills were already operating on the Vermont side.

The initial rush to capitalize on Vermont's resources died out in the early 1800s when the state's economy was affected by such national events as the Embargo Act of 1807, the War of 1812, and, finally, the Tariff Acts starting in 1816. Forges that initially produced for purely local needs now became concerned about costs of transportation needed to carry heavy iron products to marketplaces much farther away. Mining operations that at one time could just pick-and-shovel ore from an exposed ledge now were required to weigh practical and economic considerations involved in expensive shaft-digging and hoist machinery. Works operating marginally were abandoned in favor of more promising ventures that required larger outlays of capital. And though an amount of this early capital came into Vermont in the form of out-of-state capitalists who developed substantial ironworks at Vergennes, Plymouth, Shaftsbury, and Troy, other ironworks at Sheldon, St. Johnsbury, Bennington, Pittsford, Dorset, and Brandon were initially developed through local means.

The opening of the Champlain Canal resulted in a dramatic

change of commercial activity on Lake Champlain: it finally drew Vermont trade from the St. Lawrence. Whereas its timber had been choking ports at Québec, it now jostled Adirondack logs for price and position at the head of tidewater navigation at Albany and Troy, New York. Davey's ironworks at Fair Haven were unshackled from strictly local demand as a result of the canal and could now ship iron south and west. Conant's ironworks at Brandon found new markets in New York for stoves and castings. The canal also opened new paths to market for Barney's forge at Swanton (O'Hara 1984:278).

New York, however, thought it sound policy to encourage its own manufacturing production through light tolls, and to derive as much canal revenue as possible from "foreign" ones. New York interests recognized early on the potential for a major iron industry in the Adirondacks and undertook to encourage its development through a preferential canal toll system. Toll collectors classified iron, nails, etc., made in New York "not enumerated," the toll being one cent per hundredweight per mile. But non-New York, or "foreign," paid three times the rate per mile (O'Hara 1984:268-269).

The Vermont legislature had shown as much disdain toward the construction of the Champlain Canal as it had during the earlier 1792–1796 attempts. It spurned every appeal for cooperation by New York before the canal was built, yet both knew that Vermont was also destined to reap benefits that the canal would provide (Swanton's marble industry and Burlington's transshipping facilities, for example). And by the 1830s, the Lake Champlain Transportation Company, incorporated by Vermont in 1826, enjoyed a virtual monopoly of the lake business (O'Hara 1984:125). But the Vermont iron industry came under the canal's classification of "foreign iron," and so was forced to pay the higher toll. What more benefit might the industry have gained had legislators at Montpelier cooperated earlier? What might the character of the Vermont (and New York) iron industry have been had preferential tolls not been established?

It has been the contention that coincident with the opening of the canal, New York and Albany money "discovered" the iron ore and water resources of the Adirondack Mountains. The numbers of ironworks in New York's Essex County increased from 4 to 24 with the canal's opening (O'Hara 1984:310-311). The canal did in fact stimulate some renewed ironworks activity at Vergennes with the construction of Rathbone's new blast furnace there and Ward's purchase and reopening in 1828 of what remained of the ill-fated Monkton Iron Company. But Crown Point and Port Henry, New York, some 20 miles up the lake from Vergennes, came to be the new seat of the iron business in the Champlain Valley. Port Henry became the largest shipping port for ores mined in the region, and by 1865 could boast of 8 blast furnaces, 20 forges, 3 rolling mills, and 2 foundries (O'Hara 1984:269-270). Within a few years of the canal's opening, the output from ironworks on the New York side of the lake appeared to have mortally wounded Vermont's earlier, significant position in the industry. But at whose profit and at whose expense? Surely not at the expense of some sharp-eyed, ambitious Vermont industrial families, who respected no state boundaries and who eagerly made their own killing in the industrial market alongside the Yorkers.

The Marriage Connection

Family interrelationships found in industrial expansions throughout the nation were also obvious in the iron industry in Vermont. The Penfield and Hammond families, for example, both involved in mills in the Pittsford area, were also involved in ironworks operations at Crown Point. They became closely related through marriage: Allen Penfield to Anna Hammond in 1810, Thomas Hammond to Sarah Penfield Stewart about 1820, and Augustus Hammond to Mary Penfield in 1839. Whether any of these marriages were arranged with business gain in mind is unknown, but they do indicate the tendency of families with similar industrial pursuits to socialize. In the process, loose business alliances were made between families, some capital may have supported either or another in-law's pursuits, and technical "family secrets" were probably discussed and shared.

John Penfield, born in Fairfield, Connecticut, in 1747, married Eunice Ogden, also of Fairfield, in 1770. Their 10 children were born before they arrived at Pittsford in 1795, at which time they purchased some land and a gristmill. A son, Allen Penfield, built a sawmill and later a gristmill at Crown Point in 1808. Two years later he married Anna Hammond and, together with his brother-in-law Charles F. Hammond, commenced to build an ironworks empire in New York. In 1812, Allen, John, and Sturgis Penfield (brothers), Thomas Hammond (Allen's father-in-law), and others formed the Pittsford Manufacturing Company, which carded and dressed woolen cloth.

Allen sold his shares in the mill in 1827 and the next year constructed his homestead in Crown Point at Ironville. He built the first forge at Ironville that year and a blast furnace a few miles west, nearer to the mines, in 1845. The works were operated by a company formed that year and composed of Allen Penfield, his brothers-in-law Charles F. and John C. Hammond, and Jonas Tower (of New York). In 1851, Tower sold his interest in the company to William H. Dike and Edwin Bogue, both of Pittsford. Dike's mother was the former Tamesin Hammond; Edwin Bogue was Dike's brother-in-law. Vermonters all, they organized the Crown Point Iron Company, and turned much iron into gold over the next decades.

Allen Penfield died in 1871 and was buried at Ironville, and the blast furnace was soon after shut down. His shares in the iron business and properties were sold to John and Thomas Hammond, who reorganized the company, built blast furnaces along Lake Champlain, and laid dozens of miles of railroad track between the mines and the furnaces. The community of Hammondville grew around the mines, located about 4 miles southwest of Ironville. When the ore ran out in 1893, everything shut down.

Thomas Hammond, progenitor of the Hammonds of Pittsford, arrived there in 1785. He was born in Newton, Massachusetts, raised at Leicester, Vermont, and served during the Revolution in the Continental Army. Returning to Vermont, he married Hannah Cross in 1784. The marriage accounted for much of his success, although he persevered also due to his own wits and skills in the wilderness and hardships of early Vermont. An active Congregationalist, he served in many local and state offices, and rose to the rank of colonel in the state militia by the War of 1812. The Hammonds, like the Penfields, had 10 children. Besides Anna, who married Allen Penfield, her brother Augustus married Mary Penfield, Allen Penfield's niece, in 1839. Augustus and Mary stayed in Pittsford, inherited the family homestead, and eventually purchased the homestead of Mary's father, Sturgis Penfield.

Another daughter of Sturgis Penfield was Eleanor B., who married Henry F. Lothrop of Pittsford in 1848. His father, Howard Lothrop, had worked at Israel Keith's blast furnace at Pittsford, rose to be its operating superintendent, and eventually, through wise investments, became owner of the works. He sold it to Gibbs & Company in 1809, retiring with a good profit. He arranged for his son, Henry F., to manage his investments (Huntington 1884).

When 57-year-old Thomas Hammond's wife Hannah died in 1819, he married Sarah Penfield Stewart, the oldest daughter of John and Eunice Penfield. The senior John Penfield, who had only recently become father-in-law to one of Thomas Hammond's children, had finally become father-in-law to Thomas Hammond himself (Hammond 1900).

Related to Wait Rathbone, Jr., who owned a blast furnace at Tinmouth, was cousin Joel Rathbone, who owned a stove foundry at Albany, New York, along with Lewis, John F., and Clarence Rathbone. These works were in the northern part of the city, where little Rathbone Street still runs parallel to Broadway, a few blocks northeast of the Colonie Street and Broadway railroad bridge. Also operating stove foundries in Albany about the same time was John S. Perry (no known relation to Abner Perry, partner to Wait Rathbone). The wife of John S. Perry was Mary J. Willard of Plattsburgh, no known relation to Elias Willard, another blast furnace owner at Tinmouth (Tenny 1886:140-149). Elias Willard shared a common great-grandfather with Dr. John Willard, husband of Emma Hart Willard of Berlin, Connecticut; Middlebury, Vermont; and Troy, New York (Willard 1858:395). Dr. William Willard (Elias Willard's brother) was husband of Mary Rathbone, sister of Wait Rathbone, Jr. (Cooley 1898:626-627).

John Conant came to Brandon in 1784, originally planning on settling in western New York State. But when he got as far as Brandon and met Charity Broughton, his travels were over. In addition to his ironworks activities, he was a leading force in the Baptist Church in the village, held a number of elected and appointed town and county posts, and built a number of mills. He married Charity the same year he arrived in Brandon and, along with his father-in-law Wait Broughton, established his early mills and ventures into the iron business in Brandon. John and Charity had nine children; two sons succeeded their father at the ironworks. One of them, John A., was the leading stockholder of the Rutland & Burlington Railroad when it opened in 1849, held several public posts, was part or full owner of a number of industrial interests, and was president of the Brandon Bank. He married Adelia A. Hammond, granddaughter of Thomas Hammond, in 1869. This was the second marriage for both, he then 69 and she 49 years of age, each by then quite wealthy. Adelia's mother was Paulina Austin, daughter of Appolos Austin, co-owner of the ironworks at Vergennes in 1836.

Other Vermont families involved in ironworks activities in New York were the Dikes and Bogues. Tamesin Hammond, sister of Anna Hammond Penfield and Augustus Hammond, became the wife of Jonathan Dike in 1808; Francis M. Hammond, daughter of Augustus and Mary Penfield Hammond, married C. F. Dike in 1868. Jonathan and Tamesin Hammond Dike moved to Crown Point where Jonathan died in 1870. Daughter Loraine H. married Dr. George Page, brother to the Vermont governor; another daughter, Mary E., married Edwin S. Bogue, whose cousin Catherine Bogue married Dr. Ebenezer H. Drury, nephew to Abel Drury (Barker Oct. 1942).

Members of the Fuller family worked at the Lenox Furnace, Massachusetts, and left in 1785 along with Gamaliel Leonard for Hampton, New York, just across the Poultney River from Fair Haven. Roger and Harvey Fuller worked a forge at Brandon in 1810. The year 1818 found four brothers of Ferrisburgh—Stillman, Sheldon, Heman, and Ashbell Fuller—operating Herreshoff's Forge at "John Brown's Tract," somewhere deep in the northern Adirondack Mountains. They were at the Rossie Iron Works in 1820, where David Parish entered into a contract with S. Fullers & Company to run the furnace and forge for a term of five years. In 1832, the four brothers were in the Town of Fowler in southern St. Lawrence County, where they built a blast furnace that went into operation in 1833. The settlement that grew around the ironworks included Fuller's store, with Heman Fuller as Postmaster in 1832, and came to be called Fullerville, later (1848) Fullerville Iron Works. The name is still on New York State highway maps. Successive companies were S. Fuller & Company, Fullers & Maddock, Fullers & Peck, and H. Fuller & Company. Stillman Fuller was Town Supervisor in 1830 and 1833–1834; Heman Fuller served that office in 1846–1847. Under later owners, the Fullerville blast furnace ran until 1882. Another Fuller enterprise was in the Town of Brasher in the northeast corner of the county, where Stillman Fuller built a blast furnace, put into operation in 1836. He sold it two years later and the community is still known as Brasher Iron Works (R. S. Allen letter to author Sept. 20, 1988).

A ca.-1835 blast furnace north of Crown Point near East Moriah, New York, was built by a Mr. Colburn, possibly Edward or Edmund Colburn (spelled Coburn by some). This Colburn may have been related to the Colburns of Fair Haven. John Peabody Colburn built a blast furnace along the Poultney River in 1825 just below Carver's Falls in West Haven. After the death of his first wife, he married Lucy Davey, daughter of Jacob Davey who was then major owner of the vast ironworks at Fair Haven. The Colburns came to Vermont from Canada about 1787, settling in Fair Haven, and became involved with the Davey families in many activities. Descendants of John P. settled in various parts of Vermont and the United States (Gordon and Coburn 1913).

Gamaliel Leonard, whose 1788 forge in Fair Haven along the Poultney River was one of the earliest forges in Vermont, was a descendant of the same James Leonard who landed about 20 years after the Pilgrims and is credited with building the first forge in this country. Gamaliel was also involved with blast furnaces at Lenox, Massachusetts, and New Haven, Vermont. His son Charles married John P. Colburn's sister Betsey, and at her death he married the other sister (Adams 1870:428).

The first blast furnace erected in northern New York State was built about 1809 at the mouth of the Salmon River, just south of Plattsburgh. It is thought to have been the work of Alfred Keith (Israel Keith's brother), who was also involved with a furnace at Rossie, New York, in addition to his own ironworks at Sheldon. Jacob Saxe (spelled Sax by some), the son of John Saxe (Saxe's Mills, Highgate), became a partner in the furnace at Salmon River under the name Keith & Saxe. Jacob Saxe was sole owner in 1820 and acquired land up and down the west side of the lake, including an ore bed at Crown Point that supported the needs of his furnace. Saxe's furnace and works were washed away by a freshet in 1830. He married Rowena Keith in 1812. Jacob W. Saxe, one of their sons, married Grace B. Drury. Matthew Saxe, brother to the senior Jacob Saxe, was also involved in the iron business in northern New York. His family settled in the Town of Chazy, near what became Saxe's Landing, today's Chazy Landing, New York (Seavor 1930).

About the time Keith was building the furnace at Salmon River, Abel Drury was operating the first blast furnace at Highgate. The Drury family had settled in Pittsford about the same time as the Keith family, striking up an acquaintance and apparently discovering their mutual interest in the ironworks business (although no previous connection can be found between the Drury family and iron making). Hannah Drury married Alfred Keith in 1793 and within five years some of his sons plus some of the Drurys moved north to Sheldon and Highgate. In addition to Drury's 1807 furnace at Highgate and Keith's 1798 and 1823 furnaces at Sheldon, they cooperated in a furnace at Highgate in 1820. Abel Drury married Sarah Keith and two of their children, Zephaniah Keith Drury and Sarah Keith Drury married Hannah Saxe and Peter Saxe, niece and nephew to Jacob Saxe. Besides being closely related to each other, the Drury, Keith, and Saxe families were all very active in town and county government, serving in various elected and appointed posts from 1800 to 1864 (Anderson Sept. 1939; Saxe 1930). In 1798 members of the Keith, Gibbs, Leach, and other families emigrated to Canada to settle on a tract of land "on which to erect an ironworks for several persons who intend removing to the province [Ontario], 1,200 acres for the use of the works, 600 acres for Union Keith, Unite Keith, Jonathan Keith, Ruel Keith . . . Rufus Leach . . . Nathan Gibbs . . . Ebenezer Gibbs . . . Scotland Keith . . . each of these 17,200 acres . . . most all were Loyalists. . . ." (Blanchard Jan. 1956:63-64).

All these Keiths were probably brothers of Israel and Alfred Keith. Ebenezer Gibbs and Ruel Keith had land transactions at Pittsford in 1795; Ruel returned from Canada and died at Sheldon in 1837. Nathan Gibbs, who had bought Israel Keith's furnace at Pittsford in 1795, returned and died there in 1824. Rufus Leach might have been Andrew's brother, who owned the Pittsford furnace after the death of Nathan Gibbs (Chessman 1898).

Many of the individuals and families mentioned, all involved to some degree in the iron business from the 1780s to 1850s, became related or interrelated in time. With similar industrial interests, they were able to capitalize on the iron industry outside Vermont and on both sides of Lake Champlain. Table 1-1 shows these families and their family ties and ironworks affiliations in Vermont, Massachusetts, and New York State. Other Vermont families not previously discussed (for example, the Granger family) also had ironworks activities outside the states included in the table.

Up and Down the Iron Roller Coaster

By the 1840s the period of Vermont ironworks expansion had peaked and in the midst of the national economic slump of the 1850s had come to a near halt. Only the needs of the Civil War offered stimulus to drag a handful of Vermont iron-making operations along with it. The prominence of iron manufacture in Vermont had been lost (Swank 1892:99).

During its formative years, however, Vermont rivaled neighboring New York, Massachusetts, and New Hampshire in the mining and smelting of iron. It might be difficult to prove that during that early period the Monkton Iron Company was the largest ironworks in the United States, although it was so claimed (see chapter 4, AD-146); but that wrought and cast

Table 1-1. Vermont Families—Ironworks Affiliations

Vermont Family Name	Vermont Ironworks	New York Ironworks	Massachusetts Ironworks
Hammond	Bennington(?) Forest Dale(?)	Crown Point	
Austin	Vergennes		
Conant	Brandon		
Broughton	Brandon		
Penfield		Crown Point Troy	
Lothrop	Pittsford		
Harwood		Crown Point	
Bogue		Crown Point	
Drury	Highgate		
Saxe	Highgate	Plattsburgh	
Keith	Pittsford Sheldon Highgate Vergennes(?)	Plattsburgh Rossie	Easton
Page		Crown Point	
Dike		Crown Point	
Cooley	Pittsford		
Sutherland	Proctor		
Perry	Tinmouth	Albany	
Willard	Tinmouth	Albany(?)	
Rathbone	Tinmouth Clarendon Vergennes	Albany	
Davey	Middlebury Fair Haven Salisbury	Troy(?)	
Colburn	Fair Haven West Haven	Moriah(?)	
Leonard	Fair Haven New Haven		Lenox
Fuller	Ferrisburgh Vergennes(?)	Fowler Rossie Brasher Troy(?)	Lenox

iron were reduced in forges and furnaces located in over 50 towns and cities in Vermont may come as a surprise to those whose impression of this state's early history was one of strictly agriculture and rural industry. Blast furnaces and molten iron definitely are not rural industry. Yet the character of the iron industry in Vermont and in most surrounding states in that period was rural. Although physically large, blast furnaces were usually operated by workers who lived within sight of the stack, and who tended backyard gardens and animal pens to augment their needs during the non-productive winter months and the ever-threatening cycles of economic depression. These iron-works communities were located as near to the mines as available waterpower permitted, thus further isolating many of them from the centers of population growth and further contributing to their rural character.

During the 10-year period following the end of the Revolutionary War, 16 forges and 3 blast furnaces were erected in Vermont for the production of wrought and cast iron. These were this state's initial iron-making industries and they signaled the entry of the state into nearly a century of sometimes successful (but usually frustrating) battle with nature, politics, and economics. The fortunes of these works rested on 18th-century educated estimates of the probable quantity and quality of a local ore bed, and political foot-dragging that caused a 20-year delay in building the canal to connect Lake Champlain with the Hudson River. By the early 19th century, ironworks had to deal with special interests that ran import tariffs up and down, causing all manner of havoc in the national economy. In his economics analysis of 19th-century America, Stuart Fleming wrote:

More than technological limitations, however, it was

1-7. *An 1830s blast furnace deep in the Adirondacks of New York; typical of contemporary Vermont blast furnaces (Masten 1923:facing 132).*

quirks of economic events that held back the American iron industry in the first half of the nineteenth century.

Three recessions, one in 1808 stemming from the trade embargo imposed a year earlier by the Jefferson administration, and one each in 1819 and 1837 (caused by business panics), did not help. Nor did the protective tariffs enacted by Congress in 1815 to foster "infant industries" and help make the American states more self-sufficient. The tariffs actually subsidized inefficiency and technological stagnation in the iron industry, and failed to encourage the formation of the kind of corporate groups which, by 1825, made the English ironmasters such a major political force. The English could (and did) sometimes dump their iron on the iron market at below cost, just to ensure nervousness among investors in American concerns. Who was going to put up capital for a furnace of say 600 cubic meter capacity, if a year later a slackening of demand would force it to run about 60 percent effectiveness? (Fleming Sept./Oct. 1985:71, 77).

When the United States Congress directed the 1809 census to include the manufacturing companies of the country, the Vermont General Assembly appointed a committee of one from each county in Vermont to prepare a statement of the state's manufactures. Their November 7 report on ironworks included the following data:

Counties	Furnaces	Forges
Bennington	1	3
Rutland	3	6
Addison	2	15
Franklin	2	2

The furnace and forge at Vergennes, which are included in the above statement, have been erected by a company from Boston. The furnace has been in blast for some time, and it is said to yield from 60 to 70 cwt. of pig iron and ware each 24 hours. The forge is calculated for eight fires, solely for the purpose of refining, all of which fires it expected will be ready to commence the business in a few weeks. The owners of the works have it in contemplation to extend them to the manufacturing of steel and iron-mongery in their various branches. There is also a slitting mill at Vergennes, and one at Fairhaven, where the rolling and slitting of iron is carried on to a large extent, and it is believed with handsome profits to the owners. . . . Jacob Galusha (Walton vol. 5 1877:500-501).

U.S. Census returns of 1810 indicated Vermont forges and furnaces produced about 1,300 tons of pig and bar iron that year, amounting to 36 percent of New York and 55 percent of Massachusetts output. And although Vermont iron production increased more than five times by the 1840 census, it had slipped to 48 percent of Massachusetts and well back of New York, which had increased its iron output 23 times. Of its neighboring states, only New Hampshire remained behind Vermont in iron production:

	Blast Furnaces		Bloomeries		Iron Output	
	1810	1840	1810	1840	1810	1840
Massachusetts	--	48	--	67	2,340	15,336
New Hampshire	--	15	--	1	--	1,420*
New York	11	186	7	120	3,671	83,781
Vermont	8	26	2	14	1,300*	7,398

*estimated by author

Breakdown of 1840 census data of Vermont ironworks reveals the disposition of these works, but some of the data are misleading. The census listing of the furnaces, for instance, includes blast, forge, and foundry furnaces. Lack of responses from some works to census takers (usually the local federal marshal) or exaggerated claims by others (to impress the stockholders?) distort the numbers. Results of the census, however, as shown in table 1-2, do provide a sense of the disposition and magnitude of the Vermont iron industry for the 1830–1840 period.

Vermont never was destined to become a major iron-making region. Its harder magnetic ores, for example, contained just enough manganese impurity to affect the quality of the cast iron. Mountain streams that afforded some of the best water-power sites to drive waterwheels and turbines also plagued mills with flash floods:

1783: Poultney River	1830: New Haven River	1869: New Haven River
1811: Poultney River	1831: Middlebury River	1898: Roaring Branch (in
1813: Missisquoi River	1847: Middlebury River	Woodford and Bennington)
1828: Lamoille River	1852: La Platte River	

These floods, called freshets when occurring in springtime thaws, were usually triggered by heavy rains in the local mountains, which washed away everything in their paths. (One particularly devastating torrent in west-central Vermont in 1783 caused the Poultney River to flood and wash across a half-mile bend in the river and erode a new path to Carver's Falls, leaving one West Haven sawmill high and dry along the old riverbed.) Forges and mills that had been operating only marginally but might have been able to survive a pressing economic slump to better times could not afford to rebuild after being washed away.

Then there were the long Vermont winters. In the 1850s, at the end of the disastrous economic depression, James Lesley wrote: "Besides this [the Green Mountain Furnace], there have been no blast furnaces running in Vermont for some years. There stand two in Sheldon, Franklin Co., 9 miles east of St. Albans; one in Troy, Orleans Co; one in Plymouth, Windsor Co., Tysons; two in Bennington, Bennington Co., and two in Dorset, on the Western Vermont Railroad, between Bennington and Rutland. The heavy snows make it difficult to get stock and unless such lignite beds, as the one used by Conant Furnace be discovered elsewhere, the dearness of charcoal and the scarcity of ore will prevent this from becoming a principal furnace district again" (Lesley 1858:76).

Table 1-2. Ironworks Census of 1840

County	Furnaces	Tons of Iron	Number of Forges, Bloomeries, and Rolling Mills	Tons of Iron	Tons of Charcoal	Number of Workers	Capital Invested
Addison	1	100	8	360	1,716	32	$ 44,000
Bennington	5	1,829	--	--	380,880*	184	165,000
Caledonia	1	30	--	--	200	15	6,000
Orleans	1	382	1	5	930	25	100,000
Rutland	11	3,365	5	290	2,832	363	275,050
Washington	1	100	--	--	150	11	5,000
Windham	2	87	--	--	29	2	4,800
Windsor	4	850	--	--	1,670	156	64,300
Totals:	26	6,743	14	655	10,084**	788	$664,150

*most likely bushels of charcoal
**author's estimate; includes (*) above

Chapter 2
Forges, Furnaces, and Foundries

In the iron business there are blast furnaces, puddling furnaces, heating furnaces, air furnaces, cupolas, and more. Each has a size, shape, and purpose. Some are associated with each other, some are not. As if to further confuse the unwary researcher, many cartographers, historians, and U.S. Census takers right down to the present insist on identifying anything connected with ironworks as a furnace, without further qualification. These include blacksmith shops, foundries, bloomeries, and even charcoal kilns and lime kilns.

Iron was initially made in Vermont, as elsewhere, by two distinctly different processes, depending on whether the desired product was cast iron or wrought iron. Cast iron is iron that contains significant amounts of carbon and is too hard to hammer. It was molded (cast) into desired shapes such as potash kettles, tools, stove plates, machine gears, or ingots. Cast iron,

also called pig iron after being molded into ingots, was made in a blast furnace, so named for the large blast of air that was needed to maintain the high temperatures within the stack. Wrought iron, on the other hand, is a relatively soft, carbon-free iron, which can be easily hammered into horseshoes, wheel rims, or plows, or drawn into rods to make nails. It was made in a bloomery forge, so named because the initial product of the forge was an approximately 100-pound (1-cwt) bar called a bloom.

The Bloomery Forge

The availability of forests to provide fuel for making charcoal did as much to dictate location of the bloomery forge site as did the site's proximity to waterpower. Bits of slag in Near

2-1. *Refining iron with a trip-hammer. Note heavy wood beam above the hammer, which the hammer "bounced" against while being lifted upward, thrusting the hammer down on the anvil with more force than if merely dropped at its height (Diderot 1763: plate 96).*

2-2. *A working reconstruction of an 18th-century bloomery forge at Colonial Williamsburg, Virginia.*

Eastern deserts betray an ancient catastrophic loss of local forests for making charcoal, at a time when the primitive methods of iron making consumed 70 pounds of charcoal for every pound of iron produced (Fleming, July/Aug. 1983:66).

Contrary to popular thought, unlimited hardwood forests were not everywhere available in the American Colonies to supply charcoal. The expensively high ratio of charcoal consumption to iron bar production caused many to consider bloomery forges as wasteful. One of these areas was Pennsylvania, where few bloomeries existed. There the blast furnace came into use instead from almost the birth of this frontier industry. The reverse was true in New England, where bloomeries thrived (Bining 1973:65). Colonial New England iron was therefore made primarily in bloomeries (Pearse 1876:101). Vermont was no exception; there were many more bloomeries than blast furnaces.

Many of the early New England ironworks contained "complete works"—both blast furnace and bloomeries—rather than just one type of forge. These New England works were generally categorized as follows: (1) *smelting furnaces* reduced crushed rock-bearing ore into pigs, with unlimited charcoal supply; (2) *refinery forges* imported pig iron from New York, Pennsylvania, and Maryland furnaces and converted it into bar iron; (3) *bloomery forges* reduced directly from bog ore (without an intermediary furnace operation) into blooms—much inferior to those refined from pigs; (4) *"bog ore"* furnaces reduced bog ore and mainly cast hollowware (Bining 1973:28).

Few records dealing with the operations of forges in colonial America have survived but it is assumed the forge procedures and design in Vermont followed the English pattern. Generally, the English forge had two hearths (called fires in the 1780s and 1790s) to each trip-hammer. Plans of the forge at the 17th-century ironworks at Saugus, Massachusetts, contained this ratio. The 1765 forge at Charlotteburg, New Jersey, had two sets of this 2-to-1 hearth–to–trip-hammer arrangement, each

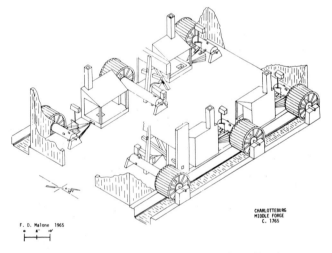

2-3. *Ground plan of a bloomery forge at Charlotteburg, New Jersey, about 1765; typical in both layout of apparatus and area as those built by Ira Allen in Vermont during the 1780s (Lenik 1974:10).*

set using about 2,000 square feet of floor space (Lenik 1974:10). Ira Allen contracted for a forge at Tinmouth in 1791 with two fires. A year later he contracted for another forge in Shelburne measuring 50 by 40 feet, or 2,000 square feet (Wilbur vol. 2 1928:6, 27). Matthew Lyon sold his "two south fires together with a hammer, anvil, and coal house" at Fair Haven in 1794 (Adams 1870:142). It seems, therefore, that Vermont's earliest bloomeries, at least, followed somewhat in the pattern of English and colonial American bloomeries.

Vermont bloomeries in the early 1800s were the latest improved version of the old Catalan forge (Overman 1850:245). No longer a small cup-shaped device, it had evolved to a 6- to 8-foot-square stonework table called the hearth, with a place for the fire 24 to 30 inches square, recessed 15 to 18 inches of the expert bloomer. When he judged the time had come, the bloomer separated the last significant parts of the slag from the charge and lifted what had now become a bloom out of the hearth with heavy, long-handled iron tongs. If the bloom was no larger than a basketball in size, it may have weighed about 100 pounds (not including the weight of the tongs) and could be lifted out by a single bloomer. But if the hearth capacity was larger, the bloom might weigh up to 500 pounds. That size bloom required lifting by two or more workers with specially large tongs that were sometimes connected waist-high by chains to an overhead support beam. The ironworkers could then swivel the bloom up and out of the hearth to an adjacent anvil where the bloom was worked on by a trip-hammer to

2-4. *Wood and leather bellows, such as this one with an iron tuyere attached, provided forced draft for many early bloomery forges.*

deep into one corner of the hearth. The hearth was 3 to 4 feet high. Through the back wall was an iron nozzle called the tuyere, which directed the preheated draft that was provided by the wooden bellows and waterwheel. These were early predecessors to the Champlain Forge, which reduced magnetic ores. The Lake Champlain region, both the Vermont and New York sides, was regarded industry-wide as containing the best-known deposits of the time.

To reduce the ore in a bloomery, first the hearth was lined with charcoal, then coarse iron ore placed against the wall of the hearth opposite the tuyere, the fire set, and the draft gently directed against the ore. Charcoal and ore were added as the process continued, 400 pounds of ore being a common charge. Charcoal was piled 2 to 3 feet high against the back wall above the hearth. After 1½ to 2 hours the charge was reduced to a hot (but not red-hot) mass, pasty in consistency, like taffy or cold molasses. It was the skill and experience of the bloomer that made the critical difference whether the soft iron mass could be separated from enough charcoal and non-iron elements to result in a bloom of marketable value. Poor iron, with too high a ratio of non-iron elements remaining in the product, resembled no more than one large chunk of slag. The resulting bloom was therefore subject to considerable variation, depending on whether the bloomer considered the economy of charcoal or ore the object. By manipulating the tuyere to save charcoal he obtained a small yield of iron; or, he obtained more iron by burning more charcoal.

Good bloomers worked the iron mass in the hearth with long iron tools, slowly applying moderate draft, and turning and folding the charge (much like a baker kneading dough). The bloomer's job was to concentrate the iron within the charge into a coherent ball of iron, working out pieces of stone and non-iron material. Some of the non-iron material might melt and run out of the charge as droplets of slag, but usually the charge looked like one large mass of debris, except to the eye

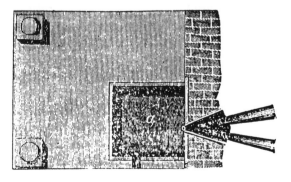

2-5. *Vertical section of bloomery fire (top); plan at hearth level (bottom). Hearth at point "a" (Overman 1850:246).*

squeeze out the non-iron particles, returned to the hearth for further heating, then underwent repeated hammering. The process eventually shaped the bloom into a long, thick bar, which could be rolled into smaller bars and cut into individual 1-cwt pieces (merchant iron). Waste material left in the hearth, although much of it contained iron, was cleaned out and discarded. The hearth was recharged before it cooled and the process repeated.

The bloomery process obviously wasted much good iron, especially at bloomeries that operated before 1800, when American bloomers had not fully developed the necessary skills and hearths had not incorporated the latest technology. The British made sure the American Colonies did not have access to the latest developments from Europe. Slag from many early bloomeries contained so much reworkable iron that some of the slag heaps were later "mined" and remelted.

Slag from many early- to mid-19th-century Vermont bloomery sites is likewise dark and heavy, loaded with wasted iron. Not shiny and light in weight like slag from blast furnaces, bloomery slag is dull-looking, appearing like something from outer space. Hefting a piece in one hand while holding a similar-size rock in the other will immediately betray the difference in weight, the heavier being the slag.

Despite later improvements, the bloomery process remained an apparently inefficient one. Yet it remained popular because the bloomery forge required a much smaller initial investment of money and labor than that of building a blast furnace. Whereas the blast furnace, once fired, had to remain in continual day-and-night operation, month after month, the bloomery cycle ended with each final removal of the bloom from the hearth. The bloomery consumed much less fuel and time to come to temperature as compared to the large blast furnace, which took days to slowly bring up to operating temperature. The bloomery could more easily respond to fluctuations in the supply of ore and fuel, and to demands of the market. And since the domestic needs of blacksmiths who were making horseshoes and door hinges could be better met by the direct ore-reduction process of the bloomery, these small ironworks tucked away in mountain hollows became more significant contributors to the market needs of early Vermont than did the blast furnace.

On an average, it took 4 tons of ore and 300 bushels of charcoal to make a ton of iron. In Vermont bloomeries, where the rich magnetic ores were worked, a ton of iron in the 1840s cost about $40 to make. An ironworker earned an average of $10 per ton (Overman 1850:247-248).

There are numerous references to trip-hammers and trip-hammer shops throughout town and county histories. Trip-hammers were large, ponderous, and noisy hammers that might have been associated with a forge, but could also have been involved in other activities, including welding, plating, hammering edges on axes and knives, or stamping out small pieces of copper, iron, bronze, or leather for various mechanical, decorative, or architectural needs. Stamping did not require much hammering force and as such, the hammers were quite small, on the order of 10- to 40-pound hammerheads and anvils. They were all waterpowered, but being small operations, could have been set up in modest shops near any small streams.

Most trip-hammers were associated with blacksmith shops or small foundries. Hammers usually did not involve any furnace beyond a small charcoal hearth to heat metal, which made it easier to plate, edge, or stamp. Welding required an intense heat, enough to bring the metal to a cherry-red brightness before hammering, requiring a larger, bellows-driven heating furnace. Small welds, such as for wagon wheel rims, could be done by the blacksmith's rhythmical hammer. Larger welds for repairing cracked or broken castings were relegated to the trip-hammer at the forge. Both were noisy and scattered many sparks, much to the amusement of spectators.

The hammers used at the forge had hammerheads weighing from 50 to 400 pounds. For drawing small-diameter iron, such as for nail rod, a hammerhead of 50 pounds was sufficient.

2-6. *Tilt hammer and foundation pilings (left) and helve ring (center). The helve ring served as the strong fulcrum on which the full weight of the helve rested (Overman 1850:335).*

Forging 60- to 100-pound blooms required a hammerhead of 300 to 400 pounds. These heads were made of strong-quality cast iron and were secured to the business end of the helve by wooden wedges. The other end of the helve was acted on by the waterwheel (Overman 1850:336-339).

In the usual arrangement, a cam wheel driven by the waterwheel struck forcibly downward on the helve, which, pivoting on a horizontal pin near its middle, raised the hammerhead end. The closer the pivot pin was located to the cam wheel end of the helve, the higher the hammerhead would be raised (much like adjusting a seesaw), and thus more striking force on the anvil would be obtained. But then a more powerful waterwheel was required (putting the heavier person at the short end of the seesaw), due to the additional torque now added to the hammer. Hickory or oak was most commonly used for making the helve.

The anvil, upon which the hammer worked the iron, equaled the hammerhead in weight. It was attached to the cut end of a 4-foot-diameter log that extended lengthwise 6 to 8 feet into the ground. Under that, a platform of pilings secured the anvil to a stable platform. At many forge sites long since abandoned or destroyed by fire, the location of the anvil is still marked by its deeply buried foundation. With that located, the rest of the forge remains can be approximated and found.

The cam wheel did not merely raise the hammerhead to let it drop to the anvil. When striking its end of the helve, it caused the opposite (bottom) edge of the helve to bounce off a large piece of timber. This bounce imparted to the hammerhead the effect of a recoil and dramatically increased its striking force on the anvil. The faster the hammering speed (either by increasing the rotational speed of the waterwheel or by additional cams on the cam wheel), the greater the hammering force due to increased recoil action.

Hammers of this type were called German forge hammers, but they were commonly known in Vermont as trip-hammers or tilt hammers, from the actions of the mechanisms. A variation of the forge hammer that was more common in Europe had the cam wheel raising the hammerhead at that end, and was known as the T-hammer. By the 1840s, when most water-driven hammers were being replaced by steam hammers, bloomeries in Vermont were still utilizing the cheap and abundant water resources of the state. Only in foundries and heavy machine shops did steam, and later hydraulic, hammers make their appearance.

The process of hammering blooms was known in some sectors of the industry as shingling. It was usually used more in terms of hammering to remove (or squeeze out) solid bits of impurities such as slag, small stones, or unburned charcoal, rather than hammering the bloom into a uniformly shaped bar. A type of hammerhead with a beveled face called a squeezer was sometimes employed for shingling. An "iron and shingle mill," therefore, did not refer to the manufacture of house shingles.

Another process of producing wrought iron was to refine pig iron from the blast furnace and convert it in the puddling furnace. Refining meant cleansing the pig iron of most of its carbon and other impurities. It was called a puddling furnace because the pig iron was melted in a reverberatory-shaped chamber and worked in "puddles" into pasty balls, similar to the bloomery process. The puddling process took advantage of a major difference between wrought and cast iron: how their carbon content inversely affected their respective melting points. Cast iron, with a higher carbon content, melted at a lower temperature, about 2,100° F, whereas practically carbon-free wrought iron melted at about 2,500°F (Schuhmann 1906). The heat in the puddling furnace was maintained high enough to melt the pig iron, but just short of the melting point of wrought iron. Additionally, by burning charcoal in one hearth and drawing the hot flaming gases over and through an adjoining hearth containing the pig iron, the iron was melted and its carbon burned away. Physical separation of the iron and charcoal in this horizontal-type furnace prevented charcoal car-

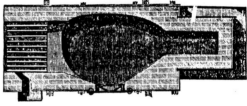

2-7. *Vertical section (above) and ground plan (below) of puddling furnace, showing the fire chamber and grate (left), hearth (center), and chimney (right). The puddler worked the iron through the door at the center, top view; and bottom, lower view (Overman 1850:264-265).*

bon from replacing burned-away carbon. In the foundry, this separation-type furnace was known as an air furnace.

Puddlers stirred the molten iron with long iron rods that reached into the furnace through little holes in its side walls. The stirring action continuously brought higher-carbon iron from below the surface to be exposed to the carbon-consuming flames. As the carbon content of the iron was reduced, and therefore its melting point dropped, the iron commenced to congeal (come to nature). Lumps of this purified iron were removed from the furnace and worked at the hammer much like the bloom of the bloomery process. The puddling furnace product, however, was much more pure than that of the bloomery. The resultant iron bars hammered from puddled iron were called puddle bars or muck bars. They were cut into pieces 2 to 4 feet long, piled in stacks weighing upward to a ton, reheated in another furnace specially designed for this purpose (called a heating furnace), and each piece was finally rolled into merchant bars.

With the development and proliferation of puddling furnaces, a controversy arose regarding the quality of wrought iron made by the direct method—the bloomery—and the indirect method—puddled pig iron from the blast furnace. In the 1850s, when the two operations were operating neck-in-neck for supremacy, the consensus was in favor of the bloomery. One reason was that bloomeries produced in smaller quantities. This was an age when small quantity was still considered superior to large; only 25 years later the theme would switch to "big is better." The puddling furnace, which was consuming much more charcoal per ton of merchant bar, would evolve into an efficient process capable of turning out a most superior wrought iron from the most questionable grades of pig iron.

One significant improvement to the Catalan forge was made

2-8. *Interior view of the forge at Jay, New York, in 1888. Man in the right foreground is lying in a charcoal basket (courtesy Adirondack Museum).*

in the Adirondack bloomeries during the early 19th century. It consisted of preheating the blast, which was never done with the earliest Catalan forges (Swank 1892:107). The improvement seems to have been copied at the Fair Haven Iron Works; an 1866 description of the bloomeries includes three arched pipes for preheating the blast above each bloomery hearth (Neilson 1866:227). Since it was an American improvement, it became known as the American Bloomery, although in the New York and New England area it was called the Champlain Forge (Egleston Sept. 1879:515). "The Catalan Forge in this country took the form of the Champlain Forge, which had the blast heated by the waste flames from the forge. These waste flames heated a coil through which the blast was blown, thereby cutting down the fuel requirement. The Champlain Forge, of considerable importance in the development of the early iron industry in the northern Appalachian areas, was capable of producing an iron with an almost complete absence of phosphorus and sulfur" (Kirk and Othmer vol. 8 1952:25).

Physical details of the Champlain Forge were described in 1879 as follows:

The furnace in which the ore is reduced and the bloom is made consists of a series of cast-iron plates, 2 to 3 inches in thickness, securely fastened together, forming a rectangular opening, which, at the bottom, varies from 24 to 30 inches, at right angles to the tuyere, and 27 to 32 inches parallel to it. On the back side, parallel to the tuyere, it is 28 to 36 inches high. On the front this plate is cut down to from 15 to 19 inches, to make a place for a small platform, or shelf, called a fore plate. The bellows space, where the operation of reduction is carried on, is thus rectangular in shape, and is called the firebox. Its walls are usually vertical, except the fore and skew plates, which are generally inclined, but sometimes they are made to incline outward at the rate of 1 inch in 7.

Each one of the plates forming the sides of the furnace had a name and a special duty. They are sometimes made of more than one piece, and are not always of exactly the same shape, nor are they always put together in exactly the

same way in different works, but the variations are not very essential. Their size varies also with capacity of the furnace, but their office is the same in all. Those plates most exposed to the direct action of the fire are usually cast with holes in them, into which pieces, called repair pieces, are made to fit, so that they can easily be removed and replaced when worn out (Egleston Sept. 1879:518-519).

Another contemporary report described the hearth area varying from 27 by 30 inches to 28 by 32 inches, with the height from 20 to 25 inches above the tuyeres and 8 to 14 inches below:

In the East Middlebury forges this bottom plate is 4 inches thick and has within it a hollow space of 4 inches. The side plates, which slope gently inward in descending, and rest on ledges on the bottom-plate, are 1¼ inches thick. A water box, measuring 12 by 8 inches, is let into the twyer-plate [*sic*], and a stream of cold water circulates through this box and through the bottom plate, as well as around the twyer. The length of the hearth, from the twyer plate to that opposite, is 24½ inches, and the breadth from front to rear is 29 inches. The twyer enters 12 inches above the bottom, and is inclined downwards at such an angle that the blast would strike the middle of the hearth. The opening of the twyer has the form of the segment of a circle, and is 1 inch high by 1¾ inches wide. In front of the furnace, at 16 inches from the bottom, is placed a flat iron hearth, 18 inches wide. The side plate beneath it is provided with a tap hole, through which the melted slag or cinder may be drawn off from time to time. The iron plates used in the construction of these furnaces last for 2 years.

At East Middlebury . . . the estimated consumption of charcoal was 270 bushels to the ton of blooms, a result which is the mean of the figures obtained at the New Russia [N.Y.] forges. Some of the ores here used contain a little phosphate of lime, and it was observed that when too hot a blast was used, although the production of metal was rapid, the iron from these ores was hot-short, while with the cold blast, formerly employed, the iron, although pro-

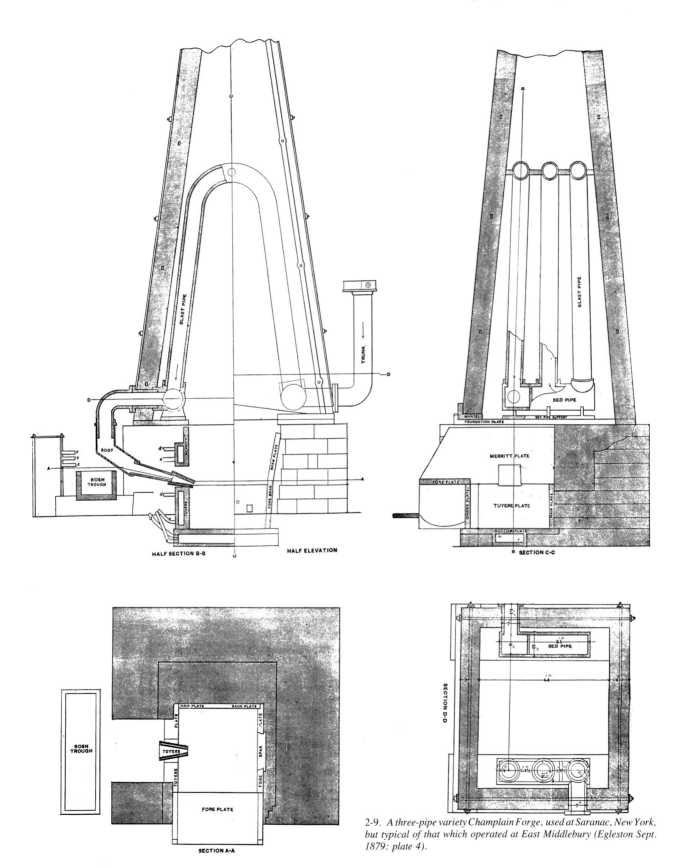

2-9. *A three-pipe variety Champlain Forge, used at Saranac, New York, but typical of that which operated at East Middlebury (Egleston Sept. 1879: plate 4).*

duced more slowly, was never hot-short. The force of the blast at these forges was equal to 1¾ pounds and even 2 pounds to the inch. Mr. Pearson, the director of the East Middlebury forges, made, in the autumn of 1867, experiments on several tons of the iron sands from Seven Islands [Sept-Îles, Québec] and succeeded in obtaining from them about ⅜ths of their weight of good iron. He, however, found it necessary in order to treat these fine sands, to reduce very much the force of the blast. . . . It appears to be from ignorance of this fact, that the bloomers of New York had always rejected the fine sandy ore separated during the process of washing, as being unsuited for treatment in the bloomery fire (Hunt 1870:277-280).

Tools required at a typical Champlain Forge (Egleston Sept. 1879:536) were:

Bloom tongs	Foss hook	Sledge, 3 pound
Turn-bat	Cinder bar	Hammer, 1½ pound
Billet tongs	Tapping bar	Fore bar
Ore shovel	Furgen	Anvil
Fire shovel	Wringer	Piggin

The U.S. Census of 1860 recorded three bloomery forges still operating in Vermont, the only report of such forges yet in operation throughout New England. The bloomeries reported an output of 1,400 tons of blooms. Neilson's 1866 report notes, however, that Vermont did not become the solitary producer of blooms until 1864, the last year that the bloomery fires ran at the Franklin Forge, New Hampshire. The only other bloomery then in New England was at Falls Village, Connecticut, which by that time had not run for some years (Neilson 1866:232-236). Vermont bloomeries were replaced by larger specialized operations such as the National Horse Nail Company at Vergennes. Some of the smaller forges continued supplying local blacksmith and foundry needs until cheaper puddled iron from outside the state closed them down. In the post-Civil War period bloomeries continued at East Middlebury, Fair Haven, and Salisbury. By the time the East Middlebury bloomery closed in 1890, the significance of Vermont's superior Lake Champlain magnetic ores had already passed into history (Swank 1892:113).

The Blast Furnace

The early 19th-century blast furnace structure, or stack, was generally 25 to 30 feet square at its base and 30 to 40 feet high. The outer walls were made of hard stone masonry and were either vertical or slightly sloping inward as they rose upward so that the top flat area was less than the base area. Rather than having the fuel and ore carried up steps and ramps alongside the stack, the furnace was built beside an embankment, with a stone or wooden bridge laid from the bank to the top of the furnace. Across this bridge, workers known as bridgemen carried ore and fuel in wheelbarrows, emptying them into the furnace through an opening at the top.

The construction of such a heavy structure required very special attention to the foundation and to the nature of the

2-10. *Typical pocket, or "testing" furnace, for testing the ore before investing in a full-size blast furnace stack. Note the foot-operated bellows at left (Fisher 1949:18).*

ground on which it was to be built. Poor ground preparation could result in the stack shifting under the combined weight of the structure plus its load of molten iron. The effect could be a fatal rupture of the blast furnace itself.

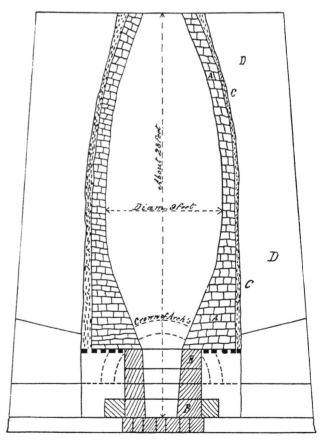

2-11. *Inside configuration of a late-18th-century furnace showing the rough nature of the stone bosh lining (Salisbury Iron 1878:4).*

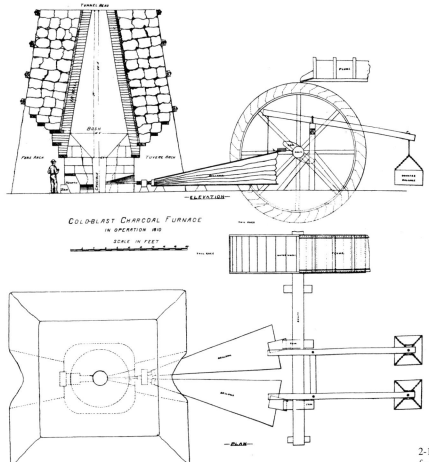

COLD-BLAST CHARCOAL FURNACE
IN OPERATION 1810
SCALE IN FEET

2-12. *Plan of a ca.-1810 cold-blast charcoal furnace showing side view (above) and top view (below) through the furnace.*

During the 1780–1810 period when Vermont was experiencing its first large influx of settlers, the iron industry nationwide still consisted of a large number of relatively small furnace and forge operations. The only major blast furnaces near Vermont in that period were situated in the vicinity of Salisbury, Connecticut. The quality of the iron demanded at that time was so poor in comparison to only a half-century later that the skills for smelting iron were not yet complex. A shrewd entrepreneur with some industrial acumen and idle capital could easily afford to speculate on the construction of a small blast furnace to "test" local ores (Fisher 1949:18). If it succeeded in producing an acceptable-quality iron, he could rebuild a larger, more efficient furnace, or reap a tidy profit through the sale of the proven site. If the furnace failed, abandonment meant the loss of a small investment and he was free to tend to other speculative ventures. Such small furnaces might have been the so-called "pocket furnaces" at Weybridge, New Haven, and Tinmouth before 1800.

The first settlers to Vermont found the land well-watered with streams, meaning an abundance of good mill sites for grinding grain and sawing wood. They also found the soil of the valley bottoms to be wet and heavy (Lamson 1922:115). This might have resulted in good farming, but would not do

for the manufacture of iron. Damp ground was cold ground, and therefore drained much heat away from the bottom of the furnace hearth. Field research has found that a number of Vermont furnaces built during that early period had been constructed on ground so damp that in springtime it was actually soggy. Some were only 10 to 15 feet from good-running streams, and the bases of these furnaces barely a foot above stream level. Others, somewhat farther from the stream but still on the same level, must also have been close to the local water table. Such furnace sites have been found in Troy, Tinmouth, Clarendon, New Haven, Orwell, and Bennington. At one of the Tinmouth sites the telltale of a cold hearth was found in the form of heavy chunks of black slag. Might these small, poorly located furnaces have been the results of some speculators' poor judgment?

The problems of building a blast furnace on damp ground were recognized by the 1840s, as instructed by Overman:

A furnace should be located on a dry spot, free from springs and water of any kind, and not exposed to floods after heavy rains. The ground should be then excavated, until the bottom is sufficiently solid to bear the heavy weight of the stack. The foundation should be at least 1 foot larger in each direction than the base of the furnace; that is to say, if the furnace is 30 feet at the base, the foundation ought to be 32 feet square. Any kind of hard, large stones may be used to fill the excavation. No mortar should be used in the stone work. We should be careful to leave some channels through which rain or spring water in case it should penetrate the foundation, may flow off. Such a drain should be carefully walled up and covered. The cavities or channels for the blast pipes are to be placed level with the ground; and the four pillars of the furnace then laid out (Overman 1850:153-154).

To hold the stack's masonry together and to protect it from shifting due to expansion when in blast and contraction when out of blast, pairs of horizontal iron rods or flat iron straps, called binders, were embedded into opposite and diagonal sides of the stack. Early furnaces used binders made of timber. The binders were connected near their ends by horizontal bars that

2-14. *A study of binders and keys at the mid-19th-century Pittsford stack, showing pairs of diagonal binders protruding from the wall and keyed securely to horizontal iron plates.*

2-13. *A unique binder assembly found among collapsed furnace debris at East Bennington. Note the key through the end of the spike (the other end of the spike is headed). Pairs of these binders were laid at right angles to each other in the corners of the stack to strengthen the walls.*

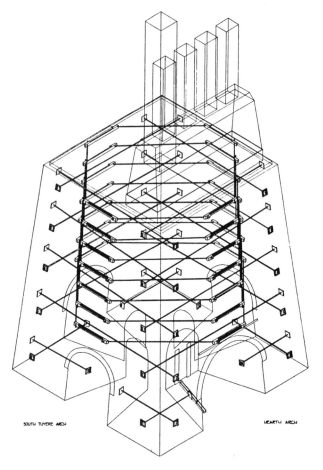

2-15. *An "X-ray" isometric view of the reinforcement binders of a mid-19th-century blast furnace (Bowie, John R., HAER, NPS 1978:8-13).*

laid up against the furnace wall. Through these bars, the slotted end of the binder protruded. A heavy iron wedge in the slot held the entire arrangement of binders together. "The strongest and most secure binders are wrought iron bars, 3 inches wide, and ¾ inch thick. They can be rolled in one length, and should be 2 feet longer than the actual length across the stack; each end of such a binder is to be bent round to form an eye.... A flat bar of the same dimensions as the binder is pushed through this eye; and sufficient room is left for a key or wedge ... the eye is formed by simply bending the bar round, and by riveting it in two places. A slight welding heat may be applied to the joint. There should be 5 binders on each side of the furnace, making 20 binders in all; as well as 8 bars reaching from the top to the lowest binder" (Overman 1850:157).

The eight bars reaching from the top to the lowest binder were laid against the wall horizontally, giving an impression of ladder rungs laying upward against the wall, rising from just above the arch to the top of the stack. Binders with slotted ends are visible at the standing blast furnace ruins at Bennington and Forest Dale; iron binders with horizontal bars at Pittsford; and remains of binders, wedges, and end plates (instead of horizontal bars) among the debris of the partially collapsed furnace at Troy. In the breakdown of the west stack at Bennington are binders that look like 2-foot-long, small iron ladders: 2-inch-thick bars bent in a U-shape, one end slotted and the other end pinned. These binders were laid flat and totally within the stonework, as no parts of them are visible sticking out through the wall.

One of the most visual characteristics of an iron-smelting blast furnace is the arrangement of the arches. These were a functional part of the furnace design and were built during the construction of the furnace proper. Early furnaces were built with only one or two arches, such as those at Bennington, East Dorset, and West Haven. The Tyson furnace at Plymouth had three arches. But the final design was four arches, one in each of the four sides, as at Forest Dale. Even New Hampshire's eight-sided blast furnace at Franconia has only four arches. One arch was usually larger than the other three to give iron-workers room to work the hearth. This was called the work arch. The other three arches provided access to the tuyeres and were thus called tuyere arches. A typical blast furnace 30 feet square at the base had a work arch 14 feet wide and tuyere arches 10 feet wide. The work arch reduced in width to 5 or 6 feet at the hearth; the tuyere arches to about 3 feet.

The arches of earlier furnaces were built of stone, as at Bennington, East Dorset, and Forest Dale. Stone arches, however, were prone to cracking, and as happened from time to time, the intense heat within the hearth would cause the blast to work its way out of the hearth and throw stones in every direction inside the work arch. The solution was to use hard-burned bricks that were strong and durable. At least one course of stonework above the brick-lined arch was also arched so as to relieve some of the pressure on the brickwork. The Pittsford furnace arch is brick-lined but there is no attached course of stone above.

The stone wall areas that made up the corners of the furnace adjacent to the arches were called the pillars. Almost any kind of hard building stone, such as granite or even slate, could be

2-16. *View into the partially collapsed ruin of the 1823 stack at East Bennington, exposing three distinct inner design details: the outside walls (left and right), a small surviving section of bosh lining (lower center), and rock fill between the bosh and outer walls.*

used to build the pillars, which were laid solid. Limestone was a poor furnace construction material. By 1850 it became the practice to mortar the stones into place, although none of the standing and collapsed furnace ruins found in Vermont show positive evidence of any outside walls being mortared or cemented (excluding mortared brick arches). The only blast furnace built in Vermont after 1850 was Henry Burden's 1863 stack at Shaftsbury, which unfortunately was completely razed sometime before 1900. Vermont blast furnaces were evenly laid with a structural balance of large and small stone, with shimming and chinking where necessary. The stacks generally maintained dressed walls, square corners, and fine symmetrical appearances considering the available working materials.

When the construction of the pillars reached about 7 feet high, construction of the arches commenced. Horizontal channels were left in the pillars and walls above to allow the binders to be pushed through after the furnace was built. Wood scaffolding surrounded the stack and gave the masons a place to stand. As the stack rose, the scaffolding followed it upward. Furnaces made of relatively small fieldstones were built by handing or hand-hoisting the stones up a scaffold and setting them into place. Those stacks made of massive blocks (ashlar) required a boom and winch to raise the stone. Such derricks were used in quarries throughout the state to hoist granite, slate, and marble, and similar devices were probably used to build the furnace walls.

Little pre-1850 furnace construction information is available, but techniques of working with heavy stones were widely known. Castles and stone bridges and aqueducts had long since been built in Europe. In New England, stone was used in house and barn foundations, root cellars, churches, bridge and road abutments, dams, canals, sea wall and dock facilities, and many 18th- and 19th-century forts in the Champlain Valley. The derrick was positioned on a platform at the ironworks site to build the furnace stack and wheel pit, plus associated retaining walls and abutments. Afterward, the derrick was disassembled and removed.

Assuming the typical blast furnace was 35 feet high, its rising walls were tapered inward such that the 35-foot-square dimension at the base reduced to about 15 feet square at the top. This resulted in a wall that sloped inward about 2½ inches per vertical foot.

Coincident with the building of the arches, the rough inner wall was laid up. This inner wall was laid vertical for 5 feet before contracting inward about 1½ inches per foot to the top, allowing for the configuration of the bosh. An internal cross-section view of the furnace would show the bosh looking much like an egg standing on its fatter end, about 9 to 10 feet in

2-17. *Massive breakdown of the Forest Dale stack conveniently exposed the in-wall and furnace lining for study, but also accelerated further deterioration in 1990.*

diameter at the widest. The bosh lining was mortared with fire clay; the lining was firebrick. The space between the bosh lining and the inner wall was about a foot wide and was filled with stone fragments. Remains of a few early Vermont furnaces

show linings made of red sandstone rather than firebrick. These are in sites at Tinmouth, Troy, Clarendon, and Dorset. No rough inner wall was found at any of these sites. At the Forest Dale furnace, firebricks were found that were made at Troy, New York, and at Brandon. Complementing the number of stove foundries in Troy at that time, the making of firebrick there was a big business. Firebricks made at Troy are common and have been found at many blast furnace (and lime kiln) sites throughout New York and New England.

2-18. *Arrangement of hearthstones: The bottom stone was bedded in fire clay and sand, tipping a bit downward toward the front of the hearth (right). Two sidestones were backed by the backstone, through which tuyere holes were cut before the stones were imbedded. The timpstone (tymph) overlapped both sidestones and extended below them. The damstone, a small triangular stone shown on the bottom stone and forming part of the forehearth, was usually laid after the furnace was completely dried and ready for blast. The tymph and damstone were sometimes faced with cast-iron plates to protect them from slag that would be apt to stick to stone and brick (Overman 1850:159).*

Directly below the bosh was the hearth, lined similar to the bosh, into which the molten iron and slag would eventually collect. The hearth, also known as the crucible, was about 2 feet square with walls 2 to 3 feet thick, flaring outward a little in its 4- to 5-foot height. It was extremely heavy when filled with molten iron and was therefore supported on a strong foundation. The top part of the bosh was called the shaft. It increased in diameter from about 3 feet at the top opening to about 10 feet at the center of the bosh. The top opening was the charge hole and was lined with curbstone, usually granite. The charge hole at the top of the Forest Dale stack is further protected by a cast-iron ring and plate.

A high-roof wooden structure called the casting shed was built against the opening of the work arch to protect the delicate and dangerous casting operations from wind and rain. The high roof allowed space for heat thrown off by the molten iron to rise and escape out the roof-top monitors. The casting shed also provided clearance for hoists and cranes that moved ladles of molten iron and finished ingots (pigs).

The three solid ingredients in the iron-making process of the blast furnace were the iron ore, charcoal, and limestone. These ingredients were prepared and mixed in ratios required to obtain iron of desired quality. Each "batch" of mixed ingredients dumped into the furnace was known as the charge, thus the naming of the charge hole at the top of the stack. The limestone in the charge acted as a flux, chemically uniting with various impurities in the iron ore under the influence of the high temperature inside the stack. The proper mix of limestone depended on the estimated quantity of impurities in the iron ore. Some furnaces averaged 6 percent limestone mixture to the ore, others as high as 10 percent. As the crushed limestone descended into the stack, it heated and released carbonic acid, which rose out the top of the stack along with other stack gases. The burned lime continued its descent and combined with silica that was present in the iron ore. Without the lime, the siliceous materials would not fuse and flow freely. With proper quantities of lime, the silica and other mineral constituents of ore and ash united to form a liquid slag that separated out to float atop the dense molten iron (Campbell 1907:43-44).

2-19. *Charging barrows in which ore, fuel, and limestone were manually pushed from the measuring house to the top of the furnace, then dumped into it* (Annual Report of . . . Pennsylvania *1894:66ff*).

The molten iron, meanwhile, collected in a growing puddle at the bottom of the hearth. As more and more iron collected in the hearth, more slag formed, requiring the ironworker to periodically open the higher of two tapholes in the hearth. Opening the higher hole allowed the slag to run out and provide space in the hearth for more molten iron to accumulate. Slag was commercially a waste by-product of the blast furnace operation, although an analysis of cooled slag by the ironmaster told him many things about the quality of the iron he was making. The color of slag was not always a safe criterion of the quality of work being done in the furnace. Gray slag, for example, might contain as much wasted iron as green or black slag. But as a general rule, gray slag did prove somewhat better.

A furnace in good condition would produce a highly glazed green slag. Perfectly gray, white, black, or olive-green slag was not a good indicator (Overman 1850:203). After being allowed to cool and solidify, the slag was broken up and carted away to be discarded, usually some distance from the immediate working area. Years later, many large slag heaps were "discovered" and used as filler in asphalt that today covers many roads in the vicinity of old ironworks.

In the early 20th century, a process was developed by which high-pressure air was blown through molten slag from steel furnaces, creating a fibrous material generally known as rock wool. This material, a forerunner of fiberglass, was used to make a fireproof building insulation. Rock wool was also made from limestone and siliceous rock.

When it was determined that enough molten iron had formed in the hearth, usually because iron was now running out the upper taphole along with slag, the lower taphole was opened and the iron ran out to the molds. There was a large, flat-edge stone called the tymph located inside the hearth. The tymph's bottom, flat edge was level with the bottom of and just behind this lower taphole. By forcing the molten iron to flow under it before passing out the taphole, the tymph stone served a dual function. It prevented hot stack gases from escaping though the taphole and splattering molten iron about the casting area, and at the same time, it blocked most of the slag that was still in the hearth and floating on the iron from running out with the iron.

The molten iron flowed out of the hearth into a central trough, where remaining slag and oxidized scum were skimmed off by ironworkers with special tools. The iron flowed from a central trough into smaller lateral troughs around it, all dug into the molding sand on the casting floor. Early ironworkers saw in the arrangement of the large central trough connected by small runners to smaller troughs a resemblance to a sow with suckling piglets around her. The heavier central casting thereafter became known as the sow and the small castings became the pigs. To this day, the general expression "pig iron" remains for the casting product of the blast furnace process.

2-20. *Casting pigs in sand at the base of a mid-19th-century blast furnace. Note that the casting area is within a building that protects the workers and castings from weather* (Chapin 1860:156).

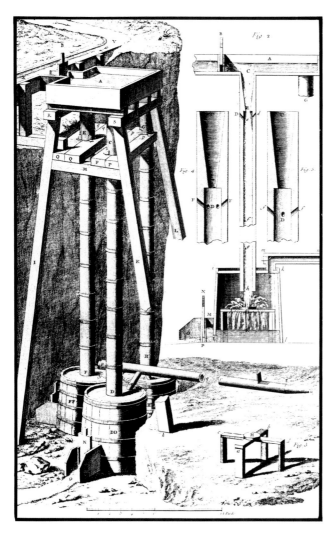

2-21. *The trompe, in which falling water draws in air (upper right). The aerated water falls into a box and the froth gives up the trapped air, which is coaxed out the end of the horizontal pipe (Diderot 1763: plate 88).*

Draft, also called blast, fanned the charge to temperatures that accomplished reduction of the ore. It was usually supplied by bellows in early times, although a device called a trompe came into use also. The trompe is said to have been invented in Italy in 1640, its use confined at that time to some charcoal furnaces and Catalan forges in Spain, Italy, Germany, and France. It was also known as the water-blast and was used in some southern states, but also in the Adirondack Mountains of New York (Allen 1983:86). Vermonter Allen Penfield from Pittsford employed a trompe (he called it a troupe) at his forge at Crown Point in 1828 (Allen 1967:4).

The trompe was essentially a 5- by 2½- by 1½-foot-deep wooden box, nearly immersed in a stream directly under the flume. Water rushed straight down off the end of the flume through an 8-inch-square, 10- to 20-foot-long wood pipe. Air

was sucked in through small holes in the side of this pipe by the action of the falling water and was trapped in the box below. In this box, water escaped out a hole in the bottom while the air was forced out a hole near the top of the box. The pressure of the collected air given up by the bubbling froth moved the air along. Although a blast provided by the trompe was very uniform as compared to the pulsating bellows, it required huge amounts of water that might be put to better use driving water-wheel/bellows machinery. The blast was also cold and damp. Its main advantage was that it was easily and cheaply constructed—ideal for a quick speculative forge or small blast furnace.

Bellows resembled common household fireplace bellows except that by the era of Vermont ironworks, they had grown to 22 feet long and 4 feet wide. Bellows date back to antiquity when slaves, standing on a pair of bellows often made of goatskin, shifted their weight so as to repeatedly step on one, then the other. This is depicted on the walls of an Egyptian tomb that dates to about 1500 BC, showing a small furnace and bellows nearby (see figure 1-1).

Waterwheels and their associated shafts, controls, and cams were developed to near perfection by the 18th century. Through innovation and experimentation, waterpower systems in New England were transformed into highly efficient sources of power. They took advantage of good running streams and powered all types of mills well after the adoption of steam power in the more industrialized parts of the United States. Cut from hardwood, usually oak, the waterwheel was carefully assembled and balanced. The shaft was cut from the tallest and straightest tree in the local forest, shaved to about 2 feet in diameter, and notched to the wheel. Waterwheels were connected to operate trip-hammers, shears, rollers, rock and ore crushers, and other devices in addition to bellows and air cylinders (blowing tubs) for bloomeries and furnaces.

The blast usually had a pressure of ½ pound per square inch. It was introduced into the hearth through a tuyere that measured 2 to 3 inches in diameter. Some tuyeres were double-walled so water could circulate through them, preventing them from melting. Early furnaces had one tuyere; later furnaces had as many as five or more for even distribution of the blast. While passing upward through the burning charge, the oxygen in the blast combined with the carbon in the charcoal to form carbon dioxide and produced very high temperatures. The hot, oxygen-hungry carbon above this combustion zone reduced the carbon dioxide to carbon monoxide and in turn reduced the iron from its ore. Hot gases vented out the top of the furnace through a flue, which protected the bridgemen from the noxious fumes. The gases usually burned on reaching the outside air above the furnace, resulting in the flaming top that was typical of early furnaces: "A translucent flame interspaced with flowing sparks rose and fell from the open trunnel head [*sic*] in harmony with the pulsations of the blast. By day it was suspended over the furnace top like a mystical oriflame, and at night it served as a beacon, lighting up the countryside" (Peters 1921:7). Patrick E. Mooney of Pittsford, in 1953 the sole surviving workman of the Pittsford furnace, remarked how the furnace sent up flame-colored gases, lighting the yard enough to read a news-paper. Sometimes it attracted people to the scene who thought a fire was raging out of control (McWhorter "Mooney" *Rutland Herald* Oct. 2, 1953:68).

The flame at the top of the furnace told the ironmaster a number of things. If the flame was dark and heavy, it indicated that the furnace was cooling and the charge was probably too heavy. A light, smoky flame throwing off white fumes indicated too much limestone, or that the charge might be too light. An almost invisible, lively flame at the top indicated a healthy state inside the furnace (Overman 1850:204-205).

As the years passed and furnace designs improved, the need for an increased volume of blast forced ironmasters to turn to other devices to replace the outdated bellows. One such device was the 1550 invention of a German organ builder, later adapted to an industrial use. The machine looked so much like a pair

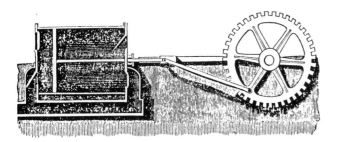

2-22. *Horizontal iron cylinder blast machine, such as operated at Forest Dale. Note double-acting valves (Overman 1850:399).*

of tubs that from the beginning it was called blowing tubs. The machine was made of two main cylinders (the tubs) with pistons connected by linkages to the waterwheel. Air was pumped from the cylinders into a smaller chamber called an equalizer (windbox), which contained a horizontal, free-riding weighted piston that maintained a steady blast at uniform pressure.

While designing the Monkton Iron Company blast furnace at Vergennes in 1808, Bradbury and Perkins considered cylinders of wood, but they had to settle on conventional leather bellows—wooden cylinders were still so new, no one was found who knew how to make them (Seaburg and Paterson 1971:203).

During a 1974 inspection of the remains of two 19th-century blast furnaces deep in the Adirondack Mountains of New York, many pieces of blast machinery were found, reflecting the state of the technology of the two sites. Near the collapsed ruins of an 1844 blast furnace (which might have been built on the foundation of an earlier 1838 furnace), pieces of wooden cylinders and their 6-foot-long piston rods with wood heads were found half-buried in dense undergrowth alongside the upper reaches of the Hudson River. The cylinders were made of laminated wood. The piston heads had a strip of leather nailed around the edge to reduce air leakage while pumping air to the furnace. Many pieces of gears, thick iron plates, and unidentified castings were also found in the vicinity. About a mile downstream and adjacent to the standing ruin of an 1854 furnace are four 46-inch-diameter cast-iron cylinders with heavy piston rods that could be adjusted to provide 36- to 66-inch strokes. Each cylinder is about the size of a 500-gallon fuel oil tank.

The accepted year for the appearance of blowing tubs in the Northeast is 1835 (Harte 1935:42), indicating the advanced state of thinking at Vergennes. Conant's furnace at Brandon was enlarged in 1839 with two 6½-foot-diameter blowing tubs, the earliest recorded use of the device in Vermont (Lesley 1858:76). The cylinder heads were double-acting (air pumped

2-23. *Ca.-1915 view of waterwheel, blast machinery, and heating ovens (top of the furnace) at Forest Dale (courtesy Vermont Division for Historic Preservation).*

with each in-and-out stroke of the piston), with both inlets and outlets closed by wood flap valves on leather hinges. The pistons were made airtight by a packing of narrow leather strips on the riding edges. Although graphite and lard were common lubricants, many residents 2 miles from the furnace would swear that on a still night the furnace was right next door. Some older residents of Tyson used to claim that when in blast, the creaking and groaning of the bellows machinery at the furnace could be heard 3 miles away, contributing in part to the name of nearby Echo Lake (Hubbard 1922:51).

Replacement of wooden cylinders with those made of iron started in the 1850s. Operation of the iron cylinders was the same as the wooden, but much quieter. They were less prone to leaking due to warped wood parts, and had better-balanced parts. They could be made to run vertically or horizontally, with the former found to work better when driven by steam engine, the latter by waterpower. Blast furnaces throughout most of New England were so large by the 1850s that they were generating enough waste heat to run small steam boilers, but Vermont's well-watered countryside continued to power its blast machines. As recently as the early 1900s a large water-wheel connected to a pair of iron cylinders could be seen at Forest Dale. Today, only the empty wheel pit and blast machine

mounts remain, next to the silent, decaying furnace stack.

Another improvement was the hot blast, first introduced by James Neilson in England in 1828. Furnaces were previously blown with unheated outside air. During winter, the cold outside air had a bad effect on both the homogeneous temperature inside the stack and the desired uniform consistency of the

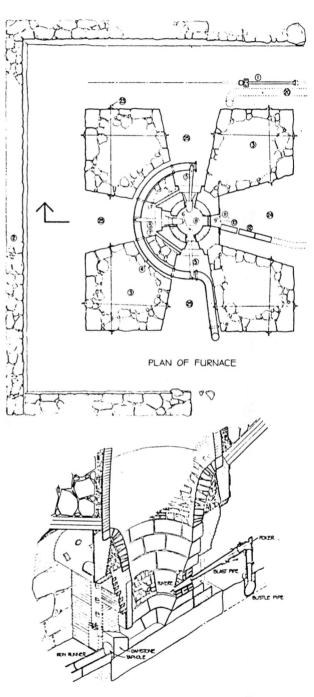

PLAN OF FURNACE

2-24. *Pressure of the air blast was regulated by use of trundle valves (top) before being fed into the tuyeres (middle). Tuyeres were made round (left) or flat (right), the latter so as to support the nozzle, but the former the most common. Both tuyeres contained hollow jackets through which water circulated (a and b) to prevent the nozzles from melting. A manometer (bottom) measured blast pressures as near to the tuyere as possible (Overman 1850:419, 423-424).*

2-25. *Blast was distributed to the tuyeres around the base of the furnace by a bustle, or "belly" pipe (Richards, B.A., and Bowie, J.R., HAER, NPS 1978:4-13, 13-13).*

smelted iron. The preheated blast not only solved most of these problems but also reduced the amount of fuel required to smelt the ore. The blast could be heated by pumping it through pipes that were either laid over an independently located fire or run over the top of the furnace. The latter, utilizing the hot waste gases of the furnace, required no extra fuel. It was the most efficient and became the accepted technique.

In practice, hot blast was created in a brick-type chamber called an oven, located at the top of the furnace stack. The cold blast was received from the blast cylinders, which were on the ground near the waterwheel, and pumped through many round pipes inside the oven. Inside the oven, some of the furnace waste gases that had been diverted into the chamber passed around the outside of these round pipes. Because cold air expands when heated, the pipes were quite large—up to 5 feet in diameter. The hot gases entered the oven at the bottom of one end, played through the rows of pipes, and, somewhat cooler, exhausted out a chimney near the top of the opposite end.

2-26. *Broken end of a bustle pipe (right) and the tuyere (center) at the Forest Dale furnace (courtesy Vermont Division for Historic Preservation).*

The pressure from the blast machine forced the heated air out of the oven and down a pipe to the tuyeres. This vertical pipe was built inside the furnace wall to insulate the hot blast from the cooler outside air. The hot blast was applied to a series of tuyeres around the widest part of the bosh by means of a circular pipe called the bustle pipe. Where a "T" connected the bustle pipe to a tuyere, a small round piece of isinglass (mica) was mounted into the pipe so the ironmaster could look directly through the inside of the tuyeres to inspect the red-hot interior of the blast furnace.

Historical consensus credits Oxford Furnace in New Jersey with the distinction of the first practical application of hot blast in the United States, in 1834 (Temin 1964:59; Swank

1892:326). But a hot-blast system was introduced at Bennington the year before (Hodge May 12, 1849:290). Perhaps one of those crumbling furnace ruins at Furnace Grove at East Bennington qualifies as a national industrial monument?

2-27. *Although not as efficient as utilizing waste furnace gas, one method of preheating blast was to pass it through a small, independently heated stove beside the stack (Overman 1850:432).*

2-28. *Tapping the hot exhaust gas just below the top of the furnace did not interfere with top doors and charge-measuring devices (Overman 1850:450).*

Initial hot blasts in New England were about 250° F with 900° F being the upper limit. The Forest Dale furnace preheated blast at 600° F in ovens that were still visible at the top of the furnace in the early 1900s.

When all worked well within the furnace, the charge moved its way down the throat of the furnace at a steady rate. The bridgemen charging the furnace top paced their efforts by the steady descent of the charge. But when they found themselves catching up too quickly, it was the sign that something was

2-29. *Cross-section of a typical mid-19th-century blast furnace showing the top heating ovens, the downer pipe, and bustle pipe feeding hot blast to the tuyeres near the bottom of the hearth. This is probably what the furnaces at Pittsford and Forest Dale looked like in their final days of operation* (Salisbury Iron *1878:7*).

amiss somewhere inside the furnace. A stuck charge usually was budged loose by turning the blast on and off a number of times in quick succession. If that did not unstick things, a bridgeman probed inside the furnace with a long iron rod. In the meantime, fuel was no longer descending to the bottom of the furnace and the furnace was starting to cool. The result could solidify everything in the hearth and in the furnace, requiring the expensive process of opening a furnace wall to remove the "frozen" charge. If probing at the top did not move things along, then more drastic actions were called for. Both tapholes were opened and slag and iron were run out of the hearth. Part of the forehearth was removed and iron rods probed up to the charge to dislodge the stoppage. Some ironworks were known to have small cannon for just such an emergency. After removing part of the hearth, small solid shot was fired upward into the charge (Harte 1935:61-63).

The problem was caused by large pieces of ore, charcoal, or limestone, which should not have been charged into the furnace in the first place. These pieces expanded when nearing the lower, hotter end of the bosh and sometimes wedged the charge by forming a bridge, or arching, across the inside of the bosh. The charge below this bridge continued to move downward, but everything above stopped. In the frenzied battle

2-30. *This evolution of Pennsylvania's anthracite-fueled blast furnace also shows the relative scale in size of Vermont's early, small blast furnaces compared to later 19th-century furnaces* (Annual Report of . . . Pennsylvania *1894:50ff*).

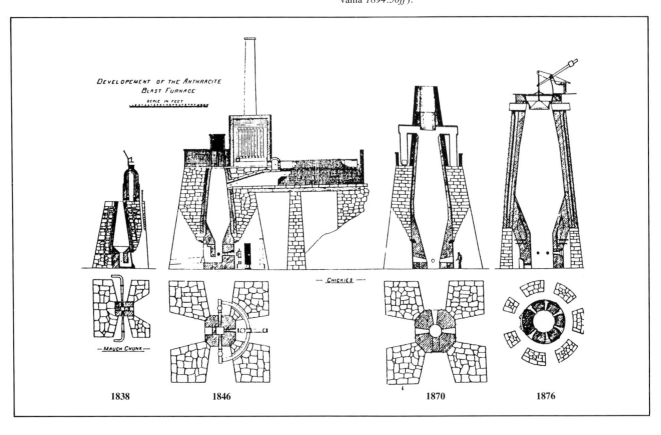

against time to save the stack, many a bosh wall was inadvertently ruptured, spilling the molten slag and iron, turning the casting shed into a miniature volcanic eruption and fatally injuring many ironworkers.

The efficiency of the blast furnace was defined in terms of how much charcoal was needed to make a ton of iron. Tyson Furnace consumed 150 bushels of charcoal per ton of iron made by cold blast but only 100 bushels by warm blast (Hodge May 19, 1849:306). In the New York–New England area, the average blast furnace consumed 120 to 130 bushels per ton of iron (Overman 1850:168). This confirms earlier statements about the apparent wastefulness of bloomery forges, which consumed about 300 bushels of charcoal per ton of blooms. But it also took additional charcoal to puddle pig iron into wrought iron. What primarily regulated consumption of charcoal in the furnace was the design of the stack. In the 1840–1850 period, an optimum furnace height was about 35 feet. Shorter stacks consumed charcoal excessively; taller stacks strained the blast. In the race to increase production some ironmasters pushed their shorter furnaces to produce beyond their natural limit rather then invest some capital to rebuild their older stacks up to "modern" 35-foot heights. A furnace that readily produced 35 to 40 tons a week could be coaxed to 50 or 60 tons. But when the consumption of charcoal outran the increase in iron output, the point of diminishing returns was exceeded.

The development and improvement of the cupola furnace at the foundry allowed cast iron to be remelted in a separate furnace and run into molds for casting operations. The importance of the cupola furnace was that it relieved the blast furnace of the job of direct casting, and allowed it to concentrate on just casting pig iron. The cupola did its casting in a foundry

2-31. View up the inside of the Forest Dale stack in 1990, showing the two side openings near the top where some of the hot exhaust gases were drawn into the blast heating ovens (courtesy Vermont Division for Historic Preservation).

built either next to the blast furnace, or remote from it near markets and transportation. Other pig iron was shipped to the puddling furnace where it was refined.

The advantage of Vermont's seemingly limitless streams to run its mills with cheap waterpower was balanced by Vermont winters, one characteristic of which is the numbing cold that froze millstreams solid for months at a time. But even before a solid freeze, ice formation and expansion did much damage to wooden sluice gates, raceways, and the waterwheel. When the time came, the last heat was drawn from the furnace, the sluice gates closed, the waterwheel slowed to a halt, and quiet once again returned to the countryside. As soon as the furnace interior had cooled, it was inspected for wear and damage. A decision was made whether to daub up the firebrick or replace the entire lining. Clinkers were coaxed out of the hearth with heavy iron scrapers, wheezing blast pipes repaired, and badly burned tuyeres replaced. There was time to patch leaks in the roof of the casting shed, replace broken windows, and make some new tools for next year. There was also time to balance the past season's profit margin against needs for improvements to the furnace hardware as the technical state of the iron-making business moved onward. The furnace owners and partners considered how the convening session of the Congress might affect the future prices of iron, costs of fuel, and the economy of the industry in general. And, after reflecting on all that, it was no wonder that so many Vermont ironworks failed to reopen the following spring.

Early Vermont Foundry Operations

Some early Vermont iron-making industries were set up so that many products that were later made in a foundry had earlier been cast right at the blast furnace. By the early 19th century, however, iron making was a blast furnace function and iron working was done solely at the foundry. In some cases, the foundry was built next to the blast furnace stack, such as at Pittsford and Tyson. Usually, the foundry was located a distance from the blast furnace, and might even have been operated by another company.

Two distinctly different kinds of furnaces, the cupola furnace (the cupola) and the air furnace, were used in the foundry to melt and work the pig iron. Which was used depended on a number of variables.

The cupola furnace was the more convenient, economical, and most generally used. It resembled a brick tower, 3 to 10 feet wide and about one story tall, or tall enough to rise as a chimney through the roof of the foundry. A late-19th-century cupola was made with a steel jacket and a firebrick lining. Charging was done through an iron door, 6 to 10 feet from the bottom, through which pieces of pig iron and coke (or charcoal) were introduced. The cupola worked much like a blast furnace, but with some significant differences.

The cupola was started by laying a bed of charcoal and scrap wood on the bottom, igniting it, and as the fire burned, adding more fuel—charcoal, coke, or coal. The time required to heat the cupola and firebrick was generally one to two hours. Tuyeres and natural draft up the tall chimney initially kept the fires going; when charging commenced, only tuyeres provided draft.

Iron was then fed into the cupola through the charging door in as small pieces as practical for the diameter of the cupola. The quantity of iron fed was dependent on the size of the cupola; the larger the diameter, the more iron. A 5-foot-wide cupola could be charged with about three tons of iron.

It took six to eight tons of coke or five to seven tons of hard coal to melt a ton of iron. Too much or too little fuel affected the quality of the iron. In cases where inferior iron (burned or dirty) was used, the charge included a flux of limestone, feldspar, or magnesia; the amount depended on the quality of the iron—worse iron required more flux to carry the impurities off as slag. But over-fluxing could attack the cupola lining and lead to premature shutdown of the cupola. The flux was added (called "slagging out") in egg-size pieces and mixed well with the iron, only after the cupola was filled to the charging door or the iron had been melting for about 30 minutes. Slag was tapped from the slag hole, located just below the tuyeres (so that the slag did not interfere with the blast). The slag hole was placed in the wall about opposite from the spout that allowed the molten iron to flow from the bottom of the cupola.

Tapping the cupola was the most dangerous part of the operation, requiring a number of tools for tapping and handling the ladles. The tapping bar was forced into the taphole to loosen the plug, and the molten iron burst out and down the spout. The iron ran directly into a mold or a ladle. The ladle, depending on its size, was hand-carried or crane-assisted to the molds. The taphole was closed with another tool, the stopping bod, which stopped up the hole with a clay plug. It took much skill to prevent the flowing iron from pushing the clay off the end of the tool, or from continuing to flow around the plug and splattering onto the floor (and the workmen). Once flowing, molten iron was not easy to stop.

The air furnace was a variation of the puddling furnace, in which the fuel and iron did not come in physical contact. It received its name from its use of natural convection rather than blast or forced air draft as used in the cupola. Air furnaces were used where melting required great purity and strength.

2-34. *Transporting a red-hot bloom from the puddling furnace to the hammer, where the bloom was worked into a manageable shape (Chapin 1860:159).*

2-32. *The puddler working the iron through a small hole in the side wall of the puddling furnace (Chapin 1860:159).*

2-33. *At the puddling furnace, where cast iron from the blast furnace was converted into wrought iron, the puddler removes a bloom with a large tongs (Chapin 1860:158).*

2-35. *After the hammer-shaped piece of wrought iron was squeezed into a rough iron bar, it was successively passed through smaller pairs of rollers, eventually formed into long, flat iron plate ready for shearing and stamping into nails (Chapin 1860:160).*

Larger pieces of scrap iron could be melted in the air furnace, and the greatest casting strength could be obtained with the air furnace because the iron could gain the highest percentage carbon with the lowest percentage sulfur.

The air furnace was generally a rectangular box, 6 to 8 feet long, 3 to 5 feet wide, and 4 to 6 feet high. It looked more like a furnace laid on its side, since the process here was more horizontal than vertical. The foundation under the furnace had to be very strong to hold up under the heavy weight and the stresses involved in the operation. It also required a much greater amount of skill to operate, and up to 12 percent of the iron was usually lost through oxidation.

2-36. *Casting at the Gray Foundry at Poultney in 1956 (courtesy Richard S. Allen).*

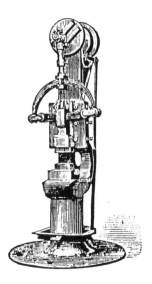

2-37. *A ca.-1880 power hammer, looking very much like those used in Trow & Holden at Barre in 1980 to forge stone-working chisels (Naujoks and Fabel 1939:10).*

One end of the furnace contained a grate on which the fuel was piled. A foot-high bridge separated the grate from the hearth, which was the middle section of the furnace. Chunks of pig iron were laid in the hearth, fed through a side door. The entire inside of the furnace was lined with firebrick. A spout was located at the lowest point of the hearth to draw off the molten iron. Other small holes in the walls were either peepholes or permitted tools to sample the molten iron. At the back end was a brick chimney, 30 to 80 feet high, sufficient to provide draft and draw air into the front (grate) end.

The air furnace required 5 to 6 hours burning before it could be charged with iron. The bars of pig iron were piled crisscross so the hot gases could be drawn between and around them and up the chimney.

Typical of Vermont's larger 19th-century foundries was the Burlington Manufacturing Company, whose rolling mill contained three trains of rollers, four heating furnaces, and a hammer in one large 75- by 155-foot wooden building. The adjoining nail shop was built of brick and housed 46 nail and spike machines. The entire works was run by four steam engines and had the capacity of making 6,000 tons of iron products a year (see chapter 4, CH-IW06).

Products made at early Vermont foundries varied with time and demand. During the early years of settling and clearing lands, the common foundry products were nearly the same as that of the blast furnace: merchant bars for the commercial trade, hand tools, parts for waterwheel systems, iron stock for blacksmiths to fashion into horseshoes, hinges, and soft nails, and also something called hollowware—pots that were used for making potash.

Potash Kettles

Although potash was used to some lesser degree in making glass, most everyone asked will respond that it was a part of the early process of making soap. And so it was. But as Dorothy Canfield Fisher pointed out: "the amount of potash you came across in old account books and commerce reports couldn't have been for making soap to wash with. Enough was sent out of Vermont every year to wash the clothes and faces of humanity all round the globe ten times a day . . . in a manner of speaking. In 1791, three hundred tons of potash were produced in one Vermont county alone. That's six hundred thousand pounds and that year two million pounds were exported from the whole state" (Fisher 1953:164).

The answer to the apparent puzzling need for such huge amounts of potash was found thousands of miles across the Atlantic in the woolen mills of England. As part of the process of converting wool from its original scratchy texture to fine soft cloth, the wool had to be finished. The process was called fulling and involved treating the raw wool with fullers soap. The chief ingredient in this soap was potash, and tons were needed every year by the English mills to finish the wool. But with the restrictions on cutting trees in England for anything except naval construction, potash had to be imported, and the seemingly endless forests of the American Colonies answered the question of supply. To further encourage the importation of potash from the colonies, starting in 1756 all potash from America was imported duty-free (Fisher 1953:163-184).

2-38. *A large heavy-duty cast-iron caldron, abandoned near one of Vermont's more remote blast furnace sites.*

The process for making potash was quite simple, and the chief ingredient, wood, was a by-product of settlers clearing their land. Essentially, logs and branches were burned and their ash collected in a trough. Water was poured on the ashes and drained through them into a large cast-iron pot. This solution was boiled until the salts—the potash (also called pearl ash)—crystallized at the bottom of the pot. Instructions for making potash were written and printed in England and sent to the colonies where they were eagerly studied. All the raw materials were here, all one needed was the patience to endure the time-consuming process . . . and a large cast-iron pot.

These pots—called hollowware, potash kettles, or caldrons in advertisements and books of the time—were usually made right at the furnace by direct casting into a mold. The typical potash kettle weighed 400 to 1,000 pounds, measured 40 to 60 inches across, and had walls 1 to 2 inches thick. Some were cast upside-down, resulting in a weak bottom that rapidly burned out during the boiling process; the better pots were cast

2-39. *Too heavy to be moved, this large cast-iron bell sits outside a former antique shop in West Rutland.*

open side up, a more difficult molding operation but one that produced a pot whose bottom was the strongest side (Miller 1980:187-208).

By 1790, with frontiers being pushed forward and forests cleared at a furious rate, potash exports from the United States had tripled that of 1770. In Vermont, where potash production was in full swing, the first award of the newly created U.S. Patent Office was in recognition of an improved potash-making process. Samuel Hopkins of Pittsford was awarded U.S. Patent Number 1, signed by George Washington (Paynter 1990:18-22). An illustration of the device is in *Pittsford: Now and Then* (Pittsford Historical Society 1980:93). Not only were more and more individual Vermonters taking advantage of the potash "boom," but large-scale commercial potash industries came into existence. They were called potasheries (also asheries). Potash Bay at Addison on Lake Champlain was the site of one such potash mill. The business in turn generated the demand for good quality, heavy-duty cast-iron kettles. In response, blast furnaces up and down Vermont turned out the kettles day and night. At Sheldon, potash kettles were so good that customers came 200 miles to choose among 45-, 69-, and 90-gallon kettles. So many people waited their turn to buy kettles hot from the mold that Sheldon pots were called Sheldon Currency.

2-40. *Remains of the waterpower system for a foundry and plow factory along the New Haven River below a washed-out dam, two miles east of Bristol village. This imposing feature housed a turbine; the inlet at the top and outlet at the bottom.*

Just as the ironworks had fully geared up for kettle production in the early 1800s, potash demand suddenly dropped off. Europeans had discovered that sodium could replace potash and could be made much more cheaply from the vast European salt deposits. In addition, the threat of renewed war between England and the United States resulted in a trade embargo that cut severely into potash exports. Although Vermonters managed to smuggle potash into Canada during the embargo, by 1810 the demand had peaked. The Monkton Iron Company at Vergennes was finally getting its troublesome blast furnace to work by then, but cast its first batch of kettles too late. So much

2-41. *Ruins of a waterpower system in the Mad River at Warren, showing the dam (lower right), machinery scattered about, and the penstock that conveyed the water (left) to a mill.*

hollowware was being made throughout Vermont that the rapidly declining potash market became saturated with kettles. They were piling up unsold at furnaces in Pittsford and Bennington. And with the end of the War of 1812, the potash demand ended. Those ironworks whose mainstay had been potash kettle production found themselves out of business. A few works continued making kettles for other domestic needs, such as Pittsford, where a ca.-1831 advertisement listed kettles from 7½ to 15½ inches in diameter priced from 20¢ to $2. But the kettle business remained a shadow of the former potash kettle frenzy.

Cast-iron caldrons and kettles can still be seen throughout Vermont performing new, non-potash functions. Some water cattle and chickens in barnyards; others provide extra-large pots for frontyard plants. Many more are in museums and in front of town halls and churches. At least one large, heavy cast-iron kettle lies partially hidden in the undergrowth of a remote Vermont blast furnace ruin, too heavy to be dragged away.

2-42. *Although many mill dams were made of stone, others, such as this washed-out artifact in the Ottauquechee River at Bridgewater, were made of wood with a stone base.*

2-43. *A relic of Manchester Center's more industrial days lying in the brook in 1981, just downstream of the marble bridge. The turbine disappeared a few years later.*

2-44. *A rusted turbine in the New Haven River at Brooksville, site of the Brooks Edge Tool Company foundry.*

Fireplaces

By the 18th century, experiments were being made to line fireplaces with cast-iron plates, rather than stone or brick. Called firebacks, these heavy plates rested against the back wall of the fireplace to provide two important functions. The obvious was the protection the plate provided to the back wall of the fireplace, by insulating the wall from the intense heat of the fire, thus reducing injury to the masonry. The second, and less obvious, was the heat radiated back out of the fireplace by the fireback, after the fire has slowed to a smolder.

Firebacks were cast about an inch thick right on the casting-room floor of the foundry or blast furnace. In time, patterns were pressed into the sand, lending artistic and decorative designs to the front of the firebacks. In houses of the wealthy, which contained many fireplaces, custom-ordered firebacks depicted coordinated themes. One such theme might be winter/spring/summer/fall-related decorations on firebacks in four first-floor fireplaces; then biblical (or patriotic) themes for the second-floor fireplaces.

Fireplace hardware also included andirons, chimney cranes, caldrons, grates, and fireplace tools. Andirons raised burning

wood off the fireplace floor to improve burning efficiency and keep the fire from smothering in its ashes. An early andiron was probably just a single iron bar on short legs, hoisting one end of the log off the floor. Eventually, pairs of andirons were used. The word is supposed to be a corruption of "hand-iron"— an iron that may be moved by hand (Kauffman 1972:262). Ends of andirons were sometimes decorated, fancier ones with brass finials. The ends of some early andirons had a dog's face cast on them, prompting the name "dog-irons." The most distinctive andirons were made of brass. Andirons were listed as products in many Vermont ironworks. Their fabrication was simple and their use a necessity in the many fireplaces that found use in the state.

A chimney crane was a triangular-shaped arrangement of iron bars, mounted on the side of the fireplace to afford a swivel and hook to hang a caldron over the fire. Although larger cranes were made in the foundry, small cranes could be made of wrought iron, welded together by the hammering.

Caldrons were a very old type of cooking pot cast similar to potash kettles, one difference being that the caldron was usually cast on three short legs and had handles to hang from the chimney crane. Ironworks that made potash kettles usually made an additional line of caldrons and cooking pots.

The grate was a basket-shaped arrangement of iron bars made specifically to hold coal, although wood was as easily used. Early grates resembled andirons with crossbars. Some modern grates include a pair of decorative front columns as a reminder of the early andirons. Fireplace tools included an ash shovel, brush, and tongs. An added touch was made by attaching brass handles to the tools to match those on andirons or grates.

By the early 1700s, experiments were made lining the three walls of the fireplace with iron plates and moving this iron "fireplace-box" into the room. The most famous experimenter was, of course, Benjamin Franklin, who published his findings on the subject of fireplace improvements in 1744 (Kauffman 1972:197). Franklin pointed out that most of the heat of the fireplace was carried up the chimney, and his solution was to build an iron fireplace that inserted into the masonry fireplace. His insert forced the heat and smoke to travel up an inner wall

2-45. *Cast-iron office front in downtown Burlington.*

of the box, down a smoke exit column behind that wall, then up the chimney through holes behind the bottom of the exit column. The roundabout route caused more of the heat to be captured by the iron while still allowing the smoke to clear from the fireplace. The front of the box remained as open as the original fireplace, which distinguished it from a stove. But the misnomer of the "Franklin Stove" continues to this day.

As modifications and improvements were made to the iron fireplace, the insert slowly crept out of the fireplace and into the room, resulting in the completely closed-in true stove. A transitional fireplace/stove was one that could be operated both as a fireplace (front doors opening the entire front wall) or as a stove (front doors shut). One modern stove made by Vermont Castings at Randolph bears a strong resemblance to these early 18th-century transitional stoves.

In an index of U.S. patents issued to inventors of fireplaces and improvements from 1790 to 1873, the following Vermonters are listed:

Date	Name	Residence	Invention
July 7, 1813	C. Guernsey	Poultney	Fireplace, stove
August 16, 1817	W. Salisbury	Derby	Fireplace
March 28, 1865	P. P. Stewart	Troy, N.Y.	Fire-pot for stoves, furnaces, etc.

Cast-Iron Stoves

As fireplaces evolved into stoves, industry in Vermont followed suit with parlor stoves and, to a lesser degree, kitchen ranges. Foundries experimented with many designs; some for simplicity, others for grace and style. The best designs combined both. The most efficient designs incorporated a balance of decorative work in the form of various motifs on front and side panels of the stove. These helped make the stove attractive and allowed it to be accepted as part of the parlor furniture; thus, the parlor stove.

The convoluted surfaces also had a practical side. They afforded more heated surface area to transfer heat from the hot interior of the stove into the air around it. Stove design took on such a state of art by the 1850s that many started looking like miniature buildings, complete with windows, archways, doorways, and all types of graceful filigree and intricate designs. They were also designed so they could be cast in sections, one panel at a time, crated, and assembled later by the customer. Many were crated and shipped by canal to western markets, which is probably where most of Vermont's stoves ended up.

Early stoves were cast right at the blast furnaces, just as the caldrons were. But after the coming of the railroad, pig iron was shipped to foundries where it was melted and cast by a cupola furnace. The cupola allowed better control than the blast furnace (Waite Jan. 1977). Air furnaces proved inefficient since they consumed greater quantities of fuel. Although castings produced from air furnaces were superior and could be drawn more readily, these characteristics were not critical in casting 19th-century stoves.

The motif on the stove panel was determined by the design carved on a wooden master, called the pattern. Because iron shrank a little while cooling (about 1/8th inch per linear foot), the pattern was made slightly larger than the size of the final casting. The carving and machining of patterns was an art in itself, requiring the skill and the patience of a sculptor. The smallest defect in the pattern would also appear on the final motif. After the pattern was pressed into molding sand and carefully removed, the impression in the sand became the mold for the molten iron. Patterns themselves were not molds and never came into direct contact with the molten iron.

Dozens of stove styles and designs were cast in Vermont during the 19th century, as well as into the current century. Cast-iron stoves were a practical alternative to smoky fireplaces as homes started to take on a more civilized appearance than early pioneering cabins. With the opening of the Erie Canal and increased settlement of the Midwest and far West, a market developed quickly at Albany and Troy, New York, the head of the canal. Most of the Vermont-made stoves found their way to Albany and Troy after being packed in flat sections in heavy wooden boxes (probably weighing tons), and went to stores in Chicago and St. Louis before their final destination in frontier homes, general stores, and schoolhouses. Museums in the Midwest, therefore, probably display many Vermont-made stoves.

Vermont foundries also turned out varieties of kitchen stoves, although none were found during this study. John Conant is widely credited with "partial success in building an out-and-out cook stove in 1818. Philo Penfield Stewart of Troy [N.Y.], may be called one of the fathers of the modern [1836] stove" (Moldenke 1930:13-14).

Philo Penfield Stewart of the Penfield and Stewart families of Pittsford patented the first of a long line of successful cook stoves in 1838 (Groft 1984:85-86). He founded Oberlin College, Ohio, in 1833 and designed his first stove there, calling it the Oberlin Stove. In 1838 he moved to Troy, New York, and perfected what became the P. P. Stewart Summer and Winter Cooking Stove (see Groft 1984:86 for an illustration and ca.-1838 advertisement). Lacking capital to cast his stove, he contracted with Fuller, Warren & Company at Troy to manufacture it. Over 90,000 stoves were cast and distributed. Stewart died in 1868 and is buried at Pittsford.

The following is from a list of patents on cooking stoves, dated 1790 through 1836. It gives a sample of by whom (and an idea of where) cooking stoves might have been manufactured.

Patent to	Location	Date
John Conant	Brandon	— — — 1819
John Conant	Brandon	December 13, 1823
Henry Stanley	Poultney	December 17, 1832
Elisha Town	Montpelier	December 16, 1833
Elisha Town	Montpelier	May 16, 1834
P. F. Perry	Rockingham	June 28, 1836

As was noted in chapter 1, many Vermont families involved in the iron business were related through marriage. Some might also have been related to similar-named families connected with the iron business in New York State:

New York Connection	Vermont Connection
John Davy Washington Foundry (Troy) ca. 1853-1861	Jacob and Israel Davey (Fair Haven) ca. 1812-1870
S. W. Gibbs (Albany) ca. 1867-1873	Nathan and Cornelius Gibbs (Pittsford) ca. 1796-1825 Cyrus Gibbs ca. 1827-1835
John Perry Albany City Furnace Perry Stove Company ca. 1849-1896	Abner Perry (Tinmouth) ca. 1800-1815
William Cobb Furnace (Albany) ca. 1838-1850	Binny Cobb Foundry (Woodstock) early 1800s
George Willard (Albany) ca. 1839	Elias Willard (Tinmouth) ca. 1800-1815

Two known New York–Vermont connections were:

Joel and John Rathbone Rathbone's Furnace (Albany) ca. 1830-1872	Wait Rathbone, Jr. (Tinmouth) ca. 1815-1837
Rensselaer D. Granger Ransom & Company (Albany) ca. 1840-1850	Simeon Granger (Pittsford) ca. 1827-1879

Joel Rathbone, related to Wait Rathbone, Jr., of Tinmouth, owned a major stove foundry at Albany: "In 1827, as one of the firm of Hermans, Rathbone & Company, he engaged in the wholesale stove business and, by modifications and improvements in the patterns of stoves made under his direction, secured a very large and lucrative trade. In 1829, on the death of Mr. Hermans, he succeeded to the entire business, which he continued in his own name until 1841, when, at the early age of 35 years, with a well-earned fortune, he retired. . . . He purchased a large estate just below the city . . . and 'Kenwood' became his residence" (Cooley 1898:115-116).

Rensselaer Dudley Granger left Pittsford, arriving at Woodstock around 1830 where he operated a foundry (sold to Daniel Taft about 1836). Moving to Troy, New York, he patented an improvement on a rotary cooking stove in 1837 (the cooking surface rotated horizontally over the burn-box). He also patented a cooking stove called Granger's Patent Air-Tight Stove in 1846. This variety stove was called a "parlor cook" because it incorporated a cooking compartment in the chimney (isolated from the smoke). It was an early pioneer of the kitchen range and was manufactured by Ransom & Company of Albany, New York (Groft 1984:28, 88).

Many early-period Vermont-made stoves continue in active service at rural general stores, post offices, small businesses, and private homes. Until he sold them in 1984, the late Douglas Cain of Manchester probably owned the best private collection of Vermont stoves in the state—stoves made at North Dorset, Plymouth, Brandon, West Poultney, and Pittsford (Curtis and Curtis 1974:11-53). Another former collector was Floyd Snow of Arlington. Most of these stoves are now at the Bryant Stove Museum, Thorndike, Maine, about midway between Augusta and Bangor. The author's small collection of Vermont stoves was recently loaned to the Farmers Museum at the President Coolidge birthplace in Plymouth. One of the largest private collections of cast-iron stoves was open to the public at The Stove Museum in North Hoosick, New York, but has been closed some years now. The status of the collection, which contained many made in Vermont, is unknown.

Table 2-1 lists 19th-century Vermont manufacturers of cast-iron parlor stoves with types of stoves cast and typical manufacture date. The data were drawn from archival sources, visits to museums and historical society stove exhibits, and stoves owned by the author. The list is incomplete but contains all Vermont stove makers known at this time. Information on actual dates of stove manufacturing by these furnaces and foundries is scant for two reasons. First, production records, where kept at all, have not survived to any great degree. Second, not all stoves were cast with dates on them. Many have only patent dates, which might or might not reflect the actual year cast. Then there were popular-selling stoves, their designs pirated by unscrupulous foundries and manufactured with neither maker nor date.

Table 2-1. Vermont Cast-Iron Stove Manufacturers

Manufacturer	Location	Type	Date
Addison County			
Monkton Iron Company, Vergennes	(none found)		1810s
Wainwright Foundry, Middlebury	Sheldon Museum, Middlebury	Box #4	1840s
Wainwright Foundry, Middlebury	Shelburne Museum	2-column box	1840s
Wainwright Foundry, Middlebury	Chimney Point Historical Site	Double high	1840s
Bennington County			
Bennington Iron Company, Bennington	Bennington Museum	Franklin	1830s
W. Allen Foundry, North Dorset	(none found)	Box #8	1874
Dorset Iron Company, East Dorset	(none found)	Large box	1850s

Table 2-1. Vermont Cast-Iron Stove Manufacturers (Cont.)

Manufacturer	Location	Type	Date
Caledonia County			
Fairbanks Iron Works, St. Johnsbury	(none found)		1823
Paddock Iron Works, St. Johnsbury	(none found)		1832
Spaulding & Fletcher, St. Johnsbury	(none found)		1874
Chittenden County			
Burlington Mill, Winooski	(none found)		1838
Franklin County			
Sheridan Foundry, Highgate Falls	(none found)		1840s
Lamoille County			
Morrisville Foundry, Morrisville	Farmers Museum, Plymouth	Box "Giant"	1880s?
Orleans County			
Murkland Foundry, Barton	The Chronicle, Barton	Box #26	1890s
Murkland Foundry, Barton	Pierce House, Barton	Parlor	1890s
Eastman Foundry, North Troy	(none found)		1870s
Boston & Troy Iron Company, Troy	(none found)		1840s
Pearson & Burnbee, Irasburg	Old Stone House Museum, Brownington	Cook and box	1840s
Rutland County			
Conant Furnace, Brandon	Congregational Parsonage, Brandon	Range	1840s
Conant Furnace, Brandon	Farmers Museum, Plymouth	Box	?
Langdon Foundry, Castleton	(none found)		1830s
Green Mountain Iron Co., Forest Dale	Farmers Museum, Plymouth	4-column	1840s
Royal Blake, Forest Dale	(none found)	Box	1840s
Rathbone Furnace, Tinmouth	(none found)		1819
Abner Perry, Clarendon	(none found)		1815
Stanley Company, West Poultney	Farmers Museum, Rutland	Box #4	1848
Stanley Company, West Poultney	Farmers Museum, Plymouth	Box #1	1845
A. J. Ruggles Company, West Poultney	(none found)	Box	1850
Pittsford Iron Company, Pittsford	(none found)	Range #3	1857
L. Prichard, Pittsford	Pittsford Historical Society Museum	Box #4	1873
Granger & Brothers, Pittsford	Pittsford Historical Society Museum	Box	1840s
Granger Brothers, Pittsford	Shelburne Museum	Box	1840s
Grimm Company, Rutland	(none found)	Range	1890s
Washington County			
Twing Foundry, Barre	Hill-Martin Company, Barre	Box	1840s
Robinson Foundry, Barre	(none found)		1840s
Wainwright Foundry, Montpelier	(none found)		1830s
Windham County			
(unknown company), Putney	(none found)		1852
Windsor County			
Tyson Furnace, Plymouth	Farmers Museum, Plymouth	Box #7	1839
Tyson Furnace, Plymouth	Woodstock Historical Society Museum	2-column	1847
Daniel Taft & Son, Woodstock	Woodstock Historical Society Museum	Box	1850s
Porter Dodge Company, Perkinsville	Woodstock Historical Society Museum	Soapstone	1859
Dodge, Henry Company, Perkinsville	Woodstock Historical Society Museum	Soapstone	1859
Vermont Snath, Springfield	Congregational Church, Peru	General #8	1859
F. Gilbert Foundry, Hartland	(none found)		1874

2-46. *Sargent, Osgood & Roundy Company's foundry (today's Vermont Castings, Inc.) as it appeared in 1980.*

Stoves are now only intermittently being made in Vermont at Vermont Castings Company, Randolph; Vermont Iron Stoveworks, Waterbury (up to 1988); and Hearthstone, Morrisville. All are presently under market pressure to diversify into other heavy iron products; the Waterbury operation might drop out of the stove-making business altogether. Hearthstone was recently acquired by Industrias Hergon, a Spanish foundry company.

In some of the same buildings at Randolph where the Vermont Castings Company used to make stoves in 1975 but now has its business offices, the Sargent, Osgood & Roundy Company foundry operated a coke-fired furnace and made agricultural

implements until the 1950s. Roger Bedell of Vermont Castings, who worked as a melter at Sargent, Osgood & Roundy from 1938 to 1941 described his days at the old foundry in a 1980 interview:

> I started working there when I was 19. We used to wheel the iron around in a wheelbarrow. We had a crane [and] we'd hitch it up to the wheelbarrow and hoist the whole thing up to the cupola. Then we'd weigh it on a big set of scales and throw the iron in. The man who taught me my job was 80 years old. That was amazing, a man that age wheeling iron around. You wouldn't see that today.
>
> I had to break up the pig iron to get it in the cupola. It comes in big flat pieces. The furnace here (the new foundry) is big enough to take care of it without breaking it up. We used scrap iron, too. The junk men brought in motor blocks, only they weren't smashed up like we get them now. We used to have a big weight out back with a gasoline engine and we'd drop it onto the motor blocks and it would smash them up.
>
> There was a clay plug in the cupola. We stood in front of it with a big rod and poked it out. Then we held the ladle underneath to get the iron and carried it to the molds. The iron was cast in flask molds on the floor. The molds were made by hand, using sand to make the cope and drag which are the lower and upper halves of the mold. The molten iron was poured in by hand and the mold removed when the iron had cooled. Then the castings were shaken out by hand, and the sand shoveled into a machine to get it ready for the next day's castings.
>
> Every morning we melted a batch of iron in the cupola. We'd start pouring at 2 p.m., and pour all the molds for

2-47. *Doing a pour in the Vermont Castings stove foundry at Bethel (courtesy Vermont Castings, Inc., Randolph).*

that day. At the end of the day I had to empty all the leftover iron out of the cupola. Then we remelted it the next day. Now everything is improved. The furnaces never cool. They go on 24 hours a day (*Vermont Castings* Spring 1980:12).

2-48. IA underfoot in Vergennes.

Vermont Castings was formed in 1975 with a handshake between Duncan Syme, his brother-in-law Murray Howell, and William Mitchell (Duffy 1985:202). Their stove parts were initially cast at a foundry in Kentucky and shipped for assembly in the rented Sargent, Osgood & Roundy Company buildings. The demand for stoves during the energy crisis of the 1970s forced the company to contract with larger foundries until its own foundry was built at the south end of the village in 1979. A new assembly plant was later put into operation at Bethel. The new foundry still melts and molds, but with a difference that Sargent, Osgood & Roundy never would have dreamed of: pushbutton computer control. One button will send a line of molds across the casting room, another button starts automatic pouring.

2-49. IA at rest along South Main Street in Rutland.

The foundry uses about 100 tons of molding sand per operating hour. The sand, from Cape Cod, is a highly processed material specifically made for foundry use. Pig iron comes from New York; scrap iron consisting mostly of crushed engine blocks comes from Massachusetts. Three electric furnaces, each with a 40-ton daily capacity, melt and mix the iron with other additives, and maintain the molten iron at 2,700° F.

In contrast to the old flask mold in which the pattern was manually sand-rammed on both sides, Vermont Castings' computer-controlled molds machine-compress the molding sand between two patterns. Each pattern represents the front and back of a stove part; the patterns' imprints on the opposite sides of each section of molding sand in reality end up being the back of one mold and the front of the next. The molds are automatically made in series, laid one against the other, leaving cavities in between that are filled with molten iron. After pouring, the molds move along a conveyor for cooling, then a vibrating track shakes the sand from around the casting. While the molding sand is recycled back on a conveyor, the casting is cleaned, machined, inspected, and assembled, thus carrying on a 20th-century version of an old Vermont ironworks tradition (*Vermont Castings* Spring 1980:1-11).

2-50. A broadax made at Brooksville, on display in the Sheldon Museum at Middlebury.

John Deere and the Lawrence Blacksmith Shop

Neither foundry nor furnace by any stretch of the imagination, the Lawrence blacksmith shop must nonetheless be mentioned because of the apprenticeship served here by John Deere, one of Vermont's more famous ironworkers. Seventeen-year-old Deere left his hometown of Rutland and went to Benjamin Lawrence's blacksmith shop in Middlebury village, apprenticing there from 1821 to 1825. He later set up his own shop at Burlington where he hammered out ironwork for mills being built at Colchester. Not satisfied, he moved to Illinois in 1837 and settled at Grand Detour, where he solved a problem.

The fertile prairie land of the Midwest continually stuck to the plow, creating a frustrating problem for the farmer, who had to stop every few feet to kick clods from the plow. Charles Newbold of New Jersey had relieved some of the early farmers' plight by patenting the first cast-iron plow in 1797, displacing the wooden plow. And in the years following, many blacksmiths tried to improve on Newbold's implement. Jethro Wood's plow patented in 1814 (and again in 1819) succeeded in improving on it by casting the plow in sections. Worn out or broken parts of the blade could be replaced more economically than replacing the entire plow. By 1830 Wood's plow had found popular use in northern and Middle Atlantic states, but its inability to cut into the tough prairie soil discouraged its use in the West (Temin 1964:39).

2-51. *Plows similar to this were made by the thousands in Vermont foundries during the 19th century.*

It was the plow designed by John Deere in his smithy at Grand Detour in 1839, not long after he arrived, that proved the most successful. Deere's plow turned the sticky bottom soil better than all other models. The next year he made 10 plows, in 1841 he made 75, and by 1846, annual production had reached 1,000 plows. Moving to Moline, new shops were built and new partners joined the booming manufacturing and sales business. In 1857 his company made 10,000 plows. John Oliver of Indiana followed in 1868 with the first chilled steel plow whose strength and self-scouring features further improved plowing efficiency. But it was Deere's earlier breakthrough that earned him the distinction of having invented "the plow that broke the plains" (*Encyclopedia* vol. 9 1938:13-15).

An archeological dig into the site of the Benjamin Lawrence shop at Frog Hollow was carried out in 1975, coordinated by Bill Murphy and assisted by his 11-year-old son Brendan, plus Bob Alcott and others. Materials retrieved included enough evidence to prove the site had been used for blacksmithing, gunsmithing, and carpentry work (Murphy ms 1975). Murphy's report and some of the artifacts from the dig are at the nearby Sheldon Museum. In the park in front of the museum is a historical marker, recognizing John Deere's contribution.

Flask Molding

The casting was made by either of two methods: sand casting or flask molding (see *Sand Cast Moulding* 1981; *Hopewell Furnace* 1983:50-51). Sand casting was the earlier and simpler of the two, requiring only that the pattern be pressed into fine sand, usually on the casting room floor. After removing the pattern from the sand, the remaining depression was the reverse of the pattern. When the molten iron was poured into the depression, the final casting ended up a nearly exact copy of the depressed pattern. ("Nearly exact" because the iron shrinks a bit as it cools.) One of the many problems with this type of molding, however, was that molten iron naturally flowed to its own level. Unless the sand depression was exactly level, the casting ended up with the "downhill" end much thicker than the "uphill" end. The result was a casting either too thick, heavy, and costly, or too thin and weak (and also costly since the casting was discarded and reworked). Flask molding not only solved these problems, but also made it possible to make three-dimensional castings, that is, design motifs on top, bottom, and both sides of the casting, if desired. The flask, however, was a more intricate device, which required skills that eventually earned a molder the reputation of a craftsman.

The flask itself was a wooden box made up of sections. Its size depended on the size of the casting. Since stoves were made in sections that were assembled after casting, the sizes of flasks could be kept manageable, about 2 feet long, 1½ feet wide, and a foot high. When assembled, rammed with special damp molding sand, and filled with molten iron, the flask was quite heavy—thus the need to carefully design stove parts and assembly procedures.

Flask molding started with the molder placing a clean, dry follow board on his workbench. The follow board was about 1 inch thick and made to the same dimensions as the flask. The flask body was made of two identical wooden sections, each resembling an open, four-sided box without bottom or top. The first of these two sections was called the drag and it was placed directly on the follow board. The wood pattern was gently placed on the follow board and centered in the drag. The pattern was then sprinkled with a light coating of charcoal dust to prevent molding sand from sticking to it.

One secret of perfect molding was to use a high-quality molding sand. The best early molding sand came to be called Albany Sand because originally it was found near Albany (Guilderland), New York. Similar-quality sand, eventually found at other places, was also called Albany Sand.

After the pattern was coated with the charcoal dust, the slightly damp molding sand was shoveled into a hand-held sieve, called a riddle, which was shaken over the pattern, sifting and spreading the fine sand evenly over the entire pattern. After the pattern was completely covered, some coarse, damp sand was added until the drag was slightly overfilled. The sand was packed down with a wooden rammer and the excess scraped away with a strike bar, by running the bar diagonally across the top edge of the drag.

Another follow board was placed on top of the drag, and the whole assembly, including the bottom follow board, was carefully turned over so that the second follow board was now on the bottom of the flask. The first follow board, now on top, was removed, exposing the pattern. Loose sand was blown away with a small hand bellows. The second of the two flask sections, called the cope, was placed squarely on the drag. Before the cope was likewise filled with sand, a hole had to be left in the sand to allow the molten iron to be poured through it and into the cavity left by the later-removed pattern. This hole was accomplished by placing a round, tapered, wooden wedge, small-end down, directly on the center of the pattern. The wedge was called the gate; the hole left after its removal was the gateway. The gate was just long enough to stick above the top edge of the cope.

As before, charcoal dust was sprinkled on the pattern, followed by fine, damp molding sand sifted through the riddle, and finally coarse sand rammed compactly into the cope and carefully around the gate. The excess sand was again cut away with a strike bar, being careful not to jar the gate sticking out of the top of the sand. The gate was then very carefully lifted straight up and away, leaving the funnel-shaped gateway through the sand to the bottom where a small part of the pattern could be seen. Loose sand was blown away with the bellows. The molding sand, being slightly damp and tightly compact, would now allow the cope and all the sand in it to be gently lifted from the drag, so that the wooden pattern could be removed. The pattern had now left both sides of its impression in the sand; on the top of the drag (the bottom half of the flask) and the bottom of the cope (the top half of the flask). Any touching up of the impression was done with a molders spoon; loose sand was again blown away with the bellows. The cope was replaced atop the drag exactly as before and two or more iron C-clamps wedged the cope and drag, along with the follow board at the bottom, tightly together. When the molten iron

2-52. *Middlebury stove marked Wainwright 4 on display in the Sheldon Museum at Middlebury.*

was poured through the gateway and into the pattern cavity, the C-clamps prevented the cope from "floating" or lifting off the drag.

Numbers of flasks were assembled and set up on strongly supported platforms or on the level casting room floor, allowing quick and easy filling with molten iron. The flasks were usually lined in rows that extended outward from the furnace so the molder could quickly walk in straight lines back and forth between the hearth and the flask without having to go around corners. When all was ready, the foundryman tapped the furnace and white-hot molten iron immediately ran out into a hand- or crane-held crucible. Steady hands, strong back, and a cool, patient mind were now necessary as the molder quickly and carefully ladled iron from the crucible to each flask. He filled the flask with one complete pour to the top of the gateway before going to the next flask or returning to the crucible for enough iron for the next complete pour. Other ironworkers kept clear of the area lest the molder become distracted, spill the hot iron, and waste time, causing the iron to "dull." With all the flasks filled, the iron immediately began to set. The flasks were unclamped and the castings removed with tongs to be air-cooled—quicker cooling than if left to cool in the flask. After cooling, the small tapered piece of iron formed from the gateway was broken off, rough edges were filed, and the casting cleaned and inspected. If necessary, screw holes or assembly slots were drilled and the finished casting buffed and sent on its way to be assembled along with other sections into a stove, or to the carpenter shop to be crated for shipment.

The Molder

The major effort at the foundry cupola evolved around the molder (see Stockton 1921). It was he who ladled molten iron into molds and was responsible for the quality of the castings. Since early furnaces frequently had no fixed time for pouring off, the molds were prepared ahead of time and the molder went home to wait to be called, and often the call would come in the middle of the night. It was not uncommon, therefore, for a molder to be seen trudging to the furnace at 4 a.m., with his helper (also known as his "berkshire") carrying a lantern beside him.

Working hours of the early molders were long and indefinite. Heats were frequently run all day and night, seven days a week. Workmen casting at night sometimes slept beside their furnaces. At some furnaces, molders were required to furnish their own tools and facing materials, and frequently were compelled to pay for broken or damaged patterns and molds, or were not paid at all for imperfect castings. Wages were low; payment made partly in money and partly in store orders or due bills. Some foundrymen fined molders for reporting late while giving nothing for overtime work.

Molten iron from the cupola was often dirty or dull. Dull iron was molten iron too cold to pour properly. There were also cases when castings were imperfect, where insufficient iron had been melted to fill all the molds, or where chill cracks developed in the castings. Prior to the 1890s, stove foundrymen often refused to pay for castings made with dull iron, placing the entire loss on the molders over their vigorous protests. At

2-53. Morrisville stove marked Giant No 2 on display in the Farmers Museum at Plymouth Notch.

times the foundry was at fault for supplying dull iron, but it was usually impossible to place responsibility for work lost due to this because molten iron lost life rapidly after being drawn from the cupola. Molten iron carried too long in a molder's ladle could also become unfit for use. It was a dispute between

2-54. Murkland stove on display in the Pierce House at Barton (courtesy Robin Tenny).

foundryman and molder that often resulted in open rupture in the normally close working relationship at the furnace. The problem of dull and insufficient iron was taken up in 1896 by the National Union of Iron Molders (the Molder's Union) with the solution that a questionable heat be poured only by a foreman's order, and any work lost by dull or insufficient iron for that heat still be paid for.

The Apprentice Molder and Molders' Helpers

As was the custom (and still is in some industries), boys were apprenticed to molding skills at an early age. Many were sons or nephews of already-skilled ironworkers (journeymen), while others had no connections at all with the business. The related apprentice obviously had the inside advantage. The practice of legally indenturing the apprentice was starting to phase out by the post-Civil War years although the molders fought to keep it as a form of job security for the apprentice. By a legal indenture the employer contracted with the boy's parent or guardian to teach him the trade, furnish him work each working day, pay him a stated wage, furnish him proper care during sickness, and be responsible before the courts. The apprentice agreed to be honest, sober, and attentive, to work each working day, advance his master's interest, and use diligence in learning the trade. Either party had the power to break the indenture for sufficient cause as determined by the court, and the indentures were recorded at county-level offices. The usual indenture period was four years. The ratio of the number of apprentices to molders in the shop, however, was always in dispute. Neither the foundry operators, the ironworkers, nor, eventually, the Molder's Union could ever agree. Apprentice-to-journeymen ratios varied from 1:6 to 1:8. Even varying the ratios per floors of the foundry was tried, with the same lack of success.

By the 1890s the age of the indenture had been generally accepted by all parties to have long-ago passed, and although the ratio problem continued as a hot issue, no strike occurred over it. Because most foundries could not provide continuous year-round employment for molders and therefore the exact method of figuring the number of molders on which to base the ratio, the issue continued to the 1920s.

In the early 1800s boys were often apprenticed to the molders trade while still children, 11 and 12 years old not being uncommon. Boys of a more advanced age, however, were usually preferred. In 1867 the Molder's Union established 16 as a minimum age and in 1870 that of 20 to be maximum age. The latter was rescinded in 1895 and the 16 minimum age held into the 1920s.

The foundry owners always insisted the apprentice serve his entire term with a single employer; the foundryman who used the apprentice during his earlier, unproductive years should also have his services during his later, productive years. The molders never made it a rule to call the apprentices out on strike since the relationship between employer and apprentice was looked on as personal, not to be interrupted by action of the journeymen. Although some shops did involve apprentices in strikes, by the 1920s it was still the exception rather than the rule.

The molder's helper was a person hired to assist the skilled journeyman under whose direct supervision he worked. In contrast to the apprentice, the helper was not engaged to learn the job, but to supply comparatively unskilled labor. The helpers were divided into three classes: remote helpers, helpers, and advanced helpers. Remote helpers were little more than laborers and came into little intimate contact with the journeymen. They cut sand, skimmed iron, and shook out castings. Helpers worked alongside the journeymen and were known as berkshires, or bucks. The term berkshire originated in Berkshire County, England, where the English molders developed the term sometime before the 19th century. Helpers handled patterns and prepared the simpler molds. Advanced helpers were helpers in transition to the status of full mechanic, or journeyman-on-probation.

The helpers were continuously in the midst of controversy, seen as a low-cost advantage to the foundryman and a job threat by the molder and apprentice. Obviously, the helpers often picked up enough of the trade to qualify for a molder's job in the event of the latter's absence from the shop due to illness or strike. If the helper became disgruntled with his molder, he frequently set up as a molder himself, thus intensifying competition within the trade. Berkshires were prohibited from joining the Molder's Union; they were barred from employment at most association shops by the early 1900s.

Railroad Iron and National Industrial Trends

The period of Vermont ironworks expansion peaked by the 1840s and in the midst of the national economic panics of the 1850s had commenced its decline. Even the coming of the railroad, which most ironworkers associated with heavy iron consumption, failed to significantly increase iron production anywhere in New England until after the Civil War.

Early railroads used little iron, except for the steam engine. Passenger cars were wooden copies of the old stagecoaches, and tracks were thin strips of iron nailed to a wood rail. As engines and cars grew in size and weight, however, an all-iron track was needed and developed. But since the railroad builders were more interested in initial costs than in long-term operation, cheaper rails of poor quality were imported from England, much to the disgust of domestic iron makers. Abram Hewitt, co-manager of the Trenton Iron Company of New Jersey, one of the largest U.S. ironworks of the time, charged: "The vilest trash which could be dignified by the name of iron went universally [in the Welsh ironworks] by the name of American rail" (Temin 1964:21-22).

The British not only supplied cheap rails, they supplied them on credit. Capital was obtained more easily in England than in the United States, and the American railroads of the 1850s were built of British iron, at least partly because they were also built with British capital (Temin 1964:22). This was also true in Vermont. When an order for rails by the Rutland & Burlington Railroad with a Boston foundry in 1847 fell through because of the condition of the money market, the railroad company immediately contracted for 2,000 tons of English rail (Shaughnessy 1964:5).

The major demand for iron in Vermont came from the non-railroad sector sector of the economy. The Civil War offered some economic stimulus to drag a handful of the major Vermont ironworks along with it. But only after the war did rolling mills in this country produce rails acceptable to the domestic industry in quantity to supply most U.S. needs. By then, the dominance of iron manufacture had already been established well away from New England, and the prominence of iron smelting and pig iron production in Vermont had been lost.

Evolution of the Vermont Iron Industry

In the 1850s the Vermont iron industry reflected changes in national industrial trends as more pig iron was run from blast furnace hearths into commercial bars. In that form the cast iron became a more versatile valuable market commodity than products cast directly at the furnace. This period saw many foundries relocating away from blast furnaces and closer to industrial consumers or transportation facilities. These foundries forced the local blast furnace to compete for business against cast iron made hundreds of miles away, thanks to canal boats plying Lake Champlain and railroads snaking up the valleys. Small trip-hammer shops found stiff competition from foundries, the latter finding molding sand significantly more adaptable to intricate patterns that ponderous forge hammers could not match. The independent foundry stole the stove business away from the blast furnace, and later the stove industry itself split off as a separate industry. By 1860 about 30 percent of the foundries nationwide specialized in casting stoves (Temin 1964:38-39).

The emphasis of the iron industry in 1870s Vermont had shifted from iron making to ironworking. All blast furnaces except one (Pittsford) had gone cold and most bloomeries were out of operation. Waterpower was still running most of the ironworks, while a few were powered by steam engine fueled by wood from the local forests or coal shipped in by train or boat from as far away as Pennsylvania. Agricultural implements, from rakes and scythes to threshing machines, were now in growing demand due to continued agricultural, commercial, and population expansion in the western farming states and territories. Heavy industry for its time was making its presence felt in Vermont through the manufacture of steam engines, boilers, machine castings, railroad track, bridges, and paper, stone, and lumber machinery. Iron foundries could be found in almost every city and major village in the state.

The first truly comprehensive list of iron manufacturing companies in the nation was published in 1874, titled *Wiley's American Iron Trade Manual of the Leading Iron Industries of the United States.* The title actually continues for another 53 words and the book contains descriptions of blast furnaces, locomotive works, foundries, stove foundries, shipyards, etc. Vermont ironworks total 173 entries, compared to 257 entries for New Hampshire and 600 for Massachusetts. The entries include everything from blast furnaces and steel mills to small general-purpose machine shops and they describe, from the commercial perspective, the state of the iron industry by 1874.

Table 2-2 presents that state of the ironworking industry in Vermont in 1874 as extracted from the book (*Wiley's* 1874:162-165). Included in the table are foundries and machine shops, large and small, in sequence by county and town.

Table 2-2. Vermont Foundry Activity in 1874

Location	Company Name or Owner	Products
Addison County		
Bristol	M. Barlow	Plow irons
	G. H. Bartlett	Iron foundry, agricultural implements
Brooksville	Brooks Edge Tool Company	Axes, hatchets
East Middlebury	Burlington Manufacturing Company	Iron foundry
Middlebury	R. Ross	Machinery
	D. Martin	Iron castings, machinery
Shoreham	E. S. Newell	Agricultural implements
Starksboro	D. Fergusson	Agricultural implements
	P. Morrison	Agricultural implements
	S. W. Nutting	Agricultural implements
Vergennes	National Horse Nail Company	Horsenails
	Vergennes Machine Company	Woodworking machinery
Bennington County		
Arlington	F. L. Ames	Chisels
	Arlington Car Manufacturing Company	Railroad milk cars
	I. McLaughlin	Machinery
Bennington	E. Adams	Patent steam governors
	Cooper & Tiffany	Knitting machines
	Putnam Manufacturing Company	Wringers, metal notions
	Bennington Machine Works	Paper and marble machines
	A. Walsh	Machinery
Dorset	W. Allen	Iron foundry
Peru	E. P. Chandler	Machinery
South Shaftsbury	Eagle Square Company	Carpenters' steel squares, cutlery
Sunderland	Douglas Manufacturing Company	Edge tools
Caledonia County		
Barnet	Smith & Galbraith	Agricultural implements
	Jas. Warden	Agricultural implements
Danville	S. Ladd	Edge tools
	J. Gould	Edge tools
Groton	M. Wild	Edge tools

Table 2-2. Vermont Foundry Activity in 1874 (Cont.)

Location	Company Name or Owner	Products
Caledonia County (Cont.)		
St. Johnsbury	J. Belknap	Knives
	L. Buzzell	Iron foundry and machinery
	E. & T. Fairbanks Company	Railroad track, platform, and counter scales
	Jas. Nutt	Files
	Paddock, Dean & Company	Machinery
	N. W. Peck	Agricultural implements
	B. F. Rollins	Threshing machines
	Spaulding & Fletcher	Stoves
	Jas. M. Warner	Mowing machines
	Connecticut & Passumpsic Railroad Machine Shop	
Chittenden County		
Burlington	Brink & Company	Iron and brass foundry
	W. G. Farmer	Machinery
	B. S. Nichols & Company	Steam engines, wood- and slate-working machinery
	P. M. Varney	Machinery, guns
Hinesburgh	J. Edwin	Machinery
	P. Rufus & Sons	Agricultural implements
Jericho	A. M. Ford	Turbine wheels, machinery
	H. S. & F. D. Wood	Agricultural implements
North Williston	H. J. Fay	Agricultural implements
	Paine & Brown	Iron foundry
Winooski Falls	R. Daniels, Edwards, Stephens & Company	Waterwheels, mill and woodworking machinery
Franklin County		
Bakersfield	Brelgham & Barnes	Agricultural implements
Enosburgh	J. Bust & Company	Machinery
	J. Parley & Company	Machinery
	Sprague & Lawrence	Machinery
Highgate	B. Olds	Machinery
	D. V. Sheridan	Iron foundry
Montgomery	Carpenter & Smith	Agricultural implements
	H. D. Sabin	Machinery
St. Albans	St. Albans Foundry Company	Railroad car wheels, agricultural implements
	Vermont Central Railroad Machine Shop	

Table 2-2. Vermont Foundry Activity in 1874 (Cont.)

Location	Company Name or Owner	Products
Franklin County (Cont.)		
Sheldon	S. S. F. Carlisle & Company	Iron foundry
Swanton	B. B. Blake	Edge tools, machinery
	J. Truax	Machinery
	Kidder & Rood	Mowing machines
Lamoille County		
Johnson	H. D. Stearns	Horse rakes
Morristown	F. F. George	Machinery
Orange County		
Bradford	R. R. Aldrich	Machinery
	H. Strickland	Iron foundry, machinery, agricultural implements
Brookfield	Locke & Company	Agricultural implements
	Brookfield Fork Company	Forks
Fairlee	H. S. Porter	Scythes, axes
North Tunbridge	R. Smith & Company	Iron foundry
Orange	D. Dinsmore	Agricultural implements
Randolph	Jas. Welch	Iron foundry, castings
Thetford	A. S. Briggs	Edge tools
	S. C. Arnold	Machinery
	O. B. Blake	Machinery
Tunbridge	J. L. Hall	Axes, edge tools
	G. H. Hacket	Machinery
	R. C. & C. B. Smith	Machinery
Orleans County		
Albany	I. H. McClary	Agricultural implements
Charleston	E. H. Goodwin & Son	Machinery
North Troy	Elkins & Braley	Stump and stone extractors, agricultural implements
Rutland County		
Benson	Dorsey & Howard	Agricultural implements
Brandon	Brandon Manufacturing Company	Howes' scales, weigh beams, store trucks
	Eagle Foundry	Bridge castings

Table 2-2. Vermont Foundry Activity in 1874 (Cont.)

Location	Company Name or Owner	Products
<u>Rutland County (Cont.)</u>		
Castleton	F. A. Barrows	Iron foundry, plows, machinery
East Poultney	M. G. Noyes	Machinery
Fair Haven	Leonard & Baldwin	Machinery
Mendon	Walker & Riley	Machinery
Middletown	A. W. Gray	Agricultural implements
	E. W. Gray	Iron foundry
	J. Granger	Machinery
	H. Haynes	Machinery
Mount Holly	M. Tarbell	Agricultural implements
Pawlet	E. Colvin & Bro.	Edge tools
Poultney	H. M. Ruggles	Iron foundry, machinery
Rutland	Mansfield & Stimson	Iron foundry, machinery
	Rutland Foundry & Machine Shop	Railroad car wheels
	A. L. Smith	Tools
	Steam Stone Cutter Company	Stone dressing, quarry machinery
	Rutland Railroad Machine Shop	
	Lincoln Iron Works	Steam engines, machinery, castings
Wallingford	Batcheller & Sons	Forks, scythes, hoes
	Globe Fork Works	Hay and agricultural implements
West Rutland	W. Graham	Machinery
	C. J. Lee	Machinery
	W. M. Tuggy	Machinery
<u>Washington County</u>		
Barre	Stafford, Holden & Company	Agricultural implements
	Smith, Whitcomb & Cook	Mill machinery, turbines
Berlin	D. B. & J. S. Boisworth	Horse rakes
Calais	W. C. Robinson	Horse rakes
	W. Chase	Machinery
Montpelier	N. P. Brooks	Tools, builders hardware
	J. L. Cummings	Edge tools
	Lane, Pitkin & Brook	Circular sawmills, waterwheels, mill gearing
	M. Wright & Son	Woodworking machinery
	Stimson & Company	Spring hinges

Table 2-2. Vermont Foundry Activity in 1874 (Cont.)

Location	Company Name or Owner	Products
Washington County (Cont.)		
Northfield	W. Briggs	Tools
	Belknap, Ely & Company	Iron foundry, circular sawmills
	J. M. Smith	Tools
	W. J. Wright	Machinery
	H. D. Bean	Machinery
Waterbury	D. K. Adams & Company	Iron foundry
	H. W. Judson & Company	Machinery
	H. Moffett & Company	Iron foundry, machinery
	A. H. Selleck & Company	Carding machinery
	Colby Bros & Company	Machinery
	M. E. Smilie	Machinery
Woodbury	J. W. Town	Machinery
Windham County		
Athens	Durham & Upton	Agricultural implements
Bellows Falls	Frost, Derby & Company	Scythe snaths
	Osgood & Barker	Iron foundry, machinery
	A. Worthington	Machinery
	Rutland & Burlington Railroad Machine Shop	
Brattleboro	Burnham & Willis	Iron foundry, machinery
	L. H. Crane	Machinery
	F. Tyler	Iron foundry, papermaking machinery
	S. M. Spencer	Dies
	Vinton & Hines	Machinery
	C. J. Weld	Wood-planing machines
	G. B. Wheeler	Edge tools, axes, skates, drawing knives
	L. Worcester	Machinery
Londonderry	Thos. Gearfield, Jr.	Agricultural implements
	H. Lawrence	Machinery
Putney	W. Parker	Rakes
West Brattleboro	J. Clark	Machinery
Wilmington	A. B. Medbury	Screws
Windsor County		
Bethel	L. W. Newton	Machinery
	J. G. Sargent & Company	Tools
Bridgewater	R. W. & F. L. Penny	Machinery

Table 2-2. Vermont Foundry Activity in 1874 (Cont.)

Location	Company Name or Owner	Products
Windsor County (Cont.)		
Hartford	French, Watson & Company	Specialty work, forks, agricultural implements
Hartland	N. F. English	Machinery
	F. Gilbert	Agricultural implements, plows, stoves
Ludlow	W. A. Patrick	Lathes, wood machinery
	Patrick & Gregg	Machinery
	J. P. Warner	Machinery
Rochester	Pearsons & Heath	Edge tools
	J. Woods	Machinery
	A. Worcester	Iron foundry, agricultural implements
Springfield	Gilman & Townsend	Last machines
	Geo. Kimball	Rakes
	Messenger & Davis	Machinery
	Parks & Woolson	Cloth-finishing machinery
	Richardson & Company	Castings, agricultural implements
Windsor	F. Draper	Iron foundry, general castings
	Windsor Manufacturing Company	Lathes, drill presses, milling machines
	Lamson & Goodnow Manufacturing Co.	Scythe snaths
Woodstock	R. Daniels Machine Company	Rag-, rope-, and straw-cutting machines, agricultural implements
	A. G. Dewey	Scythes, axes
	W. S. English	Rakes
	A. H. Wellington	Machinery
	N. Woodbury	Machinery

Transition

From the 1840s to the 1980s, the Vermont ironworks experience was varied, with many types and sizes of shops, foundries, and works. As the railroads and canals reached toward and into Vermont, they also affected the character of this industry. Some small shops moved out of the hills to take advantage of the opportunity to interface with the national market. But the transition from supplying local needs to national demands now subjected these operations to vacillations of national economics from which the small shops had formerly been insulated. Western migration and the taming of the prairie created an industry all its own. Hundreds of Vermont shops and factories turned out axes, hoes, shovels, scythes, hay tedders, potato diggers, cultivators, hay and manure forks, and plows for the prairie farms, along with nails, tools, stoves, and domestic hardware (door hinges, andirons, kettles, latches) for the prairie house and barn. Increased construction of government and commercial buildings in capital cities and financial centers resulted in the exploitation of Vermont's granite, marble, and slate resources. This in turn spawned a stone-working tool and machine industry that produced machinery for quarrying, cutting, finishing, and polishing. And even the means to transport these heavy and cumbersome products of stone and iron both within the state and to the outside world created railroad shops and foundries that made railroad cars, car wheels, track, truck castings, locomotive boilers and engines, and even the iron bridges to carry all of it over rivers, roads, and valleys.

A study of trade journals and U.S. Census returns determined

2-55. *One of the few remaining structures of the original Lincoln Iron Works in Rutland.*

trends in Vermont technical foundry operations, working conditions, power sources (surprisingly, many were still using waterpower well after much of the rest of the country had converted to steam or electricity), and factors well beyond the scope of this book. One interesting aspect of the study was that some of the businesses identified themselves by their type of operations (foundry, manufacturing, machine shop) and others by product manufactured (agricultural implements, machine castings, tools, stoves). Many identified themselves with a multiple number of operations and products, which made for difficulty in tracking them in the reference material. It raised questions as to whether something had really changed from the previous year, or whether the respondent merely answered the same question in a different way.

Table 2-3 presents a product/process-oriented listing of Vermont industries included in industrial trade journals for the years listed. Taken together with the other information in this chapter, it brings the character of the ironworking business in Vermont into better focus. For example, the decline and disappearance of waterwheel manufacture is the obvious result of conversion to more dependable sources of power. The loss of the elevator business, on the other hand, is the result of consolidation of that industry by larger companies outside Vermont (e.g., Otis Elevator, Boston).

The decline in numbers of foundry and machine manufacturing businesses year to year was sometimes the result of reorganization and consolidation into larger, more efficient operations. Smith, Whitcomb & Cook of Barre had 35 employees in 1926 but 65 in 1980, an 86 percent increase. Jones & Lamson

Machine Company at Springfield rose from 600 employees in 1926 to 1,000 in 1980, a 67 percent increase, but in the same time period employment at Howe Scales at Rutland dropped from 650 to 250.

In terms of numbers of operations, the ironworking industry in Vermont essentially doubled between the 1840s and the turn of the century. The impression that a "long Vermont winter" was experienced in the late 19th century is contradicted, at least by the ironworks sector. Activity in the peak year of 1896 reached 158 foundries, factories, and machine shops, keeping many hundred hands (and bodies) busy and warm while working hot iron (*Walton's* 1844-1984). During that hectic period, 40 percent of Vermont's ironworking production was accomplished in Rutland, Windsor, and Addison counties. Foundries and machine shops affected the economies of 120 Vermont towns. The top ten ironworks centers in the 1890s were St. Johnsbury, Brattleboro, Springfield, Barre, Rutland, Montpelier, Windsor, Burlington, St. Albans, and Bennington.

With the turn of the century, the complexion of the ironworking business in Vermont changed as the manufacture of ponderous iron castings gave way to delicate tools and electronic scales. By 1909, foundries and machine shops had consolidated or dwindled to 14 operations in just as many cities (*Walton's* 1909:184). The number of ironworking shops in the state in 1980 declined to near 1840 figures (productivity was obviously much higher). Those remaining are more in the line of space-age precision toolmaking shops rather than the traditional foundries and heavy machine shops. Windsor, Rutland, and Chittenden counties account for 50 percent of this 20th-century version of

Table 2-3. Vermont Industry Trends

Product	Number of Establishments for Year					
	1889	1893	1902	1910	1920	1926
Agricultural implements	51	31	22	16	10	6
Automobiles					1	1
Axles	2	1				
Blacksmith tools	5	2				
Boilers (steam)	7	5		1	2	2
Bridges			1	1		
Car wheels (railroad)	2	3				
Edge tools	7	4	4			
Elevators	2	2	1			
Forging machinery		1				
Foundries	39	27	18	11	12	12
Hollowware	3	2				
Heavy machinery/castings	80	56	59	36	35	41
Machine tools	6	12	15	3	12	8
Scales	3	2	2	3	3	3
Stone-cutting machines	5	16	28			3
Stoves	13	6				
Waterwheels	14	8	3			
Yearly total:	239	178	153	71	75	76

the ironworking industry. The top ten machine and tool centers have now become Springfield, Burlington, Rutland, Winooski, Windsor, Brattleboro, Barre, St. Albans, St. Johnsbury, and Lyndonville.

Epilogue

It must appear strange that some of today's quiet, pastoral Vermont towns such as Dorset, Bristol, Highgate, New Haven, Arlington, Sheldon, Tinmouth, Lincoln, and Middlebury were a century-and-a-half ago at the very cutting edge of the Industrial Revolution.

There are those communities that lost, through change, their industrial-sounding names:

Lyon's Works (Fair Haven)
Factory Point (Manchester Center)

Mill Village (Cady's Falls).
Forge Flatts (Holden)

Others have remained in name to preserve a hint of their industrial roots:

Chiselville (in Sunderland)
Graniteville (in Barre)

Mechanicsville (in Hinesburg)
Talcville (in Rochester)

And finally, there are those that disappeared altogether, along with their unique names:

Foundryville (in Hartland)
Copper Flat (in Strafford)

Old Job (in Mount Tabor)
Furnace Village (in Pittsford)

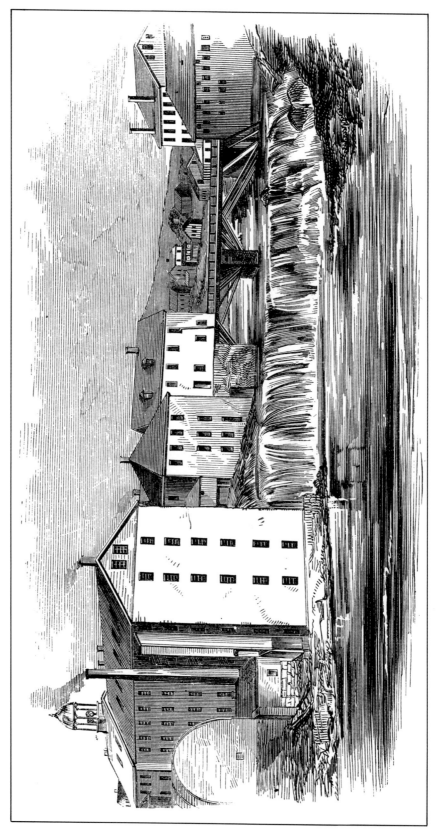

Middlebury Falls, from an engraving in Samuel Swift's History of the Town of Middlebury, 1859.

Chapter 3
Iron Mines and Ore Pits

Iron ore is found in many forms throughout the world. Long before it was being worked in primitive hearths, nodules of nearly pure iron could be found lying about on the ground. History books have numerous accounts of high-quality bar iron being made at forges from iron-rich rocks and outcroppings found up and down the mountains of western New England during colonial times. As the frontier moved slowly westward over these mountains from the early New England coastal settlements, some sharp-eyed land speculators quickly recognized the natural resources of the area. It was not only the agricultural, mineral, and lumbering resources that attracted them, but also the proximity of many of these resources to potentially excellent mill seats along the many quick-flowing mountain streams and rivers.

3-1. *After being hand-screened, the ore was shoveled onto a mechanical screen (the angled frame) and, by swaying this back and forth against the side uprights, ore was filtered through quarter-inch mesh into the pile below. Riddlings vibrated over the edge of the frame into the box at left to be discarded (Overman 1850:47).*

During and immediately following the Revolutionary War, thousands of acres of Vermont land were consolidated from numerous small holdings into large and expansive tracts, or grants. Choice grants were quickly acquired by the first to come, many of whom served in Vermont during the Revolution. Typical was Matthew Lyon, who in 1779 was arranging for the grant of the town of Fair Haven. Lyon had already inspected the town and became aware of the commercial value of the falls on the Castleton River and also the lumber and iron resources in the area. Likewise Ira Allen, who in 1783 was contracting for the construction of forges along the Winooski River to exploit the bog ore beds at Colchester. That same year, William Gilliland of New York State was contemplating the erection of an ironworks, which was eventually built in 1801 at Willsboro, New York, and was designed for casting anchors weighing from 300 to 1,500 pounds. They were shipped up the lake to Whitehall, overland to Fort Edward, thence by boat on the Hudson River to Troy.

Ore for these works came principally from Vermont, with small amounts from Canada. One of the early ore beds has historically been located at Basin Harbor. Owned by Platt Rogers, it was the only deposit worked during that period in the whole region (Watson 1869:438-439). But this bed was in fact across the lake in New York. Rogers settled at Basin Harbor at an early time, causing confusion between location of his residence and of his ore bed (Allen 1980:16). Soon after 1790 a number of ore beds were being worked along the western slopes of the Green Mountains. Samuel Williams wrote in 1794 that great quantities of iron ore were located at Tinmouth, Pittsford, Rutland, and Shoreham, the ore was melted and worked easily, and it made excellent nails (Williams 1794:316). The 1796 Whitelaw map also identified two "iron oar" beds at Bennington and another at Monkton, in addition to identifying ironworks sites. Major beds were opening in 1800 at Bennington, Highgate, Monkton, and Chittenden. By 1842 Zadock Thompson had recorded a total of 24 towns where iron ore was known to exist or was being actively mined. Two-thirds of these towns are in the western part of the state.

The earliest organized attempt to scientifically analyze the state's mineral resources was a series of reports published by State Geologist Charles B. Adams. In 1845 Adams published the first formal report on the geology of Vermont in which he categorized ores as brown iron ore and magnetic oxide (Adams 1845:17-27). The former included brown hematite, bog ore, and yellow ocher; magnetic oxides included red hematite, magnetic ore, and red ocher.

The brown ores were found in Bennington, Tinmouth, Dorset, Manchester, Huntington, Milton, Wallingford, Putney, Brandon, Pittsford, Monkton, Leicester, Bristol, Guilford, Salisbury, Chittenden, Highgate, Swanton, Plymouth, Rutland, Strafford, Colchester, and Sherburne. Hematite mined at Colchester in the late 1840s was boated up the lake to be smelted in an iron furnace at Westport, New York (Hodge May 19,

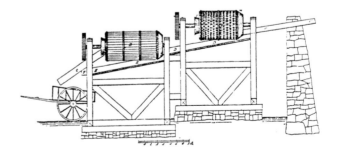

3-2. *A typical ore washer in which raw ore was washed and separated from waste by streams of water in two revolving cast-iron drums. The first (upper) drum was perforated with small holes and the second (lower) drum had long slits. Iron ore that reached the bottom was carted to the blast furnace (Salisbury Iron 1878:6).*

3-3. *The entrance to one of the Somerset iron mines at West Dover.*

1849:306). A vein of iron ore at North Dorset was described as being three feet wide and within 100 feet of the ca.-1830 blast furnace there. And a mine one mile east of Sheldon was one of many in the area that provided iron to blast furnaces in the early 1800s (Morrill and Chaffee 1964:41). Brown hematite ore was mined at Forest Dale at the foot of a sandy hill to the east of the furnace, near the base of higher mountains. Some 1849 costs were: iron ore, $1.75 per ton, at the mine; iron ore, $2.50 per ton, after washing; and charcoal, $5.00 per 100 bushels.

Before charging it into the furnace, the ore was washed to remove clay, stones, and dirt, allowing for a more efficient smelting process. Yield of the furnace was 5½ to 6 tons of iron a day. The annual capacity of the furnace was about 1,200 tons (Hodge May 12 and 19, 1849:290 and 305). Iron was also mined at "Selden's marble mill" in eastern Brandon, where the limestone contained several percent iron ore. This limestone was mined along with the iron and used for flux at the furnace (Hitchcock et al. 1861:640).

Lumps of brown iron ore were abundant in the soil of Dr. Drury's farm, two miles south of the Pittsford blast furnace. And in Chittenden, three miles northeast of the Pittsford stack, was Mitchell's ore bed, one of the most extensive iron mines. From a main shaft 60 feet deep, galleries were dug 100 feet to the north and south. The south gallery led to a solid bed of ore, two to three yards thick in limestone rock. It provided 45 percent of the iron at the Pittsford furnace. Conant's mine at Brandon had not yet bottomed out of the ore bed at 90 feet, and he improved the yield of iron to 50 percent by working the ore with a stream of water, washing it in a rotating strainer. Other iron ore diggings were found in 1987 near Beaudry Brook

on the west slope of Bloodroot Mountain in Chittenden, and also about 200 feet downhill along Steam Mill Brook. Both are associated with mound-type charcoal-making sites; the latter with stone foundation ruins of possible ore-roasting ovens.

A major hematite discovery in Sheldon in the 1830s was exploited for over 50 years. The initial outcrop, on a knoll near Black Creek, was worked (mostly by open cut) by Lawrence Brainerd and W. O. Gadcomb, both of St. Albans, who owned the property. They built a bloomery forge (location unknown) and produced blooms, working it into bar iron that was used in the vicinity, although some was shipped up Lake Champlain to Troy and Albany, New York. But lack of direct railroad connections and insufficient demand for the blooms forced abandonment of the forge. The vein was traced for nearly 20 miles, with some prospecting done on outcrops at Berkshire, Enosburg, and a few miles east of St. Albans. The vein being narrow, however, only a few carloads of ore were taken out at these places. The Keith furnace at Sheldon had also used this ore in the 1830s, mixing it with bog ore from Swanton.

A new use for the ore came with the St. Albans Iron and Steel Works, when a 10-ton Siemens open-hearth furnace was built in 1877 for the manufacture of steel track for railroads. Furnace charge consisted of pig iron, old rails, steel scrap, and magnetic ore. The ore and pig iron came at first principally from Port Henry and Crown Point, but the ore from Sheldon was successfully substituted for the magnetite and was thenceforth used exclusively. Aldis O. Brainerd, mine owner, shipped several thousand tons of ore, carried by teams three miles to the Missisquoi River and then to St. Albans, a total distance of about 13 miles.

The mine was about a mile southwest of Sheldon village, and a mile west of the St. Johnsbury & Lake Champlain Railroad, which ran along Black Creek. It consisted of two distinct parallel veins outcropping to the surface about 30 feet apart;

3-4. *An "iron bug" encountered at Fairfax, but not of the bog ore variety; rather, a creation of the modern-day Fairfax Forge, made of scrap hardware.*

each outcrop was about three feet wide. Work was done mostly on the westerly outcrop with several open cuts and two shafts over 60 feet deep. At the bottom of the shafts, the vein was 10 feet wide. Since the mouth of the shaft was about 100 feet above Black Creek, no water interfered with mining the depth of the shaft. Timbers were not required in sinking the shafts due to the stability of the walls (Brainerd 1884/1885:689-691).

Magnetic ore, so called because it could influence small magnets such as a compass, yielded over 70 percent iron, and was found mainly in Dover, Plymouth, Stockbridge, Bethel, Troy, Rochester, Rutland, Chester, Addison, Huntington, Bridport, Hancock, Jay, and Brandon (Adams 1845:21-27).

John W. Stickney (father of Vermont Governor William Stickney) was superintendent of the Tyson Iron Company at Plymouth and manager and agent for the two successive ironworks operations there, spanning a period of about 45 years and ending with the final blast in 1872. While with the ironworks, he wrote the following report on iron and other ores on the company's property in Tyson and vicinity:

Beds of brown hæmatite near Tyson Furnace, in Plymouth, Vt., were discovered by the undersigned, in company with an older brother in 1825. The main bed was opened by I. Tyson, in 1836 and was exclusively worked by him from that time until 1855. Many thousand tons of iron were manufactured from this ore, of the very best quality. Three kinds of ore are found in this bed.... The largest specimen makes white iron with good success. These ore-beds are geologically situated as follows: Beginning in a valley running nearly east and west, are bounded on the north by a ridge or elevation of talcose slate, through which passes heavy veins of dolomitic and silicious limestones, and smaller veins of the carbonate of lime. On the south is quite a large mountain, being a spur of the Green Mountains. This mountain is mainly made up of gneiss rock, and heavy veins of granular quartz interstratified with it.... The main bed, worked by I. Tyson, is not exhausted, and can be opened without much cost.

Beds of brown hæmatite, in Tinmouth, Vermont, in geological formation are not unlike the one in Plymouth, above described. They are now being worked by I. Tyson Jr., & Sons, and are situated on the west side of the Green Mountains, and within four miles of the Western Vermont Railroad.

The one mainly worked the present winter, I describe thus: It is worked on its western declivity by an adit, or level, running easterly into the hill, say sixty yards, when the ore was reached. Three hands are now raising from six to ten tons per day....

This ore bed was opened by D. Curtis, of North Dorset, thirty-five or forty years ago,—who then run a blast-furnace at that place. Mr. Curtis informed me that this ore was repeatedly tested in his furnace at that time, and found to be of the very best quality, making iron superior to any then made in this State.

I also send specimens of magnetic ores, commonly known as rock ores, from different veins in the vicinity of the furnace.

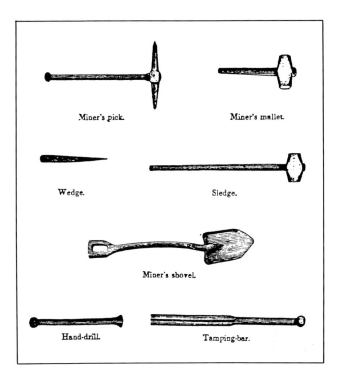

3-5. *An assortment of mid-19th-century mining tools (Overman 1850:55).*

These are largely percented with metallic iron.... Two of them, the Taylor and Hall veins, have been worked by Mr. Tyson to some extent; the others have not been explored.

Variegated marbles, soapstones, and sandstones abound in the vicinity, the latter suitable to use as fire-stone in lining the furnace. Strong indications of a copper vein are known to exist in the east part of the town of Plymouth, two miles from the furnace....

Galena (or lead ore) is also found near Plymouth, in the town of Bridgewater; being discovered when working a vein of quartz for crushing to obtain gold. This vein of quartz passes entirely through the town of Plymouth, and is the most easterly one marked on the map of said town, which is herewith sent for reference to the localities of minerals, &c., herein described.

Gold had been successfully washed in the eastern part of the town ... and exists in workable quantities on mineral rights owned in connection with the furnace property. Having no specimens of gold now on hand, I am unable to add these to this collection.

Kaolin (or pipe clay as it is sometimes called) is found in an extensive bed, immediately east of the bed of hæmatite iron ore first described in this statement, and between it and the iron ore is an extensive bed of moulding sand, which has been used for moulding purposes at Tyson Furnace, and largely sold to other foundries in New England.

I also send a specimen of carbonate of iron (or steel ore), a large vein of which is found one and a half miles east of the furnace, Strong indications of copper ore also exist in connection with this vein (*Geological Surveys* 1864:14-15).

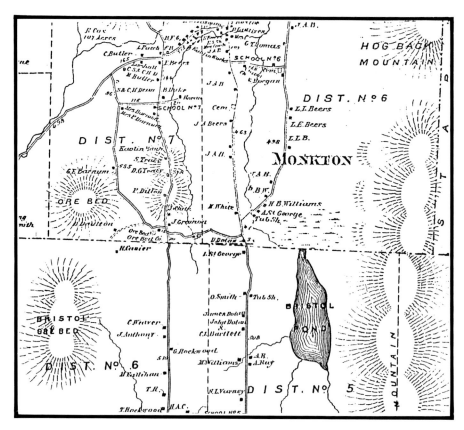

3-6. *Iron ore beds in Bristol (lower) and Monkton (upper), exploited in the early 19th century for forges and furnaces at Vergennes, New Haven, and Ferrisburgh in addition to local forges at Bristol and Lincoln. Both ore beds were part of the same mineral system (Beers* Addison *1871:11, 23).*

The "main bed" that Stickney's report refers to as worked by Tyson but not exhausted is probably that indicated by the 1869 Beers map of Plymouth on Weaver Hill, east of the furnace site. Reference to D. Curtis (Daniel Curtis?) reducing Tinmouth ore at his furnace provides important information as to a possible early date, about 1825, for the blast furnace operating at North Dorset. A collection of holes, mounds, and pieces of iron ore lying about on Caleb Scott's farm in the southwestern part of town might have been part of the Tinmouth ore bed. About two miles farther north above Route 140 where East Road tops a low rise are remains of a line of iron diggings, paralleling the road a few dozen feet on the east for about 200 feet.

When Stickney wrote his report, gold fever was sweeping Plymouth and surrounding towns. The prospects of mining gold were also evident in the iron company's assessment of its property value. The map Stickney said he was including with his report was probably the *Map of the Town of Plymouth,* drawn up in part by him and dated 1859. The map indicates all mineral locations then known to exist in the town, but it especially emphasizes gold locations. With the end of the Civil War in sight at the time of the report, and the impending loss of the works' prime customer, the Union Army, Stickney was already making preparations for inducing speculators to come and invest in Plymouth's new-found mineral wealth. When the gold fever eventually played out many years later, it was generally agreed that those working "the gold fields" could have made more money if they had spent the time doing honest labor on local farms.

Years later, Guy Hubbard of Windsor described the iron mines at Plymouth:

This first "Hæmatite mine," (now caved in [in 1922] and inaccessible because of the decay of the timbering) was but a short distance west of the furnace. Eventually this consisted of a vertical shaft fifty feet deep and a lower gallery four feet wide by six feet high running fourteen hundred feet in a northeast and southwest direction from the foot of the shaft. This gallery sloped and its lower end opened upon a brook, into which the water drained without pumping. In one part of this gallery the ore consisted of lumps of brown hæmatite, while in another part it consisted of black oxide of manganese. A bed of high grade fire clay, suitable for use in the foundry, were also penetrated in these workings, much to the satisfaction of the management. At first, the buckets of ore were raised in the shaft by a horse power windlass, but eventually a steam hoisting engine was installed at the mouth of the mine. This hæmatite proved rather refractory, but it was discovered that this fault could be remedied by allowing water to run over it for some time before smelting.

A much more picturesque mine (recently "rediscovered" by the writer [Hubbard] when he nearly fell into its abandoned vertical shaft in the midst of a clump of raspberry

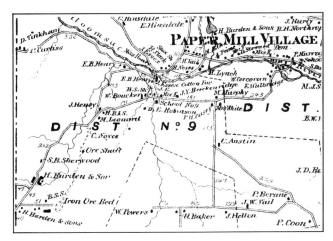

3-7. *The North Bennington Iron Works, which was the iron mining operations end of the Burden Iron Works, dug ore in western Bennington near the New York State line (lower left). Ore was carted north on Ore Bed Road to Burden's ore-washing works on Paran Creek (top center). thence two miles northeast to his blast furnace at South Shaftsbury (Beers Bennington 1869:23).*

bushes) was later opened on the rugged summit of Weaver Hill, a part of Mount Tom, about three miles east of the furnace and at an elevation of fully two thousand feet. The product of this mountain mine was locally called "Spaffic" or "Steel ore," and consists of a hard lime rock of black and brown color. It is technically called "Spathic," and is crystalline carbonate of iron. This mine . . . has part of its

vertical shaft and upper gallery still accessible [in 1922] on account of their being cut in the solid rock. The lower part of the shaft, and the deep galleries which penetrate hundreds of feet into the mountain, are full of cold, bluish colored water which has been accumulating during the many years since the pumps ceased to operate. This ore was dislodged by the use of black blasting powder, and the mine used to be a favorite gathering place for the farmers' boys, who made a practice of begging powder from the easy going foreman. In the course of time a new foreman came upon the scent, with the announcement that he was using "Kill-all Powder," a compound so sensitive that the sunlight would explode it, and so powerful that a grain of it would blow a man to "Kingdom Come." Mr. Tyson then suddenly ceased to supply the local munition market.

This Spathic ore contained a great deal of sulphur compound and green stone, and was roasted in kilns to drive off the sulphur and some of the other impurities before being smelted. It produced a peculiar iron which could be converted into steel by a single "blooming" operation—hence the name "steel ore" (Hubbard 1922:48-49).

One of the problems with the ore beds in Vermont, as well as elsewhere in the Northeast, was the proximity of the iron ore to veins of manganese. Under great heat, such as that of a blast furnace, manganese will release a large quantity of oxygen. A bed of manganese many feet wide in Bennington was separated from the iron ore by a layer of clay not more than a half-inch thick. An ironmaster there in the early 1800s thought the black manganese to be a purer iron ore and charged his blast furnace with a large amount of it. When the furnace was tapped, the molten stream burst into a furious fire, driving

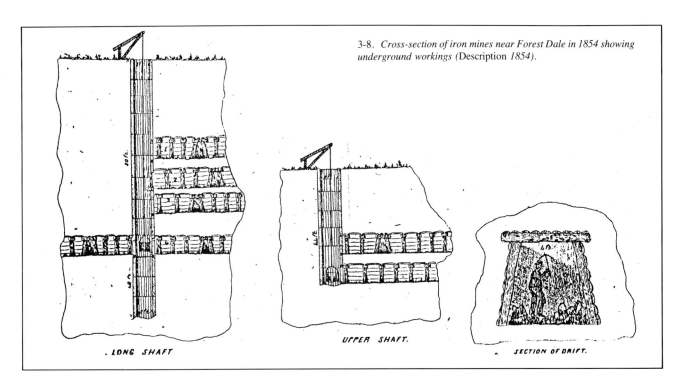

3-8. *Cross-section of iron mines near Forest Dale in 1854 showing underground workings (Description 1854).*

LONG SHAFT

UPPER SHAFT.

SECTION OF DRIFT.

63

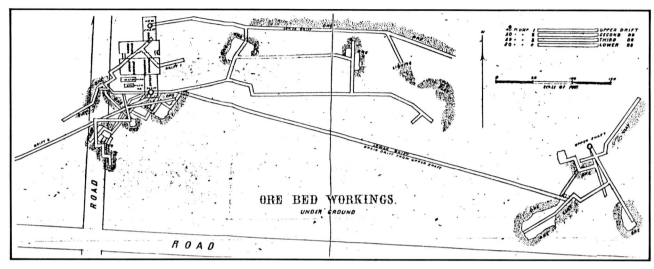

3-9. *Ore lots near Forest Dale in 1854, about a mile southeast of the blast furnace* (Description *1854*).

the workers from the building. Removal of the remaining manganese forced the expensive process of shutting down the furnace (Adams 1846:215). Another area affected by manganese was Bristol and Monkton, where extensive mining operations were carried out into the early 1800s. There were contiguous beds across the town boundaries in northeastern Bristol. The Monkton side of the beds was additionally plagued by surface water drainage problems.

English inventor Henry Bessemer's process of making steel in 1856 was to blow air through molten cast iron in a pear-shaped thick steel container called the Bessemer Converter. The blowing raised the temperatures inside the converter, causing the impurities in the iron, including carbon, to burn away, creating a pure refined iron—wrought iron—without the use of charcoal. But if the reaction were halted before all the carbon burned away, the result would then be a low-carbon iron, or steel. Another Englishman, Robert F. Mushet, found that better results could be obtained by continuing the blowing process to the complete decarbonization of the iron, then adding small amounts of carbon and manganese back into the molten iron to create steel. What this all meant was that manganese, formerly an undesired, troublesome element in iron ore, was now needed by the steelmakers as an additive to the refined iron, and the search for rich manganese deposits was on (Lewis 1976:36-37).

The manganese associated with iron ore at Wallingford drew Andrew Carnegie's attention in the 1880s (Klock 1976:42). This black ore, as it was called, was described in an 1859 analysis as having a ratio of 84.5 iron to 15.5 manganese. The chief center of the manganese bed lay about a half-mile up Homer Stone Brook from the Otter Creek, in the midst of a boulder-strewn hollow. An adit (horizontal passage) in this area passed into a hillside first through 100 feet of gravel, then 100 feet of limestone, and finally 250 feet of red and yellow ocher and white clay before reaching the mother lode of iron ore and manganese. When smelted, it made a very hard, white iron

that was also very brittle (Lesley 1859:542). Carnegie, however, worked the bed for the manganese, needed by his steel mills back in Pennsylvania. Between 1888 and 1890 more than 20,000 tons of the ore were shipped out (Jacobs 1927:211).

Another major impurity, although less dangerous than manganese, was titanium. This element did not lie next to iron ore like manganese but was part of the ore itself. Much iron ore in northern Vermont as well as the Adirondacks in New York contained titanium. Early users of cast iron ignored the titanium content, but as the state of the industry advanced and the quality of the iron became significant in more applications, the titanium became a problem. Such was the case in the town of Troy, where a three- to five-foot-wide vein of magnetic iron ore was found to be two miles long and thought to be inexhaustible. But the problem and expense of separating the titanium from the iron ore closed the blast furnace not long after it went into operation.

Most pre-1800 Vermont iron-mining activity centered around the extraction of ore from shallow, marshy areas. This ore was called bog ore and was found not only in marshes along Lake Champlain and lake-level tributaries but also in certain inland bogs a number of miles from the lake.

Bog ore consisted of various oxides of iron that had dissolved out of older, decomposed iron ore in chemical association with large amounts of sulfur or carbonate. Weathering actions slowly washed these oxides downhill from the higher, older elevations to settle and collect in marshes, and in time to accumulate in layers. The ore remained in some marshes even long after some of the more inland swamps had lost their feeder streams and dried up. There is some scientific thought that bog ore is due to actions of an "iron bacteria," whose ferric oxide and ferrous carbonate excrements resulted from the ingestion of iron from the solutions in which they lived. Whether in wet marshes or dried beds, bog ore was mined merely by shoveling up the ore-bearing soil, drying it, and feeding it into a blast furnace or forge. Depending on local stream activity, the ore

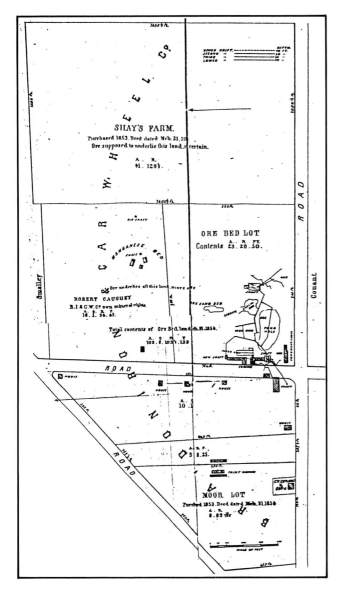

3-10. Layout of iron mines, lignite beds, and clay beds at Forest Dale in 1854 (Description 1854).

In his 1861 report on the geology of Vermont, State Geologist Albert Hager noted that much time speculating and prospecting for rich ore veins in Vermont resulted in trying to smelt tons of non-iron-bearing rock that deceived all but the educated eye. Secretly shared "Old Indian" myths hinted at locations of valuable iron mines, but the marked rocks or trees had long since been removed, so precise locations could no longer be determined. Many holes and piles of rocks up and down the state mark spots of fruitless blasting and digging in search of elusive mother lodes of rich iron ore. Hager reported that much money was expended in vain searches for a bed of ore in Ludlow and Plymouth, where horizontal exploratory tunnels called drifts were driven into terraces that showed promise. A similar prospect at Bethel proved unsuccessful in the search for iron ore and fatal to one of the miners by the premature detonation of the blasting powder.

As demand for ore increased with the construction of ironworks, activity at the mines expanded to large-scale digging operations by dozens of miners. Blasting with black powder was common, and fatal mine cave-ins such as one near Bristol were not uncommon (Hitchcock et al. 1861:816-818). As mines deepened, water seepage became a problem. This was initially relieved by waterwheel-driven pumps. With the development of steam power, machines ran the pumps, ore crushers, and washers, allowing miners to dig deeper into the Green Mountains.

As with the bog ore, initial mining techniques in Vermont consisted of nothing more than pick-and-shovel work, budging the ore out of shallow holes. The ore was separated from the excess waste rock by crushing it with sledgehammers. It was then loaded either into oversize saddlebags or horsecarts for the trip to the furnace or forge. Ore-laden boats soon were plying Lake Champlain in many directions.

In time, however, efficiency demanded that the ore delivered to the ironworks contain less waste material, leading to the invention of various ore-processing machines. One such machine was an ore crusher, or stamper, in which the iron ore was passed through in a chute while being subjected to pounding by rows of vertical hammers. At the ore washer, water played on the ore, washing away dirt and floating debris. Ores were

leached back into exhausted swamps, and after twenty to fifty years bog ore could again be "mined."

Expectations that much richer beds of iron ore existed upstream in the hills surrounding the bogs or near the source of springs usually brought disappointing results (Hitchcock et al. 1861:816). Sulfurets and carbonates of iron, the usual sources of the bog ore oxides, were of no value for smelting and even injurious when used with other iron ores. Rusty iron scum (gossan), frequently seen in pools of stagnant water or as tarnish on the face of rock outcrops or road cuts, was—and still is—a mistaken indication of the existence of good iron ore in the vicinity. Bog ore deposits were worked not only in towns that bordered Lake Champlain but also on the eastern slopes of the Green Mountains.

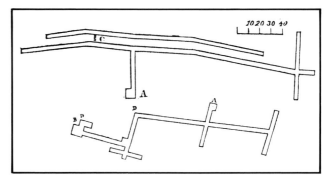

3-11. Plans of the two galleries that make up the Mitchell ore bed in Chittenden, which provided iron ore to the blast furnace at Pittsford, two miles to the south. Shaft A of the upper mine is 54 feet deep; shaft A of the lower mine is 62 feet deep. The long galleries run north-south (right-left), although the physical relationship between the two mines might not be exactly as illustrated (Adams 1846:84).

3-12. *A mid-19th-century iron miner with his pick, water jug, and barrow. Light was provided by a candle set into a holder in the brim of his hat (Orr 1860:591).*

also subjected to tumbling in a revolving wooden drum. Through small holes in the drum walls, proper-size pieces of ore fell into a waiting cart to be drawn to the furnace when filled. Pieces of ore that were too large to fit through the holes passed through the drum and out the other end, to be returned to the stamping machine. The machines were all water-driven.

The Crown Point Iron Company at Ironville, New York, separated ore from waste by use of magnets. The device that did the separation was the brainchild of Allen Penfield of Pittsford. Penfield's magnetic separator was a rotating barrel with magnetic steel points, which attracted the pieces of iron-bearing ore. Non-iron material continued through the rotating barrel and out the other end. Castings that went into the construction of the separating machine were made in Vermont by the Gibbs and Cooley foundry at Pittsford. But the problem was to keep the magnetic points strong enough to attract iron for a reasonable length of time. Professor Joseph Henry of Albany, New York, came to the rescue, connecting a galvanic cell (battery) to wire coils and wrapping the coils around the steel points in the drum, creating an electromagnet. It is generally recognized as the first practical industrial application of electricity (Allen 1967:7-9). The "henry" is today the official unit of measure for magnetic force.

It was this magnet that attracted the attention of another Vermonter, a blacksmith from Brandon named Thomas Davenport. On visiting Ironville in 1833 to buy scrap iron and seeing the separator in action, he immediately visualized the magnet's potential as a new source of motive power. Davenport and his brother-in-law, Orange Smalley, went on to experiment and eventually develop an "electromagnet engine," an early forerunner of the modern electric motor. Four years later, he and Smalley received the world's first patent on an electric motor from the U.S. Patent Office. Some disagreement exists regarding who contributed what toward the invention of "Davenport's motor." Smalley appears to have provided electrical and magnetic expertise, having dabbled with batteries; Davenport was the more mechanically minded. But the creative mind that invented the motor was not matched by practical minds that could find an application for it. Davenport's efforts kept him and his family in a continual state of destitution and he died a broken man (*Brandon* 1961:188-193).

Engineering texts generally credit the English physicist and chemist Michael Faraday (a blacksmith's son) and French physicist André Ampère with experiments in the 1820s–1830s that led to the development of the modern electric motor and generator. A monument erected in 1910 by the Allied Electrical Associations in America alongside Route 73, just south of Forest Dale, marks the site of Smalley's blacksmith shop (now a house) where Davenport did most of his work on the motor (no mention is made of Smalley). The shop originally stood near the blast furnace, across from Royal Blake's house (Mary Kennedy letter to author, April 13, 1986). Davenport's shop is now part of the general store at the intersection of Routes 53 and 73 (Mary Kennedy verbal to author, May 27, 1989).

3-13. *Although mules were used in the larger galleries, the miner pushed his own heavy-laden cart in the smaller recesses of the mine (Orr 1860:591).*

A model of Davenport's motor is in the Smithsonian Institution, together with the electromagnetic separator built by Professor Henry for Allen Penfield. In 1959 descendants of Penfield and his partners placed a tablet outside the Penfield homestead at Ironville. They formed the Penfield Foundation three years later to maintain the homestead as a museum, as it continues today. In the museum rear is a reconstruction of Henry's electromagnet, built in 1933 by General Electric Company engineers from Schenectady.

By the 1860s iron mining in Vermont centered around a few

good ore beds, as the demand for better iron closed down those beds whose ore quality was poor or marginal at best. Good ore beds lay in Chittenden, Manchester, Dorset, Brandon, Bennington, and Pittsford (Hitchcock et al. 1861:819-827). Iron ore was also being boated across the lake from the Crown Point area and mixed with local Vermont ore to impart improved characteristics in the cast and wrought iron made in western Green Mountain furnaces and forges. On the eastern side, ore from iron mines at Lancaster and Franconia, New Hampshire, was reduced by ironworks at St. Johnsbury. Bog ore from West Claremont, New Hampshire, was mixed with commercial bar iron at Windsor to produce a fine custom-quality iron.

3-14. *Typical view inside a mine, showing timbers that kept the walls from collapsing into the workplace (Orr 1860:588).*

One lesser-known source of iron ore for Vermont forges was at a major iron-producing area in Québec, at Seven Islands (Sept-Îles), located about 400 road miles northeast of Québec City on the north coast of the St. Lawrence River. A great mass of iron ore was discovered there in the early 1800s, a few hundred yards up a small stream that empties into the Bay of Seven Islands, imbedded in the labradorite rock of the land. Although magnetic, the ore contained a large amount of titanium, and when pulverized it yielded about 57 percent iron. This was not great by contemporary standards, but significant due to the quantity of iron ore available in the area, including a deposit of iron sand (black sand) that stretched along the coast from the Bay of Seven Islands to Moisie, a distance of 15 miles. Great ironworks were built at Moisie to work the ore.

Experiments made at the East Middlebury forge in 1867 on several tons of iron sands from Seven Islands succeeded in obtaining about 37 percent of their weight in good iron. This was done by following the practice of the forges at Moisie, which was to reduce the force of the blast, a fact apparently lost on ironworkers in northern New York, who usually rejected the fine sandy ore separated during the ore-washing process as being unsuited for the bloomery (Hunt 1870:260-262, 279-280).

A number of Vermont mining companies sprang into existence during the early to mid-19th century, speculating on a chance to strike it rich in iron or whatever mineral they chanced upon. Most were informal organizations with no officers or capital assets; just a few partners who either did their own digging or hired cheap labor to pick-and-shovel holes here and there. Others were formal organizations complete with officers, contracts, and substantial landholdings. They were chartered by the state legislature to sell stock and carry out the business of mining. A few were successful and evolved into smelting companies, such as the Pittsford Iron Company, and left significant records in history books and ruins of great furnace structures to study. Most of these mining companies, however, slipped into oblivion. Only an entry in the legislative record notes their existence; see table 3-1.

Table 3-1. Chartered Iron and/or Mining Companies

Year of Charter	Company Name
1810	Orange Mineral Company (Thetford)
1812	Vermont Iron and Coperas Factory Company (at Thetford, Norwich, and Hartford)
1825	Rutland Iron Manufacturing Company
1833	Bristol Iron Manufacturing Company
1836	Windsor and Plymouth Ascutney Iron Company
1845	Jefferson Mining Company (Newbury)
1845	Washington Iron Company (Brandon)
1845	Otter Creek Iron Company (Vergennes)
1849	American Mining Company (Windsor)
1862	Missisquoi Lime Company in Vermont
1864	Concord Mining Company
1868	North Troy Mining Company
1870	Burlington Prospecting and Mining Company
1872	Berkshire Mining Company (Richford)

The names of some companies might be deceiving, such as the Missisquoi Lime Company in Vermont, which was chartered to mine and smelt iron ore in addition to quarrying and burning lime. The firms covered themselves for any mining eventuality. The Orange Mineral Company at Thetford, for example, ensured that its charter provided "for the purpose of exploring and digging gold, silver, lead, iron, and all manner of mineral ores, which may be found on their lands. . . . And shall also have the privilege of making and manufacturing white lead, read lead, sugar of led [*sic*], lethridge of lead, white and blue vitrol, and allum and also for smelting of iron ore; and any other things that can be wrought from the ores and metals, which may be, or have been discovered on their lands . . . in the town of Thetford" (*Acts and Laws* 1810:13-14). One railroad company in southern Vermont drew its articles of incorporation on the broadest terms possible when it named itself the Bennington & Glastenbury Railroad, Mining and Manufacturing Company (Shaw 1952:20).

3-15. *The miners followed the vein of ore, whether it led them horizontally or vertically through the earth (Orr 1860:592).*

Mining companies speculated on a grand scale during the latter half of the century. The White River Iron Company (WN-IW01), for example, resulted from prospecting discoveries made in the 1870s by Julius J. Saltery of Boston, who claimed to have found gold in association with magnetic iron ore at many places in the White River. Saltery claimed that in some places gold and iron sand were mixed so abundantly that if both could be utilized, then "a permanent success would be gained, more so as the gold would not only pay expenses but a profit." Separation was to be by gravitation action of water, the heavy gold and iron settling out. The gold and iron were to be separated by the "California sluice process." But the company failed two years later (*Herald and News* Aug. 9, 1917:10).

Not giving up easily, Saltery organized the Pittsfield Iron Ore Company, which eventually became the Pittsfield Iron and Steel Company (RU-IW14), after buying up much of the old White River Iron Company property. Mines were opened on the Tweed River West Branch and machines were put into

place for crushing and concentrating the ores. But in 1882 this company also failed (Davis and Hance 1976:92).

Another company, the Lamoille and Elmore Iron Factory and Mining Company, was chartered by the state legislature in 1827 for "the manufacturing of iron, steel, etc., in its various branches, for and during the term of 25 years" (*Acts and Laws* 1827:89). The company operated two beds near Lake Elmore, one to the east of the south end of the lake about 100 feet beyond Route 12, the other about two miles southwest along an abandoned road (Willard Sanders letter to Richard S. Allen, October 31, 1955). The pit and signs of drilling were visible at the second mine as recently as the 1950s. It is immediately east of the old road, between the road and a brook that originates from Little Elmore Pond.

About a quarter-mile from Handle Road, up the eastern slope of Mount Snow in Dover, are the dramatic tunnel-like entrances in solid rock of two iron mines that were worked sporadically in the early 1800s. According to one reference, the mines were worked as early as the Battle of Bennington (Skelan 1961:147). More likely, the Trainor Mining Company first worked ore here around 1820, digging the ore out of the solid rock to support a forge about a mile to the southeast. But the high cost of transporting the reduced iron over the mountains to Bennington (and Troy, New York) soon closed both forge and mines. The mines were reopened in 1832 by two New York speculators, Wilder and Richards. More effort and more money were sunk into the holes to no further avail and the mines were soon abandoned again (Kull 1961:3-4).

3-16. *Replica of Professor Joseph Henry's electromagnet in the Penfield Homestead Museum at Crown Point, New York. It was a magnet similar to this that inspired blacksmith Thomas Davenport of Brandon to experiment and develop a rudimentary electric motor.*

The mines were found in 1984 among the trees between downhill trails of the Carinthia Ski Area. The mine entrances are deep within rock cavities amid breakdown and tailings, and tunnels (not explored by the author) extend hundreds of feet into the side of the mountain, one of them ending in a shaft that rises about sixty vertical feet to the surface. The former

3-17. *Two abandoned iron mines along the west branch of the Tweed River near the Pittsfield-Chittenden town line.*

owner of the ski area, Walter Strugger, preserved the mines as he found them, with the hopeful intent of somehow including them at some future date as part of his recreation area. Children who used to hike up the old Somerset Road in the early 1900s on the last day of school from nearby District School Number 8 for a picnic at the minehead would have appreciated that. It will be interesting to see what the new owners of the ski area will do with the mines.

A large mine opened between North Bennington and the state line in 1845. When Henry Burden and Sons of Troy, New York, operated it in the 1860s, it was known as the North Bennington Iron Works. It supplied ore to Burden's blast furnace at South Shaftsbury for about ten years (Lewis 1876-1877:228-229).

Some ore was also shipped to Burden's works at Troy until the mine was abandoned in the 1880s in favor of the superior magnetite ores from Mineville, New York (Jacobs 1944:39-41). The mine was a large open-pit operation and the huge hole is still visible today. Prospecting was done here as recently as World War II by the U.S. Bureau of Mines in anticipation of reopening some mines in New York and New England for the

war effort. State Geologist Elbridge Jacobs wrote in his 1943–1944 report that Vermont iron ore appeared to have been thinly bedded deposits of bog ore and hematite, often associated with manganese. The latter usually prevented the economic smelting of the ore. He also wrote that the blast furnaces seemed to have exhausted the iron deposits near them, probably because of the thinness of the beds, but that the old Burden mine at Bennington was the most promising deposit. Since the Bureau of Mines left in 1945, only the rabbits have been interested.

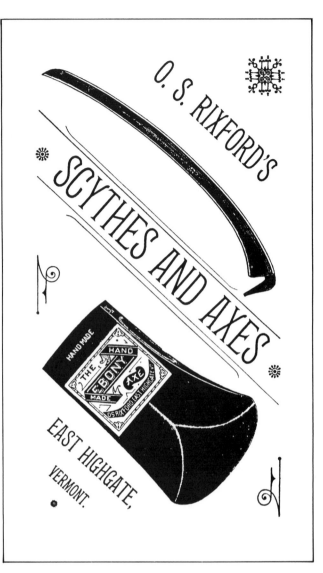

Chapter 4
The Ironworks Study

Study Methodology

Ironworks on an industrial scale commenced in Vermont a few years after the end of the Revolutionary War and ended about a century later. During that 100-year period, blast furnaces, bloomery forges, and foundries made or worked iron in all of the state's 14 counties. A majority of the blast furnaces and bloomery forges lay west of the Green Mountain range, generally in the valley of the Otter Creek.

Because few business records of these industries remain, it is not known for sure where all that iron went. Some Vermont iron found markets in local foundries and mills, but most probably ended up in works at Troy, New York, and Boston. Some iron might even have found its way to markets in Québec. Research into 19th-century canal and railroad records could provide some answers. Other sources of information might be hidden away in state or federal tax records, papers of incorporation, and banking and financial papers. All that remains now of these iron-making operations are the historical records as gleaned from dozens of town, county, and state histories, and their physical remains along mountain and valley streams.

Archival and field information that follows is the result of work done mainly from 1978 to 1988. When this project began in 1978, the author knew of only two blast furnace sites in Vermont: one at East Bennington with the ruins of two collapsed stacks and the other at East Dorset. The sites were visited, neighbors were queried, and some libraries were visited where card files were inspected for anything related with the iron industry (and card files yielded meager results). Files were eventually created while studying town, county, and state histories, trade journals, and maps. Frequent trips were made to the University of Vermont (UVM) Special Collections Library and the Vermont Historical Society (VHS) Library, with the purchase of many new and used books on local history in the process.

Trade journals and reports that provided 19th-century operating and production figures and descriptions for forges and foundries throughout the United States were of immense value. Many of these are found only outside Vermont. Also used were 19th-century county and town histories plus currently published and reprinted histories, publications of historical societies and museums, business directories, and U.S. Census reports. Much ambiguity in the historical descriptions of ironworks was encountered.

One of the more intriguing items was a short article published by the VHS in 1953 by State Geologist Elbridge Jacobs on the subject of ironworks, in which he claimed the following locations and dates of blast furnaces in Vermont:

Tinmouth	1783	Sheldon	1798	Dorset	1831
Bennington	1786	Vergennes	1799	Fairfield	1831
Pittsford	1791	Swanton	1799	Tyson	1837
Fair Haven	1797	Forest Dale	1810	Bennington	1853
Chittenden	1797	Manchester	1821	Pittsford	1859

Blast furnaces were built at many of these locations; forges were in use in others; both types were found at some of the works (Jacobs 1953:130). Jacobs' source of information was a manuscript sent to him by Charles Rufus Harte of New Haven, Connecticut. In an April 5, 1955, letter to Richard S. Allen of Albany, New York, Harte wrote that what he sent Jacobs was "a copy of a series of abstracts from various Vermont town histories, and for their accuracy—other than to the copying—I accept no responsibility, and of the furnaces I have very little personal knowledge."

Harte was otherwise an accurate and thorough historian of ironworks in New England, and authored a number of valuable articles and booklets on the subject in the 1930s and 1940s. He visited Vermont in August 1935 and photographed furnace remains at Manchester ("the merest trace"), East Dorset ("a beautiful little stack"), Pittsford ("behind a little mill on a side-road"), Brandon ("just south of where [Route] 7 crosses a big brook"), and Forest Dale "the Green Mountain stack, which was in very good condition").

Archival research has not uncovered the same historical references Harte said he was using or the photographs he took. Researching similar-named town histories in other New England states has likewise failed to resolve many of the iron-making site claims made by Jacobs and/or Harte. But this does not mean the data are incorrect. Many iron-making remains are still waiting to be rediscovered in Vermont.

Three series of maps were used to determine the existence, location, and time period of the ironworks. These were the 1796 to 1838 James Whitelaw maps of Vermont; the 1854 to 1859 Scott, Rice, McClellan, Walling, etc., county maps; and the 1869 to 1878 F. W. Beers county atlases. The Whitelaw maps used a Mars symbol ♂ (which in alchemy stood for iron) to indicate iron-making sites without differentiating between forges or blast furnaces. The county maps identify bloomeries and furnaces by owner or company name. Additionally, they display foundries, machine shops, mines and ore beds, raceways, dams, and buildings on village, town, and county scale. Maps with ironworks information were compared, site by site, directly to each other and to county, town, and state histories and gazetteers, ironworks reports, and ironworks-related articles. With this information, the sites were located as closely as possible on current USGS topographic maps and the effort then shifted out of the house and library and into the field.

At first thought, the search for an 18th- or 19th-century stone blast furnace does not seem so difficult that it requires a technique. In terms of its massive size, a blast furnace is about the height of a two- or three-story structure. Blast furnaces were usually made of large stone blocks, were surrounded by other structures and waterpowered devices, and thus should be in the midst of an acre or so of stone foundations. And some standing blast furnaces were quickly located in the field. But a collapsed furnace today resembles no more than a low, brush-covered mound. It can be as deceptively difficult to locate as a fully standing 30- to 40-foot-high stack in the heavily foliated

Vermont countryside. The location of the few obvious blast furnaces, such as Bennington and East Dorset, were made right from the truck window. The more difficult ruins resulted in many hours, and sometimes many weekends, of hiking through brush and wading in streams.

An electronic metal detector was tried with no satisfactory result. Iron-making and ironworking sites have become recipients of all manner of discarded machinery, some from later industries at the same site, some from trash dumped into water-wheel pits, cellar holes, and abandoned waterways (flumes, canals, and raceways). Searching for ironworks by inspecting the general area with a detector took time better spent looking for more accurate surface clues. One alternative to electronic metal detectors is dowsing. It was not tried but is claimed to have been used with some success around the world to find such things as buried pipes and cables, so why not a forge site (Hume 1969:36-39)?

The most obvious artifact at an iron-making site is the standing or nearly standing blast furnace ruin. The less obvious is slag, that ubiquitous waste by-product of the iron industry. But slag can be a misleading artifact. Good blast furnace slag is usually multicolored with a glassy surface. It will shatter easily if struck, and its slivers will injure unprotected eyes, hands, and feet. The slag can be shades of blue, green, black, and gray. Some slag will betray its former molten state through ripple marks on the surface or holes left by gas bubbles. Some glassy blast furnace slag might contain pieces of stone, iron, or charcoal, but most will not. Blast furnace slag is lighter in weight then bloomery forge slag, which is much heavier for the same size and much less colorful. Because the process of making bloomery iron (wrought iron) does not involve the high temperatures of the blast furnace process, bloomery slag does not appear glassy or multicolored. The lower bloomery forge temperature also results in an incomplete smelting process, resulting in a product that at one end of the bloom is more iron than slag, while at the other end is more slag than iron. Bloomery slag (the waste end of the bloom), therefore, contains much iron; the slag is much heavier and darker than blast furnace slag. Heavy, dark slag will usually indicate the site of a bloomery, and this slag is more often then not loaded with high levels of iron, unburned charcoal, and bits of stone.

Archeological analysis into historic blast furnace slag has been done by Professor John R. White of Youngstown State University, Ohio, who has shown that in addition to its chemical attributes, "the slags have visual attributes such as color, texture, and porosity which likewise provide clues to their use, temperature, effectiveness, etc. The effectiveness of the slag is a primary indicator of the efficiency of the furnace operation and the iron-making process" (White 1980:55). The type of fuel, whether charcoal or coal, for example, can be determined in the laboratory through slag analysis, thus affording further interpretive data on the state of the technology at the given iron-making site.

The extensiveness of slag heaps also indicates the degree of blast furnace activity. But slag accumulations at later blast furnaces were trucked for use as fill or mixed with tar for use in road building. Slag is useful for locating the ruins of collapsed blast furnace sites, first by finding the random pieces of slag along streambeds in the suspected area of the furnace, and

second by following the slag indications upstream until none is found. Since slag and everything else washes downstream, note the increased number of slag finds in the streambed as the inspection proceeds upstream. A marked drop in slag finds signals the time to search for the site itself. But this technique is not always foolproof: bits of slag were tracked a quarter-mile up the Konkapot River, right past the actual forge site at New Marlboro, Massachusetts, to the back fill of a stream-side cemetery. In this case, the slag existed both upstream and downstream of the forge site.

Since early blast furnaces and bloomery forges depended on waterpower to produce the necessary draft, they located alongside dependably flowing streams, usually next to a major falls or rapids. With abandonment of the operations, most of the remaining artifacts worked their way into these streams and were washed farther downstream by yearly cycles of spring freshets augmented by ice movement. The streambeds in the vicinity of mills, therefore, became the depository of all manner of industrial artifacts (and contemporary domestic trash). Inspection of suspect streambeds for artifacts is therefore an essential part of a search for and inspection of the industrial site.

The best time to inspect the stream is late summer, preferably during an extended rainless period when water level and turbidity are low. A clear, sunny day is necessary to see the stream bottom clearly, strolling knee-deep into the stream, working upstream, keeping the sun behind if possible. Each side of the stream was inspected and the middle crisscrossed. Water deeper than knee-high significantly reduced bottom visibility. Care was taken not to step on glass or trip on underwater hazards.

Since the stream probably eroded new channels in the past century, inspection of eroded shorelines and accumulating sand and gravel bars aided in determining where a previous channel might have been and, therefore, where older wash may have accumulated. Heavy iron objects such as mill machinery, gearing, large bolts, braces, and shafts were usually found in deepest midstream or stranded in deep pools. The immediate bottoms of falls, if they are accessible, were good places to inspect. Relatively lighter objects such as bricks and slag were found closer to shore, although slags loaded with iron were also found in deeper pools.

Access to streams was easiest at a bridge, but high stone abutments and steep embankments sometimes caused problems. Residents rarely refused permission to walk through a driveway or backyard to gain access to fields and streams. Neighborhood children were usually quite knowledgeable about what was in streambeds and where "treasures" could be found. At Pittsford, however, hours were spent in a fruitless search for some "old machinery" in Furnace Brook until it slowly became apparent that the kids were talking about the rusted remains of an ancient Volkswagen, partially buried in a midstream sandbar. Another good technique was to inspect stream bottoms with binoculars from the center of bridges. This was especially fruitful when the pools were deep and a bright sun was directly above (midday). Drivers do not expect to meet people standing on narrow bridges, so care was taken not to get squeezed by trucks or run down by cars. I wish I had a better answer for the Vermont State Highway patrolman who stopped and asked why I was leaning out from the middle of the concrete bridge at East Middlebury.

Scaled sketches of the streams were made as inspections proceeded. Pencil was superior to ink; water drops smeared the latter. The general shorelines and gravel bars, rapids, quiet pools, and major boulders were sketched. Landmarks such as bridges, houses, and large trees were identified for later reference. Compass checks maintained orientation of zigzagging streams. When an accurate measurement could not be made, distances were paced between dependable reference points (but not trees, which might be cut down or washed away). All artifact finds were located on the sketch whether in question or not, saving a repeat inspection months later when the water was usually higher (and colder). Special attention was paid to evidence of marks such as machined cuts and drilled holes on ledges in the stream and on the shore.

Remains of dams were evidenced by stone block or concrete abutments at facing sides of the stream, although an abutment may have remained on only one side. Early dams were sometimes indicated by only a few one-inch-diameter holes drilled into underwater ledge. When one was found, I looked for others or a series of them every few feet across the stream. They usually marked the base of a dam and usually, but not always, were located at the top of a falls to increase the head. Corroborative evidence, such as remains of an earthen dam that might still exist high up the shore adjacent to the drilled holes, was also checked. The dam might not be directly related to an iron-making site, but a documented reference to a forge built so many feet downstream from another mill and dam often proved the value of the find. And just as a good mill site may have supported a succession of small mills, so may have the dam, with washouts by periodic freshets resulting in repeated reconstructions and possible enlargements.

A knowledge of dam-building technology and water privilege rights was helpful in further interpretation of dam sites. While searching for an 18th-century iron-making site in the La Platte River at Shelburne Falls, two iron rods were discovered, securely imbedded about twelve feet apart in a ledge on opposite sides of the center of the stream. The rods might have been anchors for cables that added support for a high dam, the remains of which stood on one shore about 50 feet downstream. Although remains of three dams (and a possible fourth) were found at Shelburne Falls, the exact location of Ira Allen's 1792 forge still remains a mystery, probably because it was destroyed by freshets and a succession of mills that followed at this excellent waterpower site.

Results of the Ironworks Study

Forty-three ironworks sites were reported to the State Archeologist during the 1978–1990 period of the overall state-wide study of ironworks and are now part of the Vermont Archeological Inventory. Five other sites, at which inconclusive or no positive surface evidence was found but subsurface material might exist, have been reported to the State Archeologist in the Field Site (FS) category. In-progress archival and field work continues at 51 more sites. The total number of ironworks sites studied is therefore 99 at this writing.

Table 4-1. Ironworks Sites

Site No.	Principal Name	Blast Furnace	Bloomery Forge	Foundry	Iron Mine	Charcoal Kiln
Addison County						
AD-146	Monkton Iron Company	Yes	No		Yes	
AD-299	East Middlebury Iron Works		Yes	No		Yes
AD-300	Orwell Furnace	Yes				
AD-339	Eagle Forge		Yes			Yes
AD-340	Little Otter Furnace	Yes				
AD-404	Richville Forge	?	?			
AD-406	Sawyer's Forge		Yes			
AD-407	Salisbury Forge		Yes			
AD-414	Brooks Edge Tool Company			Yes		
AD-415	Wainwright/Davenport Foundry			Yes		
AD-416	Holley Forge		Yes			
AD-417	Lewis Creek Farm Forge		Yes			
AD-430	North Ferrisburg Forge		Yes			
AD-431	Doreen's Forge		Yes			
AD-432	Barnum/Nichols Forge	No	Yes			
AD-493	Baldwin Creek Forge		Yes			
AD-FS50	Ackworth Bloomeries		No			
AD-FS86	Franklin, (etc.) Forge	No	?			
AD-IW01	Downing Forge		No			

Table 4-1. Ironworks Sites (Cont.)

Site No.	Principal Name	Blast Furnace	Bloomery Forge	Foundry	Iron Mine	Charcoal Kiln
				Evidence of Associated Components*		
Addison County (Cont.)						
AD-IW02	Nichols Forge	No	No	No		
AD-IW03	Vergennes Iron Company			Yes		
	White's Forge		No			
	National Horse Nail Company			Yes		
AD-IW04	Belding/Drake Furnace	No	No			
AD-IW05	Brooksville Pocket Furnaces	No				
AD-IW06	New Haven Mills Forge		?	?		
AD-IW07	Barnum Forge		No			
AD-IW08	Fuller Forge		No			
AD-IW09	Scott, (etc.) Forge		No			
AD-IW10	Scott Forge		No			
AD-IW11	Burnham Forge		No	No		
AD-IW12	Munson, (etc.) Forge		No			
AD-IW13	Fergusson Forge		No	?		
AD-IW14	Upper Lewis Creek Forge		No			
Bennington County						
BE-9	East Dorset Furnace	Yes			Yes	
BE-10	Bennington Iron Company (East)	Yes	No	No	Yes	Yes
BE-11	Bennington Iron Company (West)	Yes				
BE-35	North Dorset Furnace	Yes			No	Yes
	Allen Foundry			Yes		
BE-36	Burden Furnace	Yes			Yes	Yes
BE-64	Fassett and Hathaway Furnace	Yes				
BE-IW01	Bennington Forge		No			
BE-IW02	Woodford Furnace and Forge	?	No			
BE-IW03	Nobel's Forge		No			
BE-IW04	Dorset Village Furnace	No			No	
BE-IW05	Factory Point Furnace	?			No	
BE-IW06	Sage and Olin Furnace	No				
BE-IW07	"the Pup"	No				
Caledonia County						
CA-20	Paddock Iron Works	No			Yes	
CA-IW01	Joes Brook Forge					
Chittenden County						
CH-FS70	Spafford Forge		Yes			
CH-IW01	Ira Allen Forge		No			
CH-IW02	Shelburne Falls Forge		?			
CH-IW03	Stanton Forge		Yes			
CH-IW04	Seeley Forge		No			
CH-IW05	Milton Forge		No			
CH-IW06	Burlington Manufacturing Company		No	No		
Franklin County						
FR-67	Keith Furnace (West)	Yes			No	

Table 4-1. Ironworks Sites (Cont.)

Site No.	Principal Name	Blast Furnace	Bloomery Forge	Foundry	Iron Mine	Charcoal Kiln
				Evidence of Associated Components*		
<u>Franklin County (Cont.)</u>						
FR-68	Keith Furnace (East)	No			No	
FR-149	Rock River Furnace	Yes				
FR-163	Barney Forge		No		No	
FR-IW01	Missisquoi Forge		No			
FR-IW02	Fairfield Furnace	No				
FR-IW03	Brainerd and Gadcomb Forge					
<u>Grand Isle County</u>						
GI-IW01	Goodwin Forge					
<u>Lamoille County</u>						
LA-IW01	Cady's Falls Forge		No			
<u>Orange County</u>						
OR-IW01	Randolph Furnaces					
<u>Orleans County</u>						
OL-3	Boston and Troy Iron Company	Yes	?	No		
OL-IW01	Phelps Falls Forge		No			
<u>Rutland County</u>						
RU-41	Green Mountain Iron Company	Yes	Yes	No	No	Yes
RU-57	Granger Furnace	Yes		No	Yes	Yes
RU-76	Tinmouth Channel Furnace	Yes			Yes	
RU-77	Rathbone Furnace	Yes			Yes	
RU-87	Chipman Forge		Yes			
RU-97	Chippenhook Furnace	Yes				
RU-99	Colburn Furnace	Yes				
RU-153	Gibbs and Cooley Furnace	?			No	
RU-162	Willard and Perry Furnace	Yes			Yes	
RU-171	Packard Mill/Forge		Yes			
RU-195	Gamaliel Leonard Forge		Yes			
RU-217	Conant Furnace	?			Yes	Yes
	Brandon Iron & Car Wheel Company	?		?		
	Howe Scale Company			?		
RU-FS17	Lyon's Works	No	No	?		
RU-IW01	Forge Flats		?			
RU-IW02	Miller Forge		No			
RU-IW03	Wallingford Furnace	No				
RU-IW04	Allen Forge		No			
RU-IW05	Carver's Forge					
RU-IW06	Dan Smith Forge		No			
RU-IW07	Castleton Forge		No			
RU-IW08	Joslin and Darling Forge		No			
RU-IW09	John Burnham Forge		?			
RU-IW10	Keith Furnace	No				
RU-IW11	Larnard's Forge					

75

Table 4-1. Ironworks Sites (Cont.)

| Site No. | Principal Name | Evidence of Associated Components* | | | | |
		Blast Furnace	Bloomery Forge	Foundry	Iron Mine	Charcoal Kiln
Rutland County (Cont.)						
RU-IW12	Sutherland Falls Forge		No			
RU-IW13	Spud Leonard Forge					
RU-IW14	Pittsfield Iron & Steel Company				Yes	No
Washington County						
WA-25	Rice's Furnace	No			No	
WA-IW01	Davis Forge					
Windham County						
WD-38	Somerset Forge		Yes			
Windsor County						
WN-51	Tyson Furnace	Yes	No	No	No	No
WN-FS14	Upper Falls Forge		No			
WN-IW01	White River Iron Company	No	No			

*Yes   = some surface evidence
No   = no surface evidence although component is documented
?   = questionable field evidence
(blank) = no component association, or not field-checked

Table 4-1 lists the 99 ironworks sites that have been researched. The table lists the sites by county, and numerically within county by site identification number. Sites unreported (IW numbers) are those whose ruins or remains have not been found or where inconclusive evidence exists to positively identify the site. The table lists the site identification number, its principal name, and whatever ironworks components are associated with the site. Note that the area of component association in the table disregards geographic distance: if the component can be connected to the site by documentary association or by direct physical evidence, it is an associated component.

Following table 4-1 are sections that divide the state into northern, central, and southern districts, described in the Introduction in the front of this book ("Presentation of the Study"). In these sections, the history of the ironworks site and the descriptions of whatever physical remains exist are presented, within each section by county, and within each county, either in chronological sequence when practical, grouped to reflect a geographic proximity, or in a north-to-south sequence. Grouping does not reflect any commonality that might have existed when the ironworks were in operation, but aids in describing them. Accompanying maps provide a geographic sense of the physical disposition of the sites and ruins, without compromising the exact location of the site.

WARNING to Hikers and Explorers: Although appearing sturdy, furnace ruins are in fact fragile. Climbing about them loosens stones, weakens walls, and significantly contributes to their progressive deterioration. Blast furnace ruins can collapse without warning and crush people under tons of stone.

The Northern District

This district contains 22 ironworks sites, giving it an average density for such sites in the state. No iron-making sites are known to exist in Essex County. Blast furnaces account for eight of the iron-making sites, a notably higher percentage than in the central and southern districts.

Ironworks in Franklin County were generally centered in Highgate and Sheldon. A furnace site in Highgate is supposed to have dated to the Revolutionary War period, possibly earlier according to local tradition, and might have been that found alongside Rock River in the northern part of town. The site's proximity to the international boundary coupled with confusion of the boundary's exact location during that period might indicate furnace operation by Canadians. The furnaces at Sheldon were built by Alfred and Israel Keith following successful furnace ventures at Pittsford in the 1790s; previous to that, their father operated a blast furnace in eastern Massachusetts. The Keiths were also involved in iron making in New York State. Very little of these early Vermont ironworks remain to be seen.

The town of Troy in northeastern Orleans County was a wilderness when the Boston and Troy Iron Company went into operation there in the 1830s. Yet this remote site in the shadow of Jay Peak endured long, unproductive winters and inadequate transportation to make its mark casting stoves. It also cast heavy iron posts for the boundary between the United States and Canada, some of which are still there, continuing to do their job.

Chittenden County owes most of its earliest ironworks to the efforts of Ira Allen, who sought to attract buyers for his tracts of land in northern Vermont by building mills on the many plentiful streams and rivers through rent-free arrangements for prospective buyers. Politics and bad timing eventually undid Ira Allen's plans and he lost everything. Some of his forges were built alongside the Winooski River in the vicinity of the falls, just downstream of today's Route 7 bridge. This area has undergone intensive industrial development during the past 200 years, proving the soundness of Ira Allen's choice for mill seats. In addition to mill construction on the rocky precipices overlooking the falls, blasting into the rock ledges for water-power tunnels and dams has changed the face of the falls since Allen's forges made iron there. Early-20th-century views of the falls are on display inside the west end of the main Champlain Mill building at Winooski. Across Main Street (Route 7) at the Winooski end of the bridge is stairway access to a small park and a path to the ledges overlooking the falls. The bottom of the falls (the Salmon Hole) is best accessed by walking around the west end of former mill structures (now condominiums) along West Canal Street. Care must be taken, however, not to explore during spring thaw when the swift water is high; the vertical (and sometimes slippery) ledges are not fenced.

The blast furnace site at Waitsfield in Washington County is intriguing not only for the lack of physical surface evidence but also because it was unsuspected, discovered by chance during archival research.

CALEDONIA COUNTY

CA-20 Paddock Iron Works (St. Johnsbury): In 1815 at the western edge of the St. Johnsbury village, Joseph Fairbanks built a dam across the river. By the fall of 1815 a sawmill was operating at the dam and in the following spring, a gristmill. By 1818 Joseph's nephew Huxham Paddock had a trip-hammer and foundry operating at Sleepers River. His contract called for waterpower sufficient to drive a trip-hammer, grindstone, and two pairs of bellows, indicating the possibility of a bloomery (Child 1887:327).

Thaddeus Fairbanks, Joseph's son, built the Fairbanks Iron Works in 1823, continuing the industrial development near the Sleepers River dam. The works produced stoves and plows. The next year another son, Erastus, gave up his unsuccessful general store and joined the iron company, forming the E. & T. Fairbanks Company (*Fairbanks Standard* 1980:5). It is unknown what the Fairbanks foundry contained in the way of types of hearths for melting and casting, but the smelting of ore by blast furnace is doubtful. A blast furnace had been in operation since 1805 at Franconia, New Hampshire, less than 25 road miles to the southeast, smelting iron ore that was mined in that vicinity since the 1790s (Serafini 1952:15). Iron needed

by the Fairbanks to cast their stoves and plows probably came from these Franconia forges until increased demand for iron by the new scale business encouraged Paddock to construct a blast furnace nearby. The E. & T. Fairbanks Company then went on to make its name in the manufacture of the world-famous Fairbanks Scale, operating today in St. Johnsbury as the Fairbanks Weighing Division of Colt Industries.

Across the village and up the Passumpsic River from the Moose River was Arnold's Falls, named for the builder of sawmills and gristmills here in the late 1780s. Another sawmill was built by James Ramsey and Allen Kent in 1820, and some started to call it Ramsey's Mills although references to "Arnold's Privilege" persisted to 1830 (Fairbanks 1914:146). Following Ramsey and Kent, the mills were purchased about 1822 and expanded by Hiram Jones and Sargent Bagley.

In 1828 the Fairbanks were already selling off some of their foundry work (wagon manufacture) "to concentrate on other projects—and the new scale was already being ordered by customers" (*Fairbanks Standard* 1980:7). That same year Huxham Paddock moved his foundry works from Sleepers River to Arnold's Falls where he built a blast furnace and extensive works to make bar and cast iron (Fairbanks 1914:147). Hiram Jones and James Ramsey, who had been operating mills earlier at the falls, took the contract for the construction of the main forge building, employing a large force of men. As the business expanded many houses were built about the complex and the community came to be called Paddock Village.

The rise and demise of many ironworks industries, not only in Vermont but in the entire country, were affected in large part by domestic economics and tariffs. Following the Peace of 1814, imports of English-manufactured goods reached such alarming proportions that a great protectionist tide rose, specially favoring cottons, woolens, glass, and iron goods. One of the highest import tariffs occurred in 1828, the year that the Fairbanks started shifting more of their business toward the manufacture of scales and Huxham Paddock decided to expand and relocate his ironworks to the Passumpsic.

History records that Paddock's blast furnace made a high-quality iron. Fuel for his furnace and forges was charcoal, obtained from the plentiful supply of hardwood in the surrounding hills. Most of the ore was carted in by oxen from Franconia, New Hampshire. Lesser amounts came from Piermont, New Hampshire and Troy, Vermont. Some bog ore came from Lancaster, New Hampshire (Child 1887:315). Experiments in combining these different ores resulted in an iron that was used to manufacture stoves and hollowware (Fairbanks 1914:147). "Paddock made a box stove which was safe, a good cooker and a very good heater. He made plow points and fitted them into the plows made in his wood shop. He made barrel hoops for the barrel factory where my great grandfather once worked. Andirons were a necessity as were kettles and cooking utensils. He made horse shoe irons, nails, flat iron for hinges, and even iron fences were called for, items necessary to a fast growing community unlinked as yet to any transportation system except for an occasional stage and ox carts" (Asselin Jan. 1963:34-35).

In conjunction with the blast furnace and foundry, Paddock established a machine shop which specialized in mill gearing. "The establishment of Mr. H. Paddock consists of a blast furnace, and a machine shop for finishing every description of

4-1. *Sketch by Dr. E.D. Asselin showing what remained of the foundry at Paddock Iron Works by 1910. The Passumpsic River and rapids are seen in the background (courtesy Vermont Historical Society).*

mill gear and ordinary machinery" (Thompson 1842:157). In one shop was a turning lathe considered at the time superior to any other in the state (Child 1887:315). It was capable of turning a shaft 3 feet in diameter by 14 feet long. Iron and wood turning lathes, as well as cylinders, spindles, gears, cranks, gudgeons (heavy iron pivots), pumps, shafts, hubs, and nails were all manufactured by Paddock.

Fire struck in 1841, as reported by *The Caledonian* on March 2: "Last Tuesday the quiet citizens of our village were startled by the cry of fire. It proved to be the building covering the blast furnace owned by Mr. Paddock, which was nearly all destroyed. Although there were other buildings contiguous and attached to the one on fire, no essential damage was done to them. . . . As the furnace was not injured, the loss is trifling—not more than one or two hundred dollars."

The works were operated by Huxham Paddock until his death in 1845 (Child 1887:315-316). In 1843 his only son, John H., in company with John C. Paddock and Newell Woods, assumed the business under the name of J. C. and J. H. Paddock & Company. The next year Woods retired. About 1849 Joseph Fuller (John H.'s uncle) became a partner, and the next year John C. withdrew from the firm, leaving John H. Paddock to continue the business.

In an 1849 report, James Hodge described the blast furnace at St. Johnsbury village (among 10 he listed as then existing in Vermont) as being "closed." Hodge further commented that "the number of furnaces in the state which, if not actually in blast, will probably go into operation again in more prosperous periods of the trade. . . . Several of these . . . are soon to go out of blast in consequence of want of demands for their products" (Hodge May 12, 1849:290). Two comprehensive iron trade reports of the 1850s, however, fail to mention any ironworks at all in St. Johnsbury (Lesley 1858:77; 1859:25-27).

Since Hodge listed the blast furnace at St. Johnsbury already

closed in 1849, chances are that it never again went into blast in the 1850s due to the poor economic state of the iron industry following the nationwide depressions in the 1850s. (The furnace might have gone out of operation as early as 1840 following the Panic of 1837). That the blast furnace was mentioned as being undamaged by the 1841 fire and was described in Zadock Thompson's 1842 account does not necessarily mean that it was at those times in actual blast. Because of the death of the works founder and the partnership shuffles between 1843 and 1849, however, the year 1845 is a good approximate date for the furnace shutting down, followed by Hodge's "closed" in 1849.

The 1875 Beers map shows location of the foundry, machine, and pattern shops of the Paddock Iron Works, although this was not the actual name of the works at the time. The map also indicates Paddock Iron Works buildings on the north side and just downstream of the dam. A foundry and machine shop next to Luke Buzzell's office was directly across the river from the Paddock Iron Works, but just upstream of the dam. Buzzell was one of a succession of owners after the Paddocks (Child 1887:476). The ca.-1828 blast furnace would most likely have been built downstream of the dam, on the north side of the river alongside today's Concord Avenue.

Sometime after 1870, Michael Hynes, owner of the Acme Iron Works at Paddock Village and manufacturer of brass and iron fittings, succeeded John H. Paddock, ending the Paddock connection with the iron business (Fairbanks 1914:476). Paddock's 1828 machine shop was leased in 1876 by O. V. Hooker and Daniel Thompson (Hooker & Thompson Company). Hooker formed O. V. Hooker & Son's Machine Shop, across the Passumpsic River at the north end of Railroad Street in 1878; that same year he came into control of what remained of Paddock's ironworks (Fairbanks 1914:476). The foundry continued until about 1895, replaced by Hooker's foundry across the river, nearer to the railroad siding (Asselin 1963:34-35). In 1937 it was being identified as the Hooker-Reed Company (Smith 1937:22).

What remained of the foundry on the original side of the river fell into disrepair. By 1910 only a decaying building was left: "It was torn down soon thereafter for safety reasons. It was of heavy construction and covered with wide pine boards with no shingles. The smelters must have thrown a lot of heat for the men to be able to work in such a loosely constructed building in that climate. Now all that remains of this once formidable industry is the old stone wall. The other shops are still standing and have been in use as wood working shops, once a shirt factory and the like. Paddock, which was perhaps Vermont's greatest industry, is but a legend today" (Asselin 1963:34-35).

Inspection along the river shore just off Concord Avenue in 1979 failed to locate anything positively identifiable with a blast furnace. The "old stone wall" remains of the foundry north wall prevent the street from slipping into the river. The shoreline is littered with much slag, pieces of waste iron, small castings, and firebrick. These all appear to have been associated more with the foundry. Most likely, the old blast furnace was razed and its masonry reused for additional foundry building construction. Curiously, the day the area was inspected, a small, modern-day blacksmith shop stood on the site of the old foundry.

CA-IW01 Joes Brook Forge (Danville): An ironworks operated around 1810 at Danville, about 10 miles west of St. Johnsbury. The 1810 Whitelaw map shows an ironworks on Joes Brook, a quarter-mile upstream of South Danville and associated with the names Blanchard and Lowell. Nothing more is known of this early ironworks. No attempt has been made to locate the site.

ORLEANS COUNTY

OL-IW01 Phelps Falls Forge (Troy): The first major discovery of good quality magnetite in the town of Troy was in 1833, although there had been much conjecture for two years before of the possibility of rich iron ore in the town. The ore was dug on a hill a mile east of the Missisquoi River, two miles northeast of Troy village. The next year a forge was built by local people on the river at Phelps Falls, along the River Road, a mile north of today's Route 100. Iron ore was reduced here for a year. The forge, ore rights, and machinery were sold during the winter of 1834–1835 to Binney, Lewis & Company of Boston. Binney was Dr. Amos Binney, son of Colonel Amos Binney, the navy agent at the Boston Navy Yard; both were connected with the Strafford Copper Works (Abbott 1973:2). Lewis was Samuel L. Lewis, a sea captain and shipowner in Boston.

Binney, Lewis & Company made bar iron until 1841, at which time the forge and other local mills were purchased by Cortes Phelps and Madison Stebbins (Child *Orleans* 1883:288.55). At this time in poor health, Binney retired the next year from his copper activities and died in 1847 (Abbott 1965:242). That same year the company's property was divided between Phelps and Stebbins with no mention made of the forge. It had probably never been operated during the period of this partnership, since it was reported that the works lay idle and in ruins for many years (Child 1887:288.49). No evidence of the site was found in a 1980 field inspection.

OL-3 Boston and Troy Iron Company (Troy): In November 1835 two companies were chartered by the state to make iron at Troy: the Boston and Troy Iron Company, by partners John Williamson, Hezekiah H. Reed, Thomas Reed, Jr., Augustus Young, and John Spalding; and the Boston and Vermont Iron Company, by partners James C. Dunn, Daniel D. Brodhead, Amos Binney, and Samuel L. Lewis (*Acts Passed* 1835:121-124). There is confusion over which company built the blast furnace since both were chartered by the state to make iron. But the Boston and Troy Iron Company is thought to have been connected more with the mining part of the business, and the Boston and Vermont Iron Company with smelting. Dividing the mining and smelting between two companies might have been a cozy business arrangement. The Boston and Troy Iron Company purchased over 1,200 acres of land, including 20 acres of ore beds. A blast furnace, boardinghouse, and other buildings were erected two years later, two miles downstream from the Phelps Falls forge, which was still in operation at this time.

The operations failed in 1841 after expenses outran profits. The land, ore beds, and furnace buildings passed by mortgage to Francis Fisher of Boston, who refired the furnace in 1844. That year he produced 600 tons of pig iron and castings. One chief product was iron boundary markers, which were used along the Vermont and Canadian border (Bearse 1968:373). Shortly after 1844, Fisher also built a forge to manufacture bar iron. Stoves were also cast here, but the one called the P. P. Stewart No. 6, as referenced in a town history of Troy, is incorrect; it was made in Troy, New York (see chapter 2).

By the mid-1840s a community called Troy Furnace had developed about the furnace works, complete with its own post office (Thompson 1842:174). Ore was then brought to the blast furnace from beds owned by W. W. Huse in the town of Jay, west of the furnace. In 1846, when the furnace shut down due to the unfavorable tariff, Huse was in charge of the ironworks. The Orleans Iron Company organized in 1847, attempting to get the ironworks back into operation, but nothing ever came of the iron industry in Troy again. The post office at Troy Furnace closed its door in 1851 (Swift 1977:371).

One continuing problem at the works was the high percentage of titanium in the ore (Hemenway vol. 3 1877:326). This was also a problem with the rich magnetite ores of New York's Adirondack Mountains, where similar frustrations with smelting occurred in the same period of time. The titanium made smelting difficult and expensive. It was the beginning of the time when the iron-making technology demanded a higher quality of inexpensive pig iron. The remote location of the Troy furnace from rail and water transportation, plus the short blast season, also contributed problems and led to the demise of the works.

The 30-foot-high ruin of the stack was barely standing when last inspected in 1980 along with Dr. Peter Thomas of the University of Vermont, and Vermont State Archeologist Giovanna Peebles. The site is a few minutes walk over the hill through pastures west of River Road about halfway between Routes 100 and 105. Here in the midst of caved-in cellar holes and a scattering of slag (one "bear" is about two feet wide) the stack crumbles bit by bit, visited only by fishermen and a stray cow or two. The wide flume, which leads to the furnace,

4-2. *A view of the partially collapsed ruin of the Troy blast furnace stack in 1982.*

was used around 1900 to convey logs down the river, around the falls. The flume might be a deepened and widened version of the original flume that was dug along the same path. If recent speculation on a nearby hydroelectric project becomes a fact, the remains of this rich archeological and picturesque site could become flooded. The Missisquoi Valley Historical Society on Main Street in North Troy has several relics of the industry (Butterfield 1977:1).

FRANKLIN COUNTY

FR-IW01 Missisquoi Forge (Swanton): Among all the forges and mills that Ira Allen contemplated and contracted, it is difficult to determine which actually were built and operated, built and offered for lease, or not built at all. He advertised in 1789 at Swanton to lease the lower falls of the Missisquoi for iron making with terms being the usual seven years rent-free, followed by repurchase (Wilbur vol. 1 1928:520). But the 1793 accounting of his forge holdings at Shelburne and Colchester make no mention of a forge among his sawmills and gristmills at Swanton or "Hyegate" (Wilbur vol. 2 1928:53).

Although no firm evidence has been found that iron was actually made at Swanton before Rufus Barney built his forge there in 1799, one reference had large mills and a forge at Swanton by Ira Allen in 1797 (Graham 1797:159). And the previously mentioned ca.-1772 Metcalfe map (chapter 1) also showed the possibility of forges here at that time.

FR-163 Barney Forge (Swanton): Rufus and Elisha Barney of Bennington began construction of a forge at Swanton in 1799, following purchase of a half-interest in 200 acres of land on the west side of the Missisquoi River near the falls (Aldrich *Franklin* 1891:405-406). The Barneys built a forge, a forge dam on the river, a long flume from the dam to what became the forge pond, and from there a channel to another dam below

the forge and thence downstream to the river. The channel essentially cut across a curve in the river, creating Goose Island. Whitelaw's 1810 map shows the ironworks at the site as described. The manufacture of iron commenced in November 1800. In 1803, Rufus Barney divided his half-interest in the forge between his son, Lemuel Barney, and his son-in-law. Iron was made in considerable quantities from abundant local bog ore beds. The iron was sold principally to blacksmiths in the neighboring towns. Much iron was also made into tire-iron (wagon-wheel rims), sleigh shoes (runners), plows, and mill iron. Common bar iron sold for $7 per cwt for nearly 20 years (Hemenway vol. 4 1882:1023).

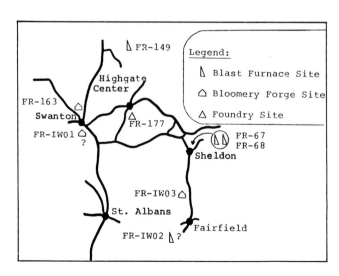

4-3. *Franklin County ironworks sites.*

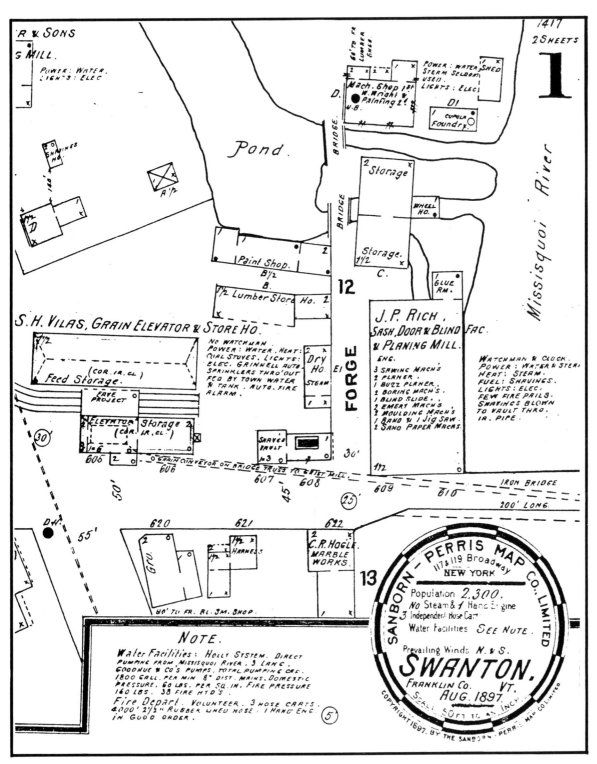

4-4. *The 1897 Sanborn map of a part of Swanton village, showing the inlet to the forge pond at the end of Forge Street (today's Foundry Street). Notice the Wright Machine Shop and foundry cupola on Goose Island (top) with notation that power was by water. The planing mill was replaced by a gunpowder factory and later by a marble plant. By that time the inlet and most of the forge pond had been filled in.*

The forge burned about 1816 and was rebuilt. It was run mostly by Lemuel Barney until 1821 when a new forge was built just west of the 1816 site. Elisha Barney and Robert Foster worked the forge until 1824 when it was purchased by R. L. and H. W. Barney. A new forge was erected by F. H. and L. H. Barney in 1849. This new forge was a better design and was acquired entirely by F. H. Barney after a few years. It made blooms "for the southern market" (Troy, New York?) until 1868, at which time the forge was removed and a circular sawmill erected in its place.

Reasons for failure of the 68-year-old forge at Swanton were claimed to have been the exhaustion of the bog ore beds, which up to 1835 could be shoveled from the surface of the ground, and also the scarcity and dearness of wood for making charcoal. But competition from ironworks in favorable locations was also a factor. The Walling 1857 and Beers 1871 maps show the main dam, forge pond, the forge, forge brook, and Goose Island. The 1871 map identified the site as "Old Forge," with much of Goose Island and many houses and lots in the area belonging to members of the Barney family.

Remains of the forge pond and tailrace that ran downstream to the Missisquoi River were still visible at the site as recently as 1985. The tailrace is marked by a distinct tree line; the forge area is filled with refuse. The old forge pond is swampy and is slowly being filled for an adjacent parking lot. Some bits of slag were found, but no other ironworks artifact. The trace indication of a foundation at the site of the forge may be forge-related or may have been associated with later mills at this site. Foundry Street, at the south end of the "island," indicates a more recent foundry operation.

FR-IW02 Fairfield Furnace (Fairfield): In a short paper published in 1953 on the subject of ironworks in Vermont, then-State Geologist Elbridge Jacobs included in the list of towns and furnaces "Fairfield, 1831" (Jacobs 1953:130). Jacobs' data source was Charles R. Harte. A thorough archival search has failed to find any forge or blast furnace in Fairfield, and the history and location of Fairfield furnace/forge remain a mystery.

FR-67 and FR-68 Keith Furnaces (Sheldon): Four years after Israel Keith sold his Pittsford furnace property, he established another ironworks, nearly 90 miles to the north. He and his brother Alfred built a blast furnace at Sheldon (FR-67) on the east bank of the Black Creek.

Some sources indicate construction date of the Sheldon blast furnace as 1798, but the consensus is 1799. The Keiths later built a forge and also made potash kettles. People came from as far as 200 miles away to line up for their kettles, loading them on wagons while still hot from the mold. The business did so well that employment exceeded 100 men, and for a long time the iron was referred to as "Sheldon currency" (Hemenway vol. 1 1867:372, 378). Ore initially came from bog ore beds in Highgate, but a large ore bed was discovered and worked 1½ miles east of the furnace.

By this time the Keith family's skill in building and working blast furnaces was so well known that their aid was sought by others. While the Monkton Iron Company was building at Vergennes in 1808–1809, a Mr. Keith was associated with the operations there. Then George Parish came to Vermont and offered Keith and two other Vermonters, Ebeneezer(?) Marvin (of Sheldon?) and (?) Sykes, the use of his furnace at Rossie, New York, and all the iron they could make in three months, in exchange for showing him how to run the furnace (Hough 1853:450). Accepting the offer, Keith "made a very handsome thing out of it, besides showing his New York friends 'how to do it' " (Hemenway vol. 1 1867:378). Keith references were

4-5. A section of the abandoned tailrace of the Barney forge at Swanton, about a quarter-mile downstream from the forge site. The race, when used, cut across an inside curve of the Missisquoi River, creating Goose Island, to the right, which has long since returned to the mainland and lost that identification.

4-6. *Is the collapsed archway of an old blast furnace in there? Did the later woolen mill here at Sheldon village build on the foundation of the earlier blast furnace?*

most likely to Alfred Keith, understood to have the technical skill with respect to building and operating blast furnaces; Israel was usually the one to bankroll the operations.

Israel Keith eventually retired from the furnace business, returned to Pittsford, and continued his law practice in U.S. and Vermont courts. Alfred Keith continued to run the Sheldon furnace business and in 1823 he built a new blast furnace (FR-68) across the river (west side). He donated the land on which the Episcopal church still stands, next door to his house.

4-7. *A large piece of cast iron, possibly a crude pig, among the foundation stones of the woolen mill ruins at the Sheldon furnace site.*

He died in 1840 at age 72 (Ashton 1979:20) and was probably buried in the church cemetery next door. A 1983 search failed to locate his gravestone, although his house is standing. His son Alfred, Jr. (there were many Alfreds in the family) continued the Sheldon family industries, running the gristmills and sawmills on the east side of the river and maybe the blast furnace on the opposite shore. By 1859 both furnaces were still standing but out of operation (Lesley 1859:25).

The site is 500 feet downstream of the concrete bridge. What is visible at the site today are the trash-filled ruins of Alfred Keith's later gristmill. As recently as 1979, what was believed to have been the remains of one arch of the furnace was hinted at beneath the north wall (Richard S. Allen to author, 1979). Partial collapse of the walls since then has made confirmation of this impossible. One interesting discovery was a piece of pig iron that is a part of one of the walls of the old gristmill. After many unsuccessful searches for blast furnace slag following the initial 1979 visit, some was finally found in 1987 on the west side of the river opposite the gristmill ruin, eroding out of the riverbank. This area contains many stone and concrete walls and features not related to the ironworks but to later industries. Exact location of the two Sheldon blast furnaces remains a mystery.

FR-IW03 Brainerd and Gadcomb Forge (Sheldon): Following a major iron ore discovery in Sheldon in the 1830s, owners of the mine property, Lawrence Brainerd and W. O. Gadcomb, built a bloomery forge to work the iron. They produced bar iron that was used in the area although some was shipped to Albany and Troy, New York. Lack of direct railroad connections and insufficient local demand for the blooms are reasons given for closure of the forge (Brainerd 1884/1885:689-691).

Exact location of the forge is unknown but most likely it was in the vicinity of the mine and near Black Creek, about a

4-8. *A view looking east at Highgate Falls, probably in the late 19th century, showing the O.E. Sheridan foundry immediately downstream of the bridge. Stoves, plows, machinery, and hollowware were cast here (courtesy Franklin County Historical Society).*

mile away. Brainerd and Gadcomb were from St. Albans and the ore was shipped to the St. Albans Iron and Steel Works in the 1870s. No field attempt has been made to locate the site. L. R. Brainerd & Company was also involved in lime kilns at a quarry near Swanton (see chapter 8).

FR-149 Rock River Furnace (Highgate): In addition to blast furnaces at Pittsford and Sheldon, either (or both?) Alfred or Israel Keith was also involved in making iron in Highgate as a part-owner with Abel Drury in an early blast furnace located in the northern part of Highgate (Hemenway vol. 1 1867:258).

There is a furnace mound ruin in northern Highgate at Rock River, claimed to date to the period of the Revolutionary War (Leader 1973:2). This might have been the "first furnace built in Highgate" but built much later, and by Abel Drury, in 1807 (Hemenway vol. 1 1867:255). Drury advertised the Highgate furnace on January 6, 1808, in the Burlington *Vermont Centinel:*

"Iron Hollow Ware. A large quantity on hand and for sale, consisting of potash kettles and all kinds of small ware."

Although there is sufficient evidence pointing to a blast furnace operating in Highgate as early as 1807, the Whitelaw map does not show an ironworks here until 1821. By 1825 ore from Highgate was being reduced at a furnace operated by Benjamin F. Hollenbeck and Luther K. Drury (Anderson 1939:142-143). Location of the furnace is unknown; it may have been the one at Rock River. The furnace was a productive operation; cast iron sold for 17¢ a pound (compared to scrap iron, which then sold for 1½¢ a pound). The advent of the railroad, which brought cheaper iron into the area, is the cause given for the furnace's demise.

Also involved in an ironworks at Highgate around the 1810–1815 period were Jacob and Matthew Saxe, sons of John Saxe (of Saxe's Mills). They learned the iron business in Highgate,

4-9. *Six-foot-diameter iron hoops are all that remains of the wood headrace that powered mills at Highgate Falls.*

4-10. *Replacing the covered bridge at Highgate Falls was this beautiful lenticular-design iron bridge, recently abandoned and replaced by a modern concrete bridge about a quarter-mile downstream.*

there being a deposit of iron ore known locally as the Furnace Lot (Saxe 1930:20). The brothers later moved to Chazy, New York and became associated with a blast furnace that was built in 1809 by Alfred or Israel Keith at Salmon River, just south of Plattsburgh. The Plattsburgh assessment roll of 1811 listed Luther Drury owning 3½ acres and half-interest in a furnace, possibly that at Salmon River. The assessment also listed "Keth & Wood" as owner of 18½ acres and a furnace (Hurd 1880:187). Another reference had Elisha Clark operating the Salmon River blast furnace in 1813 and Luther Drury manufacturing potash kettles, stoves, and hollowware in Plattsburgh in 1817 (Porter 1941:213). Jacob Saxe eventually became sole owner of the furnace in 1820. It was washed away by a freshet 10 years later (Allen 1983:86). Matthew stayed at Chazy, but Jacob moved back to Vermont, settling at Sheldon where he operated a mineral spring under the name Saxe & Company (Hemenway vol. 1 1867:380).

The Rock River furnace mound is on the west side of the river, downhill from the town road at a point about 300 feet northwest of where the road turns sharply north. The vicinity was a candidate for gas exploration in the early 1980s and when last visited in 1986 was posted against trespass. Just downstream from the furnace mound are the abutment remains of a road crossing. On a knoll across the river is the Stimet cemetery.

Remains consist of a mound-type concentration of large stones, blast furnace slag, and charcoal marking the probable furnace site. Bits of slag and charcoal were also found by shallow digging in the vicinity; larger, baseball-size slag is in the river. The vicinity of the furnace grounds, between the road (to the west) and the river (to the east), is open land. The property owner lives about a half-mile north but is extremely uncooperative.

GRAND ISLE COUNTY

GI-IW01 Goodwin Forge (Grand Isle): Out on Lake Champlain at the island town of Grand Isle, a forge was operated along Mill Brook in the early 1800s. Nothing more is known about the forge except that Isaac Goodwin produced plows and domestic utensils here until 1838 (Thompson 1842:28). No field attempt has been made to find the site.

CHITTENDEN COUNTY

CH-IW06 Burlington Manufacturing Co. (Burlington): For some years up to 1865, the East Middlebury works (AD-299) ran in connection with Israel Davey's other operation, the Fair Haven Iron Works (RU-FS17). In July 1865, Davey and Benjamin Nichols sold their bloomeries at Salisbury (AD-407) and East Middlebury to the Burlington Manufacturing Company, which had a rolling mill and foundry in Burlington. This company was formed in 1865 and went into operation the latter part of that year (Neilson 1866:235).

The Burlington Manufacturing Company also had interests in forges at Clinton County, New York. For a time in 1866, it leased the Ticonderoga Iron Company, which was formerly managed by a Vermonter, William Calkins (Allen ms 1982). Iron blooms from these forges were made into nails, marble saws, and merchant iron at Burlington.

The company's rolling mill contained three trains of rollers,

four heating furnaces, and a hammer in one large 75- by 155-foot wooden building. The adjoining nail shop was built of brick and housed 46 nail and spike machines. The entire works was run by four steam engines and had the capacity of making 6,000 tons of iron products a year. The mill and foundry were located along Champlain Street, about where the old Vermont Spool and Bobbin Company building stands (today a condominium). The company superintendent was Jacob D. Kingsland, native of Fair Haven and a former partner there with Jacob Davey in 1829. Kingsland had also been connected with ironworks at Keesville, Essex, and Dannemora, New York. After leaving Burlington, he established a nail factory at Vergennes (Allen ms 1982; Adams 1870:143).

The Burlington Manufacturing Company reorganized in 1872, dropped out of the ironworks business, and concentrated on the manufacture of marble (Child 1882:103-105). The ironworks end of the business became part of the Pioneer Mechanic's Shop Company, which came under the control of Benjamin S. Nichols in 1868. These shops were located at the foot of Cherry Street between Battery Street and the railroad tracks.

CH-IW01 Ira Allen Forge (Colchester): When Ira Allen returned to Colchester following the end of the Revolutionary War, he commenced development of the waterpower resources of the Winooski River with the construction of a dam, along with two forges "and a furnace," which produced bar iron, mill irons (machinery hardware), forge hammers, and anchors (Rann 1886:555). Allen contracted for other such mills in Vermont where waterpower and raw material made them practical. His usual arrangement was to lease the mill rent-free, typically for seven years, with an offer to buy it back at a fair market price. One lessee was Aaron Brownell, who leased three forges and an anchor shop for £5 monthly plus a part of the iron made (Wilbur vol. 2 1928:27). Joseph Mozier leased one fire in the forge for 50s. a month (*Calendar* 1939:53). Brownell then leased another anchor shop and a forge, for £60 and £50 a year

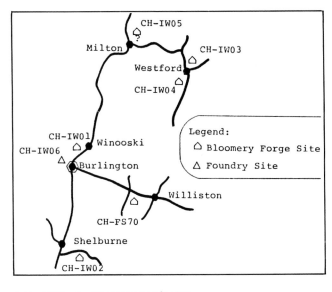

4-11. *Chittenden County ironworks sites.*

(*Calendar* 1939:55). In 1791 correspondence between Ira Allen and Jacob Johnson, the latter agreed to build a forge at Burlington (*Calendar* 1939:30). By early 1792 Allen was busy designing the largest forge he had constructed to date and he ordered a hammer, bellows, etc., from Connecticut. In March he contracted to build a large new anchor shop in Colchester.

Included in an itemized list of Allen's mills at Burlington dated November 8, 1973 were two forges and an uncompleted anchor shop (Wilbur vol. 2 1928:28). A lease offer he published January 3, 1794 mentioned the newly built college (University of Vermont) at Burlington plus mills and an ironworks at the Winooski falls within two miles of the bay. Bog ore from the nearby shores of Lake Champlain was initially used at these forges. When this was depleted, ore beds opened in parts of Colchester, most of them bog ore beds in swamps and ponds. One such bed was in the northwest corner of the town, about a half-mile west of Colchester Pond, per the 1857 Walling map of Chittenden.

The 1796 Whitelaw map indicates ironworks along the Winooski River in the vicinity of the falls on the Colchester side; the 1810 map shows them on the Burlington side. A 1986 inspection of the river below the Route 7 bridge was made and, as expected, nothing related to an Ira Allen-period ironworks was found. The falls area has undergone extensive industrial development, completely changing its appearance since Ira Allen's days. The river tumbles over some small rapids, then plummets over the major falls through a narrow gorge just below the bridge. Whole trees have been seen running this gauntlet during spring thaw. Whatever forge slag was discarded here 200 years ago has long since washed downstream to the river flats and is hidden in sand and gravel bars.

CH-IW02 Shelburne Falls Forge (Shelburne): In 1792, the day after contracting for the anchor shop at Colchester, Ira Allen contracted with Israel Burritt to build a 40- by 50-foot forge house (Wilbur vol. 2 1928:27). Allen was to furnish the boards, logs, irons, nails, and bricks for the chimney, leather for the bellows, and "two barrels of pork and 20 gallons of rum while the work is doing" (*Calendar* 1939:36). The forge was located by the 1796 Whitelaw map at a dam in the La Platte River. The forge was at Shelburne Falls, on the south side of the river opposite a sawmill; both were above the falls. In a description of a flood in 1852 that washed away all mills at this site along with many mills farther downstream, no mention is made of the forge.

The river at Shelburne Falls was inspected above and below the bridge in 1980 without locating any specific iron-making related evidence. Some bits of badly corroded iron and burnt-end brick were found, which might be from a blacksmith shop that stood just northeast of the bridge in the 1860s. A number of dam footings were found above and below the bridge.

CH-IW03 and CH-IW04 Stanton and Seeley Forges (Westford): Two forges were making iron in the early 1800s at Westford. The first (CH-IW03) was built by Joshua Stanton sometime between 1795 and 1810; it appears on the 1796 Whitelaw map. Ore for the forge was mined from beds in Colchester and mixed with harder magnetic ore from New York. Magnetite was boated to Burlington and carted to Westford. Regardless of the expense for these logistics, business was good enough to justify erection of another forge a

few hundred feet farther downstream. The final owner was Stanton's son-in-law Luke Camp, who operated both forges until his death about 1810. The ore beds at Colchester also failed at about this time (Rann 1886:696).

A field trip and interview with the late Irene Allen at Westford (May 15, 1979) placed the first forge just west of the upper bridge over Brown's River. Swimmers reported seeing some underwater machinery here, but no ironworks artifact was found. She also said that a second forge (CH-IW04), built around 1800 by John Seeley, Jr., of Westford, was probably in the vicinity of the lower bridge. Some slag, a burned hearth brick, and the underwater remains of a wood crib for a dam were found about midway between the bridge and remains of another dam.

CH-IW05 Milton Forge (Milton): A forge was in operation in Milton on the west side of Miner's (or Poor Farm) Falls on the Lamoille River (Carlisle 1975:43). The date of the forge is unknown but since it drew ore from the Cobble Hill area about 2½ miles south, the forge probably operated in the 1820–1840 period. The site was searched for in 1980 but not found.

CH-FS70 Spafford Forge (Williston): An elusive forge site was found in the eastern part of Williston, built by General Jacob Spafford, one of the town's first settlers (Rann 1886:657). The forge is identified on the 1810 Whitelaw map as "Gen'l Spafford." It appears to be on Allen Brook and to have been buried under the southbound lane of the Interstate (I-89). Site inspection in 1980 resulted in finding some bits of slag and maybe a headrace in the heavy undergrowth, about 200 feet upstream from I-89. Although a small brook today, it is generally believed that most Vermont creeks ran more heavily in earlier years judging from the numbers of mills that once operated on streams that are today only a trickle.

WASHINGTON COUNTY

WA-IW01 Davis Forge (Calais): At East Calais, Nathaniel Davis operated a nail factory along the Kingsbury Branch in 1812 (Hemenway vol. 4 1882:161). In addition to his trip-hammer shop where he turned out scythes and hoes, his forge made cut nails from iron ore that was dug from ledges a short distance west of the village (Bliss 1954:268). The ore, however, was not sufficient to justify the costs. Nail production lasted only two years. No field attempt has been made to locate the forge.

WA-25 Rice's Furnace (Waitsfield): About two miles south of Irasville, along the east side of the Mad River, Edmund Rice owned a blast furnace that may have operated here as early as 1816. Rice came to Waitsfield in 1803 from Charleston, New Hampshire, and was a cabinetmaker and early merchant, prominent in town until his death in 1829 (Jones 1909:26). Associated with Rice at the furnace were Edward Fales, Theophilus Bixby, James Selleck, and others. The furnace smelted ore that was brought in from Orange County, making iron kettles among other items. The works also included a foundry, which housed a trip-hammer. In the great freshet of 1830 the works, together with a dam, were washed away and never rebuilt. Thomas Poland later constructed a small sawmill on the site, which he operated until it, too, suffered the same fate as its predecessor (Jones 1909:66).

The site was inspected in 1986 with no visible surface indications found of the ironworks, the later sawmill, or the dam. Neither slag nor charcoal could be found on the ground or for about 100 feet along the river at the site, or at another point about a mile downstream at the Route 100 bridge. Except for good historical accounting that pinpoints the location of the ironworks, no surface remains betray the site of this furnace/forge site. The older house standing at the site was probably that of Thomas D. Poland, who ran the sawmill (Beers *Washington* 1873:55).

LAMOILLE COUNTY

LA-IW01 Cady's Falls Forge (Morristown): In 1826 when Joshua Sawyer started a plan for the opening of an iron ore bed in Elmore, he erected a forge a little south of today's hydroelectric station at Cady's Falls in Morristown (Mower 1935:67). But the operation was plagued by problems with the ironworkers, with the iron itself, and finally in 1828 with nature, as a flood brought disaster to the forge. Sawyer deeded his destroyed forge property and the ore bed to the Lamoille and Elmore Iron Factory and Mining Company. The forge site was thereafter used by various mills; the 1859 Lamoille County map shows a starch mill occupying the site and the 1878 Beers map shows it unoccupied. The village of Morrisville purchased the site in 1895 and built a hydroelectric station either directly on or very near to the north end of the old forge site.

No remains of the forge were visible during a 1979 visit although the steep shores of the Lamoille River were not checked for slag. Local residents knew nothing of any iron-making activity here, but there are locally in existence some iron implements and fireplace andirons that were made at Cady's Falls forge from Elmore ore (Sanders 1953:242).

The Central District

The central district contains the majority of the iron-making sites of the state. Addison and Rutland counties alone contain 63 sites, which is about two-thirds the number of ironworks sites in the entire state. The major blast furnace operations centered in Rutland County while the state's major bloomery forges were in both Addison and Rutland counties.

By the mid-19th century, five bloomery complexes in the central district had become nationally known for the quality iron they produced:

Ackworth Bloomeries (West Lincoln)	ca. 1828 to 1865
East Middlebury Iron Works	ca. 1831 to 1890
Fair Haven Iron Works	ca. 1812 to 1870
Salisbury Forge	ca. 1847 to 1870
White's Forge (Vergennes)	ca. 1847 to 1857

Israel Davey, owner of the Fair Haven Iron Works, bought the Salisbury Forge in 1854 and took Benjamin Nichols as a partner in 1862. These two forges then merged and became the Fair Haven Iron Company in 1867. The next year, the company became part of the Burlington Manufacturing Company, which by then also owned the East Middlebury Iron Works. The Ackworth Bloomeries and White's Forge were never part of these transactions.

A number of pocket furnaces also operated in the central

district. Pocket furnaces have been variously defined and illustrated to be about 5-foot-high stone furnaces with full-size blast furnace capability in regard to smelting iron ore. In some cases these diminutive furnaces could have been production units. They were also used to test the ore as an alternative to the expense of building a full-size furnace. For some unknown reason, there was a concentration of pocket furnaces in the Brooksville area (see AD-IW05).

Seven forges were built and operated in and around Bristol village from 1791 to the 1850s. Since no principal name could be found for some of the works, these have been arbitrarily named for owners of record. The forges were contemporary with (and probably similar in design to) the forges at Lincoln. The principal source of ore for these forges was the Bristol ore bed, on a mountain in the northwest corner of the town. Ore was mixed with magnetic ore from Crown Point and other places on the west side of the lake (Munsill 1979:107). The Bristol ore bed is a few miles south of the Monkton ore bed and part of the same geologic system (Adams 1845:22). Ore beds were found in other parts of the town but not in quality or size that justified the expense of mining them. The low price of foreign iron forced the ironworks of Bristol and Lincoln out of the business in the 1850s, never to open again. Many checks for slag were made in and along the New Haven River from Lincoln to well below Bristol village, especially during drier summer months. But the finds were relatively well-distributed small pieces of waterworn slag that could have come from any of the forges along this stretch of the river.

ADDISON COUNTY

AD-IW01 Downing Forge (unlocated): The 1832 manufacturing returns of Vermont listed a forge in Addison County under the name of T. Downing (Kelley 1969:877-907). All other forges in the county included in the returns can otherwise be accounted for. No reference to this ironworks can be found in the county. Inspection of the Downingville area does not suggest any good site for a forge. In 1792 a James Downey, Jr., was involved in a forge at Fair Haven belonging to Gamaliel Leonard (RU-195). But the location of Downing's 1832 forge in Addison County remains a mystery.

AD-300 Orwell Furnace (Orwell): It was at Fair Haven that Matthew Lyon established an industrial base around a series of falls along the Castleton River (RU-FS17). These industries, which became known as Lyon's Works, included extensive ironworks, and there is confusion about whether a blast furnace was part of it. Lyon did, in fact, build a blast furnace and it is supposed to have been in operation in 1788, doing a "considerable business" (Smith 1886:557). But that blast furnace was in Orwell, not Fair Haven. In all the information concerning Lyon's Works at Fair Haven, although there are many references to a furnace or blast furnace, nothing can be found to indicate a blast furnace erected or operating there. The Orwell furnace site is 15 miles north of Fair Haven, and the 1796 Whitelaw map shows a road direct from Fair Haven to the furnace.

During a 1981 inspection of the site along East Creek, exactly where the 1796 Whitelaw map indicates an ironworks, furnace slag was found in a pasture along with burnt bricks, waste iron,

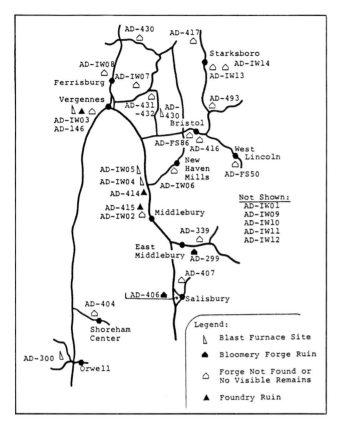

4-12. Addison County ironworks sites.

stone walls, and indications of a head- and tailrace. The site is nearly halfway between Fair Haven and Lyon's iron mine near Port Henry, and also much closer to Lake Champlain. East Creek flows a few dozen feet from the furnace site and is lake-level to within 100 feet of it. Lightly laden ore boats might have negotiated the shallow creek at one time.

A committee of the Vermont Assembly recommended in 1791 that the Lyon blast furnace in Orwell be repaired and set in blast, indicating that the furnace was out of operation at the time (Austin 1981:162). The Orwell stack probably suffered from poor ground insulation that allowed surface dampness to cause a "cold hearth," resulting in a large number of defective castings. And at some times of the year the stream ran too low to drive the waterwheel (Boltum 1881:10). Inspection in 1981 found that the ground at the suspected furnace site was only a few feet higher than the nearby pasture, which had a spongy, soggy feel underfoot. Yet at the time (Labor Day weekend) the creek was running quite low. Lyon's continuing petitions to the state assembly may, therefore, have been unsuccessful attempts to replace the ailing Orwell stack with a better site in Orwell (or maybe Fair Haven?).

AD-406 Sawyer's Forge (Salisbury): Both Connecticut and Vermont have a town of Salisbury, and both towns have an iron-making history. But one recently published history has laid claim to iron cannon and shot being cast in the Vermont town during the Revolution when in fact it was nearly deserted

for fear of marauding Tories and Indians (*Gazetteer* 1976:76). To confuse matters, Ethan Allen (of both Connecticut and Vermont fame) built the first blast furnace at Salisbury, Connecticut, at today's Lakeville village. Salisbury iron was a quality of iron unique to that Connecticut-Massachusetts-New York area and, except for Samuel Keep, has nothing to do with making iron in Salisbury, Vermont.

The first forge in Salisbury (Vermont) was built by Thomas Sawyer in 1791. He had already built a sawmill, gristmill, and tavern in the community known as Sawyers Mills per the 1796 Whitelaw map. Three years later some trip-hammers were built nearby. The works were converted to a shovel factory around 1813 by Harry Johnson, which was possibly operated 20 years later by A. Johnson (Smith 1886:605-606).

Forge construction was directed by Samuel Keep, an iron maker who was born in Salisbury, Connecticut. He arrived at Salisbury, Vermont, via Crown Point and stayed on to work in the bloomery. In 1795, John Deming of Middlebury bought the mills and tavern of Sawyers Mills; Sawyer then moved to New York. Deming and a later partner, J. Woodward, sold to Hascall and Nelson in 1813. Patrick Johnson eventually bought the forge and took Jonathan Kendall as partner, then sold to Ellery Howard and son. They operated the forge until 1853 when it closed in the midst of the nationwide slump in the iron market.

Investigations at the forge site by Salisbury historian Max Petersen in 1976 resulted in finding pieces of iron and hardware, and the collapsed chimney and hearth of the refinery part of the forge (Petersen 1976:16-17). The forge site is on the north shore of the Leicester River, just below the Central Vermont hydroelectric power generating station in Salisbury village. Much slag, charcoal, firebrick, and very heavy pieces of castings were seen during a 1986 inspection.

AD-407 Salisbury Forge (Salisbury): A more modern bloomery was built at Salisbury sometime between 1843 and 1849 by A. B. Huntley but it was abandoned due to financial reasons after making only a few hundred tons of iron (Smith 1886:607). The new forge was about a half-mile upstream of Sawyer's Forge (AD-406). Forges were described as being at many waterfalls near here in 1855, most likely all part of Huntley's forge operations (Swift 1859:15).

Israel Davey, by then owner of forges at Fair Haven, bought Huntley's forges in 1854 and took Benjamin S. Nichols as partner in 1862. The forges merged with the Fair Haven Iron Company five years later, the next year becoming part of the Burlington Manufacturing Company, which also owned the East Middlebury Iron Works, five miles north of the Salisbury Forge (Petersen 1976:25).

Like its sister operation at East Middlebury (AD-299), the Salisbury Forge contained three bloomery hearths, three waterwheels, and a side-lift hammer. Capacity of the Salisbury Forge in 1866 was about 750 tons. In 1864 some 280 tons of iron were made from 500 tons of ore and about 75,000 bushels of charcoal. Chunk iron made from Port Henry ore was used at the Burlington works (Neilson 1866:232-235).

The forge at Salisbury was one of five (others at Fair Haven, East Middlebury, West Lincoln, and Vergennes) known throughout the industry for producing a high-quality wrought iron by the direct bloomery method. Neilson reported in 1866:

Production		Production	
Year	Tons	Year	Tons
1854	200	1860	0
1855	300	1861	0
1856	300	1862	0
1857	200	1863	0
1858	200	1864	280
1859	200	1865	450

With the end of the economic stimulus of the Civil War and the postwar drop in iron prices, quality iron was yielding to cheaper iron from other parts of the country. Israel Davey died in 1869; the Salisbury Forge closed the following year.

Remains of the forge lie just downstream of the Central Vermont dam, about a half-mile northeast of the village. Slag, charcoal, and the race reveal the course of the waterpower system from the falls to its return to the river. A spool factory, which followed the forge at the site, detoured the race, visible by its extension where the race starts to turn toward the river. Ruins of a more recent mill are just downstream of the forge site.

Plough Shares.

FOR SALE at the EAGLE FORGE
100 Share Moulds,
of a superior quality.
ROGER NOBLES
Middlebury, Sept. 4, 1827. 4tf

4-13. National Standard *September 11, 1827 (courtesy Sheldon Museum)*.

AD-339 Eagle Forge (Middlebury): Roger Nobles operated an early forge along the upper Middlebury River in a deep gorge a mile upstream of East Middlebury. Dates of operation are not known for sure, but the forge was in operation as early as 1810 (Smith 1886:342). In 1827 Nobles advertised plows for sale at the Eagle Forge. The forge was abandoned soon after and was washed away by the 1831 freshet.

The river was inspected upstream of the Route 125 bridge in 1984, hiking upstream on North Branch Road and taking an old road that forks off to the right a few minutes walk from the bridge. Up the road is an area of charcoal, which extends from the trail for about 50 feet toward the river and 50 feet along the edge of the road. Other features in the area include a 40-foot-long by up to 9-foot-high stone wall; large (2- to 3-foot-diameter) stones laid in a line, possibly anchoring the shore end of a dam; two levels of ground (the trail and a lower level adjacent to the bottom of the 40-foot stone wall). A path,

cut into the face of the charcoal-covered ground, allows swimmers access through the area to the river, here about 25 feet below road level. There is much evidence of recreation activity all along the road. According to local tradition, the charcoal once burned underground for many weeks before it was extinguished (Victor Rolando paper, 1984). Slag was found in the river during a later field inspection. About 20 to 30 feet upstream of the end of the 40-foot wall, some walnut-size pieces of magnetic iron ore were found, lying where they appear to have fallen from a wagon that might have been carrying ore along the old road. The ore might have come from Crown Point, since that ore was later carted to a forge that operated a few years later below the bridge.

About 200 feet upstream, another stone wall, much less obvious (about two feet high by 10 feet long) was found. No charcoal or slag was found here. Although a narrow path continues another 100 feet, then pinches out in the narrowing gorge at the base of a high cliff, the road itself appears to end here. Topography of the opposite shoreline hints at a bridge having been here, with the low stone wall being the remains of the bridge abutment on this side of the river. No companion feature was seen on the immediate opposite shore; the river is about 15 to 20 feet wide and one to two feet deep here, but most likely much deeper during spring thaw. Farther upstream on that opposite (south) side, the road can be found again, very faintly, still heading upstream. This might have been a predecessor road to the present Route 125 highway or maybe an old charcoal road for the forge(s) below.

Could the charcoal area have been connected somehow with the forge operations at a later period below the bridge? Considering the available space to store charcoal and ore at the later downstream forge site (AD-299), it is doubtful that the downstream forge would have carted these materials upstream to store them at this space-limited location. It is possible, therefore, that this charcoal area is the approximate site of the Eagle Forge, and that this was a bloomery forge operation, since in the early 1800s plows were still being made by hammering wrought-iron plates to form mold boards. With a high cliff on the shore opposite the charcoal area, it was a good place to build a dam, hence the line of large stones along the shore immediately downstream of the site. The old road continues its level about 25 feet above the present river level for about 200 feet upstream to stay above the level of the backed-up forge pond above the dam. There might have been some connection between this forge and Nobel's Forge (BE-IW03) in Pownal.

AD-299 East Middlebury Iron Works (Middlebury): Shortly after the Eagle Forge was washed away by the 1831 freshet, another forge was built downstream and nearer the village by George Chapman (Fenn vol. 13 n.d.:30). George Chapman was followed sometime before 1846 by Middlebury merchant Asa Chapman, who along with some other Chapmans was also running a forge in Lincoln (*Walton's* 1846-1850).

Asa Chapman ran the forge at East Middlebury until about 1850 at which time the operations became Slade, Farr & Co (*Walton's* 1850). Chapman also maintained a ledger, which he titled the *Teaming Book*, in which he recorded the daily comings of wagon loads of charcoal and ore, and the departures of wagon loads of iron (Sheldon Museum Library). The period covered is from August 1845 through October 1848. In the 18 months from April 1846 to October 1847, 396 tons of ore were recorded arriving on 393 wagon loads, about a ton of ore per wagon arriving nearly every day. In the 1860s some ore came from as far away as Seven Islands (Sept-Îles), Québec (Hunt 1870:279-280). But most appears to have been dug at Crown Point, boated across the lake to Vergennes, then shipped by wagon to the forge. Shipped to Vergennes from the forge during that same period were 226 tons of iron in 249 wagon loads, or slightly less than a ton of iron per wagon leaving every other day. In a 2½- month period, it was recorded that "Coal received of John Maganity" was 1,730 bushels in 21 loads, which averaged about 80 bushels of charcoal per load. Altogether, the names of 57 teamsters are recorded hauling ore, charcoal, and iron to and from the forge. It was truly a busy place when all the woodchoppers, miners, colliers, blacksmiths (to service the horse teams and the tools of miners and ironworkers), boatmen, bloomers, and their families are considered. Forge operations either directly or indirectly affected the livelihood of over a hundred people.

The ledger recorded that a freshet destroyed the forge on October 30, 1847. The following month one iron shipment was made; no further shipments were made until May 1848. An itemized list of costs to rebuild the forge totals $1,661.47. When operations resumed, the forge received 249 tons of ore and shipped 187 tons of iron from May through October 1848. Production ratios of the older to newer forge (1.75 to 1.33 tons of ore per ton of iron) calculates to a significant 23.7 percent increase in efficiency of the forge. Technical improvements had obviously been incorporated into the new forge. The ledger bookkeeping system does not allow comparison of charcoal efficiencies.

That ratio of 1.33 tons of ore to 1 ton of iron output was quite superior in comparison to other forge outputs of about the same period. At the Salisbury Forge the ratio was 1.75:1 while at the West Lincoln forges it was 2.10:1. By comparison, at the Pittsford and Plymouth blast furnaces the ratio of ore to

iron was 2:1 (Neilson 1866:217-218, 232-233). Variations in local ore quality would have affected these ratios.

After Slade & Farr operated the forge, Israel Davey came into control. Davey now also owned the Salisbury Forge, about five miles to the south, in addition to his ironworks complex at Fair Haven. Soon after taking over the East Middlebury Forge, Davey took Benjamin S. Nichols as partner, and they sold the works in 1865 to the Burlington Manufacturing Company. According to Neilson, production through 1865 was:

Production		Production	
Year	Tons	Year	Tons
1854	50	1860	400
1855	50	1861	400
1856	300	1862	400
1857	300	1863	400
1858	300	1864	400
1859	400	1865	500

By 1866 the forge was called the East Middlebury Iron Works and had three bloomery hearths, each with its own waterwheel, and one side-lift hammer. The forge consumed 100,000 bushels of charcoal and 700 tons of Lake Champlain ore in 1864. Annual capacity of the forge was estimated at 750 tons. The main product at the time was billets, which were rolled by the Burlington Manufacturing Company (Neilson 1866:232-235).

Three large waterwheels were supplied by a head of water from a dam upstream from the bridge. Ore still came down the lake from Mineville, New York, but now traveled by railroad to Middlebury Village, and finally by wagon to the forge. The process was reversed for shipping iron to Pennsylvania and New Jersey, where it was converted into steel. The forge complex consisted of a large charcoal and ore shed, the forge building, and a smaller waterwheel house. Iron was drawn from three hearths every three hours, cooled in a circular mold, hammered into a large block 6 inches thick, then cut into 6-inch-square by 18-inch-long 1-cwt blooms (Fenn vol. 13 n.d.:30).

Charcoal was made up the Middlebury River North Branch in Ripton where 60 to 100 men worked cutting trees, tending the kilns, and driving teams. About 9,000 bushels of charcoal were made annually in kilns owned and operated by the East Middlebury Forge Company (Smith 1886:593-594). Built sometime previous to 1859, the kilns were still operating when the forge went out of business. A nearby boardinghouse fed and housed the charcoal workers.

Subsequent to the Burlington Manufacturing Company ownership, the forge continued sporadic operation. The 1871 Beers map identified the owners as Williams & Nichols. Andrew Williams was from Plattsburgh; Harvey J. Nichols was works agent. They rebuilt the works in 1880, annual capacity then being 1,300 tons of charcoal blooms for steel manufacture (*Directory* 1882:169). When it was abandoned in 1890, the forge was the last iron-making operation remaining in Vermont (Swank 1892:113). Around 1900, the hammerheads, tuyeres, waterwheel, shafts, etc., all weighing about 500 tons, were purchased for scrap. At that time, it was reported that the forge building was still standing (Patch 1918:158).

4-14. *Foundation remains of the forge at East Middlebury, possibly the waterwheel pit.*

Traces of the forge were still visible in 1985, just downstream of the Route 125 bridge over the gorge. For 100 feet below the bridge there are piles of black, rusty slag mixed with charcoal. A path leads from the highway diagonally through the site. East of the path are the stone wall remains of the forge, coal house, wheel pit, and the long tailrace. A state plan to relocate the Route 125 bridge 100 feet downstream might impact this historic site. Charcoal kilns that probably serviced the forge were found in 1983 near Dragon Brook, about two miles north (chapter 6, AD-314).

AD-IW02 Nichols Forge (Middlebury): The earliest ironworks at Middlebury village was at Frog Hollow, where Jonathan Nichols built a forge, trip-hammer shop, and gun factory in 1794 on the west side of the falls (Smith 1886:284-285). Ore for the works came mainly from Crown Point, mixed with some local ore from Monkton. Jonathan was joined by his brother Josiah two years later and, together with Daniel Pettibone and Ezekiel Chapman, discovered a process for welding cast steel, which they patented in 1802. The same year a federal contract for 1,000 guns was filled and delivered by the gun shop.

The shop was just northwest of the base of the falls under fill that today is a parking area in Frog Hollow along the Otter Creek. Three buildings identified as "Forge, Furnace & Trip Hammer" were drawn on a map in 1885 by Henry L. Sheldon of the first industries at the falls nearly 100 years before (Sheldon Museum Library). Much iron was made and worked here, and the works changed hands many times, eventually coming to Rufus and Jonathan Wainwright, Jr. They built a furnace (cupola?) on the site of the former forge soon after the end of the War of 1812, where stoves were cast (Smith 1886:325-328).

Areas of the parking lot, falls, and lawn behind the Old Stone Mill were inspected in 1984. Slag was found along the shoreline just upstream of the site of Nichols' gun shop and Wainwright's pre-1826 stove foundry. The eroding shoreline has exposed slag for 20 to 30 feet along the shore from the edge of the hillside lawn to well into the creek. Associated with the slag are firebricks of a period later than either the Wainwright or Nichols operations. The site area has been backfilled, hiding from view any slag remains on the older, now-buried shoreline. All archival references to "furnaces" at the falls hint at cupola furnaces rather than blast furnaces. But the possibility remains that for a short time around 1800 a blast furnace may also have operated near the falls prior to being displaced by a cupola.

AD-415 Wainwright/Davenport Foundry (Middlebury): Soon after the end of the War of 1812, Rufus and Jonathan Wainwright, Jr., built a furnace (cupola or air furnace?) on or very near the site of the former Jonathan Nichols forge, which had already changed hands many times (Smith 1886:325-328). In 1821 they advertised cook, parlor, and box stoves and trimmings, caldrons, kettles, andirons, and hollowware. Their offer of terms for cattle, horses, or grain with "a liberal discount for cash" reflected the continuing problem of lack of hard money, nearly 50 years after Ira Allen's similar offers in his ironworks ventures.

Fire destroyed the works in the summer of 1826 along with nearby gristmills and sawmills. A new foundry was built on the east side of Paper Mills Falls, a mile downstream. The

> **R. & J. Wainwright,**
>
> HAVE now on hand and will keep for sale, during the present season, a general assortment of
>
> ## STOVES,
>
> consisting of
> Cook, Parlour Shop and Sheet-Iron Stoves,
> —ALSO,—
> ## Stove Pipe,
>
> and Trimmings of every description.
>
> ☞ Cattle, Grain, and a few good Horses, will be taken in payment for the above articles.
>
> Middlebury, Sept. 18, 1821.   5—tf

4-15. National Standard *October 2, 1821 (courtesy Sheldon Museum).*

December 1841 issue of the *Middlebury People's Press* announced that E. & A. A. (Edward and Alonzo A.) Wainwright were selling cooking, box, and parlor stoves, plows and plow irons, and hollowware "that have been manufactured at this furnace for the last 20 years."

In April 1844, Wainwright made a detailed description of these works (which included a "new building") for fire insurance purposes:

> The following is a description of the buildings belonging to Edward Wainwright situated in Middlebury at the lower falls on the East side of Otter Creek and one mile north of the village. The buildings are situated in relation to each other as follows: —the furnace stands immediately on the bank of the creek—and is 80 feet 10 inch by 30 feet 4 inches and one story high, and the roof is covered with sheet iron plates except 17 feet of the north end. The pots for smelting iron [are] placed in the south end of the furnace and in said furnace are two stoves for heating the same. Attached to the south end corner of the Furnace is a wing 11½ feet in breadth by 16 feet 2 inches in length. This wing is a wheel house and covered with sheet iron. Within 1 foot of the wing stands over the floom [*sic*] a building that is two stories high, is 24½ feet in length by 17 feet 4 inches in breadth and within the said building no fire is kept. North end of this building 21½ feet distant stands the coal House.

The coalhouse [is] directly east of the furnace distant 41 feet 2 inches. The new building stands immediately upon the bank of the creek somewhat west of north of the furnace, 41 feet from it. It is 50 feet 4 inches by 30 feet 4 inches and 2 stories high and is warmed by three stoves. The lower story is used as a machine shop—the upper story for joiner shop for making stove patterns, &c. Northeast of this last building stands the horse shed, 11 feet from it (*Vermont Insurance* 1844:No. 502, Bk. 2).

The "pots for smelting" would appear to indicate the presence of an iron-smelting blast furnace, but no mention is made elsewhere in the description of a necessary ore house. The building dimensions and distances between buildings, to the inch, are an archeological find.

Five months later, a fire consumed the "furnace building and coal house containing Lehigh (coal) and charcoal plus valuable patterns, tools, &c." (Sheldon, Bk. 178). The loss was $2,000, of which $1,600 was covered by insurance. The loss included the 80- by 30-foot furnace building, valued at $450 (*Vermont Insurance* 1844:No. 504, Bk. 2). The works were rebuilt and continued until the death of Jonathan Wainwright in 1845, at which time Jason Davenport bought the business. An 1849 advertisement listed machine castings, mill cranks and gears, stoves, caldrons, kettles, sleigh shoes, and wagon boxes for sale at the furnace. Davenport continued the business until about 1866.

Inspection of west side Paper (Pulp) Mills Falls in 1985 indicated evidence of the many mills that operated here at one time in the form of an impressive, deep raceway cut into solid rock, scattered bricks, many dozens of nails of all sizes, and many iron rods still firmly implanted in the stream bedrock just downstream of the covered bridge. On the east side of the falls, next to the headrace that leads to the hydroelectric power station, a 1986 inspection during lower-water conditions located some surface patches of slag-appearing material and significant stone wall foundations, which could be the remains of the Wainwright/Davenport foundry operations.

Upstream at Middlebury Falls, standing evidence of the former industrial activity of the village still exists, but no surface remains of the former Wainwright Foundry (or the Nichols Forge) can be found.

AD-146 Monkton Iron Company (Vergennes): The importance of the great falls of the Otter at Vergennes was recognized at an early time. The first mill here was a sawmill constructed in 1764 (Smith 1886:642). The next year a contract to build a gristmill was made. Considerable contention for these early mills ensued between New York and Vermont interests, including quasi-military actions by Ethan and Ira Allen just previous to the Revolutionary War. Mill construction at the falls proceeded vigorously following the war.

The year 1786 is mentioned as the date of the first ironworks. This forge might have been built by Gideon Spencer of Bennington, who moved to Vergennes that year (Smith 1886:646-647). Ore came from local beds (and Skene's ore bed in New York?), mixed with magnetic ores from northern Vermont (Highgate) and New York. A description of Vergennes in 1788 includes a small forge on the east side of Otter Creek, probably Spencer's (Smith 1886:649). The works changed hands many times, coming to Jabez G. Fitch in October 1789. It was seized the next year by a sheriff's return on a writ against Fitch in favor of some Québec merchants. The property included the residence of a bloomer, one forge with "every implement necessary for operating" one coal shed, and a blacksmith shop (Smith 1886:653). Azariah Tousey operated another forge on the west side of the creek above the falls in 1799 (Smith 1886:662).

4-16. Middlebury Galaxy *August 7, 1849 (courtesy Sheldon Museum).*

These operations were all in place and operating when a gentleman arrived in 1807 from Boston to effect the transformation of the iron industry in Vergennes.

The Monkton Iron Company was exceptional not for what it did or did not do, but for the wealth of historical data the company left behind. The trials and failures of a group of Boston investors trying to turn a profit from an ambitious venture nearly 300 miles away is laid open by the record of papers and ledgers on file at the Bixby Memorial Library at Vergennes. In 1932, Adella Ingham authored an unpublished manuscript titled *In The Days of The Monkton Iron Company of Vergennes, Vermont 1807–1830*, which documented her research into Monkton Iron Company letters and ledgers that had recently come into the possession of the Bixby Library through the generosity of Philip C. Tucker III. As the assistant librarian, she took on the task for personal interest, as only so many valuable little histories are ever written. Not enough credit can be given for efforts such as these, in a period when research grants were rare and the Comprehensive Employment and Training Act (CETA) was yet a lifetime away. Through her writing we can follow the daily frustrations of the company and its few slim successes. But were these frustrations reserved for the Monkton Iron Company alone? Nowhere else has such an explicit record been found of another Vermont ironworks operation. We know only bits of information; a starting date here, an abandonment date there, some tonnages and topics of interest someplace else. Everything between this scattered information can only be conjectured. But just as we must be careful not to conclude that the Vergennes ironworks experience was typical for others in Vermont, we must also be careful not to conclude that the others were more successful. A majority of ironworks ventures in Vermont had a short life. Many died in infancy.

By 1807 Boston had become one of the busiest ports on the coast, with merchant ships carrying on trade with ports as far away as China. And though their main attention was directed out to sea, it was not uncommon for Boston merchantmen to look inland for opportunities. That summer found Perkins Nichols of Boston buying up tracts of land in Vermont. Variously identified as an engineer, lawyer, and merchant, he was impressed by the potential of the falls at Vergennes and the proximity of iron ore beds a few miles away at Monkton. He was also an associate of a group of other Boston merchants who organized themselves later that year as the Monkton Iron Company (Seaburg and Paterson 1971:199-219).

The company consisted of Stephen and George Higginson, Francis Bradbury, James and Thomas H. "Colonel" Perkins, Benjamin Welles, Perkins Nichols, and William Parsons. Colonel Perkins, the major force behind the partnership, was a Boston merchant who built a fortune in sea trade, canals, bridges, politics, land speculation, and mining. In December 1807 an embargo on foreign trade was put into effect. Shipping dropped to zero and the port of Boston was starting to take on the appearance of a ghost town. The Monkton Iron Company appeared to provide a timely outlet for the Boston money men to put now-idle capital back to work. But because they were relative amateurs when it came to the iron business, the venture proved a financial disaster. They had the political and financial acumen to become the leading spokesmen on the Boston waterfront, but did not have the skill to run a successful iron business. Their hiring of men to supervise the construction of the ironworks through secondhand advice was in complete contradiction to their methods of operating a successful shipping business and it cost them endless problems. But you could not prove it by the people in and around the little community of Vergennes, who knew a good thing when they saw it; or to the U.S. Navy, which a few years later was rewarded with an unexpected tactical coup.

By mid-1808 construction of the furnace hearth had commenced with the expectation that it would go into blast before winter. Construction took place near the southern end of the falls, right side when facing upstream. (The 1810 Whitelaw map indicates an ironworks on the opposite side, not on this side until 1821.) Attempts to speed up the work were protested by the local workers who demanded higher wages despite the high unemployment at Boston caused by the embargo. With summer, many workers left for haying. The wheelwright who had been hired in March to construct the waterwheel machinery had not yet arrived by July. Waterwheel construction went ahead anyway with local supervision. The wheelwright finally arrived in September and the next month the furnace was completed, but the December date for going into blast was thwarted by an early and unusually cold winter that froze the Otter Creek. Work shut down until spring.

The plans were to build a blast furnace, some forges, plus rolling and slitting mills and nail machines. The company was going to operate every phase of the production: from mining and charcoaling to smelting and refining, thence to casting, machining, and finally, marketing. Even a company store and employee library were planned.

Work on dams, flumes, and the beginnings of a blast furnace was begun as soon as the property came into the hands of the Company. Laborers were hired for the construction work in Vergennes and fifteen or twenty were set at work at the ore bed in Monkton. They spent much time clearing away the earth to prevent its falling in when the blasting was begun. A boarding house was built and a family hired to manage it. Irish and Canadian laborers worked for the small sum of ten dollars a month "and found" [food and lodging].

Well-wooded land was to be had at four or five dollars an acre, and that was an important consideration. The fuel used in the furnace and forge was charcoal and large quantities had to be provided. Mr. Bradbury bought up tracts of woodland in surrounding towns and hired men to cut the timber and convert it to charcoal. Some of the tracts purchased included as many as five hundred acres. He also advertised for charcoal and many settlers went into the business of making it. A boarding house for the laborers in Vergennes was built. At about this time the Company opened a general store in Vergennes.

In March 1808 we find record of a man named Butler cutting a thousand cords of wood at two dollars a cord and another gang of men cutting twelve hundred cords at the same price. How fast the original forest must have been disappearing! Houses for storing the charcoal were now necessary and eventually there were fifteen such houses. Blacksmith shops in Vergennes and Monkton were found to be needed when the ore and charcoal were being brought in to Vergennes. A farm in Ferrisburg, with a small forge near by, was owned by the Company. Here cattle, sheep and hogs were raised to furnish food for the employees.

Mr. Bradbury was a very busy man. He bought timberland, got out timber for the construction in Vergennes and contracted for charcoal, supervised the work at the ore bed and at the Ferrisburg farm, to say nothing of the building of dams, flumes and the blast furnace in Vergennes. Small wonder that he protested that he could not attend to the retail shop. He did not feel competent to select the articles to be kept in a country store and begged the officers of the Company in Boston to put in a man accustomed to such trade. This man was provided and the store stocked and in operation. This was in January, 1808. . . .

In November 1808 more than a hundred men were employed by the Company; colliers, miners, carpenters and masons, and all bought their supplies from the company store. Charcoal was bartered for store goods. . . . Many pairs of oxen and horses were used in drawing the ore from the ore bed to Vergennes and in bringing in the charcoal. . . .

The Company was now running three boarding houses and the matter of provisions was important. Evidently much wheat was then raised in the country round about and frequent mention is made of buying it by the bushel for the boarding houses. Beef, pork and shad were bought by the barrel. Candles were an important item to provide and were often mentioned.

Contracts were made for raising the ore at the Monkton ore bed for seventy-five cents a ton. At the lake ore bed it was one dollar.

Several spans of mules were bought in Hartford, Connecticut to take the place of oxen and were the first to appear in this part of the country. At one time the Company owned thirty-seven oxen, twenty-nine horses and seven mules. Great effort was made on the Ferrisburg and Monkton farms to raise hay and oats for the horses and cattle owned by the Company. Much hay had to be purchased however.

An orchard of five hundred apple trees was planted on the Monkton farm and it is said the remains of it may still be seen (Ingham 1932:5-13).

4-17. Middlebury Mercury *May 30, 1810 (courtesy Sheldon Museum).*

The furnace was fired on May 11, 1809 after the repair of the winter ice damage to some of the waterpower equipment. Nine days later the furnace was warm and stabilized. The waterwheel started turning, the bellows began their rhythmic creaking and puffing, and the blast began. An inability to control the speed of the waterwheel caused a hotter than desired blast and some small cracks in the hearth, resulting in fears that it might burn out prematurely. During the early summer the charge was slowly increased with no serious problem, and the yield climbed from 1½ tons to nearly 2 tons of iron a day. But this was far less than the 4½ tons that had been expected. On August 6 the furnace was shut down to rebuild the hearth. The chance to make a killing in the iron market was slipping away. Cheaper iron from Europe was now arriving at Boston with the lifting of the embargo the previous March. In early September the furnace again shut down for repairs.

In two months the hearth was repaired and the furnace was once more back in blast. A month later, results of the repair became evident as the yield rose to 3 tons a day, but still over a ton a day less than hoped for. And although the potash kettles being cast were not moving too well, the stoves were beginning to attract a market; some profits meant some cheerful news in Boston. But just then the tymph stone broke. Failure of the tymph stone forced another shutdown and a time-consuming cooling-down period. Furnace repairs were completed in mid-January 1810; the furnace was refired, then shut down again to replace another burned-out hearth. By June the furnace was back in operation for the fourth time in a year, surviving a leaky flume and the sudden illness of its operators. After a month the creek level dropped and the waterwheel slowed to a stop. With this stoppage, some repairs were made, one of which was to improve the regulation of the blast pressure. By the end of October, the furnace was again in blast, followed by another problem, and shut down at the end of November. A month later, ice stopped the refinery wheels from converting cast iron into wrought iron and on the first day of 1811 everything came to a halt.

So it went at Vergennes with the iron company continuing its unprofitable trial and error ways until the War of 1812 caught up with Vermont. Early in 1813, a contract was made with the government for 300 tons of shot for the small fleet of gunboats on Lake Champlain. By that summer the works were producing 7 tons of iron and 12 tons of shot a week at a cost to the government that approached four times the expense to the company. It had finally struck on a way out of the dilemma of profitless years: a U.S. defense contract! "In December 1812 the United States government ordered three hundred tons of cannon shot from the Company. In February 1813 Mr. Welles writes to George Bamford of the Ordinance [*sic*] Department [at] Albany. After a long dissertation on the sizes of cannon shot he goes on to say: 'Nothing could afford me higher gratification than to see you at our works. They are the largest in the U.S. and our stock of ore, coal and pigs is so great that we could at once go into very large business for the government' " (Ingham 1932:25-26).

The statement about the company being the largest in the U.S. has been quoted many times in books and magazines and taken as fact. Many large ironworks, however, were also operating during the War of 1812 in northwestern Connecticut, the Hudson River highlands of New York, just south in New Jersey, and throughout many parts of Pennsylvania. Almost all were situated on better transportation routes to more effectively support the American forces along the east coast. That the Monkton Iron Company might have been equal in size to some of these could be true; that it was the largest of them all is doubtful. Most likely, Benjamin Welles was "puffing" to the government agent in hopes of furthering his company's financial gain.

Commodore MacDonough's little fleet of warships went into winter quarters up Otter Creek, conveniently close to the ironworks, and in January 1814 received authorization to construct new gunboats. That September the newly outfitted and armed gunboats sailed out to the lake, thrashed the British fleet at Plattsburgh, and sent the invasion army packing back to Canada. "The battle of Plattsburg in which Commodore Macdonough defeated the British took place September 11, 1814. In October

Mr. Perkins wrote Mr. Welles: 'I believe in my heart that Macdonough saved our works, but I believe too that our works saved his ships by furnishing a large supply of shot. So that I think it is an even bargain'" (Ingham 1932:35).

Hostilities ended three months after the battles on Lake Champlain, and the sweet taste of victory at the ironworks proved short-lived when it was realized that the company had lost its most profitable customer.

> The Company was making wire of different sizes and mention is made of stoves. They are described as "common shoemakers' shop stoves, double stoves with ovens, 3 ft single stoves with ovens and mechanics' stoves." The prices were $40, $30, $28 and $12. Machines were set up for making screws, but there was no market for their product. . . .
>
> Following the period of great activity on the lake came a period of financial depression. The Company made every effort to collect bills and turn into money their varied stock of iron. Debts were put into the hands of collectors and at least one man was imprisoned for debt. The Company continued to make sheet iron and wire but could find little market for them (Ingham 1932:35-36).

The forges continued making stoves, hollowware, and other hardware. But with European iron once more arriving at Boston much cheaper than nearby Monkton iron, the works shut down in 1816. An October 2, 1816 item in a Boston newspaper noted that "the extensive Iron Works, water rights, mills, and estates belonging thereto, situated in the town of Vergennes, state of Vermont" were for sale to anyone who wanted to form a company to carry on the business. It was during this time that 15-year-old Philip C. Tucker was hired and became company assistant clerk and bookkeeper.

> [Mr.] Tucker remained in charge of the Counting-house and Works. It was a position of much responsibility and care. To enumerate the duties required of this sixteen-year-old boy: the care of the counting-house, correspondence and bookkeeping, watchful supervision over the grist mill and at least weekly division of the grain brought in, frequent visits to the Ferrisburg farm, the Monkton ore bed and farm where there was stock to be cared for, and occasional visits to the lake property to prevent depredations on the timber land. All the buildings and machinery of the Works were to be inspected and kept in repair.
>
> He made constant effort to sell iron and iron products and advertised in Burlington and Middlebury papers. The matter of the taxes on the New York lands caused him much anxiety and several trips to Essex and Albany New York. Every means was taken to collect bills and many notes were sued. Detailed accounts of all events and conditions at the Works were written to Mr. Welles in Boston, yet this very busy young man found time to read and make notes on the books read.
>
> An ironworker in Fairhaven, Vermont offered to buy the scrap iron, viz., thick and sheet iron trimmings, ends of bars and whatever blacksmiths' scraps there were at $2 a hundred weight, and it is a sad commentary on the condition of affairs that the Company was glad to accept this offer.

Some pine timber on the Company's land was sold at this time to Capt. Sherman of the Steamboat Company.

The year 1816 was a barren year. All crops were so poor that the stock on the farms could not be wintered. Mr. Tucker sold all the sheep except the merinos. There were eighteen head of cattle and no hay to feed them. On the advice of a business man, Mr. Booth, Mr. Tucker considered killing them and salting the beef to be sold in Canada, but he found there was an embargo on salt beef and pork. He then decided the thing to do was to drive them to Canada and sell them on the hoof. In November 1816 this young lad on horseback, with a drover starts on this long trip driving eighteen head of cattle. . . .

Sale 1 cow	$ 18.00	
Sale 17 beef oxen weighing 12150 lbs at $3.70	449.77	[sic]
Less exchange Bradbury	6.00	
	$461.77	

Expenses P.C. Tucker driving horse and 18 beef cattle to Montreal		
Common exps.	$ 68.19	
Ferry across Lake Champlain and River St. Lawrence	18.75	
Destruction of cabbage gardens	5.00	
Assistance catching runaway cattle	1.75	
Duties	11.25	
Stowell's bill services selling	5.00	
Drover's wages	16.00	
	$125.66	[sic]
[net]		$336.11

It is plainly to be seen that every effort to raise money on the personal property of the Company was being made (Ingham 1932:38-44).

Government thoughts for a while in 1817 of establishing an arsenal near the Canadian border stirred some hope among the Boston merchants that they might yet get bailed out. When President Monroe inspected the extensive (but idle) ironworks he was not impressed. The arsenal was built elsewhere although 11 years later an arsenal did become a reality for Vergennes. When the works closed down it consisted of the blast furnace, a cupola furnace, eight forges, a wire factory, a rolling mill, plus gristmills, sawmills, and fulling mills. An 1817 advertisement mentioned a large number of cast-iron and wrought-iron products on hand and for sale. In his travels through Vermont in 1819, Levi Woodbury arrived at Vergennes on Thursday, May 14, and made the following observation of the ironworks there: "Below the Falls, but so near as to have all its machinery turned by water from above are situated very extensive Iron works. They are at present suspended & decaying. One building contains 8 or 9 chimneys and bellows &c. for making bar-iron. The furnace, the outhouses &c. are 12 or 15 in number. Both bar and cast iron were manufactured here. The ore was dug on the New York side of the Lake & is not I should think the best quality" (Fant 1966:49).

"For a short time in August 1821 the Air Furnace was revived and moulders put to work making castings. Mr. Tucker assured Mr. Welles that he had 'furnished the furnace roof with proper ladders and kept the water buckets continually full. . . .' About this time Tucker sold for the Company a piece of land in

Notice.

The Monkton Iron Co.

Have on hand a large assortment of

BAR-IRON,

Plough Share -Moulds,

Sleigh and Cutter-Shoes,

Waggon-Tire,

10d Nail-Rods,

Horse-Nail-Rods,

Hub-Iron,

Trace and Draught-Chains,

Double, 3 feet, 2 1-2 feet & close

Cast-Iron Stoves,

Pot Ash Kettles,

Farmers' Caldrons,

4d, 8d, & 10d, Cut Nails,

A large quantity first quality

Yellow Ochre :

All of which they offer for

sale on good terms at their store in Vergennes

for cash or approved credit.

BENJ. WELLS, Agent M. I. Co.

Per PHILIP C. TUCKER.

Vergennes, Sept. 27, 1817.   6 3

4-18. National Standard *October 15, 1817 (courtesy Sheldon Museum).*

Vergennes, six rods by five, for $450 which he thought a very good price in Vergennes" (Ingham 1932:45-46).

Not until after the opening of the Champlain Canal did the iron business revive to any degree in Vergennes. By that time, Amos W. Barnum had established himself as one of the city's leaders, holding a number of political posts, including mayor from 1824 to 1828. Barnum saw the value of the Champlain Canal toward promoting the commercial interests of the city's harbor and started a Tow Path Company for towing canal boats to and from the lake, seven miles down the Otter Creek. The towpath was used for several years until the advent of the lake steamers. He and others succeeded in organizing the Bank of Vergennes, which was rechartered the National Bank of Vergennes in 1865. Besides Barnum, the directors included Thomas D. Hammond, brother of Charles F. Hammond, one of the Crown Point Iron Company founders. When Barnum resigned, William Nash replaced him. Nash was a New Haven industrialist and owned a forge at New Haven Mills. Barnum also owned interests in the Stevens House and the American Hotel.

Barnum leased some of his land on the northeast side of the falls in 1824 to Alfred T. Rathbone, who built a blast furnace on it that same year. (Rathbone's father, Wait, had built blast furnaces in Clarendon (RU-97) and Tinmouth (RU-77) some years before.) Stoves and hollowware were cast by Alfred Rathbone, who also advertised to sell tea kettles, spiders, andirons, and plow irons (*Vermont Aurora* July 15, 1824; *National Standard* July 28, 1824). Soon after, Rathbone leased his furnace to Hector H. Crane (Smith 1886:677). In the fall of 1825 and early 1826, Crane published the following advertisement:

> Vergennes Blast Furnace—The subscriber informs the public that he has put his blast furnace in complete operation, and is prepared to execute orders for machine castings, from one pound to fifteen hundred pounds, at the Troy prices. He has on hand, a complete assortment of Hollow Ware, such as kettles holding from 2 quarts to 15 gallons, pots of various sizes, Spiders, Pans, Basins, Skillets, Bake Pans, Tea Kettles, Andirons, and Cast and Wagon Boxes. He will be ready in the fall to accommodate his customers with Parlor, Shop, and Cooking Stoves, and Potash and Caldron Kettles. The above articles with the exception of the Machinery Castings will be sold upon the approved credit, or for almost any kind of country products, on as reasonable terms as they can be had at other Furnace in any part of the country. Merchants can be furnished at the Troy prices (*Vermont Aurora* Sept. 22, 1825; Jan. 6, 1826).

The reference to Troy prices reflected competition with Troy, New York, the result of the newly opened Champlain Canal.

Alfred T. Rathbone, who had built this furnace on land leased from Amos Barnum, ran afoul of the law about 1826 when he found himself "financially over-extended." His creditors had him jailed (he escaped briefly) and he lost his furnace in the ensuing court action.

Barnum's ironworks interests also included ore beds in Monkton and near Moriah, New York, and 1,200 acres of timberland near Westport, New York, where the Sisco Furnace operated (*Vermont Aurora* June 18, 1829). Yet despite his vast holdings, he died a poor—and childless—man at age 57 (Smith 1886:676).

After the sale of its property on the falls in 1831, the Monkton Iron Company still owned 2,300 acres of land in New York and 1,500 acres of timber tracts in Vermont. New York acreage no doubt was bought by iron interests there, such as Colburn who owned a blast furnace at Moriah and who bought the nearby Monkton Iron Company ore beds (Ingham 1932:49-50).

The "old furnace" was still standing at Vergennes in 1849, but it is not known for sure if it was that owned by the Monkton Iron Company (Hodge May 19, 1849:305). The 1853 map of Vergennes indicates the ca.-1830 flume cut by Ward, leading from the falls to the site of the Vergennes Iron Works.

The area suspected to have been occupied by the Monkton Iron Company is generally believed to have been on the south side of the Otter Creek, at and just below the falls, although some (or all) operations could have been on the north side as indicated by Whitelaw's 1810 map. Both sides have been thoroughly surface-inspected many times at various times of the year from 1978 to 1990 without finding anything that can be firmly associated with the Monkton Iron Company. Both

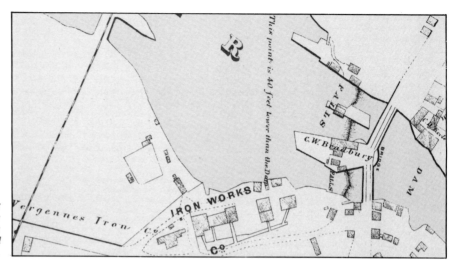

4-19. *The Vergennes Iron Company on the south bank of the Otter Creek in 1853. Note the flume which runs behind the works, the only visible remains of the works today (Wall and Forrest Map of Vergennes 1853).*

sides of the falls have undergone successions of industrial development and each have left bits and pieces of their existence behind in the form of miscellaneous castings, slag, firebrick, foundation walls, and various telltale cuts and modifications to the ledge at the base of the falls. Who knows what industrial artifacts lie at the bottom of the creek below the falls. What surface evidence remains today that can be connected with an ironworks most likely is related to the Vergennes Iron Company and/or the National Horse Nail Company (see AD-IW03, following).

AD-IW03 Vergennes Iron Company/White's Forge/National Horse Nail Company (Vergennes): When John D. Ward bought the lease of the Monkton Iron Company in 1831, he built a foundry and a flume to power it, commenced the hiring of a large number of men, and carried on a renewed iron business.

He sold the works in 1836 to Appolos Austin, William H. White, and Henry Hewitt, who formed the Vergennes Iron Company (Smith 1886:689).

One of the former owners of the Vergennes Iron Company, William H. White, built a bloomery in 1847. The forge operated marginally for 10 years, although it did become widely known throughout the Northeast. Annual production was 75 tons of iron from 1854 to 1856 and 50 tons in 1857 (Neilson 1866:232-235). These were poor economic years nationwide.

When the Vergennes Iron Company ceased operations in 1857, iron making came to an end in Vergennes. The property was bought by the Vergennes Water Company in 1866 to promote the industrial resources of the area. Two years later the National Horse Nail Company was organized, probably moving into the former buildings of the Vergennes Iron Company at

4-20. *The falls at Vergennes (left) and the south shore of the Otter immediately after the Civil War. Left-center: the National Horse Nail Company (before the first fire); right-center: the machine shop and the foundry of the Vergennes Machine Company; right edge: Kendall & Miles sash and door factory (courtesy Bixby Memorial Library, Vergennes).*

4-21. *The National Horse Nail Company at Vergennes, built after a fire in 1882 but burned again in 1902 (Geo. H. Walker & Co., Lithographer).*

the base of the falls, on the south side of Otter Creek. It continued the iron business there, much more successfully than the ill-fated Monkton Iron Company. The horse nails were made by the "cold cut" process, with nails cut out of cold iron plate. The nail was called National and was unique in being the first horse nail put on the market that was pointed and ready for driving. Previously, nails needed pointing before they could be used (Bixby Library files, p. 18). A ca.-1870 painting (by Rowland E. Robinson?) of the falls and harbor shows a cluster of industrial buildings at the site of the foundry near the bottom of the falls; the cluster includes what appears to be foundry, machine shop, and furnace buildings.

Fire destroyed the entire works on February 9, 1882. The works were rebuilt the next year, the new "hot forged" process substituted for the old, and the horse nail renamed the Champlain. When run at full capacity, the works' 80 employees could turn out 600 tons of horse nails annually.

The 1885 Sanborn map shows the main foundry building parallel to and between the Otter Creek and the raceway cut into solid rock. This race was cut in 1831 by John D. Ward, who had bought the lease of the Monkton Iron Company and built a foundry that eventually became the Vergennes Iron Company. A flume branching away at a right angle from the main raceway drove a waterwheel and blower at the east end (upstream) of the building. Sixteen forges are shown inside this end, eight to a side. The other end contained a machine shop and rooms for finishing, sorting and packing, and shipping. Two separate buildings housed a foundry and a forge for splicing the nail rods.

On Wednesday evening, October 29, 1902, another fire struck, again completely leveling the works, nearly taking the nearby shade roller factory with it: "It was a terrible but magnificent spectacle to see the rolling flames enwrapping the doomed building, everything being reflected luridly in the waters of the Otter Creek, so near at hand, yet powerless to save the works" (Bixby Library files, p. 18). This time the company chose not to rebuild, joining the many others that had succumbed to fire. The site lay abandoned for nearly 20 years until the hydroelectric potential of the falls was discovered, first by the Burlington Traction Company to power its trolleys and later by the Green Mountain Power Corporation.

4-22. *The middle section of the flume below the falls at Vergennes, tunneled through solid rock. This flume supplied water that powered the foundries at the base of the falls.*

4-23. *An abandoned turbine at the upstream end of the tunnel at Vergennes.*

Most of the flume remains are still there today, cut into bedrock in some places and tunneled through in others. The easternmost (upstream) tunnel section is about 8 feet high, 12 feet wide, and 83 feet long. There are concrete walls at the eastern end (facing the falls) that show a vertical sluice gate existed here. Some 27 feet farther west is the middle tunnel, 66 feet long. Then comes a 150-foot-long cut that ends at the entrance to the westernmost tunnel. This tunnel is also faced with concrete that indicates another sluice gate operated here. Inside the tunnel (not explored) is a six-foot-diameter iron pipe that ends 27 feet inside, beneath breakdown. It is suspected that beneath this breakdown is a vertical shaft that leads downward to the turbine. The tailrace back to the Otter Creek cannot be located and probably lies beneath fill. Total length of the tunnels and cuts is about 353 feet.

Near the western end of the raceway, much dark, heavy slag can be seen partially buried under the fill. Lighter, blast furnace slag can be found along the stream bank immediately downstream of the hydroelectric station. There are also some pieces of firebrick from Troy, New York, similar to those found at the blast furnaces and lime kilns elsewhere in Vermont. Both shores of the Otter Creek have experienced fires and floods many times, and much earth has been moved about recently to build the waste treatment facility. Closer to the falls is a modern hydroelectric generating and substation switching complex, reflecting the continued industrial vitality of the Great Falls of the Otter.

AD-IW04 Belding/Drake Furnace (Weybridge): Three miles north of Middlebury Falls is Beldens, at a falls on the Otter Creek. Joseph McKee built a sawmill here in 1791 and sold it to David Belding two years later. Belding added a gristmill in 1794 and a small furnace the next year, building up an industrial community (Smith 1886:719). Belding's furnace was one of many small ironworks that operated in this area in the very early 1800s.

Arriving here about the same time as Belding were Asoph Drake and Ebeneezer Scott. They married Belding's two daughters and became associated with their father-in-law's industrial pursuits (Smith 1886:715-716). The vicinity became known as Belding's Falls and the community was established on the Weybridge side of Otter Creek. Items cast and wrought here included nails, spikes, plow irons, and frying pans (*Drake Papers* 1802). The works may have operated until 1806. After the railroad was built north from Middlebury on the east side of the Otter, the community followed the industries to the New Haven side and became known as Beldens (Swift 1977:53).

AD-414 Brooks Edge Tool Company (New Haven): Before the disastrous 1830 flood washed away nearly all the mills along the New Haven River, a number of factories and shops thrived at what was then called Beemans Hollow. These included a trip-hammer shop, carding shop, blacksmith shop, two sawmills, two wagon shops, and two pocket furnaces. Fifteen years after the flood, an industrious blacksmith, Barzillai Brooks, moved to the hollow from New Haven Mills with his four sons, started making edge tools, and eventually established a company that produced fine axes and cutting tools (Smith 1886:537).

Barzillai and all his sons eventually became partners in a family operation, and the prosperous little community that grew around the works became today's village of Brooksville. "To the census enumerators in 1850 they reported using 40 tons of iron, 10 tons of steel, 100 tons of coal for firing the furnaces, and 20 grindstones. Eighteen men were employed, and the factory's output was 35,000 axes valued at $30,000" (Farnsworth 1984:146).

Following the retirement of the elder Brooks in 1866, one

of the sons, Norman, along with two others, organized the Brooks Edge Tool Company. They built the forge and trip-hammer shop just below the falls (remains of which exist today) and production flourished (Rucker Aug. 1981:3). "An average worker earned $225 a year in 1860, $500 a year in 1870. . . . Although a variety of edge tools were made, the company's specialty was axes—as many as 50,000 a year, sold wholesale for $11 a dozen" (Farnsworth 1984:146).

On September 7, 1877, the following description of the works was published in the *Middlebury Register*:

This is an institution. It always has been. It existed before Brooksville did. The Brookses have always run it. They probably always will. The men employed in the shop are strong, robust, healthy looking fellows, but it is an unwelcome fact that men engaged in this business seldom live to a very great age. It is unhealthy business. Where the disease known as the "grinder's consumption" fastens upon its victim, it works slowly but surely till death. There are few ax factories in America, but the few supply the great demand. This factory is not among the largest, though they sell their wares over almost all the northern states.

Persons in this vicinity having a holiday could not spend it more pleasantly or profitably than by looking through these shops. The managers are gentlemen and will treat you with courtesy.

The factory is now in full blast. The tools manufactured are axes, hatchets, and a queer looking thing with an ax on one end and a hook on the other, used by firemen. They get their "polls" from Cohoes, New York. The first forgers, those who draw out the "bit," are the veterans, Messrs James Nott [Nutt?] and John Shedrick. They are among the few who learned the business at this place, who are at work in the shop now. The most of the men came from the larger factories in New York. Mr. George Keyes and helper take the axes from the first forgers and draw the bit down finer. Mr. Tom Ryan and helper make the other tools. These men with a quick eye and ready hand make a handsome hatchet out of the rough bar of iron. The axes then undergo the inspection of the manager, Mr. Norman Brooks, who with a strong pair of glasses to detect the slightest mark of poor material or careless workmanship, looks them over, and if such is found, back it goes to the forgers. The grinders then have the axes; then the temperer, who places them over a hot fire and heats them to the right heat, which no one can tell but he. Mr. Frank Brooks is the temperer, and while watching his axes, he will tell you a jolly story.

From the tempering room the axes go to the grinders again and then the polishers. The polishing is done with emery fastened by glue upon a wheel, which at swift speed makes the sparks fly every time the axe touches it. In this room we find Mr. Tom Stringham and Sidney Raymond, the old grinder, who has taken to this branch. The axes then go into the finishing room, are wiped off, stamped "N. C. Brooks, Brooksville, Vt.," varnished and bronzed or painted, and hung upon a beam to dry. Then dusted, labeled and each done up in a separate paper wrapper, boxed up and sent to the depot or store room.

The company have two large store rooms. They make their own boxes, but get their helves from Sandusky, Ohio. They put handles on comparatively few of their tools. Mr. Will Brooks is overseer of the finishing or blacking room as it is called. Here also we find Mr. John Barton, who has worked in the shop off and on ever since he was "so high." . . . J. S.

The 1871 Beers map of Brooksville identifies the Brooks Edge Tool Company axe factory (forge) and other company buildings on the south side of the river, and a finishing and carpenter shop, the residence of N. C. Brooks, and more company buildings on the north side. Altogether, 13 buildings appear to be connected with the company or the Brooks family. A road is shown leading from the main street westward to a depot at the Rutland & Burlington Railroad.

Fire struck the works in 1881, destroying many buildings but not touching the forge. The *Middlebury Register* of May 20, 1881 described the excitement:

Fire in Brooksville—Last Tuesday morning, about two o'clock, the little hamlet of Brooksville was awakened by the alarm of fire, and turned out to find the roof of one of the buildings of the Brooksville Edge Tool Company on the east side of the dam blazing up. It had gained such headway that it was soon seen that nothing could be done to stay it and in a short time all the buildings in connection with the finishing shop, where the fire started, were blazing. The wind blew strongly from the northwest and the flames speedily lapped up the house and barn of James D. Nutt standing nearby. It was feared for a time that the fire would extend to the covered bridge, over the New Haven River, and help was sent for to Middlebury. The steamer was hitched up and had got to the further slope of Chipman Hill when word come that the danger was past, and the steamer returned to its quarters. There was from 8 to 1000 dozen [*sic*] finished axes in the building, of which all but a small portion was thrown out, little damaged so that the loss on the finished stock is not large. The total loss of the Edge Tool Company is less than 5 thousand dollars on which there is seventeen hundred dollars insurance. . . .

There will be but a short delay on the part of the Edge Tool Company in filling orders, as the vacant room in the forge shop on the opposite side of the stream will be speedily fitted for the grinders and polishers, who will probably be able to go back to work next Monday. The work of rebuilding will begin at once, and in a short time things will be as lively as ever.

Within a month, contracts had been let for rebuilding the stone- and woodwork, and in August it was reported that Norman Brooks was in Troy, New York, negotiating for several car loads of iron. The axe trade was described as being "very brisk" (*Middlebury Register* June 17 and Aug. 5, 1881); brisk enough that in 1883, Frank B. Brooks opened a store in the community, later operated by Norman Brooks (Smith 1886:537-538). Two years later when Norman Brooks retired, production was 4,000 axes per year. But the business declined soon after, closing the works sometime in the 1890s. *Walton's Vermont Register* listed the company for the last time in 1892.

Brooksville today is a small, quiet community on a section of highway called Dog Team Road, long since bypassed on the east by a two-mile stretch of Route 7. Downstream of the concrete bridge over the New Haven River are a series of low falls and rapids that, when dammed, provided power to drive the industries. Sparse indications remain of these old pursuits; however, sharp eyes and patient inspection will reveal an abandoned turbine here and there, some firebrick and slag, and pieces of coal and millstones hidden amid the thick (and thorny) underbrush along the shores of the river. Remains of the dam are seen in a line of iron rods along the top ledge at the upper falls.

At the south end of the dam site, a deep cut into ledge can be followed downstream in tall weeds for 100 feet to the stone foundation remains of the axe factory. This cut might have been for a headrace in earlier years; a ca.-1907 photo shows an approximately three-foot-diameter pipe following the cut, supplying waterpower to the turbine at the downstream end of the forge building (Farnsworth 1984:145). On each side of the river at about this place stood the Brooks' factory buildings. They were later used by the Vermont Marble Company, until 1920 (Farnsworth 1984:246).

Bits of rusted iron and slag are found in shoreline crevices; one crevice yielded a badly corroded axe head of undetermined manufacture (it looks nothing like the Brooks axe on display at the Sheldon Museum in nearby Middlebury). And a bit farther downstream, ALMON SHEDRICK VIIIC [1892?] is chiseled into the broad upstream side of a flat ledge, barely readable, having been washed and worn by nearly a century of ice and gravel flow.

AD-IW05 Brooksville Pocket Furnaces (New Haven): Many small furnaces, called pocket furnaces by some, were built to "test" the local ores as well as the local market. Two such furnaces operated just downstream from Brooksville before 1815 (Smith 1886:537). One was on the north side of the river at the village where it was run by a Mr. Aiken. Nearby was a trip-hammer shop where scythes, hoes, and other tools were made. The other pocket furnace was across the river and just downstream, operated by John Wilson who also ran the sawmill immediately upstream. Nearly all these small industries were washed away in the great New Haven freshet of 1830. The vicinity was also the site of the later Brooks Edge Tool Company foundry and operations.

Inspection of the area in 1986 resulted in finding nothing related to blast furnace operations. The New Haven River area between Bristol village and the river's confluence with the Otter Creek has yet to be completely inspected for evidence of more blast furnaces and forges. This winding 10-mile stretch plus the Beldens area of the Otter Creek could still yield sites of up to four very early "pocket" blast furnaces.

AD-IW06 New Haven Mills Forge (New Haven): A forge (possibly a blacksmith's shop) was built somewhere in New Haven by Timothy Allen and Ezekiel Buttolph "at an early year." Another forge was run by David P. Nash at the mills from about 1794 until "worn out," the last remnant—the anvil block—washed away in an 1831 freshet (Beers *Addison* 1871:4). William Nash may also have been connected with this forge.

Inspection in 1984 of the remains of the many mills that operated at New Haven Mills resulted in finding some slag at scattered locations on the shore and in the riverbed. Due to

later industrial development of the area, no positive evidence could be found of a furnace or furnace site.

AD-340 Little Otter Furnace (New Haven): Francis Bradbury of the Monkton Iron Company at Vergennes became interested in one of the small New Haven furnaces in 1808: "There is a furnace now at New Haven about 5 or 6 miles from the Ore Bed. It is small but might answer well for pigs [pig iron]. It may now be purchased very cheap" (F. Bradbury letter to T. H. Perkins, April 5, 1808). The ore bed mentioned was the company's mine at Monkton, northeast of New Haven. Belding's 1794 furnace would have been farther away, more like 10 miles, even had it still been in operable condition in 1808. Brooksville (then known as Beemans Hollow) likewise was too far away. One good possibility was a blast furnace on the Little Otter Creek, and within the stated "5 or 6 miles" of the Monkton ore beds.

Bradbury mentioned a New Haven furnace in three letters in 1808: April 5, June 9, and October 25. In the June letter a Mr. Washburn is mentioned as the owner of the furnace; the October letter states that the furnace is in blast and doing well. Bradbury further wrote in the October 25, 1808 letter that "it would have been very well in my opinion to have purchased that furnace as I recommended last spring, to have stopped the spirit of others interfering with us, they take much coal [charcoal] that might come to us & continually seeking out ore, that may eventually diminish our establishment."

Bradbury's "Mr. Washburn" might have been Abisha Washburn of Middlebury, who was engaged during the Revolution by the State of Massachusetts to cast cannon at Salisbury, Connecticut. Following the war, he returned to Middlebury and built some of the earliest mills there (Smith 1886:259, 270). He died in 1813 so he was alive when Bradbury wrote his 1808 letters. At the Salisbury Cannon Foundry (Connecticut) in 1777 were a Jonathan Washburn, molder, and also an Abijah Washburn, who performed unspecified duties (Middlebrook 1935:43-44). From an anecdote found among Henry Sheldon's notes at the Sheldon Museum: "He [Washburn] was a founder and used to cast cannon for the Revolutionary War. A neighbor coming into his furnace one day asked him which fire he thought was the hottest, this one here in the forge or that fed by the evil one in the regions below. 'Jump in sir, jump in and you can try them both in half a minute' was his instant response" (Polly Darnell note to author, March 26, 1986).

Along the Little Otter Creek in northern New Haven is the site of an early Vermont blast furnace. Remains of an earthen dam is just east of the North Street bridge. A recent history of New Haven mentions a furnace and casting house that stood here from about 1801 to 1810 owned by Gamaliel Leonard and others, and previously in 1800 by John Gilbert, Ephraim Hubbell, and Jose Gorsline (Farnsworth 1984:250-261).

If Gamaliel Leonard "and others" included the elusive Mr. Washburn it is still a mystery. Leonard previously built and operated a forge along the Poultney River west of Fair Haven (RU-195), and prior to that worked at the Lenox Furnace, Massachusetts. Hubbell was owner of the gristmill originally built by Strong & Chipman on the island in the Falls of the Otter at Vergennes. Hubbell sold the gristmill to Bradbury in February 1810 (Smith 1886:663).

John Gilbert could have been the Job Gilbert whose name

appears in 1797 in connection with a petition for relief from civil prosecution in which he stated that he "has for a large number of years been prinsaplеy imployed & conserned in erecting furnises stocking putting & continuing them in blast which has been attended with grate expense & loss" (Soule vol. 11 1962:33). Job Gilbert came from Mansfield, Massachusetts, where extensive ironworks operated before the Revolution (*Vital Records* 1933:31). During the war he was a captain and by 1781 was owner of a blast furnace at Lenox, Massachusetts (Wood 1969:67-68). He sold the Lenox works in 1783, bought them back in 1785, then sold them again in 1787, at which time he disappears from Berkshire County records. The 1797 Vermont petition, therefore, places this experienced ironmaster at Little Otter Creek. The possibility that John and Job Gilbert were the same person is further supported by another reference to John Gilbert owning the Berkshire Furnace at Lenox in 1783 (Pearse 1876:49-50). Gilbert was also involved with William Gilliland and New York tracts of ore-bearing land between Crown Point and the Bouquet River. Although he was considering digging ore in the Adirondacks in the 1780s, he was not planning to transport the heavy ore to his furnace in Lenox, some 150 miles south, at a time before the Champlain Canal was in existence. He had written to Gilliland in March 1783 that he would like "to be concerned in iron works at Lake Champlain," and doubled the offer of a competitor for an ore bed owned by Gilliland (Allen ms 1980:10). By the 1790s Gilbert was making iron in New Haven along the Little Otter Creek.

Inspection of the Little Otter furnace site in 1984 resulted in finding the remains of a dam just east of the North Street bridge. From the topography, a sizeable millpond could have been created, sufficient to power water-driven bellows machinery. The dam, however, might date to an industry that followed the furnace because slag was found in the body of the dam. Slag and charcoal were found in the vicinity and on both sides of the road. According to John Peters, a gardener plowing Ray Martin's garden across the highway to the west unearthed some slag, but this has not been confirmed.

The furnace could have been on the south side of the creek, tucked into the side of a low hill that gave charging access to the top of the furnace. At the top of this hill are the faint remains of a road. There is also sufficient flat area at the bottom for the casting shed. This is the only practical site in the immediate area considering proximity to waterpower and access to the furnace top. If this is the correct site, the furnace hearth was almost level with the creek's flood plain. Major iron ore beds existed to the northeast in the Monkton/Bristol area, and limestone for flux was conveniently available in the area, all maybe solving Francis Bradbury's "mystery" furnace of 1808.

AD-432 Barnum/Nichols Forge (Ferrisburgh): This is one of a number of small forges that operated along the many falls of the Little Otter Creek in Ferrisburgh, New Haven, and Monkton, taking advantage of local waterpower and exploiting the iron ore mined in the region: "The ore smelted in all the forges of this region was brought from the other side of the lake, except a small portion taken from an ore bed in Monkton, which was of an inferior quality" (Robinson 1934:245, writing about the forges in Ferrisburgh).

The site is along the Little Otter Creek in the proximity of

the bridge that carries the Monkton Road across the creek, three miles east of Vergennes. The present bridge is about 150 feet downstream of the old Monkton road crossing referred to in the following:

Just below the bridge was a forge built by Major Richard Barnum, longer ago then Mr. Luther Carpenter, who was born in the neighborhood, and is now in his ninety-first year, can remember. In 1805 Major Barnum sold the property here to Caleb Farrer, and he sold in April 1807, to Perkins Nichols, of Boston. Nichols sold the same year to Bradbury, Higginson, Well[e]s and others, all of Boston. A coal house, forge, and sawmill are mentioned in the deed (Smith 1886:446).

The forge belonged to the Boston Iron Company together with 400 acres of adjacent land and the Monkton ore bed, whereby hangs a tale of the Yankee smartness. While the Boston Company were negotiating for the purchase of the ore bed, some of its members met the then owners at the forge on an appointed day to see the quality of the ore tested. During the process of the smelting, 30 silver dollars were secretly dropped into the loop, one by one, by a bloomer who was in the confidence of his employer, and the product was of such excellent quality that the Bostonians at once closed the bargain, and came into possession of a mine so worthless that it was soon abandoned. The story has its moral, for the instigator of the fraud, after cutting a great figure for a time [probably Amos Barnum of Vergennes], died in poverty (Robinson 1934:245).

Many inspections were made of the vicinity from 1979 to 1987. Evidences of the forge are scattered concentrations of up to baseball-size pieces of slag eroding from the north bank of the creek, just downstream of the old crossing, and larger pieces scattered along the creek bed in the marshy field 200 feet downstream from the present bridge. The forge site would appear to be, from the disposition of the slag finds, somewhere between the present and former crossing, most likely closer to the former crossing. Associated with the slag eroding from the shore are small bits of charcoal. The slag and charcoal are located along a strata about three to four feet below the surface and run along 20 feet of shoreline. No other forge-related features were seen. The older crossing is evident on both sides of the creek. Although covered by a thick growth of brush, the old road can be followed uphill north to where it rejoins the present road near the top of the hill.

A. T. Keller toured a number of ironworks sites in New England during the 1930s, photographing what remained of them and providing a valuable record of the state of the sites during that period. One of his photos identifies this as the "site of the Monkton Iron Company's charcoal furnace" from the description on the back of the photo. Many attempts to relate the photo to specific terrain features have failed, although it does generally appear to have been taken near this crossing. Construction of the present bridge, earthen ramps leading up to it, and highway straightening in 1950 have drastically disturbed the furnace site. Freshets might have also contributed toward destroying what remained of Barnum's forge/blast furnace site.

AD-431 Doreen's Forge (Ferrisburgh): There was another

forge farther upstream of the older Monkton Road crossing: "There was a forge on the Little Otter Creek a little above where the Monkton road crosses the stream. I cannot learn by whom it was built or operated" (Smith 1886:446).

The site was found in August 1987, about 1,000 feet upstream of AD-432. Evidence of the forge is a 10-foot-square concentration of up to fist-size pieces of slag on the north side of the creek and half that on the south side. The slag is associated with the remains of what appears to be a washed-out dam. The shoreline topography does not appear more superior here than the rest of this area of the stream with respect to advantageous location of a mill seat. But a dam of moderate height at this point could back up enough water to create a significant millpond in the low-lying swamp just upstream. Lack of head to turn an overshot waterwheel was probably more than offset by quantity of water to power a breast wheel. No charcoal, iron, or iron ore could be found; a shallow depression that might be a cellar hole was found within reasonable proximity of the site.

AD-IW07 Barnum Forge (Ferrisburgh): About a mile downstream from AD-432 is Walkers Falls, the site of a sawmill and tannery works whose remains are still visible. About 600 feet farther downstream was a forge built by (Richard or Amos?) Barnum. The place was called Dover, and small hand-operated nail and axe factories operated here. By 1866 all traces had disappeared (Smith 1886:446). Field inspections in 1980 and 1983 found no slag or evidence of iron making.

AD-IW08 Fuller Forge (Ferrisburgh): Farther downstream from AD-IW07 and west of Route 7 is a major falls at the village of Ferrisburgh, known as Fraser's Falls from John Fraser's sawmill here in the 1820s–1830s. A forge was operated just upstream of the falls early in the century by one of the Fuller family (Smith 1886:446). Attempts to find this site in 1985 were foiled by high water.

The Fuller family of Ferrisburgh was involved in many ironworks exploits in Vermont and New York (see chapter 1, "The Marriage Connection").

AD-430 North Ferrisburgh Forge (Ferrisburgh): The site of a late-18th- to early-19th-century bloomery forge was located along Lewis Creek in 1987 through information provided by the following historical accounts:

> At the upper part of the falls, at Ferrisburgh "Hollow" there was a forge early in this century, owned by one of the Fullers. This was on the "minister's lot." In 1822, Robert B. Hazard leased of the Baptist Church a portion of it thereabout, and built a woolen factory, which afterward came into the possession of his brother, William Hazard who in 1832 leased it to Theodore D. and Edmund Lyman. Theodore D. Lyman leased the factory to Edward Daniels in 1864. In 1884 it was burnt, while run by John Vanduysen under lease from Daniels (Smith 1886:447).
>
> Presently, one comes to the Hollow, long ago cursed by John Nutting when he lost his holding through a defective title. But in spite of his curse, it came to have a forge, with the best and busiest gristmill for miles around. . . .
>
> The Forge, which stood thereabouts (of the woolen mill) at an earlier date, was owned by some of the Fullers (Robinson 1934:230-232).

The site is about a quarter-mile upstream of where the Hollow Road crosses Lewis Creek at North Ferrisburgh. Evidence of the forge is slag eroding out of the shoreline in the vicinity of stone walls, these most likely the remains of the later woolen mill. Some large (basketball-size) pieces of slag were found, with the slag distributed over a 50-foot section of the shoreline. No slag was found upstream of the site. No dam remains were found, although the 1871 Beers map of Ferrisburgh shows a dam at or near the site.

AD-FS50 Ackworth Bloomeries (Lincoln): In contrast to its present quiet, rural environment, nestled high up a mountain along a cold and bubbling stream, West Lincoln in the early 19th century was a major hub of industry which included a number of nationally known bloomeries among its many mills. These forges were contemporaries of bloomeries at Salisbury, East Middlebury, Fair Haven, and Vergennes.

In the early 1800s the community was called Ackworth, from a town in New Hampshire that Joseph Blanchard, Isaac Houston, and William and Andrew Mitchell left in 1827 to come to Vermont. (Esther Swift locates Ackworth at Rocky Dale, in Bristol.) About 600 feet east of the bridge at West Lincoln they built a bloomery and a sawmill. The forge started making bar iron the next year. About the same time or possibly a year earlier, Henry Soper and Philetus Pier built a forge another 500 to 600 feet farther downstream from these forges (Smith 1886:492-493). Both forges were probably on the north side of the river. They operated only a few years, being carried away in July 1830 by a flash flood, which washed away the fully stocked coal house, stacks of ore and iron, and the sawmill, as well as houses, the original bridge, and many acres of top soil. Both forges were rebuilt that same year.

The upstream forge was built on or near its former site. The 1857 Addison County map shows forges just upstream of the confluence of Isham Brook and the New Haven River. The downstream forge was relocated about 300 feet farther downstream from its original site, probably where the map indicates a forge and dam. This forge was built by Oliver W. Burnham of Vergennes, who became part owner with Pier just before the flood. He became sole owner of both forges around 1840 and continued to make iron until he died about 1860. The operations were continued by his heirs.

A thrifty little manufacturing village developed about the forges and other mills as men with capital invested here. It fast became the business heart of the town. Iron ore came from the Adirondacks across Lake Champlain, and the hauling of ore and iron to and from the forges gave steady employment to a great many people who owned teams. The charcoal was furnished mostly by those who owned and cleared woodlands in the nearby forest. The wealth of the town previous to 1850 was to a great extent due to the ironworks and it was the nucleus of about the only business in which large sums of money were annually paid to employees. When the forges were run to their full capacity, they were capable of making 300 tons of iron yearly to each fire. The forges were enlarged in 1843 and again in 1854. In 1856 the ironworks was managed by O. W. Burnham (Lesley 1859:149). In 1858 there were four fires and two hammers operated by two waterwheels (Lesley 1858:75).

Neilson reported in 1866:

Production		Production	
Year	Tons	Year	Tons
1854	672	1860	0
1855	560	1861	0
1856	616	1862	150
1857	80	1863	150
1858	0	1864	160
1859	0	1865	100

[The forges were] owned up to 1856 by Oliver W. Burnham. About [1856] the owner died, and the bloomeries became the property of the heirs. Very little was done until about 1863, when the fires in one of the bloomeries—there were formerly two—were started up. In 1864 the bloomery was purchased by Lincoln, Cain & Co., and operated by them until December 1865, when it was abandoned. A saw and stave mill now occupies its site.

In 1865 the forge contained 5 forge and 3 run-out fires, 2 trip-hammers, and 2 waterwheels (Neilson 1866:235).

Neilson also reported that in 1864 the forges consumed 34,500 bushels of charcoal, 336 tons of Lake Champlain ore, and five tons of scrap iron. In a description of another flash flood in October 1869 that carried away or damaged mills, no mention was made of the forges (Smith 1886:560). A clapboard and stave mill appear next to the dam and millpond on the former forge site in the Beers 1871 map of Lincoln village.

The stream has been inspected in West Lincoln as well as farther up and downstream many times, especially during low-water periods, but nothing significant has been found to indicate the existence of such an extensive ironworks operation here at one time. Stone walls along the shore might have been associated with the forges or with later mills. Occasional bits of slag, rusted iron, and charcoal can be found in the stream from hundreds of yards upstream of the village to places among the downstream boulders to Rocky Dale, and as far downstream as Bristol.

AD-IW09 Scott, Munsil, and Eaton Forge (Bristol): The first of Bristol's two early forges was built in 1791 by Amos and Cyprian Easton, Amos Scott, and Gordon Munsil (Munsill 1979:107-110). It was located on the west side of the New Haven River and stood near today's bridge just downstream of the village. In addition to bar iron the forge made plows, crow bars, and tire iron (wheel rims).

Remains of the forge were probably destroyed by construction of the Bristol Manufacturing Company in the late 19th century, the ruins of which still existed when inspected in 1983. No evidence of a forge was found.

AD-IW10 Scott Forge (Bristol): Bristol's second forge was built by Ebenezer and Amos Scott soon after and near the first forge, on the west side of the stream. It made similar hardware, some used locally and some shipped to Troy, New York to pay for goods purchased there (Munsill 1979:108). Its remains probably suffered the same fate as the first.

AD-FS86 Franklin, Arnold, and Hobart Forge (Bristol): On April 5, 1808 Francis Bradbury of the Monkton Iron Company wrote to Thomas H. Perkins of Boston about progress with construction of their blast furnace at Vergennes. The letter

included a reference to stone lining material for a furnace at Bristol: "I also have heard of a slate stone on the border of the lake that may answer for the lining. This can be examined when Mr. Bates comes up. I think also it best to say nothing of this slate for a furnace at Bristol, my avocations at present are so many that I cannot attend to it as it ought to be." Was Bradbury referring to the possibility of building a blast furnace at Bristol in addition to the one at Vergennes? Might he have been considering improving an existing furnace at Bristol?

This might have been Bristol's third forge, built in 1802 along the river at the base of the village by John Arnold, Henry and Joshua Franklin, and Nehemiah Hobart. It made bar iron for many years but might have had a blast furnace in addition to the bloomeries. The forge was successful in spite of its cramped location between the river and the high bank that is immediately behind buildings on the south side of Main Street. Partial and full owners included over a dozen men. Forge workers came from as far as the iron districts of Salisbury, Connecticut to work here. Seven proved an unlucky number for this forge. It burned in 1809, 1816, and 1823, and was rebuilt each time. The end came, of course, seven years later in 1830 when a freshet that ravaged the New Haven River valley finally destroyed the stubborn ironworks. Only the deeply imbedded foundation pilings remained by the 1860s to mark the spot (Munsill 1979:110).

One day in 1808, the owners of the Monkton Iron Company rode over from Vergennes to inspect their ore beds in Monkton and "a furnace in the neighborhood" (Seaburg and Paterson 1971:205). It is unclear whether "the neighborhood" meant Monkton, Bristol, Ferrisburgh, or somewhere else. The 1802 forge at Bristol was the closest one to the ore beds, but we now know that there also had been a blast furnace only three miles away along the Little Otter in nearby New Haven (AD-340).

The river and shore at Bristol village where the forge and/or furnace operated was inspected in 1983 with no evidence found of either. The river starts curving south just downstream of the site, and to reduce shore erosion here a high stretch of riprap was laid up against the shore, significantly disturbing the suspected area of the site. Disturbance has also been caused by trash dumped down the high embankment directly on the forge site. Somewhere beneath Bristol's trash and riprap might be the buried ironworks.

AD-493 Baldwin Creek Forge (Bristol): The fourth forge in Bristol was erected in 1832 by Thurston and James Chase, George C. Dayfoot, and Nathaniel Drake up Baldwin Creek in the northeastern part of town. Waterpower was poor, especially in summer months, but some profit was made at the forge by Thurston Chase and Philo S. Warner (Munsill 1979:110).

Since 1981, many checks were made for slag in Baldwin Creek in and below Chase Hollow. Chase Hollow is a deep ravine through which Baldwin Creek runs after it crosses into Bristol from Starksboro, paralleling Route 17. Up to fist-size pieces of forge slag were finally found in 1990 along the bank of the stream about 100 feet downstream of the present Route 116 bridge. A single slag find was made between the bridge and the concrete abutment of the former bridge, just upstream. All slag finds were on the east side of the stream. Along the east side of the stream downstream of the bridge is a wide, silted-in area, under which the forge site might lie. Inspection of current and older maps indicate at least three bridges were built in this proximity, all contributing in part to disturbing the forge site.

AD-416 Holley Forge (Bristol): Bristol's fifth forge was built by Enos Soper, Chester Buel, and Henry Soper (who also owned a forge in Lincoln). It was on the north shore of the New Haven River about a mile upstream of the village. The 1857 map of Addison County indicates the forge opposite the home of Winter H. Holley, who owned it for a while (Munsill 1979:111).

The site of the forge was inspected in 1980, behind and adjacent to a mobile home park on Route 17. Here were found many pieces of slag, some charcoal, and a dozen three-foot-diameter iron hoops that held a large wooden pipe together that might have powered the forge waterwheel. Further remains of the forge may possibly still lie beneath the wall of domestic trash that lines the shore behind the mobile homes, or under the woodlot adjoining the park to the east.

AD-IW11 Burnham Forge (Bristol): The sixth forge in Bristol was built by Oliver W. Burnham of Vergennes (who also operated the forge at West Lincoln). It operated briefly up Baldwin Creek near the Starksboro town line and had a brief life (Munsill 1979:111). This site also remains unlocated.

AD-IW12 Munson, Dean, and Gaige Forge (Bristol): Bristol's seventh and final forge was built a half-mile downstream of the village by Luman Munson, Bennet B.Dean, and Datus R. Gaige. A dam and flume conveyed waterpower to the forge, located about 500 feet from the main channel, safe from freshets. Ownership changed hands while bar iron production varied through good times and bad. The principal market was Troy, New York. The forge was out of operation by 1860 (Munsill 1979:112).

A few pieces of slag-appearing material were found near here in the river during a 1982 field inspection, but they could have washed down from any of the many forge sites farther upstream. The site of this forge has not been found.

AD-404 Richville Forge (Shoreham): In the kitchen of the Penfield Homestead Foundation Museum at Ironville in Crown Point, New York, is a beehive oven with a heavy cast-iron door, on which reads:

PATENT
C. RICH SHOREHAM VT.
NO. 2.

Since the Penfield house was built in 1828, a furnace of some sort was producing castings during that time somewhere in Shoreham. The 1796 Whitelaw map indicates an iron forge, gristmill, and sawmill at a point where today's Shoreham Center is. It was named Richville in earlier years.

A high dam today backs up the Lemon Fair River, creating Richville Pond. But a century ago two other dams existed a short distance farther downstream. In 1785, Thomas Rich of Warwick, Massachusetts purchased land at the falls near the upper of these two earlier dams. The next year he constructed a sawmill. Jacob Atwood moved into the community in 1788 and a few years later built a forge at the north end of the same dam. A few years later another forge containing two bellows

and four hearths was built 100 feet farther downstream where the other dam stood. In 1797 Ebenezer Markham built a nail factory and trip-hammer shop on the north side of the upper dam, possibly right on the site of the earlier Thomas Rich forge. The nail factory was later converted into a cloth factory (Smith 1886:622-623). Ore for the forge was mined a half-mile to the northeast, but the ore's high sulfur content forced its mixture with ore from Crown Point, in order to produce bar iron (Goodhue 1861:94). (Matthew Lyon also used some ore from Shoreham, making castings from it at his blast furnace at Orwell, five miles south.) Along with Thomas Rich came his 16-year-old son, Charles. In addition to owning and operating many mills, Charles Rich went on to serve in the U.S. Congress for 10 years. He died in October 1824, from complications caused by standing too long in the Lemon Fair River while fixing one of his mills (Goodhue 1861:189-190).

Charles Rich (Jr.), son of Charles Rich (the congressman), is probably the "C. Rich" whose name appears on the cast-iron oven door at Ironville, since the senior Rich died four years before the Penfield homestead was built. But nothing substantial can be found about any Richville furnace and/or foundry or the involvement of any Charles Rich with an ironworks beyond that intriguing oven door at Ironville. Charles W. Rich of the same family was born in Richville and moved to Swanton in 1840. There he opened quarries and built many lime kilns, establishing a successful lime-burning business (see chapter 8).

Ruins of the mills at Richville were inspected in 1986. High stone wall ruins and two breached dams were found in heavy underbrush, just below the modern dam. Some bits of charcoal and slag were found on the north side of the river, about 100 feet below the remains of the lower dam, but of an insufficient amount to confirm this a site of an early blast or cupola furnace. Later mills obliterated surface traces of the forge, sawmills, and gristmills that the Whitelaw map indicated here in 1796.

4-24. *Door of the beehive oven at Penfield Homestead Foundation Museum, Crown Point, New York, made in a Richville foundry at Shoreham.*

It is an interesting area to explore.

AD-IW13 Fergusson Forge (Starksboro): A forge was built in Starksboro about 1819 by Elisha Fergusson and Samuel Bushnell in the south part of the village (Smith 1886:635). The 1857 map of Addison County indicates that they also operated a foundry about a half-mile east of the village. Zadock Thompson reported in 1842 that a forge in Starksboro produced 60 tons of bar iron annually. In 1857 the village works were identified as the furnace of Fergusson & Sayles, and by 1871 only David Fergusson was associated with the village works; he consolidated the works a few years before.

The suspected site of the village works, just behind the village general store on Route 116, was visited in 1980. Some bits of slag were found along with broken pieces of a cast-iron stove, not necessarily a product of the forge/foundry. There were also some forges upstream of the village (see AD-417).

AD-417 Lewis Creek Farm Forge (Starksboro): In response to a landowner's invitation to inspect what looked like slag, surface indications of an early-19th-century forge were found at the Lewis Creek Farm in 1986 (Fred Elwert letter to author, Oct. 22, 1985). Basketball-size chunks of slag in association with pieces of red brick were found in the field downhill behind the farmyard. What appears to have been a berm or dam created a small millpond here; a forge might have stood on the low knoll. It is difficult to believe the small brook that today flows through the site had ever been sufficient to create a workable millpond, which adds support to the theory that Vermont streams and brooks ran higher in earlier times.

AD-IW14 Upper Lewis Creek Forge (Starksboro): According to an early account, Lewis Creek is formed "by the confluent waters of three springs which are not more than 20 rods apart, and which unite after flowing a short distance. Not more than a half-mile from its head, this stream once turned the wheels of a sawmill, fulling mill, two forges, and two trip-hammer shops. These have long since passed away" (Smith 1886:629).

Lewis Creek was inspected in 1990 from just below the Route 116 bridge to near its southwest source, off Ireland Road, and two places in between without finding any slag. At a point about a half-mile east of the highway, one mill foundation was found (containing a liberal amount of trash) but not of the forge variety. An early forge site might yet be waiting for discovery up Lewis Creek.

RUTLAND COUNTY

RU-IW01 Forge Flats (Chittenden): In a short paper published in 1953 on the subject of ironworks in Vermont, then State Geologist Elbridge Jacobs mentioned a number of towns where furnaces operated, explaining that blast furnaces operated at some and forges at others. The list of towns and furnaces included "Chittenden, 1797" (Jacobs 1953:130). Jacobs' data source was Charles R. Harte (see chapter 4, "Study Methodology"). Research has failed to reveal any blast furnaces in this town, but a forge and possibly an ore roaster did operate here. There are many historical references to a blast furnace being built in Chittenden in 1792 by a Mr. Keith of Boston, all of which can be traced back to Graham's 1797 history. It is unknown why Graham made this mistake, unless the exact location of the Chittenden-Pittsford town line was unknown at that time.

But the 1796 Whitelaw map clearly shows the blast furnace in question over the line in Pittsford. In the mountains near the Pittsford town line, there was extensive iron mining, and in the 1880s various companies were formed to exploit iron ore beds in Chittenden.

At Holden was a community known as Forge Flats in the 1880s (Smith and Rann 1886:553) and the town's first "iron forging plant" was located here (Swift 1977:387). Field inspection has failed to find the site of this forge although some slag was found in 1984 just downstream from the fish hatchery in Furnace Brook.

RU-IW02 Miller Forge (Wallingford): Solomon Miller operated an early forge at Wallingford, which also had some Nathanial Chipman interest (Rann 1886:705). After Miller left for Williston in 1786, his son Alexander continued to make hoes, axes, and nails (Smith and Rann 1886:835-836). The forge operated on the site of the stone shop establishment of Batcheller and Sons, on Main Street. (The "Old Stone Shop" is a common landmark to people driving along Route 7 through Wallingford village.) In 1865 good business dictated expansion into larger quarters along nearby Otter Creek and the stone shop was used for tumble-polishing the forks. The 1869 Beers map indicates the location of Batcheller & Sons Fork Manufactory between the Rutland & Bennington Railroad tracks and the Otter Creek.

RU-IW03 Wallingford Furnace (Wallingford): What was once thought to have been a high-quality iron ore deposit existed up Homer Stone Brook, east of South Wallingford. Thompson's 1824 Gazetteer mentioned a furnace in Wallingford, suspected to have been located near these iron deposits, and worked for a time in 1815 (Klock 1976:42). In the 1840s the bed was one of the sources of ore for the blast furnace at North Dorset, where the manganese in the ore in association with the iron became obvious (Hodge May 12, 1849:290). Steel magnate Andrew Carnegie bought the ore beds in 1880, built a railroad spur to the mines, and commenced digging the ore (Klock 1976:42). The iron and steel industry was finally beginning to recognize iron smelting as more of a chemical reaction, thus the need for manganese—previously considered an unwanted impurity—in steel making. Carnegie carted tons of the "black ore" to his Edgar Thompson Steel Works in Pennsylvania, forerunner to the Carnegie Steel Company (and, in 1901, U.S. Steel).

The Homer Stone Brook area was visited in 1984 and some indications of either Carnegie or earlier operations still remain. The hint of a narrow gauge railroad bed can be seen alongside the brook, and farther upstream the collapsed mines are betrayed by surface sinkholes. Here and there are high and dry raceways, probably used in ore-washing operations. But no slag or evidence of a blast furnace was found; it was most likely churned under by the Carnegie people.

RU-87 Chipman Forge (Tinmouth): Tinmouth was an early area of extensive forge and blast furnace activity. Nathanial Chipman was producing bar iron at his forge here in 1786, but difficulties with production and profits forced him to repeatedly sell his farm and forge to his brother Darius (Chipman 1846:66). He fared better in the political furnace, serving eventually in the U.S. Senate.

An ironworks site was found in 1983 near Chipman Lake,

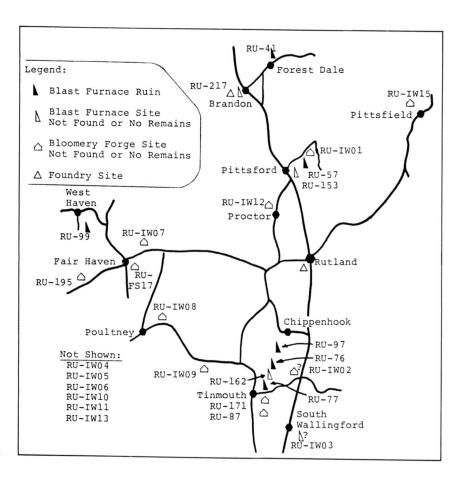

4-25. *Rutland County ironworks sites.*

leading to speculation that the difficulty with production and profits may have been caused by Chipman building it too close to the stream. The site is along Tinmouth Channel about a mile downstream from the outlet of the lake. About where the 1796 Whitelaw map indicates an ironworks, some heavy, black slag was found in the stream. Following the trail of slag a few hundred yards upstream led to the faint remains of a dam and some depressions along the shore. In the streambed where the dam would have been is a wood beam, the possible dam crib. In the middle of one depression that was partially lined with large stone blocks, some fist-size pieces of heavy, black slag were found only inches below the surface. Because the slag is heavy and black, it could indicate the site of a bloomery forge, but could also indicate the site of a poorly operating blast furnace, a blast furnace with a cold hearth. In this close proximity to the stream, its heat could easily have been drawn off by the damp ground beneath it.

An older local resident identified this place as the site of "the old pumpkin mill," where pumpkin seeds were milled at an early time (pumpkin plants were noticed growing in the vicinity of the forge site). He also remembered that most of the land in the area once belonged to members of the Chipman family.

RU-162 Willard and Perry Furnace (Tinmouth): Of the 10 to 12 forges (and/or furnaces) operating in Tinmouth in 1798 (Bishop vol. 1 1868:523), one might have been linked with a

dam on Tinmouth Channel in the northern part of town. No trace of the dam can be seen today, but there is much blast furnace slag and charcoal in the vicinity.

The original dam was an earthen affair, which backed up the channel and created a lake three miles long and in one place a half-mile wide. The dam was built at or before 1793; Tinmouth residents claimed that year the start of "fever and ague" caused by "a large pond of water in said town called the furnis pond" (Soule vol. 11 1962:350-351).

The 1796 Whitelaw map shows two ironworks just downstream of this dam. One was possibly the ca.-1793 Federal Furnace (RU-76); the other was probably that of Samuel Allen and Elias Willard, later Elias Willard and Abner Perry (Smith and Rann 1886:830). The one at the dam was probably that of Willard and Perry because it was eventually "taken away" (see later), relocated farther upstream, and later associated with Rathbone.

By 1805 Perry was in partnership with Wait Rathbone, Jr. (son of Captain Wait Rathbone), who came from Connecticut by way of Troy, New York and Middletown Springs in the late 1790s. (Rathbone initially ran a blast furnace (RU-97) with Perry at Clarendon, later opening another furnace (RU-77) with William Vaughan at Tinmouth. In 1805 and 1807 they advertised in the *Rutland Herald* for various hardware. One advertisement read: "Tinmouth: New Furnace in Tinmouth is now completed and in blast—at which place the subscriber has on hand for sale Potash Kettles and all other kinds of Hollow Ware. All kinds of machinery cast on the shortest notice. Tinmouth, December 20, 1807 Wait Rathbone."

The dam at the furnace was "taken away" in 1815, but it is not clear whether this meant intentionally (by aggravated Tinmouth residents?) or by washout. The furnace "which stood upon it" was rebuilt farther up the stream near the center of the town (Thompson 1842:172). It is doubtful the furnace was actually built directly on the dam, but rather, just beside it.

The site of the dam and furnace were initially located in 1981, followed by repeat inspections to more accurately identify the remains here. The area shows evidence of much disturbance; for example, the old bridge has been replaced by a large new corrugated pipe under the road. Nearby is a section of high, thick concrete wall, a reminder of an unsuccessful 20th-century attempt to again harness the waterpower of Tinmouth Channel. The trench for the foundation of this wall cuts through the old furnace grounds.

RU-76 Tinmouth Channel Furnace (Tinmouth): Previous to 1800, a forge and blast furnace were built in the north part of the town (Smith and Rann 1886:830). On February 1, 1793, Federal Furnace at Tinmouth advertised in the *Vermont Gazette:* "Federal Furnace now in blast, and turns out work equal to any furnace in the United States. Any kind of hollow ware, from potash kettles to the smallest article may be had at said furnace, on as reasonable terms as they can be purchased at any others. Almost every kind of country produce taken in payment." Accepting country produce in payment reflects the scarcity of hard money in Vermont, an economic condition that was to persist for another century.

A furnace mound was found in 1979 about 500 feet down-

stream from RU-162. Here on the west bank of the Tinmouth Channel is the ruin of what might have been the 1793 Federal Furnace. One furnace wall stands at this ruin with a section of the bosh lining showing through the top, similar to other contemporary Vermont blast furnaces ruins. The late Henry Potter reported finding a cast-iron kettle and other iron items many years ago just downstream of the furnace ruin. Diane and Kenneth Terminini of New Jersey, owners of the furnace site, have indicated their plans for the property will not jeopardize the furnace grounds.

4-26. *The surviving wall of a collapsed blast furnace ruin along the Clarendon River at the north end of Tinmouth.*

4-27. National Standard *September 8, 1819 (courtesy Sheldon Museum).*

RU-77 Rathbone Furnace (Tinmouth): An October 2, 1815 item in the *Rutland Herald* said that Rathbone's furnace was casting clothiers' press plates, hatters' planing kettles, close cooking and other stoves, and machinery. Wait Rathbone, Jr. had taken his oldest son, Alfred T., as partner by 1819, and Rathbone and Son cast many domestic items. On September 8, 1819, W. Rathbone & Son advertised that they had for sale potash kettles, caldrons, cooking and parlor stoves, and a general assortment of hollowware and machinery. Alfred later moved to Vergennes to sell his father's wares and ended the partnership; he eventually built a blast furnace of his own (see AD-146).

Wait Rathbone, Jr. then went into partnership with William Vaughan and continued to do a good business at their Tinmouth furnace (Smith and Rann 1886:830). It may have been from this furnace in Tinmouth that the National Hydraulic Pump Company of Windsor obtained its pig iron (Putnum Dec. 1940:365). Rathbone started selling his interest in the furnace and some of his property in 1828. The Rathbone and Vaughan partnership was dissolved two years later when what was left of the former's properties in Tinmouth and Clarendon was sold. Rathbone moved to Rutland in 1835 and died there in 1847. The last operating blast furnace in Tinmouth, probably Rathbone's, went out of blast in 1837 (Thompson 1842:172).

4-28. A collapsed blast furnace mound along the Tinmouth Channel, a few hundred yards north of Route 140, typical of what such a mound looks like in the wild. Hardly visible in even moderate underbrush, these sites can easily be missed.

Rathbone's furnace was inspected in 1979 behind the Jaquay house on Route 140. Next to the 10-foot-high mound of stones that is the furnace ruin is a stone-lined waterwheel pit with its tailrace heading to the stream. Upstream of the ruins is the dam site and the faintest hint of a headrace.

RU-IW04 Allen Forge (Tinmouth): While Ira Allen was contracting for the construction of forges in the Burlington area, he also contracted for the construction of a forge at Tinmouth in 1791. It was to have two hearths in a 50- by 40-foot building, accompanied by a 30- by 40-foot charcoal shed and housing for the ironworkers (Wilbur vol. 2 1928:6). If it was in fact built, it might have been one of the 10 to 12 forges operating at Tinmouth in 1798 as reported by Bishop in 1868, but nothing further is known of it.

RU-171 Packard Mill/Forge (Tinmouth): Surface remains of a bloomery were found in 1986 along Tinmouth Channel among a network of earthen flumes, a concrete race, and the partially standing remains of a wood and stone dam in the high brush just south of Route 140. Many pieces of bloomery slag lie along the stream bank just downstream of the dam; a thick coating of charcoal covers the nearby hillside. Could this be the site of the unlocated Allen Forge (RU-IW04) alongside

what might have been an early highway? The 1869 Beers map shows this the location of "A. Packard's Saw Mill." A cheese factory operated here later (Nelson Jaquay comment to author, Sept. 21, 1986). It was a pocket of intense industry in contrast to today's quiet appearance.

RU-97 Chippenhook Furnace (Clarendon): A furnace operated in Clarendon before 1817 doing a good business casting stoves (Smith and Rann 1886:575). *Rutland Herald* advertisements in 1805 and 1807 mention a Clarendon Furnace; in 1805 by (Abner) Perry and (Wait) Rathbone and in 1807 by Rathbone alone. Both advertisements state the furnace in blast, potash kettles and hollowware on hand, and "all kinds of machinery will be cast on the shortest of notice" (Rathbun ms n.d. 38-41).

An interview with the late Henry Potter of Clarendon (Dec. 27, 1984) followed by inspection of the Clarendon River later that day at Chippenhook resulted in finding a furnace ruin a few hundred feet northwest of the Town Road 23 bridge. The collapsed ruin is about a 20-foot-high mound of stones with the bosh lining extending upward out the top, much like the furnace at North Dorset. The furnace was built at the base of an embankment, at the top of which today are the house and yards of Mr. and Mrs. William Bauer. Near the furnace base is a slight depression, possibly outlining the casting shed area.

About 100 feet away is the Clarendon River where 20- by 20- by 6-foot-high stone foundation walls stand immediately next to the river's edge. Mr. Bauer called it "the quenching pit" although it is doubtful that quenching (annealing) was any part of the operations. The foundation looks more like the remains of a waterwheel house, especially since the base of an additional wall is near the middle of the ruin where one end of the wheel shaft could have been supported. A partially collapsed opening near the base of the downstream corner could have let spent water return to the river after turning the wheel.

This could have been Rathbone's Clarendon Furnace, but another furnace ruin might exist elsewhere in the town. While collecting information and making notes for an article on Tinmouth/Clarendon history in 1937, Wilbur Bradder wrote: "Two furnaces at bridge at Chippenhook. Can still see stacks (Herbert Best)." Does this mean that another furnace site exists somewhere in Chippenhook? Or was Bradder confusing this with another bridge a few miles upstream in Tinmouth where two furnace stacks once stood? Might there be undiscovered furnace ruins along the Clarendon River/Tinmouth Channel?

RU-FS17 Lyon's Works (Fair Haven): Born in Ireland in 1749, Matthew Lyon came to the colonies at the age of 15 and worked out his passage as an indentured servant. He was freed a few years later, settled in Cornwall, Connecticut, and married Mary Horsford (whose mother had previously been wife of David Allen, uncle to Ira Allen). He bought his first piece of property at Wallingford in 1773, took part in the storming of Fort Ticonderoga in 1775 with the Green Mountain Boys, and participated in the defeat of Burgoyne at Saratoga in 1777. Soon after, Lyon resigned his commission to attend to the military and political needs of Vermont (Austin 1981:7-32).

Taking advantage of his official position as Clerk of the Board of Confiscation, Lyon commenced to purchase land taken from local Tories and in 1779 petitioned for the grant of the township of Fair Haven in the expectation of developing the waterpower and other natural resources of that area. Within two years, he owned over 400 contiguous acres, rich in iron and lumber, all around the falls of the Castleton River. He started building mills in 1782 at the falls in Fair Haven and three years later built a dam at the upper falls.

Fair Haven grew to be a major iron-making center called Lyon's Works. The same year he built the dam, Lyon petitioned the state for the scrap iron in the old fort at Mount Independence (Grout 1927:169). Responding favorably, a 1785 Vermont law directed the sale of the remains: "Whereas there are a number of cannon, mortars, mortar beds, bumbshells, carriage wheels of cast iron in and about Mount Independence which are public property, which are rendered unfit for service and may be of service in making bar iron . . . sell the same at public vendue to the highest bidder" (Williams 1966:32).

In 1788 when his forges were busy turning out nails and other hardware, Lyon advertised the following in the October 6 *Vermont Gazette:* "The subscriber takes this method to inform the public, that he has got the nailing business going on with vigor. That he has 8d, 10d, and 20d, nails, for sale for cash, as cheap as they are to be had in Albany [New York], and of a much superior quality. . . . At said works are made for sale, blacksmith's anvils of all sizes, blacksmith's bellows and other tools, clothier screws, all sorts of mill irons, warranted chains of all sizes, most sorts of farming tools of iron."

Ore for the forges came mainly from beds across Lake Champlain near Port Henry where Lyon owned a share as early as 1785 ("Original Owners" April 11, 1885). In the October 6, 1788 *Vermont Gazette*, he published plans for building a blast furnace for casting hollowware and pig iron "without which we cannot have a complete or independent set of iron works in Vermont." A month later, the state legislature authorized him to run a lottery to raise money to erect the furnace. Needing more money to build then he could normally deduct from lottery sales, he proposed to borrow the money paid and three months after the drawing award prizes in hollowware that he would cast. William Griswold of Bennington won top prize (Nordell 1967:51).

Lyon was again searching for money to build his blast furnace in October 1789, requesting state aid for a loan of £800. Whether this was to build a second blast furnace or to finish work on the first one is unclear. The loan petition also requested a purchase of land in Orwell on which to build the blast furnace (Austin 1981:41-42). He already had a lease for the lands until 1792. He was turned down on the purchase request in October 1790, and three months later also lost the vote for his state aid. Attempts to raise money in 1793 again failed.

Did Lyon ever build a blast furnace at Fair Haven? He *did* build a blast furnace and it is supposed to have been operating in 1788, doing a "considerable business" (Smith 1886:557). But that blast furnace was in Orwell (AD-300), not Fair Haven. Lyon's continuing petitions may have been unsuccessful attempts to replace his ailing Orwell stack with another, either at a better site in Orwell or maybe at Fair Haven. In all information concerning Lyon's works at Fair Haven, although there are numerous references to a furnace or blast furnace, nothing can be found to indicate a blast furnace erected or operating at Fair Haven. Many inspections of the Castleton River have likewise failed to reveal any blast furnace slag, from the upper falls to hundreds of yards downstream. When Lyon sold two

of his forges on the south side of the Fair Haven works to William Hennessy in 1796, the sale included a hammer, anvil, and coal house (Adams 1870:142). Hennessy could not make a profit and lost the works in 1798 to Abraham Leggett of New York. Lyon, meanwhile, had left Vermont for Philadelphia and in 1800 sold the balance of his works to Edward Douse, of Dedham, Massachusetts. The transaction included the slitting mill and the ironworks, plus an extensive tract of land south and east of the river (Adams 1870:116). In November of that year, Lyon sold his remaining property in Fair Haven to Josiah Norton of Castleton. Norton had previously bought Lyon's paper mill and many acres of land. Dan Smith, who was later to build a forge at West Haven (RU-IW06), leased the ironworks from Douse in 1801. In 1801 he bought them and in 1807 sold to Jacob Davey. More people were involved in these transactions, including William Lee of Poultney who also came into ownership of the two south fires of the forge around 1800 (Adams 1870:117). No mention is made of any blast furnace in Fair Haven as part of all this buying and selling of the ironworks property. Insofar as it is known, therefore, the first blast furnace in Vermont may have been that erected by Lyon at Orwell, and not Fair Haven, as seems to be the historical consensus.

By 1812 Jacob Davey had taken control of the Fair Haven works. Born in New Jersey in 1771, Davey moved to Vergennes in 1800 and to Fair Haven in 1804 as superintendent of the ironworks. He soon purchased acreage in and around the ironworks and by 1812 was involved not only in the iron business, but also in fulling and finishing cloth and operating a sawmill. Davey also speculated in real estate and held local political office (Hemenway vol. 3 1877:732-733).

Davey's works burned in 1815 and were immediately rebuilt, implying that business was good. This was in contrast to the ironworks at Vergennes, which were languishing in the postwar depression. In 1829, Davey sold a half-interest in the works to three investors but bought it all back two years later. By 1842 the ironworks included a number of bloomeries, a rolling and slitting mill, and an extensive nail factory. The rolling mill made nail plates, marble saw blades, horseshoe rod, and bar iron (Thompson 1842:70).

In 1843 the ironworks again burned and were again rebuilt. That same year, Jacob Davey died and the works were sold at auction to Artemas S. Cushman. Jacob's son, Israel Davey, bought out Cushman in 1853 and six years later sold a half-interest to Benjamin S. Nichols, who in turn sold it back to Davey in 1865 (Adams 1870:144).

During this period the works prospered and were known throughout the industry. Production of the rolling mill and bloomery (Neilson 1866:224) was:

Year	Rolling Mill Tons	Bloomery Tons	Year	Rolling Mill Tons	Bloomery Tons
1854	700	300	1860	1,000	300
1855	700	300	1861	1,000	300
1856	700	300	1862	1,000	300
1857	700	300	1863	1,000	300
1858	—	—	1864	1,000	350
1859	1,000	300	1865	1,000	350

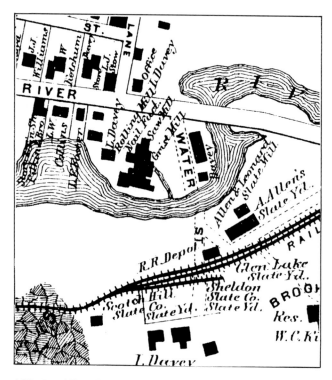

4-29. Israel Davey's rolling mill and nail factory among other mills on the north side of the Castleton River at Fair Haven in 1869 (Beers Rutland 1869:19).

The rolling mill consumed 30 tons of anthracite and 700 tons of bituminous coal from Cumberland, Pennsylvania, plus tons of scrap iron and Lake Champlain ore in 1864. That same year the bloomery consumed 80,000 bushels of charcoal and 400 tons of ore. Full capacity of the bloomery was 500 tons. The works were described in 1866:

> [The] forge, billets and bars are made from scrap and from Lake Champlain ore, and sometimes the two mixed. Blowing is done by means of a "Tyler" wheel. There are two blowing cylinders of about 28 inches diameter and 4½ feet stroke. There are two bloomery fires, and a side-lift hammer. Over each fire are three arched pipes for heating blast. There is one tuyere to each fire, nozzle [oval-horizontal] shaped, 1½ inches long and 7/8 high. Hammer weighs about 1400 lbs., and is run by a breast wheel of about 13 feet diameter and 3½ feet buckets.
>
> Charcoal is hauled on an average about 9 miles, and costs (1866) about 12 cents [a bushel].
>
> Rolling mill contains 1 heating furnace, and one 12-inch train of rolls, with which scrap bars, horseshoe, band, and round iron, nail plate, and marble saws are rolled. In the heating furnace scrap piles are heated and rolled bars are reheated. Cumberland coal chiefly is used in this furnace. Capacity of rolling mill, 1500 tons.
>
> Nail factory contains 10 machines.
>
> In all, there are 5 water-wheels: 1 for blowing forge, 1 for rolls, 1 for shears, 1 for nail factory, and 1 for hammer.

All except the last are "Tyler" wheels. The water privilege is good.

> Product of the works is in marble saws, horseshoes and other iron, and nails. Marble saws are made partly of scrap billets made in forge, and partly of bars rolled from scrap piles. Horseshoe iron is made from the scrap billets.
>
> Product of the rolling mill has for some years been about 1000 tons, about 350 of which are marble saws, some 400 are nails, and the balance in horseshoe and other iron (Neilson 1866:227-228).

Mention of the use of two bloomery fires with three arched pipes for heating the blast indicates the works employed the Champlain Forge principle of operation. The 1869 Beers map of Fair Haven shows the rolling mill and nail factory complex plus a sawmill and a gristmill on the north side of the Castleton River, east of today's Route 22A.

When Israel Davey died in 1869 he was sole owner of the vast ironworks operations at Fair Haven. His nephew, Rufus C. Colburn, continued operation of the works for the benefit of the estate, but this was the post-Civil War depression period and the slate business was fast displacing the iron business at Fair Haven. Within a few years, the forges shut down and became history.

Inspections of the site in 1978 and 1979 failed to reveal any surface indications of where specifically in that four-acre area the ironworks were located. Some forge-type slag was found near the base of the upper falls, but no blast furnace slag could be found. Debris from a succession of slate works generally buries the entire ironworks site, in the midst of which is an underground turbine and a tailrace that are most likely remains of these later industries. In 1986 there were plans for building a hydroelectric power station at this excellent mill site. A historical marker a few blocks away at the village green recognizes the ironworks heritage of Lyon's Works.

RU-IW05 Carver's Forge (West Haven?): One of the earliest settlers of the East Bay-Poultney River area was (Joseph?) Carver, who is supposed to have operated a forge in the area. Carver lived here during the Revolutionary War, and he and his forge might have been present at the time of the Hessian incursion from Lake Champlain into the Castleton area during the Burgoyne campaign the summer of 1777 (Pat Murtagh to author, Aug. 15, 1989). Whether the forge was in New York or Vermont is unknown but it probably was a bloomery, fashioning hardware and tools from local ore for local consumption. A Carver family cemetery is located in New York about a mile southeast of the Cogman Bridge, hinting that the forge might not have been in Vermont. But another cemetery containing Carvers is in Vermont just east of Carver's Falls. Close inspection of the shores of East Bay and in the Whitehall-Hampton-West Haven area might result in slag finds that could aid in locating Carver's Forge.

RU-IW06 Dan Smith Forge (West Haven): Dan Smith, nephew of Dr. Simeon Smith, came to Fair Haven from Suffield, Connecticut, probably in the early 1780s. From 1803 to 1807, he owned and operated the ironworks in Fair Haven that previously belonged to Matthew Lyon. Sometime during the War of 1812, he built a forge at Carver's Falls (Adams 1870:468). He also made nails during a later time in a factory (possibly a blacksmith shop) that was located alongside today's

Route 22A, east of the falls and just inside Fair Haven township (Smith and Rann 1886:862-864). Little else can be learned of this site.

In 1787 Simeon Smith (not Dr. Simeon Smith) came to Fair Haven from Sharon, Connecticut, settling in the west part of town. He built a sawmill on the Hubbardton River; the next year Jonathan Orms built a forge on the New York side (of Carver's Falls?) for Smith (Adams 1870:69). Orms later purchased the forge from Smith and built a sawmill and a gristmill, creating a small industrial complex near the falls that became known as Orms Mills (Smith and Rann 1886:862-864; Adams 1870:446). For a time, Smith also owned a share of the nearby Gamaliel Leonard Forge (RU-195).

RU-99 Colburn Furnace (West Haven): John P. Colburn came to Vermont from Canada with his father and family in 1808, eventually settling at West Haven and there learning the blacksmith trade. In 1817 he bought a half-interest in a scythe factory in Fair Haven where he produced axes and hoes. He married Lucy Davey following the death of his wife in 1824. Lucy was the daughter of Jacob Davey who was then operating the ironworks at Fair Haven. In 1825, Colburn, his father-in-law Jacob Davey, and James Y. Watson built a furnace stack "just below Carver's Falls" (Adams 1870:330-332).

It may be coincidence, but a few miles downstream from Carver's Falls were anchored what remained of MacDonough's victorious Lake Champlain naval squadron. After the War of 1812 the fleet was stripped of its guns and ordnance and the ships were harbored north of Whitehall. In 1819, one of the decaying ships sank at anchor; the next year another sank. The three remaining vessels were towed up the Poultney River and there allowed to sink. In 1825, the same year Colburn built his blast furnace just five miles upriver, the U.S. Navy sold what remained of the fleet for scrap, and all that remained by that time above water was broken up for the iron it contained (Cohn 1984:55). Could Colburn have had that scrap iron in mind when he built his furnace?

About a quarter-mile below Carver's Falls, the Poultney River emerges from a rocky gorge, flows rapidly through some island and shoreline sandbars, and takes a sharp right turn. The result, over the years, has been the creation of a triangular-shaped piece of flat, silted land on the inside curve of the river, the Vermont side, while the river erodes away at the outside part of the curve, the New York side. This triangular piece of land is bounded on two sides by the river and on the other by a high rocky embankment, the continuation of the river gorge. At a point some 300 feet from the river and at the base of the embankment Colburn built his blast furnace in 1825. It has to have been one of the poorest choices for a blast furnace site ever made. The late Paul Doran, who owned the furnace site, said that the river floods the entire area below the embankment every spring. The furnace ruin was found Memorial Day weekend of 1984 after climbing down the gorge by following the trace remains of a road that leads from Doran's farm to the site. (It was later learned that the furnace area is a favorite haunt of rattlesnakes.) The collapsed walls of the ruin are made of large blocks of stone and were probably hoisted into place by a derrick placed atop the nearby embankment. A 10-foot-high section of the 9-foot-diameter bosh remains, with no refractory lining or brick in evidence. Inspection of the bosh indicates two possible arches, one facing the embankment and the other 90 degrees to the northwest, facing what was probably going to be the casting floor, another poor choice considering how low and wet the ground is. The tangle of roots in the silt thwarted attempts to shallow-dig for slag. No evidence was found of head- or tailraces, cellar holes, waterwheel pit, slag, or charcoal. This, plus the lack of refractory material or evi-

4-30. *Colburn furnace ruin at West Haven. Note the lack of a bosh lining, indicating the possibility that this furnace was never fired.*

dence of burning inside the bosh, leads to the conclusion that the furnace never went into blast. Most likely, Colburn discovered his error at the first high water and abandoned the venture.

The ruin of another Colburn furnace that did see service is still standing 30 miles to the northwest at Moriah Center, New York. But this furnace operated from 1848 to 1858, some 17 years after John P. Colburn died. According to Eleanor Hall, Moriah/Port Henry historian, it was probably an Edward or Edmund Colburn (Coburn?) who ran the Moriah furnace (Richard S. Allen letter to author, April 23, 1984). Neither of those names has yet been tied to any of the Vermont Colburns. Other Colburns known to have been connected with the iron business were Charles T., brother of John P., a Pittsford blacksmith; and Rufus C., son of John P., who ran the Fair Haven works after Israel Davey died.

RU-195 Gamaliel Leonard Forge (Fair Haven): Born in Raynham, Massachusetts in 1757, Gamaliel Leonard was a descendant of James Leonard, who landed in this country about 20 years after the Pilgrims and is credited with building the first forge in this country (Adams 1870:426-427). Sometime after the end of the Revolutionary War, Gamaliel Leonard migrated to Lenox, Massachusetts, where he worked at the blast furnace. In 1785, after two years at the furnace, he moved, along with a member of the Fuller family, to Hampton, New York across the Poultney River from Fair Haven.

Leonard bought a 120-acre tract along the Poultney River in Fair Haven, alongside a small falls just upstream of where the old Skene Road crossed the river. (Route 4 today crosses about 100 feet farther upstream.) He moved to Fair Haven in 1786, built a house near the falls, and then a sawmill, the second one in the town. In company with Elias Stevens and Daniel Arnold of Hampton, he built a forge at the west end (just downstream) of his sawmill in 1788. Four years later Arnold sold his share of the forge to James Downey, Jr. In 1802 Stevens sold his share to Simeon Smith.

Downey, from Granville, New York and former worker in Lyon's forge at Fair Haven, sold his share in 1798 to Samuel Atwood (Adams 1870:352-353). Might this be the Downey/Downing who later owned a forge in Addison County (AD-IW01), as reported in the Census of Manufacturers for 1832?

The 1796 Whitelaw map does not show Leonard's forge along the Poultney River west of Fair Haven. Does this mean that the forge was out of operation at that time or that Whitelaw was unaware of its existence? The 1869 Beers map of Fair Haven shows the old Skene Road crossing and a group of buildings in the immediate vicinity, including the sawmill and house of David H. Bristol (whose father bought and rebuilt Leonard's house) on the Vermont side, and a machine shop and woolen mill owned by Bristol and two stores (one owned by an H. Leonard) on the New York side.

When inspected in 1989 a concentration of slag was found just downstream of the mill's still-standing stone foundations next to the falls, a few hundred feet north of the Route 4 bridge. Some pieces of slag were up to one foot thick. Smaller pieces were found along the bank as far as 100 feet downstream. Location of the site agrees with two historical accounts that Leonard built his forge "at the west end of the sawmill" and "below his sawmill." Luckily, the new Route 4 bridge was built just far enough upstream to preserve this interesting site.

There is much to see and learn here.

How long the forge operated is unknown. Shares of ownership changed hands up to 1802, although this does not mean the forge was in actual operation then. Speculative buying might have been afoot. Shares of Leonard's sawmill were sold, the mill was rebuilt, and a share of that was sold in 1803. More shares were conveyed and then the mill was swept away by "the great freshet of 1811" (Adams 1870:153). The freshet might have swept away the forge also, marking at least its latest operating year. During these years, Leonard was also associated with a blast furnace in New Haven (AD-340).

Leonard bought the sawmill and rebuilt it after the washout and again sold it, along with three acres of land and the old house where he had lived, to David H. Bristol in May 1842. Bristol later built a machine shop and new dwelling house on the premises, those seen in the Beers map.

Gamaliel Leonard died at Fair Haven on August 7, 1827 and was buried in Low Hampton, New York. His oldest son Charles, born in Fair Haven, married Betsy Colburn, sister of John P. Colburn (Adams 1870:428). It was this Colburn who built the blast furnace at the base of Carver's Falls (RU-99). Another son, Gilbert, operated a "small furnace near Mr Davey's works [RU-FS17] between 1812 and 1820" (Adams 1870:429). Simeon Smith, who bought Elias Stevens' share in Leonard's forge in 1802, earlier owned a forge that operated on the New York side of Carver's Falls (see RU-IW06). DeWitt Leonard, grandson of Gamaliel, published the *Fair Haven Journal*, and together with E. H. Phelps (Leonard & Phelps) published Andrew Adams' *History of the Town of Fair Haven, Vermont*.

RU-IW07 Castleton Forge (Castleton): A forge operated from the 1790s to about 1815 in Castleton, two miles east of Fair Haven (Smith and Rann 1886:541). The forge was located north of Route 4A, at a site that places it near (or maybe under) the Lake Bomoseen dam at Hydeville per the 1796 Whitelaw map. Nothing was found in a 1984 inspection.

RU-IW08 Joslin and Darling Forge (Poultney): Along the Poultney River, six miles south of Lyon's Works, Samuel Joslin and Abel Darling built a forge in 1785 (Smith and Rann 1886:772). The 1796 Whitelaw map shows it about a half-mile upstream of East Poultney. Inspections of the river in 1981 resulted in finding occasional pieces of slag but no forge site or slag concentration.

RU-IW09 John Burnham Forge (Middletown Springs): At Burnham Hollow, in today's town of Middletown Springs, a forge and foundry were operating in the 1790s in addition to a number of other mills, all built by John Burnham, who came from Shaftsbury in 1785. These were all washed away in 1811 after which the forge was rebuilt but not operated as extensively as before (Smith and Rann 1886:653). Bits of slag were found at various places along the Poultney River in a 1981 inspection but no definite ironworks site was found.

RU-IW10 Keith Furnace (Pittsford): Israel Keith came to Pittsford from Easton, Massachusetts, which was an 18th-century ironworks town in its own right. He graduated from Harvard in 1771 and joined the army at Boston two years later (Shipton 1975:549-550). Keith rose to the position of deputy adjutant general on General Heath's staff before resigning his commission in 1778 to resume the study of law. Admitted by the Suffolk County Bar in 1780 to practice before the Massachusetts Superior Court, he married Caroline Jenkins in Boston three years later. He retired from the Suffolk Bar in 1790 and the next summer he was in Pittsford, putting idle money to work building a blast furnace.

The ironworks were built on 3½ acres of land that he bought from Joseph Hitchcock, of which he paid "six pounds lawful money" (*Keith Furnace Lot* Deed, Massachusetts Historical Society, vol. 2, Aug. 3, 1791). He also purchased some land from Ira Allen, "agreeing to pay him with iron and hollowware manufactured by him which was to be delivered at Allen's house" (Wilbur vol. 2 1928:70).

Israel Keith supplied the money; his father Zephaniah and younger brother Alfred supplied the skill and ironworks know-how (Shipton 1975:553). The works made a good-quality iron that found a ready market (Caverly 1872:517). Scotland Keith came to Pittsford in 1795, purchased a share in the furnace, and joined the rest of the family in the firm of Keith & Company (Caverly 1872:270). The blast furnace was built so near the Chittenden town line that many historians, starting with Graham in 1797, credited that town with the site of Keith's furnace (Graham 1797:86). The error has been copied in a number of published histories as recently as the 1970s (Thompson 1842:55; Hemenway vol. 3 1877:547; Jacobs 1953:130; Swift 1977:388). Whitelaw's 1796 map clearly indicates "Furnace" in Pittsford.

Israel Keith sold his furnace property in 1795. Four years later he proceeded to establish another ironworks nearly 90 miles to the north, where he and Alfred built a blast furnace on the east bank of the Black Creek in Sheldon (see FR-67 and FR-68). Returning to Pittsford, he continued his law practice in U.S. and Vermont courts. He died at Pittsford on June 3, 1819 and is buried in the Congregational church cemetery where his tombstone stands in the unmaintained section, barely visible amid the high thorn bushes.

Keith's former furnace property in Pittsford had changed hands many times. These partial and full owners included men who, like the Keiths, also came from Easton. Howard Lothrop invested in the works and became superintendent (Smith and Rann 1886:902). Nathan and Cornelius Gibbs and Edward Kingman, also from eastern Massachusetts, along with Luke Reed, ran the furnace business in the late 1790s until Nathan Gibbs eventually came into full control. Gibbs enlarged the furnace in 1824, making the bosh 8 feet wide by 27 feet high. He improved the property and operated the works until he died later that year (Caverly 1872:517). Nathan Gibbs is buried next to Israel Keith. Andrew Leach, buried nearby in the same cemetery, owned the furnace from 1824 to 1826.

Although it is assumed that Simeon Granger's enlargement of Keith's furnace stack in 1827 completely razed it, an intensive search of Furnace Brook below the site has not been made to eliminate the possibility of an earlier Keith furnace ruin/site in existence. Information from the Massachusetts Historical Society, however, appears to identify the area of the Granger furnace ruin (RU-57) also as the site of the Israel Keith 1791 furnace (David Ingram letter to author, Dec. 2, 1988). Keith's house might have been where only a depression today remains, at the site of Granger's house per the 1854 map of Rutland County, although this has not been proven. Much work remains in finding the homes of Vermont's great ironmasters.

RU-57 Granger Furnace (Pittsford): Simeon Granger was born in 1770 at West Springfield, Massachusetts, moved with his parents to Sandisfield following the Revolution, and there married Phoebe Couch in 1791. In 1801 he moved to Salisbury, Connecticut, where he became involved in the iron business. In November 1826, when he learned that Andrew Leach at Pittsford had put his blast furnace (RU-IW10) up for sale, he bought it. Waiting until dark so he would not be missed, Granger left Salisbury and rode night and day to reach Pittsford and made the purchase. On his way to the town clerk to record the deed, he waved the deed to another prospective buyer just arriving from Salisbury, saying to him "You are too late, neighbor; the property is mine!" (Granger 1893:865). Granger incorporated the business on November 14, 1826 as the Pittsford Iron Manufacturing Co. Partners of record were Lyman and Chester Granger, their father-in-law Cephos Smith, and Egbert B. Smith (*Acts Passed* 1826:98-99). Histories refer to the company as Simeon Granger & Sons.

The Grangers rebuilt the furnace in 1827 and two years later built a foundry nearby and moved into Keith's former house. A number of items were cast at the furnace, including stoves. A few years later the foundry was moved some 50 to 100 feet west of its original location (Caverly 1872:518). In 1834 at age 64, Simeon Granger died, leaving two of his sons, Lyman and Chester, to continue the business.

Lyman Granger had commenced practicing law after graduating from Union College at Schenectady and the Litchfield Law School, Connecticut, moving to Rutland in 1823. With the formation of Simeon Granger & Sons in 1826, he moved to Pittsford and represented the town at the General Assembly during that and the following year. In 1837 his health had already started failing and he sold his interest in the furnace property to Edward L., his brother. Lyman Granger died suddenly two years later while visiting at Utica, New York. Chester and Edward L. Granger formed C. & E. L. Granger, and when Edward L. died in 1846, George W. Hodges came into the business under the firm name of Granger, Hodges & Company.

Due to poor economic conditions, the works partially suspended operations in 1852. At this time the business was incorporated into a stock company, the Pittsford Iron Co., and the village of Grangerville grew along Furnace Brook near the works. In addition to the blast furnace, there was a cupola furnace at the foundry, a blacksmith shop, company store (across from Chester Granger's house), the furnace school, and about 20 tenant houses for the ironworkers. In 1853, the furnace was enlarged to 42 feet high. A 24-foot waterwheel provided the heated blast of 600°F (Lesley 1858:76). Production capacity was 2,600 tons a year, but the furnace smelted only 350 to 1,757 tons a year from 1854 to 1858. The foundry cast 300 tons of stoves a year (Lesley 1859:26). There was no production from 1859 to 1863; only 400 tons were smelted in 1864 (Neilson 1866:218). Why the furnace made so little iron during the Civil War years is puzzling.

Ore for the furnace was found locally in many places. While Granger was excavating for the construction of his new furnace, good-quality iron ore was found directly underfoot (Hodge May 12, 1849:291). Ore was dug nearby on both sides of the stream and from deep mines at Chittenden, 2½ miles north. These mines remained in operation to 1872. Local ore was sometimes mixed with magnetic ore and boated and carted to Pittsford

IRON WORKS, PITTSFORD, VT.
PRICES OF STOVES, HOLLOW WARE, &C.

Numbers			Diameter of Boiler holes	Length of Fire Arch	Price
1	Farmer & Mechanic Elevated Oven Cook Stove,	3 Boilers	13 in.	22 in.	11.00
2	ditto. " " " " "	2 "	14	26	12.00
3	ditto. " with or without back Furnace,	4 "	"	"	15.00
4	ditto. " " " " "	4 "	15	28	17.00
2 to 4	Same Stoves with Mammoth Oven, additional price,				2.00
1	Square Oven Cook Stove, Oven 13 x 14 x 22 in.	2 Boilers	13	22	12.00
2	ditto. " " " 13 x 15 x 22 "	2 "	14	26	13.50
3	ditto. " " " 14 x 15 x 24 "	2 "	"	"	16.50
4	ditto. " " " same, "	2 "	15	28	18.50
2	El. Oven Parlor Cook Stove, 1 boiler 13 in. and 2 "		8½	20	9.00
3	ditto. " " 1 long " 18 " and 3 "		7½	19	9.50
4	ditto. " " 1 " " 18 " and 4 "		7½	19	10.00
7	East'n Queen Air Tight, 2 " " 17 in. and 4 "		7	16	12.00
8	ditto. 2 " " 18 " " 4 "		8	18	15.00
9	ditto. 2 " " 19 " " 4 "		9		17.00
4	Hot Blast Air Tight Cook Stove, 1 long 19 in. and 4 "		8	20	16.00
5	ditto. 1 " 21 " " 4 "		9	21	18.00
0	Air Tight Parlor Box Stove, hearth on side,			18	3.00
1	ditto. " " " hearth on the end or side,			18	4.50
2	ditto. " " " " " "			21	6.00
3	ditto. " " " " " "			25	8.00
4	ditto. " " " " " "			30	12.00
5	ditto. " " " " " "		9 in.	3 ft.	15.00
8	Rail Road ditto. " - - -			4 ft.	45.00
6	Air Tight Sap Boiling Stove for Pan 28 x 44 inches,			3 ft.	16.00
	Same Stove with false Cap for 25 inch Cauldron and for two boilers 10 x 12 inches,				20.00
	Same Stove with all the above and Large Square oven,				25.00
1	Arch Top, 26 x 30 inches - - - for Kettles of		18 in.		1.50
	Same with 4 Circles and Griddles, - -				2.50
2	ditto. 28 x 40 inches for 2 Boilers and Kettle of		25 in.		3.00
	Same with 7 Circles and 3 Griddles,				5.00
	Arch Mouth, - - - - - -				1.25
	Oven Mouth, - - - - - -				
1	Cauldron Kettle, 30 gallons, - - - -		25 in.		5.00
2	ditto. 60 " - - - -		30 "		8.00
	Flat Iron Heater, - - - - for 6 Sad Irons				2.75

Numbers		Diameter at the top	Price
2	Maslin Kettles	7½ in.	0.20
3	ditto. - -	8½	0.30
4	ditto. - -	9½	0.40
5	ditto. - -	10½	0.50
6	ditto. - -	11½	0.60
7	ditto. - -	12½	0.70
	Nest of above six Kettles,		2.70
00	Boiler - - -	9	0.40
0	do. - - -	10	0.50
0 & 1	do. - - -	11	0.60
1	do. - - -	12	0.70
	Nest of above four Boilers,		2.20
2	Boiler - - -	10	0.80
3	do. - - -	11	0.90
4	do. - - -	13	1.00
	Wash boilers - -	15½	2.00
	Pots - - -	7	0.80
	do. - - -	8	0.90
	do. - - -	7	1.00
	Tea Kettles - -	7	0.80
	ditto. - -	8	1.00
0 & 1	Spiders, Flat Bottom	9	.25
1	do. Round "	9	.25
2	do. " "	10	.33
2 & 3	do. Flat "	10	.33
4	do. " "	12½	.50
2	Grid Irons 16 in. long	9	.42
4	do. 17 "	9	.58
6	do. Square		.75
1	Bailed Basin - -	12	.33
2	do. do. - -	12	.50
	No bail do. - -	9	.42
	Bread Basins Round,	9	.33
	do. do. Square,	6 x 9	.42
	Pestle and Mortar,		.67

4-31. *Price list of ironware produced by Granger, Hodges & Co. at Pittsford in 1851 (typeset from a poor original; courtesy UVM Special Collections Library).*

from mines in New York. In order to obtain maximum yield from its ore, Granger ran the cooled slag through a stamping machine. A stream of water washed away the lighter vitreous portions of the slag and the heavier iron particles were collected and recycled into the furnace (Hodge May 19, 1849:305).

After the Civil War, a new group of owners called the Vermont Iron Company fired the furnace once again in 1865, but iron prices fell sharply during the post-war period. Jeremiah Pritchard of Boston was running the works in the 1870s when railroad wheel iron and spiegel (pig iron with high manganese content) were being made (Lewis 1876-77:234).

The Mitchell ore bed at Chittenden shut down in 1872; five years later, Chester Granger died at age 81. In addition to his involvement with the ironworks, Granger was one of the orig-

inal directors of the Rutland & Burlington Railroad, director of the Bank of Rutland, and also representative to the General Assembly from 1862 to 1865; he later engaged in an iron business in Pennsylvania but returned to Pittsford where he retired. The works were owned by Naylor & Company from 1882 to 1886; they were probably gambling on a general improvement of the iron business. The works were called Titan Furnace at this time (Child 1881:179). There is no evidence that the furnace ever operated after 1883, making it the final operating blast furnace in Vermont.

Of other Grangers, Chester's younger brother Rensselaer Dudley Granger moved to Woodstock about 1830 where he was involved in the mercantile business for several years. He later converted his mill into a foundry, making castings and

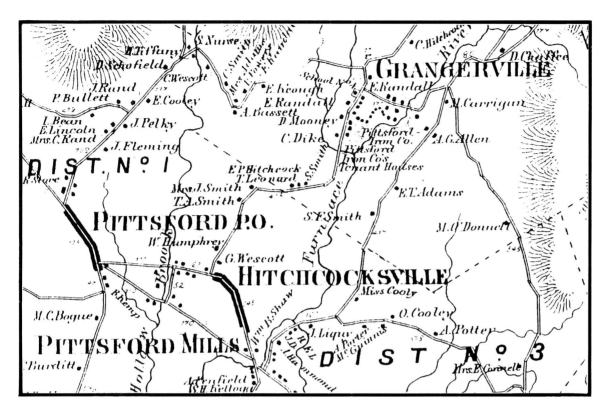

4-32. *A pocket of industry at Pittsford, including the community of Grangerville (upper right) with the Pittsford Iron Company, company tenant houses, and the furnace school along "Furnace River." Notice the family names associated with the Crown Point Iron Works (clockwise): Dike, Hammond, Penfield, and Bogue (Beers* Rutland *1869:31).*

tools under the name Granger and Swan (Aldrich and Holmes 1891:267; Watson 1967:17). He sold the foundry to Daniel Taft around 1836 (Taft at the time owned and operated foundries in nearby Taftsville). Granger then moved on to Troy, New York, where he was awarded many patents on stove designs, the most famous being Granger's Air Tight Parlor Cook (patent date 1846), cast for many years at Ransom & Company, an Albany, New York stove foundry (Groft 1984:88). William S. Granger, one of Chester's sons, moved to Providence, Rhode Island, becoming treasurer of the Cove Foundry & Machine Company. It was succeeded about 1880 by the Granger Foundry & Machine Company, of which he became president. The company later merged with three other firms to become the Textile Finishing & Machinery Company, a foundry that made machines to bleach, dye, and finish cotton goods (Dodge 1912:204).

In a 1953 interview by the *Rutland Herald,* 86-year-old Pittsford native Patrick E. Mooney related his memories of working at the furnace (McWhorter Oct. 2, 1953:68). He started work there at age 15 and was at the furnace two years until the last blast in the spring of 1883. Mooney said the works was owned by Gillman Pritchard, who lived in an old brick house (the Ironmasters Inn) across the road from the furnace. In 1953, the house was occupied by Pittsford sawmill owner Harry Smith.

Mooney said that about 60 men were employed at the furnace, the mine, and the charcoal kilns. The kilns were operated by

Bill Taylor and wood for the kilns—maple, birch, and beech—came from the surrounding hills. He said that the five kilns took 90 cords at a time (which calculates to 18 cords per kiln, low considering the usual 25 to 40 cords per kiln for the period. See chapter 5).

Charcoal and ore were hauled to the furnace by horse teams owned either by the company or by local teamsters. The wagons drew two 3-ton loads daily from a mine in Chittenden. At the furnace, the ore was dumped into a pile where 15-year-old Mooney loaded the ore on a one-horse cart and drove it to the "tophouse." Here the ore was weighed, run over the stack, and dumped in. The furnace had to be charged 13 times in each 12-hour shift. For carting ore from 7 a.m. to 6 p.m., seven days a week, Mooney was paid $1.15 a day. During this 10-hour shift, the men stocking the furnace had to draw enough ore to keep it going around the clock. The firemen and their helpers worked in two 12-hour shifts, one beginning at noon and one at midnight. They received $1.75 a day, which was considered good pay, and their helpers got $1.25 for 12 hours work. In young Patrick's day, "another day, another dollar" was no idle expression.

The furnace sent up flame-colored gases, which at night lit up the yard so one could read a newspaper, said Mooney. It sometimes brought people to the scene, thinking a fire was raging out of control. Every eight hours, men in the casting shed drew out five tons of molten iron and cast it into 100-pound blocks of pig iron: three feet long, three inches wide, and four

4-33. *The old Ironmasters Inn still standing next to Furnace Brook, across the field from the Granger furnace.*

inches deep. These were loaded into wagons and taken to the railroad at Pittsford Depot for shipment to Boston. The men led a rugged existence, said Mooney. "They could stand more in a day than they do now" was his opinion.

Mooney spent 59 years in the same house where he was born at Pittsford Furnace and received his schooling, which ended when he was 13 years old, at the Furnace School. His father was a foreman at the furnace but died when Patrick was in his teens, leaving his mother with six children to support. Pritchard, the furnace owner, "took a little compassion on my mother," said Mooney, giving him his first job.

A long-time Pittsford resident made a sketch in 1945 of the furnace in operation, based on an on-site description by Patrick Mooney. The sketch, however, bears only little resemblance to the present remains (*Pittsford Now and Then* 1980:94).

The wooden buildings where the ore was handled had been torn down by 1953 and made into a sawmill. The company store, which stood near the road, also had disappeared entirely. The blast furnace still stands off Furnace Road, about a mile northeast of Pittsford village. The stack retains most of its iron binders and arch brickwork, but a section of the top of the stack was gouged out by an earthmover about 30 years ago, exposing some of the internal structure relating to the heating ovens that once stood atop the furnace. Associated with the ruin are partially caved-in stone block walls, foundations, and the upstream remains of a dam and headrace. The remains of the Smith sawmill are immediately downstream of the furnace under collapsed boards. Under this woodpile is a large concrete foundation in which a turbine once sat, driven by water that was conveyed into it through the existing large iron pipe. Local tradition holds that Smith used the furnace stack to burn waste wood from his sawmill. The furnace hearth was still choked with rotted boards until cleaned out by owner Allen M. Hitchcock in 1990. The entire furnace area is littered with slag, burnt brick, pieces of waste iron, and charcoal. Domestic trash adorns

the embankment adjacent to the furnace. (Over the three-day Memorial Day weekend of 1991, about 30 volunteers from the Northern New England Chapter–SIA and the Pittsford Historical Society, led by Dr. David Starbuck, cut trees and brush, excavated, recorded, and surveyed and mapped the furnace grounds. This was the first of what might become an annual chapter project.)

What has been taken by many to have been the old Granger Homestead, the large brick house across the road from the furnace ruin, is now generally believed by Pittsford historians to have been an inn operated contemporarily with the works by B. H. Trowbridge (Henry M. Paynter conversation with author, May 25, 1991). Granger's house was a few hundred feet to the north, across the road from the company store, according to the 1854 map of Rutland County. Nothing remains of the house today. The old inn was bought by Charles Smith in 1883 (*Pittsford Now and Then* 1980:41). Various members of the Smith family owned it until recently, when Allen Hitchcock bought it. Hitchcock is a descendant of Joseph Hitchcock, who sold the land to Israel Keith in 1791 (Allen M. Hitchcock to author, May 25, 1991). Hitchcock sold the inn to Creg Oosterhart and Mike Greene in 1984; they embarked on the ambitious project of restoring the building to its Federal architectural style. In the process, they discovered some interesting clues about how the building was constructed, but the original construction date remains unknown. Meanwhile, they operated the house as the Ironmasters Inn, a bed and breakfast, until the house again went up for sale.

Many other structures relating to the ironworks era still stand in the vicinity. At the intersection down the highway from the inn is the old Furnace School, converted into a private residence. Westward on both sides of the highway are the former works tenement houses. Ruins of the five charcoal kilns mentioned by Mooney were found in 1986 a mile up Kiln Brook in Chittenden (chapter 6, RU-155). Many other charcoal-making sites

4-34. *Close-up view of the decorative lintels at the Ironmasters Inn, said to have been cast at the Granger furnace.*

4-35. *Front (south) wall of the Vermont Iron Company stack at Pittsford showing front ladder-like face plates, which lock the diagonal binder rods together, stabilizing the structure.*

have been found farther up Furnace Brook in Chittenden.

RU-IW11 Larnard's Forge (Chittenden): Larnard's Forge was somewhere on Furnace River (Brook) in the 1840s. It initially used ore from Granger's ore bed mixed with that from New York, but eventually used local ore alone, yielding an iron of "excellent quality" (Adams 1845:21; Lesley 1859:542). No attempt has been made to locate this forge.

RU-153 Gibbs and Cooley Furnace (Pittsford): Cyrus Gibbs and John Cooley operated a furnace at an early time near the mouth of Ripley Brook (Caverly 1872:519). It was associated with their foundry, built in 1827 on the 1808 site of Amos Crippen's trip-hammer shop, a half-mile upstream of Pittsford Mills. The Gibbs and Cooley furnace might have been one of two furnaces mentioned by Zadock Thompson in 1842 as being in Pittsford. Commonly known as "the pocket furnace," it was this works that supplied Allen Penfield at Crown Point, New York with castings for his ore-separating machines in 1831 (Allen 1967:5).

Inspection of the brook alongside River Road in 1986 resulted in finding much slag that appears to have come from a blast furnace. About a half-mile up the road from Route 7, near the remains of a dam, a high slag concentration exists, indicating a probable site of the furnace. Road construction in the vicinity might have destroyed most of the remains.

RU-IW12 Sutherland Falls Forge (Proctor): The Sutherland Falls Forge was initially owned by an early settler, Peter Sutherland. A record of deeds identifies the property as the Forge Lot and it changed hands nearly two dozen times between 1809 and 1844 (Otto Johnson letter to Richard S. Allen, Feb. 12, 1957). Owners included names connected with the Pittsford Iron Works and also works at Crown Point, New York. Ironworks at Proctor first appear on the 1821 Whitelaw map, on the east side of the falls. The forge made picks and nails in addition to producing bar iron from ore coming from local beds at first, later from Pittsford, and finally from Crown Point (Gale

1922:70). The forge was described as making bar iron and being washed away in 1840 by a freshet (Fred R. Patch letter to Otto Johnson, ca. 1956).

Confusion exists over what seems to be a blast furnace in an 1859 painting of Sutherland Falls by Ambrose Andrews. The painting shows a structure that resembles a blast furnace in configuration, but on close inspection looks more like a structure made of wooden boards and beams that probably contained a waterwheel or turbine and transmitted power by means of a vertical shaft through the middle of the building above it. Inspection of the falls in 1979 indicated little similarity between the painting and the falls. No slag was found.

RU-IW13 Spud Leonard Forge (Proctor): Another forge in Proctor, operated by Spud Leonard, made picks and nails in addition to bar iron (Gale 1922:70). Nothing more can be found of Leonard's forge, although similarity in products prompts speculation that it could have been the Sutherland Falls Forge (RU-IW12) just described.

RU-217 Conant Furnace/Brandon Iron & Car Wheel Company/Howe Scale Company (Brandon): The presence of iron ore in Brandon was recorded in 1787 when a town meeting voted to build an ironworks if sufficient iron ore was found to supply it (Smith and Rann 1886:485). No record of construction follows, but the next year there was a request by the town to lease the ironworks site and its waterpower. It may have been near what was then called the School Falls. By 1790 a forge built there by O. Blake was bought by Simeon Avery, John Curtis, and James Sawyer. A few years later it was reported that Brandon had iron foundries and forges where good bar iron was being made (Graham 1797:83).

One of the first lessees of the forge, Penuel Child, operated it until about 1810, the forge at that time being sold to Roger and Harvey Fuller. The Fullers manufactured shovels at the forge from ore mined at Forest Dale, about two miles east of Brandon village. From their two factories, at Forest Dale and Brandon village, the Fullers' shovels found markets as far away as Boston (*Brandon* 1961:44).

John Conant, age 23, purchased half of the mills and waterpower in Brandon in 1796, soon after he arrived from his hometown of Ashburnham, Massachusetts. He quickly distinguished his presence by founding a congregation of Baptists and holding posts in church and local government. In 1809 he began his first of four terms in the state legislature and in 1841 was a member of the Electoral College that elected President William Henry Harrison (*Brandon* 1961:210-211). Yet for all his community involvement, Conant also found time to become an early industrial leader in his adopted town.

Conant and his father-in-law, Wait Broughton, worked together in their early years in Brandon building mills along the Neshobe River (*Brandon* 1961:44). All this time, a forge was operating nearby, making bar iron from ore that was mined near Forest Dale. About 1810, a major iron ore discovery occurred at Forest Dale that started a significant series of events (Thompson 1842:28; Smith and Rann 1886:490).

The forge changed hands and shovel making became one of the town's major industries. Conant and Broughton also made their first venture into the iron business, building a poorly designed furnace that failed to draw. There is reason to believe they may have planned this to be a blast furnace, but due to the defect converted it into a melting furnace that cast stoves from iron smelted at Pittsford furnace. Conant finally succeeded in putting a furnace into blast in 1820. On October 2, 1821, he advertised that he had on hand a variety of stoves, potash kettles, hollowware, and machinery.

Conant took his two sons, Chauncey W. and John A., into partnership in 1823, forming the company of John Conant & Sons. Cooking stoves remained the main product, while potash kettles, castings, and even some cannon were cast (Hitchcock et al. 1861:824). As recently as the 1960s one of the Conant cooking stoves—"the wonder of the farmer's kitchen" as Abby

John Conant's
FURNACE
is now in successful blast.

HE has a great variety of
STOVES
of the most approved patterns, now ready for sale.
—ALSO.—
A quantity of
Ornamental Parlour Stoves, of
Lanes' Pattern,
with *Brass Trimmings.*
—LIKEWISE,—
Pot-Ash Kettles,
Hollow Ware,
AND
Machinery.

The IRON needs no *recommendation* where his castings have been proved.

N. B. All kinds of Produce will be taken in payment for Ware, and a *liberal discount* made for CASH. ☞ Also, a few good Horses will be received in exchange for Stoves if offered within a few weeks.

Brandon, Sept. 10, 1821.   5tf

4-36. National Standard *October 2, 1821 (courtesy Sheldon Museum).*

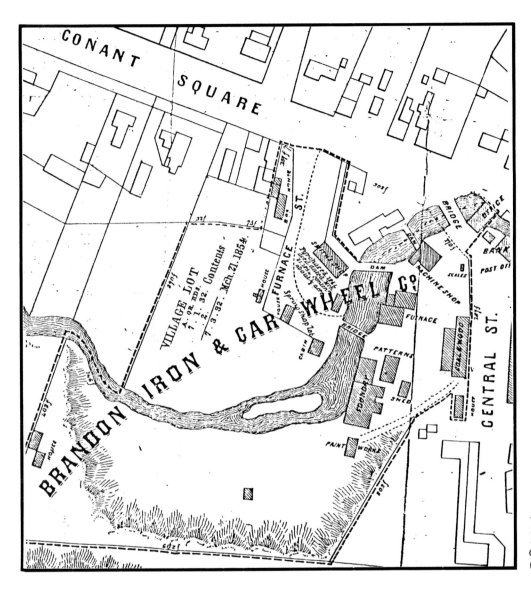

4-37. *Map of the furnace, foundry, and machine shops of the Brandon Iron & Car Wheel Company in Brandon* (Description *1854*).

Hemenway described them—was still being used in the kitchen of the Congregational parsonage in Brandon. It was described as having "a firebox, box oven, a large circular opening in the rear for griddle and wash boiler, and doors at each end" (*Brandon* 1961:46).

The furnace was enlarged in 1839 to keep up with the demand for stoves. Its 25-foot-diameter by 8-foot-wide waterwheel turned 2½ times a minute, driving a pair of 6½-foot-long by 30-inch-diameter blowing tubs (Lesley 1858:76). When John Conant retired in 1844 the company became C. W. & J. A. Conant, but by 1851 the demand for railroad iron displaced the stove business and the company was sold to the Brandon Iron & Car Wheel Company.

The car wheel company was incorporated in 1851 and eventually owned all the former Conant ironworks property at Brandon village in addition to the mines at Forest Dale. The company's 1851 report listed the furnace property in the center of the

village, the ore beds 2½ miles east, the Rutland Foundry next to the Rutland & Burlington Railroad at Rutland, and woodlands for making charcoal and lumber in Brandon, Goshen, Hancock, Ripton, and Chittenden. The company made railroad car wheel iron, car wheels, firebrick, paints, and paper clay, all at Brandon.

The 1852 report described a steam engine at the ore bed fueled by lignite, which was dug nearby. The steam engine raised 3,984 tons of ore that year. The 45½-acre ore-bed property consisted of a 15-horsepower team engine plus shafting, two sets of hoisting apparatus, two chain pumps, an ore-washing machine, and three mine shafts, one 80 feet deep and the others 120 feet deep. There were also four tenement houses.

The 7½-acre furnace property at the village included a store, a waterpowered machine shop, the blast furnace and waterwheel house, coal shed, foundry and waterwheel, furnace cabin, dwelling house, tenement boardinghouse, and barn.

When it ran, the blast furnace averaged about 6 tons of iron

4-38. *The Brandon Iron & Car Wheel Company foundry building at Brandon (Description 1854).*

Foreman	$700.00 per year
Fireman	$ 1.50 per day
Molder	$ 1.125 per day
Miner	$ 0.725 per day
Miner's helper	$ 1.00 per day
Woodcutters, teamsters, and ore washers	$ 0.77 to $1.00 per day

The Brandon Iron & Car Wheel Company foundries sold many railroad wheels to the Gilbert Company, which made railroad cars at Brandon in large buildings west of the tracks. Car shops also extended along the east side of Center Street, where other iron parts for the cars were made.

A part owner in the Brandon Iron & Car Wheel Company was Nathan Washburn of Connecticut, who invented successful improvements in railroad wheel designs and manufacturing processes, and owned several foundries in New England and New York in the 1850s that cast railroad car wheels. His design produced a wheel of great strength for the state of the industry

a day, but problems with the furnace lining and the blast machinery caused a number of stoppages. The Rutland Foundry property consisted of the foundry, machine shop, steam engine, office, storehouse and boardinghouse, plus tools, patterns, etc., on 2¾ acres of land near railroad tracks.

The 1853 report noted that 4,343 tons of ore were raised and the ore lots increased to 102½ acres. The furnace property at Brandon was then 7¾ acres and included two new tenements. Blast furnace repairs were made and in one 118-day run the furnace made 842 tons of iron, a 12 percent improvement over the previous year, while burning 35 bushels less of charcoal per day (*Description* 1854:3-41). Wages at the blast furnace were:

FOUNDRY & MACHINE SHOP. RUTLAND.

4-40. *The Brandon Iron & Car Wheel Company foundry at Rutland in 1854. Soon afterward, the entire works moved out of Brandon to Rutland, although the Brandon identification remained in the company name. Fire destroyed these buildings in 1856 (Description 1854).*

4-39. *The blast furnace of the Brandon Iron & Car Wheel Company at Brandon (Description 1854).*

of the time. Instead of cooling the wheels by immersing them in a pit of white sand, as was then the practice, Washburn cooled them slowly, annealing them in his specially designed ovens. But the year 1856 brought significant changes to the ironworking business at Brandon. A destructive January fire left the car wheel company in ruins (*Brandon* 1961:94).

The Gilbert shops moved to the Troy, New York area in 1857, eventually resulting in the large Gilbert & Company, which made heavy gun carriages during the Civil War. Railroad cars and trolleys were made at its New York shops at Green Island (near Cohoes) until 1893.

Associated with the Brandon works might have been the American Paper Car Wheel Works, which made railroad wheels at Pittsford, and the Hudson Paper Car Wheel Company which also manufactured this wheel at Hudson, New York. This unusual variety of railroad wheel was invented by Richard N. Allen and consisted of a paper disk built up by successive layers

122

of pasteboard and straw, pressed into hardboard, and dried. The board was then enclosed between two wrought-iron plates under hydraulic pressure and firmly secured with bolts. Last, a steel tire was bolted to the flange of the hub (Ellis 1878:167-168). This incredible design stood up under the vibration and stress of use better than previous cast-iron wheels, averaging 300,000 miles without a failure and adopted by the Pullman coaches for their long New York to Chicago run. (One of these "paper wheels" is on display at the National Museum of American History, Washington, D.C.)

After the fire in 1856, the company ceased making railroad wheels in favor of manufacturing paint and kaolin clay (used in fine porcelain and chinaware). Washburn relocated the car wheel part of the business to his foundries in Worcester, Massachusetts, and later to Troy and Schenectady, New York (Bishop vol. 3 1868:348).

The next year John Howe, Jr., another partner in the old car wheel company, purchased the patent rights of a weighing scale and began manufacturing Howe Scales (*Brandon* 1961:47). The Howe Scale Company moved into the property vacated by the car wheel business, but financial problems bankrupted the company in 1869. Under the name of the Brandon Manufacturing Company, it continued to manufacture scales until political pressure in 1877 moved it to Rutland, ending Brandon's connection with the heavy iron industry (*Brandon* 1961:52).

Few remains identifiable with an ironworks can be found along the base of the falls of the Neshobe where the works were. The usual scatter of slag and pieces of castings remain along the riverbank, in the roadbed alongside, and in parking areas behind buildings along the main street. Foundation stones of the foundry and blast furnace buildings that survived the transitions from the Conant stove to Brandon car wheels and finally to Howe Scales seem now to serve as river shoring and riprap. Even little Furnace Street no longer has a street name sign. A few buildings along the Neshobe date to the period of the ironworks: a ca.-1830 shop on the east side of the brook at Center Street and a ca.-1881 factory building on the opposite side of the brook. The red brick hydroelectric plant on the east bank, approximately where the Conant furnace might have been, dates to about 1912.

RU-41 Green Mountain Iron Company (Brandon): A few years before Conant built his blast furnace at Brandon village, iron making had commenced near an ore bed located at Forest Dale. John Smith's forge made iron here in 1810 with ore that came from beds dug locally and at Leicester Hollow (Smith and Rann 1886:514; *Brandon* 1961:48). A blast furnace went into operation about 1823 at Forest Dale, smelting ore that was mined a half-mile away (*Brandon* 1961:47). The major output of the furnace was pig iron, but a variety of ornamental iron such as statues, vases, and chairs were also cast. In 1845 the output of the furnace reached 1,200 tons, not including 800 stove castings (Kellogg Nov. 1897:293). This generally equaled the output of the Conant furnace at Brandon for the same approximate time period.

Some names connected with the Forest Dale furnace operations during this time were Stephen Smith of Leicester and Samuel Buell of Brandon in 1824; Royal Blake and Barzillai Davenport in 1827; and Royal Blake and (?) Hammond in 1836. Mr. Hammond might have been Charles Hammond, who

4-41. *A 1915 photo of the blast furnace at Forest Dale showing how it appeared before its casting arch was dynamited for building stone in the 1950s. Note the heating ovens on top (courtesy Vermont Division for Historic Preservation).*

a few years earlier was part owner of the Bennington Iron Company, or possibly Charles F. Hammond who operated ironworks at Crown Point, New York, in the 1840 period (or both?). An 1827 record mentioned the ore bed, furnace, and a coal house with 5,000 bushels of charcoal. The diary of DeWitt Clinton Clarke, a relative of J. A. Conant and partner in the Brandon works, mentioned an "Upper Furnace," called the Hammond and Blake Furnace, which was most likely the furnace at Forest Dale (*Brandon* 1961:46-47).

Brown hematite ore was mined at the foot of a sandy hill to the east of the furnace, and smelted to cast tools, fireplace furnishings, kettles, wagon equipment, and stoves. Even small cannon were cast; all sold throughout the Northeast as far away as Ohio. One shipment to the Chipman Point landing included a number of stoves, 59 axes, 12 draft chains weighing 2,400 pounds, and 5 two-horse wagons, plus an assortment of kettles, skillets, five dogs (heavy iron rods), flat irons, and spiders (cast-iron frying pans with legs), for a total value of over $1,000

4-42. An impressive 1915 view of the waterwheel and blowing machinery at Forest Dale (courtesy Vermont Division for Historic Preservation).

(*Brandon* 1961:48-49). At this time beef cost 5¢ a pound.

From original papers at the Vermont Historical Society Library (Jones VHS MSS21 #85), Alvin B. Jones was found to have hauled the following "to the lake" for Royal Blake:

Date	Long Tons Shipped
September 1844 to January 1845	9.93
May 1845 to June 1845	6.99
October 1845	2.31
October 1846 to November 1846	2.43
September 1847	0.98

The record also showed that Jones hauled 201 loads of flux for the furnace from April 1844 through January 1845, which gives additional information on production dates for the Forest Dale operations.

By 1854, when the Green Mountain Iron Company had been organized and the Forest Dale furnace works had been acquired, parlor stoves became the mainstay of production. The company enlarged the inside of the stack to operate it with anthracite coal instead of charcoal, but the experiment was apparently unsuccessful because the furnace shut down that same year. Anthracite fuel gave the iron different characteristics than charcoal, for example, a higher sulfur iron. Many ironworks throughout the country were trying to convert to coal at this time and

finding it difficult. More successful were those who completely razed and rebuilt their stack, redesigning it specifically to burn coal. Failure of the company, however, could have been for economic as well as technical reasons. The 1850s were difficult economic times and many ironworks throughout the country were being abandoned.

The Brandon Iron Company built three bloomery forges and a 1,500-pound trip-hammer in 1864, about 400 feet east of the furnace. Blast temperature at the time was 600°F (Neilson 1866:215). The blast was heated by ovens at the top of the stack, which were still visible in the early 1900s. These forges worked ore beds that were located a half-mile away and produced 85 tons of bar iron during their brief two months of life in the spring of 1865. The blast furnace, fired up for the first time since 1854, made 784 tons of cast iron (Neilson 1866:218). By year's end, however, the forges and furnace were quiet, never again to operate. These as well as other buildings of the Brandon Iron Company are located on the 1869 Beers map. A half-mile south, the map shows the shafts of the iron mines where ore was at that time being processed into paint pigment.

The blast furnace stands today, however precariously, in the midst of a growing underbrush. The three smaller, tuyere arches are still relatively intact with some internal breakdown. But the major damage is the breakdown from the north arch, the casting arch. This collapse was not due to natural deterioration but to intentional human destruction. While working on nearby

4-43. *The cavernous stone-lined waterwheel pit at Forest Dale, and the blast furnace standing in the background.*

Route 73 in the early 1950s, a highway construction company needed a source of rock. Told about the old, stone-built furnace, they dynamited it. Mr. Welland Horn, owner of the property, heard the blast and ran over in time to prevent further destruction (Welland Horn conversation with author, May 29, 1989). But the damage had already been done, and over the ensuing years, the forewall collapses bit by bit.

Adjacent to the stack are the stone-block mounts of the blowing tubs, and beyond is the deep, stone-lined waterwheel pit. The 100 old auto and truck tires that were at the bottom of it gave "wheel pit" a whole new meaning before they were removed in 1989. The headrace with its dozens of iron pipe hoops can be followed east to the Neshobe River. The dam site lies 100 to 200 feet farther upstream, marked by iron reinforcement rods deeply imbedded in the ledge.

All around the area and across Route 73, which parallels the former road on the north, the barest remains of cellar holes can be seen, vestiges of the community that at one time thrived about the works. Across the highway from the works stands the beautiful stone house built by Royal Blake, where hinges in the rear, wooden part of the house were made at the ironworks (*Brandon* 1961:157).

On the north side of Route 73, just uphill from the state highway shed, remains of what local residents claim was a "cup" or a casting furnace lie under roadside fill. It has also been described as having been a stone tower that was similar to the blast furnace but much shorter (*Brandon* 1961:48). Could it have been part of the stonework associated with the charging bridge? Whatever it is (was), it remains protectively buried for future study. John Smith's ca.-1800 forge was probably located about 100 yards northwest of the furnace stack, near where the present-day dirt road leads into the furnace property from the hollow.

4-44. *In 1991 the Vermont Division for Historic Preservation timbered up the archways and roofed the top of the Forest Dale stack.*

4-45. *Hardware inside the top of the Forest Dale furnace before it was roofed in early 1991 (courtesy Shelley Hight).*

4-46. *Resurgence tunnel of the Forest Dale stack, about 100 yards northeast of the wheel pit. The large, dark object in the foreground is a "bear."*

4-47. *Upper wall section of Forest Dale furnace, showing protruding stones that supported a building housing the top of the furnace.*

In 1974, a few years after the furnace and approximately 10 acres of furnace grounds were donated to the Vermont Division for Historic Preservation by Mr. and Mrs. Welland Horn, the furnace property was placed on the National Register for Historic Places through efforts of Chester Liebs (and some assistance by the author). The stack was fenced off following the continued deterioration of its north wall but, until recently, the division was unable to do much toward protecting the furnace grounds due to budget constraints. Trash along the stream reflects the numbers of campers who annually use the grounds at will; in the cellar hole of one of the works' tenements was a plastic sheet lean-to. Renewed interest in the furnace and property by the division led to significant activity at the furnace grounds in 1989 in the form of a week of technical recording. A year later another section of the stack, an approximately 10- by 12-foot-square piece of the in-wall, fell out the front of the stack, an ominous sign of the fragile nature of the structure. In late 1990, the division had the stack roofed and the archways timbered. By November 1991, an architect had been contracted and plans were drawn for the stabilization of the stack with an eye on eventual full restoration for an interpretive park.

It has often been difficult to distinguish between some historical references to ironworks at Brandon village and Forest Dale. Ore from the Forest Dale area was used in furnaces at both Forest Dale and Brandon, and corporate ownership and leasing of the mines sometimes overlapped the same time periods. They had similar names: Brandon Iron Company, Brandon Mining Company, and Brandon Iron & Car Wheel Company. DeWitt C. Clarke bought stock in the Brandon Iron Company in 1837, John A. Conant then being the manager. In 1841 the

4-48. *Ornate stove made by the "G.M. Iron Co."*

company ceased to be, appearing to be insolvent, inferring operations at the Brandon village. But at that time the works there were also known as John Conant & Sons, becoming C. W. & J. A. Conant in 1844.

At Forest Dale, the Brandon Iron Company reactivated the furnace in 1864 and built bloomery forges, producing cast and wrought iron. About the same time at Forest Dale the Brandon Mining Company was extracting kaolin and paint pigments from the ore beds nearby. Both are indicated on 1869 Beers maps. Did Conant have some connection with the Forest Dale works in the 1830s through the Brandon Iron Company? Was the Brandon Iron Company of the 1860s a return of the old company or a new company with the old name? Did, in fact, an iron-smelting blast furnace operate with the Howe Scale Company and later with the Brandon Manufacturing Company at Brandon village? Or, after 1856 when the Brandon Iron & Car Wheel Company ceased making car wheels, did the Brandon village works use pig iron made elsewhere, such as from Pittsford or Crown Point?

RU-IW14 Pittsfield Iron & Steel Co (Pittsfield): After the failure of the White River Iron Company (WN-IW01), Julius J. Saltery organized the Pittsfield Iron Ore Company, incorporated March 1880 at Hartford, Connecticut for the purpose of mining ore at Pittsfield and Chittenden (Hyzer 1954:132-133). With capital of about $2,500,000, buildings and machines for crushing and concentrating the ores were put in place and 1,400 acres of the defunct White River Iron Company property was bought. Roads were cut up and down the valley, connecting the mines and charcoal kilns with the main works, which were just over the town line in Chittenden. Eight hearths and one hammer made charcoal blooms, which were shipped out for making steel. The iron was "made by improved Catalan forges from magnetic ore existing in gneiss formation." Officers were William G. Bell, president, and J. Foster Clark, treasurer, of Boston; Julius J. Saltery, superintendent, of Pittsfield (*Directory* 1882:169). When completed, the works were expected to produce about 10 tons of blooms per day at a cost of $35 per ton (including freight) delivered to the railroad at Bethel. The blooms were to have been especially adapted for making a fine grade of steel by open-hearth furnace or for fine-tool crucible steel. The weekly payroll was $400 to $500 in 1881. That same year, the Pittsfield Iron & Steel Company, with Saltery as president, bought the White River Iron Company. French laborers were brought in from Canada in 1882, but a few months later the company shut down, changed hands, and the stockholders were left holding an empty bag. A more sane logging and lumbering operation succeeded in later years, connected by a four-mile railroad to the junction at Stockbridge (Davis and Hance 1976:92).

Inspection of surface remains of iron-mining operations up the Tweed River West Branch at Pittsfield in 1988 found only a cave-like hole in the side of a low cliff and a small stone foundation nearby (the mine is marked on the USGS topographic map). No hearth foundations or charcoal kilns were found nor are their locations known by a local historian.

ORANGE COUNTY

OR-IW01 Randolph Furnaces (Randolph): Ironworks are documented to have been operating in Randolph before 1800,

although no firm field or archival evidence of this has yet been found (Swank 1892:132-133). Two furnaces operated in the town in 1842; they could have been either foundry or blast-furnace variety (Thompson 1842:147). The town had two forges and a slitting mill 25 years later, however, supplied by ore mined in the vicinity (Bishop vol. 1 1868:528).

WINDSOR COUNTY

WN-FS14 Upper Falls Forge (Weathersfield): When an ironworks along the Black River burned sometime before 1792, Weathersfield's connection with the iron-making industry of Vermont ended. As early as 1786 an ironworks operated at what later came to be called the Upper Falls. That year Levie (also Levy, or Levi) Stevens sold his interest in the ironworks to Nathan Deane of Cavendish, the agreement mentioning "the new fire . . . cole House and ore houses and lot of land belonging to the works" (Hunter 1984:7). The "cole House" of course referred to a structure where charcoal was either made or stored; the ore houses stored iron ore. The mention of the "new fire" clearly indicated a bloomery forge operation, a "fire" then the common name for a bloomery hearth.

Information provided by Edith Hunter of Weathersfield placed the site of the forge along the north shore of the Black River, within a quarter-mile upstream of the covered bridge. An area up to a half-mile upstream of the covered bridge was inspected in 1985 without finding any ironworks artifact. No slag was found in the river or along the shore; no charcoal, burnt brick or stone, nor pieces of waste iron, flume, or ironworks foundations along the steep riverside embankments on either side of Route 131. The valley is quite narrow here, making a fine location for a dam, one of which stood from the 1830s to 1890s, giving the place its name, Upper Falls, and supporting a number of mills. Ruins of a mill exist on the southern shore, but any mill site on the northern shore anywhere near the river most certainly was destroyed by construction of Route 131. Slag that found its way into the Black River from the ironworks in the 1790s has most likely been thinly scattered by 200 years of water and ice action between Upper Falls and the Connecticut River.

WN-51 Tyson Furnace (Plymouth): In 1922 the Town School District of Windsor published an industrial history of Windsor, researched and written by Guy Hubbard. It was one of a number of social and economic essays and works written by Hubbard that delved into Windsor's heavy industries during the period between the two world wars. As part of his 1922 industrial history, he devoted an entire chapter to the subject of the ironworks at Tyson (Hubbard 1922:47-54), parts of which follow:

In the latter half of the 18th Century there flourished in Baltimore [Maryland] a wealthy Quaker family, the head of which—Mr. Isaac Tyson—was a merchant and owner of a line of fast "Baltimore Clippers" in the overseas trade. His son, Isaac Tyson, Jr., the greater part of whose long life was to be spent in the study of geology and in the practice of mining and smelting, was born in Baltimore, on October 1, 1792. He began his active career as Supercargo on one of his father's Clipper Ships, and as such it was his bad fortune to be wrecked, and his good fortune to be rescued, on the coast of the south of France.

4-49. *Former works office (left) of the Tyson Iron Company in Tyson.*

While waiting at Bordeaux for the Yankee Consul to arrange for his return passage to Baltimore, young Tyson visited a profitable mine where chrome yellow was being dug. He remembered having noticed a mineral like this during his rambles in the hills of Maryland, so upon returning to his native State he at once investigated the matter, and the result was that he discovered valuable deposits of chromate of iron at Bare Hills, Maryland and in Chester County, Pennsylvania. His father bought up these deposits and in the year 1816 they began the manufacture of chromate pigments, medicines and chemicals in a laboratory on Pratt Street in Baltimore. This proved to be a prosperous business, and in 1822 they removed to a much larger manufactory on Washington Avenue, mentioned by Bishop as one of the large industries of Baltimore. [Bishop was author of a history of American manufacturers in 1868; see Bibliography.]

On February 15, 1827, Isaac Tyson, Jr., patented a method of making copperas by smelting copper pyrites, and in 1829 extensive works were erected at Strafford, Vermont, for the application of this invention and for the production of copper.

In 1833 the younger Tyson sold out his interests in the Baltimore concern, in order to become manager of this new Vermont industry. . . .

In the fall of 1835 when Mr. Tyson, on horseback, was crossing the mountains at the headwaters of the Black River in Plymouth, Vermont, he chanced to notice outcroppings of what to his practiced eye appeared to be rich iron ore of the micaceous and black oxide variety. Early in the following spring he dispatched his confidential agent and mining expert, Mr. Martin of Strafford, to make a careful examination of the Plymouth region, and this gentleman not only located several rich ore beds, but also found near by plenty of limestone for flux, in the midst of forests where high grade charcoal for smelting could be easily and cheaply made—a combination as interesting to an Iron Master of those days as were the discovery of the joint coal and iron deposits of Pennsylvania and Alabama to those of later years. As a result of Mr. Martin's report, Mr. Tyson at once bought up the promising ore beds, the nearby lime quarries, and hun-

dreds of acres of the surrounding heavily forested mountain sides. . . .

On November 10, 1836, Mr. Isaac Tyson Jr., of Strafford, and Messrs. Thomas Emerson, Albert G. Hatch, and Jonas G. Dudley of Windsor, incorporated a company with the ambitious title, "Windsor and Plymouth Ascutney Iron Company," for the purpose of digging ore, and manufacturing and vending iron. . . . Tyson Furnace, like a typical Western mining town, had sprung up almost over night in the wilderness beside picturesque Echo Lake in Plymouth. Here in 1837, Mr. Tyson opened his "Hæmatite Mine" and in the fall of that year put his furnace in blast. . . .

The furnace was of the economical "hot blast" variety and was a handsome stone structure thirty-four feet high and thirty-two feet in diameter at the base, where it rested on three heavy arches. This stack was surmounted by a rounded cupola and a tall chimney. The stack was lined with fire brick and its inner sides sloped together toward the bottom like the inside of a lamp chimney so that the charge could settle freely. A strong tramway led from the bank back of the furnace to a roofed platform called the "top house" about the cupola, so that the carts of charcoal, limestone, and iron ore could be drawn to the top of the stack.

The charging was done by the "top man" through a door in the cupola, the charcoal being first thrown in from large flat flaring baskets upon a two-wheeled barrow. On top of this was placed a layer of broken limestone for flux, then followed the iron ore, dumped in from boxes with handles for convenience in lifting. Several such courses, or charges, four or five feet thick, were added until the stack was filled to the cupola floor.

The ordinary "charge" for the Tyson furnace was twelve bushels of charcoal, from eight to fourteen boxes (about one hundred pounds each) of iron ore, and two similar boxes of crushed limestone. The Plymouth ore contained fully fifty per cent of iron, and under favorable conditions the burning of one hundred bushels of charcoal produced one ton of iron. The blast was run night and day by two groups of men who worked on twelve-hour shifts, and from three to five

4-50. *The photo of Tyson furnace from which Myron Dimmick might have done his painting of the works about 1900 (compare with photo at beginning of chapter 1). The three furnace-like structures in right background are unidentified but could be charcoal or lime kilns (A.A. Baldwin photo; courtesy Barbara Chiolino).*

tons of iron were run off in twenty-four hours.

The "blowing engines" of the Tyson furnace consisted of a pair of enormous tub bellows, pumped by cranks fastened to the opposite sides of an overshot waterwheel, in a wheel house back of the Furnace. The air was delivered by a hundred foot wooden stave pipe fifteen inches in diameter, to a large wooden tank or equalizing reservoir beside the furnace building. From this the compressed air was conducted through a coil of iron pipe in a small heating furnace where it was raised to approximately the temperature of melting lead. This heated air was blown into the furnace through two water-cooled blast nozzles, or "tuyeres," two and a quarter inches in diameter. These entered at opposite sides of the stack, about four feet from the bottom.

The overshot wheel which operated the bellows was thirty-two feet in diameter and five and a half feet wide. It was provided with sixteen buckets, each of which would hold about a hundred gallons of water, which were filled at the top by a wooden flume, and the wheel revolved by the weight of the water, which was emptied out as the buckets approached the bottom. This flume was thirty inches wide and carried the water from the reservoir in the brook half a mile west of the furnace. When the water ran twelve inches deep in the flume the big wheel developed about sixty horse power.

The hub of the water wheel was an iron hooped log thirty inches in diameter, having wrought iron trunnions at each end to which were keyed the bellows cranks. The trunnions ran in wooden bearings and at first much trouble was caused by the friction of the heavy mechanism setting these blocks afire. Finally some rustic genius conceived the idea of drilling the bearing surfaces full of holes, driving hemlock knots endwise into these holes, and reboring the combination to a smooth bearing. These peculiar "oilless bearings" proved entirely effectual in solving this mechanical problem, as they ran for years with but little friction or wear. . . .

As described by the old residents thereabouts, Tyson Furnace, when in blast, was an awe inspiring sight. The bellows made a dismal groaning and creaking sound which, in damp weather could be heard three miles away, and the flames leaped twenty feet above the top of the stack with a roaring which made Echo Lake a realistic name. While the top man tested the height of the charge with a sort of an iron flail, adding new material as it settled, two furnace men stripped to the waist stood in the arches at the base of the furnace and peered in at the tuyeres to watch the progress of the smelting in order to control it properly. The molten iron gradually collected in the bottom of the furnace while the slag floated to the top and ran over a dam into a slag pit.

When time came to pour off, one of the furnace men would blow a horn, which was a signal for a gathering of the natives to see the molten metal rush forth into the "pig bed." The sight was especially stirring during the hours of darkness, when the flames and glow of the metal illuminated the whole neighborhood. The metal was released by drilling out a fire clay plug in the base of the furnace, and was shut off by an insertion of a fresh one, immediately baked in place.

The pig bed was an open sand mold under cover of a shed, and had a central channel leading from the outlet of the furnace, with basins the size of hundred pound pigs branching out from it.

Some of this pig iron was sold to other foundries, of which there were in olden times numerous ones of small size scattered about the country for supplying the local trade with stoves and hollowware. The sows, as the masses of iron in the central channel of the pig bed were called, and a considerable amount of pig iron, was remelted in a smaller cupola furnace in the Tyson Foundry. This was molded into all kinds of machinery castings, hollow ware and cooking utensils, and into "Parlor Fireplaces," with elevated ovens, which were extensively advertised by Mr. Tyson as an improvement over primitive fireplaces (then commonly used for cooking and heating) and widely sold in northern New England. Box stoves of the "Steamboat" variety were also made in large numbers and may still be found in use in the country districts of Vermont where wood is the popular fuel. One of the vivid recollections of the writer's [Hubbard's] father was his experience sometime about 1850 when as a boy of 14 he was driving a pair of horses attached to a wagon loaded with Steamboat Stoves from Tyson Furnace over the mountains to a store at Windsor. On a steep hill the horses ran away, but he managed to guide the crashing and banging load of stoves at full speed down the mountain until the horses tired themselves out. This was a frequent happening in those days of heavy freight teaming, yet the drivers usually managed to come out on the "top of the heap" in spite of the narrow rocky roads and their primitive wagons, with wheels held by linch pins on wooden axle trees.

The various kinds of ore found in Plymouth in apparently inexhaustible quantities, rendered the location one of the most favorable in the entire country, and as the iron produced by compounding the different ores was considered equal to the best foreign importations, Tyson Furnace was for many years one of the most important iron works in New England. For this reason, very complete accounts of it may be found in some of the older books on metallurgy, and from these accounts much of this information has been obtained.

The Tyson works in the heyday of their prosperity are described as comprising two blast furnaces for smelting and a cupola furnace for remelting, a wheel and bellows house, four charcoal houses, a saw mill, carpenter, pattern, machine and blacksmith shops, a large ware house and office building, a store, a tavern, two barns, two wagon sheds, and sixteen houses containing twenty-three tenements. As many as a hundred and seventy-five men were employed in good times, there being among others; twenty charcoal burners, twenty molders, two firemen, two top men, two plate brushers, one founder, one coal man, one ore picker, one ore roaster, six blacksmiths, ten miners, six teamsters, six farmers, three clerks, an agent and a manager. Others were employed as quarrymen, wood choppers, road builders, etc. The ordinary workmen received from $14 to $18 per month; ordinary molders $1.25 a day; first molders $1.50 a day; and foremen $500 a year. In 1840, six hundred tons of iron were produced at Tyson Furnace, which sold as pig iron at $35 per ton and as castings at from four to five cents per pound [$80 to $100 a ton]. The workmen were a mixed lot—French wood choppers from Canada, charcoal burners from the Black Forest in Germany, Irishmen and negroes. The Irishmen predominated and the remains of the collection of workmen's houses is called "Dublin" to this day.

Isaac Tyson, Jr., operated the Furnace continuously until 1855, when he retired from the business, and returned to Baltimore, where he died in November 25, 1861. The works were idle from 1855 until 1864, when on account of the demand for iron created by the Civil War, they were reopened by the Tyson Iron Company, a Boston corporation who purchased them from the Tyson estate. This concern furnished much of the iron used in construction of the "Monitors."

After the close of the Civil War, this company sold out to the Spathic Iron Company, a Hartford, Connecticut corporation manufacturing edge tools. This company controlled the only other bed of spathic ore then known to exist, this being in Connecticut. This company ran the Tyson Furnace and the Spathic Mine under a German iron master and instead of pig iron, they produced a product called "spiegeleisen" which they converted to cutlery steel at their Connecticut plant. The last blast was run in 1872. . . .

Today [1922] all that remains of "Tyson's Furnace" is the name of the scattered village, which is one of the beauty spots of Vermont; the old warehouse; traces of the flume and waterwheel; a few weather-beaten houses in the settlement of Dublin; an oil painting of the furnace made many years ago by Mr. Myron Dimmick (a workman at the furnace who became a landscape painter); and a few of the old employees over eighty years of age who prefer to end their days amidst these familiar haunts. The stacks have entirely disappeared and their site is occupied by a saw mill.

Plymouth recently has been much in the public eye as the birthplace of Vice President Coolidge, and his father is one of the old gentlemen who find the town still good enough for them.

When the writer [Hubbard] and others visited the village of Tyson sometime since for the purpose of digging up facts . . . rumors of the revival of the iron business began to fly thick and fast, and the villagers probably saw in imagination their beautiful valley darkened by clouds of smoke, and their peaceful mountain sides torn up by mining operations.

The only possibility of the revival of this extinct industry probably lies in the very "impurity" which caused the old-time iron masters so much annoyance by rendering their castings hard and brittle. I refer to the manganese, now extensively imported for use in making alloy steels, and which exists in great quantities in the abandoned ore beds of Plymouth. As this actually does furnish a possibility of revival I should have used the word dormant instead of extinct in referring to the present conditions. The old time iron masters of Plymouth were exceptionally highminded and public spirited gentlemen, so the people of that town have a good reason to regret their departure (Hubbard 1922:47-54).

In the preceding, Hubbard accounts for *two* blast furnaces during the "heyday of their prosperity," which is the only known reference to two blast furnaces at Tyson. The following 1864 geological report includes descriptions of a hot-air furnace and a cupola furnace. Hubbard might have mistaken reference to the hot-air furnace as being another blast furnace.

The furnace is a heavy stone stack 34 feet high to the tunnel head, with a cupola of six feet, is 32 feet diameter at base, and is in good working condition, and will be ready for a blast by the first of May. The tunnel head is 2¾ feet in diameter, boshes 8½ feet and slope 50 degrees, and lined with sandstone which is obtained near the works. The crucible, or hearth, is of sandstone, 20 inches on diameter at top and 15 at bottom. The tuyer [*sic*] arch is 8¾ feet wide 7 feet high. The main blast pipe is 15 inches diameter and 103 feet long, and is entirely new. The tuyers are 2¼ inches, the waterwheel is a new overshot, 30 feet diameter, with 5-feet buckets and 10-inch rim, made of wood, bolted and strapped with iron.

The cost of making [one ton of] pig iron is estimated as follows: –

130 bushels of charcoal	$ 7.80
2¼ tons of ore	$ 5.06
12 laborers	$ 3.00
1 iron master	$ .75
Flux	$ .08
Superintendence	$ .50
Contingencies	$ 1.00
Transportation to Boston, Springfield, or Albany	$ 5.25
Incidental expenses	$ .50
Cost on market	$23.94

This estimate is based upon the supposition that none of the material is now owned by the Company, instead of which there is now on hand and paid for more than 2000 thousand [*sic*] tons of ore, 100,000 bushels of charcoal, 200 cords of wood, 100 tons of castings and scrap iron, 50 tons of shot iron and 60 tons of flux. The capacity of the stack is 7 tons per day, but if its average yield should not exceed 6 tons, and if the price of iron should not exceed $60 per ton, we have a daily profit of $216, which would give a dividend of more than 3 per cent a month upon the whole capital stock, or over 36 per cent a year (*Geological Surveys* 1864:5-7).

(At Binney Cobb's foundry in English Mills, about 25 miles to the northeast, small machinery, fire doors, and grates were cast in the early 1800s [Dana 1887:69]. Cobb obtained pig iron from the blast furnace at Tyson [Warren Wood letter to author, Jan. 19, 1986]. No foundry remains or slag were found in a 1987 inspection of English Mills; no further information could be provided by Phyllis Cobb, current owner of the old Cobb homestead.)

Much of the technology of furnace operations at Plymouth came from Tyson's experiences and observations elsewhere. For example, he did much experimenting with sizes and shapes of furnaces and hearths for smelting copper at Strafford. He tried various fuel/flux/ore mixes, searching out improved hearth-lining materials. By the end of 1833 he had a copper-smelting blast furnace in operation using anthracite. The coal was boated down Lake Champlain and went over the mountains by wagon to Plymouth. He borrowed from what he observed at a furnace near Albany, New York, and made a new method of diverting some of the hot exhaust gas from the top of the furnace to preheat the blast.

Tyson pumped blast into his iron furnace at Plymouth at 1½ pounds per square inch. Magnetic ore from Lake Champlain was mixed with local ore and hematite from Tinmouth. The Tinmouth ore was hauled four miles by wagon to Wallingford, then by railroad 34 miles to Ludlow, finally the last few miles by wagon to the furnace. Local magnetite contained too much manganese to make it economical to use. Charcoal was hauled an average of three miles (Neilson 1866:220).

The 1855 map of Windsor County shows the furnace works, the furnace and flume, the line of workers' houses, and the schoolhouse opposite the furnace. The iron mine on Weaver Hill, a small iron ore bed near Plymouth Union, plus vast company-owned woodlands southwest of a small ore bed are depicted on the 1869 Beers map of Plymouth.

Hubbard's 1922 description of the area still describes it today. The District 12 schoolhouse stands up Dublin Road; the old works office is today a residence near Route 100. Next door, another old works structure is the little Tyson Library. Slag and other ironworks-related debris litter the stream down to beyond the highway. The Echo Lake Inn completes the transition from industrial to resort area. Dimmick's painting, referred to by Hubbard, is part of the Vermont Historical Society collection.

WN-IW01 White River Iron Company (Bethel): As a result of Julius J. Saltery of Boston's discovery of gold and magnetic iron ores at many places along the White River, the White River Iron Company was formed in 1878; Saltery appointed himself superintendent. The company purchased property in Chittenden, Bethel, and Pittsfield (possibly Stockbridge?) with plans to construct the reduction works at the junction of Locust Creek and the White River, about two miles west of Bethel village. Saltery worked out of his office at the nearby Locust Creek Hotel. Supposedly, the works consisted of a steam engine and boiler; shipments of hot-blast pipes, liquidizer, blowing apparatus, and steam hammer were en route. Washing and separator works were complete; foundations for the furnace and liquidizer were nearly ready. The concentrator castings had also arrived.

It was expected that the iron ore would yield 68 to 75 percent iron, adaptable to a high-grade steel. Two tons of magnetic iron sand were expected to produce a ton of iron blooms, fueled by about 150 bushels of charcoal. The magnetic sand was to be run through a concentrator and brought to the furnace by a car. Separation was to be by gravitation action of water, the heavy gold and iron settling out. Gold and iron were to be separated by the "California sluice process." The freed iron sand would be mixed with a measured amount of carbon (charcoal), hoisted to the deoxidizer (sinter) and remain for 24 hours under high heat until thoroughly deoxidized, and finally fed into the open-hearth furnace.

The operation failed two years later when it was discovered that the gold was not sufficient to pay expenses, let alone make a profit. And the iron ore was not in sufficient quantity of the quality needed to justify continued investment. The Edmunds estate at the mouth of Locust Creek was known as the "forge property" until 1917. That same year, F. G. Dutton bought the estate and used the last surviving forge building as a barn ("White River Iron Works . . ." *Herald and News* Aug. 9, 1917:10).

The site of the White River Iron Company, along Locust Creek between Route 107 and the White River, was inspected in 1986. No physical evidence remains to indicate the ironworks activity that took place here just over a century ago. Not even the barn remains today. Washouts, such as that in 1927, succeeded in erasing surface evidences of the industry. The Locust Creek Hotel still stands, today included on the National Register of Historic Places.

The Southern District

Visible ruins of four blast furnaces exist in Vermont's southern district. Of the other six blast furnace sites, half might be archeologically accessible while the other half are probably lost forever due to land development or other site disturbances. No bloomery ruin has been positively identified in the southern district to date although slag finds point to one possible site at Dover.

Major iron making in the the southern district occurred in the Bennington-Woodford-Shaftsbury area, where blast furnaces operated from about 1793 to 1873. Proximity to sources of good ore coupled with mountains of forests for charcoal and fast-running streams for waterpower made this area natural for the iron industry. Good roads also connected Bennington with Troy, New York, only 30 miles away.

Remains of the Bennington Iron Company are seen daily by alert drivers about two miles east of downtown Bennington. Just off the north side of Route 9 on private property stands one of the oldest blast-furnace stacks in New England and New York. And at Shaftsbury, after the demise of the Henry Burden & Sons furnace and works, the Eagle Square Company moved

in to occupy some of the furnace grounds. But most of what remains of that works is hidden by heavy overgrowth and fill, waiting to be rediscovered.

BENNINGTON COUNTY

BE-IW01 Bennington Forge (Bennington): In 1775 George Keith was mixing ore and making nails at a shop beside Mill Stream in Bennington (Niles 1912:446). This may have been nothing more than a blacksmith forge, since it was not uncommon for individuals to forge small items, mixing local ore with wrought iron to obtain desired metal characteristics. In 1786 he built a forge on land he leased from Eldred Dewey, located about a quarter-mile east of the Dewey house. This forge might have been the first bloomery in the Bennington area (Hemenway vol. 1 1867:137). That same year William Blodgett advertised for sale: "[The] best refined bar iron, per ton or less quantity . . . the above articles will be given for good coal, ore or Pot Metal delivered to the forge" (Spargo 1938:27).

Coal was a reference to charcoal; pot metal was scrap iron (burned-out iron pots). Although physical location of this forge site is not known, historian John Spargo placed it in the village somewhere east of Route 7. The 1796 vonSotzman map of

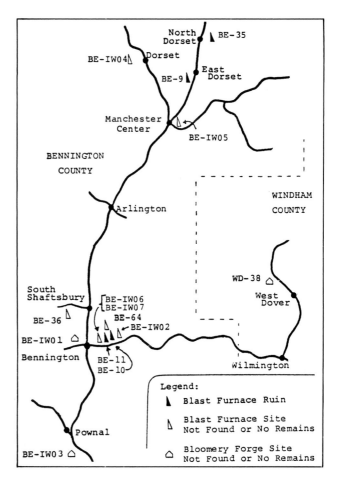

4-51. *Bennington and Windham County ironworks sites.*

Vermont indicated a forge with names "Blodgete" and "Deweys" at what appears to be the Walloomsac River near the middle of the village. This could have been at the millpond, northwest of the main village intersection (Routes 7 and 9). The 1856 Bennington County map shows this pond with a variety of mills, including two foundries immediately downstream of the pond. The area coincides closely with the location of Keith's 1786 forge. Both the Keith and Blodgett forges are given 1786 starting dates, so it is possible that Blodgett bought Keith's forge that year. Ironworks had a history of changing owners many times, sometimes many times in the same year, even cycling between the same pair of owners.

Inspection of the area just a few blocks from downtown Bennington, in 1983, resulted in finding pieces of slag in the brook next to the Catamount School, immediately above the North Street bridge. This would have been upstream from the millpond and came from foundries that operated in this area in the early 19th century.

BE-64 Fassett and Hathaway Furnace (Bennington): Benjamin Fassett and Simeon Hathaway began building a blast furnace in 1793 along what came to be Furnace Brook. The 1796 Whitelaw map indicates an ironworks along this brook, about 1½ miles south of the Shaftsbury town line where the brook enters a narrow valley. A 1797 advertisement stated the furnace "is now in blast . . . they will begin to cast this day" (Spargo 1938:8).

Spargo insists in his history of iron making that this is not the first furnace in Bennington. Since he does not differentiate between a blast furnace and a bloomery forge, he could be interpreted as stating that the first blast furnace in Bennington was Blodgett's, and thereby, the first in the state. But Blodgett advertised bar iron and Spargo did not seem to be aware of this crucial difference in his analysis of the word forge, reading into the word a definition that encompasses a process that produced both cast and wrought iron.

By 1799 the blast furnace of Fassett and Hathaway came under the control of Moses Sage, Paul Cornell, and Caleb Gifford who operated it until ore beds in nearby Shaftsbury became unprofitable to work. The blast furnace was probably abandoned in 1803, which was the year before Sage and his son-in-law Giles Olin commenced operation of a new blast furnace a mile east of the village.

During the summer of 1981, an attempt was made to locate the site of the 1793 blast furnace along Furnace Brook. Beginning at Kocher Drive, a trail of bits of slag was followed upstream in the brook, past the landfill, to the remains of a washed-out dam, about ¾ of a mile to the north. In addition to the slag ending here, finds of slag and charcoal were located among collapsed stone walls immediately southeast of the dam. Here also is what appears to have been an earthen charging ramp that led to the furnace top. More low stone walls, a possible flume, and the barest remains of a ca.-1835 east-west road can be found about 100 feet farther upstream. No slag was found upstream of the dam site; no firm remains of the actual blast furnace were found.

It is possible that the site was later used for a sawmill and both eventually destroyed beyond recognition by nearly 150 years of spring washouts and ice movement. It appears that the furnace was built within 30 feet of the streambed and with its hearth nearly level with the local water table, thus probably accounting for the unprofitable operations here.

BE-IW06 Sage and Olin Furnace (Bennington): After the abandonment of their works on Furnace Brook about 1803, Moses Sage and Giles Olin built a new blast furnace east of the village of Bennington, near some newly discovered ore beds in Woodford. The new Sage and Olin furnace, called Bennington Furnace, commenced operation in 1804 or 1805. Two advertisements by Sage in 1806 offered work for woodchoppers and the sale of potash kettles and hollowware at the Bennington Furnace (Spargo 1938:12). The business continued until 1811 when it was purchased by Thomas Trenor (Trainor?) who ran the furnace on and off until 1819, about which time he probably abandoned it. Spargo wrote that Sage moved to Pittsburgh, Pennsylvania in 1816, possibly building the first blast furnace there. (Research has failed to confirm either his being there or building the first furnace at Pittsburgh.) About 1821, the business was acquired by Seth Hunt who razed the Sage and Olin stack and built a new furnace. As far as is known, later blast furnaces at the site destroyed evidence of this earlier furnace.

BE-10, BE-11, and BE-IW07 Bennington Iron Company (Bennington): The year after he razed the Sage and Olin furnace, Seth Hunt built a new furnace (BE-10) to specialize in the production of pig iron. Soon after he sold the furnace to the Bennington Iron Company (1822). This is the easternmost of the two stacks standing at Furnace Grove off Route 9, east of the village. Partners of record were "Charles H. Hammond, Nathan Leavenworth and their associates and successors" (*Acts and Laws* 1825:87-88). Hammond and Leavenworth are supposed to have been "New York City men." (No connection has been found between this Hammond and those associated with the Crown Point Iron Company, New York, or the furnace at Forest Dale.) Hammond served as Town Representative from Bennington in 1826 although for some unusual reason he does not appear in census reports for 1820 or 1830. Spargo said that Leavenworth and Hammond were Yale College graduates and were "fast friends" before coming to Bennington, but he also believed Hammond did not reside in Bennington (Spargo 1938:19, 23). Charles Henry Hammond and Nathan Leavenworth did in fact graduate from Yale, Hammond in 1815 and Leavenworth in 1778, but the latter died in 1799. Another Charles Leavenworth graduated in 1815 with a Charles Henry Hammond; this Leavenworth died in 1829, C. H. Hammond died in 1850 (*Catalogus* 1886:16, 34).

The Bennington Iron Company also acquired the furnace property of Robinson and Lyman, just over the town line in Woodford. The company erected two more furnaces: a large one, the westernmost of the two at Furnace Grove (BE-11), and later a smaller one about 40 feet away and between the two stacks (BE-IW07). This smaller furnace was referred to as "the Pup." This might have been the cupola built in 1824 to remelt pig iron to cast hollowware and plows in addition to filling orders for custom work. (Two stoves cast here are at the Bennington Museum.) An 1831 advertisement noted the addition of a refining forge to the Bennington Iron Company whose two blast furnaces were then making seven tons of pig daily. This calculates to about 1,000 tons a year, about average for blast furnaces in New England at the time.

4-52. *Joseph Hinsdill's 1835 sketch of the Bennington Iron Company looking north from across Roaring Brook (foreground). A forge dam and four charcoal kilns are at left, two blast furnace structures behind the company office at center, and Nathan Leavenworth's house in the right background (courtesy Bennington Museum).*

The first hot blast in the country might have been introduced at Bennington in 1833 (Hodge May 12, 1849:290). Hot blast was the system of preheating the blast air, initially at 250°F, later to near 900°F. James Neilson of England patented the technique in 1828 and William Henry was experimenting with it in New Jersey in 1834 (Harte 1935:47).

A map of Bennington with some accompanying history and a panorama of the Bennington Iron Company was published by Joseph N. Hinsdill in 1835. The view was drawn from across the south bank of Roaring Brook looking north, viewing the forge, two blast furnaces, what appears to be four charcoal kilns, the business office, and other buildings. The year 1835 would seem to be somewhat early for the charcoal kilns, but Isaac Doolittle patented a charcoal kiln design at Bennington in 1829 (Hodge May 12, 1849:290).

The sketch is a valuable historical and archeological resource for interpreting this early-19th-century Vermont iron industry. It also shows buildings around the furnace stacks, nearly hiding the furnaces from view. These buildings housed the charging and casting operations in addition to blast-producing machinery.

The two furnaces were described in 1849 as being 40 feet high, one 9 and the other 9½ feet across the boshes. They were blown with hot blast, the blowing apparatus consisting of eight tub bellows (probably two pair per furnace). The tubs were

four feet in diameter with a 22-inch piston stroke working alternately, driven by a single waterwheel 22 feet in diameter with 12-foot-wide buckets (Hodge May 12, 1849:290).

The Bennington Iron Company failed in 1842 by which time the price of iron had fallen from $66 to $22 per ton. Creditors included banks and merchants in Bennington and in Albany and Troy, New York, plus unpaid employees and farmers. Much litigation followed with the property eventually being purchased by Captain Hamilton L. Shields who leased the furnace to Brock and Hinsdill for three years. They made enough profit to renew the lease another three years to 1853 but then lost it all. No part of the ironworks operated after that. In 1866, the last of the wooden portions of the three furnace stacks burned. "The Pup" collapsed later and was removed in 1890.

Two furnace stacks remain in varying states of collapse at Furnace Grove, off Vermont Route 9 in East Bennington. The large stack, the westernmost of the two, stood in good condition until the early 1900s when the south facade collapsed in the middle of the night with a roar that wakened nearby residents to fears of an earthquake (Van Santvoord 1958:92). It continues to crumble a few stones at a time each spring such that what remains is very unstable. The easternmost stack is the oldest standing blast furnace ruin in Vermont and it too is in poor condition. (The oldest standing furnace ruin in New England

4-53. *The Bennington Iron Company remains about 1880 with "the Pup" in between and the works office at left (courtesy Richard S. Allen).*

4-54. *View of the furnaces at East Bennington, just after collapse of "the Pup" between the two stacks. Note that track for the railroad and trolley had not yet been laid down (courtesy Tordis Isselhardt).*

4-55. *The ca.-1823 (left) and the 1822 (right) stacks about the 1890s, after collapse of "the Pup." Vibrations from the trolleys probably did much to accelerate collapse on the left stack (courtesy Richard S. Allen).*

4-56. *The old works office, now a private home at Furnace Grove in East Bennington; the 1822 stack in the background.*

might be the Falls Brook Furnace at Middleboro, Massachusetts, built in 1735 [David Ingram letter to author, Dec. 2, 1988].) North of the stack are the remains of the headrace and waterwheel pit where the blast machinery was found. The tailrace from this stack goes underground, then resurges beneath the west archway of the western stack. Atop the rise behind

this stack is a tall iron shaft made of pig iron, standing vertically in the yard.

In addition to these two furnace stacks, the old company business office still stands at the entrance to Furnace Grove, where account books were maintained for incoming and outgoing supplies and goods. Now a private residence, it looks

4-57. *Ruin of the 1822 stack, the easternmost of the two standing ruins at East Bennington.*

4-58. *Ruins of the ca.-1823 Bennington Iron Company blast furnace, the westernmost of the two standing stacks at Furnace Grove.*

much the same as it did in 1835, with the exception of the missing rooftop tower and bell. The ironmaster's house, built in 1824 and also appearing in Hinsdill's 1835 drawing, was in 1987 The Captain's House Bed and Breakfast, most likely named for Captain Shields.

BE-IW02 Woodford Furnace and Forge (Woodford): Robinson and Lyman were operating a forge and blast furnace at Woodford Hollow sometime around 1802. The works made pig iron, plows, and other agricultural implements. During the Jefferson administration (1800–1808), a large contract was filled, supplying a considerable number of anchors for U.S. Navy gunboats. The ore also came from Woodford, near the furnace and forges. The 1810 Whitelaw map, however, does not indicate this apparently large ironworks complex.

Following acquisition of these works by Hunt and Quimby (the proprietors of the nearby Bennington Furnace), the Woodford operations concentrated on supplying charcoal to the Bennington Iron Company for as long as the latter remained in business, although a forge at the Hollow continued to produce bar iron. Another forge was built later and was operated during the period of operation of the furnaces at East Bennington (Child 1880:26).

A search made in 1983 for the furnace was complicated by remains of a railroad, which was built through here in the 1870s and used slag as fill on which to lay the tracks. The slag might have come from either (or both) the East Bennington and the Woodford Hollow furnaces. There was also some 1950s highway realignment in the area. About 100 feet north of the old railroad bed, nearly on the Bennington-Woodford town line, a possible furnace site has been identified by the amount of slag and brick found there. Much domestic and construction debris is mixed with the slag and brick, further confusing the site. A system of raceways leads uphill from the site to a stream a quarter-mile to the northeast.

BE-IW03 Nobel's Forge (Pownal): The 1796 Whitelaw map indicates a forge in Pownal; it is further identified as "Nobles" on the 1810 map (see AD-339, Eagle Forge). The forge is shown along the Hoosic River at a point that appears to have been near today's Green Mountain Racetrack (dog racing). Comparison of today's Hoosic River bed to that in 1869 indicates the riverbed has shifted westward (Beers *Bennington* 1869:27). One curve of the river that passed east and under the railroad tracks in 1869 now runs alongside the western edge of the tracks. The bypassed river curve is an isolated swamp immediately east off Route 7. Similarly, the next downstream (north) mile of the river has shifted many hundreds of feet westward, hugging the base of the hill on that side of the valley.

Inspection of the river behind the racetrack grandstand in 1983 disclosed a six-foot-high riverbank on the eastern shore containing such mixed fill as contemporary asphalt, brick, concrete, conduit, and glass. This fill might have been dumped here as part of a Hoosic River flood control project, and has served as the base for the construction of the racetrack and its associated facilities. The site of Nobel's forge most likely is under much of this fill, near a small pond at the eastern edge of the racetrack where the riverbed was in 1796. It certainly has gone to the dogs.

BE-35 North Dorset Furnace/Allen Foundry (Dorset): This blast furnace operated at North Dorset as early as 1825, about

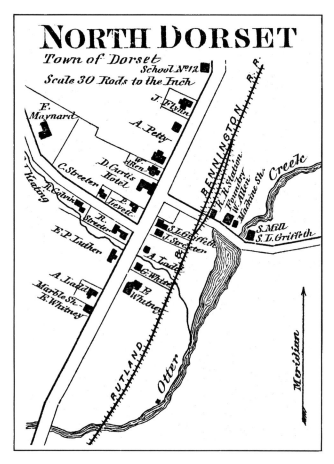

4-59. *The W. Allen Foundry and Machine Shop at North Dorset in 1869 (center-right). There was a small iron-making and ironworking community in the early to mid-19th century. Note the sawmill of Silas Griffith (Beers Bennington 1869:10).*

a half-mile northeast of today's Emerald Lake near the head of the Otter Creek. Daniel Curtis ran the furnace, initially obtaining his ore from a hematite bed some 10 miles away in Tinmouth (*Geological Surveys* 1864:14-15). The ore later came from a bed near East Dorset, and eventually from a mine Curtis opened about 100 feet from the furnace stack (Adams 1845:18).

The 12-foot-high stone mound remains of the collapsed furnace was found in 1981 in the Emerald Lake State Forest. Its outside masonry was probably used in the construction of a later foundry and/or sawmill, whose ruins are also nearby. The furnace bosh rises above the collapsed walls about it, and standing atop the fallen-in stack with its waist-high glazed walls, one feels as if standing atop a castle battlement. The bosh lining is a rough-lain, red-color sandstone. Similar stone has been seen in furnace ruins at East Dorset, Tinmouth, Clarendon, and Troy. Some pieces of red brick lie among the collapsed walls, but none appear burned. There is no visible evidence of an archway; the collapse is too complete. No binding rods or end plates were found.

North and west of the furnace ruin is an area 50 by 70 feet and many feet deep of slag. A hundred feet southwest of the ruin is the possible site of a mound-type charcoal-making area where chunks of charcoal were unearthed by modern heavy equipment in the process of working a logging road in 1983. Farther up the road are the barest remains of a headrace, starting at a small brook but ending downhill beneath more earth disturbances caused by the same logging operations. The raceway heads toward the blast furnace site, but does not appear to reach it. It may have been used for washing ore or to augment the sparse amount of water in Otter Creek.

Daniel Curtis was also owner of a once-famous hotel at North Dorset, succeeding his father, Elias, at the hotel. Elias was the son of Zachariah Curtis (buried at Pittsford) and a pioneer settler of Manchester who moved to Dorset in 1794. Daniel was in turn succeeded by son John (Aldrich 1889:420).

On the west side of the Otter Creek from the ruin of the North Dorset blast furnace are the remains of the Allen Foundry. Here are various foundation walls, more blast-furnace slag, and bits of iron. Much of the foundry site has been used as a dump for trees, brush, and trash. Remains of the foundry are visible for about 50 feet along the dirt road that passes through the area, east off Route 7. Foundry artifacts lie scattered from this road to about 120 feet north. The entire west bank of the creek at the foundry site is a 6- to 10-foot-high wall of slag. At the north end of this slag is glassy, blue furnace slag. Why the blast furnace slag is found on the opposite side of the creek from the actual furnace site is not known. Did an earlier blast furnace operate on this side?

Welcome Allen came to Dorset and purchased "the old foundry property" in 1847 or 1848. This infers that a foundry already existed there, possibly built and operated by one of the Curtis family that previously owned the nearby blast furnace. Wel-

come Allen operated the business until 1869 and was followed by his son, Florez R. Allen (Aldrich 1889:419). The foundry last appeared in *Walton's Register* in 1894.

The foundry produced various styles of cast-iron stoves (Curtis and Curtis 1974:15). The need for cast iron therefore made a next-door blast furnace practical, at least in the 1840–1850 period before railroads could supply large quantities of cheaper pig iron. The annual capacity of the blast furnace was reported in 1849 to be 1,000 tons, although the furnace was not at that time in blast (Hodge May 12, 1849:290). An 1856 report referenced it as one of "two blast furnaces in Dorset on the Western Vermont Railroad" (Lesley 1858:76).

The 1856 Bennington County map indicates "Allen's Machine Shop & Furnace" at two buildings, side by side but opposite the Otter Creek from today's blast furnace ruin. The Allen "furnace" on this map might have been a cupola for remelting pig iron for casting stoves and tools. The 1869 Beers map of Dorset indicates "Foundry W. Allen Machine Sh." adjacent to two buildings, directly across Otter Creek from S. L. Griffith's sawmill. Griffith was a major producer of lumber and charcoal at Mount Tabor from the 1870s to the early 1900s.

BE-IW04 Dorset Village Furnace (Dorset): Near Prentiss Pond on the western outskirts of Dorset village, a smelting furnace operated "at an early date," of which little else is known (Humphrey 1924:116). Remains may have been scattered or cannibalized for construction of a gristmill which later occupied the approximate site, per the 1869 Beers map of Dorset. The area was inspected in 1984 but no slag or ironworks artifacts were found. This early furnace might have been built a few hundred yards downstream of the pond to take advantage of

4-60. *The mound remains of the Curtis blast furnace along the upper reaches of the Otter Creek in North Dorset.*

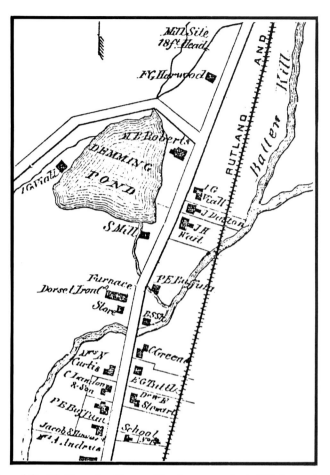

4-61. *The Dorset Iron Company blast furnace complex in 1869, just south of Deming Pond (Beers Bennington 1869:10).*

the narrowing little valley and permit a shorter dam than the present one.

BE-9 East Dorset Furnace (Dorset): About the time the North Dorset blast furnace closed, another was being built by Francis Draper around 1846 or 1849 near East Dorset at South Village (Neilson 1866:217; Child 1880:130). The furnace made iron for eight years, after which it lay idle. It was purchased by the Dorset Iron Company in 1864, possibly the result of demand for iron during the Civil War. By 1866, however, it was still out of blast but reported being in fair operating condition (Neilson 1866:220). The facilities included a 100-foot-long casting house made of marble. This building also contained a large waterwheel and a cupola furnace that was designed for casting stoves. Although the company owned 100 acres of woodland, there was some consideration given in 1866 to converting the stack to burn anthracite. It was still out of blast in 1874 and the following year Draper bought it back, expecting to repair it and resume smelting. He might have planned to use the furnace to support a cupola furnace he owned in Windsor. Draper also owned ore beds a mile north of the furnace. There is no evidence that the furnace was ever fired up after its initial shutdown in 1854.

The furnace stack was still standing in relatively poor condition in 1989. Cathy and Dennis Conroy, owners of the stack, live in the house directly next to it. They cleaned out the interior of the stack in 1987, finding many pieces of tools and a bar of pig iron in the process. During the next year, however, the stack resettled and new cracks opened in the outside walls, causing concern that the stack might collapse at any moment. Stabilizing efforts by the owners are now under way.

The stack can be seen east from Route 7A just south of Morse Hill Road during periods of thin foliage. Much of the bosh and hearth lining is missing, but enough remains intact to see that the lining was of stone rather than firebrick. The front (east) archway is of stone block construction; the south

4-62. *Blast furnace and foundry at East Dorset in the 1890s. The foundry was built of marble; only foundations remain (courtesy Cathy and Dennis Conroy).*

4-63. *The East Dorset stack at South Village in 1991, next door to the owners.*

4-64. *A piece of pig iron (center) found inside the East Dorset stack while it was being cleaned out by the owners.*

4-65. Details of the hearth at East Dorset after loose breakdown had been removed.

and north archways have become blocked with stones from the collapsed wall behind the stack. There does not appear to have been a west archway.

The hint of a road can be seen behind the stack leading to the top where a charging platform once stood. The stone embankment wall has collapsed against the back wall of the furnace so that one can now walk from the charging hill to the furnace edge and look directly down into the furnace interior. Some charcoal has been found on the charging hill, probably remains of coal sheds that stood here. Slag from the furnace litters the area and can be found as far away as in the stream under the highway bridge, just to the south.

The forge pond still remains, 100 yards north of the furnace. No trace of the flume that carried water to power the furnace bellows is visible today. All surface evidence was removed by a sawmill that operated later at the pond outlet, and by gravel quarrying in the 1940s just north of the furnace. Foundation remains of the casting house were found in the thick brush adjacent to the stack.

BE-IW05 Factory Point Furnace (Manchester): An 1828 petition for a post office at the "North Village in Manchester" (later Factory Point; now Manchester Center) described the community, which contained "more than thirty families, three retail stores, two tanneries, one Blast Furnace. two woolen factories, and one distillery, all in actual operation besides shoe makers, cabinet and chair makers, blacksmith and other merchants" (Bigelow and Otis 1961:101).

This furnace was also probably that which Harry Whipple of Manchester knew about. Whipple, who delved into local history, had some handwritten papers dated 1829 that discussed "iron furnaces" here. In 1955, it was stated that he could identify the exact spot where the "iron furnaces" (more than one?) were located (Anna B. Buck letter to Richard S. Allen, July 8, 1955). Visits to the local library and research at historical society

archives have failed, however, to locate these papers.

The furnace might have gotten ore from an iron mine at Lye Brook, which supplied ore to an iron company in the lower Hudson River Valley a few years later. There was also an iron foundry at the Center, which used scrap iron (Bigelow and Otis 1961:152). No physical remains of the mine or foundry have been found.

During many summer weekends in 1981, all sides of the (then) Route 7 and 30/11 junction were closely inspected, including the streambed in the proximity of the marble bridge in Manchester Center. Fortunately, the sluice gate at the dam was open that summer and the bottom of what is usually a deep millpond was accessible for inspection. On this bottom, downstream of the marble bridge, many bits of blue slag were found. A few larger, walnut-size pieces were found downstream of the dam and the falls. This would normally indicate the former presence of a blast furnace in the vicinity. The upstream trail of slag ended in parking lot fill immediately northeast of the bridge. The slag in the stream had washed out either from the parking lot or from the fill used to raise the approaches to the bridge many years ago. Inspection of the stream for 100 yards upstream of the bridge netted no further slag finds. Slag associated with charcoal, bits of rusted iron, an industrial-size iron-toothed gear, and other unidentified domestic and industrial hardware were found one day in 1987 eroding out of the high embankment behind the Sirloin Saloon Restaurant, about 700 feet east of the bridge.

A succession of bridges existed at the Center, starting with a wooden bridge, an iron bridge in 1884, and finally the present marble bridge in 1912, which was widened in 1942 (Bigelow and Otis 1961:20-22). Each bridge was built a little higher over the creek than its predecessor, requiring its approaches to likewise be raised. It is possible that slag from a nearby blast furnace was in part used as fill under these approaches. It was not an uncommon industry practice to use slag for fill, or mixed with asphalt or cement as a filler.

In a short paper published in 1953 on the subject of ironworks in Vermont, then State Geologist Elbridge Jacobs included in the list of towns and furnaces "Manchester, 1821" (Jacobs 1953:130). Jacobs' paper referenced a "manuscript" supplied to him by Charles R. Harte (see chapter 4, "Study Methodology"). According to Harte, if you traveled up Route 7 (today's Route 7A), you would find only the "merest trace" of the Manchester stack (Charles R. Harte letter to Richard S. Allen, April 5, 1955).

There were also lime kilns in Manchester, which have nothing to do with ironworks, but it does offer a possible explanation for seeing "blast furnaces" in the town in the 1950s (see chapter 8). Lime kilns are another type of furnace whose ruins are sometimes mistaken for iron furnaces. One kiln stood at a place known as Purdy Hill (Purdyville), about two miles south of Manchester Village, which may be one answer to Harte's "merest traces of a stack up Route 7" in Manchester (if in fact Harte ever went to Manchester to see the remains in person, or was told this secondhand).

BE-36 Burden Furnace (Shaftsbury): On April 30, 1827, the *Vermont Gazette* contained an advertisement for the firm of Douglas & Bangs, offering for sale at their Shaftsbury furnace cast-iron plows and castings of any size (Spargo 1938:21). This might have been a cupola furnace, operated by Norman Douglas and Rufus Bangs, both involved in the manufacture of carpenters' squares in Shaftsbury before the Civil War.

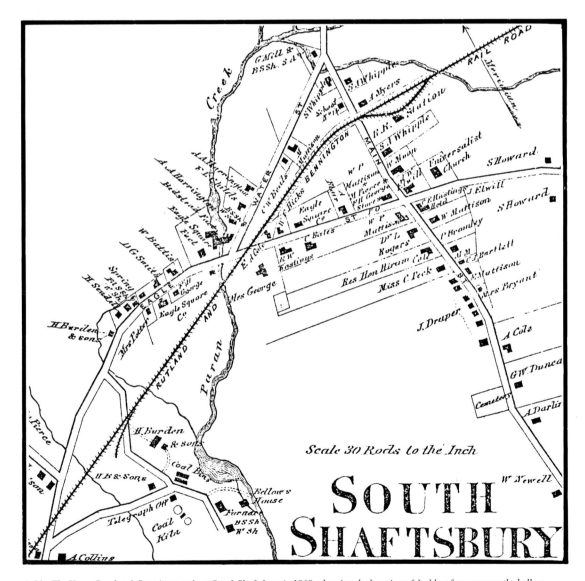

4-66. *The Henry Burden & Sons ironworks at South Shaftsbury in 1869, showing the location of the blast furnace near the bellows house along a flume parallel to Paran Creek. Only stone and concrete foundations and walls and scattered slag and brick in an area of heavy brush known locally as the furnace grounds remain today to mark the site* (Beers *Bennington 1869:21*).

A blast furnace was, however, built in Shaftsbury in 1863 by Henry Burden & Sons of Troy, New York. It was located west of today's village of South Shaftsbury on Paran Creek. Ore was dug locally and in Bennington. Pig iron from the furnace was shipped to the Burden foundries and to mills along the Hudson River at Troy, where it was used to make railroad spikes, horseshoes, stove castings, and machinery. The 1869 Beers map of Shaftsbury shows the works contained charcoal kilns, coal sheds, bellows house, and buildings that were residences and offices. Production of pig iron was 149 tons in 1863, 1,602 tons in 1864, and 2,315 tons in 1865, the Civil War years. The furnace was 28 feet high by 10 feet across the bosh. The hot blast was driven by an overshot waterwheel by means of two 30-inch-diameter blowing cylinders placed directly over the waterwheel. The blast of 1¼ pounds per square inch entered the furnace through two 4-inch-diameter tuyeres. The furnace consumed 210,160 bushels of charcoal and 3,779 tons of ore in 1864 (Neilson 1866:218-220).

The principal source of ore for the works was an area near the border with New York State about five miles southwest of the furnace. The mine has been variously called the Burden Iron Works and the Burden Iron Company. The ore was transported to North Bennington where it was washed in mills along the Paran Creek.

After the Civil War, Burden leased the works to Troy, New York stove manufacturer George W. Swett who operated it until the business panic of 1873 (Levin 1978:50). At that time the furnace capacity was 3,000 tons a year, making it the largest-capacity blast furnace ever fired in Vermont. Swett continued ownership of the works until 1877, hoping for better times that did not return (*Walton's* 1877:141).

The stack and buildings were razed sometime before 1900. The field of slag and bricks became slowly overgrown and by 1955 the burnt mound that marked the furnace base was barely discernible (Richard S. Allen ca.-1955 note to author, August 1979). An inspection of the furnace grounds was made in 1979 and only the usual slag, pieces of brick, and the dam could be found. Heavy vegetation kept the location of the burnt mound completely hidden from sight.

WINDHAM COUNTY

WD-38 Somerset Forge (Dover): The Somerset Forge was built in 1820 by the Trainor Mining Company, possibly by the same Thomas Trenor who ran the old 1804 Sage and Olin blast furnace from 1811 to 1819 before moving to Somerset (Hemenway vol. 5 1891:350). The forge and mine were in a part of the town of Somerset that later became part of the town of Wilmington and is today the western part of the town of Dover. The October 17, 1826 *Vermont Gazette* noted in an editorial that bar iron made at the Somerset Forge was being sold to a machine shop in Bennington. The forge was apparently competing directly with the local Bennington Iron Company's forges. The costs of transporting the heavy bars over mountains to Bennington and to Troy, New York eventually forced the forge to close (Spargo 1938:22). A tannery was built on the site of the forge, which operated to 1861. The tannery was demolished in 1867 and replaced with a sawmill (Kull 1961:3-4). The 1856 Windham County map locates the tannery where the old road

to Somerset crosses the brook, about two miles northwest of West Dover.

Extensive remains of a high, long stone dam that probably powered the sawmill (and maybe the tannery before it) were found here in 1984. Much slag and charcoal were also found along the stream between the dam and the road, betraying the approximate site of the forge on ground disturbed by later industrial activity.

Ore for the forge came from iron mines found in 1984 about two miles northwest on the property of the former Carinthia Ski Area. After failure of the forge, the mines were reworked by some New York businessmen in 1832. They also abandoned the mines after spending much money and effort (see chapter 3).

Note that heavy clothes-pressing irons marked DOVER seen at antique shops or used in homes as doorstops were not made at Dover, Vermont, but most likely at the Dover Furnace in New Jersey.

Summary of Results

Forty-three ironworks sites were reported to the State Archeologist during the 1978–1990 period of the overall statewide IA study and are now part of the State Archeological Inventory. Five other sites have been reported to the State Archeologist in the Field Site (FS) category. Inconclusive or no positive surface evidence was found at these sites, but further study might determine them to have potential archeological value. Archival and field work continues at 51 more sites in the work-in-progress (IW) category. The total number of ironworks sites studied is 99 at this writing. Ironworks include blast furnaces, bloomery forges, and foundries. While some ironworks sites contained one or more of these, other sites contained as many as all three.

A breakdown of the results and distribution of the sites and remains by county is presented in table 4-2. Ruins/remains include standing or partially collapsed ruins, mound remains, or any visible, identifiable surface evidence such as slag, bits of charcoal, or pieces of brick. As the table indicates, a majority of the ironworks were found in Addison, Bennington, and Rutland counties. Although the study identified no ironworks

Table 4-2. Summary of Ironworks Sites and Remains

County	Sites	Blast Furnace Ruins/Remains	Bloomery Forge Ruins/Remains	Foundry Ruins/Remains
Addison	32	3	10	4
Bennington	13	6		1
Caledonia	2			
Chittenden	7		2	
Franklin	7	2		
Grand Isle	1			
Lamoille	1			
Orange	1			
Orleans	2	1		
Rutland	27	9	5	
Washington	2			
Windham	1		1	
Windsor	3	1		
Total:	99	22	18	5

in Essex County, many early foundries are known to have operated there.

The sites of 36 blast furnaces and 66 bloomery forges were researched. Furnace ruins or remains were found at 22 sites (61 percent) while forge remains were found at 18 sites (27 percent). This discrepancy is probably due to a forge's ruin being smaller and easier to raze than a furnace's towering and imposing bulk. Of the 22 blast furnace ruins/remains, 3 were found to be wholly or substantially standing, 6 were partially standing, 3 were mound remains, and 10 had only trace surface remains. Except for a partially standing blast furnace ruin at Troy, the 12 furnace ruins and remains were found along the western slopes of the Green Mountains or in the Champlain Valley. Bennington and Rutland counties account for the most blast furnace ruins; those in better condition are at East Bennington (two), East Dorset, Pittsford, and Forest Dale. All furnace sites are private property except those at North Dorset (Emerald Lake State Forest) and Forest Dale (Vermont Division for Historic Preservation). Table 4-3 shows the distribution of blast furnace ruins and remains by county.

Of the 66 bloomery forge sites researched, only 18 sites yielded any surface evidence. No field evidence was found at 32 sites and 16 more sites have eluded attempts at discovery. Almost all forge sites researched were along the western slopes of the Green Mountains or in the Champlain Valley. Many more operated at an early time west of the Green Mountains and in the Connecticut River Valley; only those at Calais, St. Johnsbury, Cady's Falls (Morristown), and Weathersfield are included in this study. Table 4-4 shows distribution of bloomery forge ruins and remains by county.

Table 4-3. Distribution of Blast Furnace Ruins or Remains

County	Fully Standing Ruins	Partially Standing Ruins	Mound Remains	Trace* Remains	No Field Evidence	Total
Addison				3	2	5
Bennington	1	2	1	2	5	11
Caledonia					1	1
Franklin			1	1	2	4
Orange					1	1
Orleans		1				1
Rutland	2	3	1	3	2	11
Washington					1	1
Windsor				1		1
Total:	3	6	3	10	14	36

*Slag finds only.

Fifteen foundries were also researched although this category of ironworks was not a major thrust of the study. Thirteen foundries were identified through archival and field work to be integral parts of blast furnace and bloomery forge sites. They were researched along with the other ironworks components of these sites and were included with their associated furnace or forge site reports. Two foundry sites not directly associated with furnace or forge sites were researched and included in the study because of their proximity to other ironworks, the amount of archival material found, and the wealth of their field remains.

4-67. *Alluded to be a scene at Burden's iron mine in western Bennington, this 1865 painting by I. Sackett is a romanticized view of the Burden Iron Works at South Shaftsbury, showing the blast furnace and its top oven under the tall, smoking chimney (courtesy Bennington Museum).*

These two were assigned their own site numbers and reported individually. Additional foundries associated with 19th-century stove manufacture included in chapter 2 (table 2-1) are not included in the table 4-2 foundry category.

Almost all ironworks ruins were found to be extremely fragile. Walls of fully and partially standing blast furnaces can collapse without warning on anyone exploring them, crushing a person beneath tons of rock and brick. These stone ruins are especially precarious in springtime when the melting winter ice can cause the collapse of numbers of large, heavy stones and possibly whole sections of the wall. Illegal trespass can complicate attempts to recover medical expenses from injuries. Legal action can also be brought against those who vandalize archeological sites. Those sites on public property are protected by a variety of state and federal regulations. Both the state of Vermont and the federal government actively prosecute violations of historic preservation laws.

Table 4-4. Distribution of Bloomery Forge Ruins and Remains

County	Ruins/Remains	Trace* Remains	No Field Evidence	Unsure of Location	Total
Addison	3	7	15	2	27
Bennington			2	2	4
Caledonia			1		1
Chittenden		2	4	1	7
Franklin			2	1	3
Grand Isle				1	1
Lamoille			1		1
Orleans			1		1
Rutland		5	6	6	17
Washington				1	1
Windham		1			1
Windsor			1	1	2
Total:	3	15	32	16	66

*Slag finds only.

Three conical-type charcoal kilns that supposedly operated somewhere in Stamford. Note bottom sections made of stone and upper sections of brick; the vaulted top is probably brick. These kilns are claimed to be those near the Haskins mill, but appear more like the remains of kilns found up Crazy John Stream (courtesy Stamford Community Library).

Chapter 5
Historical Overview of Charcoal Making

The Charcoal-Making Process

Whereas iron mining was more or less connected to a blast furnace or bloomery forge, charcoal making was not. The iron industry, not only in Vermont but in neighboring New York and Massachusetts, did in fact consume much of the charcoal made in this state. Much charcoal also found markets in the copper-smelting operations at Strafford and Vershire, in iron and brass foundries that dealt with metals requiring special qualities, and also in glass foundries.

Charcoal was used because it is nearly 100 percent pure carbon and burns hotter than wood. There are other reasons why the ancients chose charcoal over traditional fuels (wood and baked dung, for example), but to understand why, exactly what happens during the smelting process must be understood:

> Combustion is an oxidation process. That is, oxygen must combine with the carbon, hydrogen, and hydrocarbons of which all fuels are made in order for the fuel to burn. In many pyrotechnological processes, such as ceramic production and metallurgy, the atmosphere in which combustion occurs is critical. There are two extremes. We speak of a reducing atmosphere when oxygen is insufficient for complete combustion; we speak of an oxidizing atmosphere when the draft in a furnace is strong enough to provide more air than necessary for the fuel to burn. The excess oxygen will combine with any other suitable substance it finds, for example, the metal being smelted.
>
> Roasting in an open container over a wood fire is an oxidizing process. The aim is to drive off the sulfides or other impurities in the ore and replace them with oxides. However, the problem in smelting is one of reduction. The aim is to *remove* oxygen from [ore]-bearing compounds, not add more. [Closing] the draft would create a reducing atmosphere, but it would also probably lower the furnace temperature below the point where smelting takes place. There is, fortunately, an alternative. Instead of closing the draft, a reducing fuel can be used, and that is precisely where charcoal comes in. Unlike wood, charcoal is composed largely of pure carbon, the other elements having been burned off in the charring process. It produces quantities of carbon monoxide gas when burned and creates an oxygen-starved atmosphere (Horne 1982:7-8).

Exactly when in history charcoal making (also called coaling) started is not known. Charcoal sometimes results from incomplete burning of wood in a fireplace. In reburning it, ancient man might have noticed that the charcoal emitted no smoke and burned hotter—an obvious improvement over burning wood. It was probably trial and error that resulted in the use of charcoal for smelting ores. Feeding charcoal into the primitive forge, early humans knew nothing about chemistry, oxidation, or oxygen-hungry atmospheres.

Even the ash of the charcoal was a desirable element in making iron due to its fluxing qualities. Mineral coal was ex-perimented with and tried in iron furnaces many times through the ages, but it contained too many impurities that adversely affected the quality of the metal reduced in the furnace. Until 1735, when Abraham Darby successfully coked coal in his furnace at Coalbrookdale, England, the iron industry fueled its furnaces and bloomeries with charcoal.

Charcoal making in Vermont descended from a long history of the industry that reaches into ancient time. Charcoal was made by the reduction of timber, and Vermont, like most of New England and New York at the time, abounded in what were once considered to be boundless forests. Charcoal was cheap and easy to make (as long as the forests remained boundless) and being light in weight, large quantities of it could be transported great distances with moderate effort. Since most early ironworks were built next to good running streams, they were also usually situated in or near a good stand of forest. Thus the distance and time was small between chopping trees, charring the wood, and delivering the charcoal to the works in the very early days of the industry.

Only live trees were cut for making charcoal, and they were best cut in winter while the sap was held in the roots. This reduced the amount of pitch that had to be burned off and increased the quality of the charcoal. It also reduced the weight of the logs, lessening the woodchoppers' efforts. In addition to stimulating woodchoppers to work to keep warm, the cold winter snows eased the transportation of heavy loads of wood by animal-drawn sleigh. Leaves, small branches, and sometimes the bark were stripped away, making more efficient use of the space in the kiln for more solid pieces of wood. The wood was cut into exactly 4-foot lengths. Diameter was not considered of much importance except that it be as uniform as possible. Very large pieces were split.

At 17th-century Saugus, Massachusetts, woodchoppers for the ironworks were prisoners brought by England from Scotland for that specific purpose (Clarke 1968:17). During the colonial and post-colonial period, slaves chopped wood at southern ironworks. By the Vermont ironworks era, woodchopping for the charcoal industry provided off-season work for farmers, some of whom periodically harvested stands from their own wood lots. Woodchopping also provided employment for ironworkers who might otherwise be unemployed during winter shutdown periods due to frozen, ice-covered waterwheels.

The price paid per cord for woodcutting varied with place and time. A woodchopper in Vermont was considered making good wages at 25¢ per cord, while the chopper in Missouri thought double that was still poor compensation. Cutting saplings and crooked timber cost somewhat more. Tall timber one to two feet in diameter were more profitable to cut. Hardened wood, maple, sycamore, and knotty timber were more expensive to cut than oak, beech, hickory, and pine. Hillsides were cleared with more difficulty than level ground and demanded higher wages.

A good woodchopper was expected to average three cords

Vol. I. Oeconomie rustique, Charbon de Bois, Pl. I.

5-1. *Charcoal making in Europe during the mid-1700s. The upper sketch shows the four stages of ground preparation for the mound, then the laying up of the cordwood. Note the collier's cabin and stacks of cordwood in the background. The lower sketch shows the mound in operation with stages of settling and, finally, to the right-center, a mound of charcoal (Diderot 1763: plates 24 and 25; courtesy Dover Publications).*

Vol. I, Oeconomie rustique, Charbon de Bois, Pl. II.

a day, a cord being a stack of logs 4 feet wide and high by 8 feet long, but a great deal of deception was practiced by the choppers. They cut the wood too short, laid up the wood in crooked and hard-to-measure rows, did not pile the wood tight, or set the cords on hidden rocks and stumps. An acre contained an average of 30 cords of wood and the price of wood in the 1850s was 5¢ to 10¢ a cord (Overman 1850:84-85). Ten years later, at Tyson furnace, good hardwood suitable for making charcoal delivered at the furnace cost $2.00 to $2.25 per cord (*Geological Surveys* 1864:13).

Some woodchoppers were expected to pile the wood in round piles ready for coaling. Wood was stacked on end, each piece being the standard 4 feet long. The pile was tighter at the top than the bottom (the pieces of wood leaned toward the center of the pile as they were stacked), so the measurement of the pile was made at the top. Capen Leonard of Chittenden published a small pamphlet in 1848 which contained a complex formula for calculating how much wood was in a pile: "Multiply together half the diameter and half the circumference, divide the product by 32 (if the wood be four feet in length), and the quotient will be the number of cords" (Leonard 1848:3). A table in the booklet that translated piles of wood with circumferences from 20 to 160 feet into cords of wood made everything much easier for the collier. It took much of the guesswork out of the problem and bypassed the formula. In the table, for a typical 4-foot-high woodpile measuring 30 feet in diameter (94 feet in circumference) the yield was 22 cords.

By the 1850s, special attention to analyzing the results of charring various species of wood resulted in a number of interesting conclusions. Of greatest importance to the ironmaster was the specific gravity of various kinds of wood. Hardwood weighs more than softwood and was preferred by blast furnace operations over softwood. Bloomeries preferred charcoal made from softwood. Since the quality of the iron produced in a blast furnace was limited by the height of the stack (for better draft), this in turn was limited by the crushing resistance of the charcoal. A successful iron production was possible only where the hardest woods were used, resulting in the hardest and heaviest charcoal.

The higher the specific gravity, the more dense the charcoal, and therefore the less tendency for the charcoal to crumble in the blast furnace. Dense charcoal maintained air spaces around itself and allowed for more efficient combustion. Compare the specific gravity of some samples of wood (where water = 1.0000) after the wood had been kiln-dried (Overman 1850:81):

Wood	Specific Gravity
Oak, white or red	0.6630
Sugar maple	0.6137
Beech	0.5788
Birch	0.5699
Poplar	0.4464
Pine, red	0.4205
Pine, white	0.3838

Another interesting evaluation of charcoal is to compare its relative heating ability to other fuels (Overman 1850:136):

One pound of:	Heated this many pounds of water:
Oil, wax	90 to 95
Ether	80
Pure carbon	78
Charcoal	75
Alcohol	67.5
Bituminous coal	60
Kiln-dried wood	36
Air-dried wood	27
Turf	25 to 30

The following, from the Fletcherville furnace near Mineville, New York, across Lake Champlain from Addison, presents weights of charcoal in pounds per bushel (lbs/bu) made from various types of wood (Egleston May 1879:384):

Wood	Lbs/Bu	Wood	Lbs/Bu
Sugar maple	19.0	Hemlock	12.8
Yellow birch	18.8	Poplar	12.3
Beech	17.0	Spruce	11.2
White ash	16.3	Basswood	10.6
Black ash	14.5	White pine	9.8

Note the density of the sugar maple charcoal relative to a majority of the other woods. The loss of huge stands of sugar maple in New York, Massachusetts, and Connecticut to the voracious appetites of charcoal-eating blast furnaces virtually wiped out the maple syrup industries in these states.

Charcoal was made by controlled burning of the wood. The burning was not allowed to progress beyond active smoldering, otherwise the entire effort would be consumed in flames. Properly controlled smoldering provided enough heat to burn off all the spirits and pitch in the wood, resulting in nearly 100 percent carbon remaining as charcoal. The uniformity of the charring process also guaranteed the uniformity of the charcoal's quality. Various configurations of wood stacking and techniques of wood burning were tried in the quest for both quality and predictable uniformity. By the post-Civil War period, a more permanent structure called a kiln was used, with a firing and operating procedure that approached an exact science.

Pits and Mounds

In the days before permanent kiln structures, wood was charred in earth-covered mounds. Thomas Egleston, who wrote many papers in the late 19th century on iron manufacture and charcoal making, called the mound types "meilers," a German word for charcoal kilns or piles. In his 19th-century dictionary of manufacturing arts, Andrew Ure described making charcoal in heaps, which he also called "meilers" (Ure 1854:397). Mound types were also called heaps, pits, and kilns. Heaps was synonymous with mound. Pits has been explained by some as an anachronism from the coal-mining industry—from days when coal was mined in pits. Kilns better define the later brick and/or stone structures. Other coal-mining expressions such as collier were carried over to the charcoal industry.

The most likely explanation for "charcoal pits" is based on

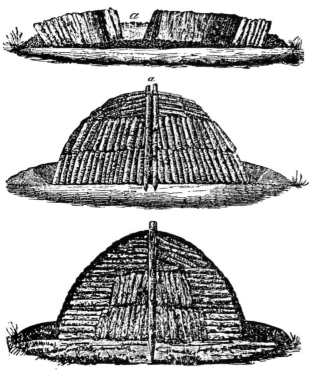

5-2. *A charcoal mound was built by first piling the cordwood vertically around the circumference (top) and continuing in alternate horizontal and vertical layers (bottom). A chimney was formed either by a number of small-diameter logs (center) that created a vertical airspace between them, or by a single large-diameter log placed vertically in the middle (bottom) to be removed later (Overman 1850:104, 105, 107).*

5-3. *A charcoal mound of cordwood ready to be covered with sod (courtesy* Berkshire Eagle, *Pittsfield, Mass.).*

the charcoal-making process employed by the Romans to manufacture charcoal for their forges. Charcoal making in mid-19th-century America differed little from that in use at the time of Pliny in AD 23–79. Historians believe these ancients made charcoal simply by digging a hole in dry ground, filling the hole with wood, setting it afire, and immediately covering it with sod (Overman 1850:104, 109).

The pit method is still used to make charcoal in parts of the Middle East, where the pits are small, bell-shaped, and lined with stone to prevent earth from mixing with the charcoal. The top opening of the pit is the only opening for air. After the wood inside the pit is set afire, this opening is sealed to allow the wood to smolder into charcoal. The typical pit takes one day to dig and line, one day to carbonize, and two days to extinguish and cool the charcoal (Horne 1982:10).

In the charcoal mound, wood was stacked in a 30- to 40-foot-diameter mound, leaving an approximately one-foot-diameter space in the middle to act as a chimney. When stacked, the wood was 10 to 14 feet high at the center. A mound of these dimensions used about 30 cords of wood, the equivalent of an acre woodlot. After all spaces were filled with smaller pieces of wood to make the mound compact, it was covered with a fine layer of charcoal dust, then earth and leaves. A hole was left at the top for the chimney and small 3- to 6-inch-diameter vent holes were opened around the sides, about a foot above the ground. When all was ready, burning ashes and tinder were dropped into the center chimney and the side vents alternately

opened and closed as needed to supply a natural draft and draw the burning from the middle of the mound to the sides. It took about a week to char the wood, depending on the type of wood and the skill of the collier.

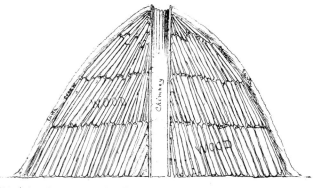

Making Charcoal — Section of coal pit ready for burning —

5-4. *Rowland E. Robinson sketched this cross-section of a mound that was probably in the Ferrisburgh area during the mid-18th century. The center chimney was formed by a narrow circle of tall, straight wood. Cordwood was tightly stacked outward from the chimney and upward to the top of it. The pile was covered with a layer of straw, and finally a layer of earth that was sometimes mixed with coal dust. Comment at bottom reads "Making charcoal—section of coal pit" (courtesy Rokeby Museum, Ferrisburgh).*

5-5. The Charcoal Burners, *by Rowland E. Robinson, from the original drawing (courtesy Rokeby Museum, Ferrisburgh).*

Men as black as the devil.

no smoke.

Making Charcoal.

Raking out the coal.

The tenders of these charcoal mounds were called colliers, after English coal miners of the same name. It was the job of the collier to build the mound, stack and cover the wood, correctly ignite the mound, and control the charring. As the wood was reduced to charcoal, the mound contracted and opened holes in the covering. This made for an undesirable job for the collier, that of walking about the top of the smoldering mound, closing the holes, and pushing the earth down by jumping up and down on it while prodding beneath with a long iron rod to settle the coals. Holes in the covering were of the utmost concern to the collier since openings would allow fresh air to enter and burst the charcoal (and himself) into a conflagration. Such activity soon covered the collier with black soot, lending more similarity than name only to his coal-mining cousins.

The charring was complete when the smoke stopped and the shrinking ended. As the earth covering was pulled away, barrels of water were kept handy in case a spark restarted the burning. Only a little water, when used, was needed. The charcoal was still very hot and the water immediately saturated the burning coals with scalding steam trapped within the quickly covered mound. After cooling, the charcoal was carefully shoveled into wagons with wood shovels and rakes to reduce breaking the pieces of charcoal, then taken to the forge. Some teamsters gave the charcoal an extra watering, just to be safe. There is one story of a burning charcoal wagon seen many miles away at night rolling downhill out of control, looking like a comet. Another story describes one hapless New England driver who left a load of charcoal in his wagon for the night. The next

5-6. *This rough sketch by Rowland E. Robinson might have been a preliminary for* The Charcoal Burners, *probably done on-site in or near Ferrisburgh during the mid-19th century. The sketch shows two colliers raking charcoal from a cooled mound. Comment at top left is "Men as black as the devil" from the charcoal dust. The colliers' rakes and carrying baskets (lower right) are non-metal, to avoid unnecessary charcoal breakage (courtesy Rokeby Museum, Ferrisburgh).*

morning he found only warped hardware on the blackened ground where his load of charcoal had been the night before (Hubbard 1922:49-50).

The collier's burning season ran from the end of one winter to the start of the next. Charcoal would deteriorate if left to accumulate, so it was made only a few weeks before it was needed at the forge (Bining 1973:64). It took a well-organized and alert collier to master the operation of the number of mounds he had to tend. Should he lose a mound through accidental fire, he was fined the value of the wood. A good collier had to juggle a number of duties, alternately charging and discharging mounds while tending to the vent holes of others. Since the mounds were built 100 or so feet from each other (to give working room and prevent the spread of fires), charcoal tending was difficult (Walker 1966:242). The collier spent the entire charcoal-making season on a mountainside, living in a small hut among his mounds. He kept a small vegetable garden when his day and night duties permitted, and sometimes augmented his diet with small game when he had the chance to check his traps.

5-7. *A burning charcoal mound, covered with earth and emitting a wisp of visible smoke, at a 1939 reenactment of the ancient art (courtesy Hagley Museum and Library, Brinton Coll., Wilmington, Del.).*

5-8. *A charcoal mound site near Adler Brook in Ripton, showing its distinctive raised, circular shape, which is typical of most mound remains found in Vermont.*

The process of making charcoal attracted many visitors, some of whom would beg some choice chunks of charcoal to bring home and drop down their well to "sweeten" the water. It was also a time when many people believed that drinking the most foul-smelling spring water cured any manner of ailments, or that sitting seminude in hot mud did wonders for their skin. So why not hike up to the charcoal mounds, stand downwind in the "purifying" white smoke, and breath deeply the exhilarating benefits of the pyroligneous vapors? Emphysema was a word a century yet to come into common usage, as tar, acetic acid, creosote, and naphtha liberally coated the lung tissues of all who were exposed to the charring fumes.

Producing charcoal in earth-covered mounds, however, had a number of drawbacks. Some of these were the amount of time and labor required to produce the charcoal, the difficulty of maintaining complete control of the burning process, and the high amount of dirt that usually mixed with the charcoal from the earth cover. The mound method also produced a weak charcoal, one that crumbled relatively easily in the blast furnace and sometimes choked the blast. By the end of the Civil War, a solution to these problems was the increasing use of more permanent kiln structures.

Charcoal Kilns

Initially, kilns were rectangular or round, and usually of red brick on a stone foundation. Firebrick was sometimes used but was not necessary as long as the red brick was hard enough to resist fire. A typical rectangular kiln in New England measured 40 to 50 feet long, and 12 to 15 feet high and wide. Capacity was 55 to 70 cords of wood, nearly double that of the mound process. The yield of 30 to 35 bushels of charcoal per cord of wood in the mound increased to 45 to 50 bushels in the kiln, a significant jump in efficiency. The rectangular kiln, however, was not as common in New England as in the South. Although some rectangular kilns were found in Vermont, round and conical kilns were the enduring configurations.

A 20- by 30-foot-rectangular charcoal kiln had essentially the same capacity as a 28-foot-diameter kiln of the same height. The rectangular kiln, given its straight lines and right-angle corners, was much easier to construct than the round kiln. Fitting square doors on curved lintels was avoided, and cordwood stacked easier inside the rectangular kiln. Then there was the problem of constructing an arched, corbeled roof atop the round walls. Why, then, were there not many more rectangular than round charcoal kilns? The answer: incomplete combustion took place in the square corners of the rectangular kilns, and this waste more often offset all the benefits of its simpler construction.

Round kilns, also known as round furnaces, were typically 28 to 30 feet in diameter at the base and 12 to 16 feet high at the center. Some were built with vertical walls, others with battered walls. In the battered-wall design, the diameter at the top of the wall was a few feet less than at the base, approaching a conical shape. Round kilns required two to three heavy iron bands around the wall in addition to the usual braces. The few iron bands found in the field varied from 28 to 30 feet inside diameter, indicating the outside diameter of the kiln where it was placed. These heavy iron bands were not carried up the

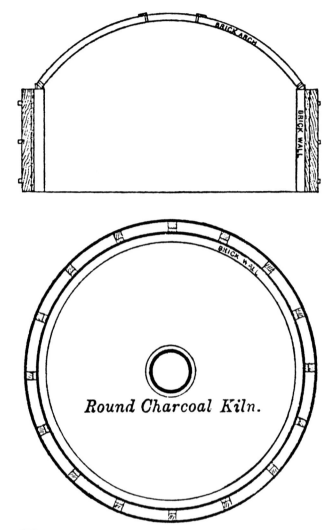

5-9. *Round charcoal kilns were made of vertical brick walls and outside iron binders supported with outside wooden posts. These were most commonly used in the Adirondacks of New York State (Egleston May 1879:386).*

mountain to the kiln construction sites in one piece, but assembled in sections with ½-inch-diameter bolts pushed through pre-holed and preformed joining ends, and attached with 1⅛-inch-square iron nuts (without washers). Small iron bands up to 2 inches wide were single-bolted; 4-inch-wide bands were bolted three at a time in a triangular pattern at joining ends of the bands. These joining ends consisted either of angled and overlapping sections requiring one set of three nuts and bolts, or of butted ends connected together with an iron plate against the outer side of the joint and bolted together with two sets of three nuts and bolts, each set at the ends of the two butted iron bands. The bolts were always placed so that their heads were nearly flush with and on the inside of the joint assembly (bolt head against the kiln wall), and the nut on the outer side of the joint facing away from the kiln wall. In this manner, little

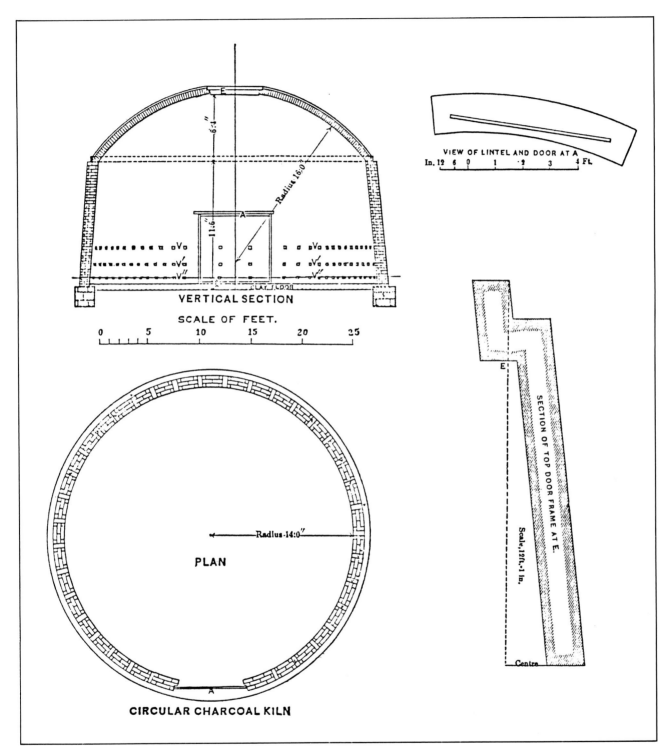

VIEW OF LINTEL AND DOOR AT A

VERTICAL SECTION

SCALE OF FEET.

PLAN

CIRCULAR CHARCOAL KILN

SECTION OF TOP DOOR FRAME AT E.

5-10. *The circular charcoal kiln, most commonly found in Vermont, was built with battered brick walls and iron hoops. The battered-wall design was more stable than the straight wall of the round kiln and permitted the construction of a slightly larger-capacity charcoal kiln. Notice the top loading hole; ankle, knee, and waist vents; and vaulted brick roof. The design of a sill plate is at upper right; design at right shows the angular pitch of the top door frame (Egleston May 1879:387).*

5-11. *This charcoal kiln typifies the round brick types that operated in 19th-century Vermont. Probably photographed about 1890 and already showing some decay, this one operated at Fayville, an industrious 1870s–1880s logging community in the northwestern corner of Glastenbury (courtesy Shaftsbury Historical Society).*

mechanical damage was done to the kiln wall and the banding nuts could be tightened from time to time as necessary. These iron bands aided significantly in stabilizing the kiln structures during the heating and cooling cycles of operation.

The kiln had about 300 vents around the lower wall in three rows of 100 vents each. Some kilns had cast-iron vents, others merely holes left by deletion of a brick during construction. The vent hole opening could be closed by inserting a brick lengthwise. The 3- to 5-foot-diameter vent at the top was lined with a cast-iron ring which, together with the heavy doors and cast-iron bands, weighed about 3,000 pounds. It took about 36,000 bricks to build this type of charcoal kiln (Egleston May 1879:388).

The 40 to 50 cords of wood took four or five men one day to load. The kiln was ignited with a long-handled torch at the bottom, in space below the wood that was left by the skids. This was usually done at night so that the progress of the flame could be seen and better controlled. When the kiln was lit, all

5-12. *Cast-iron kiln vent from a brick-type charcoal kiln site at Ripton.*

5-13. *A heavy iron casting that protected the top loading hole of a brick-type charcoal kiln at Glastenbury just south of "the forks." The casting protected the top inner circle of bricks from burning out prematurely, and also from damage through loading cordwood down into the kiln. The casting was made in one solid piece, with thick, reinforced supporting tabs at every quarter which held it firmly in position. To the right is another casting, upside-down on the ground; both castings have been stolen since this 1982 photo.*

5-14. *One of the better remains of a brick-type charcoal kiln, showing the black pitch still coating the inside wall. This site is near the old Greeley Mill at Mount Tabor.*

side vents were open, but as soon as the wood was burning, the two lower rows of vents were closed. During the first four days, the heavy white smoke coming from the upper vents indicated water being driven from the wood as steam. This was followed by blue smoke, indicating that the kiln was very hot and the charring nearly complete. When the charring was complete, all vents were closed to suffocate the fires, followed by five to six days of cooling. Water was generally no longer used to extinguish the fire and reduce cooling time because the water was found to impair the value of the charcoal for blast furnace use. It took four men one day to unload the kiln. The entire cycle took 10 to 12 days.

Historical records indicate that by the late 1870s, small conical kilns had gradually and generally replaced the larger kilns of other shapes everywhere except in Vermont. Generally 25 to 30 feet in diameter at the base and 25 to 35 feet high, conical

kilns were designed for 25 to 45 cords of wood. Some were built into hillsides so that a charging door was near the top; others had a door only at the bottom. Although an overwhelming number of charcoal kilns located in Vermont have been of the round variety, at least one brick-type and numbers of stone-type conical kilns have also been found. Typical of stone-type conical kilns are those atop East Mountain (Bald Mountain), about three miles east of South Shaftsbury near the Shaftsbury-Glastenbury line. They are 30 feet in diameter with walls 2½ feet thick. Wall thickness diminished with height. Kiln doors were ⅜-inch-thick iron sheets measuring 6 feet wide by 5 feet high. The brick-type conical kiln was found in Readsboro. It measured 28 feet across at the base with walls 1 foot thick. It was reported that although it took about 33,000 bricks to build a conical kiln at Plattsburgh, New York, the conical kiln at Readsboro required 40,000 bricks (Egleston May 1879:393). Kilns of a third variant design found at Readsboro, Stamford, and Shaftsbury were built of stone up to about 4 feet high and then brick the rest of the way.

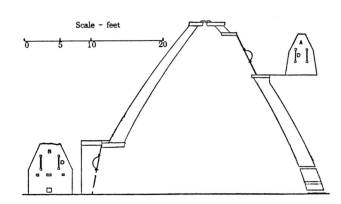

5-16. *Plan of a conical charcoal kiln at Wassaic, New York, whose top-loading opening is a transitional feature from the circular kiln (Egleston May 1879:390).*

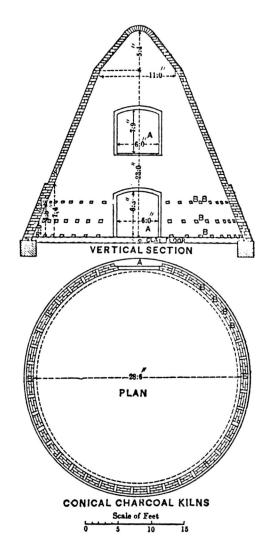

CONICAL CHARCOAL KILNS

Scale of Feet

5-15. *The most efficient design of a charcoal kiln, with an upper side-loading door replacing the round top-loading hole. This conical charcoal kiln operated at Readsboro in the 1870s to 1880s (Egleston May 1879:391).*

Typical conical kilns held about 35 cords of wood, which took four men 12 hours to load, and the efficient charcoal yield of 50 bushels to a cord was maintained. It was generally conceded by 1880 that the smaller conical kilns holding 25 to 35 cords were the most profitable. They were less expensive to build, more easily charged (loaded) and managed, gave an improved yield, and could be cycled more frequently than any other type of kiln. Some representative costs to charge, burn, and empty a conical kiln per 1,000 bushels of charcoal in 1879 were $7.50 at Plattsburgh (Norton Ironworks), $7.00 on Lake George (near Roger's Rock), and $6.00 in some Vermont localities. Statistics of some typical conical kilns were:

	Charge	Burn	Cool	Discharge
Time (hours)	10	192	72	10
Men per day	6	1	0	4
Horses per day	1	0	0	2

Extrapolation of some of the meager charcoal production data in published histories of Vermont does not indicate a

5-17. *Conical charcoal kilns that still stand at Wassaic, New York, which supplied charcoal to ironworks in the Hudson Valley in the 1870s–1880s (courtesy Richard S. Allen).*

5-18. *A side-loading door, similar in configuration to doorways of the standing conical kilns at Wassaic, New York, found near the ruin of one of the Readsboro charcoal kiln sites west of Route 8, indicating this kiln might also have been conical in construction.*

5-19. *A rectangular-type charcoal kiln, made of brick, showing cast-iron external binders and vent holes along the bottom (Overman 1850:110).*

5-20. *Charcoal was transported from the kilns in wagons that could be quickly emptied either by dropping the side panels or sliding out the bottom boards. Since charcoal lost value if broken into small pieces, the teamster shoveled as little as possible (courtesy* Berkshire Eagle, *Pittsfield, Mass.).*

5-21. *Transferring charcoal from wagons to railroad cars at Danby Station. Note how bins are lifted from the wagon, hoisted above the railroad car, and dumped into it, avoiding unnecessary shoveling of the charcoal (Chapin 1885:16).*

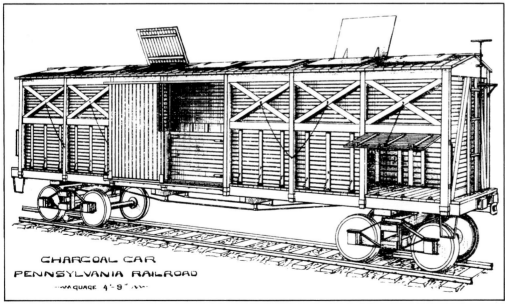

CHARCOAL CAR
PENNSYLVANIA RAILROAD
—GA GUAGE 4'-9"—

5-22. *A typical charcoal railroad car used in Pennsylvania in the 1880s (*Annual Report of . . . Pennsylvania *1894:35ff).*

5-23. *Logging in winter, when the trees contained less sap (top), hauling logs down treacherous trails in Mount Tabor (middle), and "Kiln ready for firing—showing the fore arch." The man with a high hat, standing on top of the kiln, was probably Silas Griffith (Chapin 1885:11).*

5-24. *Vent hole construction (center) in the wall of a stone-type charcoal kiln, north of Old County Road in Stamford. Note the two standard bricks (center) holding up a flat lintel stone. The resultant hole allowed a third brick to be inserted to control the draft.*

5-25. *Griffy doing her part inspecting a charcoal kiln ruin atop Berlin Mountain in New York. Note non-brick-type vent hole construction, although single bricks that controlled draft were found still in place.*

consistency in yield (bushels of charcoal per cord of wood). The Barnum Richardson Company's eight kilns in Winhall produced an average of 2,000 bushels of charcoal per kiln; each kiln cycled 15 times a year. The Bennington & Glastenbury Railroad, Mining, and Manufacturing Company's 18 kilns in Woodford produced 1,600 bushels per year with a yield of 40 bushels per cord. Fourteen of its running kilns produced 28,000 bushels per month. Analysis of this data shows that each kiln cycled about every 24½ days. Using this as a basis, the following yields of some charcoal-making companies in southern Vermont were calculated. Note that the bushels of charcoal per kiln indicates relative size of the kiln:

Company	Average Bushels of Charcoal per:	
	Kiln	Cord
Morehouse & White (Woodford)	2,760	25
Barnum Richardson Co. (Winhall)	2,000	40
Bennington & Glastenbury Railroad, Mining, and Manufacturing Co. (Woodford)	1,600	40
Beckley & Adams (Woodford)	1,470	36
Maltby (Peru)	1,000	29
Root & Jones Chemical Works (Bennington)	?	45

Although the Morehouse & White kilns produced the most bushels of charcoal per kiln, the yield of their kilns was relatively low compared to the others.

The Root & Jones Chemical Works at Bennington was a chemical company interested mainly in the distillates in the wood; the charcoal was strictly a by-product of the process and the high charcoal yield indicated an efficient extraction process. The first successful distillation factory in the country was built in 1850 in New York, and principal products of these distillation factories were acetic acid and methanol. After the 1920s these could be made synthetically and the distillation factories disappeared. Factories such as this burned nearly 100,000 cords of wood annually, making about 35,000 tons of charcoal in the process (Simmons 1960:10).

Consumption of charcoal by ironworks varied from operation to operation. As iron production increased, ironworks were forced to look farther each year for quality woodlands from which to draw charcoal. Once stripped of timber, it took 20 years for regrowth to be sufficient for another clearing. A blast furnace making six tons of iron a day consumed 270,000 bushels of charcoal annually. This calculates to 6,750 cords of wood. At the average rate of 30 cords to the acre, access to 225 acres per year was needed (1849 figures). And for a constant supply, therefore, a typical blast furnace required 4,500 acres of woodland to keep up with consumption. (Hodge June 9, 1849:354). Since few ironworks owned such acreage of woodland, proximity to the railroads for delivery of charcoal from outlying areas to augment local charcoal production became important.

In the 1850s ironworks in Vermont were drawing charcoal from an average of 10 to 14 miles away. The expense of hauling charcoal greater distances placed a higher expense on the cost of making and working iron. Works that could not stay competitive closed. When the Barney forges at Swanton closed after 68 years of operation, the expense of charcoal was blamed (Hemenway vol. 1 1867:1022-1023). And by the early 1900s

when charcoal was being shipped north to ironworks in Connecticut, New York, and Massachusetts from as far away as North Carolina, blast furnaces and bloomery forges had long since ceased operating in Vermont.

Transition

The charcoal industry in Vermont was a reflection of the iron industry, typically rural in the sense that only a few operations approached organizational efficiency. Most were scattered up and down the high western slopes of the Green Mountains in pocket industries that supported purely local needs. Up to the early 1800s when much of the countryside was still being cleared, farmers were able to lay away substantial amounts of money or credit by making and selling charcoal (Smith 1886:493). The stone- and brick-type kilns made their appearance by the mid-1800s and charcoal making shifted from pin money to industrial profit. Kilns on the eastern side of Lake Champlain competed with those on the western side as the charcoal market put better profit position before local loyalties.

Although mainly distributed among eastern townships in Addison, Rutland, and Bennington counties, early charcoal making was also carried on in a few isolated places to the east and north. And by the late 1880s, the charcoal industry was transformed into just a few highly organized operations. Their efficiencies reflected what was quickly happening to Vermont's "boundless forests."

What became of the charcoal industry in Vermont? Historians have traditionally blamed such things as the scarcity of quality woodlands or the increasing cost of making charcoal for the charcoal-burning blast furnaces for the failure of the charcoal industry. A great area of forest land *was* cut for charcoal; and the price of charcoal *did* rise through the 1880–1900 period. But to understand why the charcoal industry died, one must look at what was happening nationwide to its most profitable customer—the charcoal iron industry.

Up to the 1830s all iron made in the United States was charcoal iron, that is, iron made in furnaces and bloomeries fueled solely with charcoal. Soon after the Civil War, significant numbers of furnaces started burning coke, which was made from coal by a process somewhat similar to that of making charcoal in a kiln. The production of charcoal iron continued to increase, however, reaching peak production of about 710,000 tons in 1890 (Schallenberg 1975:342-343). Hardware produced in the late 19th century required a general-purpose iron, not brittle for pounding tools, sharp-edged for cutting tools, and strong for large tools and castings. Charcoal iron was ideal for all these applications. Charcoal was also so relatively easy to burn that blast furnaces did not require strong blast equipment. There was never a shortage of woodland for making charcoal. The countryside abounded in forest land in the 19th century in spite of lumbering and clearing land for farming. The charcoal iron industry continued on in this country for over a century after it ended in forest-poor England.

Following the Civil War, technological innovation in the coke and charcoal industries increased apace, with innovation in the coke industry keeping well ahead of charcoal. By 1910, the heyday of the beehive coke ovens, there were 100,362

5-26. *An itinerant charcoal burner at his trade at one of the charcoal kilns at North Leverett, Massachusetts, which operated up to 1980.*

individual ovens in the United States according to the Federal Bureau of Mines. By the early 1900s coal barons built tens of thousands of red-bricked ovens right outside the mouths of coal mines. They were "hellish pillars of fire" that burned 24 hours a day, seven days a week, to fuel the booming steel mills. ("Beehive Coke Ovens. . ." *New York Times* Sept. 12, 1982:73).

Innovation in blast furnace technique and design also moved onward as newer furnaces were built higher in order to increase iron production. But as the furnaces grew higher, the charcoal, being brittle and weak, crumbled into small particles in the tall furnace stacks with the weight of additional fuel and iron ore piled above it. Though most charcoal furnaces were kept small and squat, severely limiting their ability to keep pace with the trend of increased iron output, by 1900 some charcoal furnaces managed to reach up to 60 feet in height.

Technological innovation in the iron industry itself also advanced at an increasing rate after the Civil War, and by the 1890s, significant quantities of open-hearth steel were starting to appear on the market. Although still several times more expensive than charcoal iron, products made from open-hearth steel lasted several times longer than those made from charcoal iron. This, coupled with the decreasing cost of making coke, spelled the beginning of the end of the charcoal iron industry, and thus the end of the charcoal-making industry. The total number of 500 charcoal furnaces in the 1860s dropped to half that in the 1880s, to less than 100 in the 1890s, and less than 50 after 1900 (Schallenberg 1975:346).

Inventories of freight cars owned by the Rutland Railroad also reveal what was happening to the charcoal industry in Vermont. In 1905 and 1910 the Rutland owned nine charcoal cars. Two cars were 33 feet long (inside) with 12- and 15-ton capacities; the other seven were 37 feet long with 15-ton capacities. No charcoal cars appear on Rutland inventories after 1910 (Bill Badger letter to author, May 5, 1991).

In the 1960s the demand for charcoal for use in backyard grills encouraged a renewed market for the fuel. Charcoal production nationwide was about 200,000 tons in 1950, up to 350,000 tons by 1956, and approached 500,000 tons by the 1960s, nearly equaling turn-of-the-century production figures (Simmons 1960:10). The art of charcoal making had revived in many states, especially in Michigan, Arkansas, Tennessee, and West Virginia.

In an effort to capitalize on this new demand, authorities in New York and New Hampshire who were conscious of forest resources issued many small booklets and bulletins to would-be charcoal burners on how to build efficient kilns from ordinary inexpensive materials and how to make the charcoal. One such kiln was made of sheet metal, forming a miniature beehive-type structure. A variation of this design employed a crane to lower steel kilns over stacks of wood; it then lifted the kiln after the wood had charred. Another kiln that found popular favor was a rectangular unit made of cinder block, designed for one and two cords of wood. During and after World War II many of these cinder-block kilns were built around the country, including the one that was found a few dozen feet off the road to Pikes Falls at Stratton.

Kiln Touring

For the venturesome, there are operating charcoal kilns in New England within a 2-hour drive of Vermont. At Union, Connecticut, about a 15-minute drive south of Old Sturbridge Village, Massachusetts, on and visible from Route 171, the Connecticut Charcoal Company operates seven 30- to 35-foot-diameter brick-type kilns. The originals of these recent-vintage kilns were built in 1939 to take advantage of local forest damage caused by a hurricane the year before. One of the 1939 kilns is still standing and operating. The kilns today burn slab wood, waste from lumbering operations. Charcoal is made by the traditional process, with the most obvious exception being the pollution-control device attached to the kiln. The device looks like a giant vacuum cleaner. Charcoal yield at the kilns is a surprising 45 to 50 bushels per cord of wood, comparable to yields at 19th-century coaling operations for similar-design kilns. Customers for the charcoal are various foundries in New York, New Jersey, Massachusetts, and Connecticut. The charcoal is also sold to individuals (about $2.00 a bag) who find it aids in starting their coal stoves in winter. The company has established a retail barbecuing market for the "clean coal" (versus so-called "briquette coal," which usually contains large quantities of non-charcoal material and toxic industrial waste).

In Massachusetts, modern charcoal found its way to Boston's better restaurants and steak houses (Woolmington Dec. 1979:80-85, 132-134). At Leverett, charcoal was made at two brick-type kilns until they were closed in 1980 due to air-quality laws. The kilns are about a mile south of the village of North Leverett along Old Coke Kiln Road, an area where charcoal making dates to about 1825. And in the Dubuque State Forest near East Hawley there is a fully standing stone-type conical kiln, which made charcoal from 1872 to about 1900.

5-27. *Charcoal kilns at the Connecticut Charcoal Company in Union, showing vent holes and kiln door plastered shut and whitewashed to contain heat and shut off draft at the end of the burn. The water on the black ground, sticky with pitch, is moisture liberated from the charred wood that seeped through the kiln walls. The walls were hot to the touch and the air carried a pungent naphtha odor.*

5-28. *Tools of the trade at the Connecticut Charcoal Company: charcoal fork, picks, and shovel; a wheelbarrow of whitewash to seal the kiln walls; and a face mask/filter (hanging with the sweater).*

Chapter 6
Study of Charcoal Mounds and Kilns

Study Methodology

Initial charcoal making in Vermont coincided with initial iron making. As settlements grew, foundries and blacksmith shops added an additional demand for charcoal. Whether smithies or foundries operated first can be argued either way (in early times there was often little difference between the two), but charcoal was a requirement for both. Each made its own charcoal, usually locally, until land clearing pushed the forest line back into the mountains.

The problem encountered while researching for ironworks production records was reflected in the search for records of charcoal production: little has survived. Exceptions are some one- or two-page accounts in library archives and the usually vague references in published histories. Much of what has been learned about the charcoal industry in Vermont came from finding the charcoal-making site, estimating its period of operation, and trying to guess where all the charcoal went. Estimating the period of operation, when no documentation was otherwise available, was done after field inspection of the physical remains, not always an accurate method. What was discovered about charcoal making in places outside Vermont was usually applied to the data found in Vermont. As realistic an idea as possible was thus strived for with regard to what was going on in this state.

No doubt there is much "undiscovered" archival information in ledgers stacked on shelves of libraries and bookstores, as well as passing references in personal and business letters saved in family Bibles or note boxes. Likewise, many hundreds of remains and ruins are still hidden in the mountains, waiting to be found and assimilated into the growing bank of knowledge, for reevaluation and reinterpretation of the Vermont charcoal-making experience.

The search for brick-type charcoal kilns was similar, yet somewhat different, than the search for furnaces and forges. Charcoal kilns were not always built near streams and rivers because waterpower was not required in the kiln operation. But the kilns were usually built near sawmills, and these mills did have a need for water. By the period of the major charcoal industry in Vermont (1860–1900), steam-powered sawmills had arrived. And although steam sawmills continued to operate near streams, water now was required only to replace that lost by the boiler in the form of steam. It was a small amount compared to the amount of water previously required to power a large waterwheel or turbine-powered sawmill.

Mounds and kilns were built as close as possible to the source of their wood supply. Rather than build kilns at the foot of the mountain, near flat roads and local transportation, it was determined early on that hauling heavy logs to the kilns should be minimized and effort concentrated on carting the lighter-weight charcoal. Thus, most charcoal mounds and kilns are found well up the higher elevations, near barely visible roads. Hauling tons of iron reinforcement bands, doors, covers, and other hardware in addition to thousands of bricks up steep mountain roads in the days of non-mechanized transportation must have been a sight. It brings to mind a vivid definition of the term "labor-intensive."

Brick-type kilns in Vermont were each made from 33,000 to 40,000 bricks, depending on various design features. Bricks, therefore, are obviously one of the things to look out for when in the field searching for charcoal kilns. Most of the kiln's bricks tend to remain where they have been since collapse of the kiln structure, except for those moved through flood and ice action or bulldozing as part of nearby trail or road maintenance. A number of kilns were built of stone, and probably because stone is everywhere available in Vermont, stone-built kilns are less vandalized than brick ones. And not all charcoal kilns in Vermont were round or conical. Four ruins found at two sites in Chittenden were rectangular.

Most kiln sites have long since become buried under heavy brush and tall grass. Some kiln ruins are so leveled that the sites can be walked through without being seen. At Ten Kilns Meadow in Mount Tabor, we discovered one morning that we had pitched our tent the day before in thick grass directly on top of the leveled five-kiln site that we were going to spend the day in search of. We had slept all night inside one of the ruins.

If a stream is nearby, a close inspection of the streambed and shore may reveal pieces of brick that worked their way downhill or were thrown into it. If you are in the vicinity of a suspected charcoal kiln site and there are pieces of red brick in the stream or along the trail, keep a sharp eye out for the kiln ruin. Since objects wash downhill with time, search directly uphill from the exact point of the find, regardless of the direction from which the area was approached.

Another clue in the search for a charcoal site is charcoal itself. In the process of discharging the kilns and loading and driving the charcoal wagons, much spillage occurred. The closer to the kiln, therefore, the darker the soil. But black soil can also be caused by things such as rotting vegetation. Charcoal does not significantly disintegrate over centuries, otherwise the process of carbon dating prehistoric sites would today be impossible. But charcoal can be made by other ways than a prehistoric cooking fire or a charcoal kiln. Finding a badly burned tree stump beneath some charcoal could indicate evidence of a forest fire. Nails and domestic debris mixed with charcoal could mark the site of a house or barn fire. Camp fires usually leave charcoal. The presence of charcoal, therefore, does not always indicate a charcoal mound or kiln site. Check the soil for actual bits of charcoal; they can be as small as grains of sand. Having accumulated through dozens of years of kiln operation and being light in weight, much charcoal has washed downhill from the kiln sites in the past century over the ground, along hiking trails, and onto roads.

The third clue to consider is the terrain. Kilns were usually constructed into 15- to 20-foot-high embankments. A single-kiln site may have a single concave depression cut into the adjacent low hill; an eight-kiln site may have eight such concave depressions. These concave cuts into embankments were sometimes reinforced with 3- to 5-foot-high stone walls at their highest point, where the kiln was built farthest into the embankment. While the kiln was standing, the distance between the concave wall and the kiln wall was 3 to 4 feet, enough space to allow a kiln tender to walk behind the kiln to maintain vent hole operations or repair the walls. The concave stone-lined embankment is a positive indication of the kiln site.

The hint of an old road might be found leading uphill to the kiln site. Another road might lead around the hill to the top of the embankment. Here, above the kiln, was a wood ramp that allowed access to the charging hole in the roof of the kiln. But some kilns might have been built so far from the embankment that no concave depressions or wall exist. This is true of the site of eight kilns at Old Job in Mount Tabor. And at Ten Kilns Meadow, not far away, the embankments have flat walls instead of concave for each individual kiln. Although the process of making charcoal was generally consistent from operation to operation, field evidence shows that certain specific techniques varied.

A kiln ruin itself can be characterized by anything from visible brick or stone walls 3 to 6 feet high, complete with vent holes, large kiln-girdling iron hoops, and mounds of charcoal, to no walls but a low 30-foot-diameter circular mound of thousands of bricks, or only a circle of very black ground. The nearer the kiln ruin is to public visibility and motorized access, usually the less the remains to view. Also, the nearer to road and heavily used trails, the more evidence of discarded trash (beverage cans, bottles, automobile parts) in the sites and potholing in the walls. Over the years, many kiln sites have become the source of brick for chimneys and backyard fireplaces of nearby residents. Since most kiln sites in the Green Mountain National Forest are on U.S. Forest Service property, they are actively protected by forest rangers. Violators are arrested and prosecuted. But this does not entirely prevent sites from being vandalized for brick and scrap iron. The dollars made stealing and destroying a site do not come close to compensation for the loss of a historic and educational resource to the general public.

Aerial photo inspection for charcoal kiln sites was tried at the Vermont Mapping Program, Waterbury, with no success. Photos inspected were 1:1250 to 1:5000 scale orthophotos of Vermont taken at about 30,000 feet (1 inch of orthophoto equals about 416 feet on the ground). After spending hours squinting through a magnifying glass at dozens of these 3-foot-square black-and-white photos and then weekends field-checking some possibilities, the only sites confirmed were those already known. Visible kiln ruins measure less than $\frac{1}{16}$th of an inch in diameter in the orthophoto and look like tiny moon craters. It was one thing to know where they exist and find them in the orthophoto; it was another to determine whether that tiny round feature was in fact a kiln ruin or an empty swimming pool (Stamford), a circular depression (Tinmouth), a frozen puddle (Winhall), a silo foundation (Panton), or just a pile of manure (Shoreham).

Searching for the earth-covered mound was much more difficult because no bricks or iron hardware were used in its construction and, therefore, no hardware remained to guide the way. Neither were they usually built into an embankment as were the structure-type charcoal kilns. And having predated the brick-type kiln, nature has had much more time to hide the evidence with more trees to disguise the site, more leaves and soil to cover the burned pitch floor, and more rains and spring thaws to reconfigure the site and scatter charcoal more thinly over a wider area. One clue to a mound site was the presence of lush vegetation. An 1851 agricultural journal noted that the effect of charcoal dust resulted in the "quickening" of vegetation: "The spots where charcoal pits were burned 20, and some say even 30 years since, still produce better corn, wheat, oats, vegetables or grass, than the adjoining lands" (Carey 1851:516). The preference of white birch and yellow birch for charcoal-making (and lime-burning) areas was noticed while doing fieldwork in the Green Mountains.

Ground preparation for mound construction in areas liberally covered with surface stones required clearing the area first. The result was a denser distribution of stones in the circular area immediately outside the perimeter of the mound site than the area farther out. A shallow, circular ditch, called the gutter, was dug around the perimeter but outside the mound floor. The gutter and area of stones were good indications of a mound site. Charcoal was made inside the gutter area and this floor was saturated as deep as a foot with charcoal and pitch. Charcoal spilled during unloading was also found outside the perimeter. The gutter was sometimes more obvious in spring and fall, when leaves had blown into it and became trapped in the depression.

The lack of hardware and bricks made finding a charcoal mound site in a random search almost impossible. Since charcoal mounds took longer to prepare, charge, burn, and discharge than the later brick-constructed kilns, the need for a sawmill to cut wood and keep up with the charring had not yet become a necessity. Wood was cut by axe, so the mounds could be remote from a waterpowered sawmill. The site of a number of charcoal mounds was discovered by U.S. Forest Service personnel high up the slopes of Worth Mountain in Hancock and Bloodroot Mountain in Chittenden, far from any obvious sawmill site. They were found during routine surveys of forest tracts for logging potential. Sharp-eyed forest rangers first noticed cellar holes at both sites with scattered bits of charcoal nearby. The remains of six charcoal mounds were found in the immediate vicinity at Worth Mountain and 20 more at Bloodroot Mountain.

Historical references to charcoal making in the early 19th century are skimpy. Statements that charcoal was made "in the nearby woods" define neither distance nor direction. What might have been nearby woods for the forge at Swanton in 1810 could today be someone's backyard in the village. Conversations with older, longtime residents within a 10-mile radius of an ironworks produced some results. One farmer remembered plowing soil that was especially black just after a light spring rain. Another remembered a family tradition of ancestors making charcoal while clearing farmland.

Ironworks in the 1790–1800 period consumed less charcoal than those of the 1870–1880 period. As such, charcoal was made from forests that were closer to the ironworks in 1800 than in 1870. By the 1880s, the brick-type kilns were located well up in the mountains, attacking last stands of hardwood forest. As the charcoal industry swept across the valleys and up into the mountains, the clearings behind became farmland in many places. The passage of time, therefore, became the measure of distance; the terrain defined the direction.

Results of the Charcoal Kiln Study

Fifty-seven charcoal-making sites were reported to the State Archeologist during the 1983–1991 period of the overall statewide IA study of charcoal kiln ruins and mound remains and are now part of the Vermont Archeological Inventory. Forty-two sites contained 130 kiln ruins: 108 were made of brick, 9 of stone, 12 of a combination of stone and brick, and 1 of concrete block, while fourteen of the sites contained remains of 51 mounds (one site contained both a brick-type and a mound-type). Analysis of the kiln ruins determined that 122 were round, 5 were rectangular, 1 was conical, and 2 remain unidentified. All except two sites are within the new (1991) proclamation boundary of the Green Mountain National Forest; a majority are on federal property. Two other sites have been reported to the State Archeologist in the Field Site (FS) category. There was inconclusive or no positive surface evidence at these sites, but subsurface material of 4 charcoal kilns and an undetermined number of mound remains might exist. Archival and field work continues at 12 more sites in the work-in-progress (CK) category. The total number of charcoal-making sites studied is 71 at this writing.

Brick-type ruins found in Vermont were generally laid up in a modified common bond with headers laid every third course. The walls were laid three bricks thick on the stretcher courses and 1½ bricks thick for the header courses, generally measuring 17½ inches thick. The walls and their reinforcing hardware supported the vaulting brick roof and compensated for the kiln's heating and cooling cycles, which caused the structure to expand and contract slightly with each of these cycles.

In addition to the heavy cast-iron bands that reinforced the brick walls, other hardware found included large front charging doors made of sheets of about ½-inch-thick iron bolted together to form one unit measuring up to 6 feet high by 7 feet wide, iron wall binders with end plates, heavy iron lintels which provided a platform across which the iron doors slid, and cast-iron vent hole linings. Inspection of the few pieces of hardware that have survived scrap drives indicated little similarity between hardware designs and dimensions, suggesting that hardware for the kilns was made "on order" at a foundry. Some front charging doors had U-shaped iron handles bolted or welded to them; other handles were a U-shaped section of long iron bars that reinforced the entire height of the door.

Variability in design of hardware for charcoal kilns was also obvious in the configurations of the round covers that closed the top charging holes by laying flat on the round holes in the tops of the kilns. These 6- to 7-foot-diameter by ½-inch-thick iron covers displayed varieties of vent holes. Most covers had nearly brick-size holes cut lengthwise into the cover so the holes could be closed simply by bricks laying flat on them. One cover found at Peru had holes with small, sliding iron doors that could be opened and closed to control the draft allowed to enter the kiln through these top vents. A few covers had no holes at all. Cover handles varied from pairs of U-shaped

iron units bolted or welded to the covers to U-shaped sections of long iron bars that reinforced the entire diameters of the covers (similar to variations of handle designs on the large iron doors). Probably because of their round, flat shape, these covers escaped detection of scavengers. Except for their uniquely shaped iron doors, no hardware was found associated with stone-type kiln ruins because their beehive design created a much more stable structure.

All kiln ruins, whether brick- or stone-type, contained vent holes that conveniently allowed the lengthwise insertion of an ordinary red brick to close the hole. Stone-type kiln ruins used a pair of bricks set lengthwise side by side with another lengthwise brick-size space between them. These were laid over and under with large flat stones. Variations in vent holes were found at two sites of brick-type kiln ruins that had cast-iron vent linings. At one stone-type kiln site, vent hole linings were found made of an unidentified tile material.

Kiln ruins and mound remains were found at elevations from 660 to 2,400 feet above sea level. Vermont's lowest elevation is 95 feet, at Lake Champlain; the highest point is Mount Mansfield at 4,393 feet. The average state elevation is approximately 1,000 feet. In the area of the most kiln finds, 12 mountains rise to between 3,000 and 3,800 feet. Brick-type kiln ruins averaged 1,815 feet in elevation at a range of 660 to 2,360 feet. The largest concentration of 59 brick-type ruins was found between 1,500 and 2,000 feet. Stone-type ruins averaged 2,057 feet in elevation with a range of 1,560 to 2,400 feet, somewhat higher in elevation than the brick types, but significantly compacted in a tighter range. The largest concentration of 10 stone-type ruins was found between the 2,000- and 2,500-foot level. Mound-type remains were found at the lower average of 1,336 feet in elevation, at a range of 700 to 2,360 feet; there was no significant concentration at any elevation. Most kiln ruins were found in proximity to good-flowing streams.

Table 6-1 lists the charcoal kiln and mound sites that have been researched alphabetically by county and numerically within county by site identification number. Sites unrecorded (CK numbers) are those where ruins or remains either have not been found or inconclusive evidence exists to positively identify the kiln or mound site. The table lists the sites' identification numbers; their principal names; number of units (mounds and/or kilns) per site; whether the site is mound-type, made of stone, brick, or a stone-and-brick combination; and if in the Green Mountain National Forest.

Following table 6-1 are three sections that divide the state into the northern, central, and southern districts, as described in the Introduction in the front of this book (see "Presentation of the Study"). In these sections, the history of the charcoal-making site and a description of whatever physical remains exist are presented. Table 6-2 at the end of the chapter summarizes the results of the charcoal kiln study.

Presentation of sites within each section is by county, and within each county, sites are presented either in site number sequence or grouped to reflect a geographic proximity. Grouping does not reflect any commonality that might have existed when the kilns were in operation, but aids in describing them. Accompanying maps provide a geographic sense of the physical disposition of the sites and ruins, without compromising the

Table 6-1. Charcoal Kiln and Mound Sites

Site No.	Principal Name	Units per Site	Type	Green Mountain National Forest
Addison County				
AD-16	Huntley Island	1	Mound	No
AD-314	Dragon Brook	4	Brick	Yes
AD-315	Widow's Trail	3	Brick	Yes
AD-338	Billings	3	Brick/Stone?	Yes
AD-341	Keewaydin Camps	4	Mound	Yes
AD-348	Adler Brook-East	3	Mound	Yes
AD-351	Adler Brook-West	1	Mound	Yes
AD-356	Sandusky	?	Brick	No
AD-395	Worth Mountain	6	Mound	Yes
AD-405	Leicester Hollow	3	Mound	Yes
AD-467	Barker Brook	1?	Stone?	Yes
AD-FS85	Mt. Fuller	?	Mound?	No
AD-CK01	Cobble Mountain	?	Brick?	Yes
Bennington County				
BE-37	Red Cabin	5	Brick	Yes
BE-39	Mad Tom Lower	3	Brick	Yes
BE-40	Mad Tom Middle	1	Brick	Yes
BE-41	Mad Tom Upper	5	Brick	Yes
BE-42	Winhall River	4	Brick	Yes
BE-43	Bromley Brook	4	Brick	Yes
BE-44	Bourn Brook	8	Brick	Yes
BE-45	Bickford Hollow	3	Brick	Yes
BE-46	East Fork	3	Brick	Yes
BE-47	West Fork	5	Brick	Yes
BE-50	Heartwellville-Stone	1	Brick/Stone?	Yes
BE-51	Heartwellville-Brick	2	Brick	Yes
BE-52	Heartwellville-Conical	1	Brick	Yes
BE-53	Cotykilns	4	Stone	Yes
BE-54	Dutch Hill	2	Brick/Stone?	Yes
BE-55	Gully Brook	2	Stone	Yes
BE-56	North Glastenbury	1	Mound	Yes
		1	Brick	Yes
BE-57	Hager Hill	2?	Brick	Yes
BE-58	Bacon Hollow	1	Mound	Yes
BE-61	East Mountain	1	Mound	Yes
BE-62	Burden Lots-South	2	Brick/Stone	Yes
BE-63	Burden Lots-North	2	Brick/Stone	Yes
BE-105	Kennedy	1	Brick/Stone?	Yes
BE-106	Cardinal Brook	4	Brick	Yes
BE-107	Crazy John Stream	3	Brick/Stone	Yes
BE-108	Thompson Farm	2	Mound	Yes
BE-134	Old Route 30	1	Brick	Yes
BE-142	Sylvan Ridge	2	Stone	Yes
BE-143	Southwest Corner	1	Brick	Yes
BE-153	Harmon Hill	6	Mound	Yes
BE-190	Northwest Corner	1	Brick	Yes
BE-191	Benedict Hollow	2?	Brick	Yes
BE-CK01	Snow Valley	?	Brick?	Yes

Table 6-1. Charcoal Kiln and Mound Sites (Cont.)

Site No.	Principal Name	Units per Site	Type	Green Mountain National Forest
Bennington County (Cont.)				
BE-CK02	Barnumville	2?	Brick	Yes
BE-CK03	Root & Jones Chemical Company	?	?	Yes
BE-CK04	Red Mountain	?	Brick?	Yes
BE-CK05	Sandgate Charcoal Plant	?	?	Yes
BE-CK06	Fayville	?	Brick	Yes
Caledonia County				
CA-CK01	I. N. Hall & Son	?	Brick?	No
Chittenden County				
CH-1	Pine Island	2	Mound	No
Orange County				
OR-CK01	West Braintree	?	Brick?	No
OR-CK02	Ely	?	Brick?	No
Rutland County				
RU-78	Old Job	8	Brick	Yes
RU-79	Ten Kilns Brook	10	Brick	Yes
RU-84	Black Branch	9	Brick	Yes
RU-85	Four Kilns	4	Brick	Yes
RU-86	Greeley's Mills	?	Mound?	Yes
RU-108	Kiln #36	1	Brick	Yes
RU-155	Kiln Brook	5	Brick	Yes
RU-156	Lampman	1	Stone*	Yes
RU-160	Danby Mountain Road	4	Brick	No
RU-188	Beaudry Brook	20	Mound	Yes
RU-190	Furnace Brook	3	Brick*	Yes
RU-FS19	Danby Station	4	Brick	Yes
RU-CK01	Dugout Road	1?	Stone?	Yes
Washington County				
WA-21	Stevenson Brook	?	Mound?	No
Windham County				
WD-66	Harold Field	1	Concrete block*	Yes
Windsor County				
WN-CK01	Salt Ash Mountain	?	Not known	No

*Rectangular kiln

exact location of the site.

For the purpose of this study, remains and ruins are used to differentiate between non-structural and structural surface evidence. Remains include charcoal mounds that have no structural elements and are relatively flat, circular areas with other mound-type characteristics (see chapter 5, "Pits and Mounds"). Ruins include charcoal kilns that are standing or partially standing structures, and might also include visible sections of brick and/or stone walls (see chapter 5, "Charcoal Kilns"). Remains are therefore associated with surface evidence of charcoal mounds while ruins are associated with surface evidence of charcoal kilns (whether of stone, brick, or combination). A charcoal-making site can be an area with or without any visible surface mound or kiln features.

WARNING to Hikers and Explorers: Although appearing sturdy, kiln ruins are in fact fragile. Climbing about them loosens stones, weakens walls, and significantly contributes to their progressive deterioration.

The Northern District

CALEDONIA COUNTY

Charcoal was being made in Barnet, Groton, and Walden in the 1880s, possibly to support foundries in St. Johnsbury and along the Connecticut and Passumpsic rivers. Charcoal customers in St. Johnsbury were the Paddock Iron Works and Fairbanks Scales. The scale company annually consumed 100,000 bushels of charcoal in addition to 300 tons of anthracite for working its 2,500 tons of pig iron, 200 tons of bar iron, 38 tons of steel, and 20 tons of copper (Hemenway vol. 1 1867:407; Child 1887:315). Some of the county charcoal burners were Felix Many of East Barnet, John B. Rogers and Frank M. Shaw of Walden who made charcoal about a mile north of Joes Pond, and Thomas B. Hall and Albert S. Clark of Groton (Child 1887:267).

CA-CK01 I. N. Hall & Son (Groton): In 1876 Thomas B. Hall started a charcoal business with his father under the name I. N. Hall & Son (Child 1887:196). Albert S. Clark of Groton also made charcoal for the company. Location of the kilns is not recorded but is suspected to be near Route 302 near West Groton, possibly toward the abandoned railroad grade. No attempt has been made to physically locate the site.

CHITTENDEN COUNTY

CH-1 Pine Island (Colchester): Chittenden County may contain one of Vermont's earliest charcoal mounds remains at Pine Island just north of Burlington. Excavations here in the late 1960s by the Vermont Archaeological Society suggest this is the site where Ira Allen contracted Aaron Brownell about 1794 to make charcoal for the former's forge and anchor shop at Colchester (chapter 4, CH-IW01). The two low mound remains were about 33 feet in diameter with shallow ditches circling them. The center of one mound revealed a center hole, which at one time held the center vertical chimney log. Also excavated was a large charred log. The mounds were covered from inches to a foot with layers of charcoal (Haviland 1973:1-4).

WASHINGTON COUNTY

WA-21 Stevenson Brook Charcoal Mounds (Waterbury): The Waterbury Last Block Company operated a sawmill a few miles east of the county line in the Little River State Park during the 19th century. According to a state park map, charcoal mounds were associated with the mill. The map shows "Coal Pit Bottoms" and "Former Charcoal Pit Burnings" about two miles up Stevenson Brook and west of the main park area near the dam (William Gove letter to author, Nov. 1, 1985).

The trail to the site, which parallels the brook on the west, was hiked in 1986 with no remains of charcoal or mounds being found. Evidence of the sawmill are cellar holes, a large rusty boiler, saw blades, part of a turbine, and unidentified castings. A wood marker "8" on a nearby tree correlates this area to the charcoal and sawmill site number on the map. Sides of hills in the area of the mill as well as potential areas on the way back down the trail were inspected with no evidence of charcoal found.

The Central District

ADDISON COUNTY

Early-19th-century charcoal making in Addison County generally centered around the needs of the Monkton Iron Company at Vergennes. Initial needs were satisfied from charcoal made in fields in the immediate area. One of these areas was Mount Fuller, in western Monkton, where charcoal making is an oral tradition. As charcoal needs grew, it forced expansion into tracts of land in the nearby towns of Panton and Addison (Smith 1886:666). In time, the Monkton Iron Company looked across the lake for better prices (Seaburg and Paterson 1971:207). So great was the company's expected need for huge amounts of charcoal that when it advertised in January 1808 that it would purchase charcoal in large quantities, it also built large barns for storing it. Eventually, there were 15 charcoal storage barns in Vergennes (Smith 1886:665).

Several mounds, oval to round, were found many years ago at Cornwall with ditches around them. One contained charcoal 18 inches deep (Haviland 1973:1). The remains of another was found about the same time in the middle of a swamp in northern Leicester. Charcoal was made up the North Branch of the Middlebury River in Ripton from 1859 to the 1880s in kilns owned by Williams & Nichols of the East Middlebury Forge, which made 9,000 bushels of charcoal a month (Smith 1886:593-594). Using Hodge's June 9, 1849 figures (see chapter 5, "Charcoal Kilns"), this calculates to the destruction of about 90 acres of forestland per year, from just this one moderate-size operation alone. According to research done by State Archeologist Giovanna Peebles, a possible charcoal mound site "on the highway from Bristol to Burlington, in Edgewood" was found to be in Bristol and Burlington, Connecticut, and not Vermont as the reference alludes (Haviland 1973:1).

Sites of charcoal mounds have been found by Green Mountain National Forest personnel in Hancock and Ripton, north of Ripton village near Huntley Brook, and on the western slopes of Worth Mountain near the Goshen line. Dick DeBonis of the U.S. Forest Service generously spent his weekends guiding us to many northern district sites. Two miles northwest near Dragon Brook are ruins of four brick-type kilns. The ruins of three more lie well hidden atop a mountain a mile southeast of Ripton village. Ruins also lie alongside Forest Road 32 just south of Route 125. At East Granville, kilns at the now-abandoned village of Sandusky made coke from coal that was mined nearby before the 1860s. The remains of mound sites were recently located on the east side of Lake Dunmore, and also a few miles southeast, in Leicester Hollow.

Northern Addison County Charcoal Sites: Because of the number of forges and furnaces that operated in northern Addison County in the early 1800s, significantly more charcoal-making sites existed than have been found in the field or in the archives. Ironworks along the Little Otter, for example, must have made large amounts of charcoal in the surrounding area, which was

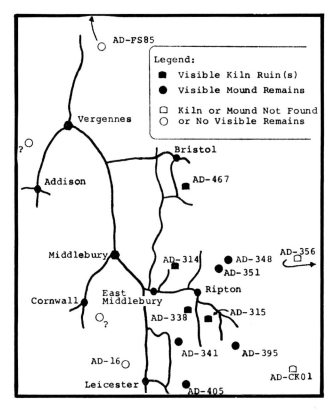

6-1. Addison County charcoal-making sites.

forested at the time. Crop and pastureland that replaced the harvested forests erased the surface evidences of these charcoal-making sites. The upper Lewis Creek area east of Route 116 might be another undiscovered charcoal-making area.

AD-467 Barker Brook Charcoal Kiln (Bristol): There are a number of published references to a charcoal kiln along the west side of South Mountain, about two miles south of Bristol village: "Midway between the Money Diggings and Rattlesnake Den, at the foot of South Mountain, lies the ruins of the Barker Charcoal Kiln, so-named from the small stream of that name, on which it was situated.... The Barker kiln was more extensive than the usual type being a stone enclosure, laid up with mortar, about 10 feet high and 20 feet square. Openings the size of bricks were made on all four sides for drafts and bricks kept on hand to fill these openings when it was necessary to close the drafts. The south side of this kiln is still in almost perfect condition" (Harvey and Kellogg 1941:94-95).

The west slope of South Mountain has been inspected many times since 1986, and the "money diggings" and "rattlesnake den" have been found based on information provided by John Peters of New Haven, and Bob Carpenter and Ted Lylis of Bristol. John Peters, who knew where the diggings were, felt that the stream shown on the USGS topographical map was Barker Brook (John Peters letter to author, Sept. 6, 1986). If this is true, a stone ruin found about a 10-minute hike uphill from Town Road 23 at the double culvert (top of the rise) could possibly be the so-called Barker charcoal kiln. An arrow drawn

on a copy of the topographical map by Bob Carpenter, pointing out the trail to the kiln, further reinforces this.

The ruin looks more like the stone foundation of a cellar hole for a small building then a charcoal kiln, and no charcoal was found inside, the hole or associated with the foundation. Charcoal was found, however, in a depression about 50 feet north and along the steep trail leading up to this flat area. Whether the Barker charcoal kiln ruin has been found or not remains a mystery.

AD-FS85 Mt. Fuller Charcoal Area (Monkton): North Ferrisburgh resident Fred Royce remembers visiting Mt. Fuller many years ago, taken there on walks by his mother and seeing areas of black soil and charcoal (Fred Royce to author, April 20, 1985). The charcoal area is up Jackey Lane near the south end of the mountain, just north of the Collins Cemetery. Inspection of the USGS map shows a somewhat level area about a half-mile up the south side of Mt. Fuller from the jeep trail, which could be the charcoal area.

An attempt was made in 1986 to inspect the charcoal area, but a barking reception from free-running dogs of all sizes and persuasions (plus my own barking dog in the pickup) and no response from a nearby house to my beeping discouraged further exploration.

The proximity of Mt. Fuller to ironworks that are documented to have operated within a few miles at a number of places along the Little Otter Creek in Ferrisburgh and New Haven, and the Otter Creek at Vergennes, give credence to charcoal being made here at an early time.

Ripton Area Charcoal Sites: Charcoal operations in the Ripton area most likely were connected with the forges at Middlebury village, and later at East Middlebury. Mound remains up the side of Worth Mountain show how deeply the forests were penetrated and exploited in early times. Local tradition indicates that the road between Ripton and Lincoln, which has not been fully inspected as part of this study, was an area of early charcoal making.

AD-314 Dragon Brook Charcoal Kilns (Ripton): This four-kiln site was initially found with the assistance of Dick DeBonis (U.S. Forest Service) in 1982 and revisited alone in 1985 to inspect results of logging operations nearby. The ruins are about two miles up Dragon Brook from the North Branch of the Middlebury River, near the end of a logging road and about 200 to 300 feet east of the brook.

Nothing historical is known about the kilns, but their proximity to the East Middlebury ironworks makes them candidates for providing charcoal to these works. Some interesting cast-iron vent liners were found here, seen at only one other charcoal kiln site (AD-315) in Vermont.

AD-315 Widow's Trail Charcoal Kilns (Ripton): Ruins of three brick-type charcoal kilns were found in 1982, with guidance to the site by Dick DeBonis (U.S. Forest Service), about 1,700 feet up an unnamed mountain a few miles southeast of Ripton village. The ruins are at the top of a cross-country trail named Widow's Trail, in a wet, swampy bog. Two ruins lie together; the other is about 50 to 60 feet to the east. Interesting hardware was also found here, similar to that at the Dragon Brook ruins (AD-314). DeBonis said he believed these kilns were operated by Parsons Billings. Nothing further is known about this site.

AD-338 Billings Charcoal Kilns (Ripton): The remains of one of the Parsons Billings charcoal kilns indicated on the 1871 Beers map of Ripton were found in 1984, just off the west side of Forest Road 32. The map shows what appear to be three kilns southeast of Ripton village, identified "coal kilns." Nearby is the residence of "P. Billings." A business notice on the map identifies him as a "Farmer and Manufr of Clapboards, Shingles, and Charcoal, and Dealer in Coarse Lumber." A number of other buildings plus a clapboard and shingle mill are also identified along this stretch of the South Branch on the map.

The ruins are about 100 feet west of the road through some thick berry bushes, about 750 feet south of the upper bridge over the South Branch. One ruin is a semicircular stone wall built into a partially caved-in embankment. Pieces of red brick and charcoal are within the ruin. A large mound of stones lies south of the ruin; there is no known connection with the kiln ruin. The other two kiln ruins might lie north of the located ruin, but poor visibility due to density and height of the thorny berry bushes in the vicinity made complete inspection impossible.

AD-348 and AD-351 Adler Brook Charcoal Mounds (Ripton): Sites of three, possibly more, mound-type remains were found in 1985 along the sides of a trail a mile south of Adler Brook. Dick DeBonis (U.S. Forest Service) led the way to the vicinity of the mound remains (AD-348). He had discovered them as part of a survey of the trail, which might be used by logging operations later in the year. The trail skirts the south side of an unnamed mountain (elevation 1,645 feet) just southeast of the juncture of the North Branch and Adler Brook.

Charcoal-making activities here might have been those of Parsons Billings, who operated a sawmill about one mile northwest of the charcoal area and was a dealer in charcoal (Beers *Addison* 1871:36). Some cellar holes and charcoal-bearing depressions were found in the vicinity, possibly indicating charcoal storage sheds.

The site of a single mound-type remain was found on the return hike down the trail from inspecting the previous kiln ruins (AD-351). It is along the same trail, uphill from the outside corner where the trail turned sharply south on its way back to the highway. A pile of small stones attracted an uphill inspection; some charcoal indications in the vicinity of the stones encouraged a broadened inspection (reason for the pile of stones is unknown). In the process the mound remain was found.

AD-395 Worth Mountain Charcoal Mounds (Goshen/Hancock): Sites of six mound-type remains were found up the west slope of Worth Mountain in 1980 by U.S. Forest Service personnel as part of a cultural resource reconnaissance survey. The remains range from 34 to 39 feet in diameter, lying in no definite pattern. Associated with the remains is a nearby cellar hole, which probably housed the collier. Because the site is some distance from any recognizable landmark, it is not certain if the site is in Goshen or Hancock.

Granville Area Charcoal Sites: Discovering that charcoal was made in this area was surprising until proximity to the railroad that ran through the valley was apparent. The railroad placed these charcoal kilns within an hour's haul to foundries at Randolph and points south, and Montpelier and points north. The "coal mine" at Sandusky (East Granville) sounds exciting and some day might be "rediscovered."

AD-356 Sandusky Charcoal/Coke Area (Granville): You would not know it today when you drive by, but at one time, Sandusky, Vermont was a bustling industrial community. The 1871 Beers map of Granville shows 15 structures including two "coal kilns," a "coal and acid house," a railroad depot, the property of Webb, Chaffee, Cummings & Company, and a sawmill:

There used to be a village called Sandusky just out of what is now East Granville village in the extreme northeastern corner of town. About 1850, a good vein of coal was discovered there. A mine was opened, kilns were built for burning coke, and a village made it profitable to ship both coal and coke. In 1857 the post office of Sandusky was opened, and for a decade the community flourished. Vermont's Sandusky unquestionably took its name from Sandusky, Ohio, where the name derives from the Iroquois and means "source of pure water." Many young Vermonters had gone west earlier in the 19th Century, and in 1868, Hemenway's Gazetteer reprinted several letters from that period that had been written from Sandusky, Ohio, to the folks back home in Vermont. Soon after the Civil War, the coal vein petered out, and the village went out of existence. Today only a few foundations and the abandoned coal mine mark the location of Sandusky in Granville (Swift 1977:41)

The area of the "coal kilns" was inspected in 1985, along the Third Branch of the White River, a few hundred feet east off Route 12A. The site is in a small patch of dense brush, next to the stream. Surface scratching revealed rusted cans, old shoes, sheet metal, nails, broken glass bottles, and some creamware. Testing in spots inside and outside the wooded area unearthed pieces of usual-looking charcoal, nothing at all like coke. No kiln-type brick or charcoal kiln artifact was found.

Inspection of the stream revealed the wood remains of a bridge that carried a spur track from the main line on the east side of the stream to the west side, just as indicated in the Beers map. The map also shows a road crossing to the east side, where the depot stood, but no evidence of either road or bridge could be found. Inspection of the stream for 100 feet upstream and downstream yielded various pieces of rusted iron castings and rod, most apparently connected with the railroad. Some pieces of red brick were found, although none appeared burnt as would charcoal kiln bricks. Railroad tracks lie just a few feet from the east side of the stream, and pieces of ties, spikes, etc., lie along the embankment on that side. Today's tracks, however, might not be where tracks are shown in the 1871 Beers map. If coke was in fact made here, it might have been the only coke made in Vermont.

Between the highway and the falls is the remains of a dam, possibly that of the sawmill. Just upstream, a 5-foot-square thick iron sheet that looks like a door of a charcoal kiln (coke kiln?) was found. A wide inspection around and above the falls area failed to reveal any kiln evidence. More "coal kilns" are shown on the Beers map about three miles south in Braintree (see OR-CK01).

AD-CK01 Cobble Mountain Charcoal Kilns (Hancock): Charcoal kilns were supposed to have operated somewhere up the west slope of Cobble Mountain but a search through the area in 1989 resulted in no kiln finds. According to verbal directions by Dick DeBonis (U.S. Forest Service), the subject area is west of Route 100 and "a bit south" of the Route 125 intersection. The section of the mountain inspected yielded some old cellar holes many hundreds of feet up the steep slope and some suspicious black dirt, but no positive charcoal finds. We might not have been "a bit south" enough (see also chapter 8, AD-LK02).

Salisbury Area Charcoal Sites: The most interesting mound finds in the county were those made on tiny Huntley Island in the middle of Salisbury Swamp, in the midst of cabins and a rifle range at Keewaydin Camps, and up Leicester Hollow one hot, muggy day amid clouds of mosquitos. The hike up the trail through the hollow is a must for anyone who wants to see a real piece of Vermont wilderness. That pioneers could have eked out a living in this narrow gorge by farming and charcoal making reflects on the character of the people who settled the land.

AD-16 Huntley Island Charcoal Mound (Leicester): Huntley Island is a slight rise in Salisbury Swamp, one of a group of swamps extending from Middlebury on the north to Sudbury and Brandon on the south. The island is small and during spring floods it probably disappears. It is located in northwest Leicester and borders on the south side of Leicester Creek about a mile before it flows into Otter Creek.

The site was inspected in 1978 by archeologists William Bayreuther, Cindy Cook, Frank L. Cowan, and James B. Petersen of the University of Vermont while canoeing the river. The charcoal remains were described as being a 4- to 6-inch-high 20-foot-diameter mound with a 1- to 2-foot wide rise at its outside edge, resembling a low-profile donut on a level tree-covered area. How and why charcoal was made on an island in the middle of a swamp is unknown unless the area was sufficiently tree-covered and dry at one time to make the effort worthwhile.

AD-341 Keewaydin Camps Charcoal Mounds (Salisbury): Surface remains of four mound-types were recorded in 1985 on the grounds of Keewaydin Camps, about 100 yards from the northeast corner of Lake Dunmore. The site was found through information provided by Polly Darnell of the Sheldon Museum Library, Middlebury.

Israel Davey (of the Fair Haven Iron Works and eventual owner of the Middlebury Iron Works) purchased the former forge (1849) of A. B. Huntley, and "bought a portion of mountain land, across from Keewaydin Camps, where wood was burned to make charcoal for his furnace [forge]. That area is still known by some as Coal Kiln Flats" (Petersen 1976:25). The "across from Keewaydin Camps" had me searching the west side of Lake Dunmore until Polly directed me to the east side.

The remains are on a relatively flat area east and uphill of Route 53, near the end of a trail that joins the highway at the abandoned red schoolhouse. Some of the kiln remains are integrated into camp structures. The remains are characterized by 40-foot-diameter circles of stone plus the round "gutter" at the outside edge. Some remains are more obvious than others. Since three of the remains are grouped relatively close together, with the fourth somewhat isolated, one or more kiln remains might have existed in the area between at an earlier time. There

are many more remains uphill from these (Barry Schultz King to author, May 26, 1989).

AD-405 Leicester Hollow Charcoal Mounds (Leicester): Hiking up Leicester Hollow during bug season must be experienced to be appreciated. A search for a reported rectangular charcoal kiln was undertaken in the hollow the first June weekend of 1986. To make conditions worse, it was a very muggy day and sprinkled on and off just enough to increase the discomfort. As it turned out, the rectangular-shaped kiln was not found, but remains of three mound-types were.

The hollow is a seven-mile-long north-south ravine that is drained by Leicester Hollow Brook. Silver Lake, elevation 1,250 feet and headwaters of the brook, is at the northern end. At the southern end the brook joins Neshobe River. The sides of the hollow are generally steep and rocky, yet the hollow was not only settled from about 1820 to 1900, but industry of sorts was carried on here (Peleszak 1984:6, 11).

The valley floor widens a bit at "the Greenings," halfway up the hollow, where three mound-type remains were found. A cellar hole and some fruit trees indicate where the widow Glynn lived. Charcoal might have been used by a forge that operated in Goshen at an early date; the mounds were most likely connected with blast furnaces in Forest Dale and Brandon village. The remains are 30 to 100 feet east of and parallel to the trail. They are 30 feet in diameter and cut somewhat half-moon-style into the rising embankment.

About 500 feet north of the cellar hole on the same side of the trail is supposed to be remains of the rectangular charcoal kiln. It is "bermed up and the ground surface inside is covered with charcoal" (Billee Hoornbeek letter to the author, March 2, 1986). Inspection of the area turned up nothing. (Iron was also discovered in the hollow in 1815 but it is unknown where or if the ore was exploited.)

ORANGE COUNTY

OR-CK01 West Braintree Coal Kilns (Braintree): The 1871 Beers map of Braintree indicates an "Acid Ho. & Coal Kilns" in northwest Braintree, at the junction of the White River Third Branch and Brackett Brook. Webb, Chaffee, Cummings & Company might have had something to do with this operation since that name is indicated a bit upstream along the brook, and is also associated with "coal kilns" in Sandusky (AD-356).

Inspection of the area in 1985 resulted in finding no charcoal or anything associated with coal kilns.

OR-CK02 Ely Charcoal Kilns (Fairlee): Charcoal kilns operated in the village of Ely in the vicinity of what is now a lumberyard along the Connecticut River (Collamer Abbott to author, May 19, 1990). These kilns made charcoal for the copper furnaces at Vershire. No attempt has been made to inspect the site.

RUTLAND COUNTY

A variety of coal then called brown coal was mined at Brandon and used to drive steam engines associated with providing blast to the furnace at Forest Dale. Not hard coal, it was more of an intermediate between peat and bituminous, known as lignite, and was not an uncommon occurrence in New England. The lignite vein was a half-mile south of the Forest Dale Cemetery

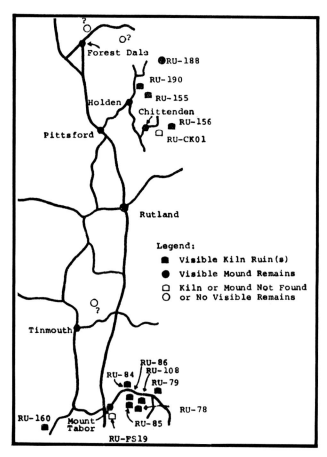

6-2. *Rutland County charcoal-making sites.*

off Route 73, descending obliquely, 20 feet wide by 14 feet thick, to as deep as 90 feet (Thompson 1842:50). As recently as 1911, many hundred tons of it were mined during a coal shortage (*Brandon* 1961:58).

Some charcoal might have been made right at the Forest Dale ironworks site. Six 4- to 5-foot-high and 85- to 14-foot-long (bottom to top) terraced stone walls just west of the furnace mark where the hillside was reinforced to prevent crumbling into a possible charcoal-making area below. Much charcoal was found on the ground in front of these walls during the three-day cooperative recording project in May 1989 by the Vermont Division for Historic Preservation, the Northern New England Chapter–SIA, and the Vermont Archaeological Society.

Charcoal for Conant's furnace at Brandon village came from a settlement called New Philadelphia, about five miles to the southeast. Here, a community of charcoal burners lived, making charcoal by the old mound method and socializing little with the outside world. Many communities made up chiefly of char-coal burners in New York and New England shared the custom of keeping to themselves (see Blanchard 1960:1-22, about Dud-leytown, Connecticut, a fascinating story of an isolated charcoal-making community). The town of Philadelphia was absorbed into Goshen and Chittenden in 1814 and 1816, respectively, but the cellar holes of the community still remain. Prices of

charcoal recorded at Forest Dale were "$3.00 in cash, $3.50 in trade, for a bushel of charcoal." Receipts read "cole" for charcoal. Some charcoal was made in an area near the Brandon-Goshen line called "the basin"—a natural hollow into which Basin Brook flows (*Brandon* 1961:45, 48). During logging operations in this vicinity in 1991, much charcoal was reported churned to the surface due to the skidding of logs (Henry Paynter to author, June 8, 1991). Charcoal was also made on the slopes of Miller Hill in Sudbury (Mary Kennedy to author, April 13, 1986).

Local tradition in Tinmouth is that charcoal was made up and down the Channel for furnaces operating in the vicinity during the early 1800s. No wonder then, when Nelson Jaquay plowed the large field behind his house, a number of black, charcoal-bearing patches were exposed in various parts of the fields, formerly well hidden beneath sod and tall grass. How many more fields in the valley are withholding secrets?

In parts of Pittsfield and Chittenden, the Tweed River Iron Company (successor to the Pittsfield Iron and Steel Company) operated an extensive mining and charcoal-making business in the 1880s to support a bloomery forge in Hartford, Connecticut. Ore and charcoal were shipped from the mountains by wagons to Bethel, then by rail to Hartford (Smith and Rann 1886:551-552).

The 1854 map of Rutland County indicates "coal kilns" in Chittenden, east of the old mountain road from East Pittsford to Chittenden village. Farther east near Lefferts Pond are the partially standing remains of a rectangular-shaped charcoal kiln. The ruins of five brick-type kilns were also found up Kiln Brook in Chittenden; nearby along Furnace Brook are ruins of three brick-type separate-bay kilns.

Charcoal kilns operated near the West Castleton-Fair Haven town line in the late 1860s (Beers *Rutland* 1869:18). Kilns might also have been located about a mile northwest of Beaver Pond at Proctor, atop a high bluff. There were also charcoal kilns along the slopes of Dorset Mountain in southern Danby (Crosby et al. 1976:7). Mountain areas behind Ruth Foy's property and also on the east slope of the mountain above the quarry might yet reveal some charcoal kiln surprises.

Chittenden Area Charcoal Sites: Charcoal making in the uplands of Chittenden provided fuel for ironworks at Holden in earlier days, and at Pittsford in later days. Remains of mound-type operations can be found almost at will up any small valley in the upper Furnace Brook area. One of the most remarkable finds was that of three brick-type rectangular kilns, only a stone's throw from River Road. Discoveries such as this show that much more is waiting to be found in that area, and also along the ridge farther to the south (as shown by the charcoal that George Butts digs up in his garden).

RU-188 Beaudry Brook Charcoal Mounds (Chittenden): Sites of 20 charcoal mounds about 2,000 feet up the west slope of Bloodroot Mountain in the town of Chittenden were inspected in 1988. Information leading to recording this site was provided in late 1987 by U.S. Forest Service archeologists Billee Hoornbeek and David Lacy. Although Billee reported finding "a field of kilns" in the vicinity of a cellar hole, the majority of the finds we made were well outside the immediate area of the cellar hole. We did notice much surface disturbance in this area, as if made by tree-throws, which more and more started looking like what Billee might have been describing as kiln sites.

Billee said that the kilns were small, disturbed, and possibly used once. I feel that a mound-type charcoal kiln might be small and disturbed, but considering all the work that goes into site preparation (stump and rock removal, leveling, rain gutter around base), no mound site would be used just once. And why up to 30 of these "one-time" kilns in such close proximity?

The period of making charcoal in this area is unknown, but charcoal made here probably supported blast furnace, forge, or foundry operations in Pittsford (see chapter 4: Keith-Granger blast furnaces 1791–1880s, RU-57, five miles south along Furnace Brook; and the ca.-1820 Cooley and Gibbs furnace/foundry, RU-153, about six miles downstream). The late Patrick E. Mooney recollected the hillsides above Pittsford aglow at night from the charcoal kilns (McWhorter Oct. 2, 1953:68). Note that Kiln Brook, site of brick-type charcoal kilns (RU-155) is about two miles south of the Beaudry Brook kilns. It is generally felt that brick/stone-type charcoal kilns began to replace mound-type kilns during the Civil War period. But some mound operations might have continued into the 1870s and 1880s. There is a local tradition in Monterey, Massachusetts of mound-type charcoal kilns operating into the early 1900s (Richmond Furnace, near Pittsfield, operated to 1923).

The mound remains were generally found within 100 feet either side of a trail; most within 50 feet. The trails are narrow and probably contemporary with the charcoal mounds. Bits of charcoal can be found almost anywhere in the trail beds, probably having spilled from charcoal wagons. Some remains are better defined than others. Identification of a potential mound remain was made by locating an approximately 25- to 30-foot-diameter oval, flat area, free of large stones, and circled by a relatively higher concentration of stones (probably increased by stones thrown or removed from the kiln area proper). Some hillside remains were dug slightly into the uphill side with the downhill side built up. On these, much charcoal could be found eroding out of the built-up circular embankment. Some remains on level ground were slightly built up. Each site was tested with a trowel in at least two places to determine whether the soil was naturally black or contained bits of charcoal. Charcoal found without associated kiln surface features was determined to be spillage or the remains of charcoal piles.

RU-190 Furnace Brook Rectangular Charcoal Kilns (Chittenden): Collapsed remains of a multi-bay charcoal-making site were found in 1988. Discovery was made while driving along River Road on the way to Steam Mill Brook, and stopping to inspect some "foundation walls."

The site is located about 150 feet up a side road that runs northeast off the south side of River Road, about 1½ miles north of Holden and 600 feet north of the concrete bridge over Kiln Brook. The site is bordered on three sides by a wall of heavy stone, 8 feet at highest (north corner), the open end facing southwest (downhill). It contains three charcoal kiln ruins, each made of brick. The westernmost ruin is about 14 feet wide by 56 feet long; the middle ruin is 12 feet wide and about the same length; the easternmost ruin is about 10 feet wide and 50 feet long. The ruins lie parallel to each other about 15 feet apart. The area was heavily covered with leaves and branches in November, and with the bricks so randomly dis-

tributed in the direct kiln vicinity, it was difficult to determine exactly where kiln wall foundations lay underneath it all. Two pieces of hardware were found in the site.

In his paper on the manufacture of charcoal in kilns, Thomas Egleston dimensioned two types of rectangular kilns in New England:

	Type A	Type B
Length	50	40
Width	12	15
Height	12	15
Capacity in cords	55	70

Egleston described a number of construction techniques, none specific to New England (or Vermont) kilns (Egleston May 1879:378-386). Since finding the Furnace Brook rectangular separate-bay kilns is thus far a unique discovery for Vermont, the site warrants close study and attention to historic preservation.

RU-155 Kiln Brook Charcoal Kilns (Chittenden): Five kiln ruins were found up Kiln Brook in 1986 per directions given by Harley Smith of Proctor. He had not been to the site in 60 years but his directions were right on the money. The ruins are about a one-mile hike up Kiln Brook, which is a tributary of Furnace Brook. They lie in a line, parallel to and about 250 feet back from the north shore of the brook. Here the little valley widens, resulting in a sort of flat-bottom basin with little tributaries entering from the north. A snowmobile trail marked VAST (Vermont Association of Snow Travelers) enters this valley from the south, crosses Kiln Brook over a plank and log bridge, curves north across a tributary on a shorter bridge, and passes directly between the ruins and the brook. The five ruins are set back into a low embankment, the top of which would have been level with the tops of the kilns when standing. Stone walls (foundations?) lie about 100 feet behind the ruins.

A kiln door was found that looked much like that of a conical kiln after it was cleaned of leaves and dirt. In a 1953 interview by the *Rutland Herald*, then 86-year-old Patrick Mooney described working at the Pittsford furnace when he was age 15. He said that the charcoal came from five kilns, which took 90 cords at a time to charge (McWhorter Oct. 2, 1953:68). This calculates to about 18 cords per kiln, low for the usual 25 to 40 cords per kiln for the time. But if these were conical kilns the low cordwood figure would be more in line with charcoal kiln practice. Reinspection of the ruin foundations in 1987 did not, however, reveal conical walls.

RU-156 Lampman Rectangular Charcoal Kiln (Chittenden): The stone-type ruin of a rectangular charcoal kiln was found in 1986 on the property of Ken Smith, about a mile southeast of Lefferts Pond (about three miles east of Chittenden village). Directions were given by some residents of Dugout Road while I was involved in trying to find another kiln site in the vicinity.

Child's gazetteer indicates that Benjamin N. Lampman was a manufacturer of charcoal (Child 1881:310). Local historian Bert Muzzy confirmed that the ruin is on property once owned by Lampman.

The most striking feature of this ruin is its rectangular shape:

16 feet wide by 37 feet long. It is made of stone with walls generally 4 to 6 feet high; one corner is about 10 feet high. Walls are about 2 feet thick, with signs of mortaring.

Vent holes suggest the use of bricks for draft control. The inside walls are black and hard; black pitch is accumulated at the vent holes. All collapsed stone appears to have fallen into the kiln; none of the floor is visible due to the amount of stone piled inside of the ruin.

Charging and discharging seem to have been carried out at one end of the kiln, suggested by what appears to be an opening at the back (uphill) end. Some bits of charcoal were found on the ground outside this opening. A large flat sill stone makes up the base of this opening, suggesting a ramp from it to the slightly elevated ground adjacent. At this end of the ruin, a 2-foot-wide ditch runs the width and a few feet around each corner of the base of the walls, probably to keep rain runoff from leaking through the base and into the kiln floor.

There is no indication of how the kiln was roofed. The walls are vertical with no visible reinforcement to support a peak- or arch-type roof. The roof might have been large, flat, cast-iron or steel sheets, maybe removable to facilitate additional loading and unloading access. A section of railroad track sticking up through the stone wall breakdown outside the front (downhill) end of the ruin further suggests how a flat roof might have been supported. Or the kiln could have operated with no roof (open top), the cordwood covered with wet leaves and earth, much the same as in mound-type kilns.

In his report on rectangular kilns, Egleston described kilns made of brick with arch roofs. The rectangular kiln was reinforced by wood beams mounted vertically along the outside walls. Cast-iron rods bolted at the tops and bottoms of opposite beams ran widthwise through the inside of the kiln. Although this technique could have been used at this site there is neither evidence of any wood beams having stood outside the walls nor rods seen in the remains. Additionally, there does not appear to be enough collapsed stone inside the ruin to have been used for an arch roof (assuming all the collapsed stonework still remains).

RU-CK01 Dugout Road Charcoal Kiln (Chittenden): A charcoal kiln site (and possibly ruin) exists somewhere east of Dugout Road, about a mile southeast of Chittenden village, but a search of the area in 1987 failed to locate it. It is indicated as "coal kiln" on the 1854 Rutland County map. A road was recently cut through the area of interest and might possibly have destroyed any existing ruin, although much charcoal and/ or black soil would usually have remained. A field site sketch map of RU-FS117 (not included in this study), which is in the vicinity of Dugout Road, shows a 20-foot-diameter feature that might be the kiln remain. Both 1854 county map and the RU-FS117 sketch map indications are quite vague, however, and the ruin might yet be waiting to be found.

Silas L. Griffith, Vermont's Charcoal Baron: One of the most concentrated areas of charcoal making in Vermont, on the scale of an industrial operation, was at Mount Tabor during the 1870–1900 period. Silas L. Griffith, resident of the bordering town of Danby and a descendant of one of the town's earliest settlers, acquired a significant interest in logging and lumbering mills in the Danby/Mount Tabor/Dorset area. Born at Danby on June 27, 1837, the son of David Griffith, he attended the district school until about age 16, then became a clerk in the general store of Lapham & Bruce (Silas L. Griffith biography is generally from Benton 1917:215-218 unless otherwise noted). Two years later he became clerk at the P. D. Ames store in East Dorset and the following year he attended Kimball Union Academy at Meriden, New Hampshire. Age 20 found him traveling west to become a teacher, but while visiting on the way at Buffalo, New York, the financial panic of 1857 hit, his money became severely depreciated, and his westward trek ended. He got a job logging.

Returning home to Danby, he opened a general store with the financial assistance of his father's endorsement of a security note. But the New York City merchants withheld credit until his cousin, H. G. Lapham, guaranteed his accounts. He eventually succeeded as a general merchant and within four years was one of Danby's more substantial businessmen. His store operated under the name of S. L. Griffith & Company, although he had no partner; the "& Company" permitted him to keep his store and his lumber business accounts separate. During this time he married Elizabeth M. Staples, on May 20, 1863.

In 1864 (at age 27) his business was worth $48,000; the next year he sold the store part of it to his brothers C. H. and W. B. Griffith. Through foreclosure of a mortgage, he took possession of a vast tract of land in Mount Tabor, bordering Danby on the east and characterized by its mountainous terrain. Griffith now pursued the business of logging and lumbering, acquired additional land, and built many sawmills. Noticing the amounts of slash, cull logs, and other discarded waste wood from the sawmills, in 1872 he began to use this to make charcoal.

He initially contracted with the Barnum Richardson Company, which operated a number of blast furnaces and forges in northwestern Connecticut. Barnum Richardson Company was founded by Milo Barnum of Dover Plains, New York and Leonard Richardson, Milo's brother-in-law. By the 1880s, the company was run by William H. Barnum, and by then it owned and operated five foundries in Chicago, Jersey City, and Lime Rock, Connecticut, plus eight blast furnaces, each needing 1,200 bushels of charcoal per day (Cantwell July 1989:21). In addition to the many charcoal kilns it operated in other parts of Vermont (see Mad Tom Brook Area Sites), the company operated two charcoal kilns at Barnumville just west of the railroad siding (Child 1880:142). The contract called for Griffith to produce a million bushels of charcoal at the selling price of 13½¢ per bushel ($135,000) on board railroad cars at Danby Station. The contract was subsequently increased by Mr. Barnum to 13¼¢ per, for 1,250,000 bushels ($165,625) for his own Lime Rock Iron Company. But after receiving less than half of the charcoal, the Connecticut companies refused any further shipments, claiming the charcoal was not up to their specifications, when actually a disastrous drop in the selling price of pig iron had hit the market. Griffith responded by suing the firms for $100,000, but an agreement was worked out. Barnum continued to buy charcoal with contracts made orally each year thereafter, and in time, Griffith and Barnum became trusted businessmen and good friends. Griffith said later that Mr. Barnum and also Philip M. Moen of the Washburn & Moen Wire Works at Worcester, Massachusetts, were his two best friends.

In time, Griffith developed the largest individually owned

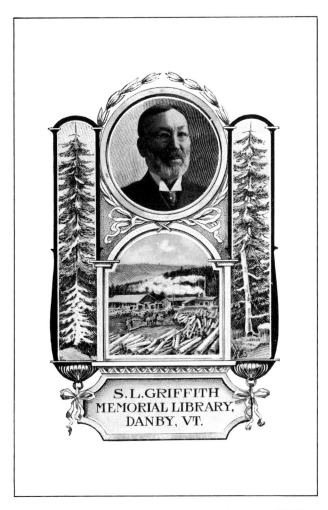

6-3. *Silas L. Griffith and his logging and charcoal works at Old Job as illustrated on a library bookplate (courtesy S. L. Griffith Memorial Library, Danby).*

business in Vermont. In addition to his charcoal and lumbering businesses, he had large property and business interests with Eugene McIntyre and others in Peru, Arlington, Dorset, Manchester, and Wallingford. He also owned a large tract at Groton in partnership with Charles L. Sowle. His total property exceeded 50,000 acres, he owned more than 200 horses, and his payroll included over 600 people, which calculates to the equivalent of a moderate-size contemporary Vermont township. He cut about 24,000 feet of spruce and a million feet of hardwood for lumber, and 1,000 cords of fuel wood, most of which became charcoal.

He owned nine sawmills, at least three dozen charcoal kilns, and maintained six general stores. From the large stock maintained at his main store at Danby, other smaller stores at his logging villages and camps drew their supplies. Connected with his works at Danby Station he had a large steam mill for grinding feed; adjoining this mill was another for making shooks (barrel staves) and boxes made from lumber not suitable for other purposes. Another shop repaired wagons and sleds; yet another

repaired harnesses. He was a pioneer in the use of saws in place of axes to cut down trees, reducing waste wood. All lumber not marketable became charcoal. He even found a market for all the sawdust (possibly for packing and storing blocks of ice). Each of his mills was connected to his main office at Danby by a private telephone wire, generally thought to have been the earliest use of the telephone in Vermont. His office was very modern and elegant for the time—lighted by acetylene gas and heated by hot water. To satisfy his needs and those of the town he built a waterworks, drawing from a spring two miles from the village. And in response to an expressed need by the village, he opened a public meat market at Danby.

At Buffum Pond, renamed Lake Griffith, he built a summer home and in his later years owned a winter residence called The Palms at National City, south of San Diego, California, where he died on July 21, 1903 at age 66. He had served in the Vermont Senate and was often mentioned as a candidate for governor, but always declined. He left a number of benefactions on his death in which Mount Tabor and Danby shared, including a fund to provide support for schools and purchase of shoes and clothing for poor children. He also left money for annual Christmas gifts for the children of Danby, which continues to this day (Daley Winter 1986:8). His desire to sponsor construction and maintenance of a public library was fulfilled by his family: the S. L. Griffith Memorial Library still serves the town. His grave is at the south end of the Scottsville cemetery, about two miles north of the village and across the valley from Mount Tabor.

Griffith's charcoal-making areas were mainly in the town of Mount Tabor. Here he operated at least 36 charcoal kilns located at many sites: Mill Glen (Old Job), Ten Kilns Meadow, Four Kilns (near Greeley Mills), the Black Branch Job, and at the railroad station down in the valley at Danby village (the depot and kilns were just inside the Mount Tabor town line). Each of these operations supported settlements of varying sizes consisting of woodchoppers, colliers, teamsters, and their families. The Mount Tabor kilns annually converted 20,000 cords of wood into 1,000,000 bushels of charcoal, shipping it all from tiny Danby Depot to customers throughout the northeast.

Griffith's initial venture into the charcoal business began at a small settlement called Mill Glen where a sawmill had been built and operated by Frank Butler in 1854. The sawmill burned sometime after coming into the possession of Griffith, who rebuilt it to operate by steam engine. The mill had an annual capacity of two to three million feet of lumber. Lath and shingles were also cut here. These were all cut from the better grades of wood. In the lesser grades and the immense amount of scrap, Griffith recognized additional profit, and in 1872 it prompted him to build his first six charcoal kilns, at Mill Glen. In time, two more kilns were added to these operations which, by the late 1880s, were described as comprising 40 to 50 structures and buildings. These included the steam-operated sawmill measuring 40 by 80 feet, which made lumber from the choice hardwood and cordwood of the balance for the kilns. There were also a large boardinghouse for single men, tenant houses and cottages for families, a schoolhouse, general store and office, harness shop, wagon shop, blacksmith shop, and stables for the animals. The houses were furnished rent free, supplies near cost, and as many needs as possible met on the spot. When

179

the post office opened the community was known as Griffith, and so identified on the 1893 USGS topographic map. From this settlement, a hundred men in gangs of 12 to 15 men each cut wood from October to April. Some remained in the woods living in log shanties (note Three Shanties Brook about a mile south) while others returned nightly to the settlement.

Mount Tabor Area Charcoal Sites: The Big Branch, formed by the juncture of Ten Kilns Brook and Lake Brook, originates where the community of Griffith once stood. About a mile up Ten Kilns Brook was a second extensive charcoal-making settlement containing 10 kilns at two sites, five kilns at each. It was also known as the Summit Job, in reference to being uphill from Griffith, although "summit" here is misleading. It is only about 300 feet in elevation higher than Griffith, with much higher hilltops all around. Initial date of operation at Ten Kilns is unknown, but is was described as well under way by 1885.

A mile downstream from Griffith was a third charcoal-making operation known as Four Kilns, named for the four kilns there. The ca.-1840 Greeley sawmill was built a bit down and across the stream. When the sawmill passed to Silas Griffith, it was reported no longer in operation.

About a mile farther downstream is the juncture with the Black Branch Brook, and a half-mile up this brook was the Black Branch Job, where a fourth charcoal-making settlement existed. Here were nine more kilns at a community that was about the size of the little village of Griffith. By 1885, the settlement included a blacksmith and wagon repair shop, a school, and some 20 tenant houses. Operations probably ended the same time as the others at Mount Tabor, although many people continued living in the vicinity until the 1940s.

A fifth group of charcoal kilns was at Danby Depot. Four kilns operated here, alongside a railroad siding just northeast of the railroad station.

The lumber and charcoal industry at Mount Tabor made a fortune for the Griffith and McIntyre partnership. The operations also attracted the attention of writers and artists, one publishing a romanticized illustrated description of the charcoal business in an 1885 magazine (Chapin April 1885:9-10). In 1893 Griffith charred a whole maple log many feet in diameter in one of his kilns and shipped it nearly a thousand miles for exhibition at the World's Columbian Exposition in Chicago (*Inventory* 1941:10). The log was probably charred at one of the kilns at the depot, since they were directly adjacent to the railroad tracks.

Within a few years, the efficiency of the woodchoppers at Mount Tabor resulted in the depletion of the forest. The sawmill at Griffith closed about 1905, the kilns cooled, and in seven years, the village was nearly deserted. A 1912 photo shows the kilns still standing along with some other structures. The property was sold to a New York lumber company and later the second-growth timber was cut to fuel a lime-burning business at South End (chapter 8, RU-157). It was probably about this time the abortive attempt was made to build a railroad up the Big Branch from the main line near South End. The old right-of-way can still be seen east off Route 7, just south of the cemetery. By 1930, the population of Mount Tabor had dropped to 130 and a few years later most of Silas Griffith's original holdings in the town became part of the newly created Green Mountain National Forest.

The sites of the charcoal kilns were inspected in the summer of 1982 when 33 of the 35 documented kiln ruins were found. The 34th was located in 1983 and the 35th in the spring of 1985. Not a total surprise, an undocumented 36th kiln ruin was found in the summer of 1985 northwest of Old Job.

RU-78 Old Job (Mount Tabor): The ruins of seven charcoal kilns were found at Old Job in the summer of 1982. Surface

6-4. A ca.-1910 postcard showing the four charcoal kilns (arrow) at Danby Station.

remains of the eighth were found the next spring, astride the alternate Lake Brook Trail immediately southwest of the juncture of Ten Kilns Brook and Lake Brook.

Inspection of the site resulted in finding seven of the ruins in high brush and trees northwest of the trail. On the opposite side of the trail from the ruins is a mound of sawdust. There are also cellar holes to the west of the kiln ruins. At the northwest end of the seven ruins the eighth kiln site was found the following spring before the high brush season, barely a circular rise on the ground.

Some collapsed bricks were cleared from facing sides of one ruin in order to study wall design, course structure, vent location, and depth and design of the kiln foundation.

6-6. *A top-loading-hole cover, unearthed at the Four Kilns site in Mount Tabor.*

6-5. *One variety of charcoal kiln top-loading-hole cover at Old Job.*

wall that provided loading bridge access to the tops of the kilns. No iron bands or vents were found, but other hardware lies in the vicinity. Large 2- by 3-inch pieces of charcoal lie about the ruins.

The lower set of ruins is located on the opposite side of the

At Griffith, now identified as Old Job on the maps, the eight kiln ruins are in dense brush a few dozen feet south of the Lake Brook Trail. On the opposite side of the trail is a 30-foot-high by 200-foot-diameter mound of sawdust, a giant artifact of a more recent woodworking operation; there is no connection to the charcoal kilns. Cellar holes in the high grass still contain broken domestic remains of the settlement and evidence of potholing for bottles and souvenirs is widespread. Badly rusted horseshoes and cracked axe heads are found lying about everywhere. No kilns remain standing anywhere; all are collapsed, leaving approximately 28-foot-diameter circles of brick walls, a foot or two high. In some walls the ankle vents can still be seen. Most iron hardware (iron bands, doors, lintels, rings, etc.) has disappeared, probably collected for scrap during World War II. Much brick is also gone, scavenged by collectors and campers through the years.

RU-79 Ten Kilns Brook (Mount Tabor): The ruins of the Ten Kilns Brook sites were found in two groups of five ruins each in the vicinity of the Forest Road 10 bridge at Ten Kilns Brook, about a mile upstream from Old Job (RU-78). The upper set of five ruins is located on the north side of Ten Kilns Brook, about 100 feet east of the road. The round brick ruins lie in a generally east-west line parallel to the stone retaining

6-7. *A very heavy cast-iron sill plate for a front-loading door, unearthed near the remains of a charcoal kiln at the Little Black Branch site in Mount Tabor.*

6-8. *Old Job, high up in the Green Mountains at Mount Tabor in the 1880s, showing: (top) the sawmill at right, charcoal kilns at left, and housing in between; and (bottom) charcoal kilns along the Big Branch (Chapin April 1885:15).*

road and about 100 feet southwest of the concrete bridge. Except that these ruins lie in a generally north-south line, the character of the ruins is about the same as the upper set. A possible cellar hole is located near the road, and there is a length of railroad track in the proximity of the ruins. The track was probably left over from construction of the concrete bridge (track can be seen as part of the bridge reinforcement). The usual kiln hardware also lies scattered about the site.

Between the ruins and the brook is a small camping/picnic area. Camp was set up here the day before in anticipation of finding the area kiln ruins. The upper site was found later that first day; the search for the lower site was left for the next day. What a surprise to discover the next day that the tent had been pitched the previous day in thick grass straddling the ground-level wall of one kiln remain of the lower site. We had slept the night before half in and half out of what was left of the kiln ruin.

Across and below the brook are some features that might relate to an earlier blacksmith shop and a sawmill indicated here in the 1869 Beers map of Mount Tabor. Ten Kilns Brook flows down a series of good falls, beginning at the bridge and continuing for about 150 feet. A cellar hole that contains charcoal is near the upper falls. About 50 feet west a flume runs

parallel to the brook, containing 13 iron hoops that might have held a circular wood pipe. All the iron hoops are flattened; diameter is estimated at 18 inches. The flume ends at the brook next to another building feature. Domestic debris lies scattered about the surface. Closer to the road is a low mound of red brick.

No cellar holes to support a work force could be found in the vicinity of the ruins. There has been recent logging immediately north and northwest of the ruins and any cellar holes here might have been destroyed.

RU-84 Black Branch (Mount Tabor): Ruins of the Black Branch kilns are a one-minute walk north along the Long Trail from the Forest Road 10 parking area, between the two concrete bridges. Here at Black Branch Job are the remains of nine kilns. Seven of the ruins lie along the Long Trail north of the road. The first pair of ruins lie about 250 feet up the trail from the road, the next five in another group about 300 feet farther up; the first three are on a lower level and the other two on an upper level. On the embankment behind the higher two ruins are the stone wall remains of a charging and loading platform.

An old road atop this embankment parallels the ruins back downhill to the road. It can be picked up continuing south of the road below the parking area along the east bank of the Little Black Branch to a crossing at the Big Black Branch juncture.

6-9. *In the lower right corner it reads "Carting Coal down the Mountain." This was once a common scene along the high trails in Mount Tabor (Chapin April 1885:13).*

There are no visible remains of a bridge here but the road can be seen continuing downhill along the west bank of the Black Branch, and probably connects with the old road along the Big Branch that connects Danby Station with Old Job and points east. South of the parking lot area and alongside the old road are stone walls and hardware. These might mark the site of the sawmill.

The eighth and ninth ruins of this group are less visible to the west along the Little Black Branch. The ninth is only barely visible just downstream of the eighth.

Much of the brick from these ruins, as with others, was used for trail maintenance, as evidenced by the red bricks that lie in the trail. No cellar holes of this once-bustling community have been found.

RU-85 Four Kilns (Mount Tabor): The site consists of two sets of two ruins each, on about an east-west line and 160 feet apart. The west pair have only small sections of foundation stones to mark the sites of two kilns. The east pair are more obvious with their brick walls and vent holes. Much of the brick from these kilns was used in the maintenance of nearby Lake Brook Trail, which passes between the ruins and the embankment of Black Branch Brook, and also along the trail about a quarter-mile to the east near a spring. (The U.S. Forest Service dynamited the standing kilns years ago, considering them at the time hazards to hikers, who camped in some of them.) Below the embankment are partially buried remains of kiln hardware, parts of stoves, and other unidentified objects.

At Four Kilns, the Lake Brook Trail joins the Long Trail. Northward and across the trail suspension bridge from Four

Kilns are the cavernous foundation hole remains of the Greeley sawmill.

RU-86 Greeley's Mills Charcoal Area (Mount Tabor): The remains of Greeley's Mills are located on the north side of the Big Branch Brook, just downstream from the Long Trail suspension bridge over the brook and a few hundred feet downstream of the charcoal kiln ruins at Four Kilns. The mill was built in 1840; the 1869 Beers map of Mount Tabor indicates Greeley's Mills at the site, a sawmill, and the names O. and A. Greeley. By 1885, the mill had passed into the hands of Silas Griffith.

Remains of an approximately 20-foot-deep sawmill cellar hole and foundation are visible about 120 feet downstream of the Long Trail suspension bridge. The trail barely squeezes between the deep foundation hole on one side and the steep bank of the brook on the other. Upstream of the foundation are dozens of partially buried iron hoops, all nearly in a straight line and about 6 to 12 inches apart. One iron hoop measured about 8 feet around the outside, which calculates to a 27- to 28-inch-diameter pipe, depending on the thickness of the pipe wall. The race connected the mill to an upstream flume, foundations of which lie precariously close to the concrete footing for the trail bridge.

Immediately uphill of the mill site are hundreds of feet of stone wall and within the walls are two cellar holes, a cemetery, and an area of ground near the center covered with charcoal. No cellar holes appear in the immediate vicinity of the charcoal, and the charcoal resembles that at kiln sites, ruling out a possible burned-down structure. A low stone wall directly uphill from the charcoal forms a definite boundary between the charcoal

6-10. *Charcoal kilns in operation at Old Job during the 1880s; note the schoolhouse at left (courtesy John Griffith, Jr.).*

6-11. *Smoke-shrouded charcoal kilns in operation at Old Job. Note cordwood on the hillside waiting to be loaded into the kilns, and a charcoal wagon in the foreground (courtesy John Griffith, Jr.).*

184

6-12. *The abandoned charcoal kilns at Old Job about 1912, looking west-ward. Although the kilns were shut down, intermittent logging continued and the houses in the background were still occupied (courtesy UVM Special Collections Library).*

and non-charcoal areas. Leading west from the charcoal area is a faint road. The road passes south of a cellar hole about 100 feet away from the charcoal area. No charcoal of any significant amount was found in this road, nor in the cellar hole it passed by. The charcoal is at least a foot deep in some places, as measured in three places. No kiln bricks were found on the ground or in any test pit. Since the charcoal area is 200 to 300 feet from and about 50 feet higher than the mill area, it is difficult to understand why charcoal might have been hauled up to this place. It is also difficult to understand whether the charcoal on the ground just downhill from the concentrated charcoal area was dropped there from wagons hauling it up (or down), or merely washed downhill over the years. The charcoal might have been made by the mound method, but if so, why is the charcoal uphill from the sawmill, if in fact the mill was where the remains are today.

RU-FS19 Danby Station (Mount Tabor): Although they were still fully standing in the 1950s, no ruins exist of the four kilns Griffith operated at the Mount Tabor railroad siding, just north-east of the station (called Danby Depot or Danby Station due its proximity to the town of Danby, although it is in Mount Tabor). Only the outline of the siding can be detected where railroad cars once lined up to load logs and charcoal. The siding was just northeast of the old railroad station, which today houses general businesses. The actual site of the kilns is the front yard of the late Ralph Carvage, who had always wondered why his soil was so black and why so many bricks surfaced in his garden every spring.

RU-108 Kiln #36 (Mount Tabor): The Rutland County his-tory published in 1886 mentions that 35 charcoal kilns were constructed by Silas Griffith at Mount Tabor (Smith and Rann 1886:696). That number has been quoted in later histories as if no other kilns were built after 1886. Since charcoal operations did not end until 1905, there was the chance that Griffith might have built other kilns. And as a result of searching the area for additional ruins, one was found in the fall of 1985 about 100 feet downstream of the "old wood road" crossing at Big Branch.

The ruin is on the north side of the brook, the opposite side from the trail between Old Job and Four Kilns. The ruin is a brick-type with walls about 3½ feet high. A large quantity of brick forms a talus slope outside the walls and nearly fills the inside of the ruin. Much hardware is in the ruin plus metal trash scattered about the immediate vicinity. Roads leading east and west seem to end in washouts.

The site is in marked contrast to those found elsewhere in Mount Tabor and would make an excellent study site. The remoteness of the ruin from well-traveled trails has apparently preserved it from scavengers and dynamiters as well.

RU-160 Danby Mountain Road Charcoal Kilns (Danby): A site of four charcoal kilns was found in 1986 from information provided by Nelson Jaquay of Tinmouth. The site is about 50 feet southeast of a cabin, east off and visible from Danby Mountain Road, about a quarter-mile down the Danby side of the top of the hill. It is uphill and on the opposite (east) side of the road from a spring, running into the roadside through a pipe. The kiln remains are in moderately heavy brush, off the south side of the driveway, at a point about opposite the halfway point between the Danby Mountain Road and the cabin.

Three of the four 28-foot-diameter brick-type ruins lie in about an east-west line, about 10 feet apart. The fourth kiln is dogleg to the south from the easternmost kiln ruin. They are nestled into the base of a low knoll, near the top of which is a low stone wall. Neither supporting nor reinforcing hardware were visible on the surface; no vent holes could be seen. The tops of the walls were nearly at ground level with only a low circular mound to indicate the approximate location of the wall.

Atop the knoll above the kiln ruins is what appears to be a base for a sawmill, possibly a boiler. The faint indication of a road leads from uphill to the south from this possible sawmill base. Another road appears to lead uphill a few dozen feet west of the base.

No history is known of this charcoal kiln site but proximity

to Danby Station hints at a possible connection with the Griffith and McIntyre charcoal operations across the valley at Mount Tabor. According to local tradition, much charcoal was made on the slopes of Dorset Mountain, meaning that many mound remains and kiln ruins are still there, waiting to be rediscovered.

WINDSOR COUNTY

WN-CK01 Salt Ash Mountain Charcoal Kilns (Plymouth): The 1869 Beers map of Plymouth indicates "Spaffic [*sic*] Iron Co's Wood Land" on the north slope of Salt Ash Mountain, where the Spathic Iron Company obtained wood for making charcoal for its furnace at Tyson. The Spathic Iron Company succeeded the Tyson Iron Company at the close of the Civil War (see chapter 4, WN-51). No attempt has been made to inspect the area.

6-13. *It is not known for sure, but these might have been the easternmost five of the eight charcoal kilns at Old Job, determined by matching the number of iron bands in this photo with those on the kilns in figure 6-12. Notice the wicker scoop at left, used instead of iron shovels to remove charcoal from the kiln so as not to break the charcoal into small pieces (courtesy Mr. and Mrs. Karl Pfister).*

6-14. *The four charcoal kilns at Danby Station as they appeared about 1950 (courtesy U.S. Forest Service, Manchester).*

The Southern District

BENNINGTON COUNTY

The county with the largest number of charcoal remains/ruins found in the state was Bennington County. This could be interpreted to mean that the highest amount of charcoal-making activity occurred in this county, although this might or might not be so. Many more ironworks are known to have operated in Addison County, for example, whose charcoal-making areas have yet to be accurately determined or found. Charcoal in Bennington County, therefore, was made both for local demands and for export to outside markets.

Those outside markets existed in Richmond, Massachusetts, where the Richmond Iron Works leased large tracts of forestland in mountainous Stamford. Charcoal kilns in Peru were owned or leased by owners of blast furnaces in the Millerton, New York area. The Barnum Richardson Company of Salisbury, Connecticut operated many charcoal kilns in northern Bennington County (in addition to buying charcoal from Silas Griffith in Mount Tabor). Barnumville is a small community a few miles north of Manchester Depot on the Vermont Railway that took its name from the two Barnum Richardson Company charcoal kilns that operated just west of the railroad siding. McNaughton and Lawrence also made charcoal at Barnumville during the earlier 1870s.

About a hundred feet southeast of the collapsed blast furnace ruin at North Dorset is the site of a mound-type charcoal-making area. Recent logging operations bulldozed a roadway through the area and much charcoal was unearthed. No kiln brick was found (the furnace dated to the 1840 period, well before brick kilns were seen in the Green Mountains).

The 1875 Root & Jones chemical works in Bennington village produced charcoal as a by-product of wood distillation. The

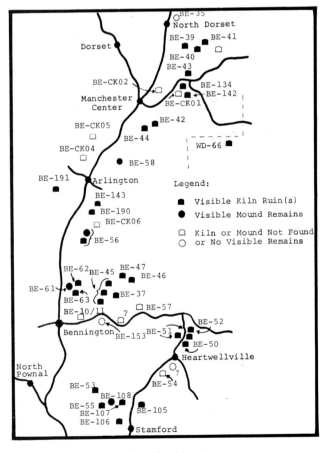

6-15. *Bennington County charcoal-making sites.*

village was also site of a charcoal kiln patented in 1829 by Isaac Doolittle (Hodge May 12, 1849:290). A sketch of the ironworks at East Bennington shows the four kiln buildings in the background, west of the furnaces (Hinsdill 1835).

Charcoal-making areas in the county were many. Some 28 ruins/remains were found in the Manchester-Winhall-Peru area; 26 in the Sunderland-Arlington-Glastenbury-Woodford area, and 23 more in the Stamford-Readsboro area. Many more kilns are known to have operated in the county, and a hike up most draws will probably reveal telltale mound remains if not more circular walls of stone or brick that mark the little pockets of early industry.

Mad Tom Brook Area Charcoal Sites: Some time before 1880, C. S. Maltby of New York purchased a sawmill in the western part of town near "the notch" where two brooks meet to form the Mad Tom Brook (Batchelder 1891:113-114). Earlier mills had sawed railroad ties out of thousands of birch trees here, sliding them down the two-mile-long water flume to the railroad siding below at East Dorset. Maltby, who owned a blast furnace at Millerton, New York from about 1864 to the 1880s, eventually built a number of charcoal kilns in Peru. There were at least 10 kilns operating in Peru at this time (Aldrich 1889:461; Child 1880:151). The kilns probably changed hands within a few years because in 1889 it was reported that charcoal was being made for Barnum Richardson Company, owner of ironworks in Connecticut and New York (C. S. Maltby and Barnum Richardson Company were competitors while the Millerton furnace was in operation; Barnum Richardson Company continued to make iron until 1920 in Canaan, Connecticut). The kilns were also reported to have made 1,000 bushels of charcoal from 35 cords of wood, significantly below the typical 40 to 50 bushels of charcoal per cord yield of kilns for the time. Barnum Richardson Company also made charcoal at Barnumville (see BE-CK02).

Nine kiln ruins were located in 1983 at three sites along a one-mile stretch of the Mad Tom Brook, and might have been part of the charcoal-making operations of Maltby or Barnum Richardson Company (leaving at least one kiln ruin not found).

The ruins are at three sites of five, one, and three ruins west of the Notch in Peru along a mile stretch of the upper end of Mad Tom Brook. The sites are identified: Mad Tom Upper Kilns, Mad Tom Middle Kiln, and Mad Tom Lower Kilns. All were found in 1983 a few minutes walk off either side of an abandoned road that forks northwest off Forest Road 21 (Mad Tom Road), about 500 feet west of Forest Route 58 (Griffith Pond Road) intersection. The old road travels downhill most of the way, becoming more and more of a trail, and meets the Mad Tom Brook in about a mile. The trail is then identified as Forest Trail 5, continuing down the Mad Tom gorge to East Dorset.

BE-41 Mad Tom Upper Charcoal Kilns (Peru): This site of five kiln ruins lies about a half-mile west of the abandoned Mad Tom Road. A trail leads northeast off this road for about 300 feet to the site, which lies to the east of the trail. The kiln ruins lie in two groups, 100 feet apart, of three and two ruins each. Domestic trash and sheet metal lie in and about the kiln ruins, not related to the kiln operations but probably to recent logging in the area. One significant kiln-related artifact is a 5-foot-diameter iron charging hole cover, much different than those found at other sites. The cover has four 2- by 4-inch vents that can be opened and closed with a sliding iron plate.

All kilns in this complex were built into an embankment. Uphill from the kilns is an open field, probably used at one time for stacking cordwood for feeding the kilns. The trail from the road to the kiln site continues through the site, crosses a small brook, and continues (more kiln ruins beyond?). At the

6-16. *A top-loading-hole cover found near Mad Tom Brook in Peru, showing one of four vent holes with a small sliding door that controlled draft into the charcoal kiln.*

brook, another trail forks back around the westernmost kiln ruin to the clearing behind and above the site.

BE-40 Mad Tom Middle Charcoal Kiln (Peru): This single-kiln site lies about a half-mile farther west of the old abandoned road from Mad Tom Upper Kilns and immediately south of the road, which is now more of a trail than a road. The ruin is well hidden in heavy trees and brush and was found only because a piece of metal, which turned out to be part of a kiln door, was found sticking out of the ground along the south edge of the trail (it always pays to check everything out). On the opposite side of the trail is a pond; about 50 feet farther west down the trail is a small log bridge over the Mad Tom Brook. Some red brick was found in the brook near the bridge.

Finding the kiln had its humorous moment. After Bob West watched me dig the piece of kiln door out of the trail and inspect it, he chided me as I went into the woods to reconnoiter. On finding the kiln ruin I called to Bob, who refused to believe I had found anything. He had gotten directions to the other two kiln sites (BE-41, -39) from local hunters who frequented the area but said nothing about a kiln ruin in the woods here. It took some coaxing to get Bob to see my "discovery." A search in the immediate area failed to locate another kiln; no clearing was found above the embankment into which the kiln was built. It is unknown if this ruin is the single charcoal kiln illustrated in a recently published town history (Beattie 1977:17).

BE-39 Mad Tom Lower Charcoal Kilns (Peru): This site of three kiln ruins lies less than a mile west of Mad Tom Upper Kilns. At this point, Mad Tom Brook is joined by a tributary from the south and the old road crossed (no bridge) Mad Tom Brook to continue along its north bank. The three-kiln site is across the tributary just downstream from the juncture, and some 300 feet uphill in a west-southwest direction. The kiln ruins lie in a triangular pattern; the two uphill ruins each lie about 20 feet from and about 12 to 15 feet higher than the center ruin. Faint trails leading upward and sideways from the site seem to peter out. No clearing was found above the site, but there does appear to be a clearing between the site and the brook. Much kiln brick lies near the brook but appears part of debris (stumps, slash, oil cans) dumped here. There might have been a logging bridge here.

While at the site, two men from Manchester drove down the trail in a jeep and joined us in inspecting the site. They listened intently as we explained the reason for all the bricks and the function of the charcoal kilns after which the father indicated his intent to return soon to "get all that free brick."

Snow Valley Area Charcoal Sites: The Snow Valley area is generally the mountainous northwestern corner of Winhall, its name taken from a ski resort that once operated here. Charcoal kilns in this area operated at near the 2,000-foot elevation and were part of the broader charcoal-making region extending from the north at Peru and Mount Tabor to the south along the west flank of the Green Mountain Range. Most ruins in this area are within a few minutes walk along established trails from Routes 30 and 11.

BE-CK01 Snow Valley Charcoal Kiln (Winhall): One unlocated kiln site hides somewhere along the north-northeast ridge of a mountain in the vicinity of the old Snow Valley ski area. Numerous hikes on the mountain in search of the elusive ruin led to finding other kilns in the general area, but not the one

that local tradition insists is nearer to the now-quiet ski lifts. The search continues.

BE-CK02 Barnumville Charcoal Kilns (Manchester): This small community two miles north of Manchester Center got its name from the two charcoal kilns operated here by Barnum Richardson Company of Salisbury, Connecticut. The kilns were located west of the railroad track a short distance south of the south crossing. The McNaughton & Lawrence Company also made charcoal here during the earlier 1870s (Bigelow and Otis 1961:147,151). At least one kiln was still operating on November 28, 1890 according to a Montpelier newspaper of that date, which said "The business of Barnumville is in lumber and the burning of charcoal in a large brick furnace constructed from a portion of the bricks of the old church in Manchester village of twenty years ago" (Mary Bort letter to author, June 12, 1991).

The area of the railroad tracks in the center of Barnumville and areas well north and south were inspected in 1985 with no kilns or signs of charcoal found. Most likely, later development along the railroad tracks obliterated any surface signs of the charcoal operations here. Local residents knew nothing of charcoal kilns.

BE-43 Bromley Brook Charcoal Kilns (Winhall): Four kiln ruins lie along the Long Trail about five minutes hike north of the parking area along Routes 11 and 30, about four miles east of Manchester Depot. The ruins are in two groups of two each, about 30 feet apart a dozen feet south of the trail. They were found in 1982 with the guidance of Sandy Partridge of Proctor. The ruins are not difficult to find since the trail here is black with charcoal runoff from the ruins.

6-17. One of four brick-type charcoal kiln ruins along Long Trail at the 1,900-foot elevation, just north of Routes 11 and 30 in Winhall.

Tradition has it that the bricks initially came from the First Congregational Church in Manchester: "In April 1871, laborers found the old brick edifice so well and strongly built that it was difficult to tear down. Some of the bricks are supposedly still in the woods north of the Peru Road on the Long Trail where they were used for charcoal kilns" (Bigelow and Otis 1961:45).

BE-134 Old Route 30 Charcoal Kiln (Winhall): The ruin of a single brick-type charcoal kiln was located in 1988. Bob West found the ruin based on information from a U.S. forest ranger in the process of relocating a section of the Long Trail south from Route 30.

The site is situated in the inside curve (east) of the Long Trail, about a quarter-mile south of Route 30. About 100 feet farther south of the site, the Trail crosses a small brook on a wooden trail bridge, the first such bridge south of the highway. A few hundred yards west of this area is the old Vermont Route 30 and 11 junction (now replaced by the newer junction, about a mile northeast).

The ruin is a rough circle of broken red brick, about 3 to 4 feet thick and 3 feet high. Some of the bricks are coated with burnt-on pitch. Along the northwest periphery of the ruin is a low stone wall, possibly a kiln foundation or retaining wall. The rise behind the ruin is cut into and probably provided support for a bridge to the top of the kiln. A round kiln cover was the only hardware found. Brick and charcoal also lie scattered outside the ruin and over the bank west of the ruin to the side of an old southeast-to-northwest running road. About 100 feet north of the ruin is a small cellar hole, possibly connected with the kiln operation.

The 1869 Beers map of Winhall shows a sawmill along Bromley Brook, a few hundred yards west, which might have been contemporary and/or associated with this kiln.

According to Bob West, the old Routes 11 and 30 were in use until about 1946 or 1947. Due to bridge washouts, the adjacent parallel road was later built and this avoided two bridges. The present highway takes a more gradual, if circuitous, route to the top of the mountain. The area is an interesting study of how the wilderness has taken over after 30-plus years of abandonment.

BE-142 Sylvan Ridge Charcoal Kilns (Winhall): Ruins of two stone-type kilns were found by Bob West in May 1989 in the woods a few hundred feet behind the home of a part-time resident on Sylvan Ridge Road. The site is about a quarter-mile west of the Signal Hill Road intersection.

The ruins are side by side, on a narrow rise of ground cut into the hill behind. The wall of one ruin stands 6 feet high with bricks still in their vent holes. The bare hint of an ancient road leads from the narrow flat in front of the ruins, around the northernmost ruin, and uphill behind the ruins. Nothing historical is known about these ruins although they most likely predate the brick-type kilns in the area.

Rootville Area Charcoal Sites: Near the southwestern corner of Winhall near Bourn Brook and the abandoned mountain community of Rootville, 12 kilns were operated by Barnum Richardson Company. A row of eight kiln ruins are at one site west of the brook and four ruins are about a mile to the east across the brook and over the hill. These kilns made an estimated 240,000 bushels of charcoal annually (Child 1880:211).

Typical of many mountaintop industrial hamlets in Vermont, the village of Rootville was 2,256 feet high up the mountain,

6-18. *The eight charcoal kilns near Bourn Brook in 1893, a few years after they ceased operation and became overgrown with brush. Note that two kilns, in the middle and rear, had already collapsed (courtesy Mr. and Mrs. Daly Rizio).*

near the source of Bourn Brook. Named after Henry Root, the community came to life in the mid-1800s around his lumber and sawmills (Swift 1977:110-111). The 1869 Beers map of Winhall shows three sawmills, a shop, and five houses at Rootville. During 1912–1919, the area resounded to the huff and puff of a logging railroad. All that remains of the Rootville area today are cellar holes and mill foundations, and the old railroad right-of-way that makes today's excellent hiking trail.

BE-44 Bourn Brook Charcoal Kilns (Winhall): The size of this site bears witness to the extensiveness of charcoal making in the Lye Brook wilderness area. Ruins of eight kilns were found a few hundred feet west of Bourn Brook in 1983, after miles (and weekends) of unsuccessful searching that started the year before. Final location of the site was provided by Bob West's uncle, who indicated that *two* bridges had to be crossed to get to it (we had been crossing only one bridge).

No historical documentation is known in connection with the ruins except that they might be part of the overall operations of Barnum Richardson Company. The site might also have been related to logging operations at Rootville, less than a mile to the southeast, and also to the four-kiln site (BE-42) about a half-mile west.

The eight kiln ruins lie in a north-south line beside a broad clearing. The brick walls of some ruins are up to 4 feet high; most are about a foot high. Much iron hardware is in evidence: charging hole covers, iron bands, rods, and a section of railroad track (from the logging-train era?).

The site is two miles up the old Rootville road, which runs from the base of Downer's Glen, across the footbridge just downstream of a private hunting camp, and along an abandoned section of the Long Trail to the Douglas Shelter. About a

half-mile south of the shelter, just short of abandoned Rootville, the trail curves to within sight of Bourn Brook. Here is a

6-20. *A top-loading-hole cover with another smaller, removable cover, found at the Bourn Brook site.*

single-log footbridge across the brook near an abandoned bridge abutment, across which is a barely visible trail on the left that climbs uphill for a quarter-mile to the broad clearing on the left.

6-19. *Ruins of one of the eight charcoal kilns in figure 6-18 in the 1980s. Nearby is the abandoned logging village of Rootville.*

BE-42 Winhall River Charcoal Kilns (Winhall): The Long Trail was rerouted a few years ago and now hikers pass within a hundred feet of four charcoal kiln ruins. They were found in 1983, up a seasonal brook that drains the kiln area. The kilns were probably operated by Barnum Richardson Company.

There is a broad clearing in front of the ruins and a cellar hole at the south end of the site, but the ruins lack the usual amount of hardware. According to local tradition, bricks from these ruins were used by the Swezey Lumber Company for construction of a nearby sawmill. The mill ruin (it burned in 1921) is about 100 feet southeast of the footbridge, near where the old and new Long Trails meet. Many bricks from both ruins have also been scavenged for use in fireplaces and chimneys in some East Manchester homes.

An old road runs uphill south of the site, at right angles from the Long Trail, and intersects Dufresne Road, an older Trail alternate. Bushwhacking across the road and westward will intersect with the old Long Trail near the Bourn Brook crossing to BE-44.

Green Mountain Ridge Charcoal Sites: Henry Burden & Sons operated two charcoal kilns near his blast furnace at South Shaftsbury (Beers *Bennington* 1869:21). Burden also operated along Fayville Branch (Peter's Branch) in northern Glastenbury. One brick and one mound-type kiln were found in this area. Four stone-type kilns and a mound-type were found 2,200 feet up East Mountain near the Shaftsbury-Glastenbury line.

According to historical accounts, Henry Burden obtained charcoal from hundreds of acres of hardwood on East Mountain (Levin 1978:49). The area of the stone-built kilns ruins was once known as "the Burden Lots" (Edwin Colvin to author, May 12, 1985). There are probably undocumented ruins and remains of many stone- and mound-type kilns in these mountains.

Other charcoal makers in Shaftsbury included C. Harrington and L. Twitchell who lived in the eastern part of town and almost in the shadow of East Mountain (Child 1880:458).

BE-58 Bacon Hollow Charcoal Mounds (Sunderland): Well up Bacon Hollow, east of Sunderland village alongside a trail that leads south from Mill Brook, are the remains of a charcoal-making area, and downstream are the remains of a sawmill and the community that once thrived around it.

The area was inspected in 1985 and one mound-type remain was found along a high, level ridge, about a mile east of Route 7. Charcoal was also noticed associated with disturbed earth in the vicinity of summer cabins along the main Hollow road and alongside Mill Brook. There are probably many more mound remains farther up the various draws of this mountain.

BE-143 Southwest Corner Charcoal Kiln (Sunderland): This single kiln ruin was found in 1991 by Dave Lacy, forest archeologist, while marking the boundary of a tract of forest for logging. The site is about a mile southeast of the Arlington exit of Route 7, in the southwest corner of the town of Sunderland near the base of a ridge. It is well uphill and about a half-mile east of the highway.

The ruin consists of a collapsed circle of brick and one 4-inch-wide by ½-inch-thick reinforcement iron band that briefly sticks up through the circle of brick in three places. Nearby is a 54-inch-diameter top hole cover. The ruin is not well defined and shows evidence of having been eroded by spring freshets. The hint of a road leads downhill from the site,

connecting about a quarter-mile away with a road from the direction of another kiln ruin (BE-190). This downhill road contains pieces of whole and broken brick from the ruin.

BE-190 Northwest Corner Charcoal Kiln (Glastenbury): This single kiln ruin was found while searching for BE-143, about a half-mile north and probably at the same elevation. It appears much more remote than BE-143, however, which probably accounts for its much better condition. Two iron reinforcement bands of the same dimensions as that at BE-143 are here, and the circle of brick is better defined. No other iron hardware was in evidence.

BE-56 North Glastenbury Charcoal Kiln and Mound (Glastenbury): Reference to a resident of Glastenbury who built a swimming pool on a charcoal kiln site sounded a bit too intriguing to ignore (Levin 1978:93). The area was inspected in 1984 and the ruins of one brick-type kiln and a mound-type remain were found, within 100 feet of a small dammed pond. From the pipes, it was obviously the water supply for Dr. Sterba's summer home and probably the earlier swimming pool.

A kiln ruin and a mound remain almost side by side is interesting. Did the former replace the latter; did they operate simultaneously? The mound-type measured 40 feet in diameter. A local resident talked of kiln ruins both above and below Dr. Sterba's house, but inspection failed to uncover anything further.

BE-CK06 Fayville Charcoal Kiln (Glastenbury): Fayville was an 1870s logging community, deep in the woods and mountains about five miles southeast of Arlington village. There are hints of charcoal having been made at Fayville but a 1984 inspection of the site revealed a large clearing with many pieces of whole and broken red brick, unidentified hardware, and the usual surface scatter of domestic discard one finds at an abandoned 19th-century village. One blackened area on the western edge of the clearing looked intriguing but this was too little surface evidence to conclude it was either a charcoal kiln or mound site, or the remains of a burned structure. It was not until 1991 that a turn-of-the-century photo of a charcoal kiln appeared, attributed to Fayville (Robert Williams photo to author, Dec. 14, 1990). The obvious next step is to hike back to abandoned Fayville and attempt to orient the landscape in the photo to that of the area, and determine if that blackened area found seven years ago was, in fact, the kiln site.

BE-61 East Mountain Charcoal Mounds (Shaftsbury): While searching for kiln ruins in 1985 along the 2,200-foot level of East Mountain, a site of one or more mound-type remains was found. Information that encouraged us up the side of this steep mountain was provided by Rob Woolmington of Bennington and Ed Colvin of Shaftsbury.

The site straddles a trail to two stone-type kiln ruins (BE-62) about 300 feet farther to the west. The mound remain is round with its usual outer, circular gutter depression. One corner is truncated by the trail; the opposite side cuts slightly into the hillside. Remains of either a smaller stone kiln or possibly a charcoal storage structure are about 25 feet to the southwest. Much charcoal is scattered about the entire area.

BE-62 and BE-63 Charcoal Kilns at "the Burden Lots" (Shaftsbury): The first site (BE-62) contains two stone-type kiln ruins, found previously by Rob Woolmington (Woolmington July 7, 1977:17-20). Each ruin is about 200 feet off opposite sides of the trail and in relatively good condition, with the wall of one ruin 7 feet high. Both ruins measure 30 feet in diameter with walls up to 2½ feet thick near the base. Vent holes, some with bricks still inserted, are at ground, 2-foot, and 3-foot levels. The quantity of rock inside the kiln indicates the whole kiln, from ground up, was made of stone. The stone appeared uncut, the builders probably utilizing the abundance of stone lying about the area. The faint remains of a road leads from the main trail to each ruin. A kiln door was found in the proximity of each ruin, each with heavy iron handles attached. Its shape resembled that excavated from the conical kiln site at Readsboro.

The next site (BE-63) was found about an estimated half-mile north of the first (BE-62). No known trail leads from one site to the other; the site was found through verbal directions by Ed Colvin. The ruins are about 100 feet northeast of the tree marked KLN with an arrow pointing to the ruins, next to a small seasonal brook.

These two ruins appear to have the same dimensions as the previous two, although they are in much worse condition. Birch trees have fallen into each ruin, further collapsing the walls beneath them. The interior of each kiln contained much more brick than can be accounted for by vents, but little remains of any collapsed stone. The only hardware found was one piece of rusted sheet iron, possibly the rotted remains of a door. A trail leads west from the site headed for the side of the mountain, probably the route taken by the charcoal wagons.

Arlington Area Charcoal Sites: Benedict Hollow is a two-mile-long cleft between 3,109-foot Grass Mountain and 2,338-foot Big Spruce Mountain, about two miles west of Arlington village. Charcoal was made at the Pitman Farm in at least five kilns, "three in the upper clearing and two in the center clearing" per a ca.-1935 paper by Fred Bush (Russell Collection, Arlington). The original operator was John Smith, who sold to Eugene McIntyre, then in turn to Frederick Miles. McIntyre owned vast forest tracts in southern Vermont and might have been involved in charcoal operations there also. (The abandoned logging village of MacIntyre, named for Eugene McIntyre, is still identified on USGS topographical maps along the Sunderland-Glastenbury line, about two miles northeast of Fayville.) Miles was operator of blast furnaces at Salisbury, Connecticut and Copake, New York from the 1860s to his death in 1896. William and Frederick P. Miles continued the Copake operation until it was closed, probably about 1903. Since Frederick P. Miles operated the works only marginally with his brother and for only five years (it was leased from 1901 to 1903), it is assumed the Frederick Miles who operated the Benedict Hollow charcoal kilns is the Frederick (K.) Miles who died in 1896, giving a bracket of time, 1860s to 1896, when these charcoal kilns might have been in operation.

Miles eventually moved his charcoal operations about two miles north to the eastern slope of Red Mountain on "property above Mrs. Fisher's" where he operated several more kilns (Russell Collection, Arlington). He transported the charcoal down the mountain by means of a half-mile-long cog railway that was controlled by a drum at the top, alternately operating a pair of cars that had a capacity of 350 bushels of charcoal each. It is unknown for sure, however, whether this cog railway was built for Miles' Benedict Hollow or Red Mountain operations.

BE-191 Benedict Hollow Charcoal Kilns (Arlington): The remains of one or two brick-type charcoal kilns were found in 1991 at about the 1,400-foot elevation, two miles up Benedict Hollow Road, then another mile farther up a newly constructed logging road from where it branches west (uphill) from the main hollow road. The logging road continues uphill past two hairpin turns, the first doubling back uphill to the north, the second to the southwest. Just as the road starts to level a bit, red brick and black charcoal can be seen on both sides of the road. The road was cut directly through the site, destroying the ruins and making it impossible to determine whether this is Frederick Miles' two- or three-kiln site (or another?). The only hardware found was an 8-inch fork prong. Local resident Danny Andrews, who lives near the bottom of the hollow, gave directions to the site.

BE-CK04 Red Mountain Charcoal Site (Arlington): Archival data indicate that Frederick Miles of Copake, New York also operated one or more charcoal kilns about a half-mile up the east slope of Red Mountain (Russell Collection, Arlington). An area of the mountain about a half-mile up Fisher Road was searched in 1989 for a lime kiln ruin identified on an annotated 1900 edition USGS topographical map in the possession of Nancy Otis of Manchester. After a five-minute walk up a wood road that forks south from Fisher Road, what was initially thought to be the lime kiln ruin was found (see chapter 8, BE-LK07). But the "ruin" was later determined to be a stone-lined, 6-foot-deep cistern, associated with the remains of a foundation just uphill from it. A charcoal kiln top hole cover, complete with its original pair of iron handles and a small center hole, was found jammed inside the cistern under branches and leaves. A red brick was found in 1991 about 100 feet away in a small brook. At the time the cover was found, the possibility of charcoal kilns being in the vicinity was not known (we had a lime kiln ruin on our mind), so the discovery of a charcoal kiln cover was treated as an anomaly to be investigated later. The charcoal-making site has not been found at this writing. (The lime kiln ruin has not been found either, leading to speculation that a charcoal kiln ruin might have been misidentified on the annotated USGS map as a lime kiln ruin.)

BE-CK05 Sandgate Charcoal Plant (Sandgate): A "charcoal plant" operated in the Wilson Hollow area of Sandgate according to a 1950 letter to the late Dr. George Russell from the mayor of Cohoes, New York (Russell Collection, Arlington). The reference hints that Wilson Hollow is the Green River valley in Sandgate, but no Wilson Hollow can be found on any current or early maps. There is, however, a Wilcox Hollow in the town, well up the Green River valley. No attempt has been made to explore Wilcox Hollow for the charcoal plant.

Bolles Brook Area Charcoal Sites: About the same period that Burden's works at Shaftsbury were declining, the Bennington and Glastenbury Railroad, Mining, and Manufacturing Company was organized (Levin 1978:87-89). The company name was an attempt to cover all business eventualities in one collective title. Originally chartered in 1855, the company did not lay track until 1872, along the side of County Street in Bennington, over the stream, through private property, and directly in front of the old furnace stacks at Furnace Grove. The tracks continued to Woodford Hollow, thence up Bolles Brook to the forks. One track continued up the east fork about a quarter-mile, and the other went up the west fork about a half-mile. Diagonally across the forks was another track that allowed trains to back up from one fork to the other so the engines could remain at the head of the train for the return run to Bennington. The tracks climbed over 1,200 feet in the eight miles from Bennington to the forks. The steepest grade on the main line was 230 feet per mile; one branch grade was 250 feet per mile, which at the time was considered to be the steepest grade of any standard gauge railroad in the country (Shaw May 1952:19-27).

The railroad company had purchased 18,000 acres in Woodford, Glastenbury, and Somerset, and constructed 18 charcoal kilns. At the end of the line at the forks the community of South Glastenbury developed, made up of loggers' housing, a boardinghouse, the steam-powered sawmill, blacksmith shop, company store, and a schoolhouse. The sawmill cut 1,000 board feet an hour and the charcoal kilns turned out 28,000 bushels of charcoal a month, all hauled out of the wilderness by the railroad. Alcohol to lubricate the woodcutters, some mail, goods for the store, and an occasional passenger came in on the return run. Within 20 years the mountain woodlands had been stripped. The Blizzard of '88 shut the railroad down for three months, and the next year the entire logging and charcoal operation closed for good.

With goals other than lumber and charcoal in mind, a new company replaced the track a few years later with heavier rail to support electric trolleys. The large boardinghouse was renovated and painted, becoming a hotel for vacationers. The old company store was converted into the Glastenbury Inn and the machinery removed from the sawmill to make room for a bowling alley, dance floor, and amusement hall. Trolleys initially ran from Bennington village to camps in lower Woodford Hollow in the mid-1890s. The new track reached the forks in 1898, where the hotel, inn, and dance hall were finished and the entire line once again ran under the name of the Bennington & Woodford Electric Railroad. But only a few months after the first excursion run to the forks, a flash flood washed out every bridge along the Roaring Brook from the Hollow to Bennington village. And along with the washed-out bridges went the fortunes of the trolley line and the Glastenbury Inn.

The return of logging to the forks in the 1950s resulted in the cellar holes of structures—including the boardinghouse/pavilion, sawmill, schoolhouse, etc.—being bulldozed (Charles Dewey to author, July 31, 1983). Only cellar hole remains that lie outside the immediate area of the forks (the east fork sawmill, the casino, and the kiln sites) can be found.

Most of the old right-of-way can still be hiked, some of it snaking its way out of Bennington, and here and there as it

6-21. *The loggers' boardinghouse, which later became a hotel for vacationers at "the forks" in Glastenbury. The village schoolhouse is to the right, and railroad tracks head to the right and also up the far (west) draw to charcoal kilns, just out of sight around the curve (courtesy Tordis Isselhardt).*

climbs up through Woodford Hollow to the forks. Much of the fill that makes up the track bed is slag, hauled from the blast furnace sites at East Bennington when the right-of-way was built. The slag can still be found in the track bed well up the hollow, miles from Furnace Grove. At the forks, the sites of the hotel, amusement hall, and schoolhouse have been back filled and leveled. Up the east fork are ruins of three charcoal kilns, and up the west fork are five ruins. A half-mile back down the trail at the head of an old railroad siding are five more kiln ruins. No tracks remain, having been pulled up for World War II scrap; but spikes, plates, and small sections of rail lie about in the underbrush and in the nearby brook. Fortunately, the scrap collectors forgot the kiln ruins, some of which still have their large iron bands and top vent hole castings.

The next valley west of Bolles Brook is Bickford Hollow. Where Bickford Hollow Brook passes from Glastenbury into Woodford there are three single-kiln sites, each on the west side of the brook and about a quarter-mile from each other. Farther downstream in Woodford Hollow, seven or eight kilns were operated by James Beckley, who ran blast furnaces at North Adams, Massachusetts and Chatham, New York (Aldrich 1889:478).

BE-37 Red Cabin Charcoal Kilns (Glastenbury): This site was found in 1982. The site is named for the red cabin located about 200 to 300 feet south of the charcoal kiln ruins. The five kiln ruins are in a generally north-south line, about 30 to 40 feet east off the old railroad bed.

The upper road joins the old railroad bed (main trail into this area) north of the kiln ruins. This upper road might have been a railroad spur, used to deliver cordwood and/or pick up charcoal. The road is a gradual climb from its northern junction with the main road. A piece of track was found protruding from brick rubble at the southern kiln ruin. Since the base of this kiln is many feet above the old (lower) railroad bed, it would more likely have worked its way downward from a higher place (the upper road bed?).

Between the upper road and the kiln ruins is a level strip,

slightly lower than the upper road, possibly an area to afford space for a charging bridge to charge the tops of the kilns.

Inside the ruins of the extreme southern kiln were two cast-iron pieces of a top vent hole lining found about 15 feet apart. They were dragged together and found to fit. The combined casting was about 5 feet in diameter, about an inch thick, and flared inward about 6 inches deep. There appeared to be another in the same ruin, buried upside down. There also were many variously dimensioned kiln-girdling iron bands that had been used to hold the kilns together around the middle and at the top. (All this hardware had disappeared when the site was revisited in 1991.)

A possible flume to the south of the ruins may be the site of a sawmill. On that side of the tributary to Bolles Brook, there is sufficient level space to have had a mill. No foundations could be found, but there appears to be a hint of a wheel pit near the downstream end of the flume.

The upper roadbed was searched for railroad artifacts but none were found. No complete piece of railroad tie could be found, so as to accurately determine the gauge of the track. The opposite side of the brook was inspected, and no charcoal or railroad-related features were found. An upside-down wreck of an automobile lies near the brook, just north of the culvert. Beverage cans and plastic containers give witness to the recreational activity of the area. A pothole is in the wall of the southern ruin.

BE-46 and BE-47 Charcoal Kilns at The Forks (Glastenbury): Ruins of the first three charcoal kilns at the forks (BE-46) were found in 1982 about a quarter-mile up the east fork of Bolles Brook. The kiln ruins have the normal amount of brickwork and hardware (bands, top hole lining), similar to BE-37, about a half-mile south. The scrap drives luckily forgot the kiln sites.

Five more charcoal kiln ruins (BE-47) were found about a half-mile up the west fork later the same day. The ruins are immediately downhill of the road leading up the west fork of Bolles Brook. The ruins appear in much the same condition

6-22. *Charcoal kilns up the west draw at "the forks" in Glastenbury. Only circles of brick remain at this site today (courtesy Tordis Isselhardt).*

6-23. *Vacationers visiting a long-abandoned charcoal kiln up Bolles Brook in the Glastenbury-Woodford area sometime before World War I (Lester B. Nichols photo; courtesy* Bennington Banner).

and hardware content as the east fork ruins.

By this time it was late in a long day spent thrashing through brush and water in the search for kiln remains, and many false kiln-appearing features were being encountered. Kiln ruins were being imagined everywhere. When the five ruins were finally found, they were seen in a hollow, looking down from a road high up the embankment. They were nearly ignored for looking too much like just another mirage.

BE-45 Bickford Hollow Charcoal Kilns (Woodford): These three single-kiln ruins were found in 1983 thanks to Charles Dewey of Bennington, retired lumber company owner who logged in and around the Bennington-Woodford area. He remembered seeing kiln ruins when logging the area many years before and guided us to the ruins.

The first ruin was found about an hour's hike up Bickford Hollow Brook from where it joins Bolles Brook. The second and third ruins are each a few minutes hike farther upstream from the first and from each other. All ruins are of brick and are on the uphill side of the trail, which follows the west side

of the brook. Each is also at the junction of an old road coming down from the mountain. The northernmost ruin may in fact be in Glastenbury; the woods are so heavy here that actual location as regards town lines is hard to determine. The ruins contain many 20- to 30-foot-diameter iron bands complete with adjustment hardware.

Bickford Hollow is a short hike up Harbor Road from Route 9 (Woodford Hollow) to the dam (right) and Bickford Hollow Road (left), following the older road northwest to the first crossing of Bickford Hollow Brook (no bridge). About a quarter-mile farther the trail recrosses to the west side. The first kiln ruin is a two- to three-minute walk upstream.

Woodford Area Charcoal Sites: Woodford City had two kilns operating in the 1890s by A. W. Hager (Aldrich 1889:480). J. J. Morehouse of Amenia, New York and E. C. White of New York City owned five kilns west of the village. Three kilns had a 40-cord capacity and two were 50-cords, all producing 12,000 to 15,000 bushels of charcoal a month. Harbour Brothers also operated kilns nearby, producing 25,000 bushels

196

6-24. A ca.-1900 view of a charcoal kiln and collier's house (?) reportedly in Woodford. This might have been one of the three single-kiln ruins found up Bickford Hollow in 1983 (courtesy Bill Gove).

a year. The Beckley & Adams Company, associated with a blast furnace at Chatham, New York, built six kilns in 1873, each with a 40-cord capacity. Later worked by Freeman S. Houghton of Bennington, the kilns made 10,000 to 12,000 bushels of charcoal per month (Child 1880:24-25). Exactly where in the Woodford area all these kilns were is unknown; most were probably very near Route 9. Inspection of both sides of the highway and up some nearby draws resulted in inconclusive finds; any surviving ruins were probably destroyed by highway widening and realignment.

Members of the Park family, some of the earliest settlers in Woodford, made charcoal for the nearby Bennington Iron Works. These kilns might have been the site of mounds found up Harmon Hill.

BE-57 Hager Hill Charcoal Kilns (Woodford): Sparse remains of charcoal kilns were found in 1984 alongside Route 9 in Woodford in the Hager Hill Road vicinity. The site was found after two hikes up Hager Hill Road (one nearly to Little Pond), but finally from information by local residents that led to Jesse Bugbee, who remembered the kilns being "very near to Route 9."

Some 100 feet off the highway in the Hager Hill Road some bits of red brick were found; adjacent to the north side of the road under heavy thorn bushes, whole bricks, some with burned ends, were found, along with bits of charcoal mixed into the very black soil, and an iron handle to a kiln door. No circles of brick were found; the immediate area was relatively flat. All these were found protruding out the southern edge of a low embankment that parallels the highway.

Local history reports charcoal made by A. W. and J. W. Hager in Woodford (Child 1880:n.p.). One of the Hager family was contacted and he remembered his father being somehow connected with the charcoal business.

BE-153 Harmon Hill Charcoal Mounds (Woodford): Re-

mains of up to a half-dozen charcoal mounds were found at about the 1,200-foot elevation, northwest of the peak of Harmon Hill in western Woodford. The mound remains were found as the result of logging in the area and were inspected by Dave Lacy and Shelley Hight, forest archeologists (Shelley Hight to author, July 2, 1990). The site of the mounds is in the vicinity of a woods trail that leads up a west nose near East Bennington and eventually joins the Long Trail about a mile east of the site. The mound site probably provided charcoal to ironworks at nearby Bennington and Woodford, and is representative of the many charcoal mound sites that exist in the vicinity and have yet to be found and documented.

Heartwellville Area Charcoal Sites: The 1856 Bennington County map indicates "coal kilns" at Heartwellville but repeated attempts to locate the site have failed. The kiln area has become a vast gravel quarry.

More coal kilns are indicated on the 1869 Beers map of Readsboro at three sites a few miles north of Heartwellville. Readsboro was densely forested and in nearly a straight line to North Adams 10 miles south; most of its charcoal found ready market at furnaces and foundries in that northern Massachusetts industrial city (Hemenway vol. 1 1867:220). The E. P. Hunt Company formed in 1868 at Heartwellville, operating a sawmill and making charcoal adjacent to the village along the Deerfield River. The kilns were conveyed to the Vermont Lumber and Coal Company in 1972. It continued to operate the kilns for a short time (Ross 1936:40). Charcoal making ended near Heartwellville by 1880 (Aldrich 1889:486).

Reinspection of kiln ruins previously found in the vicinity resulted in unearthing a conical kiln door, hinting that these also must have been conical kilns. Careful excavation of a wall section of one of these kilns proved fruitless because the bricks lay scattered all the way down through some 2 feet of debris. It looked as though the kiln had been dynamited.

Fieldwork at these interesting sites ended with the first snowfall in mid-November 1983. While digging without gloves alongside Grace in the cold, wet ground 100 feet west of Route 8 on a damp, overcast, bone-chilling day through alternating sunshine and blowing snow squalls, a state game officer drove by and spotted our unusual activity. He turned around and stopped, inspected the little excavation, and drove off, apparently satisfied we were not jacking deer.

BE-50 Heartwellville-Stone Charcoal Kiln (Readsboro): Finding this ruin in 1983 caused no small amount of excitement because it was the first stone-type kiln ruin encountered at that stage of this study. Dozens of stone-type ruins have since been located and recorded. The ruin was found while searching the area of other ruins. It measured 32 feet in diameter, making it one of the widest kilns found thus far in this study. Walls were 2½ feet thick and about 2 to 3 feet high. Vent holes had red brick in them. (The ruin bore a strong resemblance to a stone-type kiln found near the top of Berlin Mountain, southwest of Pownal in New York State. That kiln ruin is a few dozen feet off the Crestline Trail and has stone walls of similar thickness and height, but its floor is littered with brick.)

Inside, a small trench was dug into the floor down to outside ground level, 1½ feet deep and 2 feet back from the wall. Only small bits of red brick and stones were found, which raised the question of what happened to the material above the existing walls of the ruin. Speculation is that the missing material was brick and that the ruin's proximity to the highway and to Heartwellville made it an irresistible source of "free" brick. (In contrast, location of the lofty Berlin Mountain kiln in New York State was not conducive to removing quantities of brick.) If the material was stone, most likely it would still be collapsed inside the ruin. The brick scavengers obviously missed the few bricks still in the vent holes.

The ruin is a few dozen feet east off Route 8, about a mile north of the Route 8 and 100 intersection at Heartwellville. It sits on a narrow piece of ground between the brook and a low rise, into which the ruin is slightly cut, and is one of three indicated on the 1869 Beers map of Readsboro as "coal kiln."

BE-51 Heartwellville-Brick Charcoal Kilns (Readsboro): Remains of two brick-type kilns were found in 1983 about a mile south of the Searsburg-Readsboro town line. One is about 100 feet northwest of the large culvert at the pull-off; the other is about 500 feet south of the culvert on the opposite side of the highway. These are the approximate places indicated as "coal kiln" on the 1869 Beers map of Readsboro.

The upper remain is a scattered circle of brick across the brook and cut into the embankment. Lining the bottom of the embankment is a 2- to 3-foot-high stone wall. Much red brick also protrudes from the opposite bank of the stream from the kiln remain.

Shallow digging between the back of the kiln and the stone retaining wall uncovered an iron kiln door, similar in shape to kiln door openings seen at conical kilns in Wassaic, New York. This raised speculation that the remain might be that of a conical kiln (a confirmed conical kiln was found later across the highway; see BE-52 following). Excavation into the foundation of the remains failed to confirm any conical configuration of the walls since the bricks were jumbled down to their foundation stones.

The remains of the second kiln, farther south along the highway, are immediately adjacent to and cut into by the highway. Kiln brick at this site was also scattered such that exact edges of the remain were difficult to determine. This site is also cut into the side of a low hill.

BE-52 Heartwellville-Conical Charcoal Kiln (Readsboro): The same day, after finding the previous kiln remains, a search was made in the general area for any undocumented ruins, wood roads, or anything that might shed light on the ruins that were found. In the process, a flat, circular feature was discovered, cut slightly into a low rise about 300 feet northeast from the culvert and parking area adjacent to BE-51. Troweling into the ground revealed a circle of red brick, and digging deeper revealed that each successive layer of brick had been laid about an inch outward from the one above. A conical kiln ruin had been found and confirmed in Vermont!

No known documentation references this specific kiln, although a conical kiln is documented at Readsboro (Egleston May 1879:393). This ruin, unlike the three others nearby, probably dates to post-1869 because it is not indicated on the Beers map. In his paper on conical kilns, Egleston described the one in Readsboro to be 28½ feet inside diameter at the base. This kiln ruin measured 30½ feet in diameter at the base. But the wall thickness agrees, as does his sketch, which shows a row of vent holes at the base. In the excavated section, a brick-size vent hole was uncovered in the second tier of brick from the bottom. A 1-foot-diameter test hole near the center of the ruin reached the kiln floor through 2 feet of brick, burnt pitch, and charcoal. Since the base diameters disagreed, BE-51 (where a conical-type kiln door had been found nearby) was rechecked with no positive results; the walls have been too badly disturbed.

The year after the site was found it was inspected by U.S. Forest Service personnel because this forest tract had logging potential. Personnel included the forest supervisor, a Forest Service soil expert, forest archeologist Billee Hoornbeek, and a local state forester who hunted and fished the area for many years and had never noticed anything here (he knew of the other obvious ruins nearby). Puzzled, he asked Billee how anyone could find undocumented remains hidden under all that surface growth and dead leaves. Billee's answer was simply that archeologists are gifted with "finding things in places that most others see nothing at all." We are not sure if the old forester ever understood.

County Road Area Charcoal Sites: Two Massachusetts ironworks, the Ames Company of North Adams and the Richmond Iron Works of Richmond, made 20,000 bushels of charcoal a month in 14 kilns in the Stamford area. Ames owned 2,500 acres of woodland and employed 30 woodcutters and colliers (Child 1880:203). The exact locations of these kiln sites are unknown but fieldwork in the County Road section near the Pownal-Stamford line hints at this area.

The Richmond Iron Works was a major iron furnace operation near Pittsfield, Massachusetts, which by this period of time employed 700 people at its furnaces, mines, and the charcoal kilns. The company also owned furnaces at Cheshire and Great Barrington, Massachusetts, and as many as 28 tracts of land as far away as Stamford and Woodford, Vermont. Its landholdings as of 1870 are recorded in the *Doomsday Book*, on file in Pittsfield at the Berkshire County, Massachusetts, Registry of

Deeds. One 3,500-acre tract in Stamford includes 31 plots, mostly in the north-central and northeast parts of town. Ames Company holdings are indicated bordering to the west along with plots owned by other charcoal makers. The Richmond Iron Works' landholdings in the northeast corner of town border with an additional 4,520 acres (38 plots) in the southeast corner of Woodford. The company essentially owned the equivalent area of a whole Vermont township.

Rob Woolmington of Bennington, one-time avid hunter of charcoal kiln ruins in that area, found some stone-type kiln ruins near Roaring Brook (known locally as Coal Kiln Brook) in the 1970s. Two similar kilns were found two miles to the southeast in Gully Brook with walls 9 feet high. According to local tradition there are many more undiscovered kiln ruins in Stamford and Pownal, possibly on the northeast slope of a nearby mountain called The Dome. Charcoal was also made in Stamford village at a chemical works that operated there. Remains of mound-type kilns were found near the end of Maltese Road, and about a half-mile up Coal Kiln Road near Cardinal Brook, four brick-type kiln ruins were found.

The photo introducing chapter 5 shows three unidentified,

operating, century-old, conical-shaped charcoal kilns. The kilns' 5-foot-high bases are made of stone; brick continues the structure upward, in conical shape, nearly to a point at the top. These three kilns, which might be those at Crazy John Stream (BE-107), show what Green Mountain stone-and-brick conical charcoal kilns looked like in their day.

BE-53 Cotykilns/Haskins Kilns (Stamford): They are called Cotykilns (or Coty kilns) because Peter Coty operated them and transported the charcoal by horse and wagon to North Adams, Massachusetts, about 10 miles south (Woolmington July 7, 1977:17-20). They were found in 1984, with help from Bob Neville of Clarksburg, Massachusetts, about two miles north of County Road along an old section of Long Trail.

The four stone-type ruins were in fair to good condition, ranging from fully collapsed to having walls up to 8 feet high, and stand in a row a dozen feet downstream from the Roaring Branch trail crossing. Mortar and cement were used to seal the walls and bricks to control the vents. Additionally, the inside walls were coated with as much as an inch-thick layer of burnt pitch, which must have aided in keeping the kiln walls airtight. The main kiln openings faced on the brook. Hardware found

6-25. *Three of the four charcoal kilns north of Old County Road in Stamford, photographed near the turn of the century and about 50 years after the kilns had gone out of business. Notice tipped-over charcoal cart at left (courtesy Eugene Farley, Andrew C. Rumgay, and* The Transcript, *North Adams, Mass.).*

6-26. *Another view of the charcoal kilns north of Old County Road, showing wood tracks on which the charcoal cart ran (courtesy Eugene Farley, Andrew C. Rumgay, and* The Transcript, *North Adams, Mass.).*

was one shovel and a 66- by 80-inch iron kiln door (both reburied in situ).

These might also be the so-called Haskins kilns (Haun March 30, 1966). The 1869 Beers map of Stamford shows Haskins' sawmill about halfway between the kiln site and County Road, near what was then called Broad Brook. This part of the mountain was called Scrub Hill. Stone walls and some brickwork indicate the possible sawmill site. A photo of the kilns shows complete stone construction, in three stages. The lower stone wall rises with only a slight inward pitch about half the height (6 to 8 feet). The next section of wall dips inward more steeply to about three-quarters of the height. The final section is a roof, rising about another 3 to 4 feet in a concave configuration. A wide iron band girdles the kiln at the beginning of this roof section, probably to counteract the outward forces here. A relative of one of the charcoal workers connected with this site

was contacted in North Adams, but no response to a request for further information was received.

BE-55 Gully Brook Charcoal Kilns (Stamford): With the help of Bob Neville's directions, kiln ruins were found just a few minutes walk north of County Road. Up the trail alongside the east branch of Cowan Brook (locally known as Gully Brook) are the ruins of two partially standing stone-type kilns. The walls of one ruin were 9 feet high and the top took on a beehive shape. Few bricks were found inside this ruin; more were found inside the other.

The site is just west of Klondike Road and this section of County Road is drivable only in dry summer weather. It is easiest accessed from the Stamford side (upper Mill Road). My first drive up County Road was from the Pownal side in the late spring and some brooks were still overflowing the road in places. Two men in a four-wheeler grinding their way down the same road were taken by surprise at the sight of this strictly flatlander's car, feeling its way up the narrow, muddy mountain road, and weaving around boulders, fallen trees, and pond-size puddles.

An interesting feature of these kilns is their vent holes. Similar to the cast-iron vent hole linings found at Dragon Brook in Ripton, these Stamford kilns also had preformed vent holes, but made of tile. Although the inside ends of the vents were partly blocked with a thick layer of burnt pitch, the outside ends still permitted the full length of a brick to be inserted, effectively closing the vents just as it did when the kilns were in operation.

BE-106 Cardinal Brook Charcoal Kilns (Stamford): The remains of four brick-type charcoal kilns were found in 1986, about a half-mile up the Roaring Brook road from County Road. The unmaintained rough road is locally known as Coal Kiln Road. The ruins were found a one-minute walk after the Cardinal Brook bridge, immediately east (right) off the road. (Some local residents claim that the USGS Stamford topographic map is incorrect, that what the map identifies as Cardinal Brook is in fact Nunge Brook.)

Information leading to location of the kiln remains was provided by Ira and Anna Whitney, long-time Stamford residents I had visited earlier in the day. Mr. Whitney said that the site was obvious from the charcoal that ran down the embankment onto the road, but that nothing remained of the kilns themselves.

The embankment at the side of the road was indeed black with charcoal spilling down from the kiln site. Also visible in the road, as the site was approached from the downstream side, were numbers of red bricks. These are the only all-brick-constructed charcoal kilns found thus far in Stamford; all others found have been at least partly stone-built.

The kiln remains lie in a row, north to south, parallel to and about 15 feet east of the road. The northernmost ruin is on a slightly raised elevation from the other three, making it about level with the adjacent road. As the road drops off downhill and the ruins remain level, the southernmost kiln site ends up atop a 7-foot-high embankment. The hill behind the kilns appears cut into and remains of a low stone wall can be seen at the top of this charging hill, which probably supported platforms from which to gain access to the tops of the kilns. The hill behind the kilns is flat, but soon drops off on the other side (east) into Roaring Brook.

Much brick lies scattered about the site; no kiln walls remained intact. But the circles of the brick where the walls once stood could be made out, measuring approximately 28 feet in diameter. The three northernmost kiln remains are the most obvious. The southernmost is not as obvious since the remains of some of its southern and southwestern walls have eroded downhill. No iron hardware was found. In the process of inspecting the area for hardware and any associated features, some brick and charcoal were found immediately across the road, but appear to have been pushed there by some road-grading operation. Much brick also is scattered in the streambed for about 100 feet downstream.

Uphill is a small clearing with an adjoining logging road curving through it, dropping off to cross Roaring Brook on the other side of the hill. This area appears to have been associated with a recent logging operation from the depth of the wheel

tracks and amount of slash, tree bark, and sawdust. Signs of logging could be seen on that side (east) of the brook. Where the road drops downward to the brook, however, there is a high concentration of charcoal and brick. The road appears to have been cut directly through the charcoal and brick deposit. Inspection of the area revealed no charcoal kiln ruin although one might have existed here before getting plowed under by logging operations.

This mile stretch of Coal Kiln Road from its juncture with County Road a half-mile south uphill to the power lines (not shown on the USGS maps but are on the U.S. Forest Service maps) is a high-development area. During the afternoon spent at and around the kiln site, a number of overland vehicles churned up and down the road with agents and prospective buyers apparently inspecting building plots.

BE-108 Thompson Farm Charcoal Mounds (Stamford): Sites of two charcoal mounds were found on the Thompson farm in 1986. Information leading to location of this site was provided in part by Anna Whitney of Stamford, who lived on the farm as a little girl and related how she used to play on a patch of charcoal-covered ground; by Sandra Thompson, who told me of a recent visit to her farm by Mrs. Whitney and pointed to the north-northwest where she used to play in the charcoal; and also Nancy Bushika, librarian at the Stamford Community Library, who contacted Mrs. Thompson and relayed pertinent information to me.

The Thompson farm is located near the end of Maltese Road, which heads north off County Road about two miles northwest of Stamford village. A few dozen feet beyond the Thompson house, the remains of a continuation of the road can be seen going up the hill, eventually intersecting with another, more obvious, "old logging road." The charcoal-making areas are located up (north) this road about a quarter-mile, and generally fit the directions to the site as provided. Accompanying me on the search, location, and inspection of the site was 11-year-old Hawk Thompson.

The charcoal-making area was found to contain two mound-type remains. One mound remain is about 30 feet in diameter, slightly larger and more round than the other. The 1-foot-high concrete wall of an abandoned well is just southwest of the site. Physical confirmation of the site beyond the circular flat area on the slight incline was made by digging two shallow holes at each mound site with a trowel. Black soil and bits of peach-pit-size charcoal were found at both sites without digging deeper than 6 inches. Areas between and around the sites were also tested but with negative results, isolating charcoal finds to the mound sites proper. Walkover inspection was made in the surrounding area with no further finds, although many old roads in the area were not hiked to their limits. Due to the hunting season, we decided not to venture too far away from the farm and into the woods.

Dutch Hill Area Charcoal Sites: The 1856 Bennington County map indicates "coal kilns" by today's Route 8, just downhill from the old Dutch Hill ski area south of Heartwellville, at a roadside spring. And a Sunday afternoon tour of kiln ruins in the area, organized by Nancy Bushika of the Stamford Community Library, resulted in finding a kiln ruin behind Hank Kennedy's house, east of the highway, and more ruins up Collins Road near the upper end of Crazy John

Stream. The informal tour included Stamford residents Betty Vadnais, Irving (Red) Call and the late Betty Call, and Pat Rondeau with her little boy (plus Nancy Bushika and Bob West). The kiln on Hank Kennedy's property was known by the local people; Mr. Kennedy guided us to the ruin. The kiln ruins up Crazy John Stream were known by Pat Rondeau, who guided us to them, a lot less leisurely hike than the stroll to Mr. Kennedy's kiln ruin.

BE-105 Kennedy Charcoal Kiln (Stamford): This single-kiln ruin was found in 1986 about a 15-minute hike east of the Kennedy house and barn, east of Route 8, and probably within about a hundred feet of the Readsboro town line (farther to the east). The ruin measured 82 feet around the outside. It has approximately 2-foot-thick by up to 89-inch-high stone walls. Pieces of charcoal and pitch rest inside on the kiln floor along with many pieces of red brick, too many to have all been used for vents, indicating that the kiln might have had a dome-shaped brick roof. Vents in the kiln wall were made in many cases with two bricks between two large, flat stones, above and below, with space between the bricks to admit another brick for draft control. No hardware was found in or around the ruin or the nearby brook. The hint of a road could be seen leading from the ruin back toward the Kennedy house; a short way from the ruin, it joins a better-defined trail.

Mr. Kennedy said he thought that a family named McGraw owned and operated the kiln, although that name does not appear in the 1869 Beers map of Stamford. The ruin falls within the area owned/leased by the Richmond Iron Works (Massachusetts) in 1870 (*Doomsday Book* 1870:26). The company operated nine charcoal kilns in Stamford, making 5,000 bushels of charcoal per month (Child 1880:203).

BE-107 Crazy John Stream Charcoal Kilns (Stamford): The ruins of three stone-type kilns were found about 1¼ miles up Collins Road in Stamford. The road to the site is twisting and uphill most of the way, but on that day rewarded us at various intervals with large, ripe blackberries. The kiln ruins are off a side trail to the right that rejoins the main trail a short distance uphill.

The ruins are in a very advanced stage of collapse, making accurate measurements difficult. Inside diameter is 24 to 26 feet; inside wall height is about 5 feet. Walls are made of stone, about 2 feet thick. The ruins lie in an approximately northeast-southwest line, 10 and 20 feet apart. Much charcoal, burnt pitch, and pieces of red brick lie mixed inside the kiln area along with stone wall breakdown. The amount of red brick may indicate the kilns had dome-shaped brick roofs. Could this three-ruin site with kiln bases of stone and probably tops of brick possibly be those in the photo that introduces chapter 5?

Inspection of the kiln walls indicated ground-level openings faced the trail. The only hardware found was a flat iron bar woven into roots of a birch tree on the northerly wall of the center ruin. The iron rod appears similar to hardware seen on parts of iron doors at other charcoal kiln sites.

The kiln site lies within the area owned or leased by the Richmond Iron Works during 1870–1880 as a source of charcoal for its furnace at Richmond, Massachusetts (*Doomsday Book* 1870:26). The company operated nine charcoal kilns in Stamford, making 5,000 bushels of charcoal a month (Child 1880:203).

BE-54 Dutch Hill Charcoal Kilns (Readsboro): Alongside a spring that Route 8 travelers have been drawing water from for years are the collapsed remains of two charcoal kilns. The site is identified on the 1856 Bennington County map as "coal kilns," astride the Stamford-Readsboro town line. But the actual site is a bit west of the line, well in Readsboro.

When found in 1984, all there was to identify the kiln remains were some bits of charcoal, some red brick, and one large stone with a burnt, blackened end, all from a small 20- by 40-foot area between the highway and a cut-into embankment. The site is buried under an estimated 6 feet of gravel fill, which was probably done at the time of highway realignment. The area is large enough to have contained two kilns (the map indicated "kilns"). Directly across the highway are more red brick and charcoal.

BE-CK03 Root & Jones Chemical Company (Bennington Village): In Bennington village, the 1875 chemical works of Root & Jones produced charcoal as a by-product of wood distillation. From the 150 cords of wood consumed monthly in their ovens, they extracted 225 pounds of lime, 4 gallons of alcohol, 12 to 15 gallons of tar, and 40 to 50 bushels of charcoal per cord of wood (Child 1880:95-96).

WINDHAM COUNTY

WD-66 Harold Field Charcoal Kiln (Stratton): The standing remains of a concrete-block charcoal kiln were located in Stratton in 1986 based on information from Bob West's uncle. He said that on Pike's Falls Road, at the Stratton-Winhall line, a charcoal kiln could be seen standing alongside the road. The ruin was found on the second try.

The structure stands about 60 feet off the west side of Pike's Falls Road in a pine forest, about 850 feet south of the Winhall-Stratton town line. It is visible from the road only if you know exactly where and when to look. The ruin is made of modern, standard-size concrete block. It stands 8 feet high, 12 feet long, and 7 feet wide. A short chimney made of more standard chimney block is at the rear of the kiln. The front opening is 4 feet wide, and the roof made of a 4- by 8- by 16-inch concrete block, held up in position by iron pipes horizontally run in parallel through the holes of the blocks, with the blocks snugged against each other across the roof. All blocks in the roof, walls, and chimney are mortared. The entire structure is constructed on a concrete slab that extends an undetermined distance into the ground (at least 6 inches, as can be seen at one corner). Vents are provided at the corners by poking through two adjacent holes in each pair of diagonally opposing corner blocks. Vent control is by bricks placed in the holes. The kiln, as found, was about 20 percent filled with charcoal.

A local resident said that the property owner lived somewhere in Wisconsin and that the kiln was built sometime about the middle to late 1950s by Harold Field. The kiln design and period of estimated operation generally agree with the description of the mid-20th-century revival of charcoal burning for the backyard barbecue market (Simmons April-May 1960:10-12). Many small cinder block charcoal kilns were built and operated during and following World War II, their construction encouraged by bulletins and booklets published by various state resource agencies. And many modern, industrious charcoal burners did manage to put away profits against small financial investments, but with a lot of hard work and patience. People living near Field's charcoal kiln said that he apparently thought he'd found an easy way to get rich quickly, but after making only one load he quit, moved to Colorado, and has not been seen or heard from since.

Summary of Results

The quantity of kiln ruins and the variation of their design and construction material indicate that charcoal manufacture was a major 19th-century Vermont industry. The charcoal not only fueled local furnaces, bloomeries, and foundries, but after the demise of the Vermont iron industry in the mid-19th century, it found markets in Massachusetts and Connecticut, and possibly New York and New Hampshire. Charcoal also found markets in Vermont copper-smelting operations at Strafford and Vershire, iron and brass foundries that dealt with metals requiring special qualities, and glass foundries. A summary of charcoal-making sites and types of remains found in Vermont is presented in table 6-2.

Table 6-2. Summary of Charcoal-Making Sites and Types of Remains

County	Sites	Brick	Stone	Brick/Stone	Concrete	Mound
Addison	13	7		1		18
Bennington	38	53	8	11		11
Caledonia	1					
Chittenden	1					2
Orange	2					
Rutland	13	48	1			20
Washington	1					
Windham	1				1	
Windsor	1					
Total:	71	108	9	12	1	51

Anyone familiar with Vermont's landscape is aware of the rocky nature of the land. Vermont is still known for its marble, slate, and granite industries, but Vermont farmers would rather forget the miles of stone walls they have built down through the 200-year history of the state. Stone-built furnaces and kilns reflect, therefore, the adaptive use of a natural resource to answer a need for a practical building material. The stone-type kilns are built of unfinished stone, but are laid up carefully in up to 3-foot-thick walls to prevent as much air as possible from leaking into the interior of the kiln during the combustion process. Most brick-type kiln ruins have long since been cannibalized of their useful brick and hardware. Stone is such an available resource in Vermont that the best charcoal kiln (and lime kiln) ruins in the state are those made of stone.

The variability of 19th-century charcoal kiln ruins in Vermont reflects, therefore, the ability of charcoal makers to adapt the needs of the basic kiln design to the resources that were available. The consistent 28-foot inside diameter of the brick-type kilns, for example, indicates a common knowledge of one aspect of the technology. But the variability in hardware at these same brick-type kiln sites testifies to the individuality of at least one of the number of choices that enterprising Vermont charcoal makers appeared to make the most of.

*A partially standing lime kiln ruin near Cavendish Station, showing
advanced breakdown of the front arch and the iron binding holding together
what remains.*

Chapter 7
Historical Overview of Lime Burning

Lime, Cement, Mortar, and Concrete

What is lime? What is the difference between lime, concrete, mortar, and cement? Any child knows the answer: lime is that little green fruit that makes such great-tasting 7-Up. Concrete is what she roller-skates on. A mortar is a small cannon, and cement holds model airplanes together. It is not all quite that simple, of course. Yet lime, concrete, mortar, and cement all have one very important thing in common: they are all made from limestone.

Lime is made by the process of calcining limestone, that is, burning the limestone without fusing (melting) it. Pure lime (quicklime, burnt lime, caustic lime) is composed of calcium oxide. When treated with water, lime gives off heat, forming calcium hydroxide, and is sold commercially as slaked (or hydrated) lime. It is used in the manufacture of paper, glass, and whitewash, in tanning leather, sugar refining, and as a water softener and a bleach. It is also used in making mortar and cement, and as an agricultural neutralizer of acid soils. Lime water, an alkaline solution of slaked lime in water, is used in medicine as an antacid and for other alkaloid uses. In earlier days, lime was used by gas companies to cleanse coal gas that was burned in lamps to light the streets at night.

Cement, commonly called portland cement, is made by combining limestone with clay, shale, or blast furnace slag that contains alumina and silica in proportions of 60 percent lime, 19 percent silica, 8 percent alumina, 5 percent each of iron and magnesia, and 3 percent sulfur trioxide. These are all ground together, heated in a kiln at temperatures in the 3,000° F range until fused, then quickly cooled into a "clinker" and ground into powder to be packed away for storage. Although cement dates to Roman times, the name portland cement dates to 1824 when an enterprising British cement maker decided to capitalize on the similarity between the color of his cement and that of portland stone, a much-used building stone in England at the time.

Mortar is a mixture of lime or cement with sand and water. Lime mortar consists of slaked lime and sand. Cement mortar is made by mixing cement and sand with water, and is the stronger of the two; the best is made by combining portland cement, sand, water, and a small amount of lime. Concrete is a mixture of cement and coarse sand, broken stone, gravel, or cinders. Better concrete is made with portland cement.

The words marble and limestone are many times used synonymously, although each is a name for a distinctively different stone. In an earlier time in Vermont it was the custom to call nearly all stone that was not granite marble if it could be carved or polished. This meant that even schist, which is more or less crystalline, was considered a marble at one time.

Some of Vermont's finest and most attractive marbles are not, technically speaking, true marbles. These include the limestones of Isle La Motte and Swanton; the breccias of Plymouth and Manchester; the dolomites of Swanton, Malletts Bay, and Manchester; the serpentine verde antique of Roxbury; and others. All of these could be cut, polished, and sold as marble and were popularly regarded as such.

Marble is limestone that has been metamorphosed—that is, changed in nature due to the effects of heat and pressure deep within the earth. Limestone is an earlier phase of marble and it was formed under ancient seas from the residue of corals, shellfish, lime-producing plants, and lime carbonate. Limestone takes its name, therefore, from the large proportion of lime in the stone, which every lime burner knows (Perkins 1933:11-12).

Many of Vermont's early limestone quarries were opened for the intent of making marble. But as the nature of the stone was better understood and the market demanded true marble, some of these quarries switched from making "marble" to burning the stone for quicklime. And in time, even these pocket industries ceased as the demand increased for a high-quality lime and the kilns evolved into complex furnace-type operations.

The Lime-Burning Process

History does not share who first burned lime, when, or why. Lime burning certainly dates to antiquity, and it is thought that subsequent to the discovery of brick making ancient people arrived at the art of lime burning.

Assyrians and Babylonians used moistened clay as a cement but it is doubtful that they ever really used mortar. Egyptians used mortar in the construction of the pyramids. Scientists analyzed mortar used in building the pyramid Cheops and results showed that the Egyptians possessed nearly as much practical knowledge of the subject as did the mid-19th-century lime burners (Burnell 1870:1-2).

At some early period, the Greeks used compositions with lime as the base to cover walls constructed of unburned brick. And the Etruscans (700–500 BC) were the first Italians who employed mortar in building. The Romans probably derived all their knowledge of the arts from either the Etruscans or Greeks and added little to the general stock of knowledge regarding the use of limes.

Various early recorders of history acknowledged the subject of lime. One of the earliest was Marcus Vitruvius Pollio, a 1st-century BC Roman artilleryman who wrote 10 books on architecture (*De Architectura*). The oldest surviving work on the subject, its dissertations include architecture, engineering, and practical hydraulics. Pliny (the Elder, AD 23–79) and St. Augustine (AD 354–430) wrote occasionally about limes and cement, the former to complain of the malpractice of the builders, the latter to seek metaphysical comparisons.

Pure lime, or calcium, is chemically regarded as a metallic oxide, having strong alkaline properties. It is caustic but it never occurs in nature. It is found in the state of a bicarbonate, the carbonate and sub-carbonate of lime. Commercial lime is obtained by calcining these carbonates and the process consists of driving off the carbonic acid gas with which it is in combination.

The mineral that contains this carbonate of lime is given the generic name of limestone, and there are many and various forms in nature. Limestones are generally composed of carbonate of lime, magnesia, oxide of iron, manganese, silica, and alumina, and are combined in variable proportions. They are also found with a mechanical mixture of clay, of quartzite sand, and of numerous other substances. The name limestone is more especially applied to such of the above mixtures that contain at least one-half their weight of carbonate of lime. Mineralogists make a distinction between the subdivisions of limestones, which are characterized by varieties of form and structure. This nomenclature is important because every description of limestone yields a lime of different quality, distinct in color and weight, its avidity for water, and especially in the degree of hardness it is capable of assuming when made into mortar. But the physical and mechanical natures of limestone are far from being certain guides as to the quality of the lime it can yield. A chemical analysis frequently gives different results from those obtained in practice (Burnell 1870:9-10). When found in a pure state, for example, Vermont limestone contains about 56 percent quicklime and about 44 percent carbonic acid (Hitchcock et al. 1861:746).

Carbonate of lime occurs in nearly all the geological formations, but it is scarce in the primary ones. Limestone is worked largely for obtaining building stone or for burning and obtaining lime. Calciferous rocks (containing calcium carbonate) of the primary formations and of the early transition series furnish

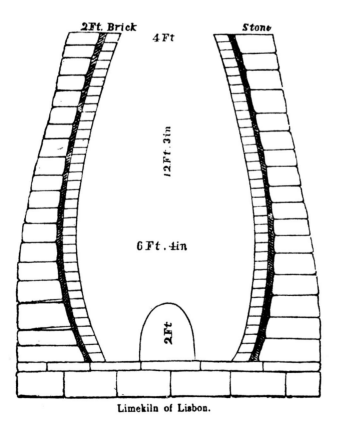

7-1. *Cutaway view of a mid-19th-century, brick-lined, stone-type lime kiln that operated at Lisbon, New Hampshire (Jackson 1844:174). Compare with figure 2-11.*

the greater number of stones that are worked under the name of marble. Secondary and tertiary calciferous rocks contain mixtures of clay and other ingredients that render them most adapted to furnish lime.

After a calcining sufficient to free the carbonic acid gas, the limestone significantly diminishes in weight. The resulting material possesses the property of absorbing water, either with or without the influence of heat. It cracks and falls to pieces while combining with the water, or slaking (spelled slacking in older books), as the process of passing into the state of hydrated lime is called. The principal characteristics of hydrate of lime are that it is white and pulverized and much less caustic than quicklime. It parts easily with the first portions of its water of combination if exposed to fire but requires a very high degree of heat to cause it to part with all of its water.

Calcining limestone can physically be done a number of ways, all of which have in common certain basic requirements. Carbonate of lime must be brought to a red-hot heat in order to free the carbonic acid gas. It must also be maintained in a continued and uninterrupted manner at that heat for several hours in order to allow all the gas to escape. The time needed for the complete expulsion of gas is in proportion to the size of the pieces of stone being heated. Large stones take a longer time; stones broken into smaller pieces, of a lighter nature, and moist take a shorter time.

The stones were broken into smaller pieces to allow the interior, insulated by the poor conductivity of the stone itself, to receive heat and to allow escape for the carbonic gas from the center of the stone. Lime burners watered the stone if prevented from using it fresh from the quarry. Moistening the stone caused the water to act on the carbonate of lime by formation of a temporary hydrate, which replaced the carbonic acid for a very short space of time in parts of the limestone first affected by the fire.

To obtain lime for water cement, the impure limestone should be broken into small pieces and subjected to a heat sufficient to expel the carbonic acid, which will require a high heat from two to five days. But care must be taken that the heat is not too intense, for if it is, the rock will become partially fused, and a glassy substance will result from the alkaline and silicious constituents of the rock. After calcination, the rock should be thoroughly pulverized and mixed with sharp sand, after which water may be applied till the mass assumes the consistency of common mortar, when it should be used immediately, especially if it possesses the setting property of some cements. The proportion of sand to be used with the cement, varies with the composition of the lime (Hitchcock et al. 1861:782).

When the limestone could not be broken into small pieces, the lime burner placed the largest blocks in the center of the kiln where they were exposed to the greatest heat. The temperature of the kiln was then raised to compensate for the larger stones. It became a question of economy—whether saving fuel compensated for the expense of breaking the stones into smaller pieces.

The color of the stone when in the kiln played an important part of understanding what was going on and when. Blue limestone became yellow if burned to a slight degree. Continuing the process, the color passed to a deep yellow, an ash gray, and finally a slate blue when the heat was very intense. There was some controversy as to whether color played any part in determining quality of the product. Some burners felt that the best hydrated limes, when properly burned, were a light straw color.

It was important to determine the proper time to stop the calcination when it became apparent that some limes, if over-burned, lost all their useful properties and were, in the work-man's phrase, killed. If under-burned, they had other undesired properties. Likewise, no comprehensive rule could be deter-mined as to the fuel used, except that the choice of fuel was reflected in the design of the kiln. In areas where wood abounded, such as Vermont, kilns were made with hearths on which the wood was burned separately from the limestone. Wood, however, was not well-adapted for operation of running-type kilns, that is, kilns that were designed to be operated continuously (called perpetual kilns in Vermont). Fresh coal often caked, impeding calcination and contributing impurities to the lime. Coke was considered the best since it gave good heat nearly at once. To produce 35 cubic feet of lime it took about 60 cubic feet of oak, 117 cubic feet of fir, or 9 cubic feet of coal. Perpetual kilns required less fuel. Heavy smoke escaping from the kiln indicated wasted fuel.

Limestone was sometimes openly burned in large piles, called heaps, consisting of alternate layers of stone and fuel, similar to the mode of burning bricks in clamps. The same care was taken as in the latter in coating the sides of the heap with clay so as to retain as much heat as possible. The heap required strict attention to obtaining proper draft so that the whole mass would be equally burned. This method was usually restricted to coal-fueled kilns, due to the amount of fuel needed to com-pensate for radiated heat loss.

The Lime Kiln

There is not a lot of information available about the history and description of lime kilns. One archival source described lime kiln configuration in terms of "a cylindrical form," "in-verted frustum of a right cone," etc. (Gillmore 1874:127). Another source, published in England, described lime kilns in terms of their shapes: rectangular straight prism, cylinder, cyl-inder surmounted by a truncated cone, reversed straight-sided cone or funnel, and a cone of different diameters (Burnell 1870:30-38).

Rectangular prisms were used for the purpose of simulta-neously burning lime and bricks or tiles. Limestone occupied the lower half of the kiln; the upper half was filled with bricks or with the tiles placed on edge. Cylinder kilns were principally used in situations where large quantities of lime were required in a short time. They were rarely constructed for definitive use; rather, they were built cheaply for a short period of use. An archway was made first to form the hearth. A round tower was built atop to form the kiln itself, which was made of limestone, brick, or any material of those natures. The outside was coated with clay to stop all holes, and the whole was covered with a hurdle, which was a coating of earth, leaves, and/or branches that insulated it, taking care to leave a hole for access to the hearth. They were constructed of more solid materials and in

7-2. A 19th-century lime kiln with stone or brick walls, showing how larger pieces of charge were arched to hold up smaller stones above (Gillmore 1874:139).

a more permanent manner, and served only for burning lime. The largest stones were placed at the bottom of the kiln with smaller ones placed in the straight cylinder at the top. These kilns were superior to previous ones because heat reverberated from the sides and could not escape into the outside without producing its useful effect. The kilns were used mainly for intermittent burning where wood or rich coal was available for fuel.

Lime kilns were later classified by types of operation: inter-mittent or continuous. Intermittent kilns were those in which each burning of limestone was a separate operation, that is, the kiln was charged (loaded with limestone), burned, cooled, and emptied, and then the cycle repeated. The advantage here was that the kiln was operated only when a demand existed; the disadvantage was the irregular quality of the product from burning to burning. Intermittent kilns were usually small and were operated by local farmers as local demand required. These were the 19th-century so-called "pot kilns" that were the har-binger of new advances in the industry (Eckel 1922:100-109). In continuous kilns, also called running or perpetual kilns, limestone and fuel were charged in alternate layers, and as the burning progressed, burnt lime was removed from the bottom while fresh layers of limestone and fuel were added to the top. The process was similar to that of the blast furnace.

The inside walls of some early kilns were protected from the extreme heat by a lining of refractory stone, usually a good-quality sandstone. When the kilns were worked by inter-mittent fires, the limestone charge rested on arches built up from pieces of stone to be burned and laid dry. A small fire was lit below these arches toward the back. The fire gradually worked its way toward the front as the draft increased. The opening was regulated to obtain the required degree of combustion and new fuel added as necessary to maintain the fire. Outside air, which entered through the fire door, carried the flames to all parts of the arch and gradually brought the whole mass of limestone to a state of incandescence. As the heat increased, the larger stones cracked and burst with loud explosions. The use of large stones was therefore avoided when building arches.

When the upper part of the kiln was smaller in diameter than the lower, the draft sometimes drove the flames out through the fire door. Very early kilns were built by trial and error, making the upper part larger or smaller, as required, to control the draft of the kiln. At some places, the lime burners placed pieces of wood vertically around and in the charge to facilitate the circulation of air and heat. These pieces of wood burned in the early stage of the process but left spaces that acted as miniature chimneys inside the charge. However, they also produced an unequal calcination.

The degree of heat required varied, depending on the density and humidity of the limestone. Likewise, the time necessary for perfect calcination was determined through trial and error. Such variables as the nature of the limestone, quality of the fuel, draft of the kiln, and direction and force of the wind all came into play. Before the process was complete, the charge in the lower part of the kiln gradually shrank. The stones that formed the arches cracked and the charge settled and lost from 15 to 20 percent of its height. Limestone generally lost about 45 percent of its weight by calcination through loss of water and carbonic gas. A simple way to determine if calcination was complete was to drive an iron bar down into the center of the charge. If the bar met with considerable resistance or struck firm, hard materials, the process was not yet complete. But if the bar penetrated easily, as if passing through loose, dry gravel, the process was considered complete. Another method was to draw a sample of the lime and directly analyze it, but this depended on where in the charge the sample was drawn.

As the character of the lime business changed from a local to a regional market, both the quantity and quality of demand increased. In many places, intermittent kilns were merely lined with firebrick and built a little higher to meet these new demands. In most places, however, kilns of new, technologically advanced designs were built.

These new kilns were 25 to 28 feet high with inside diameters of 5 to 6 feet at the top, 10 to 11 feet near the middle, and 7 to 8 feet near the bottom. The inside generally appeared similar to the inside configuration of early blast furnaces—like an egg standing on its fatter end. They were lined with regular brick or firebrick, set 14 to 18 inches thick into fire clay. Choice of firebrick was influenced by its ability to conduct as little heat as possible, yet retain the high-temperature heat. There was a 5- or 6-foot-high arched opening at the bottom through which fuel was loaded and burned lime was removed. About 1 or 2 feet above the bottom was an iron grate on which the fuel burned. The grate provided means for a good draft and space beneath for easy removal of ashes.

Limestone nearer to the fire still tended to over-burn while that near the top of the kiln might not be calcined enough. Then there was obviously a large loss of heat in intermittent kilns as the inside walls cooled while the lime was removed and the kiln was prepared for the next charge, as Vermont State

Geologist Charles B. Adams wrote in 1845:

> In burning lime the intermittent kilns only are used in this State, so far as we have seen. There is of course a great waste of heat in cooling off the kiln for every charge of limestone. Where fuel is abundant, and the demand for lime is small, this may be the best method. Common bricks are found to answer for lining, although fire bricks, such as are made at Bennington, and may be made from any of the numerous beds of kaolin, would probably be best adapted to a kiln in constant use. Between the bricks and the outer wall there should be a space filled with ashes, to confine the heat and to prevent fracture of the outer wall by sudden heat.
>
> The egg-shaped kiln is now preferred, having to some extent the properties of a reverberatory furnace.
>
> The kiln should be built against the side of a cliff on which the stone can be drawn to the top; or on the side of a steep hill, raising the ground between the hill side and the kiln.
>
> Where wood costs $2.00 per cord, the expense of burning lime in an intermittent kiln is about 8 cents per bushel. But in a perpetual kiln ... the expense is about 2 cents per bushel (Adams 1845:47-48).

The problems associated with trying to increase the output of intermittent kilns while improving the quality of the product were solved in the 1860s by the introduction of perpetual kilns. These were categorized by their three types of operation: mixed-feed (limestone and fuel fed in alternate layers), separate-feed (limestone and fuel not in direct contact), and rotary kilns.

The advantage of mixed-feed over separate-feed kilns was that they were cheaper to build, were fuel-efficient, and yielded more product for the same size kiln. But lime produced by mixed-feed discolored through contact with the fuel, the fuel ashes were difficult to separate from the burned lime, and some ash formed hard clinkers on pieces of lime that prevented a satisfactory burning.

> These [mixed-feed perpetual kilns in Vermont] are so constructed that fuel and the rock from which the quicklime is obtained are put in at the top, and the quicklime is obtained through a door at the bottom of the kiln.
>
> The space in the kilns containing the fuel and stone is egg-shaped, or like two truncated cones placed base to base, by which shape the material in the kiln is supported or kept up while the removal of the quicklime is being carried on from an opening at the bottom. It is quite necessary that good draught be maintained during the time of burning, in order that the disengaged carbonic acid gas, which is heavier than common air, be carried off—hence an orifice should be left at or near the bottom for the entrance of air (Hitchcock et al. 1861:748).

At a 1920 mixed-feed lime plant in Pennsylvania it took six quarrymen to keep three kilns supplied, each kiln taking 24 tons of stone per day. The kilns burned 26 pounds of bituminous coal per 75-pound bushel of lime produced, or 34.7 percent on weight of lime produced. This was considered an enormous ratio since mixed-feed kilns were expected to produce lime with a fuel consumption of 15 to 25 percent per weight of lime burned.

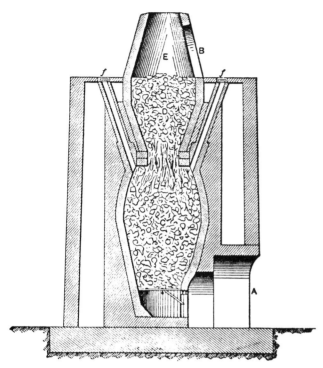

7-3. *The Aalborg lime kiln, showing side flues "f-f" leading downward to the combustion area in the middle of the kiln. Gate at bottom released burned lime and ash for removal at "A" (Eckel 1922:104).*

One type design of mixed-feed kiln was known as the Aalborg (or Schöfer) kiln. In cross-section, this kiln appeared as two smaller egg-shaped chambers standing vertically atop each other. In the upper chamber the limestone was heated, dried, and partially calcined. Fuel combustion occurred at the juncture of the two chambers, and in the lower chamber the lime cooled. Angling downward into the juncture of the two chambers, in the middle of the kiln, were a number of narrow chutes which drew fresh outside air down from the top of the kiln. This fresh air, introduced directly into the narrow juncture of the upper and lower chamber, made the juncture the hottest part of the kiln, where the fuel was consumed and the lime was burned to completion. Aalborg kilns produced 15 to 20 tons of lime a day, consuming 220 to 260 pounds of coal per ton of lime, and making for an efficient 10 to 12 percent operation.

Mixed-feed kilns were the most difficult to manage with certainty, although when running favorably were the most economical. A mere change in wind direction (which affected the draft), a falling in of some inner part of the charge, or irregularity in the size of the pieces of limestone were some of the causes sufficient to retard or accelerate the draft and produce irregular movements in the descent of the charge within the kiln, causing either an excessive or defective calcination. At times, a kiln would act perfectly for several weeks, then suddenly be out of order for no apparent reason. A mere change in the nature of the fuel would produce so great a difference in the process that it defied all calculations of the lime burner. The practice of operating running mixed-feed kilns still resulted in little predictability of product quality.

The most favorable conditions to ensure a successful burning were: the thickness of the charge did not exceed 12 to 14 inches, the charge was not higher then the top of the kiln, and the fuel was well distributed through the charge. The supervisor of kiln operations had to carefully watch the top of the kiln and have fresh currents of air opened where gases did not pass. This was determined by noting whether the stones were blackened by the smoke escaping through the top, which could only take place in the direction of the escape of the gases. Wherever the stones of the charge were not blackened, therefore, the lime burner passed an iron bar through the charge to open a new chimney.

The second type of perpetual kiln, the separate-feed, became the first truly modern lime kiln, with its distinctive steel shell rising some 25 to 35 feet above the kiln base. The rusted steel shells of these kilns can still be seen among ruins at Leicester Junction, New Haven, Swanton (Fonda), across Lake Champlain at Chazy, New York, and at Cheshire, Massachusetts. These kilns rose from 35 to 50 feet in total height above ground level. The insides of the 5- to 8-foot-diameter shells as well as the kiln areas below were lined with firebrick. Around and outside the bottom of the shell were little furnaces, also known as fireplaces, in which the fuel was burned. Fuel in the furnaces was coal or wood, whose flames were directed through two large openings around the side of the shell and directly on the limestone passing downward past the openings. In this manner, the fuel and limestone did not come in contact. Fresh limestone was fed in at the top of the shell, at some plants by small cars that ran on tracks directly from the quarry to trestles on the tops of the kilns. Burned lime was removed through draw gates opened by turning a hand wheel at the bottom of the kiln; the burned lime fell through the draw gate into railroad cars that ran on the floor beneath the kilns.

One typical kiln of this type was called the Keystone kiln. Although this kiln did not have the fuel efficiency of the mixed-feed kiln, it did make a lime of much higher quality, with 90 percent being well-burned, clean, white lime (compared to the 75 to 80 percent from the mixed-feed kiln). The fuel burned being separate from the kiln also provided better control of the burning and the reduction of under- and over-burned material. Many patents were issued for improvements to various details of this lime kiln. One such patent was for boilers inserted in the kiln arches, utilizing the waste heat of the kiln to provide power to drive drills, hoists, crushers, and other machinery associated with the quarry operations.

One frequent problem associated with lime burning was "clinkering" or the burning of clay impurities—silica, alumina, iron oxide—in the kiln, caused by the high temperature reached in the kiln combining the limestone with these compounds. The result was the sintering of the clinkers with a portion of the product, which in reality was a form of natural cement called grappiers. In this country these over-burned portions were merely discarded; in Europe they were carefully saved and ground to make "grappier cements." Clinkering could begin at very low temperatures in lime with 5 to 10 percent clay impurities. It was also caused by combining the lime with the coal ashes in mixed-feed kilns. In some types of kilns, the high-temperature attack of the lime on the firebrick lining also caused clinkering.

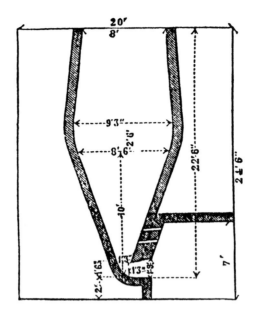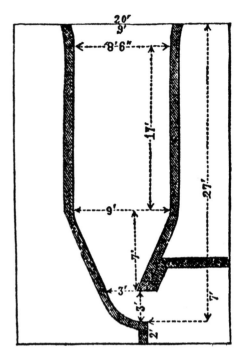

7-4. Cross-section view of two types of 19th-century lime kilns: left kiln used in Maryland and Virginia, and that on right in New York and Ohio (Gillmore 1874:128).

Generally, the lime was drawn every morning and evening, day after day. When complete, the lime had to be drawn from the kiln with caution, otherwise the charge might drop unevenly and cause a bad shift of fuel in the remaining charge. The process continued on an average of three days and nights, but it varied according to local circumstances and weather.

By the 1860s, there were general rules for construction of a lime kiln. The lining of the inside should be made of firebricks, because this material resisted the action of the fire better than any other known material. The interior opening had to be high enough to allow the heat existing at the top to calcinate the stone placed there. Calcination was attained when the ratio of height to the largest diameter was in the order of 2:1 (2 feet of height to each foot in diameter at the widest). For perpetual kilns, this ratio increased to 3:1 or 4:1, with some kilns attaining 5:1. In intermittent kilns, the best upper opening was found to be about one-third the greatest diameter, and the fire opening about one-quarter of the same dimensions in both height and width. The thickness of the walls was not invariable, but walls had to be as thick as possible to maintain mechanical stability of the kiln and retain the greatest quantity of heat. It was unwise to scrimp in the construction to save costs since these savings would quickly be absorbed in heat loss and increased fuel costs.

The third type of perpetual kilns were rotary. These were an outgrowth of the portland cement industry, which required this distinctive kiln. Rotary kilns were essentially horizontal kilns, resembling a long, large-diameter pipe, which rotated slowly on driven rollers. The charging end of the kiln was slightly higher than the discharge end so the charge could slowly move through the kiln. Its chief disadvantage when applied in the lime industry was its high fuel consumption. For best operation, rotary kilns required that the limestone be crushed to fairly even size, preferably finely ground. These conditions provided

steady operation of the kiln with a large output. But it was difficult to maintain the heat inside the kiln at an economical temperature, reducing the amount of clinkers formed from impure limestone. The use of rotary kilns grew slowly and by the 1920s there were 30 in the country (one at West Rutland and possibly another at Colchester).

Early American Lime Kilns

An essential requirement in agriculture and industry, lime was made in the first American settlements by burning oyster shells that were plentiful along the seacoasts. With the discovery of limestone outcrops, lime was widely made by frontier farmers. By the end of the 18th century, lime burning began in earnest (Long 1972:469).

One of the earliest lime kilns in the country was operated in Rhode Island. It is described in old land records that mention the Indian name Setamachut, a hill on the west shore of the Wanasquatucket River near Manton, about three miles due west of Providence. Papers dated 1662 present Thomas Hackleton's request to the town to "burne lime" and to "take stones and wood for the same purpose." "I here present the dimensions of the kiln on Setamachut—16 feet diameter at the top; 13 feet diameter at the center; and 10 feet diameter at the bottom. It is 15 feet in depth. This was the earliest form used.... These facts show that the kiln at Setamachut is the rudest and most ancient now in existence in Rhode Island" (Rider 1904:266, 268).

Pennsylvania Governor Pownall reported in 1754 that there were lime kilns on every farm he visited in Lancaster County (Williams 1952:77-78, cited in Long 1972:469). In Vermont, many hillside outcrops of limestone in Clarendon and Wallingford have been found accompanied by remains of small lime kilns used at one time by local farmers for fertilizing their fields. "There is plenty of limestone for manure on every field and it does not cost much labor or expense to come at it and it can be burned from the wood which we grub up when we clear the land" (Thompson 1884:317, cited in Long 1972:469).

Early-19th-century farmers built kilns for their own or local use either on a lot near the limestone quarry or on a woodlot, depending on the owner's judgement whether to carry the stone or the fuel to the kiln. It involved as much labor and expense to haul the wood as it did to haul the limestone. Lucky was the farmer whose kiln lay on the uphill edge of a quarry, yet downhill from a woodland so the wood cart could be rolled downhill to the site. Many lime kilns found in Vermont were on hillsides, at the edge of a quarry and downhill from forest. Lime not produced for one's self was a valuable barter item, although neither the raw limestone nor wood had as much value. Quarry workers received about 50¢ a day and the lime burner received about 75¢. Liquor was a common lubricant that kept everything running smoothly.

The early farm kiln was usually built into a hillside. Where no hillside was available, the stone kiln structure was banked up with earth, with an earth ramp leading to the top from the uphill side. Heights ran from 10 to 20 feet. Thickness of the stone walls were from 18 to 24 inches. Insides varied from square to round to rectangular and opened up from 8 to 9 feet inside diameter. Front (downhill) walls sometimes curved slightly inward at the edges according to the contour of the hill, and were laid up to the full height of the kiln in the middle to provide bank support for a road to the top of the kiln. The openings at the bottom varied in size and style. Earlier kilns had smaller openings, to protect the burning from sudden drafts lest the whole burn too rapidly. These openings were simple holes at the bottom of the front wall supported on the top by a heavy lintel stone. Later kiln openings were arched, similar to those of small blast furnaces. (Two Vermont kilns, at Jamaica (WD-68) and Wilmington (WD-89), display Gothic-style triangular openings with pointed tops.) A foot or two above the bottom of the shaft was an iron grate, above which the limestone was stacked and below which wood was piled for fueling the kiln. Grates were sometimes made so they could be shaken from the outside, as on a coal stove, to assist in removing burned lime from the stack. As the lime fell to the bottom of the stack, it was removed by hoe or shovel.

The shaft of the kiln was egg-shaped, with the larger diameter closer to the top; this was the reverse of the blast furnace, in which the larger diameter was nearer to the bottom. If a refractory stone such as sandstone was available, it was used for lining the inside. Mortaring was unnecessary if the kiln was constructed correctly and properly balanced.

The kiln was fired by placing a small pile of kindling on the grate at the bottom of the shaft. Firewood was placed on this about a foot high, then limestone in alternate layers with wood, being careful not to pack too tightly and choke the fire. When all was ready, the kindling was lighted, and the bottom and top openings were closed with an iron door or laid up with stone. All holes were mortared or plastered with clay or mud to control the draft. After running a week, depending on wind and weather, burned lime was removed from the bottom; fuel and stone were added to the top each day or two. The farmer

could count on a continuous supply of lime and still have time for farming.

It is unknown what temperatures were reached in these early lime kilns, but calcium carbonate will disintegrate at about 1,600° F, making the ideal temperature for burning lime in the range of 1,650° F to 2,200° F. Lime burned at the lower temperature proved to be the best, and the most efficient kilns burned lime at lower temperatures accompanied with steam forced into the kiln.

While vacationing in western Massachusetts in 1838, Nathaniel Hawthorne gathered ideas for a short story, titled "Ethan Brand," about a lime burner. To get his information, Hawthorne inspected some lime kilns in the vicinity of North Adams, possibly venturing north into Vermont.

> September 7th.—Mr. Leach and I took a walk by moonlight last evening, on the road that leads over the mountain. Remote from houses, far up on the hill-side, we found a lime-kiln, burning near the road; and, approaching it, a watcher started from the ground, where he had been lying at his length. There are several of these lime-kilns in this vicinity. They are circular, built with stones, like a round tower, eighteen or twenty feet high, having a hillock heaped around in a great portion of their circumference, so that the marble may be brought and thrown in by cart-loads at the top. At the bottom there is a doorway, large enough to admit

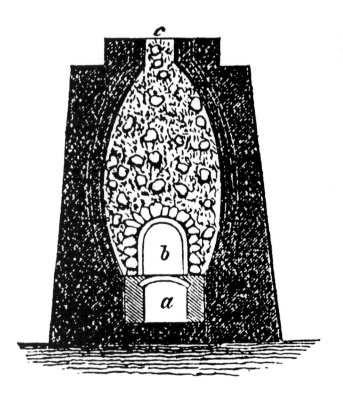

7-5. *A type of intermittent lime kiln in which the walls are firebrick-lined and the charge is still laid in an arch at the bottom. Fuel burned in compartment "b" and the lower compartment "a" provided unobstructed draft (Gillmore 1874:140).*

a man in a stooping posture. Thus an edifice of great solidity is constructed, which will endure for centuries, unless needless pains are taken to tear it down. There is one on the hill-side, close to the village, wherein weeds grow at the bottom, and grass and shrubs too are rooted in the interstices of the stones, and its low door-way has a dungeon-like aspect, and we look down from the top as into a roofless tower. It apparently has not been used for many years, and the lime and weather-stained fragments of marble are scattered about.

But in the one we saw last night a hardwood fire was burning merrily, beneath the superincumbent marble,—the kiln being heaped full; and shortly after we came, the man (a dark, black-bearded figure, in shirt-sleeves) opened the iron door, through which the chinks of which the fire was gleaming, and thrust in huge logs of wood, stirred the immense coals with a long pole, and showed us the glowing limestone,—the lower layer of it. The heat of the fire was powerful, at the distance of several yards from the open door. He talked very sensibly with us, being doubtless glad to have two visitors to vary his solitary night-watch; for it would not do for him to fall asleep, since the fire should be refreshed as often as every twenty minutes. We ascended the hillock to the top of the kiln, and the marble was red-hot, and burning with a bluish, lambent flame, quivering up, sometimes nearly a yard high, and resembling the flame of anthracite coal, only, the marble being in large fragments, the flame was higher. The kiln was perhaps six or eight feet across. Four hundred bushels of marble were then in a state of combustion. The expense of converting this quantity into lime is about fifty dollars, and it sells for twenty-five cents per bushel at the kiln. We asked the man whether he would run across the top of the intensely burning kiln, barefoot, for a thousand dollars; and he said that he would for ten. He told us that the lime had been burning for forty-eight hours, and would be finished in thirty-six more (Hawthorne *Chronicle* Dec. 1983:82-83).

Lime kilns also operated in New Hampshire at Haverhill, Lisbon, Franconia, and Lyme during this period. Limestone beds at Haverhill were near the base of Black Mountain, about 6 miles northeast of the village.

The country around is thickly wooded, so that an unlimited supply of fuel is readily commanded. The proprietor of the limestone owns 900 acres of woodland on the hill-side adjacent to the quarries, and he estimates the cost of wood fuel only at 50 cents per cord. His first kilns were badly constructed, and required from 18 to 20 cords of wood to burn a kiln of 60 tierces of lime; but the new ones, built according to the plan described to him, will require but 8 or 10 cords of wood to produce the same result. He makes two different kinds of lime, the first quality selling at $1.50 per tierce, the second at $1.25. Each tierce contains six bushels.

When it is considered that the principal expense of making lime consists in the cost of fuel, and that wood sells for $3 per cord in Thomaston, Me, and $5 per cord in Smithfield, Rhode Island, it will be perceived that the business of making lime at Haverhill, even at the low price above stated, cannot

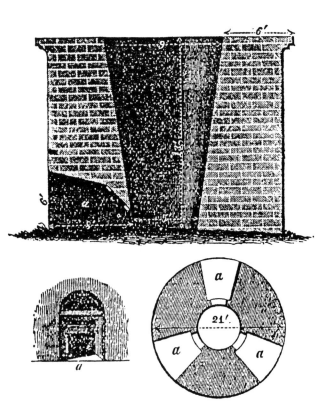

7-6. *An early attempt at continuous operation that provided three arches for the removal of burned lime (Gillmore 1874:141).*

fail to be profitable, and that great advantages will accrue to the purchaser from the cheapness of the article. Heretofore the lime used upon the borders of the Connecticut River, in New Hampshire, was brought exclusively from Vermont, and immense sums of money must have been expended in its purchase. So long as it could be obtained at a lower price from the Vermont kilns, it was natural to depend upon them; but now Haverhill lime is destined to supply that region.

The kiln [at Lisbon] is egg-shape, and measures twelve feet three inches in height, four feet in diameter at the top, six feet four inches in diameter at the boshes (a little below the centre.) Arch for fuel, two feet high. The walls of the kiln are two feet thick, and are made of mica slate lined with common bricks. It cost $150.

The common bricks soon glaze over on the surface, and withstand the heat sufficiently well. Four days and three nights are required for burning a kiln of lime, and ten cords of wood are consumed in the operation. From two to three men are employed. The cost of wood, cut, split and delivered at the kiln, $1 per cord. The lime sells for $2 per tierce at the kiln.

Mr. Oakes' quarry is situated two miles west from Franconia [iron] furnace, and is wrought to some extent for lime. This kiln is built like the one before described, but is of larger dimensions, containing 100 tierces of lime. It is built of common rocks found in the vicinity, and is lined with mica slate. The walls are from two to three feet in thickness, and the lining one foot thick. He sells his lime for $1.50 per tierce, without the cask, and for $2 when packed in them. Wood, cut and delivered at the kiln, costs $1 per cord. Fifteen cords of wood are required to burn a kiln of lime. Burning requires four days and three nights. Three men are employed at the kiln.

Estimate of cost and profits on one kiln of lime:

Cost of quarrying and hauling	$ 41	
Breaking and filling in	6	
Filling out	10	
15 cords of wood	15	
Labor	7	
100 casks at 42¢	42	
Interest and incidental	5	
Total costs	$146	[$126]
100 casks of lime sell for	$200	
Profit on one kiln of lime	$ 54	[$ 74]

Mr. Oakes has employed his lime successfully in agriculture, as a top dressing, in the proportion of one tierce to the acre. He has mixed it with compost manure and applied it to his potato crop, which, he says, appears unusually flourishing (Jackson 1844:172-175).

By the 1860s, burned lime was used:

[To] clarify the juice of sugar cane, generate heat and absorb the volatile gases in a compost heap; to purify the coal gas that illuminates our cities, bleach the rags of the papermaker and the cotton and linen fabrics of the manufacturer; to render potash and soda caustic in the soap manufacture, and used in water to restore health to the invalid; to free the hide from hair in the tanner's vat, and when mixed with litharge to dye the gray whiskers of the bachelor; to stop the stench that might arise from the slaughter-house, and to aid the chemist in his researches; and were the soil deprived of it entirely, large tracts of country now supporting luxuriant vegetation would become desolate and barren wastes (Hitchcock et al. 1861:746-747).

Although attractive on cold days for their warmth, lime kilns could be killers: "Deadly gases were frequently given off in the process of burning lime. A limeburner . . . told of a vagrant who was found dead from asphyxiation one morning near the shelter covering the shaft opening of the kiln on his father's farm. Although the area around the kiln shaft provided warmth on cold nights, the gases which escaped were extremely dangerous" (Long 1972:473).

Burned lime was usually sold by the bushel, the definition of which varied from place to place and time to time. In late-19th-century Pennsylvania, a bushel of lime measured 1¼ cubic feet which weighed about 80 pounds (Long 1972:481). In 1795 the Vermont General Assembly defined a bushel of lime, charcoal, or potash to be 2,592 cubic inches, which calculates to 1½ cubic feet (Williams 1967:414). This law was repealed in 1816 in favor of a law that defined a bushel of lime, charcoal, or potash to equal 38 quarts of ale, or Winchester measure (*Laws of Vermont* 1816:139). By 1839, Vermont defined this bushel to be a standard bushel plus ¾ of a peck (*Revised

Statutes 1840:369). Bargaining between merchants and lime or charcoal burners in the 19th century must have been an ordeal with constantly changing standards.

Lime sold for 3¢ a bushel at the kiln in the 1700s and by 1800 rose from 8¢ to 12¢ at the kiln. A farmer could pay up to 25¢ if it had to be transported any distance, quite an expense for anyone not willing or able to produce his own (Long 1972:482).

7-7. *Threaded ends of iron binding, with nuts and washers intact, extending out of the walls of a kiln ruin at Cavendish.*

The lime was carried into the field in a wagon or cart, there unloaded in spaced piles as needed, and left for slaking, which caused a chemical reaction in the lime that sometimes gave off large amounts of heat. It was not uncommon for wagons of lime to catch fire if caught outside in the rain. John Catlin's house at Richville (Shoreham Center), Vermont accidentally burned due to the heat of some slaked lime stored in the building (Smith 1886:623). Piles of lime in the field gave off steam after a rain and sometimes glowed at night.

[Benjamin Hauer] started burning lime with his father Amos Hauer, when he was thirteen years of age and burned lime in kilns in the Harpers [Pennsylvania] area as late as 1951. He told that the burning lime was done primarily between farm chores. Usually, after seeding time in spring until hay making and from late summer until about Christmas, depending on the weather, the kiln was in continuous operation. He said they burned very little lime during the hottest and coldest months.

The time required to fill the shaft in preparation for burning depended on the help available. He stated that it took one and a half to two weeks and occasionally longer for his father and him to fill a kiln. He said they frequently filled in one or two layers a day depending on time available. The stones were usually found right on the farm; sometimes they were brought there from the surrounding areas. He stated

7-8. *Variation of iron binding on the side of a kiln ruin in New Haven. The vertical plate connected the ends of the kiln-girdling iron rods and added support to the stone walls.*

7-9. *Broken wood beam that had supported upper wall section of the lime kiln ruin at Bristol.*

that within one area the quality and color of the stone could vary considerably and that it was important for the lime burner to know the stone. The stone varied in hardness and in color from shades of blue to yellow and white. The quality of the stone determined to a large degree the amount of coal required to complete the burning process. More or less coal was also required depending on the air movement and draft.

Occasionally, limestone was bought. He recalled paying one quarter cent per bushel or four bushels for one cent and from $1.60 to $1.85 a ton in later years. He stated it was common practice for a farmer who had limestone on his farm to build a kiln near the outcroppings and then hire someone to burn the lime. The limeburner may have been paid for his services or there may have been a barter arrangement allowing him to sell some lime in return for his efforts.

He said he helped fill some kilns that had a capacity of only two hundred to three hundred bushels of lime and others that had a capacity of fifteen hundred bushels. The average capacity of the kiln at which he worked was three hundred to six hundred bushels. He told of removing as many as fifty bushels of lime a day from the kiln and as few as one or two wheelbarrows depending on combustion. He recalled that his father sold lime for five and one-half cents a bushel during his first years of burning and for eighteen cents a bushel in 1951, the last year he burned lime.

He related that lime was used in large amounts for mortar between stone and brick for the erection of the exterior walls of barns, houses, and out buildings. The stone were burned in the limekiln until they became fragile and calcified. The resulting lime when slaked in water made an excellent mortar and enhanced the appearance of masonry buildings.

Considerable quantities of lime were sold for white-washing, a common practice during earlier years. Since paint was scarce and expensive, walls, ceilings, stables, fences and tree trunks were frequently white-washed. As many as two hundred to three hundred bushels of lime were sold each year for white-washing. Some buyers bought as little as a peck at a time. Lime to be used for white-washing, he stated, was best obtained from good quality white stone.

He told of applying from seventy-five to one hundred bushels of lime per acre on their land and usually one field on the farm was limed each year. He recalled a Holstein cow that fell into a lime kiln and having to tear the bottom out of the kiln to remove the dead cow. [The owner of Maplebrook Farm in Tinmouth, Vermont said the lime kiln ruin on his property had its front wall missing because he had to rescue a cow that had fallen into it. The kiln was built into the side of a slight rise at the edge of his pasture.] In addition to vagrants who slept by the kiln, he told of a basket maker who lived in and about the kilns during the decade of the forties.

Another informant told of a limekiln which was used for the storage of ice during his youth on his parents' farm. A peak roof was constructed over the shaft and ice from a nearby pond was stored in sawdust within the interior. He said the ice kept well from one season to the next.

The entire process of changing limestone to lime was an arduous task and frequently became a cooperative enterprise. It was not uncommon for neighboring farmers and friends to gather together and jointly share the task of hauling limestones and wood or attending the fire. This was particularly true when the kiln was located some distance from the quarry.

The area around the kiln frequently became a scene of many types of amusement and merriment during the early autumn evenings and nights. Corn roasts were common. Sometimes chickens were roasted and potatoes baked, making a suitable feast for a keen appetite at the end of a working day (Long 1972:474-481).

National Trends

The first national view of the lime business came about as the result of the 1900 U.S. Census. Statistics were gathered on lime plants throughout the country regarding operating expenses, production figures, fuel consumption, etc. Table 7-1 presents various statistics gathered for Vermont and four other New England states in the production of lime (Eckel 1922:114):

Table 7-1. Costs of Lime Manufacture during 1900

	Conn.	Maine	Mass.	R.I.	Vt.
No. of plants	11	20	11	3	13
Officials	12	34	3	1	2
Laborers	171	582	130	40	182
Capital	$250,392	$1,942,007	$115,639	$26,150	$256,860
Wages	$ 71,938	$ 248,371	$ 69,823	$16,230	$ 57,257
Limestone	$ 86,759	$ 347,344	$ 67,826	$ 8,314	$ 36,804
Fuel	$ 59,005	$ 196,991	$ 54,257	$ 8,700	$ 45,112
Freight	$ 2,025	$ 68,803	$ 310	—	$ 6,000
Product value	$286,640	$1,226,972	$261,477	$48,089	$207,524

Analysis of table 7-1 in terms of total operating costs (not all the census data are included) resulted in learning that Vermont costs in 1900 ran close to the average of its New England competitors, as shown in table 7-2 (Eckel 1922:115):

Table 7-2. Percentages of Total Operating Costs

	Conn.	Maine	Mass.	R.I.	Vt.
Salaries	3.6	2.3	1.3	0.8	0.8
Wages	26.8	21.9	33.3	36.1	32.9
Limestone	32.5	30.6	32.4	18.4	21.1
Fuel	22.1	17.3	25.9	19.3	25.9
Freight	0.8	6.1	0.1	—	3.5

In theory it took about 100 pounds of coal to burn a ton of limestone; in practice, however, fuel consumption was higher or lower depending on the design of the kiln and the skill of its operation. Table 7-3 shows the results of a survey of fuel consumption in the early 20th century (Eckel 1922:111). Table 7-4 shows the trend of the national lime industry from 1909 to 1920 (Eckel 1922:115).

Table 7-3. Type of Fuel Used at American Lime Plants

Kilns Using	1913	1917	1918
Coal	1,334	1,138	885
Coke	123	189	151
Coal and coke	22	51	37
Oil	54	27	24
Natural gas	30	25	21
Producer gas	76	86	76
Wood	479	268	194
Coal and wood	220	182	182
Total kilns reported:	2,338	1,966	1,570

7-10. *View of the binder assembly in the kiln ruin at Bristol, showing the flat iron binder extending out through the wall and its flat iron face plate held in place by beveled key inserted vertically through the binder hole.*

Table 7-4. Lime Burned and Sold in the U.S. from 1909 to 1920

Year	Tons of Lime	Value	$/Ton	Plants
1909	3,484,974	$13,846,072	$ 3.97	1,232
1910	3,505,954	$14,088,039	$ 4.02	1,125
1911	3,392,915	$13,689,054	$ 4.03	1,139
1912	3,529,462	$13,970,114	$ 3.96	1,017
1913	3,595,390	$14,648,362	$ 4.07	1,023
1914	3,380,928	$13,268,938	$ 3.92	954
1915	3,622,810	$14,424,036	$ 3.98	906
1916	4,073,433	$18,509,305	$ 4.54	778
1917	3,786,364	$23,807,877	$ 6.29	595
1918	3,206,016	$26,808,909	$ 8.36	496
1919	3,330,347	$29,448,553	$ 8.84	539
1920	3,570,141	$37,543,840	$10.52	515

Note that from 1909 to 1920 the tonnage of lime produced increased only about 2.5 percent, but the value of the lime through inflation caused by World War I increased 171 percent, while the number of plants producing the lime decreased by 58 percent. The industry was fast becoming highly competitive as kilns operated more and more efficiently.

Vermont Lime Kilns

The first comprehensive study of the Vermont lime industry was included in *Report on the Geology of Vermont* (1861) authored by Edward Hitchcock, his sons Edward, Jr. and Charles, and Albert Hager. In their 988-page, two-volume work, the authors stated that "to undertake the enumeration of all the places from which good material for quicklime could be obtained, would be a difficult task and one which will not

be attempted. Old limekilns abound in the vicinity of nearly all outcrops of limestone, but of late much of the lime manufactured is from perpetual kilns" (Hitchcock et al. 1861:748). Although some of the lime kilns already considered "old" by these authors in the 1860s have survived to the present day, it is too bad that some attempt was not made to record their locations while this information was still relatively current.

The earliest recorded lime kiln in Vermont (GI-27) was that at Isle La Motte, where the French burned lime to make mortar in 1664 or 1666. The date varies depending on the reference, although 1664 appears to be the date of the initial French settlement, and 1666 the construction date of Fort Sainte-Anne for which the mortar was used, and so also the lime kiln. The kiln operated to at least 1796 when it is recorded that "Royal Corbin of Windmill Pt., Alburgh, Vt., [told] Pliny Moore of Champlain, N.Y. to get some Lime at Fisk's" (Stratton 1984:118). The kiln, or at least modifications of the kiln at the same site, operated under the French, British, the Republic of Vermont, and the State of Vermont, which adds up to about 130 years of operation.

Although a marble quarry at Dorset lays claim to being the first in the country, there are many references to a quarry (later called Fisk quarry) at Isle La Motte being older (Adams 1845:45; Child *Grand Isle* 1883:226; Swift 1977:265; Meeks 1986:106). Meeks wrote: "Depending on how marble is defined, the earliest quarrying probably was at the south end of Isle La Motte as early as 1761." Stone might also have been taken from the Fisk quarry by the French in 1666 for construction of Fort Sainte-Anne. The confusion was probably caused by Fisk quarry operators calling its limestone a black marble. The Fisk quarry, however, was continuously worked longer than any other in Vermont (Perkins 1933:145).

Lime kilns started appearing in numbers with the opening

of farms and the discovery of good-quality limestone. The many small ruins found in the Vermont countryside bear witness to the amount of lime burning that took place in the early to mid-19th century. Lime kiln remains found in Vermont can be categorized, both by physical appearance and estimated use of the produced lime, as follows: farm, early and later commercial, early modern, and modern.

The farm kiln was built to fulfill strictly local demands for agricultural lime and building mortar. What surplus of production existed was sold for use in tanneries, paper mills, and chemical factories. The kilns were small relative to the size of later units, generally measuring about 6 to 8 feet inside diameter. They were built into the sides of a low rise near an outcrop of limestone and the sides of the kilns were covered with earth, leaving an opening in front to draw out the burned lime. The top kiln opening was level with the ground at the upper level, for ease in dumping limestone into it from an animal-drawn cart. Such kiln remains were found at Brandon, Tinmouth, Clarendon, and Wallingford and are some of the earliest types found thus far in the state, operating up to the 1840s.

Some kiln ruins found at Clarendon, Plymouth, Weathersfield, Jamaica, Cavendish, Whitingham, and Richford are in the early commercial category. They are somewhat larger and made with more massive-sized stones. Some, such as those in Plymouth, have front walls 8 to 10 feet high with wide ramps leading to the top from the uphill side. Plymouth limestone was considered a "very peculiar brecciated stone" which was formerly sawed and polished for marble, but later burned for

lime. It made strong and durable lime, but it was not very white (Perkins 1900:36).

Kiln ruins found at Arlington, Bristol, Castleton, Cavendish, Mendon, Benson, New Haven, Stratton, Weathersfield, Whitingham, Wilmington, and Jamaica are a later commercial-type lime kiln and start to hint at a more "furnace" appearance. These kilns still operated intermittently but were the final design before the advent of the early modern kiln. To the unwary field explorer, these squat, square stone structures could be confused with iron smelters due to their similarity in appearance. They usually displayed iron binding rods to reinforce the outer walls as in the blast furnaces. Some, however, also incorporated horizontal wooden beams built into the stonework to support the wall above the work arch, unlike blast furnaces. These kilns were most likely in operation during the immediate post-Civil War period, and up to the early 20th century.

Early modern kilns were those ruins found at New Haven, Swanton, Danby, Highgate, and Leicester. These are distinctive by their construction type and location, and have approximately 30- to 40-foot-square (or 30-foot-diameter) concrete and/or stone bases with up to 10-foot-diameter steel shells rising as high as 25 feet above the base. They are multi-unit operations and stand adjacent to railroads for access to out-of-state markets. The only truly modern-type lime kilns known to have operated in Vermont were the abandoned works at Winooski Park, razed for scrap in 1990.

Two variant modern-type kilns were Vermont's only rotary kilns, which operated at West Rutland in the 1920s (RU-LK01)

7-11. *A simple binder (right) in the corners of the kiln ruin at Amsden. This flat iron strip, bent downward at right angles at each end, lies diagonally across the corners of the kiln, holding the horizontal wooden sections in place. Hidden inside the corners, between the binder and the corner, are vertical iron rods that run the height of the stack and hold the binder tight against the horizontal wooden sections.*

7-12. *A few kiln ruins of a large lime-burning complex at Chazy, New York, inspected in 1982 before they were razed and used for fill in nearby Lake Champlain. In the ruin at the left, the shell was insulated with additional stonework. The bases of these kilns were of reinforced concrete. A quarry immediately to the south provided the raw limestone; the burned lime was carried away by railroad.*

and possibly at Colchester (CH-284), and two concrete-section kilns at Highgate Springs (FR-225).

A large portion of limestone in the state is highly crystalline, which made the Vermont marble industry so successful. Attempts to make this particular kind of marble into lime in vertical kilns of any sort, however, usually met with failure. The difficulty was that the crystalline limestone, on being heated, broke into granular form instead of keeping its shape as ordinary limestone did when burned in the vertical kiln. The result was that the draft in the vertical kiln was choked and the burning stopped. The rotary kiln, which looked like a long smokestack laying on its side, provided the solution to this problem. It opened the way for burning waste marble for manufacturing lime. Nationally, rotary kilns were used in the cement industry, and the rotary process was tried for manufacturing lime as early as 1885. Not until 1916 did this new method of manufacturing lime become one of Vermont's industries, at West Rutland.

The cars loaded with blocks, spalls, or any suitable class of marble waste from the quarries and mills are delivered under a crane runway equipped with a twenty-five ton electric crane and this equipment unloads the raw material and delivers it to a 48″ by 60″ Superior jaw crusher. This crusher weighs 105 tons and is operated by a one hundred and fifty horse power motor. The swinging jaw moves only about three or four inches but this is sufficient to crush any block that will go into the four by five foot opening, at the rate of two hundred forty tons an hour or four tons a minute.

These chunks of marble that are discharged at the bottom slide directly into a gravatory crusher. The crushed stone is then elevated and discharged by a conveyor into two stone storage bins which permit a forty-eight hour supply of raw material ahead of the kiln.

The kiln, which measures eight feet in diameter by one hundred twenty feet long and resembles a huge stack on its side, was built by the Vulcan Company. It is constructed of ⅝-inch steel plates, and the kiln equipment complete weighs 118 tons. It is lined with firebrick and revolves on two bearings at the rate of about one revolution every three minutes, a thirty horse power variable speed motor furnishing the power. This motor regulation enables the speed of the kiln to be adjusted to suit the conditions of burning and the feed is operated by a rope drive on the same motor so that any change in speed of the kiln automatically changes the rate of the feed of the crushed stone to the kiln.

The heat for burning is furnished by a Chapman mechanical 10-foot gas producer, situated in a separate building. The incoming fuel is dumped through the car bottoms into a hopper under the track from which it is conveyed to coal crushing rolls. This crushed coal is elevated and discharged directly into the coal bin over the gas producer or into the large concrete storage building with a capacity of about 300 tons. From this storage building it may be withdrawn through tunnel gates and a belt conveyor to the original elevator and thus taken to the coal bin over the producer. The producer shell is in two sections. The bottom section, to which are fastened plows for the automatic removal of the ashes, revolves slowly while the top section revolves at a faster rate of speed. The twyere [*sic*] is stationary and through it a jet of steam is admitted. A mechanically water-cooled poker fastened in the stationary top, aided by the circular motion of the shell, keeps the mass of the fire agitated and compact. The whole is water-sealed and has a capacity of gasifying about one ton of coal an hour. One pound of coal when gasified will produce from three to five pounds of lime, depending on the quality of the gas and the character of the stone. From the producer, the gas is conveyed to the main building in a large steel flue, varying from three to four feet in diameter, and delivered into the lower end of the kiln where it ignites, producing a temperature of about twenty-two hundred degrees Fahrenheit. A Westmoreland County [Pennsylvania] gas coal is used in this process, the requirements being that the coal must contain not over 1% of sulphur and be very low in ash.

The kiln is set at a pitch of one-half inch to the foot. It can thus be readily seen that the mass of broken marble

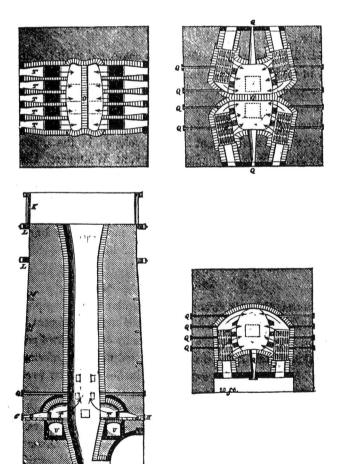

7-13. *Varieties of multiple-unit lime kilns. Left to right (top): cross-section view downward of an anthracite-fueled 10-kiln unit, and a 4-unit wood-burning kiln; (bottom): cross-section view of a wood-burning 2-unit kiln and downward view of same (Gillmore 1874:135).*

being admitted at the upper end will gradually travel toward the lower end—it taking about four hours to pass through. Surface moisture is driven off early in the kiln and as the stone approaches the lower end the pieces are broken down and the balance of any moisture and the carbon dioxide gas is driven off and carried with the combustion gases up the stack. The actual burning of the limestone is probably limited to the last or lower thirty feet in the kiln known as the burning zone. A series of baffling walls in the stack chamber prevent the fine stone particles and lime from being drawn up the stack by the draft and any of this material which collects at the base of the stack chamber is removed by a screw conveyor and deposited in the stone bins, thus being returned to the kiln.

The lime oxide or burned lime discharges at the end of the kiln through a chute directly into a cooler situated at a lower level in the cooler pit. This is a stack-like cylinder on its side similar to the kiln but without any brick lining and measures five feet in diameter by fifty feet long. The cooler equipment weighs about 27 tons. Lifting angle irons are bolted to the inside of the cooler so that as it revolves the fine granular lime is raised and dropped through the air and thus the cooling operation is facilitated. A draft through the cooler is induced by the kiln stack and the burning process in the kiln and thus the air passing over the hot lime in the cooling process is preheated for the kiln. The cooler is mounted on two bearings pitched at the same grade as the kiln and operated by a ten horse power motor. The granular lime which entered the cooler at approximately twenty-two hundred degrees is discharged at the end sufficiently cooled so that it can be safely elevated to the two large steel oxide bins of approximately two hundred fifty tons capacity each. From these bins the quick lime can be loaded in bulk into cars or barreled as the trade demands.

From these bins the lime may be taken by still another elevator to the six cylinder Kritzer hydrator. This machine scientifically slakes the lime adding the proper amount of water to exactly hydrate and yet have the product come out exactly dry. The water is admitted in a spray to the stack of the hydrator through which the heat generated by the chemical reaction is carried off and this not only keeps the light hydrate from being drawn up the stack but the water in turn is preheated thus assisting the action of the hydration. Revolving beaters or paddles assist the movement of lime and water through the series of six cylinders thoroughly mixing the oxide with the water and insuring complete hydration and the absolute drying so that the material is discharged to a screw conveyor at the bottom as an impalpable flour. This passes to Raymond mills and beaters where any core, unburned material or foreign substance of any kind is separated and discharged permitting the pure, white, fluffy hydrate to be raised in the air separators to the storage bins from which it is bagged in valve paper sacks by an Urschell-Bates valve bagging machine. A dust collecting system at the bagger removes the fine material that is spilled in bagging. The paper sacks are made with no opening except for a small hole in a fold at one end. Through this hole a tube about one inch in diameter is inserted and through this the hydrate is forced into the bag. The flow of hydrate is automatically stopped when the bag contains fifty pounds. No sealing or tieing of the bag is necessary for the pressure of the contents seals the opening in the fold and then the bags are trucked and piled in the stock house.

7-14. *Cross-section view of a Keystone lime kiln, showing firebrick-lined iron shell, fireplaces (middle), and hand-operated draw gates (Eckel 1922:106).*

The capacity of the plant as it is now equipped is about 60 tons of oxide a day or 75 tons of hydrate. The operation is continuous night and day except for forced shutdown for repairs. As many operations as possible have been made automatic thus reducing to a minimum the item of labor (Smith "Description" 1916:102-106).

The preceding report also includes pictures of the rotary kiln,

jaw crusher, gravatory crusher, gas producer, hydrator, and valve bagging machine.

In addition to the five circular stone-type kilns that the Missisquoi Lime Works operated at Highgate, the company must have experimented with kilns made of concrete sections, based on ruins found at the site in 1990. These concrete-type kilns were built in vertical half-sections that were held together with iron bands (only the impressions of the bands remain). The inside might have been lined with firebrick but none was found inside, possibly indicating that these "newer" kilns were never actually fired.

Regardless of the nationwide acceptance of the use of limestone in agriculture, 19th-century Vermont farmers were not to be immediately convinced that spreading pulverized limestone in their fields would increase crop yield. At a series of conferences held in 1871–1872 in Vermont, the recently formed Board of Agriculture, Manufactures, and Mining met and presented the following papers on the problems of farming in the state: "Exhaustion of Soils" and "Rotation of Crops" by Samuel W. Johnson of New Haven (Conn.) and William S. Thorp of Morristown; "Commercial Fertilizers" by Peter Collier of Cornwall; "The Relation of Science to Agriculture" by Henry M. Seely of Middlebury; and "The Fertility of Our Soil—How Lost, and How Restored" by Jonathan Lawrence of Passumpsic. All looked at what was happening to farming in the state, and how to turn the overused earth back into gainful production. As the nature of elements were studied, became better understood, and were more widely accepted, the nature of agriculture as a form of chemistry started taking hold. Soil exhaustion, once believed irreversible, was not necessarily the end of the world (Collier 1872:344-487). An understanding of soil nutrients and the chemistry of mineral replenishment were published in journals and preached to progressive-thinking farmers as the way to return once-dead fields to life. Henry Miles of Monkton wrote:

> No soil is productive which does not contain a considerable proportion of carbonate of lime. A productive soil may be reduced to barrenness by abstracting its lime by incessant cropping. An unproductive soil may, in many cases, be rendered productive by the addition of lime.
>
> The statement of Dr. Hitchcock is as follows: "First and most important of all, we think we have discovered the reason why Vermont so excelled all other New England states in the agricultural capabilities of her soil. It is the existence, in almost all her rocks, of lime in such a state that natural processes bring it out in just about the quantity needed by vegetation. This is the case in many parts of the state where inhabitants hardly suspect the existence of lime, and those places of the state most fertile are just the places where lime is most abundant and decomposable" (Miles 1876:271-273).

Another lime-related material that proved to be a valuable fertilizer when burned was marl. Usually found in the beds of ponds and bogs (not to be confused with peat), marl is a mixture of sand, clay, or silt that contains substantial amounts of calcium carbonate. The latter is known as shell marl and is the remains of shellfish deposited in layers in an ancient time when the area was the floor of a warm, shallow ocean. It was known as

7-15. *Approximately 10-foot-tall concrete half-sections show innovation at work in new lime kiln designs by the Missisquoi Lime Works at Highgate Springs. These units were probably built in 1918.*

marlstone when found in a solid form. Shell marl was dug and burned in a kiln the same as limestone. Important marl deposits were found in the early 19th century at Holland, Derby, Salem, Albany, Craftsbury, Glover, Greensboro, Hardwick, Walden, Sutton, Lyndon, Barnet, St. Johnsbury, Peachem, and Calais (Hitchcock et al. 1861:725).

Marl from Alburgh, Williamstown, Peachem, and Monkton was analyzed in 1847 and found to contain from 73 to 89 percent carbonate of lime, of particular value for use as fertilizer (Hitchcock et al. 1861:697).

Two marl beds worked profitably in mid-19th-century Vermont were at Marl Pond in Sutton, where digging and burning marl was a business for many years, and at Lime Pond (Limehurst Lake) at Williamstown. The marl was molded into bricks and dried; then the bricks were burned (Hitchcock et al. 1861:805).

The 19th-century Vermont farmer's ethic, however, was generally that "early rising and hard work" were the chief ingredients in the improvement of agriculture. It was especially hard to persuade him that simply broadcasting ground stone would profit where labor had failed. Despite the concentrated campaign to convince farmers that there was no real conflict between science and labor, as recently as 1929 only Maine was lower than Vermont regionally in the use of limestone for agriculture (Meeks 1986:149). And this at a time when the lime-burning industry in the state was also declining. (Today we think nothing of buying a bag of lime to balance the pH of our lawn or swimming pool; a century ago it was a revolutionary thought.)

By the 1890s, lime burning in the state became centralized at only a half-dozen operations. The discovery of the process of making hydrated lime in large quantities meant the product could be stored for long periods of time without suffering from the absorption of moisture and causing fires. The simple process

consisted merely of mixing quicklime with water and keeping the solution in constant agitation. The end result was a packaged powder product capable of withstanding long-distance shipment without losing its property for use as mortar or other industrial purposes. The production of hydrated lime led to the closing of many small kilns that once dotted the state. State Geologist Perkins reported production during this period as:

Year	Value of Production	Year	Value of Production
1893	$400,000	1896	$147,000
1894	$151,000	1899	$300,000

Perkins also stated that in 1894, six companies reported making 30,280 tons of lime; the next year eight companies made 38,720 tons.

Never in the major business category in Vermont, lime burning was most active from the turn of the century to the 1930s, reaching its peak in terms of kilns in operation in the 1920s. In 1900, the limestone quarries at Highgate and Swanton were among the oldest in the state, having been worked since the early part of the 1800s. The Highgate quarry was run by L. E. Felton and those at Swanton by J. P. Rich and W. P. Fonda. "All of these furnish the stone for extensive kilns in which lime is made" (Perkins 1900:32). The State Geologist reported the following as constituting the lime industry in Vermont during 1918: Missisquoi Lime Works (Highgate Springs), Fonda Lime Kilns (Swanton), Swanton Lime Works, Champlain Valley Lime Corporation (Winooski), Green Mountain Lime Company (New Haven Junction), Brandon Lime and Marble Company (Leicester Junction), Vermont Marble Company (West Rut-

221

7-16. *Close-up view of the side draft vent design at the base of one of five kiln ruins near New Haven Junction, showing the double arch of firebrick and single support column in the middle. Vent hole today is choked with collapsed firebrick that formerly lined the inside of the tall iron shell above it.*

land), and Pownal Lime Company. Notably missing are the Amsden Gray Lime Company (Weathersfield) which shows up in the 1924 and 1926 reports, and the Vermont Lime Products Company (Mount Tabor), which appears in no reports. By the 1930 report, only lime operations at Highgate Springs, Swanton, Winooski, New Haven, Amsden, Rutland, and Pownal are listed. That same year, the State Geologist wrote: "In going over Vermont in order to examine the ledges or outcrops, one comes across many old lime kilns of very simple construction and evidently used in old times for burning small quantities of limestone. Good limestone is not abundant in Vermont except in the vicinity of Lake Champlain on the western border. All of these primitive kilns have long since been abandoned, as new and far more efficient furnaces and new machinery have been invented and become available. It has required only a small number of these lime works to supply a much greater need than formerly existed and, of course, with far better results" (Perkins 1930:259).

By 1935 quicklime was made only at Swanton, Fonda, and New Haven, and hydrated lime at Winooski and West Rutland. Lime production varied during the seven years from 1929 to

1935 (Jacobs "Mineral Industries" 1937:19):

Year	Short Tons	Value
1929	43,923	$362,169
1930	40,648	$319,108
1931	31,218	$236,508
1932	29,027	$194,359
1933	30,753	$200,582
1934	38,015	$252,731
1935	44,599	$286,006

Vermont Associated Lime Industries bought the quarries and kilns at Leicester Junction about 1947, at Winooski Park in 1948, and the Green Mountain Lime Company east of New Haven Junction in 1950. Whether a speculative venture or an honest attempt to consolidate the industry in Vermont so it could operate more efficiently, the company soon came apart. Operations at New Haven and Leicester Junction shut down in the early 1950s. Those at Winooski Park, the last lime kilns

7-17. *Hydraulically operated draw gates at the bottom of the lime kilns at Winooski Park. When these gates were opened, the burned lime fell into waiting railroad cars below. What might have been a rotary kiln is in the background.*

to operate in the state, were sold in 1960 and closed altogether in 1971 (Carlisle 1975:13).

At New Haven Junction, only a mile west of the ruins of the Green Mountain Lime Company's five lime kilns, the White Pigment Corporation (OMYA, Inc.) carries on a somewhat modern version of the 19th- and 20th-century lime-burning business. With sophisticated computer-controlled technology, calcium carbonate filler and extender is produced from limestone that comes from a quarry near East Middlebury for paint, plastic, paper, and foodstuffs. Limestone is crushed at its Florence plant, about 10 miles north of Rutland, where production capacity is 500,000 tons of the fine powder per year. Average particle size for the different products ranges from 0.000001 to 0.000021 inch in size, a very fine product similar to talcum powder. The beginnings of the company date to a time when lime and oil were mixed for whitewash and caulking. White Pigment is owned by Vermont Marble Company, itself a subsidiary of Pluess-Staufer of Switzerland (James Stewart letter to author, Dec. 6, 1989).

At Swanton village, limestone is still quarried and processed by Shelburne Limestone Corporation (since 1987), although hydrated lime is no longer made and the kilns have long since disappeared. Giant computer-controlled machines now produce various grades of crushed stone (Douglas "Swanton Limestone" 1988:61). Only large circles on concrete platforms show where the tall kilns once burned lime.

Lime Kilns Outside Vermont

Lime kilns of all makes, ages, and states of survival dot the entire New York-New England countryside, and wherever limestone is seen in hillside escarpments or highway cuts, there is probably a lime kiln ruin or remain nearby. Some noteworthy kiln ruins not far from Vermont are just across Lake Champlain in New York, about a mile south of the village of Chazy. Here stood the impressive ruins of a half-dozen early-20th-century lime kilns whose tall, rusted iron shells swayed and groaned in the lake-driven wind until they were toppled, leveled, and carted away for lakeside fill in the early 1980s. The property owner felt that an enlarged boat landing on the lake far outweighed the historical resource value of the site. Luckily, some measurements and photos along with a firebrick inventory were made only a year or two before. Point aux Roche, about five miles to the southeast, was known nationwide for high-quality limestone quarried here and burned for cement, but it is unknown if there are any kiln ruins or remains; the site has not been visited.

At the New York end of the Champlain Bridge from Chimney Point is the Crown Point State Historic Park, site of the ruins of Fort St. Frederic where the French burned some lime during their 18th-century occupation of this part of the country. In an open field about a mile south of the park's reception center and museum is the ruin of a more modern kiln where lime was burned for industrial interests at Port Henry. Remains of the railroad that ran from the kiln across shallow Bullwagga Bay to Port Henry are still visible. When the State of New York acquired the kiln property someone started demolishing the stack and managed to open the top half of the east wall before being stopped. That opening today exposes the colorful stone lining that would otherwise remain hidden to all (except the author, who braved spiders and bees' nests to crawl inside the kiln through its ground-level openings). The remains of the charging ramp to the top of the kiln are visible just uphill of the ruin.

Twenty-five miles west of Bennington is Bald Mountain, in the western part of Greenwich (Washington County), New

7-18. *Collection of firebricks lying on the floor of the main kiln building at Winooski Park after having fallen out of the stacks above.*

York, the site of a large lime-burning complex which started burning lime as early as 1785. By 1849 there were 16 kilns in operation (*N.Y. State Agricultural Society* 1850:851). Three years later, under new ownership, 10 new kilns were built, producing 160,000 barrels of lime a year (Johnson 1878:355). Two towering ruins were still standing when inspected in 1991.

At Adams, Massachusetts, 10 miles south of Stamford, Vermont, are the operating lime kilns of Pfizer, Inc. These tall, ancient-looking, but really modern concrete-wall kilns are gas-fired units that burn a particular quality limestone for a specialized product. Lime made here is used in soil stabilization, acid neutralization, and desulfurization of steel. It is also used in the treatment of industrial wastes and sewage and proved to be a cure for an odoriferous problem at a nearby landfill. The better lime, called PCC, is used in sealants and plastics, papers, paints, rubber, and drywall compound and is sold worldwide ("Pfizer Completes a Major Face Lift" *Berkshire Eagle* May 14, 1991:D2).

A few miles farther south in the town of Cheshire, the ruins of a spectacular multi-kiln plant stand at the west end of the causeway near the south end of Cheshire Lake, at what was once known as Farnums. This plant closed about the same time as the one at Winooski Park (and might have been owned by the same firm), yet much can still be learned about the technology of the industry from the abandoned machinery that is now inhabited by birds and animals.

7-19. *Four active lime kilns (background, right) at Adams, Massachusetts, operated by Pfizer, Inc.*

224

Chapter 8
Study of Lime Kilns

Study Methodology

The study of lime kiln ruins and sites in Vermont started with the inspection of a ruin in Leicester Junction in 1984, where attention was directed by a friend who claimed that large blast furnace ruins were to be seen. Inspection confirmed suspicions that the ruin was that of a lime kiln, not a blast furnace. But the physical similarities between blast furnaces and some early commercial lime kilns encouraged further archival research and field inspection of the latter.

Information regarding location of lime kiln ruins and remains came from maps, archival references, and informants. A few kiln ruins were found by chance. Maps include the 1854–1859 series county wall maps, which indicate lime kilns presumed active or recently active at time of publication. Likewise, some 1869–1878 Beers maps also indicate lime kilns. The Doll geology map shows various limestone outcrops, which indicate areas of probability for finding limestone quarries, but was not detailed enough to provide specific surface information for finding lime kiln ruins.

The Vermont lime business has received minimal recognition in many local histories written in the 19th century. Incredibly little beyond a few words has been written about availability of limestone in the state. At best, a few histories make a statement or two alluding to lime burning at some obscure time in the past. It was not until the merits of using lime as an agricultural additive were recognized that lime burning in Vermont took on an "industrial" stance and histories written in the late 19th century reflected this. State geology reports during and after that period also included much information on the economics of the lime industry. They reported on locations of quality limestone, annual production capacities of lime works, and regional and national trends of the industry.

Archival material included state, town, and county histories and business journals. Of special help were the 1861 *Report on the Geology of Vermont* by Hitchcock et al., the 1899 through 1934 biennial reports of the State Geologist by George H. Perkins, and the 1915 U.S. Geological Survey Bulletin on the geology of Vermont dolomite and marble by T. Nelson Dale. The latter included small detailed maps of quarries discussed in the text, which greatly facilitated the search for lime kiln sites.

While using the Dale material to find the kiln ruins in the field, it was noticed that some of the descriptions referred specifically to a lime kiln in the vicinity of a quarry, but other references were merely to lime having been burned in the vicinity at one time. Field work resulted in finding ruins at 13 of 14 sites (93 percent) at which lime kilns had been specifically referenced, but at only 4 of 7 sites (57 percent) at which only vague references were made of lime burning. It is not known whether Dale could not find some of the kilns or perhaps did not intend to accurately reference kiln ruins; the reports were mainly about the geology of the state's marble industry and not about the manufacture of lime. This could mean that lime kilns might have also operated at some of the many marble quarries he discussed (and maybe at some quarries he did not discuss) but at which no mention of lime burning or lime kilns was made. Information from Dale got us into the vicinity of a kiln but it usually took local inquiry and hours of bushwhacking to get us exactly to the kiln ruin.

Informants included friends, property owners, and those who gave directions or shared thoughts on the subject along the way. Some knew only where a suspicious pile of stones was to be found; others knew a lime kiln ruin when they saw one and were specific with directions and descriptions. Most property owners and local residents were very generous with their time and knowledge of where things were and what they knew of them. Many were surprised that anyone was interested at all in "that old pile of stones."

Chance finds were also made, such as discovering Lime Kiln Road in Charlotte while driving up Route 7 one Sunday afternoon, or Arnold Kingsley's directions to a lime kiln in his Whitingham pasture instead of the one being sought farther down the road. Although not a common occurrence, a few kiln ruins were discovered while driving by or just by having glanced in that direction at the right moment. There was also much useless stopping and hiking into pastures and fields to check out suspicious-looking mounds of stones or clumps of white birch. Many ruins still lie out there along sides of roads and trails, however, waiting to be discovered and interpreted.

Finding a kiln ruin in the field, even with good archival reference to its existence and indication on a 19th-century map, was not easy. The best time of year for field work was, of course, before or after foliage season. Each was not without its hazards, however. In mid-spring there was still cold surface water and mud to be dealt with; snow and ice at higher elevations. In the post-foliage season shot and arrows were flying about, and some of the smaller ruins and features were obscured by fallen leaves.

Farm-type kilns were usually found at the base of a hill, sometimes just below a limestone outcrop. Attention was paid to ledges in suspected areas and also for indications of former roadbeds that preceded present roads, alongside which the lime kilns would have been operating.

The dividing line used in differentiating between early and later commercial ruins was the use of firebrick. Large kiln ruins near extensive quarries were obviously not farm kilns but more of a commercial operation, and these ruins, in which internal lining is made of stone, are in the early commercial (1850s–1900s) category. Those in which firebricks were found are in the later commercial (1870s–1920s) category. The presence of firebrick is taken to indicate a definite technological step forward.

Their markings indicated that most firebricks probably came from Troy, New York. A common firebrick mark was McL&H CO TROY NY, which was McLeod & Henry Company, manufacturer of stove linings and firebrick. The company was founded by Jacob Henry in 1871; Bacon & Henry succeeded him, and in turn were succeeded by Harvey S. McLeod in

1882. McLeod & Henry Company was founded February 1, 1887. Bussey & McLeod also cast stoves in that same period (Anderson 1897:313). Correlating firebrick markings with firebrick manufacturers can provide valuable kiln operating dates. Other firebrick marks found associated with ca.-1880s to -1920s lime kiln ruins were: H. W. SPEC; BOSTON [FIRE?] BLOCK CO; U.S.A.; and BRANDON VT. Among the tons of firebricks lying around the razed lime works at Winooski Park are firebricks marked LEHIGH, BESSEMER, POWER, TYRONS, D-TYRONS, and ALUSITE 81. Some of these firebricks are quite large, on the order of a cubic foot. Some red bricks found at many sites were identified DRURY (of Essex Junction); many, however, contained no markings at all.

Another indication of technological progress at kiln sites was the use of binders to stabilize the stack and keep the stonework together. Most common bindings were one-inch-diameter iron rods, threaded at ends that protruded out the walls. The rod ends had large nuts screwed on with washers that snugged the assembly against the kiln walls. At some collapsed ruins, the internal lateral crisscross pattern of these binders was revealed once the tangle of bent and intertwined hardware was figured out. At the Lyman-Martell ruin in New Haven (AD-494), a double set of bindings across the outside wall of the kiln was reinforced by a flat iron plate bolted to the rods. Nowhere did the strength of the lime kiln binding approach that of binding used at blast furnaces, however, which were much more massive in size.

Kiln ruins were anything from a 20-foot-square stone base with 25-foot-high iron shells (AD-355) to a barely distinguishable grass-covered stone mound in a pasture (WN-124). Depending on which direction a ruin was approached, it could appear to be no more than a hole in the ground from the uphill side, or an entrance to a crypt or stone chamber from the downhill or front side. One stone feature initially taken for a lime kiln ruin turned out to be an abandoned stone-lined cistern (BE-LK07).

The general configuration and character of the ruin differentiated it from, for example, a charcoal kiln or blast furnace, as did the presence of burnt lime in the form of a gray-white grainy powder or small, cracked, white stones in the direct vicinity of the kiln ruin. Because the bottom opening in the front wall of the kiln created a built-in weakness, the front walls of many early ruins were found collapsed and their stonework slumped outward to the ground, hiding any burnt lime in this area and giving the ruin a random stone mound appearance. At Scotch Hill (RU-98), moving a few stones from a collapsed front wall during a reinspection of this previously unidentified ruin exposed a hidden archway, confirming its past use as a lime kiln.

While studying lime kiln ruins, finding limestone and marble quarries was inevitable. Quarries that provided stone for the earlier lime kilns were small, appearing in many cases no more than natural outcrops. They were sometimes overgrown in summer and required some effort to find. A few were reputed by owners or local residents to be infested with rattlesnakes.

Quarries that provided stone for lime kilns (and marble) operating after the mid-19th century have left significant scars on the landscape. In most cases, the remains of ironworks and charcoal kilns left little physical disturbance to the landscape.

Soil erosion and vegetation quickly re-covered ground lost to furnace mounds, ore pits, and kiln remains. Forests cut for cordwood consumed in charcoal and lime kilns renewed themselves in a few dozen years. But quarry operations, whether slate, granite, or marble, by their nature have left gaping holes in the ground. Like railroad cuts still visible along long since abandoned rights-of-way, quarries will remain forever to remind the explorer what the 19th and 20th century did to the landscape.

Results of the Lime Kiln Study

Seventy-one kiln sites were reported to the State Archeologist during the 1984–1992 period of the overall statewide IA study of lime kilns and are now part of the State Archeological Inventory. These sites contained 93 fully or partially standing ruins or mounds (something visible on the surface). Twenty-nine sites were found within the new proclamation boundaries of the Green Mountain National Forest. Visible ruins include 71 made of stone, 13 of a combination stone and concrete, and 9 made of concrete. Thirteen stone and/or concrete types displayed remains of their tall iron shells in various stages of deterioration. Forty-three kilns probably operated at one time with iron shells.

An additional 14 sites at which inconclusive or no positive surface evidence was found but subsurface material might exist were also reported in the Field Site (FS) category. Archival and field work continues at 33 more sites in the work-in-progress (LK) category. The total number of lime kiln sites studied is 118 at this writing; 160 lime kilns are estimated through archival work to have operated in the state.

Lime kiln ruins were generally found associated with limestone outcrops or quarries. Although the earlier primitive farm-type lime kilns were usually found well away from the nearest farmhouse, almost all later commercial-type lime kiln ruins were found near roads, highways, and railroads. Farm-type ruins were the smallest type found; commercial-type ranged from much larger round shapes to imposing square structures, some with their rusting iron stacks wholly or in part above stone and/or concrete bases. One lime kiln site was found associated with an early-20th-century calcium carbide plant.

Many lime kilns were built of stone from the same quarry where they obtained stone to burn. Although appearing to be a peculiar practice, the insides of these kilns soon glazed over from the heat of burning, which protected the walls from further heat effects. The glaze also sealed the kiln from outside drafts, keeping the heat inside and reducing fuel consumption. At some ruins, the glaze was observed as being all that remained to hold small sections of inside walls intact, long after major sections of the outside walls had collapsed. Concrete kilns and combination stone-and-concrete kilns were those usually found associated with firebrick, although two stone-built kiln ruins were also found with firebrick. All combination stone-and-concrete kilns were the base for iron shells.

Lime kiln ruins were generally round or square. Some kiln ruins were built into a hillside or slight rise and their front side (that is, the opening side) was faced with a stone wall. This wall was as high as the kiln and extended up to 20 feet on either side to act as a retaining wall to support the work area

Table 8-1. Lime Kiln Sites

Site No.	Principal Name	Kilns per Site	Type	Green Mountain National Forest
Addison County				
AD-318	Huntley	2	Stone/Concrete*	No
AD-355	Green Mountain Lime Company	5	Stone/Concrete*	No
AD-409	Bristol	1	Stone	No
AD-494	Lyman-Martell	2	Stone	No
AD-FS95	Powers Lime Works	1	Stone?	No
AD-FS96	Swinington	3	Stone/Concrete*?	No
AD-FS97	Plank Road	1?	Stone?	No
AD-LK01	Quarry Road	1	Stone?	No
AD-LK02	Marsh	1?	Stone?	Yes
AD-LK03	Chaffee	1?	Stone?	Yes
AD-LK04	Peake	1?	Stone?	No
AD-LK05	Gibbs	1?	Stone?	No
Bennington County				
BE-109	Barnumville	1	Stone	Yes
BE-117	Manchester Depot	1?	Stone?	Yes
BE-118	Pownal Lime Company	1?	Stone/Concrete*?	Yes
BE-141	North Dorset	1	Stone	Yes
BE-144	Judson-Howell	1	Stone	Yes
BE-192	Martin	1	Stone	Yes
BE-FS7	Amaden & Son	1?	Stone?	Yes
BE-LK01	North Pownal	1?	Stone?	Yes
BE-LK02	Dorset Mountain Road	1?	Stone?	Yes
BE-LK03	Purdy Hill	1?	Stone?	Yes
BE-LK04	Hopper Brook	1?	Stone?	Yes
BE-LK05	Equinox Mountain	1?	Stone?	Yes
BE-LK06	Readsboro	1?	Stone?	Yes
BE-LK07	Red Mountain	1?	Stone?	Yes
BE-LK08	Lawrence	1?	Stone?	Yes
Caledonia County				
CA-LK01	Marl Pond	1?	Stone?	No
Chittenden County				
CH-282	Weston Lime Works	2?	Concrete?	No
CH-284	Champlain Valley Lime Company	4	Concrete*	No
CH-365	Laberge	1	Stone	No
CH-FS118	Bates	1?	Stone?	No
CH-LK01	Stave Point	1?	Stone?	No
Franklin County				
FR-178	Fonda Junction	6	Stone/Concrete*	No
FR-179	Joyal	1	Stone	No
FR-224	Missisquoi Lime Company	1	Stone	No
FR-225	Missisquoi Lime Works Incorporated	5	Stone(*?)	No
		2	Concrete(*?)	No
FR-226	Bancroft	1	Stone?	No
FR-227	Richford	1	Stone	No

Table 8-1. Lime Kiln Sites (Cont.)

Site No.	Principal Name	Kilns per Site	Type	Green Mountain National Forest
Franklin County (Cont.)				
FR-228	Swanton Lime Works	6	Stone(*?)	No
		5	Concrete*	No
FR-FS24	Rich Lime Works	2?	Stone?	No
FR-LK01	Ferris	1	Stone?	No
Grand Isle County				
GI-27	Fort Sainte-Anne/Fisk Point	1?	Stone?	No
Lamoille County				
LA-LK01	Benjamin Thomas	1?	Stone?	No
LA-LK02	Tillotson	1	Stone?	No
LA-LK03	Shattuck Mountain	1?	Stone?	No
LA-LK04	Bradford	1?	Stone?	No
LA-LK05	Butler	1?	Stone?	No
Orange County				
OR-FS12	Limehurst Lake	1?	Stone?	No
Rutland County				
RU-98	Scotch Hill	1	Stone	No
RU-154	Maplebrook Farm	1	Stone	No
RU-157	Vermont Lime Products Corporation	3	Concrete*	No
RU-161	Crow Hill Farm	2	Stone	No
RU-165	Bromley Farm	1	Stone	No
RU-166	"The Cobble"	2	Stone	No
RU-179	Mendon	1	Stone	Yes
RU-180	River Road	1	Stone	Yes
RU-194	Seager Hill	1	Stone	No
RU-196	Briggs	2	Stone	No
RU-197	Devils Den	1	Stone	Yes
RU-198	Howard Hill	1	Stone	No
RU-260	Bomoseen	1	Stone	No
RU-261	Chippenhook	1	Stone	No
RU-FS48	Village Lime Kiln	1	Stone?	No
RU-FS49	Kelley and Wellman	1	Stone?	No
RU-FS50	Doran	1?	Stone?	No
RU-LK01	Vermont Marble Company	1	Rotary	No
RU-LK02	Fuller	1?	Stone?	?
Windham County				
WD-67	Greene Farm	1	Stone	Yes
WD-68	Thayer	1	Stone	No
WD-69	Haven	1	Stone	No
WD-70	Twitchell-Howard	1	Stone	No
WD-87	Bemis	1	Stone	No
WD-88	Pike-Bills	1	Stone	Yes

Table 8-1. Lime Kiln Sites (Cont.)

Site No.	Principal Name	Kilns per Site	Type	Green Mountain National Forest
Windham County (Cont.)				
WD-89	Grimes-Fitzgerald	1	Stone	Yes
WD-90	Kenfield-Kaufmann	1	Stone	Yes
WD-91	No. 9 Brook	1	Stone	No
WD-92	Gray-Holt	1	Stone	No
WD-126	Vermont Lime Company	1	Stone	No
WD-127	Kingsley	1	Stone	Yes
WD-FS13	West Wardsboro	1?	Stone?	Yes
WD-FS14	Lime Hollow	1?	Stone?	Yes
WD-LK01	Merrifield Road	1?	Stone?	Yes
WD-LK02	Windmill Mountain	1?	Stone?	No
Windsor County				
WN-58	Upper Falls	2	Stone	No
WN-104	Amsden	2	Stone	No
		1	Concrete*	No
WN-108	Burnt Mountain	1	Stone	No
WN-109	Campground	1	Stone	No
WN-110	Rice	1	Stone	No
WN-111	Grace's	1	Stone	No
WN-112	Knapp	1	Stone	No
WN-113	Brookwood	1	Stone	No
WN-114	Money Brook	1	Stone	No
WN-118	Felchville	1	Stone	No
WN-119	Grass Pond	1	Stone	No
WN-120	Frog City	1?	Stone?	No
WN-121	Ward Lime Works	2	Stone	No
WN-123	Lower Branch Brook	1	Stone	No
WN-124	Liberty Hill	1	Stone	Yes
WN-128	Messer Hill Road	1	Stone	No
WN-133	Lower Grand View Lodge Road	1	Stone	No
WN-134	Upper Grand View Lodge Road	2	Stone	No
WN-135	Upper Branch Brook	1	Stone	No
WN-136	Cavendish Station	1	Stone	No
WN-137	Stearns	1	Stone	No
WN-138	Moore-Calkins	1	Stone	No
WN-139	Plymouth Notch	1	Stone	No
WN-185	Reservoir Brook	1	Stone	No
WN-FS18	Hall's	1	Stone?	No
WN-FS19	Jewell Brook	1?	Stone?	No
WN-LK01	Black Pond	1?	Stone?	No
WN-LK02	East Bethel	1?	Stone?	No
WN-LK03	South Woodstock	1?	Stone?	No
WN-LK04	Shattuck Farm	1?	Stone?	No?
WN-LK05	Hutchins	1?	Stone?	No
WN-LK06	North Andover	1?	Stone?	No
WN-LK07	Adams	1?	Stone?	No

Table 8-1. Lime Kiln Sites (Cont.)

Site No.	Principal Name	Kilns per Site	Type	Green Mountain National Forest
Windsor County (Cont.)				
WN-LK08	Knapp Pond Road	1?	Stone?	No

* Commercial-type lime kiln with high, round iron shells

above and around the top of the kiln. A majority of the lime kiln sites found ranged up to seven ruins per site. Fifty of the sites (70 percent) contained one ruin. All were made of stone and were mostly of the early-19th-century "pot kiln" variety.

Table 8-1 lists all kiln sites that have been researched by county, and numerically within county by site identification number. The table also lists the site's given name, number of kilns per site, the construction type, and if in the Green Mountain National Forest. Three sections following divide the state into the northern, central, and southern districts, as described in the Introduction of this book (see "Presentation of the Study"). In these sections, the history of the lime-burning site and descriptions of whatever physical remains exist are presented. Table 8-2 at the end of the chapter summarizes the results of the lime kiln study.

Presentation of sites within each section is by county, and within each county, sites are presented either in site number sequence or grouped to reflect a geographic proximity. Grouping does not reflect any commonality that might have existed when the kilns were in operation, but aids in describing them. Accompanying maps provide a geographic sense of the physical disposition of the sites and ruins, without compromising the exact location of the site.

For the purpose of this study, remains and ruins are used to differentiate between nonstructural and structural surface evidence. Remains include kiln mounds that have no structural elements and are relatively caved in, yet are otherwise identifiable as a lime kiln. Ruins include individual kilns that are standing or partially standing structures, and might also include visible sections of brick and/or stone walls. A lime-burning area, whether containing ruins, remains, or no visible surface features or evidence, is referred to as a site.

WARNING to Hikers and Explorers: Although appearing sturdy, all kiln ruins are in fact very fragile. Climbing about them loosens stones, weakens walls, and contributes to their progressive deterioration. Collapse of larger ruins can cause personal injury.

The Northern District

The only counties in the northern district where lime kiln ruins have thus far been found are Franklin and Chittenden counties. Ruins might also exist in Grand Isle, Lamoille, and Caledonia counties per archival sources. Lime was burned at Isle La Motte in 1666. Lime kiln remains in Franklin County center in the

Swanton-Highgate area, following an almost straight north-south limestone ledge. Major kiln remains in Chittenden County center on both sides of the Lime Kiln Road bridge over the Winooski River between Colchester and South Burlington, where limestone burning and processing was carried on commercially for about 150 years. Farther south in Charlotte, a moderate-size lime kiln probably operated until nearly the 20th century.

CALEDONIA COUNTY

CA-LK01 Marl Pond Lime Kiln (Sutton): In the northwest corner of Sutton near Lime Pond (known as Marl Pond in the mid-1800s), shell marl was dug and burned at an early time for use as fertilizer. It proved to be a valuable business for many years (Swift 1977:149). No attempt has been made to inspect the site.

GRAND ISLE COUNTY

GI-27 Fort Sainte-Anne/Fisk Point Lime Kilns (Isle La Motte): The earliest known date for burning lime in what is today Vermont is 1666, when a lime kiln was built by the French to make mortar that was used by Captain De La Motte in the construction of Fort Sainte-Anne. Archival references vary as to the construction date of the fort. A plaque at the north end of the island claims the fort was built in 1665 and dedicated in 1666. The initial French settlement probably dates to 1664 and the construction of the fort to protect the settlement in 1666. The settlement and fort were abandoned four years later. The kiln was also operated by the British and, eventually, by Vermonters as late as 1796 (Child *Grand Isle* 1883:18; Perkins 1933:145; Stratton 1984:118). In 1779–1780, Captain William Chambers of the British Navy made soundings off the shores of Lake Champlain to afford safe anchorage points should hostilities demand renewal of naval warfare on the lake. The maps of these soundings were recently published, and one of the charts identifies "Lime Kilns" at what is today Fisk Point. The bay immediately south of the point is named Lime Kiln Bay (Chambers 1984:8). The lime kilns were an obvious landmark in 1779 if they appeared on the map. Another map, drawn from a 1786 survey by John Clark, clearly identifies "Lime Kilns" at today's Fisk Point (Stratton 1984:14-15). It is improbable, however, that the same lime kiln that burned lime in the mid-17th century was one of those still operating in the 1780s–1790s. It is also unknown whether the original Fort Sainte-Anne lime kiln operated at Fisk Point or somewhere farther north, nearer

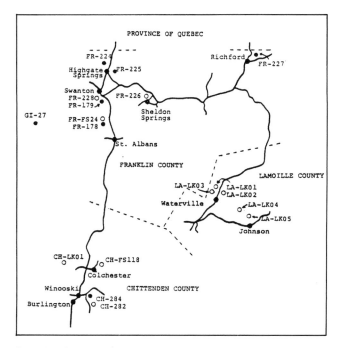

8-1. *Grand Isle, Franklin, Lamoille, and Chittenden counties lime kiln sites.*

to the fort.

Fort Sainte-Anne was at Sandy Point, near the northwest corner of the island, where today's Saint Anne's Shrine is a popular religious, picnicking, swimming, and tourist attraction. The fort faced north and west at a point where guns of "good calibre" could command passage on the lake (Child *Grand Isle* 1883:227). A priest queried at the shrine had no knowledge of exactly where the fort stood and knew of no archeological work done to accurately locate it. (Another fort was built in 1812 about 1½ miles south.)

Limestone burned for mortar (and possibly the stone for the fort itself) might have come from the vicinity of the Fisk quarry, about 4 miles south of the shrine, as indicated on the Chambers map. "The quarry is not deep, tracks for a small railroad running from the back wall of the quarry directly to the dock on the shore of the lake" (Perkins 1933:145). "The stone from this quarry known as Chazy Limestone, has been quarried continuously for over a hundred years. An immense quantity of stone has been removed. The quarry walls are over 2000 feet long and 30 feet high. The piers and abutments of the Victoria Bridge across the St. Lawrence River at Montreal were built of this stone" (Stratton 1984:118).

Three generations of the Fisk family worked the quarry, starting ca. 1802 and ending soon after 1905. The old gray-stone Fisk house is a few hundred yards north of the quarry, today owned by the Fitch family. The quarry is owned by the Vermont Marble Company.

The Fisk Point area was inspected in 1991 and about a dozen summer cabins and mobile homes were found occupying the space between the island's west shore road and the point. Two roads into the area as well as most of the cabins are on fill,

two to three feet above the local ground level. The ground between the shoreline and the road is quite low, and one vacationing resident said that in spring it is not uncommon for the lake to flood to the edge of their road (about 100 feet from the lake shore). Another resident showed where two very old barns burned to the ground two years before, and where the stone foundation remains were scattered by bulldozer. He said that 26 loads of fill were used for landscaping the yard following the fire. No one remembered seeing anything resembling a lime kiln or burned limestone. The ground rises slightly at the shore where ledge rock outcrops. Lime kilns would either have been built at these outcrops or well back of the point on higher ground to escape annual flooding, unless the lake ran lower 200 to 300 years ago. The low areas are wet and are probably the sole survivors from that time, before the point was developed. Limestone outcrops were found in the fields immediately east of the road, opposite the point, but no indications of quarrying were seen.

At the dock area, immediately south of Fisk Point, bits of burned lime were found eroding out of a 10-foot-high embankment on the east side of the road and about 25 feet south of the road to the Fisk quarry. The possible kiln site here is a mound or low rise of broken stone, some of which might have been part of the lime kiln. No burned, glazed stonework was found although some flat pieces of red-stained stone were found, appearing to have been burned. This low embankment is the only rise in the immediate area and might have been significantly disturbed by improvements to the road, which curves gently to the southeast around the rise. Directly behind (east) through a heavy tangle of trees is a small, early quarry. The main Fisk quarry is about 100 feet northeast, now flooded to approximately lake level. It was the oldest continuously operated quarry in Vermont (see chapter 7, "Vermont Lime Kilns").

The dock is a small point of land extending into the lake south of Fisk Point and was probably built during the mid-19th century from quarry tailings. At the shore of the dock are huge reinforced concrete blocks imbedded with heavy-gauge steel rods. Jammed under the blocks are sections of severely rusted and corroded narrow-gauge railroad track (smaller than 30-pound track), all that remains of the quarry railroad. At the edge of the dock are partially submerged log foundations that supported a large crane. Lake steamers docked here up to the early 20th century (see photo in Perkins 1898:41).

FRANKLIN COUNTY

FR-224 Missisquoi Lime Company (Highgate): The 1871 Beers map of Highgate shows buildings of the Missisquoi Lime Company on a small point on Lake Champlain, about a half-mile north of Highgate Springs. The lime kiln was in operation at least 10 years earlier, making an excellent quicklime, "large quantities of which are annually manufactured and sent to market" (Hitchcock et al. 1861:285). The company was incorporated in 1862 by Harvey Phelps, A. H. Barrows, Dana R. Bailey, Andrew A. Mason, D. A. Bartlett, William Fiske, and David Cross, for quarrying, mining, and working iron, copper, and other minerals, and manufacturing lime and cement (*Acts and Resolves* 1862:93). The kiln, owned by Boston interests, operated until 1888, at which time it was abandoned in favor of a newer site (FR-225) a mile south (Jacobs 1918:161).

8-2. *Inside one of seven lime kiln ruins of the Missisquoi Lime Works at Highgate, showing firebrick lining and multiple arches for draft.*

8-3. *The opposite side of the wall shown in figure 8-2, showing the brick arch, through which draft was drawn into the kiln.*

8-4. *Workers gather around the lime kiln for the photographer in this ca.-1900 photo. Note the railroad cars under scaffolding at left, possibly indicating this kiln is either at Fonda or beside the spur track at Highgate Springs. The wheelbarrow was used for carrying the burned lime from the kilns to the barrels (courtesy Bob Douglas).*

8-5. *Another early view of lime kilns in Swanton or Highgate, showing horse and wagon atop wood scaffolding between two kilns at left, small door and iron binding around kiln at right, and young boys standing beside the stack. The wagon carried off the burned lime in barrels.*

The lime kiln ruin was found in 1990 on the northeast end of the point, about a quarter-mile west from Route 7. The ruin is about 25 feet from the shore of Lake Champlain on what the USGS topographical map identifies as Limekiln Point. The kiln was probably built near the shore to be serviced by lake commerce. The dirt road leads to the point, which is owned by Barbara Updike (per Harold D. Campbell IV of Highgate Springs). The kiln ruin was found at the north edge of a quarry, associated with a manmade ramp of talus that would have allowed a bridge to service the top of the kiln.

The ruin is a brick- and stone-strewn mound, about 12 to 15 feet high. It is about 20 to 25 feet in diameter at ground level, 5 to 6 feet in diameter at the top, and well hidden from lake view by evergreen trees. At the top of the ruin are the three-sided rectangular remains of the inside lining, measuring 64 inches by over 15 inches (the fourth side does not stick out and no attempt was made to uncover it). This lining is made of firebrick, laid end- and crosswise. A glassy coating on the lining varies from ½ to 1 inch thick. Firebricks marked BRANDON VT measured 8½ by 4¼ by 2½ inches. A broken firebrick was marked BOS[TON?]. Unmarked red brick measured 7⅜ by 3¼ by 2 inches. To the southwest of the ruin is the limestone quarry and between the quarry and the lake (to the west) are the possible remains of an earlier lime kiln.

FR-225 Missisquoi Lime Works, Inc. (Highgate): When the operations closed at Limekiln Point in 1888 (FR-224), the Missisquoi Lime Company built five kilns about a mile east of Highgate Springs. The move was probably made to be nearer to both a new quarry and the railroad, and to have more land to allow construction of the five kilns. A horse railroad carried the rock from the quarry to the kilns, about 1,200 feet west of the quarry. L. H. Fenton operated the company until his death in 1914.

The company was reorganized in 1916 as the Missisquoi Lime Works by F. B. Wright, President; C. H. Schoff, Vice-President; E. Deschenes, Treasurer; and O. H. Parker, Superintendent, with company offices at St. Albans. The Works' five wood-burning kilns produced about 45 tons of lime per day. They produced over 100,000 barrels (9,000 tons) of lime in 1917. Production in 1918, with a new, modern plant expected to be in operation, was expected to exceed 130,000 barrels. Prices varied from $6.00 to $11.00 per ton in bulk and from $1.10 to $1.60 per barrel. The lime, which ran from 95 to 99 percent calcium dioxide, was held in high reputation in the lime industry (Jacobs 1918:159). The company was described as still operating in 1937 (*Vermont* 1937:276).

Remains of the Missisquoi Lime Works were inspected in 1990 after finding and inspecting the lime kiln ruin at Limekiln Point (FR-224) earlier in the day. The site is identified by "Ruins" on the USGS topographical map although this spot is somewhat south of where Jacobs described the site as being. Specific guidance to the ruins was provided by young Harold D. Campbell IV, who was riding a trail bike in the vicinity.

Mound remains of five stone-built kilns were found in a generally east-west row with each ruin about 25 to 30 feet apart. At the east end of the row is a dirt mound that appears to have been a ramp from which tracks were built over the tops of the kilns so a small rail car could deposit quarry stone directly into them. The condition of the ruins improves from east to west, with the western ruin having enough wall section standing (about 8 feet high) to indicate that the outside walls of these kilns were round. Firebrick was scattered about the ruins. One firebrick measured 9 by 4½ by 2½ inches and is marked H. W. SPEC. A broken firebrick marked BOSTON [FIRE?] BLOCK CO measured 4½ inches wide by 2½ inches thick. A wedge-shaped firebrick was marked U.S.A.

The surprise of the day was finding two more kiln ruins, not exactly in line with the five stone ruins, but in a line and offset slightly to the southwest. These kilns were made of concrete, cast solid in approximately 10-foot-high vertical half-sections. The inside diameters of the concrete ruins were estimated to have been 8 feet when both sections were standing and intact. The sections had been banded together around the middle, probably with a heavy-duty iron ring, similar to that used on brick-type charcoal kilns. One ruin had only a single section standing; the other half-section had toppled and broken. Both concrete halves of another ruin, about 40 feet away, were lying on their backs. These two kilns, which were attempts to improve the design of the five stone-built kilns, are probably the remains of Jacobs' referenced modern plant constructed in 1918. Hardware and trash were found associated with these two concrete kiln ruins, which sit in a slight depression, and within a few feet of a large concrete foundation that appears to have been the storage building and railroad loading platform.

Bordering on the south sides of the five stone-type ruins are square concrete pedestals, about 1½ feet square, 1½ to 2 feet high, and in a row about 6 feet apart. Since they are about midway between, and line up with, both the ramp and the concrete kiln ruins, it is guessed that these pedestals supported tracks that switched from the main quarry track at the ramp and allowed quarry cars to supply stone to the concrete-section kilns.

A spur track connected the plant to the Central Vermont Railroad (on what is today the dirt road into the site). The railroad no longer runs north of Swanton. Interstate 89 now generally covers the old railroad bed and a section of old Route 7 at Highgate Springs.

FR-227 Richford Lime Kiln (Richford): Limestone was quarried and burned before 1861 about two miles east-northeast of Richford, between the old road to East Richford on the north side of the Missisquoi River and the upper, parallel road (Golf Course Road). The property was identified as that of O. W. Corliss. A tunnel was also begun near the quarry before 1861 with the intention of mining copper that was in association with the limestone (Dale 1915:10).

The kiln ruin was found on the second try in 1990, about a mile south of the Canadian border alongside a rustic north-south road. Leon Carr, who was haying in the vicinity, gave directions to the ruin. The ruin is an approximately 15-foot-high mound of collapsed stone with about a third of a circular section of its inside lining sticking above the mound, enough to see that there was a light, reddish glaze on the lining. The glaze is probably all that is holding this section of wall together. No firebrick was found associated with the ruin, but five yellow birch grow atop the mound. The site is in the wooded hollow beyond the open pastures between Golf Course Road and the lower east-west road.

FR-226 Bancroft Lime Kiln (Sheldon): Among his other industrial pursuits at Sheldon Springs (known earlier as Olmstead Falls), George Bancroft operated a lime kiln. The 1871 Beers map of Sheldon shows the lime kiln and quarry on the sharp inside bend of the Missisquoi River, identified "Missisquoi Falls."

The site of this lime kiln was identified in 1990. The inside curve of the Missisquoi River at Sheldon Springs is occupied by the many buildings of the Specialty Paperboard Company, whose permission was obtained to search for the lime kiln remains. The limestone outcrop shown in the Beers map was found about 50 feet due west from the plant office. At the base of this cliff are pieces of lime powder, tightly compacted into a hard crusty composition. One could easily imagine a lime kiln having operated here. Adjacent to the kiln site is a path and the stone-wall foundation building that was one of the original buildings of the pulp company, built about 1900 (per a land surveyor who happened to drive into the area.) Although no positive surface remains exist, archeological remains of the kiln might be hidden under the path. The Beers map shows a gristmill and sawmill along the river at this point. The whole landscape of this side of the "point" has changed with the construction of the pulp mill. There are no references to this lime kiln in either the 1861 geology report of Vermont or in any of the State Geologists' reports of the early 1900s.

FR-179 Joyal Lime Kiln (Swanton): Remains of a lime kiln were found near the old John's Bridge crossing in 1987. The site is about 200 feet west of Route 7, and is 500 feet northwest of the Missisquoi River. It was found from information provided by the following historical account: "Lime was manufactured to a considerable extent before 1800. The first limekiln it is believed was built at the lime rock ledge near John's Bridge" (Aldrich 1891:406). "The writer can well remember over 60 years ago there was a lime kiln at the edge near the entrance to the old covered 'John's Bridge'; Benj. Joyal carried it on for years" (Hemenway vol. 4 1882:1024). Hemenway's 60 years before 1882 dovetails well within the period of the Ferris lime kiln (FR-LK01, following), which was erected contemporaneously with Joyal's; both appear to have been operating in the 1820s and possibly earlier.

The kiln remains were found along the lime rock ledge southwest of the bridge on the village side of the river, and consisted of a low, circular feature, about a foot high by 12 feet in diameter. The back (east) side is the natural ledge wall. Bits of burned lime and white stone made up part of the circular feature.

FR-LK01 Ferris Lime Kiln (Swanton): Another lime kiln operated near John's Bridge contemporaneously with Benjamin Joyal's, built by Jonathan Ferris (1765–1829) north of the bridge. It was described as being large and "near the one run by Benjamin Joyal" (Ledoux 1988:26-27). The possibility exists that the lime kiln remains found near John's Bridge in 1987 (FR-179) could be that built by Jonathan Ferris.

FR-228 Swanton Lime Works (Swanton): Today it is known as the Jewett Street Plant of the Shelburne Limestone Corp., but in its lime-burning days, it was the Swanton Lime Works. The company started in 1847 near Fonda (Swanton Junction; see FR-178), and in the village in 1877 by A. B. and E. W. Jewett and C. W. Rich (see also chapter 4, AD-404). The latter coincided with the completion of the Portland and Ogdensburg

Railroad. In 1888, ownership passed from C. W. Rich to his son, John P. Rich. Limestone came from quarries just south of the plant and also from Fonda. Blasted rock was carried from the local quarry to the kilns by an aerial tramway. The plant had five gas-burning and nine wood-burning kilns, but the diminishing supply of wood forced use of gas-burning kilns only by 1918. The gas was converted from soft coal to gas by a Bradley Gas Producer. The plant was considered one of the most modern and best equipped in the state. Daily production of the gas kilns was 10 tons each; yearly capacity was 15,000 tons. Average price per ton in 1916 was $5.00; in 1917 $8.00; and in 1918 $11.00 (Jacobs 1918:161). The lime was bought for the manufacture of paper, leather, and mortar, and for agriculture (Jacobs 1937:20).

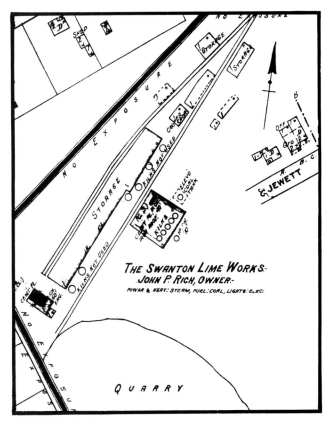

8-6. *The 1920 Sanborn map of Swanton Lime Works showing the six "kilns not used" next to the storage shed, the five new kilns on the opposite side of the tracks, and the limestone quarry just south of the kilns.*

The five gas-burning kilns were still in operation in 1932 (Perkins 1933:149). A few years later, John P. Rich passed ownership of the plant to his sons Davis, Charles, and John. With the advent of the USDA Agricultural Stabilization Program in 1937, a modern plant was built with machinery to grind the limestone (Douglas 1988:60-61).

The 1920 Sanborn map shows five kilns in a building just at the end of Jewett Street. Six more kilns are shown across

8-7. *The Swanton Lime Works lime kiln shed at left housed five kilns, as seen by their tops visible through the roof. These kilns operated from the early 1900s to about the 1970s (courtesy Bob Douglas).*

8-8. *Quarry workers at Swanton Lime Works in pre- mechanization days (courtesy Bob Douglas).*

the railroad tracks adjacent to a storage building, with the notation "kilns not used." The 1930 Sanborn map still shows the five kilns but not the six unused kilns. The storage building is gone in the 1953 map. In a 1987 visit, only a modern lime-processing operation was seen; no lime kilns. But inspection of the ground in the vicinity of the former gas-burning kilns showed large circles, hinting at the exact location and diameters of the units. This also matched their proximity to the railroad tracks as shown in the Sanborn maps.

It is unknown for sure exactly where the original nine wood-burning kilns were located; these nine plus the five gas-burning kilns total 14 kilns. Since later accounts mention only 11 kilns, which can be confirmed on-site by the Sanborn maps, the nine wood-burning kilns might have been located elsewhere. They could have been earlier kilns that operated at Fonda Junction (FR-178), or those lime kilns owned by C. W. Rich (per Beers) at another site about a half-mile farther south, whose remains have not been found (FR-FS24).

FR-178 Fonda Junction Lime Kilns (Swanton): Partially standing/collapsed mound ruins/remains of six lime kilns were found in 1986, about a quarter-mile west of Route 7 at the west end of Lime Kiln Road in the south part of Swanton. The 1871 Beers map of Swanton shows the St. Albans Lime Works on a railroad siding at Swanton Junction near a "lime stone quarry."

8-9. *Lime operations at Fonda (Swanton Junction) in 1871, showing (north to south) the "St. Albans Lime Works," the "C. W. Rich Lime Works," and "Lime Kilns" west of the railroad tracks and surrounding the limestone quarry (Beers Franklin 1871:14).*

In 1850, C. W. Rich, esq., erected some kilns of an improved kind, from which great quantities [of lime] have been made and shipped to market and are still in successful operation, being run by John P. Rich, son of C. W. Rich. W. Beecher Fonda has carried on an extensive lime business on what is called the Gadcomb farm for 20 years past (Aldrich 1891:406-407).

The quarry has been worked about ten years, the product of lime averaging about 15,000 barrels annually. At the time of our visit (1858) the kilns were producing lime at a rate of 25,000 barrels per annum. About twenty hands were employed, exclusive of coopers (Hitchcock et al. 1861:750).

Swanton Junction had a post office from 1867 to 1909. The hamlet was sometimes called Fonda Junction and now is generally known as just Fonda. The name came from the lime-burning kilns of W. Beecher Fonda, which once employed over 30 men and manufactured 60,000 or 70,000 barrels a year of what was known as St. Albans Lime for bleaching (Swift 1977:255).

The works are located just west of Fonda Junction. Lime

8-10. *An advertisement (and endorsement) for St. Albans Lime, made at Fonda (*Walton's *1876:26).*

8-11. *A ca-1915 view of railroad cars lined up on a spur track of the Central Vermont Railroad at Fonda taking on lime. Name on left car reads "National Despatch—Lime" (courtesy James A. Murphy).*

8-12. *A 1986 view of kiln ruins at Fonda, showing disposition of their crumbling stone bases and rusted iron shells.*

burning was begun in 1846 by Chas. W. Rich, following the building of the Vermont Central Railway. . . . It was continued in 1850 by Lawrence Brainerd and Edward A. Smith. The works were acquired in 1872 by W. B. Fonda. The present management (Leo F. Willson, Manager; offices at St. Albans) took control in 1917. . . . The quarried rock is hoisted up an inclined railroad and trammed to the works, where it is burned in five vertical kilns fired by soft coal (Jacobs 1918:160).

Remains in 1986 consisted of three standing ruins with their tall, round (and rusting), firebrick-lined iron stacks in varying degrees of decay; one collapsed ruin at the southern end without any iron stack and two completely collapsed remains at the northern end (six total, versus five reported by Jacobs in 1918). The most northerly remain has the least surface evidence. Indi-

cations can be seen of a railroad bed running north, possibly to another quarry.

FR-FS24 Rich Lime Works (Swanton): There were more lime kilns about a half-mile south of the Fonda lime kilns, per "C. W. Rich Lime Works" and "Lime Kilns" indicated on the 1871 Beers map of Swanton.

Inspection of this area in 1987, about a half-mile west of Route 7, resulted in finding an abandoned quarry but no kiln remains. The property owner knew of no lime kiln or ruin in the vicinity. Operations here might have been connected with those at Fonda Junction.

LAMOILLE COUNTY

LA-LK01 Benjamin Thomas Lime Kiln (Waterville): This kiln is indicated in the 1878 Beers map of Waterville, about a

8-13. Firebrick lining inside one of the kiln ruins at Fonda.

half-mile west of today's Route 109 between Codding Hollow Road and Belvidere Junction. This might also be at the quarry referenced by Dale as being "4,000 feet west of the Waterville-Belvidere road, on the second farm south of Wescott's" (Dale 1915:12). Many hours driving up and down roads and querying residents in the vicinity in 1990 failed to accurately locate the site, let alone find a ruin, due to the age of the USGS 15-minute topographical map used. New roads and homes in the area make it difficult to relate features in the Beers map with today's physical lay of the land.

LA-LK02 Tillotson Lime Kiln (Waterville): There was a marble quarry about two miles north of the village on the road to Belvidere, 500 feet to the east on a brook flowing southward in the hollow and separated from the road by a small schist ridge. Lime was burned here about 1865 (Dale 1915:11). The USGS topographical map shows a quarry symbol on the east side of Route 109 at this point, between the road and the brook (North Branch), but this is a gravel pit. The quarry was known as the Tillotson prospect. A brief search of the area in 1990 failed to reveal any evidence of a lime kiln. As far as is known, no limestone quarried in Waterville was used for marble (Perkins 1933:236).

LA-LK03 Shattuck Mountain Lime Kiln (Waterville): While querying local residents about the whereabouts of the Benjamin Thomas kiln (LA-K01), Mr. Maxfield of Maxfield Road said that there is a lime kiln ruin "over the other side of the mountain," while pointing to the west at the southern nose of Shattuck Mountain. The peak of this mountain is about a mile north and is a point on the boundary between Franklin and Lamoille counties. No attempt has been made to inspect this site.

LA-LK04 Bradford Lime Kiln (Johnson): Marble was burned for lime many years before the turn of the century four miles north-northwest of the village. The locality was a quarter-mile northwest of the Bradford house, with the lime kiln described as being near the south end of the quarry (Dale 1915:12-13). This appears to be somewhere near the upper reaches of Foot Brook at about the 1,300-foot elevation and near the trail to Waterville via Codding Brook. No limestone in Johnson was quarried for marble as far as is known (Perkins 1933:227). No attempt has been made to inspect the site.

LA-LK05 Butler Lime Kiln (Johnson): Another lime kiln in Johnson operated in the 1860s about two or three miles north of the village near a 100-foot-long cave (Hitchcock at al. 1861:558). The quarry was described as being 15 feet wide and about 35 feet long; the limestone was white with varieties of blue, pink, and light brown. The kiln was described as being downhill from a quarry near a brook flowing south-southeastward (Dale 1915:13). The quarry was on the George Butler farm, adjoining and northeast of the Bradford property (LA-LK04). No attempt has been made to inspect the site.

CHITTENDEN COUNTY

CH-FS118 Bates Lime Kiln (Colchester): A perpetual lime kiln operated near the quarry of Alphonse Bates in the 1850–1860s, not far from the railroad in the village. Bates' kiln made about 150 bushels of lime per day (Hitchcock at al. 1861:750).

The 1857 map of Chittenden County shows a lime kiln a few hundred feet northeast of the Bates house, near the corner of Depot Road and East Road. A two-hour search in a low, rocky, forested rise behind houses at the intersection resulted in finding some deep quarries but no evidence of the lime kiln. From the position of the kiln in the 1857 map, the ruin might have been destroyed with the construction of the barn/carriage house behind one of the houses along East Road. The structure is well back of the house at the edge of the woods and within a few dozen feet of the rock outcrops behind it. Another possible kiln site is the vicinity of some burnt lime, found on the north side of Depot Road, just inside the woods beside an unpaved side road (a remnant of the old Depot Road before it was straightened). Although this is not exactly where the kiln is indicated on the map, there is no other logical answer for burnt lime being here.

A small brook, today called Cold Brook, flows northwesterly between Route 2A and Depot Road; it is identified as Lime Kiln Brook on the 1857 map.

CH-LK01 Stave Point Lime Kiln (Colchester): Marble quarries opened on both sides of the Malletts Bay outlet in the 1850s, most actively on the southern side at Malletts Head (also known as Marble Head). On the north side of the outlet at Stave Point a lime kiln burned some of the marble for making quicklime (Hitchcock et al. 1861:318; Perkins 1933:155).

Location of Stave Point is unknown at this writing. Maps, histories, lake charts, and personal queries have not uncovered Stave Point. Why the State Geologist used such an uncommon name for this piece of geography in 1861 is puzzling. Inspections of various places along the north shore of Malletts Bay in 1991 showed many marble/limestone ledges but no sign of lime burning.

CH-365 Laberge Lime Kiln (Charlotte): The ruin of a mid-19th-century lime kiln was found in Charlotte along Lime Kiln Road in 1988. The kiln ruin is in a cow pasture on the south side of the road, about a mile east of Route 7. From the road it appears no more than a 20-foot-diameter mound of stones. But closer inspection in 1991 revealed the four marble corners of an 18-foot-square base protruding out through the approximately 5-foot-high mound of collapsed rubble. At top-center is a slight depression. Firebricks associated with the ruin are marked McL&H CO TROY NY, which dates the kiln to the 1880s. These firebricks were both rectangular (9⅛ by 4½ by

2¾ inches) and wedge-shaped (9 by 2⅜ by 4⅝ inches at the wide end and 3⅞ inches at the narrow end; and 9⅛ by 2⅝ by 4⅜ inches at the wide end by 2⅜ inches at the narrow end). Some red bricks were also found (7½ by 1⅞ by 3⅜ inches). About 50 feet uphill of the ruin is a small limestone outcrop, which provided stone that was burned in the kiln. Some crushed stone was seen near the foot of the quarry.

Property owner Mr. Laberge (86 years old in 1991) said that he thought the kiln operated to the 1920s because he remembers a neighbor who sold wood that was used to fuel the kiln. He said that the kiln closed because the burned lime contained too much slate. Margaret MacDonough, who lives across the road from the Laberge farm, remembered climbing to the top of the 6-foot-high ruin about 70 years ago and peering down into its round "mysterious" interior. It was her recollection that the kiln had been out of operation long before that. She also remembered a stone crusher in operation at a more recent time, which explains the crushed stone at the quarry.

Winooski Park and South Burlington Lime Kiln Sites: At the end of the War of 1812, lime extracting commenced on the Colchester side at today's Winooski Park by Sidney Weston. A few years later, Jabez Penniman, husband of Ira Allen's widow, commenced lime-burning operations on the Burlington side of the Winooski River. It was all known as The Lime Company and it covered about 22 acres of land on each side of the river. In 1858, Penniman and Noyes were operating the Winooski Limekiln Company, the first inference that kilns were by then in operation on the Colchester side (Carlisle 1975:10). Four perpetual kilns of the current design were then in operation; limestone was conveyed on tramways to the tops of the kilns. From 25 to 30 hands were employed at the works where 4,000 cords of wood were annually consumed for fuel. Production was 700 bushels of lime per day, or about 250,000 bushels (10,000 tons) of lime per year (Hitchcock et al. 1861:750).

The 1869 Beers maps of Colchester and Burlington show S. H. Weston associated with lime works on the Colchester side and "E. W." (E. Weston?) associated with a lime kiln on the South Burlington side. The 1857 map of Chittenden County also shows the lime kiln here. It is indicated just southeast of the juncture of the road and the river. At that time (1869), operations on both sides were probably owned by Sidney H. Weston, who purchased the kilns from Robert Jackson and Alexander McGregor (Carlisle 1975:11). Weston also owned businesses in Burlington and in Wilmington, New York, and eventually became the president of the Winooski Savings Bank (Child 1882:302). Operations on both sides of the river were probably collectively known as the Weston Lime Works. Business was run at the kilns by George Catlin, son-in-law to Sidney H. Weston (Carlisle 1975:13). Harvey S. Weston, who owned a 1,000-acre dairy and sheep farm, later managed the kilns on the Burlington side (Child 1882:390).

In 1907 the operations on the Colchester side were known as the Champlain Valley Lime Company, and in 1920 they were sold to a Massachusetts-based firm (Carlisle 1975:13). The works then consisted of three wood-burning kilns with an annual capacity of 3,000 tons; a considerable amount of crushed limestone was also produced for the agricultural market (Meeks 1986:148). Sanborn fire insurance maps first show these operations in the January 1926 issue, on the Colchester side only,

8-14. *Lime kilns at Winooski Park just before the site was razed in 1990 for scrap metal. Limestone was raised from the quarry, at left, to the top of the kilns via a skip car.*

8-15. *From the kilns shown in figure 8-14, lime was crushed and ground into a fine powder by machinery in this building, located just south of the kiln building (background). Only the foundation remains of this structure today.*

possibly indicating that the kilns in South Burlington had shut down by that time (about 1907 when the company name changed?). The map shows the four-kiln building with its steel conveyer to the nearby quarry, a railroad siding trestle for supply of coal to fire the kilns, and another structure directly east, which on the 1942 Sanborn map is indicated for "Lime Ore Grinding & Bagging."

In 1948 the works were sold to the Vermont Associated Lime Industries, in 1960 to Merritt L. Hulett of Granville, New York, and in 1970 to William W. Magnus. The works closed in December 1971 with the loss of a U.S. government contract for supplying lime for agricultural purposes. At the time, the plant's 20 employees produced 20,000 tons of lime per year. In 1975, the property was owned by Richard Villeneuve of Greenmont Lumber Company, Underhill. In 1975 the South Burlington property was owned by Raymond R. Unsworth of South Burlington. At the time of his purchase, Unsworth planned to develop the property into a residential area. The South Burlington Zoning Commission, however, has since zoned the property "airport-industrial" (Carlisle 1975:13). The S. H. Weston & Company papers are at the UVM Special Collections Library, donated by Miss Ruth Boardman Catlin, descendent of S. H. Weston.

Following is a description of these two lime works sites; the Colchester side (CH-284) and the South Burlington (CH-282) side.

CH-284 Champlain Valley Lime Company (Colchester): Standing and other surface remains of lime kiln operations at Winooski Park were first inspected in 1978 and again many times later, noting each time the increased amount of vandalism and destruction of the structures and grounds. The standing ruins appeared about the same in 1989 as in the 1942 Sanborn map. Since abandonment in late 1971, the structures fell into such disrepair and desolation that resurrection of any operations

8-16. *Remains of the lime kiln building at Winooski Park after the site was stripped for scrap iron.*

would have required complete rebuilding. But in 1990, while the site was in the process of being nominated to the National Register of Historic Places for the significant quality of the ruins, the kilns and structures were completely destroyed for scrap. The buildings contained many pieces of machinery, gearing, heavy steel shafting, and possibly a rotary kiln. In another building were rolling and grinding machines. Some of the tons of firebrick that had fallen to the floor beneath the kilns were identified LEHIGH, BESSEMER, POWER, D-TYRONS, TYRONS, and ALUSITE 81 96. Many red DRURY bricks were also found among the debris.

Lime Kiln Road, which intersects Route 15 at St. Michael's College, leads southward toward the site. About 800 feet south of Route 15, the road is straddled by the two large, deep quarries. The quarry to the west is not as visible from the road. The bottoms of both quarries contain water, hiding the quarry floors from view. The white quarry walls rise horizontally from the dark water. At the eastern quarry, nearest the kilns, the water edge can be reached with little difficulty nearly beneath remains of the steel conveyer. An approximately 100-foot-long, 50-foot-wide tunnel was dug beneath Lime Kiln Road at one time to connect the two quarries (Carlisle 1975:13). The tunnel was not visible the day of inspection, however, due to the height of the water in the quarries. No fences guard the quarries; it is a dangerous place to wander about.

At the west end of the main kiln furnace building, where the steel conveyer reached the tops of the four kilns, was a five-story spiraling, rusted, steel stairway that groaned and swayed in the breeze. (In 1978, Chester Liebs climbed to the top; I climbed halfway. In 1986 I was not even tempted.) A number of poured concrete foundation holes were partially hidden in high grass and brush in the immediate surrounding area. Huge, rusty pieces of steel machinery (containing many beehives) of undetermined use and a smaller kind of firebrick-lined furnace also stood in the surrounding area; log and stone abutments hinted of possible loading platforms.

No surface evidence of the 19th-century lime kiln, which operated previous to the present structures, was found. The construction (and destruction) of the present structures, the exploitation and enlargement of the nearest quarry, and the original laying and periodic improvements of the nearby railroad, which passes between the kiln and quarry sites and the Winooski River, all combined to destroy any surface features of the former operations. The 1869 Beers map of Winooski Park shows the "S. H. Weston Lime Works" exactly on the spot of today's cavernous easternmost quarry. Archeological remains of any former operations, therefore, might not exist.

CH-282 Weston Lime Works (South Burlington): Surface remains of lime kiln operations at the north end of Airport Road near the Winooski River were also inspected in 1986. The area immediately east of Airport Road (it becomes Lime Kiln Road on the north side of the bridge) revealed many surface features relating to the lime kiln and quarry operations that existed there. This area is adjacent to the roadside pull-off area, along the border of which much domestic trash has been dumped. Just inside the trees from the parking area are the remains of an approximately 500-foot-long by 4- to 5-foot-high earthen tramway, running generally north-south and somewhat parallel to Airport Road.

At the south end of the tramway is the quarry, where the tramway gently slopes downward to ground level and the remains of a road continues the gentle downward slope into the quarry. The road proceeds into the quarry through a cut in the bedrock, then curves westerly and downward at a gentle slope to the floor of the quarry. The many small trees growing on the floor of the quarry indicate the number of years since abandonment; the quarry is not as wide or deep as those on the Colchester side of the river.

The top of the tramway is wide enough for carts to have been horse-drawn from the quarry to the lime kiln indicated by the Beers map as near its northern end. No surface remains of the lime kiln could be found at the north end of the tramway. A few dozen feet east, however, there is a wide, deep depression near the bottom of which are pieces of concrete abutments, recent trash, and some burned lime. A dozen feet southeast of the depression is a concrete foundation of undetermined use. The wide, north end of the depression drops off to the Winooski River; directly across the river are visible the remains of the

lime kilns that operated on that side. Considering the location of this depression nearly adjacent to where the lime kiln stood at the northern end of the tramway, could burned lime have been carted from the bottom of the kiln to a structure that stood in this depression, and then transported across the river by cable and cart arrangement to the railroad on the other side?

Southwest of the southern end of the tramway are some large stones that at first inspection appear to be foundation walls. But any pattern to the stones' placement seems to have been caused by their having been pushed or bulldozed. Truckloads of trash and earth have also been dumped in the proximity so that the stones may have been dumped here from someplace else and have no connection with the kiln operations. Just north of the stones and between them and the roadside parking area is a 35-foot-diameter concentration of white birch, but surface inspection and shallow testing failed to reveal any charcoal deposits.

Southeast of the tramway are pieces of glazed stone and red brick that appear similar to lime kiln lining material seen at other lime kilns in Vermont. The material is in about 6-foot-diameter surface concentrations, lying here and there in this area. No kiln foundations were found in the area of these finds; no surface features or depressions appeared to indicate a lime kiln existed here. From inspection of the area immediately adjacent and over the edge of the steep, 40-foot-high embankment it appeared that debris in this area had at one time been plowed over the edge, as if the whole area had been surface cleared except for the raised tramway. The kiln lining debris found here might have been dumped here after razing the kiln stack at the north end of the tramway.

The Central District

The central district, which consists of Addison, Orange, Rutland, and Windsor counties, contains 66 lime kiln sites, over half of all the known kiln sites in the state. Windsor County contains 34 sites, with 18 sites in the town of Plymouth alone.

ADDISON COUNTY

AD-409 Bristol Lime Kiln (Bristol): A standing lime kiln ruin was found a mile west of Bristol village in 1986. Information leading to the kiln was provided by Bob Carpenter of Bristol.

> The Lime Stone is found in many different parts of Bristol on the west side of the mountain and especially along near the West line of the town is to be found a broken disconnected range of ledges of an inferior quality of Lime, where Lime Kiln[s] have been built and lime burned, which was a substitute for a better article in an early day. But the best quality of lime is now to be had from Middlebury and New Haven, two adjoining towns, and of a quality so far superior to ours in Bristol that no kilns have for many years been burned. The time may come when these Lime Ledges may be considered valuable to be burned for agricultural purposes. There has no good marble as yet been discovered in Bristol (Munsill 1979:10).

The stack is an early commercial type measuring 20 by 20 feet square at its base and 20 feet high. Flat iron rods slotted near their ends are laid in the stonework at corners. There are

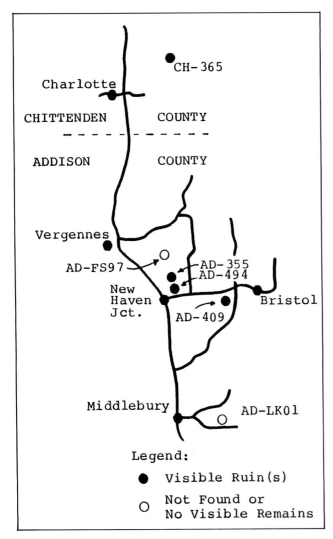

8-17. *Southern Chittenden and northern Addison counties lime kiln sites.*

8-18. *A magnificent lime kiln ruin at the end of a private driveway just west of Bristol village.*

face plates snug to the stone walls with beveled iron pins inserted into the slots, keeping the face plates, and thus the stone walls, from shifting outward. This type of iron binding, face plate, and beveled pin is similar to that found on blast furnaces at Troy, Pittsford, and Forest Dale.

Wood beams support the roof of the west archway, possibly the work arch, if the amount of burnt lime, stone lining, and brick found outside this arch for a number of feet is an indicator. The beams extend the width of the kiln and lie horizontally side by side, measuring about 10 by 12 inches thick.

Included in the breakdown of the stack were some firebrick and some red brick. On the face of the firebrick is marked McL&H CO TROY NY, indicating that the kiln operated into the 1880–1890 period.

AD-494 Lyman-Martell Lime Kilns (New Haven): Ruins of two lime kilns were initially visited on the property of Alson Martell on Quarry Road in the northwest part of New Haven in early 1990 in company with Mr. Martell, Bob West, and John Peters. John knew of the kilns and led us to Mr. Martell's house. The ruins were reinspected and recorded later in 1990.

Lime works along Quarry Road were developed as early as 1810, and land records refer to a quarry in operation in 1811. Thomas Perkins of Boston, one of a three-man partnership, may have provided the initial capital. John Lyman was owner in 1816, and Meeting house accounts show that he furnished most of the lime used for plaster and masonry. Quarry and kiln were used intermittently through the 1800s (and there may have been some connection with a kiln located not too far distant, in the corner of Ferrisburg south of Plank Road). Joseph W. Palmer listed a lime kiln in the county directory of 1881 (Farnsworth 1984:147).

Thomas Perkins of Boston, mentioned by Farnsworth, was one of a consortium of entrepreneurs who formed the Monkton Iron Company at Vergennes in 1809–1816 (see chapter 4, AD-146).

Limestone burned in these kilns came from the south-most of the two quarries identified in this vicinity on the USGS Monkton topographical map. The 1871 Beers map of New Haven indicates "Lime Ledges" directly in the vicinity of the quarries and lime kilns. The lime industry was reactivated early in the 20th century with an expansion to the west and construction of what became the Green Mountain Lime Company (AD-355). Limestone for burning in these later kilns came from the north-most of the quarries indicated on the USGS topographical map. The ruins are about 100 feet north of the Martell house, and between the house and Quarry Road. The area of the ruins is overgrown with dense undergrowth, making measuring and photography difficult. The undergrowth also makes it hard to see the perspective of the entire site. Between the kiln ruins and the Martell house are several hundred feet of exposed escarpment, up to 20 feet high in some places, which was probably an early quarry that provided limestone that was burned in the earlier of the two kilns at this site. The two kilns are built into an approximately 20-foot-high escarpment, which generally runs southwest-northeast.

The northerly ruin appears to be the older of the two lime kiln ruins, being more primitive in construction. It is made from coarse, smaller stones than those of the other ruin, and is a circular collapsed ruin with the usual round depression in the middle. Measurement of the ruin is difficult due to the degree of collapse and difficulty of determining wall locations, but it is estimated that the ruin is about 5 feet high from local ground level (local ground area is covered with scattered stonework) and about 9 feet inside diameter. Stonework connects the ruin to the escarpment behind it. Height of the escarpment here is about half as high as for the southerly ruin, about 20 feet away. No red brick, firebrick, or bindings were seen in association with this northerly ruin.

The southerly ruin is the more obvious of the two, standing about 12 feet high and 18 to 20 feet across the front. The outer wall is made of fine cut ashlar. Although the ruin is partially collapsed in the center, in many respects it resembles the Bristol lime kiln (AD-409). Breakdown is more severe on the southwest wall, where much red brick and firebrick lie about the sides of the ruin. One-inch-diameter iron binders protrude out the upper sides of the breakdown. The rods are end-threaded and contain 1¾-inch-square by 1-inch-thick nuts. On the northeast wall is a unique binding arrangement. Across the front of the kiln are two wood beams; the outer beam about 12 by 12 inches square, and the inner beam about 6 by 6 inches square. The beams supported the kiln wall above the archway, which is now collapsed behind the beams and slumped outward below them. Red bricks measured 8 by 3¾ by 2⅜ with no markings. The wedge-shaped firebricks measured 9 inches long by 2½ inches thick, 4½ inches wide at the wide end and 3¾ inches wide at the narrow end. All firebricks appear to be marked McL&H CO TROY NY.

About 10 feet north of the older ruin is an approximately 20- by 15-foot foundation wall, which served an unknown purpose. No obvious domestic or industrial materials were

8-19. *Spectacular ruins of four lime kilns just east of New Haven Junction. The base of the fifth kiln is at the left.*

found on the surface inside the foundation walls.

These lime kilns are two of many similar lime kilns that operated in Vermont in the 19th century and were predecessor operations to the Green Mountain Lime Company (AD-355), just west over the hill about a half-mile away.

AD-355 Green Mountain Lime Company (New Haven): Ruins of the Green Mountain Lime Company were found in 1985, about a mile east of New Haven Junction. The kilns are about a quarter-mile south of Lime Kiln Road, on the property of Dennis Sparling.

Early in the present century the industry was revitalized. The Brewer family purchased another 64 acres lying west of the Palmer lot and went into business as the Green Mountain Lime Company in 1907. At this time a spur track was built to connect the quarry with the Rutland Railroad. After World War II, the property passed to John Dalglish and in 1950 to Vermont Associated Lime Industries, a company with plants at several other locations in western Vermont. For a decade or so the business flourished. Eight men under foreman Howard Beckwith could produce 6 to 10 tons of agricultural lime in an hour and 15 tons of hydrate in an 8-hour day. Powered machinery included quarry equipment and rock crushers. In the production of hydrate, finer pieces of rock were subjected to a hammer mill crusher and then conveyed to an upstairs air separator, which pulled fine materials to the top and deposited waste at the bottom. Water was then mixed in (at an approximate rate of 50 gallons to 1900 pounds), the product machine-bagged, and shipped by rail. Kilns for burning the stone were abandoned when wood for firing them became hard to get, but materials were trucked to a coal fired kiln at Winooski. Business faltered in the mid-1960s and closed soon after (Farnsworth 1984:147).

In 1910, Perkins reported three kilns in operation, capable of producing 350 barrels of lime per day (Perkins 1910:349). Operations in 1916 were owned by The Brewer Company of Worcester, Massachusetts, with W. J. Dandrow, Superintendent. The limestone quarried was difficult to burn but yielded the best-quality lime. By now, five wood- and coal-burning kilns were in operation, using the Eldred Process by which the

kilns were closed at the top and "down-comers" brought the carbonic acid to the hearths. This partially checked the combustion to give a more uniform heat. The quarry was connected with the kilns by a horse tramway. The kilns had a production capacity of 12 tons each per day, but labor shortages prevented maintaining that capacity (Jacobs 1918:162-163). Among brands produced by the company were Chemical Hydrate, Mason's Hydrate, Snow Fluff Spraying Hydrate, Agricultural Hydrate, and Sure Crop (Jacobs 1937:19). It was not long before limestone was shipped in from Winooski because the local quarry could not keep up with the demand of the five kilns.

Stone Lime.

THE subscriber has on hand and will keep constantly for sale, at the marble quarry, about a mile and a half east of this village, near Millan Stowell's, on the road to Dea. Boyce's, a first rate article of Stone Lime, which will be sold on reasonable terms. NATHAN MYRICK.
Middlebury, June 30, 1841.   8tf.

8-20. Middlebury People's Press, *Middlebury, Dec. 14, 1841.*

The steel shells of four of the kilns still stand in an east-west line; the fifth ruin, at the eastern end, is totally collapsed. Much brickwork and hardware remain to aid in interpretation of the ruins. Concrete foundation slabs mark the locations of buildings that once were associated with the operations.

Uphill and immediately south of these ruins (between the five iron shell ruins and the water-filled quarry) are possible collapsed remains of two earlier kilns. These could have operated transitionally between the demise of the Lyman-Martell kilns (AD-494) and the more modern five lime kilns at this site.

The 1963 USGS Monkton map shows a spur track leading east from the main line to the kiln site; only an isolated trestle now stands in the middle of the field to mark where the track ran. The four tall, surviving, rusting iron shells are visible southward across the valley from Lime Kiln Road.

AD-LK05 Gibbs Lime Kiln (New Haven): East of Beldens

STONE LIME

Kept constantly on hand and for sale by the subscriber. Kiln two miles east of Middlebury village near David Boyce,s. The Public may be assured in the purchase of Lime this Kiln that they will get a first rate article, equal in all respects to any in the County and in whiteness far surpassing any other.

NELSON CHITTENDE N.

Middlebury Oct. 23· 1846.

8-21. Northern Galaxy, *Middlebury, June 15, 1847.*

Marble Works.

THE subscribers respectfully inform the public that the Marble works lately occupied by Caso & Spalding, are now in operation, and they are prepared to furnish all kinds of

Sawed Marble, caps and sills,

Tomb-stones, Monuments,

&c. &c.

at short notice.

STONE LIME,

Kept constantly on hand.

GIBBS & CHITTENDEN.

Middlebury, July 19, 1843.   11;y1

8-22. Northern Galaxy, *Middlebury, Feb. 7, 1844.*

was a marble quarry known in the late 19th century as the Cutler marble quarry, where Isaac Gibbs burned lime at an earlier time. The quarry was also known as the North Middlebury quarry and also the Old Middlebury quarry (*Marble Border* 1885:24, 48). The quarry was reported as "celebrated for furnishing excellent lime" (Adams 1846:234-235). Theodatus Phelps originally opened the quarry in 1830 and built a mill for sawing and processing the marble. Gibbs owned the quarry from 1851 to 1861, followed by others until the marble was exhausted and the quarry abandoned about 1885 (Farnsworth 1984:148, 231).

The 1871 Beers map of New Haven shows "Old Middlebury Quarry Co." about two miles east of Beldens on the north (New Haven) side of the Middlebury-New Haven town line. The quarry is not identified on the current USGS map, which does show Muddy Branch flowing northward through the quarry area.

Inspection of the area in 1991 resulted in finding the main quarry, stone tailings, and foundation remains of the marble mill, but no evidence of a lime kiln.

AD-FS97 Plank Road Lime Kiln (Ferrisburgh): An unsuccessful search for a lime kiln in the vicinity of a quarry along the Old Plank Road was made in 1987. A kiln is indicated in the 1871 Beers map of New Haven, but just outside in Ferrisburgh. Only the quarry is indicated in the Beers map of Ferrisburgh.

The site is a low limestone escarpment that might have been worked at an early time. There was no sign of a kiln ruin or remains. The immediate area of the site is about 100 yards south of the Old Plank Road; the intervening area is a cornfield. Reclamation of the land for farming and plowing probably destroyed any surface remains. There might have been some connection with this kiln and those of the Green Mountain Lime Company (AD-355) about a mile south.

AD-LK03 Chaffee Lime Kiln (Granville): Limestone on William C. Chaffee's farm in the north part of the town was analyzed in 1857 as being good for the manufacture of lime (Hitchcock et al. 1861:695). Although this is a vague reference to a lime kiln somewhere, there might still be a kiln ruin nearby waiting to be found. No attempt had been made to inspect this site.

AD-LK02 Marsh Lime Kiln (Hancock): Lime was burned south of the village due west of the bridge over the White River and about 750 feet above the valley floor, on the property of D. G. Marsh (Dale 1915:19-20). The Beers map indicates a limestone ledge at approximately this location.

This kiln site is suspiciously close to a reported and yet unlocated charcoal kiln site (see chapter 6, AD-CK01). There might be both charcoal and lime kiln ruins here, or maybe just the lime kiln ruin. When the area was unsuccessfully searched for remains of the charcoal kiln in 1989, it was not known that a lime kiln site was also here.

AD-LK01 Quarry Road Lime Kiln (Middlebury): A lime kiln is shown on the 1857 map of Addison County, about two miles east of Middlebury Village on the south side of Quarry Road. The site appears to be about 500 feet west of Muddy Brook. The kiln is not shown in the 1871 Beers map of Middlebury although the map does show the Vermont Marble Quarry just northwest, on the north side of Quarry Road, which might have had some connection with the kiln.

A drive-by inspection of the site was made in 1991 and nothing resembling a kiln ruin could be seen from the road. The field is fenced and permission will be obtained at a later date for closer ground inspection.

AD-318 Huntley Lime Kilns (Leicester): The lime kiln reported built by J. E. Higgins, John B. Matot, and L. P. White in 1852 might have been the first lime kiln in town. Higgins eventually ran the operation alone, and after his death the business was run by Conant & Bascom. John A. Conant managed the business and eventually took Charles Dennison as a partner, who in 1883 controlled the interest alone (Smith 1886:480).

The 1857 map of Addison County shows the marble quarry and lime kiln on the south side of the road, just west of the railroad station. By 1861, two kilns were operating, run by the Brandon Lime and Marble Company and making 25,000 barrels of lime annually. The lime was sold to the Boston Gas Light Company (2½ tons daily usage), the Waltham Bleachery Company, the Somerville Bleachery Company, and soap manufacturers at the Rumford Chemical Works at Providence (Hitchcock et al. 1861:750-751). Owners in 1886 were J. W. Buell of Orwell and O. C. Huntley, who operated the kilns under the name Huntley & Buell, making an average of 75 barrels of lime a day (Smith 1886:480).

245

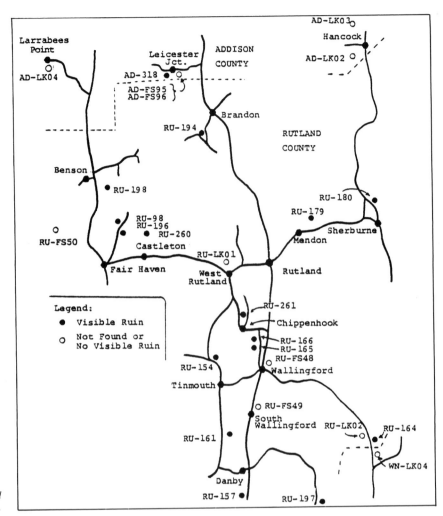

8-23. *Southern Addison County and Rutland County lime kiln sites.*

8-24. *Lime kiln ruin at Leicester Junction, which operated in the 1850s to the 1930s.*

In 1918 the operations were owned by Harry B. Huntley and the quarry had grown to 450 feet long, 125 feet wide, and 75 feet deep. The two kilns were fueled by wood and had a daily capacity of 10 tons each. Burned lime was used mainly for chemical purposes but the finer quality went for fertilizer. Price was $11.00 per ton and $2.00 per barrel (Jacobs 1918:163).

The kilns operated into the 1930s, burning dolomite from a quarry that was located immediately south of the kiln. Lime from the kiln was used at tanneries for preparing hides, at paper mills, for fertilizer, and for mortar. Annual capacity of the works was 7,000 tons (Oliver Huntley to author, March 11, 1984). It was shipped west on the Addison Railroad to Larrabees Point, thence over a wood trestle across Lake Champlain to Ticonderoga, New York. The railroad was abandoned in 1951 (Shaughnessy 1981:164).

The ruins are on the south side of the highway, west of the Otter Creek, and were inspected in 1984. They are characterized by stone walls, foundations, and the remains of two brick-lined iron shells. One shell is standing; the other has tipped over and rests on its side. The bases of both kilns are intact. The late Oliver C. Huntley, descendent of O.C. Huntley mentioned earlier, lived just northeast of the kiln site and was interviewed about the ruin. He worked at the "newer" lime kilns (AD-FS96) located just southeast, which he managed for a number of years. Students from Middlebury College frequent the ruins as part of their geology studies, courtesy of the owner who preserves the ruins.

AD-FS95 Powers Lime Works (Leicester): About 100 yards south of the highway at Leicester Junction, on the east side of Otter Creek, George Bascom and W. Powers built a lime kiln around 1876, which was immediately purchased and operated by George O. Swinington. It produced about 20 barrels of lime daily (Smith 1886:480). The 1871 Beers map of Leicester shows the Powers Lime Works just south of the road and the quarry about a half-mile south. In 1910, the Leicester Marble-Lime Company, managed by Swinington, produced about 25,000 barrels of lime per year (Perkins 1910:351). The site was not inspected because the access road was chained and posted (1985).

AD-FS96 Swinington Lime Kilns (Leicester): The three lime kilns of this company were erected in 1925, a half-mile south of AD-FS95.

We found a small compact plant where they quarried, burned, and packed in bags a variety of products made from select limestone.

The quarry has been in operation intermittently, ever since 1800 when they used ox carts to haul stone to the retort where it was baked. This original retort, or kiln, is still on the property [AD-318] and although not in use still looks good. It is of stone construction and was used from 1800 to 1863 when it was replaced by a steel kiln.

In 1925 new owners erected three new lime kilns and these are operating 24 hours per day, 7 days per week, and 52 weeks per year.

The stone is quarried in small pieces, loaded in dump carts by two Oliver tractor loaders, one a model 70 wheel tractor with Ware loader and the other a model A crawler with Ware loader, and hauled out of the pit over rails on a steep incline.

The best of the stone is used to make chemical lime for the paper industry; the next grade is used for agricultural quicklime; and what we assume are "leavings" are used as crushed rock for road building and concrete.

The best stone is dumped into the top of the kilns and baked at 2300 degrees for four or five days; that is, they dump continuously into the top and draw off the finished product continuously, taking the required time to pass through the furnaces.

Two firemen are on shift at all times to keep the fires going, using about 100 cords of wood and 25 tons of coal per week.

The plant loads about 200 tons of bagged material into [railroad] cars each week for shipment to many parts of the country. The plant is owned by Dallock Sales Co. of New York City and they do all the merchandising from the main office (*New England Construction* Oct. 1947:39).

The kilns operated to the 1950s and only the kiln bases remain (Oliver Huntley to author, March 11, 1984). The site was not inspected because the access road was chained and posted (1985).

AD-LK04 Peake Lime Kiln (Shoreham): The history of Shoreham discloses that "at an early day there were several kilns for burning lime, but none is now made" (Goodhue 1861:94). One of these early kilns might have been that south of Larrabees Point, on Lake Champlain 12 miles west of Leicester Junction. In a discussion of the value of firestone, its use in the arch of a lime kiln at Larrabees Point is also mentioned (Adams 1845:37), providing a possible early date for the kiln. Although the 1857 Addison County map shows "Marble Quarry & Lime Kiln, R.W. Peake" at the south end of the point, it was referred to as "an old limekiln" only a few years later (Hitchcock et al. 1861:286). Some limestone quarried here was also used as a flux for smelting by the ironworks at Port Henry, New York (Perkins 1933:146), but no mention is made of lime production here in various early-19th-century agricultural and industrial census reports.

Permission to visit the quarry in 1991 was denied by the property resident so confirmation cannot be made whether any kiln remains exist in the vicinity of the quarry. The few residents queried at Larrabees Point knew of no history of lime burning and did not remember seeing any resemblance of a kiln ruin in the vicinity. Larrabees Point became a major lake port and trading center with the opening of the Champlain Canal, and except for the modern cable-guided ferry that still operates between the point and Ticonderoga, New York, the little historic community has retained most of its 19th-century character.

At the state boating access area on the south side of the cove, south of the point, the Addison Railroad once crossed Lake Champlain to Ticonderoga on wood trestles and a floating barge. North from the access across the shallow cove toward the quarry, the tops of wood pilings protrude from the water, possible remains of a small tram railroad that carried marble from the quarry across the cove to the Addison Railroad.

ORANGE COUNTY

OR-FS12 Limehurst Lake Lime Kiln (Williamstown): During the mid-19th century, the bottom of Lime Pond and an area for several acres around the pond to the depth of 18 feet were found to contain an extensive bed of shell marl, which was dug and burned for fertilizer (Hemenway vol. 2 1871:1140). In the 1830s a mill operator widened the outlet of the pond in hopes of adding power to his waterwheels, only to have the pond run away and empty (Swift 1977:332). Might this event have exposed the marl? The marl was molded into small bricks and dried before burning (Hitchcock et al. 1861:805).

Lime Pond was about two miles south of the village and was renamed Limehurst Lake; today it is a popular private campground and swimming area. While camping there in 1985, no evidence of shell marl or a lime kiln was found.

RUTLAND COUNTY

RU-194 Seager Hill Lime Kiln (Brandon): A lime kiln was found in 1989 at the base of the southwest slope of Seager Hill, five miles southwest of Brandon village. Information leading to location of the kiln came from the lime kiln indication on the 1854 map of Rutland County. There is no indication of the kiln in the 1869 Beers map of Brandon.

The ruin is directly visible from the roadway; the center of the ruin being about 10 feet from the edge of the pavement and built into the side of Seager Hill. It measured 11 feet in its widest diameter; depth to the floor of breakdown is about 7 feet. A small quarry lies about 50 feet uphill from the kiln, but a much larger quarry lies another 50 to 100 feet to the southeast. A narrow path leads from one quarry to the top of the lime kiln.

RU-179 Mendon Lime Kiln (Mendon): Ruins of a mid-19th-century lime kiln were found in Mendon in 1987 through the 1869 Beers map of Mendon. The kiln ruin is about two miles north of the intersection of Old Turnpike Road (Elbow Road on the USGS map) and Route 4 in northern Mendon, and is a half-mile beyond the developed section of road.

The ruin stands on the side of a hill that drops off at the edge of the road. Its square stone walls are about 10 feet high; the east wall is collapsed. Approximate interior width is 8 feet. A small quarry, which possibly provided stone for construction of the kiln, is about 50 feet to the northeast. The quarries are 500 feet east of the road, and because of the magnesia in the marble, it was shipped to a paper mill at Bellows Falls (Dale 1915:20). As far as is known, the limestone was never used for marble (Perkins 1933:228).

RU-180 River Road Lime Kiln (Sherburne): The ruin of an early lime kiln was found in 1987 alongside River Road. General information about this site was provided by Sandy Partridge of Proctor. Specific directions were given by Charles Prior at the Sherburne Grange, where we stopped for directions.

The kiln ruin was found two miles north of the River Road and Routes 4 and 100 intersection. It is in a clearing, very visible from the road, and is built into the side of the hill. The ruin consists mainly of what appears to have been the final charge, still in the kiln, with almost all stones that made up the kiln structure missing (most likely cannibalized due to the kiln's proximity to the road). Only a part of the back wall appears to remain, the top of which is about flush with the surface of the ground. Mr. Prior said that he was born in 1906 and does not remember the kiln ever being in operation.

RU-198 Howard Hill Lime Kiln (Benson): The ruin of this lime kiln was found in 1989 through the 1854 map of Rutland County, which shows a lime kiln next to the house of "A. Pitts." The kiln is on the Walker farm, immediately across the road from the large barn, about a quarter-mile southwest of the tiny community of Howard Hill. The kiln was apparently square when in operation although fill and hillside collapse cover the back and side walls. The front (south) exposed wall measured 20 feet wide, with the lower half-dozen layers of cut stone still in place. The inside lining rises behind and above the front wall, indicating that the kiln stood at least 12 to 15 feet high at one time. Quarry for the kiln is a limestone ledge that parallels the north side of the road. Dates of operation of the kiln are unknown except for the notation on the 1854 map. From the size of the ruin, this appears to have been more of a commercial operation than a local farmer's lime kiln.

RU-260 Bomoseen Lime Kiln (Castleton): A lime kiln ruin was pointed out to Professor Bill Jordan of Castleton State College in 1991 by a realtor who referred to it as an "Indian oven." The site is about a quarter-mile southwest of the vacation community of Bomoseen, on the east shore of Lake Bomoseen.

The ruin is on the west side of a low hill, about 50 feet south of a private dirt road between Lake Bomoseen and Pine Pond. It measures 15 feet wide across by 7 feet high, in reasonably good condition. Inside is an intact 8-foot-diameter by 5-foot-deep hearth, sections of which are glazed. Around the front and sides of the ruin is breakdown, about four to five feet high, which indicates that the kiln was much taller when in operation. It was built either into the side of the hill behind it, or with a small space between it and the hill; it is difficult to determine which from the amount of loose stone about. On the ground above and behind the ruin is what appears to be a pile of stone waiting to be charged into the kiln. About 100 feet further behind and uphill from the kiln is an overgrown limestone quarry. The kiln appears to have been one of an early commercial variety, possibly operating before the Civil War period.

8-25. *Scotch Hill lime kiln ruin, found alongside the road amid slate tailings.*

No reference can be found regarding limestone quarrying or burning in the vicinity. The ruin stands on a 100-acre tract that was for sale at the time of the inspection. Bomoseen is a high recreation and development area.

RU-98 Scotch Hill Lime Kiln (Fair Haven): This ruin is five miles north of Fair Haven, next to a slate quarry on the west side of Scotch Hill Road. The Fair Haven history mentions a "lime kiln quarry" that operated near the town line toward West Castleton (Adams 1870:214). But it is unknown for sure whether this or another quarry is the object of the statement since there are many quarries in that area and many of the referenced names are associated with more than one slate quarry.

The kiln ruin was initially found in 1985 as part of a search for charcoal kilns that are indicated in the 1869 Beers maps of Fair Haven and Castleton (the charcoal kiln ruins were not found). No limestone quarry could be found in the area of the ruin. Might slate-quarrying activity in the vicinity during the ensuing 100 years have excavated and/or buried it?

8-26. *Lime kiln ruin at Fair Haven, made of some of the abundant slate in the vicinity.*

RU-196 Briggs Lime Kilns (Fair Haven): Ruins of two lime kilns were found east off Scotch Hill Road in 1989, about a half-mile south of RU-98. The ruins are adjacent, about 50 feet off the road in a low brush area directly across the road from a long-abandoned slate quarry. This might have been the lime kiln referenced in Adams, the "lime kiln quarry," except that the kilns do not appear directly associated with any quarry (Adams 1870:214).

The ruins sit at right angles to each other. The northern ruin faces east and is made more of flatter stone; the southern ruin faces south and is made more of rough stone. The latter ruin also has what appears to be a collapsed opening inside the back wall, as if connected underground at one time to the adjacent kiln or maybe to some draft-producing shaft. No obvious limestone quarry or outcrop could be found in the vicinity.

RU-FS50 Doran Lime Kiln (West Haven): Lime was burned about 1,000 feet west of Mrs. Paul Doran's house, just off Doran Road, based on information she provided. Inspection of the site and vicinity in 1985 turned up nothing directly related to a lime kiln, but there is a limestone ledge and a surface feature that appeared to indicate the existence here of a structure at one time. The site is about a half-mile north of RU-99, a blast furnace ruin.

RU-LK01 Vermont Marble Company (West Rutland): Marble dressing produces a large amount of waste marble, some of which was shipped from the Vermont Marble Company (Vermarco) to the blast furnaces at Port Henry, New York. Attempts to burn the marble waste in vertical kilns were unsuccessful because the rock became granulated by the heat and choked the kilns. The rotary kiln, which looked like a long smokestack lying on its side, was installed in 1916 by Vermarco at West Rutland. It converted the waste marble into burned and hydrated lime on a large scale under the name Vermarco Quick and Hydrated Lime. The main kiln building, which stood on the east side of Marble Street about a mile north of Route 4, was made of steel, and was 48 by 422 feet. Two other buildings 30 by 48 feet and 20 by 32 feet housed the gas producer equipment and coal storage. The rotary kiln was 8 feet in diameter by 120 feet long, made of 5/8-inch steel plates, and was lined with firebrick from one end to the other. This 118-ton unit revolved on bearings at about one revolution every three minutes, driven by a 30-horsepower motor (see chapter 7, "Vermont Lime Kilns," for a complete description of this rotary kiln).

The 1922 Sanborn fire insurance map of West Rutland shows the lime plant north of the main marble mill with the long rotary kiln inside. The rotary kiln also appears in the 1929 map but not in later maps. A second rotary kiln that was planned for the plant was obviously never installed. Lime was last mentioned being burned at Vermont Marble Company in the 1925–1926 *Report of the State Geologist.* No attempt has been made to inspect this site.

RU-261 Chippenhook Lime Kiln (Clarendon): The collapsed ruin of a lime kiln was found just north of Chippenhook village in 1991, through a reference in the history of Clarendon, which stated that "The remains of a lime kiln and several foundations exist north of the present McLellan property where the early Wescotts and Priests supposedly lived" (Potter 1982:102). The ruin was pinpointed to the north side of a knoll, about a half-mile north of the McLellan property (David E. Potter letter to author, October 1, 1990).

The ruin was found about a half-mile northeast of the West Clarendon Cemetery. It is 200 feet into the pine woods that border the western edge of an open meadow. In the woods are many north-south outcrops of limestone, some of which show signs of having been worked. The kiln ruin is on the larger outcrop, about 100 feet from its northern end. The ruin is circular with its walls caved in. Excavating could probably determine an accurate diameter but there is no visible border to the ruin as it was found. The overall ruin is about 6 to 8 feet in diameter and is depressed in the middle about 2 to 3 feet below the sides. All about the ruin are pieces of white, burned limestone. Some of the limestone that made up the walls of the kiln is pinkish in color. What remains of the ruin

8-27. *A lime kiln ruin in a pasture at the Maplebrook Farm in Tinmouth. The front wall was opened several years ago to rescue a cow, which had fallen through the hole at the top of the kiln.*

appears to indicate that it operated more as a farm-type lime kiln.

RU-154 Maplebrook Farm Lime Kiln (Tinmouth): Ruins of a small lime kiln were found in 1986 in northwestern Tinmouth. The kiln ruin stands in the woodland fringe of a pasture, a mile east of the junction of Routes 133 and 140, and about 200 feet north of Route 140. Information about the ruin was provided by Trip Westcott (Pittsford), met a week before while searching for the Gibbs and Cooley ironworks at Pittsford Mills.

The kiln ruin is conical-shaped and constructed of stone. Inside height is about 8 feet from the floor, which contains stones from partial breakdown of the front wall. Inside diameter at this false floor is about 8 feet; at a point 3 feet above the floor, inside diameter is about 7 feet. Inside diameter of the top opening is 4 feet. A vertical hole the height of the kiln cut into its north wall is 28 inches wide. Wall thickness at the opening is 41 inches. The kiln is constructed of what appears to be slate. Mortar can be seen between some of the stones.

A sketch made by Westcott showed the kiln built into an embankment, with a "keyhole" opening and circular hole at the top. The owner of Maplebrook Farm said that about five years previous (1981), one of his cows fell into a round stone-lined hole in the ground and he had to break through one wall to free her—thus the front top-to-bottom opening today.

RU-161 Crow Hill Farm Lime Kilns (Tinmouth): The ruins of two stone-built lime kilns incorporated into a single unit were visited on Clark Mountain in southeastern Tinmouth. Guided to their "pile of stones" by Caleb and Louise Scott, owners of Crow Hill Farm, we inspected the site in 1986.

About 200 to 300 feet west of the kilns are some holes and a large depression set back into the hill that appear to be remains of iron mining in the area. Local tradition indicates a number of iron mines operating along this ridge in the 19th century, and we found many pieces of iron ore in the vicinity of these holes. It was initially thought that the kilns might have been roasting ovens, to burn impurities and moisture out of the iron

ore so it could be pulverized and separated. But the kilns are somewhat uphill from the mines, which would mean carrying the heavy ore uphill. No iron ore or charcoal was found in the immediate vicinity of the kiln ruins.

The ruins are generally 3 to 6 feet high. Inside diameter of the north ruin is 9½ to 10½ feet (oval) and that of the south ruin 6½ to 8½ feet. The entire two-kiln ruin is about 35 feet wide, not counting an 84-foot-long stone wall that extends south from the ruin. The insides of the kilns show no signs of charring or glazing, but the face of the stone lining does appear parched, more so than the faces of stones on the outside walls.

Quarry for the kilns is a limestone escarpment immediately adjacent to the kilns. Small nugget-size pieces of burned lime were found a few inches below the surface, a few feet in front (west) of the kilns. It was probably a farmer's lime kiln, providing lime for fertilizer for farming operations. Except that it is a two-component kiln, it bears a strong resemblance in size and appearance to the Maplebrook Farm lime kiln (RU-154).

RU-166 Lime Kilns at "The Cobble" (Clarendon): The ruins of two associated lime kilns were located in 1986 about 1¼ miles northwest of Wallingford village. "The Cobble" is the property of Castleton State College, donated by Bud Crossman, who owns the adjoining farm on the south. According to Crossman, the heavily wooded cobble contains a rare type of fern that inhabits the boundary of the base of the cobble, where the shady hilly cobble interfaces with the sunny, flat land. He said that the college students visit the cobble annually.

The two kiln ruins are on the steep southwest slope of the cobble, at the edge of an open hay field. The larger, which is in better condition, is 8 by 12 feet inside diameter (oval-shaped) and lined with stone. Its highest wall section is 8 feet high (from the inside floor); the inside walls are glazed. The lining appears to be sandstone. The smaller kiln is about 20 feet east, on the same general slope, and is 4½ by 6 feet in diameter (also oval) and about 2 feet deep. This smaller unit may have been the original kiln, and its stone walls cannibalized for construction of the second, larger unit. No burned lime was found in the direct vicinity of the kilns.

About 50 feet immediately uphill of the kilns is an outcrop of limestone showing tool-working marks. A road leads from the west side of the kilns, uphill past the quarry, and ends about 50 feet farther uphill. Limestone might have been quarried immediately west of this uphill area also.

Crossman said that his 83-year-old mother (in 1986) remembers as a little girl the burning of lime here (1915–1920?). He guessed that some of the lime was made for mortar, used in construction of local stone houses.

RU-165 Bromley Farm Lime Kiln (Wallingford): A lime kiln ruin was found in 1986 on the farm of Steve Bromley from information provided by Bud Crossman, owner of the adjoining farm to the north (RU-166).

The ruin was found on the south slope of a gentle hill in a cow pasture, on top of which is a cornfield. The ruin is about 9 by 12 feet in diameter (oval shape), lined with glazed stone, and is approximately 6 feet deep. A small tree grows inside the ruin and some burnt lime is on the ground beside the ruin. From its small size and proximity to farms, it appears to have been an early- to mid-19th-century farmer's lime kiln for burning limestone for fertilizer. Quarry for the kiln is about 40 feet uphill of the ruin. Bromley was unaware of the existence of the ruin, but very interested in finding out about it.

RU-FS48 Village Lime Kiln (Wallingford): The 1869 Beers map of Wallingford shows a lime kiln in the village, on the east side of the main street (Route 7) between Franklin and Maple streets.

Although just north of the center of the village but still within Wallingford (and probably because of that), no kiln remains were expected to be found when searched for in 1990. On the east side of the intersection of Maple Street and Route 7 is a significant limestone outcrop about 25 feet east of the highway, behind a low stone wall and some dense underbrush. About 50 feet south is a house. The vicinity of the limestone outcrop would appear to have been a logical site for the lime kiln to operate and this area coincides with the indication in the Beers map. But much slash and debris are piled at the base of the outcrop, preventing any surface analysis. Highway widening, yard landscaping, and construction of the low stone wall (cannibalized from the lime kiln ruin?) probably contributed to the destruction of the kiln ruin.

RU-FS49 Kelley and Wellman Lime Kiln (Wallingford): The 1869 Beers map of Wallingford indicates the lime kiln of (W. W.) Kelley and (A. J.) Wellman about a mile north of South Wallingford, between the railroad and the Otter Creek. A. J. Wellman is listed in the Beers business notices as a South Wallingford lime dealer.

The area between the Otter Creek railroad bridge and Route 7 was inspected in 1990 without finding any evidence of the lime kiln. Sometime after 1871, Kelley and Wellman probably decided to exit the lime-burning business and concentrate on quarrying marble. At this time a spur railroad track was laid southward from the main line on the west side of the Otter Creek. This abandoned bed with its pattern of railroad ties was followed from the main line south about a quarter-mile to the backyard of a house near Route 7. The main quarry is just on the other side (west side) of the highway. The abandoned kiln either got buried under the railroad bed or, more likely, was razed and used for fill on which the spur track was laid. The main line also appears to have been raised to allow for the higher bridge over the Otter Creek. Local residents and property owners who are familiar with trails in the vicinity and local traditions know of no lime kiln ruins nearby.

RU-157 Vermont Lime Products Corporation (Mount Tabor): The ruins of three lime kilns were found in 1985 west of Route 7 in Mount Tabor, a mile south of Danby village. The kilns were operated by the Vermont Lime Products Corporation, and operated from 1922 to the early 1930s:

The Vermont Lime Products Corporation was organized in 1922. The three controlling directors were J. Frank Burke, P. F. McCormack, and J. W. Linnihan. The business was located about a mile south of Danby Village, in that part of Mt. Tabor called the South End. Some of the property was purchased from Mr. and Mrs. John Zulinski but the major portion was purchased from the Danby Marble and Lime Company, whose agent was Clark M. Potter. The quarry

8-28. *The Vermont Lime Products Corporation at Mount Tabor in this 1920s–1930s view. Note rail car above middle kiln. Road at right is today's Route 7 (courtesy Vermont Historical Society).*

was opened and the kilns and buildings were erected on the west side of Route 7. The office was on the east side of the highway. There was a railroad siding from the Rutland Railroad across the highway to the storage buildings. The business consisted of the quarrying of limestone and manufacturing of lime products. This operation was carried on until the early 1930s. In 1949, the town of Mt. Tabor took the property over for delinquent taxes (Crosby et al. 1976:45).

The ruins consist of the bases of the three kilns, made of poured concrete. Each base is 12 feet square and about 7 feet high. The north and south walls have 6-foot-wide by 6-foot-high openings, arched at the top. The east and west walls have 3-foot-wide by 2½-foot-high openings, square at the top. A round, approximately 8-foot-diameter vertical hole extends completely through the base. The ruins are in an east-west line, about 5 feet apart, and 76 feet west of the highway in tall brush behind a line of trees. About 15 feet south of the ruins is an approximately 12-foot-high concrete wall that parallels the kiln ruins. The immediate vicinity of the kiln ruins is littered with automotive and other miscellaneous hardware discard, but no obvious lime kiln hardware.

A large excavation a hundred feet north is today the town's trash center. No evidence of the other lime works buildings and the spur railroad that serviced the kilns was found, destroyed by Route 7 construction and later by earth moving for the trash center. The property owner in 1985 was the late Alfred Bushee, who lived in a house behind the ruins (the house burned to the ground sometime before 1990). Mrs. Breton, who lives about a mile south, said her house was formerly the old marble and lime company office, and was moved as part of highway realignments in the 1950s. Why this lime works was not mentioned in Perkins' or Jacobs' reports on the state's lime industries for the 1920s and 1930s is a mystery.

RU-197 Devils Den Lime Kiln (Mount Tabor): A lime kiln ruin was found near Devils Den in Mount Tabor in 1989 from the lime kiln indication on the 1854 map of Rutland County. Specific information that located the ruin was provided by Bill Badger of Manchester, who had previously found it while hiking in the area. This small ruin lies just downhill and around the corner from the Devils Den escarpment, alongside U.S. Forest Road 10 and a few dozen feet uphill from the old road to Weston.

The kiln was built into the hill with its opening facing downhill. A tree is growing directly out of the kiln opening. The ruin is about 4 feet wide by 6 feet long; walls on the better side rise about 2 feet. Stone for the lime kiln most likely came from the nearby limestone ledge.

RU-LK02 Fuller Lime Kiln (Mount Holly): Marble was burned about four miles southeast of Mechanicsville (today's Belmont) on the road to Weston. The locale was known as the Fuller farm, which later became the C. D. Edgerton farm. Marble openings were on both sides of the road: northwest, southeast, and southwest of the house (Dale 1915:21-22). The kiln operated in the 1860s and intermittently afterward (Perkins 1933:228).

This description might explain an unidentified circular stone ruin (VT-RU-164) that Noel Fritzinger of Weston led us to in 1986, about 50 feet off the east side of Route 155 just north of the county line. The ruin is about 10 feet in diameter, and

built into a small rise. The eastern section of wall, which appears more flat than circular, rises about 7 feet above the inside floor, in which wall breakdown has accumulated. An approximately 1-foot-diameter tree is growing in the 3- to 4-foot-thick north wall. What appears to be an entrance way is in the south wall, which faces on the dirt road that leads uphill behind the ruin. The general configuration of the ruin suggests a lime kiln, but no burned lime or quarry (or charcoal or slag) was found in the vicinity, nor are the inside walls of the structure parched or burned. Cheese being a popular product in the early history of Mount Holly prompted the thought that the ruin might have been used for roadside cold storage. The farm of D.W. Fuller is indicated in the 1869 Beers map of Mount Holly, about a quarter-mile north on the west side of the highway, where a cellar hole was found in 1990. Outcrops of limestone are everywhere in the vicinity of the cellar hole.

WINDSOR COUNTY

WN-LK04 Shattuck Farm Lime Kiln (Weston): Lime was burned at the Shattuck farm, which was about three miles south-southwest of the Fuller farm (RU-LK02) in Mount Holly (Dale 1915:24). According to the 1869 Beers map of Weston, however, the Shattuck farm is three miles south-south*east* of the Fuller farm. Could this be a typographical error in Dale's report? The area three miles south-southwest was inspected in 1990, and turned out to be just south of the Weston Priory. Inspection of an area in the vicinity of the Shattuck farm was made in the spring of 1992. No evidence of the lime kiln was found in either inspection. Work continues on finding this site.

WN-LK02 East Bethel Lime Kiln (Bethel): A lime kiln ruin remains hidden about a mile southwest of East Bethel, near a crossroads and the Quarry School (Dale 1915:22). Another reference has the kiln a bit farther south, west of the brook and southwest of the crossroads (Morrill and Chaffee 1964:7). Inspections of the area in the fall of 1989 and spring of 1992 showed some limestone ledges but no lime kiln ruin. Work also continues on finding this site.

WN-124 Liberty Hill Lime Kiln (Rochester): This kiln site was found in 1989 from information provided by a reference in a Vermont geology guide (Morrill and Chaffee 1964:37).

The kiln remains were pointed out by Robert Kennett, owner of the site (Liberty Hill Farm), after we had walked by within a few feet without seeing it. The site consists of a low, grass-covered mound. Kennett said that the kiln's iron grates were nearby at one time but we could not find them. The quarry is just uphill and visible farther down the road. According to Kennett, the kiln was operated by the Emerson family, after whom this part of the town is named. A descendent of the family lives a quarter-mile farther south along the road in the still-standing Emerson homestead. Another reference has lime burned here on the F. F. Kezer farm (Dale 1915:23). "Eastman & Keizer" is indicated here on the 1869 Beers map of Rochester. There might be more lime kiln ruins in this vicinity (Perkins 1933:232).

Plymouth Area Lime Kiln Sites: Plymouth marble is mainly the dark, almost black variety when polished. Beds from which marble was quarried for many years were a source of lime more than marble, keeping lime kilns in the town busy for a long time (Perkins 1933:147). Eighteen lime kiln sites have been

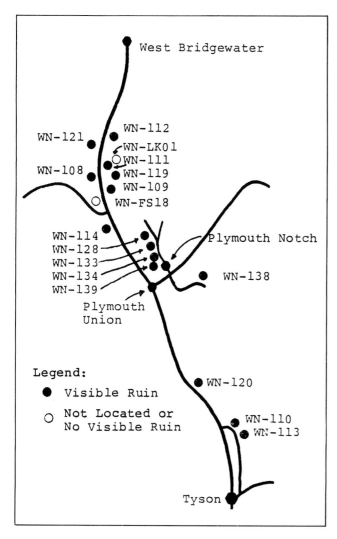

WN-112 — Knapp lime kiln
WN-113 — Brookwood lime kiln
WN-114 — Money Brook lime kiln
WN-119 — Grass Pond lime kiln
WN-120 — Frog City lime kiln (no ruin)
WN-121 — Ward Lime Works (2 ruins)

The following sites were found in the process of additional archival and field work:

WN-108 — Burnt Mountain lime kiln
WN-109 — Campground lime kiln
WN-128 — Messer Hill Road lime kiln
WN-133 — Lower Grand View Lodge Road lime kiln
WN-134 — Upper Grand View Lodge Road lime kilns (2 ruins)
WN-138 — Moore-Calkins lime kiln
WN-139 — Plymouth Notch lime kiln
WN-185 — Reservoir Brook lime kiln

The following sites, either indicated on the 1859 geologic map or discussed in the 1913–1914 *Report of the State Geologist*, have not been found:

WN-FS18 — Hall's lime kiln
WN-LK01 — Black Pond lime kiln

The sites are presented in a generally north-to-south sequence.

WN-185 Reservoir Brook Lime Kiln (Plymouth): The ruin of this lime kiln was discovered in late fall of 1991, while driving slowly north on Route 100 and glancing into the barren forest on both sides of the highway. The ruin is downhill, off the east side of the highway and on the east side of Reservoir Brook, about 500 feet south of the Bridgewater town line. Due to snow flurries and the cold-running brook, the ruin was inspected from the highway by binoculars and not physically inspected until the spring of 1992.

The ruin is on the uphill side of an old abandoned section of road. The 1869 Beers map of Plymouth shows the road north of Woodward Reservoir crossing the brook twice before reaching the Bridgewater town line. Because the map shows road at this point on the west side of the brook, the road at the ruin is probably earlier than that on the map, dating the lime kiln to pre-1869. Short sections of this road appear and disappear along the east side of the brook north of the reservoir. Today's Route 100 is completely west of the brook.

Appearing merely to be a stone mound from the highway, the ruin's inside is relatively intact with little internal breakdown. The inside looked only slightly egg-shaped, possibly because a section of the front wall had given way and fallen outward. Inside diameter is about 8 feet near the top; inside heights are about 8 feet in front and 12 feet in back. From the amount of breakdown about the ruin, the kiln must have been much higher when operating, possibly 14 to 16 feet internally. Most of the stone lining was glazed; no firebrick was in evidence. The front opening, buried under the collapsed front wall, was only visible inside and appeared to be about 2½ to 3 feet wide by high. Due to inside heights, no attempt was made to jump inside the ruin for close inspection and accurate measurements.

8-29. *Plymouth area lime kiln sites.*

documented for Plymouth, at which 17 ruins were found. Little is known, however, regarding the specific history of these kilns. Those of Christopher C. Hall, E. A. Hall, Horace N. Ward, P. P. Crandall, and H. P. Crandall were still burning lime about 1886 (Aldrich and Holmes 1891:399). Limestone from a quarry at the northeast end of Amherst Lake owned by the Neshobe Marble Company in the 1850s was burned and "produced as good lime for mortar or whitewash as can be found in the State," known as "Plymouth White Lime" (Hitchcock et al. 1861:749, 775). The 1880 *Vermont Register* (p. 130) lists C. C. Hall, manufacturer of lime. Kiln ruins found in the Messer Hill Road and Grand View Lodge Road area still display heavy coatings of a very fine, white powder. Most kiln ruins were found through lime kiln symbols on the 1859 geologic map of Plymouth. This map provided information that directly led to the following sites, generally found on both sides of Route 100:

WN-110 — Rice lime kiln
WN-111 — Grace's lime kiln

Except for the northwest corner of the ruin, all outside walls were buried from view. The visible corner showed the kiln to have been rectangular if not square, but at least not circular. No reinforcement binding or any other iron hardware was found. The rear (east wall) of the ruin was built into the steeply rising hillside, where scattered bits of burned lime were found. Too large to have been a farmer's kiln, this ruin is one of the early commercial variety.

Although in good view from the highway, this is one of the better lime kiln ruins found in Plymouth, probably due to its being across a well-running, cold stream (which had to be waded) and in a less-developed part of town. The nearest resident assumed the ruin to have been a root cellar and could shed no further light on the history of the kiln. It appears in no known archival material.

8-30. *Bottom opening of the Knapp kiln ruin near Woodward Reservoir at Plymouth.*

WN-112 Knapp Lime Kiln (Plymouth): This lime kiln ruin was found in 1987 about 50 feet east of Route 100, just north of the southwestern end of Woodward Reservoir. Owners of the adjacent campground property, Charles and Keith Knapp of Pittsfield and Rutland, said they felt the ruin was on highway property. The ruin appears more primitive than those found elsewhere in Plymouth due to the nature of its small, stone archway at the base, which faces south. White burned lime is scattered on top of the ruin, which makes it readily visible from the highway.

Due to its proximity to public view and possibility of already being on state property, this ruin, which appears stable and in relatively good condition, might be a good candidate to mark with a historical/educational marker.

WN-121 Ward Lime Works (Plymouth): Two kiln ruins of the Ward Lime Works were found in 1988 about 100 feet west of Route 100 and about a half-mile south of Woodward Reservoir.

The Ward Lime Works are on the 1869 Beers map of Plymouth; also as "W. Ward" on the 1859 geologic map of

Plymouth. No quarry could be found nearby, but recent highway realignment made some new cuts through limestone in the vicinity; an older quarry could have been affected in the process. The two kiln ruins are about 50 feet apart, in dense brush along the side of a low hill.

The largest ruin has a front stone wall about 10 feet high at highest and 22 feet wide at widest. Its hearth is accessed through an opening about 32 inches square about midpoint in the front wall at the bottom. The inside is about 9 feet in diameter and about 4 feet back from the front wall. A scatter of domestic trash litters the front of the kiln.

The other ruin is not as well defined as the first, with no obvious front stone wall. The kiln hearth is about 8 feet in diameter and caved in, but about 2 to 3 feet deep.

A woods road leads from a point about 20 feet from Route 100 (at a small concrete highway boundary marker) to the ruins, then turns north and around the low hill to a cul-de-sac.

WN-111 Grace's Lime Kiln (Plymouth): A lime kiln ruin was found about 300 feet east of Route 100 in Plymouth in 1987, from information provided by the 1859 geologic map of Plymouth.

The lime kiln ruin is an approximately 10-foot-high mound of collapsed stones alongside an abandoned segment of Route 100. The ruin is downhill of the highway, about where power lines cross the highway at a diagonal from southwest to northeast. It is nearly hidden from the highway (but Grace spotted it as we drove by). The field between the highway and the forested kiln site is clear of trees but loaded with high vegetation and berry bushes.

Broken bottles, sheet metal, and an old automobile engine were found in association with the ruin, indicating this was once a trash disposal site. The ruin is about 6 feet high and 6 feet wide, although degree of collapse made measurement difficult. Some burnt lime is visible in the area. No archway or bottom opening was apparent; they were probably located facing the old roadway, about where there is the least kiln breakdown.

WN-LK01 Black Pond Lime Kiln (Plymouth): Another lime kiln is indicated in the vicinity of WN-111 on the 1859 geologic map of Plymouth, but a search on both sides of the Black River (about 200 feet east) proved fruitless.

WN-108 Burnt Mountain Lime Kiln (Plymouth): The ruin of this lime kiln was found near the base of Burnt Mountain in 1987, while driving north along Route 100. Thin foliage along the highway made this find possible.

The ruin is about 50 feet west of the highway, about a quarter-mile south of a power line crossing, and about the same distance diagonally south across the highway from Grace's lime kiln ruin (WN-111). The ruin, built into the side of the hill, consists mostly of side and back walls with enough of the front wall standing to identify the opening. A front lintel stone remains. The remains appear similar in size and configuration with other kiln ruins found in the town and are probably contemporary with them.

WN-119 Grass Pond Lime Kiln (Plymouth): The ruin of this lime kiln was found in 1988 through the 1859 geologic map of Plymouth. It is located at the 1,320-foot elevation on the southwest slope of an unnamed 1,849-foot mountain, and about a half-mile due west of Grass Pond. The ruin is about 400 feet east of Route 100, although it is easiest reached by crossing

Black River about a quarter-mile north and working south along the ridge. A snowmobile trail (VAST) passes a few dozen feet southeast of the ruin; thus, this must be the kiln ruin in which a snowmobile got stuck, per Mr. Harootunian (see WN-109).

The ruin is characterized by an approximately 9- by 9-foot-square by 6- to 7-foot-deep hearth. The outside walls and hearth arch are almost hidden by fallen stone of the collapsed upper portion of the structure. What little of the outside wall could be seen disclosed use of horizontal wood beams in the wall construction. The large mound was estimated to be about 30 feet in diameter and 15 feet high. It was built into the side of the rise with the kiln top only slightly below ground level on its northwest side, but about 15 feet aboveground on its front (or where we estimated the front/opening side to be). About 75 feet southeast of the kiln were the collapsed remains of a wooden cabin.

WN-109 Campground Lime Kiln (Plymouth): This kiln mound is about 1,200 feet east of Route 100 in the northeast corner of the Plymouth Village Campgrounds. It was found in 1987 while searching for another ruin in the vicinity (WN-119), into which a snowmobile had gotten stuck, according to Rick Harootunian, campground owner.

Dimensions of the mound could not accurately be made due to the scattered nature of the mound debris and the nature of the topography. It was difficult to determine what was natural and what was man-made (or disturbed). The mound contains burned lime and stone from the kiln structure. Beyond the mound is low, swampy area. Immediately east of the mound is what could have been the base for an inclined tramway, leading to the top of the kiln.

WN-FS18 Hall's Lime Kiln (Plymouth): A lime kiln indicated on the 1859 geologic map of Plymouth turns out to have been located somewhere downhill and northeast of the Round Top Mountain Ski Area. It is also described as being Hall's lime kiln, about a half-mile north of Plymouth Union and about 600 feet north of a schoolhouse, some 850 feet west of which are several small quarries (Dale 1915:27)). The area pinpointed by the map in Dale's report is leveled and on it are the town garage, a shed and parking area for trucks, the elementary school, and the school bus parking area. To the west in the woods is a high, steep, rocky escarpment that could have been the source of stone for the kiln; however, no trace of stone working could be found among the outcrops.

The area was inspected in 1987 without finding any trace of the kiln. Landscaping on the lower grounds of the ski area has significantly disturbed that area. The schoolhouse indicated on the Beers map north of Plymouth Union is approximately where the map indicates it should be although it is not certain this is the schoolhouse that Dale was using as his reference to Hall's lime kiln. It is the only schoolhouse we could find in the immediate vicinity. Pacing off 600 feet north of it in 1990 brought us almost to the Route 100 bridge over Great Roaring Brook, well outside the vicinity Dale pinpointed in his map. There are five houses plus associated buildings on the west side of the highway, the construction of any of which could have destroyed the kiln, had it been near here. A local resident remembered nothing of a kiln or ruin. All things considered, Dale probably meant to write that the lime kiln was 600 feet south, not north, of the schoolhouse.

WN-138 Moore-Calkins Lime Kiln (Plymouth): A lime kiln operated about a half-mile south of Plymouth Church, on the north side of the old road to Five Corners, near a small dolomite quarry (Dale 1915:26). Plymouth Church today is known as just plain Plymouth, or sometimes Plymouth Notch.

Dale's report indicates a small dolomite quarry and remains of a lime kiln about a quarter-mile northeast and across the road from the outlet of Moore's Pond. Field inspection in 1990 turned up neither quarry nor kiln ruin. Local inquiry, however, directed us to a kiln ruin on William Calkins' (formerly Milton Moore's) property, about a quarter-mile east, 300 feet northeast of the dirt road where it sharply turns south and uphill. The ruin is at the edge of the forest line and marked with some white birch trees growing out of it, and contains some recently dumped trash. Sections of the wall are missing, apparently vandalized for other uses. The kiln lining is heavily glazed. The inside is about 8 feet square by 10 feet high. Much lime was obviously burned here.

WN-114 Money Brook Lime Kiln (Plymouth): This kiln ruin was found in 1987 about 50 feet west of Route 100, a mile south of the Route 100 and 100A junction. It is identified on the 1859 geologic map of Plymouth. The ruin measured 16 by 8 feet inside, one of the largest lime kilns encountered in Plymouth. The front wall is 25 feet long and 8 feet high at its center. The archway, facing east toward Route 100, measured 26 inches wide by 32 inches high. Stone walls crisscross the area adjacent and behind the kiln. The ruin appears stable and in relatively good condition. It is not easily visible from the highway, being set back in trees. The woman who lives across the road, however, knew exactly where it was.

WN-120 Frog City Lime Kiln (Plymouth): Surface remains of the Frog City lime kiln were found in 1988 through the 1859 geologic map of Plymouth and a photo caption that mentioned the kiln, but did not illustrate it: "Just up the lower road, out of this picture, was the Frog City School, and beyond it a sizeable lime kiln" (Ward et al. 1983:57).

The site was found while driving north on Route 100; the remains are merely a small patch of burned lime on the roadside embankment. It is about 300 feet northeast of the Frog City Road and Route 100 intersection. Directly uphill of the site is a narrow woods road that leads to a small limestone quarry and continues eastward into the woods.

There are no stone walls or holes associated with the kiln site. The ruin must have been very close to the road and destroyed during highway improvements some 20 to 30 years ago.

WN-128 Messer Hill Road Lime Kiln (Plymouth): This was the first of four lime kiln ruins found alongside this road in 1990. Three other lime kiln ruins were found later the same day farther north up the road (WN-133 and WN-134). All were discovered through information provided by William Jenney, State Historic Sites Administrator at Plymouth Union, and an archival reference: "Christopher C. Hall's lime kiln, on road 3, burns 1,600 barrels of lime per year" (Child 1884:173).

Road 3 is today's Messer Hill and Grand View Lodge roads according to the county map in Child. Any of these four lime kiln ruins might be that referenced in Child; or Hall might have operated them all at one time or another.

The kiln ruin was found less than a one-minute drive north on Messer Hill Road out of the Historic District and about 500

8-31. Other than the lime kiln ruin itself (this one at Plymouth Notch), its most visible indication was the burned lime residue that was sometimes noticed before the actual ruin was found. Yellow birch and white birch were also found in association with many lime kiln and charcoal kiln ruins.

feet north of the stone house, both on the west side of the road. The kiln ruin is about 30 feet from the road in an open section of land, very obvious to anyone driving or walking along the road. High voltage wires pass just over and between the ruin and the road.

The ruin measured about 16 feet inside diameter. Accurate measurement was difficult because trash littered the bottom of the ruin, burned lime thickly coated the inside edges, and half of the front (east) section of the ruin was collapsed. The white birch tree inside the ruin and another about 25 feet southwest were the only ones in the immediate vicinity. Standing inside, the ruin was about waist high. Pieces of red brick were found 6 feet west of the ruin.

The area immediately uphill and between the kiln ruin and road has been disturbed, possibly by bulldozing associated with the high voltage transmission lines that parallel the road. Rusted cans, bottles, paint cans, and miscellaneous hardware lie inside and around the ruin. A rusted culvert section lies nearer to the road. Some farm-type hardware lies beside the ruin and just in the woods to the southwest. Small quarries, some exhibiting white limestone and filled with stagnant water, exist just behind (northwest) of the ruin in the woods. At the nearest quarry is what appears to be a drainage ditch leading eastward to the road, just north of the kiln ruin. Many other quarries and small diggings (test holes?) continue along this side of the road northward for about one-half mile.

The whiteness of the lime in and around the ruin reflects that discussed in the 1861 state geology report and called "Plymouth White Lime," which was produced in the town during that time (Hitchcock et al. 1861:775). "[Before] railroads were introduced, no town in the State furnished more lime for market or of as better quality for mortar, than Plymouth; but since that time the foreign demand has not been so great, and being six or eight miles from the railroad, other manufacturers of lime, where the kilns are contiguous to the road, have an advantage in the cost of freight, hence the manufacture is somewhat limited, as compared with former years" (Hitchcock et

al. 1861:749).

Since there are no indications of lime kilns on the Plymouth map in the 1861 geology report, the kilns along this road probably were closed by that time. No doubt young Calvin Coolidge played in these ruins.

WN-133 Lower Grand View Lodge Road Lime Kiln Ruin (Plymouth): This was the second of four lime kiln ruins found alongside this road in 1990. It was less than a one-minute drive north of WN-128 and just northwest of the intersection of Messer Hill Road and Grand View Lodge Road. Messer Hill Road continues north up the east leg; Grand View Lodge Road starts at the junction as the west leg. The ruin is about 50 feet west of the road, uphill, and barely visible in the foliage from the road (we found it because we were driving slowly and examining the woods carefully). The ruin was betrayed by its coating of white lime, inside and out. The ruin is built into the steep hillside, its circular stone wall about 4 to 6 feet high on the downhill side and the wall continuing around and into the hillside on its uphill side. It measured about 15 feet inside diameter although accurate measurement was difficult due to the amount of burned lime coating the inside edges. Small quarries exist uphill, north and south of the ruin.

WN-134 Upper Grand View Lodge Road Lime Kilns (Plymouth): These were the third and fourth of four lime kiln ruins found alongside this road in 1990. The two ruins were found less than a one-minute drive north of the junction of Town Roads 4 and 9 and observed from the vehicle. Both ruins are on the left (west) side of the road, easily visible in low scrub brush and trees, and about 50 feet apart from each other. The southern ruin is about 50 feet from the edge of the road and the northern one is about 30 feet from the edge of the road. The bottoms of the ruins are about level with the road. Both ruins contain a covering of white lime. The inside of the lower ruin is somewhat rectangular, measuring about 10 feet wide and 12 feet long. Standing inside, it is about waist high. Its front opening is the best defined of the four kiln ruins found along the road. The inside of the upper ruin is more circular and measured about 13 feet in diameter. Again, as with the other kiln ruins along this road, measurements were difficult due to the quantity of lime covering the top edges of walls. There are small quarries west and south of the site.

WN-139 Plymouth Notch Lime Kiln (Plymouth): While photographing one of the lime kiln ruins along Messer Hill Road in 1990, Mark Shiff pointed out another kiln site behind his stone house, just up the road from the President Coolidge Birthplace at Plymouth Notch. The kiln site is near the uphill edge of the pasture and in a small grove in the open pasture. The grove is about 60 feet across its long axis by about 30 feet wide. At the northeast corner where some white birch stand is the ruin of a lime kiln. Adjacent to the ruin are two depressions containing some trash. The reason for the depressions, which do not appear natural, is unknown.

The ruin is generally circular in shape, about 8 to 20 feet across and 4 to 5 feet high. It is not as well defined as others in the vicinity, appearing more of a mound than a ruin. No firebrick was found and only a very slight glaze was on the inside lining surface, which was buried a few inches below the ground. The kiln was probably operated contemporaneously with the others in the vicinity.

WN-110 Rice Lime Kiln (Plymouth): This beautiful lime kiln ruin was found in 1987 on property owned by Anna Rice of Bethel. Information leading to the site was obtained from archival references (Ward et al. 1983:11) and the 1859 geologic map of Plymouth.

The ruin is about 1,000 feet north of the Amherst Lake public access area on State Road 22, just before the bridge over the river. It is approximately 10 feet high. Internally, it has a square front and rounded rear, is stone-lined from bottom to top, and is in good condition. The 14-foot-wide face of the ruin, with its bottom opening, faces on the road. The bottom opening measured 46 inches total height and 28 inches wide. The archway is made of 17 courses of firebrick that appear to be of a much later date than 1859. The bricks have burned ends, similar to those seen at blast furnace sites, and might have been cannibalized from the abandoned Tyson blast furnace about 2 miles south.

The archway at present appears somewhat delicate, with one smaller lintel stone precariously hanging over the opening; another, larger, above it is severely cracked. Further movement of the smaller stone could result in collapse of the entire front wall of the kiln. A simple vertical wood or steel post, wedged under the smaller stone, could delay further deterioration. Limestone burned here might have come from a quarry about two miles southeast (WN-113).

Mrs. Rice was interested in selling the property but was also concerned for the safety of the ruin. She asked the state to erect a historic sites marker at the ruin, hoping that would contribute toward its preservation. According to local tradition, the old military road to Crown Point passes through the property.

An undated photo of the lime kiln shows the archway in much better condition than it is today, with brick visible to the outside wall. Many rows of brick have since been removed and the scattered few pieces on the ground in front of the ruin account for only a small percentage of them. The missing bricks can probably be found in local backyard fireplaces. The ruin is very obvious along the inside curve of the road, and with no appreciable foliage to conceal it, it has high vandalism potential.

WN-113 Brookwood Lime Kiln (Plymouth): A lime kiln mound was found along the northeast shore of Amherst Lake in 1987 through the 1859 geologic map of Plymouth.

The ruin is an approximately 10-foot-high mound alongside the road that skirts the east shore of Amherst Lake. It is on the east side of the road and between it and the base of the hill is an older lake road. A slight depression at the top of the mound could mark the collapsed interior. Except for bits of burned lime, no other obvious surface features could be found.

8-32. *The Rice lime kiln at an earlier time, showing the decorative brick arch which is missing today.*

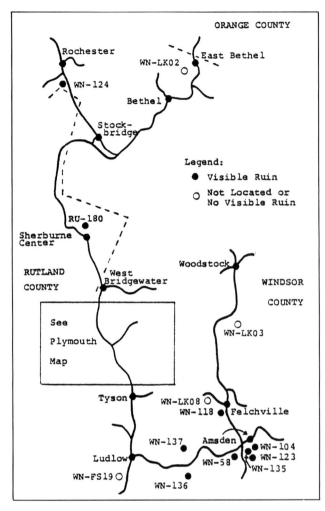

8-33. *Windsor County lime kiln sites.*

A few hundred feet directly uphill of the mound is a limestone quarry, approximately 50 feet wide and 50 feet deep into the mountainside, about where indicated on the 1859 map. This quarry was owned by the Neshobe Marble Company in the 1850s and the lime produced from it made a high-quality mortar (Hitchcock et al. 1861:749). The quarry might have supplied both this lime kiln and also WN-110, about a quarter-mile north. The quarry trail leads north, gently downhill, reaching the lake road about 100 feet north of the kiln mound. Directly across the road from the mound are summer and vacation homes and cottages, including a mobile home named Brookwood.

WN-FS19 Jewell Brook Lime Kiln (Ludlow): Dale reported the remains of a lime kiln "about 2 miles south of Ludlow, on the east side of the road to Andover, a little south of a road leading to Weston and about 3 feet north of a brook crossing" (Dale 1915:28). The road to Weston is now a trail that follows Grant Brook. The old road to Andover now parallels Route 100 about 500 feet downhill to the west.

The vicinity of Jewell and Grant brooks was inspected twice in 1990 without finding any evidence of the lime kiln, although

limestone outcrops abound. One particularly picturesque limestone escarpment is along Jewell Brook a few hundred yards upstream of Grant Brook. The 40- to 60-foot-high limestone cliff extends 100 feet upstream, creating a miniature chasm.

Enough houses have been built in this hollow to significantly modify the landscape and destroy the kiln site, especially in the specific area described by Dale. One resident remembered a lime kiln ruin being in the vicinity many years earlier.

WN-LK07 Adams Lime Kiln (Ludlow): A lime kiln operated in the south part of town in the 1860s near a limestone quarry that was on the property of A. Adams (Hitchcock et al. 1861:556). The 1869 Beers map of Ludlow shows A. Adams and N. Pettigrew at the end of a road in southern Ludlow, which might be the site addressed. The road is just east of and parallel to Route 100. Driving to the end of the road in the spring of 1992 led us to the residence of Harold Welch, who has lived here for about 20 years but knew of no lime kiln ruin or limestone quarry in the area. He did confirm that Pettigrew was a former owner of the property. Work is continuing on finding this site.

WN-LK05 Hutchins Lime Kiln (Andover): A lime kiln operated on land owned by Mr. Hutchins in the west part of town about 1860 (Hitchcock et al. 1861:556). The 1869 Beers map of Andover shows the farm of W. Hutchison in District 4 in south central Andover, but no indication of the kiln. No attempt has been made to inspect the site.

WN-LK06 North Andover Lime Kiln (Andover): In the north part of town a lime kiln operated in 1860 (Hitchcock et al. 1861:556). No attempt has been made to inspect the site.

Amsden Area Lime Kiln Sites: The Amsden group includes lime kiln remains in Weathersfield (WN-58, WN-104, WN-123, WN-135), Cavendish (WN-118, WN-136, WN-137, WN-LK08), and Woodstock (WN-LK03). Kiln ruins here follow the limestone ledge shown on the Doll geology map in a north-south direction.

Weathersfield and Cavendish have in them extensive beds of limestone, being generally in the western part of the former and in the eastern part of the latter town. Before the introduction of railroads much lime was manufactured in these towns, but recently less has been made, especially in Cavendish. . . .

The lime produced in Weathersfield is of a dark color, and does not produce mortar so white as many other localities; but when used in exposed situations it is found to be very durable, in many cases being nearly equal to water cement. It has been used much in the construction of railroad culverts, piers for bridges, &c., and in the railroad tunnel in Burlington this lime was used instead of water cement. . . . C. Amsden and Azro Craigue, of Upper Falls, are the principal manufacturers (Hitchcock et al. 1861:749).

It is a well-known fact that the dolomitic lime of Plymouth, Cavendish and Weathersfield, makes a mortar that is much more durable for situations exposed to moisture and the weather, than that made from pure carbonate of lime (Hitchcock et al. 1861:781-782).

There were lime quarries all over the west part of town [of Weathersfield]. In the land records . . . on October 1, 1848, John Dunbar was involved in a transaction in which he was going to let Samuel Alford and Roswell Downer dig and use lime rock "so much as they can burn at one kiln on his land . . . at only one place at a time" (Hunter Nov. 1984:7).

Cordwood for the kilns caused many forests in the area to be clean-cut. Charles Amsden owned much of Hawks Mountain for the wood needed to fuel his kilns. The center of the commercial lime-burning business appears to have been in the Downers-Amsden area. There are probably many more kiln ruins in this area. The ruins are described in a generally north-to-south sequence.

WN-LK03 South Woodstock Lime Kiln (Woodstock): A lime kiln ruin was reported to have been seen up a side road east of Route 106 near South Woodstock. This might have been mistaken identity with a cellar hole near a stone chamber ruin known to be in this area or possibly with the stone chamber itself. No attempt has been made to inspect the site.

WN-118 Felchville Lime Kiln (Cavendish): This lime kiln ruin was found in 1988 on the property of Mr. Taylor, on Route 106 in the northeastern corner of Cavendish. It is about 30 feet west of the edge of the highway, and just inside the edge of the woods behind a wire fence. The front wall of the ruin is about 25 feet wide and 8 feet high; its inside is collapsed but circular and about 6 feet deep. Structurally, it appears contemporary with the Plymouth kiln ruins.

WN-LK08 Knapp Pond Road Lime Kiln (Cavendish): In the northeast corner of Cavendish is the ruin of a lime kiln, somewhere north of what is today the junction of Knapp Pond Road and the Felchville Gulf Road (Dale 1915:31). Dale reported that "marble outcrops cover over an area extending 600 feet across the ridge and 700 feet on it." The marble was quarried on the west side, where the lime kiln is. No attempt has been made to inspect the site.

WN-137 Stearns Lime Kiln (Cavendish): The partially collapsed ruin of this lime kiln was found in 1990 through archival reference: "About 3 miles N. 13° E. of Cavendish village, south of a road fork, a few hundred feet northwest of the old Stearns farmhouse and west of the road, white calcite marble was formerly quarried and burned" (Dale 1915:28).

The ruin is about 400 feet west of Atkinson Road, at a point about opposite the northwest corner of Dale's referenced "old Stearns farmhouse," which is the only stone house in the immediate vicinity. The ruin is across a wet bog and at the base of a low knoll among some trees. It stands about 6 feet high and is estimated at 10 feet wide (north-south) by 12 feet long (east-west). It appeared in relatively good condition, compared to usual lime kiln ruins. No vast amounts of burnt lime were present.

WN-136 Cavendish Station Lime Kiln (Cavendish): This barely standing ruin was found in 1990 through archival reference: "About half a mile southeast of Cavendish station, just south of the sharp railroad curve and a little east of the track are a disused limekiln and a quarry" (Dale 1915:29).

Dale's "a little east" was found to be in error; the ruin was found a little *west* after spending an hour searching up and down the wrong side of the tracks. Local inquiry directed us to the kiln ruin.

The ruin is south of Cavendish village, across the bridge to the south side of the Black River, through the Green Mountain Railroad underpass, and along the road that parallels the railroad tracks. Just past where the road and tracks cross, the tracks cut a sharp angle southerly through the side of the mountain. The road continues to parallel the tracks, eventually both heading due south. About 1,000 feet south of the curve is a nearly hidden road leading due west, over the tracks, and into the lime kiln ruin, about 100 feet east of the tracks at the eastern edge of a clearing.

When first sighted, the kiln ruin stack appeared to be fully intact. But on inspection, only the front and some of the side walls are partially standing, much of the structure having collapsed into itself. Nonetheless, it is a strikingly beautiful ruin. (A camper's fireplace in front of a small shack next to the ruin is made of loose stones pulled from the ruin.) The highest point of the ruin is the northeast corner, estimated at 16 to 18 feet high. The front (east) archway, much of it collapsed up to the lower iron binding rod, measured about 8 feet high. The ruin measured 18 by 18 feet outside, at about 3 feet above local ground level. The stonework was mortared. Inside dimensions are unknown due to amount of breakdown inside the ruin.

Running through the ruin at right angles (wall to wall) are 1-inch-diameter iron binding rods, end-threaded, with a 5-inch-diameter binding plate and 1-inch-thick, 2- by 2-inch iron nut. There are an estimated 10 such binding rods; six running between the north and south walls (three each inside the front and back walls running side to side), and four running between the east and west walls (two each inside the side walls running front to back). The existence of these rods most likely accounts for the quality of the ruin still standing.

The back wall of the ruin is about 16 feet from the cliff, and its top at one time probably was level with the top of the cliff to afford access for charging the kiln. A road leads north out of the clearing and doubles back to the ledge above and behind the ruin. Rock outcroppings here and perhaps farther down the road probably provided limestone that charged the kiln.

Dale reported a number of outcrops of dolomite in the vicinity. This, plus the late-19th-century design of the lime kiln, lead to the belief that the ruin of an older and smaller lime kiln might yet exist in the vicinity.

WN-58 Upper Falls Lime Kilns (Weathersfield): A dual lime kiln ruin was found in the Upper Falls section of Weathersfield in 1985 while searching for a ca.-1790 bloomery forge site in the vicinity (chapter 4, WN-FS14). The kiln appears in the 1869 Beers map of Weathersfield identified as "Martin & Gould," about a quarter-mile west of the south end of the covered bridge.

The ruin contains two stone-built kilns, both part of a single structure. The top of the ruin is level with the dirt road that runs just behind it. A side road dips away from the main road accessing the front of the kiln units and returns to the upper road. Because the top of the ruin is level with the upper road and the openings face away from it, the ruin is relatively hidden from the upper road.

Both kiln openings are roofed by single lintel stones; the eastern unit lintel is broken but the western unit stone is intact. These flat stone lintels with their stone side supports look much like various stone chambers found elsewhere in Vermont (Neudorfer 1980:16). Some wood beams appear in part of the ruin, hinting at possible structures once associated near or on

8-34. *Partly hidden by tree roots, this primitive-looking lime kiln is one of a pair built into a common structure, just west of Downers.*

the kiln. The ruin is 40 feet wide by 10 feet high. The eastern opening is about 5 feet wide; the western opening 4 feet wide. Inside diameters are about 11 feet; the two units are about 12 feet apart. (When revisited in early 1991, the massive lintel of the western unit had broken and fallen in.) Downhill from the ruin are the remains and stone walls of a ca.-1830s to -1840s cotton mill that gave Upper Falls its name.

WN-104 Amsden Lime Kilns (Weathersfield): The standing ruins of two lime kilns were located in 1986 in the village of Amsden through information provided in part by Eric Gilbertson, Director of the Vermont Division for Historic Preservation, and Edith Hunter of Weathersfield.

The ruins stand side by side just east of Route 131, and between it and a side road that dips down into the hollow and parallels the highway for about 1,000 feet. The top of the south kiln is just below highway level and about 16 feet from the edge of the pavement. The north kiln structure has deteriorated and is not as high. The side facing the highway is partially buried. The ruins are hidden from Route 131 by their low profile and by the roadside trees.

The south kiln measured about 18 feet square, and was estimated to be 18 feet high. The north kiln measured 18 feet across the visible front wall; its side walls extend into the collapsed bank between it and the highway. This kiln appears about three feet shorter than the other. Both otherwise appear similar in configuration and in design of their courses of stone and reinforcing wood beams. At the corners of both kilns, vertical, ½-inch-diameter iron binding rods run up the stacks about 6 inches inside each corner. Diagonal iron braces 2¼ inches wide by ¼ inch thick were bent over at each end on the wood beam, 30 inches from each corner of the kiln. The kiln walls are 4 feet thick.

It is unknown when the lime kilns were built. "C. Amsden, lime, Upper Falls" first appears in *The Vermont Directory* in 1869 (p. 85). But this might have been other lime kilns also found in the vicinity. The 1869 Beers map of Weathersfield indicates kilns at Upper Falls P. O., later called Amsden, and mentions "Chas Amsden . . . Manufacturer of best quality of Diamond Lime, in Shermans Patent Kilns." The kilns produced 10,000 barrels of lime annually, widely considered to be of a superior quality (Child 1884:243). In 1910, limestone was burned in two stone perpetual kilns and the lime was hauled by teams to Cavendish for shipment. A new, modern steel kiln was also under construction that year (Perkins 1910:351). The lime owed its peculiar properties to the combination of two carbonates, calcite and dolomite, and its cement color probably to the presence of hematite (Dale 1915:33).

The stone quarried at Amsden was much better suited for burning into lime for use by masons than as an ornamental stone and has always been used and valued for producing lime.

8-35. *Ca.-1920s view of lime kilns at Amsden, showing tall iron shell above kiln in background. Whether the two foreground units were in operation at this time is unknown (courtesy Edith Hunter).*

8-36. *View of lime kiln operations at Amsden, date unknown (courtesy Edith Hunter).*

As far as is known, the stone was never used for marble. Four quarries were worked for many years by the Amsden Company; the oldest was worked for 100 years. They were about a mile east of Perkinsville, and the largest was a half-mile south of Amsden on the east side of Branch Brook. Lime made from these quarries could be cast in blocks like cement and it was claimed that no reinforcement was required. The lime was dark, about the color of portland cement (Perkins 1933:217-218).

The post office at Amsden closed in 1914 (Swift 1977:557-559), but the lime company continued to operate for many years. The great flood of 1927 nearly wiped out the lime kilns,

but the company made a large investment in new equipment. By the next summer 125 tons of Amsden Gray Lime were ready for market. This was during the time when the construction industry was shifting from plastering walls with wet lime to nailing drywall sheets (Hurd 1978:128). The Amsden Gray Lime Company was last listed as active in 1930 (Perkins 1930:259).

An undated postcard (1920s?) shows the two kilns in what appears to be a quiet, non-operating period (Hunter Nov. 1984:9). Also in the postcard is the third, modern lime kiln which was built in 1910. Its iron shell extended upward above

8-37. *The two surviving lime kiln ruins at Amsden in the spring of 1991.*

the kiln to a charging ramp and bridge that ran up to the top of the kiln from the embankment above and west of the highway. No charging ramps can be seen leading to the tops of the two stone kilns.

No surface evidence of the third kiln or of other structures shown in the foreground of the postcard could be found the day of the inspection, although a concrete-block foundation building stood on one of two older-appearing concrete slabs in the vicinity. The office building that housed the works offices still stands at Route 131, just north of the ruins.

WN-135 Upper Branch Brook Lime Kiln (Weathersfield): This lime kiln ruin was inspected in 1990 although located in 1981 by Peter Thomas (University of Vermont) as part of a survey for the U.S. Corps of Engineers. The ruin is about 30 feet off the east side of Branch Brook Road (Town Road 34), opposite the driveway of the first residence (mobile home) encountered after entering the road from Route 131. The ruin is not visible from the road due to its having been built below road level.

This structure is east of Town Road 34, on the edge of a steep bank above Branch Brook. The kiln is built into the bank. Only the back wall remains, and is farthest into the bank. On either side of the back wall the bank slopes considerably, to ground level closer to the brook edge. The kiln was oval in shape before the front wall was removed or collapsed, and is U-shaped in cross section. It is 10 feet wide on the largest axis (east-west) and 5′ 8″ wide on the north-south axis. The back wall apparently is preserved to its maximum height, which is 8 feet before being capped with larger stones which may have been the vent hole. The kiln is constructed of several courses of stone. The inner wall is approximately 1 foot thick, and is made of dry laid gneiss or schist small stones. The outer wall is made of rocks up to 2 feet in cross section and 1½ [to] 2 feet broad. The total thickness of the wall is about 3 feet. Former owner Mrs. Betty Murray did not know anything about the limekiln.

Walling's 1860 map lists A. Craigue of Upper Falls as a producer of diamond lime. Hitchcock (1861) says that Azro Craigue was 1 of the 2 principal manufacturers of lime in town. The kiln was apparently of the intermittent type, requiring filling after each firing. It is not known if this is Craigue's kiln [or] if the lime was produced for local or commercial use (Thomas *North Springfield Lake* 1981).

The kiln ruin was found generally as described by Thomas when inspected in 1990. Barbed-wire fencing, possibly new since 1981, separates a horse pasture from the kiln ruin. The fence passes within a few feet of the south edge of the ruin, making the steep downhill passage narrow and hazardous between the fence and ruin.

WN-123 Lower Branch Brook Lime Kiln (Weathersfield): This kiln ruin was found in 1988 through the 1869 Beers map of Weathersfield. Two previous attempts to find and record this ruin were thwarted in 1986 and 1987 by the high water of Branch Brook. This time we did not even get our ankles wet.

The ruin is 200 feet east of the Branch Brook, about a half-mile south of Route 131. It is situated on the first rise from the river plateau in a moderate forest and facing westward toward an open field. Front and inside walls of the ruin are

collapsed, but enough fabric of the structure exists to identify it. Inside dimensions are 7 feet wide by 6 feet deep. A long, low stone wall, most likely built after demise of the kiln, runs along the ridge that had been level with the top of the ruin, and a section of the wall runs directly on the edge of the ruin's back wall. A small quarry lies east of the ruin just past a north-south road. About 100 feet south, the trail disappears in an open field. At that point, what appears to have been a narrow inclined tramway leads uphill from the old road eastward for about 30 feet, dead-ending in another small quarry.

The Beers map shows a short, dotted-line road leading from the Branch Brook Road to the river's west bank. A hint of the road can still be seen, leading right up to the edge of the river where there might have been a bridge. No bridge abutments were found.

The Southern District

The southern district consists of Bennington and Windham counties, and accounts for 31 lime kiln sites, or about 27 percent of the known sites in the state. Some of the most impressive 19th-century kiln ruins in the state were found in Windham County at Stratton (WD-88), Wilmington (WD-89), and Whitingham (WD-91).

BENNINGTON COUNTY

BE-141 North Dorset Lime Kiln (Dorset): The ruin of a lime kiln was found in 1989, about a mile northwest of the entrance to Emerald Lake State Park in North Dorset. Information leading to the ruin was provided by Edward Eno, park caretaker.

The ruin was identified by the general configuration of the structure and a patch of burned lime in and around the ruin. Inside dimensions measure about 8 feet wide by 6 feet deep (front to back). The front arch is 22 inches high and 21 inches wide. Thickness of the front wall, which is 8 feet from the road, is 44 inches. The ruin appeared to be just outside of the state park boundary.

The kiln's period of operation is unknown, but from its similar appearance to lime kiln ruins in Plymouth and elsewhere, pre-1860 operation is suspected. State park records might shed some light on the history of the ruin.

BE-LK02 Dorset Mountain Road Lime Kiln (Dorset): Unsuccessful searches for a lime kiln ruin along the Dorset Mountain Road were made in 1986 and 1989. Reference is made to a kiln ruin here in 1964 (Morrill and Chaffee 1964:17). Nothing further is known about the kiln.

Dorset Mountain Road dead-ends about three miles north of Route 30; the kiln site should be about a mile from the end. The ruin would appear to have been in a low ravine behind some homes in the vicinity. Property owners in the vicinity of the site knew nothing of the kiln or ruin.

BE-109 Barnumville Lime Kiln (Manchester): The ruin of the Barnumville lime kiln was found in 1983, based on information in a history of Manchester (Bigelow and Otis 1961:147).

The ruin is in the woods about 30 feet west of Beech Street, north of Barnumville. It is a shallow, caved-in circular wall of stones, directly across the street from the residence of Allie Hart. The ruin, which measured about 8 feet in overall diameter, is so collapsed that no inside depth measurement could be

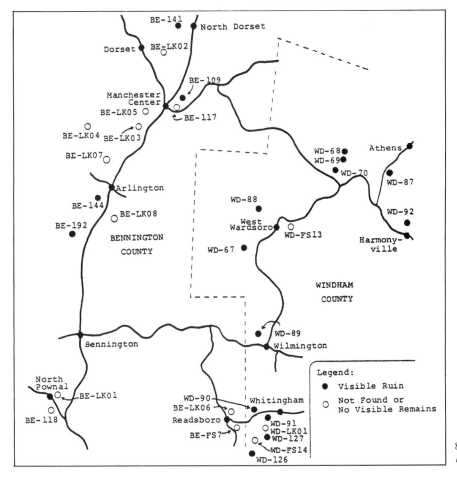

8-38. *Bennington and Windham counties lime kiln sites.*

8-39. *Collapsed ruin of a small lime kiln near North Dorset showing section of the front archway.*

made. Only one course of kiln wall is visible, and this course does not go completely around the circumference of the kiln.

BE-117 Manchester Depot Lime Kiln (Manchester): The site of a 19th-century lime kiln was found in Manchester Depot in 1987 through the history of Manchester, which mentioned a lime kiln having operated on what is now the property of Dr. Edwin K. Treat (Bigelow and Otis 1961:151).

The kiln site is about a mile east of the Routes 7A, 11, and 30 intersection (known locally as "malfunction junction"). As in the historical account, a surface deposit of white limestone residue is visible under thin foliage cover on the side of the embankment that leads uphill from the highway to Dr. Treat's house and the buildings of the Green Mountain Veterinary Hospital. No surface evidence of an actual kiln ruin can be seen. Archeological remains of the kiln might lie buried or might have been totally or partially removed during highway work or landscaping. Neither Drs. Robert or Edwin Treat could provide any information regarding the history of the lime kiln.

BE-LK03 Purdy Hill Lime Kiln (Manchester): A lime kiln operated on Purdy Hill, about a mile south of Manchester Village, but has not been found despite many searches since 1985. It was near Route 7A (Bigelow and Otis 1961:151), and was probably destroyed when the highway was rebuilt in the 1950s.

BE-LK05 Equinox Mountain Lime Kiln (Manchester): A lime kiln is supposed to have been at the foot of Equinox Mountain west of the Center Reservoir (Bigelow and Otis 1961:151). Center Reservoir, at the west end of Witherall Road, was abandoned many years ago. A 1990 search uphill of the reservoir proved unsuccessful, although some small quarries were found.

BE-LK04 Hopper Brook Lime Kiln (Sandgate): Somewhere in the wilds of Hopper Brook, east of Sandgate village, a lime kiln operated at an early time (Renner 1961:50). This brook drains the southeast quadrant of the town through some high, steep gorges.

The winding road that parallels Hopper Brook was inspected in 1990 without finding any evidence of the lime kiln. Houses, garages, and driveways dot the road, which has also been widened and straightened here and there. This might have contributed to the destruction of the kiln site, although it might have been missed in some of the heavier roadside underbrush.

BE-LK08 Lawrence Lime Kiln (Sunderland): Edgar Lawrence, who lives at the northeast corner of Bacon Hollow Road and the old Sunderland Road, said that a lime kiln ruin was in the woods about a quarter- to half-mile west of his house. The kiln was operated by his grandfather and made plaster for the walls of the house still standing just southwest of the intersection. The kiln ruin was last seen many years ago and it is believed that little if anything remains of it.

Running parallel to, and approximately a third of a mile west of, the Sunderland Road is a quarter-mile-long limestone ledge, 1 to 2 feet high at the northern end but up to 20 feet high in places at the southern end. A trail (called "the lane" by Mr. Lawrence) that leads to the northern end of the limestone ledge parallels an east-west stone wall indicated on the USGS topographical map, although the eastern half of the wall no longer stands today. The northern end of the limestone ledge, where the trail starts downhill, is the approximate location of the lime kiln. Inspection of the vicinity in 1991 with Mr. Lawrence

failed to reveal any lime kiln evidence. Immediately downhill (west) of the ledge are recently built summer homes. In the landscaped backyard of one might be the buried and scattered remains of the lime kiln. A second inspection after the foliage lessened turned up nothing new.

BE-LK07 Red Mountain Lime Kiln (Arlington): A "Limekiln" is identified on an early-20th-century annotated USGS topographical map owned by Nancy Otis of Manchester. The site works out to be about a half-mile up Fisher Road on the east slope of Red Mountain in Arlington.

The vicinity of the kiln indication was inspected in 1989, about a five-minute walk up a woods road that forks left from Fisher Road. A dozen feet of this woods road is a small cave, and another dozen or so feet downhill from the cave is a 6-foot-diameter by about 6-foot-deep stone-lined cistern, found in association with an abandoned building foundation. The cistern was at first taken to be the lime kiln, but a modern tile pipe leads from the foundation to the cistern and there is no bottom access to the cistern as a lime kiln normally would have. Nearby are limestone outcrops that show signs of being worked. Inside the cistern was a circular iron plate with a pair of heavy iron handles, looking for all the world like a modified top-hole cover from a charcoal kiln (see chapter 6, BE-CK04). Attempts to pull it out for inspection failed since it was securely jammed inside the cistern. The lime kiln ruin has yet to be found.

BE-144 Judson-Howell Lime Kiln (Arlington): The ruin of this lime kiln was found July 4, 1989 at the Howell Campground through information provided by Ken Nickerson who camped there.

The campground surrounds a small pond about a half-mile southeast of Arlington village. The kiln ruin is between the pond and one of the campsites appropriately named Limekiln Site (campsite no. 72), on the west shore of the pond. Walls of the ruin are over 6 feet high but were difficult to accurately measure due to the density of vines on the wall and breakdown at the bottom. It is a large ruin, about 10 feet across, and probably extended 10 feet into the embankment when in operation. The campsite sits directly atop the filled-in ruin, and borders three sides of the top edge of the ruin.

The campground owner said that there was a quarry just uphill, operated by Judson, where marble for a church in the village was quarried. The name Judson appears in various histories dealing with Arlington but in no connection with lime or marble manufacturing. Arlington marble was described as not of fine quality but good for building stone (Perkins 1933:164).

BE-192 Martin Lime Kiln (Arlington): The ruin of a large lime kiln stands in the southeast corner of the Arlington State Forest. It is about a quarter-mile north of Wilma and Al Rice's house, which stands at the end of Timber Trail Road, west off Route 7A in northern Shaftsbury. Mrs. Rice, who guided us to the ruin in 1991, said that the kiln was operated about 150 years ago by a Mr. Martin. The E. R. & S. E. Martin house is shown here on the 1869 Beers map of Shaftsbury although neither that map nor the 1856 map of Bennington County show the lime kiln.

The ruin is on the west side of a trail that runs across the southeast segment of the state forest property. According to Mrs. Rice, the trail was the road down which wagons carried the burned lime from the kiln. Burned lime is seen scattered all along the roadbed. The ruin is 8 to 10 feet high and over 12 feet across the front. The collapsed condition of the ruin's corners make it difficult to measure overall dimensions. Inside the ruin is a round, 8-foot-diameter, concave-wall-shaped stone-lined hearth. Only the lower half of the glazed lining exists. Burned lime of a sandy consistency is scattered throughout the interior of the ruin. No firebrick or red brick were in evidence. The front archway is completely collapsed. The exterior walls are made of relatively large blocks of stone, reflecting the labor-intensiveness of the construction effort.

Directly uphill of the ruin is an approximately 100-foot-long limestone ledge and huge piles of stones that were quarried from the ledge. Several quarries were opened in north Shaftsbury well into the early 19th century, but were all closed by 1857. A quarry opened in 1861 by Samuel Cranston was referred to as an old quarry that had been abandoned for several years (Perkins 1933:164).

BE-118 Pownal Lime Company (Pownal): The abandoned ruins of a lime kiln works and quarry were found and inspected in 1987 just south of the community of North Pownal, per the indications in the 1869 Beers map of Pownal.

The remains straddle Route 346 approximately 2½ miles northeast of Pownal village. The quarry is among the Kreiger Rocks formation, mentioned in many town and county histories. The rock formation is visible from Route 7 as far as five miles down the valley.

Surface remains of the quarry and lime-processing operations are many. Starting uphill at the quarry, on the east side of the highway, are the surface indications of a narrow-gauge track leading from near the east end of the quarry, around a curve, and downhill at a relatively steep slope to near the highway, then apparently over the highway on a wood trestle (Parks 1977:101). Where the track bed curved out of the quarry to start downhill are the mounts of steam engine cable hoist machines for raising and lowering the cable cars up and down the tracks between the quarry and the lime-processing buildings below. Steam engine cinder is found in the vicinity. On the west side of the highway and between it and the railroad tracks and the Hoosic River are crumbling concrete and stone wall remains of the lime-processing facility. These ruins are devoid of all hardware except a few mounts that probably supported crushers, rollers, etc. The site of the kiln was found near the southwest end of the remains, as indicated by a circular pattern of firebricks.

In 1918 the Pownal Lime Company had a Boston address and advertised ground limestone for liming purposes (Jacobs 1918:164). The company was still listed as active as late as 1930.

BE-LK01 North Pownal Lime Kiln (Pownal): The 1869 Beers map of Pownal indicates a lime kiln at North Pownal, at a point on land that is in proximity to a quarry on the east side of the village. A search for the kiln ruin in 1987 resulted in finding no ruin or kiln remains. From the size and disposition of the quarry, the kiln ruin was probably razed during expanded quarry operations in the later 19th century, at which time limestone was probably shipped for burning at the lime works a mile south (BE-118).

BE-FS7 Amaden & Son Lime Kiln (Readsboro): A lime kiln is indicated on the 1856 map of Bennington County about a half-mile southeast of Readsboro village, east of the road that follows the Deerfield River. An adjacent building is identified "A. Amaden & Son," which might be connected with the kiln. Beds of limestone in Readsboro, although mostly small in size, often supplied large lime kilns (Hitchcock et al. 1861:600).

A 1989 search of the area below the village resulted in finding no lime kiln evidence, although there are many limestone ledges in the vicinity. Railroad construction might have destroyed the kiln. There were other lime kilns about a mile south along the east side of the Deerfield River in Whitingham (WD-FS14 and WD-126). The vicinity from Readsboro village south to the Whitingham town line was once known as Lime Hollow.

BE-LK06 Readsboro Lime Kiln (Readsboro): Dale mentioned that a quarter-mile north of the Readsboro dam, on the north side of the Deerfield River, marble was quarried and burned (Dale 1915:52). The area northeast of the North Hill Road and School Road intersection was inspected in 1991 and no remains of a lime kiln were found. The area is now built-up with houses, driveways, and village streets.

WINDHAM COUNTY

Turkey Mountain Road Lime Kiln Sites: Standing ruins of three lime kilns (WD-68, WD-69, WD-70) were found along Turkey Mountain Road in Jamaica in 1986. Information leading to the first ruin was provided by Bob West, who learned of it through one of his students at Burr and Burton High School, Manchester. We were further aided that day in the field by Amos Newton, another student who lives nearby and whose house we visited during the day for more definitive directions.

The 1869 Beers map of Jamaica indicates two lime kilns along the north end of a road that parallels Sharp Brook farther south. The name W. Thayer is associated with the northernmost kiln and A. Howard with the other kiln. Another undocumented lime kiln ruin was found about a mile to the south. The brook is identified on current USGS maps as Little Turkey Mountain Brook; the road at its southern juncture with Route 30 is Turkey Mountain Road.

The 1961 Doll geologic map of Vermont indicates a very narrow northwest-southeast line of "buff dolomite, white to pink calcite marble" running nearly parallel to, or directly on, the road along which the lime kiln is located. Outcrops of limestone were observed at a few distinct places along the road, but not in any great quantity, possibly reflecting the narrow band shown on the geologic map. Except for making lime, limestone from this area was of little commercial value as marble due to the frequent joints in the beds by which solid blocks were spoiled (Perkins 1933:226). There is no known connection between making potash in Jamaica and the lime kilns.

WD-68 Thayer Lime Kiln (Jamaica): This ruin is generally in good condition, and lies about 10 feet east off the road. It is not very obvious when traveling north on the road due to its being tucked behind a low rise, but is very obvious when traveling south. It is probably the kiln reported to have burned local dolomite and associated with small quarries (Dale 1915:41). W. Thayer Esq. was connected with quarry here in the 1850s (Hitchcock et al. 1861:556). The 1869 Beers map

265

8-40. *The graceful ruin of the Thayer lime kiln at Jamaica, showing the decorative Gothic arch and front portal.*

8-41. *Close-up view of the front opening of the Thayer kiln. Note cracked lintel stone still holding up the heavy stonework above; early Vermonters built well.*

of Jamaica indicates the name W. Thayer next to the lime kiln.

The structure is made of flat stone, accounting for its stability down through the years. Its most distinctive feature is its front Gothic-like arch (lancet arch), built up by successive layers of flat stone. The archway faces northwesterly and is 8 feet wide at the bottom and closes to a point 8 feet high. The highest part of the kiln is 11 feet above the base. The inside walls are glazed. In contrast to the usual circular inside shape of most

other lime kilns, the inside of this kiln is square, measuring 9 by 9 feet. An opening in the wall is in the center of the front archway; the opening measured 2 feet wide by 5 feet high. Wall thickness at the opening is 3 feet. Total outside base dimension is probably 16 feet square (only the front wall was measured; the kiln is built into a low rise so that the base of the other three walls cannot be measured).

A small brook winds in front of the kiln, rising from a beaver pond about 1,000 feet to the southeast. It runs through a relatively deep gully, forming an S-curve just east of the kiln. About 15 feet in front of the kiln an unidentified iron casting was found, as was a piece of red brick. About 25 feet northeast of the kiln is an outcrop of limestone, which appears to have been worked. The outcrop continues upstream along the brook. At the base of the outcrop, small cave-like openings exist. A mound of tailings lies just north of this outcrop; another lies about 50 feet up the gully.

About 100 feet to the east, near the base of the mountain, are two small isolated stone walls of no known connection with the kiln, but possibly remains of a small dam or bridge abutment over another small brook in the area.

WD-70 Twitchell-Howard Lime Kiln (Jamaica): This kiln ruin was found about 500 feet south of the Thayer lime kiln, and is circular in shape in contrast to the Thayer ruin. It was not very obvious the day it was found, being covered with leaves. But a small section of stone wall that peeked through the leaves, plus the shallow depression immediately north of the kiln mound, caught our attention. The mound is about 10 feet high. Its circular inside, which projects through the top, measured 6 feet in diameter. It looks like a majority of the smaller lime kilns found elsewhere in Vermont. No glazing could be seen on the inside surfaces, but then, very little of the inside surface is visible. Most of it is hidden by breakdown.

Directly across the road is what appears to be some limestone outcrop. No other potential quarry was visible in the vicinity.

In 1861 the kiln belonged to A. Twitchell (Hitchcock et al. 1861:556). In the 1869 Beers map of Jamaica the name A. Howard is associated with the kiln. Howard is also indicated at a number of other places in the vicinity, one about ¾ of a mile south along the road from the lime kiln site, hinting of the possibility of more lime kiln ruins.

WD-69 Haven Lime Kiln (Jamaica): Grace spotted the Haven kiln ruin while we drove by, about a mile south of the Twitchell-Howard ruin (WD-70). It is circular in shape, similar to the WD-70 ruin but not as high. It has an 8-foot inside diameter, and no glaze coating was seen on the inside walls.

There is stone breakdown on the inside floor of the ruin, along with recent domestic party trash. The front opening, facing east toward the road, is 42 inches wide. The highest section of the north wall at the opening is 36 inches; of the south wall, 44 inches. A large stone slab, which appears to be part of a capstone, lies across the back section of the ruin. The top of the kiln ruin is level with the ground behind it, and the sides of the earthen area behind the kiln are reinforced with stone wall. Both the capstone and the ruin being level with an earthen ramp behind it appear to indicate that the top of the existing ruin is the true top of the kiln.

The kiln is not identified on the Beers map, but a cellar hole adjacent to it is identified on the map as P. A. Haven.

No quarry was seen in the vicinity, but to the north, along the east side of the road, large pieces of limestone can be seen near the base of the escarpment.

WD-87 Bemis Lime Kiln (Athens): A lime kiln operated in the northwest part of the town of Athens, just north of the Townshend line on the east side of the road from Athens to Townshend, on the Bemis farm (Dale 1915:34-35). The kiln was in association with several quarries. Stone from these quarries was never used for marble but only as material for making lime (Perkins 1933:219). William Holbrook, proprietor of the kiln, made 600 to 800 barrels of lime annually (Hitchcock et al. 1861:618).

Dale reported "several old openings and the remains of a kiln" at the southeast intersection of Route 35 and the old road heading northeast to Athens village. The intersection is about a mile north of the Athens-Townshend line. During one false start we found a neat rock cairn in the middle of a wooded pasture (it looked very much like a lime kiln ruin from the road, 100 feet away), but we beat a hasty retreat back to the road when we found we shared the pasture with two large bulls. Inquiry at the Bemis farmhouse from the safety of the pickup directed us to the kiln ruin, about 300 feet east of Route 35 and the same distance north of the town line. The ruin is a 15-foot-high, hollowed-out mound built into the hillside, and is in an advanced state of collapse. Three large white birch grow out of the kiln walls. In a collapsed building immediately north of the ruin are rusted hardware parts of a large rotating sieve and a heavy cast-iron pulverizer, made by the Holland Pulverizer Company of Holland, Pennsylvania. Uphill of this machinery is a small quarry with an old, rusted truck inside. Many small pieces of stone are scattered about the area. Was limestone being pulverized and sifted here after abandonment of the kiln?

WD-92 Gray-Holt Lime Kiln (Townshend): Lime was burned in the 1860s about a mile east-southeast of Townshend village and about 500 feet above it on the Horace Gale farm, formerly the Sharon Gray farm (Dale 1915:35-36). Dale shows the quarry at a point at the top of a mile-long steep and rutted road, northeast from Route 30 at Harmonyville. At the top of the climb in 1989 was the Dan Holt farm. Another reference places the kiln about 250 yards southeast of the road junction near the farm (Morrill and Chaffee 1964:45).

Inspection of the area in 1989 resulted in finding a partially filled-in quarry 200 feet east of the abandoned road to Brookline, southeast of the farm, and a possible kiln ruin about 50 feet up the road to Simpsonville, just across from the Holt farmhouse. The ruin is about 8 feet high by 25 feet wide. The center section of the ruin is slumped out, hiding any evidence of an archway. On top is a circular stone feature that could be the top of a lime kiln. Bits of what appear to be burnt lime are on the ground downhill of the ruin. A hint of a road leads from below the ruin, around the north side of it, and up to the main road.

WD-LK02 Windmill Mountain Lime Kiln (Westminster): A few years ago a small lime kiln was seen deep in the forest about "a mile or two into the woods" west-southwest of the village of Westminster West (Collamer Abbott letter to author, July 8, 1991). The ruin is within a one-mile-wide band of limestone that cuts north-south through the western part of the town and slightly north of a small tributary of Putney Brook. No attempt has been made to find the site.

WD-88 Pike-Bills Lime Kiln (Stratton): An extensive amount of lime was burned from an early time up to about 1910 at a kiln a quarter-mile south of the home of A. J. Pike. The kiln was associated with a quarry that is between the forks of a small brook, a quarter-mile southwest and 100 feet in elevation above the kiln (Dale 1915:43-44). Dale placed the quarry about a quarter-mile southwest of Pike's house, across a small brook and just below the quarry.

When inspected in 1990, the kiln ruin was found exactly where Dale had it, about a five-minute walk along the active logging road southwest of the former Pike house, today owned by Lee Bills. The ruin is about 300 feet beyond a small brook (Pike Hollow Brook?), and 100 feet southeast off the road at an overgrown clearing. The day of the inspection, this small clearing was covered with head-high goldenrod, making walking difficult while tripping over fallen trees and stepping into small depressions, all well hidden from view.

The ruin is a huge, intact 40-foot-wide by about 20-foot-high and 25-foot-deep stonework edifice. At ground level are three openings, about 6 to 8 feet deep into the front kiln wall, the weight of the kiln above each held up by short sections of old railroad track. The track measured 3½ inches high by 3 inches across the base (30- to 40-pound track). All pieces of track were bent downward under the weight of the stone wall above. The openings were about 4 feet wide at the bottoms, 3 feet wide at the top, and about 6 feet high. Thinking this was a three-kiln unit built into a single structure, we were surprised after climbing to the top to find that it was, in fact, a single kiln unit with one large oval opening. Mr. Bills said that the rotted logs inside the kiln were from years ago when his father built a ramp over the top of the kiln and used the ruin as a loading platform for a logging operation (probably in the 1940s). No firebrick or binding were found associated with the ruin. A trail leads uphill from the top of the ruin in the general direction of the quarry. The limestone was carried from the quarry on small rail cars, probably powered by steam-operated cables, per a photograph that Mr. Bills showed us.

This kiln ruin is one of the more impressive lime kiln ruins found in the state so far. It reflects the labor-intensiveness of the industry at one time, which, when considering the wilderness surrounding of so many of these remote sites today, makes a profound statement about the degree of industrial activity that went on during Vermont's earlier years.

WD-FS13 West Wardsboro Lime Kiln (Wardsboro): The 1869 Beers map of Wardsboro shows a lime kiln east of West Wardsboro and south of Route 100. The area was inspected in 1990 without finding any surface trace of the kiln. A moderate amount of development in the area plus highway work probably accounts for the ruin's demise, although subsurface remains might yet exist.

WD-67 Greene Farm Lime Kiln (Dover): This lime kiln ruin was found in 1986 on the Greene Farm in northwest Dover on the north bank of the North Branch Deerfield River, known locally as Limekiln Brook. Initial information about the ruin was provided by letters between the late Stephen Greene, Chester Liebs (University of Vermont), and Giovanna Peebles (State Archeologist). Specific directions were provided by Janet Greene on the day of the visit and telephone conversations two days earlier with Mark Sprague, her farm manager.

The ruin, which has only one corner of wall visible, is approximately 10 feet high with three trees growing out its northwest corner. It appears to have been out of operation for at least 100 years. It is about 20 feet from the brook, in which are outcrops of pinkish-white marble. Dale made mention of the kiln mound and the colorful marble outcrops in the vicinity (Dale 1915:45-46).

> Two marble beds lie close to Mt. Pisgah (Mt. Snow), in the north-west corner of the town. The first bed is about one third of a mile north of the mountain on Lime Kiln Brook, and about one fourth of a mile southwest of the farm long known as Edwin J. Bartlett's, now Stephen Greene's. The marble outcropping measures 47 feet in width and 19 feet in thickness. This Dover marble, coarse-grained, pinkish in color and streaked with green and white dolomite, was never quarried for commercial purposes. For many years the stone was burned for lime, hence the name of the brook (Kull 1961:3).

The 1869 Beers map of Wilmington shows part of Dover then in Wilmington and a limestone ledge indicated near the location of the lime kiln. The map also indicates the home of N. A. Kennon and a sugar house just east of the ledges. Both buildings still stand, the former being Mrs. Greene's house today. No evidence of a quarry was noticed the day of the inspection. The ruin appears to be too deteriorated to justify restoration, as suggested in Mr. Greene's 1978 letter, but it was a nice thought.

WD-89 Grimes-Fitzgerald Lime Kiln (Wilmington): Near an outcrop of marble about two miles northwest of Wilmington village, lime was last burned about 1850. The kiln is described as being just north of the outcrop, which is about 700 feet west

of the W. S. Grimes house at the 1,800-foot level of the mountain. Dale showed it about a mile north of Route 9, west of Haystack Mountain Road, near the end of what is Beebe Road (Dale 1915:47-48).

The site was found in 1990 on Tom Fitzgerald's farm, which includes the old Grimes farmhouse, at the end of Beebe Road. The ruin is a quarter-mile north of the dirt road that leads slightly uphill west of the farmhouse. Between the ruin and the road is a quarry, approximately 200 feet long by 6 to 8 feet deep/wide, looking like a meandering World War I infantry trench.

The kiln ruin has a Gothic-type opening, rising from about 3 feet wide at ground level to a point 4 feet 9 inches high. The outside wall measured about 18 feet square at ground level, which was difficult to measure due to the amount of breakdown. The inside of the ruin, however, is relatively intact, and displays a definite egg shape, measuring 9 feet in diameter at the widest, narrowing at the top and at the bottom. The inside walls are reddish from the heat of burning lime. Walls measured about 3 to 4 feet thick. No firebrick or binding were found associated with the ruin. The front opening faces to the east, on the downhill side. A tree (not birch) was growing inside the ruin.

Mr. Fitzgerald said that the farm was formerly owned by author Elswyth Thane, who wrote many books while living there. One book mentioned the old lime kiln ruin (*The Strength of the Hills* 1950, 1976). Her husband was Dr. William Beebe, the famous explorer and naturalist who headed worldwide scientific expeditions, made a record descent of 3,028 feet into the Atlantic Ocean in 1934 in a diving chamber he designed, and wrote many books on his experiences (e.g., *Half Mile Down* 1934). Although Dr. Beebe did spend some time with his wife at the farm, she and the remote farm were apparently not enough to distract from his main interests in New York City. She built a special room for him in an unsuccessful attempt to entice him to stay more, but he must have considered the rustic old Vermont farm to be the end of the world.

Whitingham Lime Kiln Sites: Nine lime kilns were reported to be in full operation in the town of Whitingham about 1830: three at Lime Hollow, three in the Dix neighborhood, two in the vicinity of the Timothy Jillson place, and one at the Newell place. John Parsons and Benjamin Battles were the "lime kings" of Lime Hollow, and the common at the center of the town was the "grand receptacle" for casks of lime awaiting transportation. The lime business flourished in Whitingham from 1820 to 1840 but by 1894 only two kilns remained in operation (Jillson 1894:46).

Although four lime kiln ruins were found in Whitingham, many more remain to be discovered and recorded. Finding the various houses referenced in the 1894 town history could go a long way toward locating the missing lime kiln sites. The 1869 Beers map of Whitingham shows the residence of T. Jillson in the vicinity of an unlocated kiln on Merrifield Road (WD-LK01), and the "Dix neighborhood" seems to be in the vicinity of today's Route 100, where a kiln ruin was found nearby alongside No. 9 Brook (WD-91). The Newell place might be today's residence of Arnold Kingsley, near another lime kiln ruin (WD-127).

WD-91 No. 9 Brook Lime Kiln (Whitingham): About a mile southwest of the village, about where No. 9 Brook empties into the Harriman Reservoir, a lime kiln and quarry operated on the west side of the brook (Dale 1915:49-50). Dale shows the site about a mile upstream from Route 100, but the best approach to finding the ruin was downhill, east from the highway.

The ruin was found in 1990 based on specific directions from Robert Filler who lives on Route 100, due west from where the site was thought to be. It turned out to be on the east side of the brook, not the west side per Dale. The ruin stands intact about 18 feet high and 20 feet across the front at ground level, narrowing slightly toward the top. The opening at the bottom measured 4 by 4 feet high and wide, leading inward to a smaller opening, about 3 feet high by 2 feet wide, which opens into the kiln proper. Although the lintel stone above the opening has about a 1-inch-wide vertical crack through it, the stone is still holding up the wall. The ruin faces directly toward the brook, about 40 feet away, and is built into the side of the steep embankment. Extending outward about 6 to 8 feet toward the brook on each side of the ruin are 2-foot-high stone walls, probably to keep the working area at the opening clear from hillside material that might work its way down the steep embankment on each side of the kiln. At the edge of the brook, in front of the ruin, is a low stone wall. This wall might be what is left of a bridge that crossed the brook.

The top of the ruin is relatively intact, showing little sign of stone movement. Two white birch grow out the top; one inside of the ruin and the other outside. The inside of the kiln is about 5 feet deep at the top, and has been the recipient of branches and much domestic trash. The inside diameter measured 11 feet at the widest, but gave indications of becoming wider farther down the reddish inside of the ruin, probably having the same egg-shaped interior as does WD-89. No firebrick or iron binding were found associated with the ruin. One piece of unmarked red brick was found on the ground in front of the opening but appears to be a stray piece, possibly having fallen out of some of the refuse that was dumped into the top of the ruin. The ruin is another magnificent example of 19th-century workmanship. The hint of a trail leads uphill to the southeast from the top of the ruin, somewhat paralleling a rusted barbed-wire fence.

While returning to the west side of the brook, the remains of a road were found opposite the kiln ruin, leading uphill toward limestone outcrop, confirming that a bridge connected the kiln to the west side of the brook. Directly above the outcrop and running north-south at the top edge of the steep incline is a 4- to 5-foot-high stone wall, most likely built to keep cattle from falling over the edge and into the limestone outcrop.

WD-90 Kenfield-Kaufmann Lime Kiln (Whitingham): Two miles southwest of Whitingham village and 1,000 feet south of the highway, a quarry provided limestone for Kenfield's lime kiln, which was near the road (Dale 1915:49). Lime was reported to have been burned here in the early 1860s. Limestone from Kenfield's quarry (spelled Kentfield in the reference) was analyzed at 97½ percent carbonate of lime (Hitchcock et al. 1861:748, 555). The 1869 Beers map of Whitingham shows the J. Kentfield house on the north side of the highway. Dale showed the quarry site just south of Route 100, about 1½ road miles east of the county line.

After spending an hour searching the heavy underbrush on

both sides of the brook south of the highway in 1990, only the quarry was found. Close inspection of a small grove of trees and brush in the open field north of the highway and just east of Bob Kaufmann's house (the old Kenfield homestead) revealed the barest traces of a lime kiln ruin. Most of the kiln's stonework is missing, but enough pieces of burned lime and the general configuration of a lime kiln were found to make the identification. The ruin, only about 50 feet uphill from the highway, must have been very visible in days when most of it was intact. Stonework at each end of the culvert that conveys the brook under the highway about 60 feet away hints at where some of the missing stone went, although close inspection of the culvert failed to reveal evidence of any burned stones. A fine stone wall across the highway, running diagonally southwest behind the barn, could be where more of the stone from the ruin came to rest.

WD-127 Kingsley Lime Kiln (Whitingham): During a repeat search for WD-LK01 in 1991, Arnold Kingsley gave directions to a kiln ruin on his farm, which is about a mile up Merrifield Road from Route 100. The kiln ruin is in a small grove of trees (containing the usual white birch) immediately across the road from the Carley Cemetery. The ruins measure about 12 feet square but are otherwise vague in configuration. There was much burned lime but no firebrick or red brick in evidence. Mr. Kingsley knew nothing about the age of the kiln or who operated it. He said that the farm was bought by his grandfather from Mr. Fortner, who had bought it from Mr. Newell. The 1869 Beers map of Whitingham shows C. B. Newell at the farm, who might have been the kiln operator. The Kingsley house dates to 1799 or 1800.

WD-LK01 Merrifield Road Lime Kiln (Whitingham): Lime was burned about a quarter-mile southwest of WD-90, where marble outcrops occur on both sides of the road (Dale 1915:49). Dale indicated the outcrop in the middle of the road. Inspection of the area in 1990 found stone outcrops everywhere, especially on the west side of the road, but no evidence of a lime kiln. Mr. Kingsley (see WD-127) also confirmed a lime kiln ruin in this vicinity, about a half-mile south of Route 100 on the east side of the road.

WD-FS14 Lime Hollow (Whitingham): A lime kiln is indicated on the 1869 Beers map of Whitingham, just downstream of the county line. Names associated with the kiln are L. and M. B. Bishop. The 1870 issue of *Walton's Vermont Register* listed W. Pike and Luna Bishop manufacturing lime at Sadawga.

The area was inspected in 1990, with no evidence of the kiln found, although the limestone outcrops of the hollow were very obvious. The site is close to the old Hoosac Tunnel & Wilmington Railroad right-of-way in the area of the Harriman Power Plant, either or both of which might have destroyed any kiln remains. This area was once known as Lime Hollow, from the amount of limestone quarried and burned in the vicinity (Swift 1977:514). The railroad bed and present road crisscross south from Readsboro, past the power plant to a gravel pit about a half-mile south of the plant. In some places, the present road was seen about 10 to 15 feet higher than an older road running back and forth beneath. Ruins that might have been here have long since been destroyed by either the road, railroad, or power plant, but subsurface remains might yet exist.

Since it was impossible to relate the present surface topography to roads and landmarks in the Beers map, even a remote guess as to the location of the kiln site could not be made. (Lime kilns also operated about a mile to the north; see BE-FS7 and BE-LK06.)

WD-126 Vermont Lime Company (Whitingham): The Vermont Lime Company operated a lime kiln along the east shore of the Deerfield River at Shermans, a station along the route of the Hoosac Tunnel & Wilmington Railroad. The site of the kiln ruin is about three miles south of Readsboro village, or about two miles north of the Massachusetts line. In the vicinity are also the extensive ruins and remains of the Sherman Carbide Company. The lime company is said to have operated ca.1890 to 1900, but possibly also operated earlier. "The company's logo was the strongest lime in Vermont. In the woods there were about five kilns. The largest of these kilns is oval in shape. If you go around this kiln you will find a hole which you can climb in. Mr. Henry Oakes, who is now 97 years old [1984], used to draw the cord wood that was once used in the kilns" (Lefebvre 1984). Lefebvre mentioned five kilns although only one was found. Dale wrote about the marble outcrop at this site but mentioned neither the lime kilns nor the carbide company that was in operation at the time.

The marble at Sherman has been shown by actual use to be valuable for the manufacture of calcium carbide. During the early part of the war [World War I] a plant for its manufacture was constructed at Sherman at a large cost. A very excellent product was made for six or eight years, but about a year ago the plant shut down and now it is being dismantled. There seems to be no local reason why the process should not be successfully carried forward. But the place is some distance from a coal supply and out on a stub railroad expensive to operate and these things are handicaps. On the other hand the plant is far enough from industrial centers to have little or no detrimental contacts with the large labor problem. Further, the product is claimed to be very superior. The marble is abundant and very easily gotten from quarry to plant. The geologic and geographic conditions may be considered very satisfactory (Hubbard 1924:342).

Three inspections were made, one in 1990 and two in 1991; the kiln ruin was found the third time with the assistance of Readsboro resident and former GE associate Bob Dion. The 20-foot-square and 5- to 6-foot-high stone ruin is uphill and east of the only major brook crossing a mile south of the power station, on the east side of an old road that climbs to eventually overlook a major portion of the carbide works ruins. Because it was pouring rain and conditions were near impossible, accurate measurements were left to another day. No firebrick was found associated with the ruin.

Downhill to the north, west, and south of the kiln ruin are nearly a dozen stone, brick, and concrete ruins of the carbide works on various levels of the hillside that rise steeply immediately east of the abandoned railroad right-of-way. There are three magnificent stone archways, one lined with three tiers of red brick, hinting at some kind of furnace operation; four oval, 1½-foot-high by about 6-foot-deep concrete ovens placed on a high platform of flues; at least two high, square, poured-concrete water towers that look like lime kiln ruins to the

unwary eye (and could account for some of the five kilns referred to by Lefebvre); many, many foundations of varied shapes and undetermined functions; and many cellar holes of houses and at least one hotel. One of the ruins associated with the carbide works might be a more modern lime kiln but this needs further study. One poured-concrete foundation is probably 50 feet square with walls that reach 25 to 30 feet high and reinforcement rods sticking higher at the tops of columns and corners. The building was obviously abandoned in mid-construction. Hundreds of firebricks of many configurations and brand names lay about. Noticeably missing was iron hardware, such as oven doors. Pieces of marble found at the quarry associated with the carbide works were found to contain graphite crystals. The whole area was heavily forested, which reduced visibility and prevented appreciation of the total range of the ruins.

Something very labor-intensive went on here at one time, and it will probably take an intimate knowledge of early-20th-century carbide making to be able to specifically interpret the function of each of the ruins. It is a fascinating site to explore and it begs for serious archeological study.

Summary of Results

The variability in design of lime kilns ranks just behind the variability in design of charcoal kilns. As is the case with charcoal kilns, ruins and remains of lime kilns reflect the various construction materials used, the configurations of the kilns, and the numbers of kilns at each site. Of the 118 lime kiln sites researched, 85 sites were found, and 64 of these (75 percent) yielded 93 ruins. Thirteen out of a possible 43 ruins still contained remains of their tall iron shells. Thirty-four ruins were found to be internally lined with firebrick. Table 8-2 presents the distribution of lime kiln sites and types of ruins by county.

The largest concentration of lime kiln ruins was found in Windsor County at Plymouth, where 17 ruins were found. These ruins are adjacent to outcrops of limestone that were considered in the early 19th century to be of exceptional quality.

Table 8-2. Distribution of Lime Kiln Sites and Ruins

| County | Sites | Type of Ruins | | | |
		Stone	Stone/ Concrete	Concrete	Total Ruins
Addison	12	3	1 + 6*		10
Bennington	15	4			4
Caledonia	1				
Chittenden	5	1		4*	5
Franklin	9	8	3 + 3*	2	16
Grand Isle	1				
Lamoille	5				
Orange	1				
Rutland	19	16		3	19
Windham	16	12			12
Windsor	34	27			27
Total:	118	71	4 + 9*	5 + 4*	93

*Contained remains of iron shells.

Glossary of Ironworks, Charcoal, Lime Kiln, and Brick-Making Terms

The following is a list of terms used in association with blast furnaces, bloomery forges, foundries, mining, charcoaling, lime burning, and brick making. Sources include dictionaries, encyclopedias, technical manuals, and professional papers, many of which are included in the Bibliography. While some of the definitions are taken from sources of the time, note that the meanings of some terms changed through the years with the technology.

Aalborg kiln: A lime kiln with two vertical inner chambers; also known as a Schöfer kiln.

Air furnace: A horizontal reverberatory furnace in which the metal is melted by the flame from fuel burning at one end of the hearth, which passes over the iron toward the stack (chimney) at the other end. See puddling furnace; reverberatory furnace.

Alloys: Metallic substances composed of two or more elements and processing properties different from those of their components.

Ancony: An unfinished bar of wrought iron, narrow in the middle but thick and coarse at the ends.

Ankle vents: The lowest row of vents in a charcoal kiln, at ankle height.

Anneal: Heating iron to above a critical range, holding it at that temperature for a required time, and slowly cooling it to make the iron less brittle.

Annealing pots: Iron boxes or containers in which castings are packed for protection against the furnace atmosphere during the annealing operation.

Anthracite furnace: An iron-smelting blast furnace that uses anthracite coal as its fuel.

Anvil: The base of a hammer into which a sow block and die are set; a block of iron or steel on which metal is forged.

Anvil cap: See sow block.

Arch bricks: Bricks that surround fire holes, or arches, on temporary kilns or clamps.

Ashlar: Cut-and-finished stone building blocks.

Bats: Broken bricks with one entire end.

Bear: A large unmelted mass of furnace charge. See salamander.

Bellows: A box with flexible sides in which alternate expansion and contraction draws air through a side valve and expels it through a nozzle.

Belly pipe: The air pipe that supplies blast from outside the furnace (from the bellows) to the dropper and bustle pipes from beneath the hearth.

Bessemer process: A process of making steel from cast iron through burning out carbon and impurities by blasting air upward through the bottom of the molten metal. It heralded the age of cheap steel in the U.S., beginning in 1865. Because it was not suitable for all iron, it was suspended in the early 20th century by the open-hearth or Siemens-Martin process.

Billet: Iron stock with a round-cornered square or rectangular cross-section, to which further processing, such as forging or rolling, is given.

Binder: Cross-rods and hardware that hold the blast-furnace masonry from shifting while settling.

Blacking: Carbon facing for foundry molds or cores consisting of charred wood, coal, coke, or graphite ground to a powder. See foundry facing.

Blacksmith: A smith who forges by hammering (black; the color of the metal). See whitesmith.

Blast: A continuous blowing, to which the charge of ore or metal is subject in the furnace.

Blast furnace: A tall-shaft variety of furnace operated by forced draft.

Bloom: A mass of wrought iron from a Catalan forge or a puddling furnace, deprived of its dross and shaped in the form of an oblong block by shingling; metal that has been somewhat reduced from an ingot by rolling or cogging, but which receives further work by rolling or forging. See loop.

Bloomer: One who works blooms at the forge. See puddler.

Bloomery: A forge that makes wrought-iron blooms directly from ore, or more rarely from cast iron.

Bloomsman: See bloomer.

Bloom tongs: See tongs.

Blow: The impact or other pressure produced by the moving part of any forging unit.

Blowing in: Starting up the blast furnace.

Blowing out: Shutting the blast furnace down.

Blowing tubs: Blast-producing machinery consisting of water-wheel-driven pistons and cylinders, which replaced bellows.

Blows: Trapped gas bubbles in castings, causing voids in the metal.

Bod: A cone-shaped lump of clay attached to the end of a stick to close the furnace taphole.

Bosh: The bottom inward-sloping surfaces of the furnace cavity.

Boss: A projection on the main body of the forging, generally cylindrical in shape.

Bottom board: A wood board which acts as a base for the mold.

Bottom sand: The layer of sand with clay rammed on the bottom doors of the furnace to form the sloping hearth or crucible bottom.

Bottom stope: See underhand stope.

Brand: Incompletely charred wood in a charcoal kiln.

Breast: Part of the furnace lining connecting the spout with the bottom and made up with a taphole for every heat.

Breast wheel: A waterwheel, driven by water passing behind and below the wheel, driving it in opposite direction from the overshot wheel. See undershot wheel.

Bridge: An obstruction within the blast furnace that prevents the charge from moving downward.

Bunny: A mass of ore, as distinguished from a vein. See horse.

Burnt lime: See quicklime.

Burrs: Bricks that stuck together during heating; also called clinkers.

Bustle pipe: A pipe that partially or fully encircles the stack to supply blast air to two or more tuyeres.

Calcining: Heating to high temperatures without melting, to remove volatile matter. See sinter.

Carbonate of lime: Chemical name for limestone.

Carbon steel: Steel in which the physical properties depend primarily on the carbon content, other elements not being present in appreciable quantities.

Carburize: Adding carbon to low-carbon iron or steel by heating it to above critical range when in contact with some carbonaceous material (charcoal, coke).

Case harden: A method of hardening the surface of the metal.

Casting sprue: See sprue.

Cast iron: An iron containing so much carbon, usually above 1.7 percent, that it is not usefully malleable at any temperature.

Catalan forge: A bloomery that produces wrought iron from ore and has a siliceous bottom lined with charcoal and a tuyere inclining downward. The front is piled with ore and the back with charcoal and the whole covered with a fine mixed ore and charcoal dust moistened with water. So named from the area of Spain (Catalonia) where it evolved.

Caustic lime: See quicklime.

Cement: Mixture of lime, clay, and shale or blast furnace slag that is ground together, heated to fusing, quickly cooled, and ground into powder.

Cementation: A steel-making process dating back to the late 16th century, in which wrought-iron bars were held at high temperature in a closed oven (furnace) in the presence of carbon-rich material (charcoal). If left long enough, the carbon penetrates the iron, converting it to steel.

Cement mortar: Mixture of lime and cement with sand and water. See lime mortar; cement.

Champlain Forge: A modification of the Catalan forge, developed in the Adirondack district of New York, in which blast was preheated.

Char: To reduce to charcoal or carbon by burning in the absence of air.

Charcoal: Carbon prepared from vegetable or animal substances, as by charring wood in a kiln from which air is excluded.

Charcoal furnace: A blast furnace that uses charcoal as its fuel.

Charcoal kiln: Round, rectangular, or conical structures made of brick or stone for charring wood. See kiln.

Charge: A given weight of metal, stone, and/or fuel introduced into a furnace or kiln.

Checkerwork: A firebrick structure built so that the bricks alternate with open spaces, permitting the passage of gases which give heat, or receive heat from the firebricks. See recuperator.

Chill: A properly shaped casting forming part of the entire interior molding surface, intended to draw heat from the molten metal so rapidly it solidifies faster at that point and becomes sound.

Chipping: Removing fins and gates from castings with a chisel; the process of chipping slag and refuse attached to the lining of the furnace after the heat has been run.

Chuffs: See shuffs.

Cinder: Unburned or unreduced charge or fuel.

Clamp: A temporary-type brick kiln; variant of a scove kiln.

Clinker: A brick heated to near or actual melting or vitrifying; also hardened, burned impurities in a lime kiln.

Coal blacking: An iron founder's blacking made from ground coal. See blacking.

Coal off: To cut a forest for charcoal wood.

Cogging: The reducing operation in working the ingot into a billet by the use of a forging hammer or a forging press.

Coke: Residue of coal remaining after high-temperature heating, used as a fuel in furnaces and forges.

Cold blast: Furnace blast at air (outside) temperature.

Cold-short: Metal that is brittle when heated below a red-heat. See hot-short; red-short.

Cold shut: An imperfect junction between two flows of metal in a mold.

Collier: A coal miner or a charcoal maker.

Concrete: Mixture of cement and gravel.

Cope: The upper or top-most section of a flask, mold, or pattern.

Core: A separate part of the mold that forms cavities and openings in castings, which are not possible with a pattern alone.

Crib: Timber framework support or foundation for a structure such as a dam.

Crucible: A vessel with a refractory lining used for melting or calcining iron or steel.

Crucible steel: A type of steel made by melting steel that is made in cementation furnaces in clay crucibles. It produced a better-quality steel with a more even distribution of carbon. The process originated in the 18th century.

Culls: Bricks so defective they cannot be sold.

Cupola: A type of blast furnace for melting metal (as compared to smelting ore), which consists of a vertical cylinder lined with refractory material and provided with openings for the entrance of a blast. In the cupola furnace, metal is melted in direct contact with the fuel.

Cwt: A hundredweight; 100 pounds (or 112 pounds if in long tons). The common unit of weight at an ironworks. See long ton; quarter.

Daub up: The process of applying a mixture of clay and sand to the defective parts of a furnace lining after a heat, to restore the original lining.

Die casting: Pouring metal into a metallic mold or die and holding it there until solidification takes place.

Dies: Steel blocks into which desired impressions are machined, and from which forgings are produced. Forging dies usually come in pairs, with part of the impression in one of the blocks and the balance in the other.

Downcomer: See downer.

Downer: The pipe or chute that conducts blast down to the bustle pipe or tuyere inside an early blast furnace, or draws air down to the charge in a lime kiln.

Draft: The stream of air blast delivered by the bellows or air pump that maintains combustion in the furnace.

Drag: Lower or bottom section of a flask, mold, or pattern; also called nowel.

Draw: See temper.

Draw bar: A bar used for lifting the pattern from the sand of the mold.

Drift: A mine passageway driven on, or parallel to, the course of a vein of rock stratum.

Drop forge: The shape obtained by working metal in a pair of dies to produce the form in the finishing impression under a drop hammer.

Dropper: An air pipe that supplies blast from the belly pipe under the hearth to the bustle pipe.

Dross: The solid scum that forms on the surface of a metal when molten or melting, largely a result of oxidation, but sometimes dirt and impurities rising to the surface.

Dumb stove: A fireless, sheet-metal stove that radiates heat received from a fired cast-iron stove that is usually on the floor below.

Dump: The fuel bed and slag that falls out of the furnace when the bottom is dropped after a heat has been run.

Equalizer: See windbox.

Fag-end: The part of the bloom cut off when cutting it in half by drop hammer.

Fagot: Pieces of wrought iron, bundled together, for rolling or hammering at high temperature.

Fillers: Ironworkers who charged ore, fuel, and flux into the top of the blast furnace.

Fin: See flash.

Finery: See refinery.

Firebrick: Brick made of highly refractory clays.

Firebridge: A short wall inside a reverberatory furnace, made of highly refractory material, which separates the fire from the molten metal.

Fire sand: A sand so free from fluxes that it is highly refractory.

Flash: The metal that is in excess of that required to fill out the final impression in a pair of dies, and moves out as a thin plate through the parting line of the dies. Also called fin.

Flash pan: The machined portion of the die that permits the excess metal to flow through.

Flask: A metal or wood box without top and without fixed bottom, used to hold the sand in which a mold is formed. It usually consists of a cope and drag, which remain on the mold during pouring.

Flop forging: A forging in which the bottom and top die impression parts are identical, permitting the forging to be turned upside-down during pouring.

Flume: An inclined channel for conveying water from a distance to supply power to a waterwheel, turbine, reservoir, etc. See race.

Flux: The basic material added to the furnace charge that unites with sand, ash, and dirt during melting to form slag.

Forehearth: A stationary covered container directly attached to the furnace, into which the metal flows as fast as melted, and from which it is tapped for distribution.

Forge: Usually, a general term that includes a furnace, or a shop with a hearth, where wrought iron is produced directly from the ore, and is rendered malleable. See bloomery.

Forging: Metal that has been worked to some definite predetermined shape by a process of hammering, upsetting, or pressing, either hot or cold, or by a combination of several of these processes.

Foss hook: An iron rod with a loop at one end and a handle at the other; used at the forge for handling the bloom.

Foundry: An establishment in which metals are molded or forged for production of castings.

Foundry facing: A ground carbon (coal) material applied to the surface of a sand mold to prevent the molten metal from penetrating and reacting with the sand of the mold. See sea coal.

Friable ore: Ore easily crumbled into small pieces. See shot ore.

Furgen: A 4-foot-long straight iron rod used for sounding the fire in the bloomery forge. Also called a tempering bar.

Fuse: To heat to melting temperature.

Gabbro: A dense igneous rock containing low quantities of iron and lime. It was unsuccessfully burned in some 17th-century New England blast furnaces for ore; later used for flux.

Gangue: Non-iron mineral matter associated with the ore.

Ganister (gannister): A fine-grain quartzite used in the manufacture of refractory brick.

Gate: The end of a runner where the molten metal enters the mold.

German steel: Also called natural steel, produced by interrupting the refining process in a forge before all the carbon was removed.

Giant: A large nozzle used in hydraulic mining.

Gossan: Decomposed rock or vein material of reddish or rusty color caused by oxidation (as in a road cut).

Grampuses: Four- to five-foot-long tongs for handling the red-hot bloom.

Grappier: A form of natural cement made in a lime kiln by sintering clinkers.

Gray stock brick: Good bricks but irregular in color.

Grissel (grizzel) bricks: Slightly better-burned bricks than place bricks.

Grizzly: A coarse screen grating used in hydraulic mining for keeping large stones swept down by the current out of the grizzly box; also, a mechanically actuated type having moving chains, disks, rings, etc.

Grizzly box: A large box, usually of wood, to collect ore washed into it, the result of the hydraulic mining process.

Grizzly elevator: An ore-washing device operated by a hydraulic giant (nozzle; see giant), consisting of a long, wide chute with an approaching apron, and a short bottom section followed by a long grizzly.

Grizzlyman: A miner who operates the grizzly.

Headrace: That part of the race that conveys water to the waterwheel. See tailrace.

Hearth: The floor or sole of the furnace.

Heat: A stated tonnage of metal obtained from a period of continuous melting in a furnace.

Heat treat: Any operation of heating metal and cooling it in order to bring out desired physical properties.

Helve: The heavy wood boom of a forge hammer, with the hammerhead at one end, being raised by cams at the other end.

Hollowware: As distinguished from flatware, an article that has volume and significant depth (cups, bowls, pots, kettles, etc.).

Horse: A large mass of ore, parallel to the walls of the mine. Also, a large body of useless rock within an ore deposit. See bunny.

Horse whim: See whim.

Hot blast: Furnace blast preheated to 400° F or more.

Hot-short: Metal that is brittle when heated beyond red-heat. See red-short; cold-short.

Hot spruing: Removing castings from gates before the metal has completely solidified.

Hurdle: An outside covering of earth, leaves, or brush that insulates the kiln.

Hydrated lime: Lime that is treated with water after burning in the kiln; forms calcium hydroxide. See lime water.

Ingot: The casting from which the rolled or forged iron is to be produced.

Iron: Fe, atomic number 26, atomic weight 55.847; fourth most common element, second most common metal behind aluminum; a heavy, malleable, ductile, magnetic element that readily rusts in moist air; occurs native in meteorites and combined in most igneous rocks; is the most used metal and is vital in biological processes.

Jigging: Process by which ore and rock are separated after crushing, through mechanical water separation.

Jinker: See whim.

Keystone kiln: A separate-feed-type lime kiln.

Kibble: An ore bucket, or tub, hoisted by means of a waterpowered windlass.

Kiln: A large stove, oven, or furnace of brick, stone, or clay; a heated chamber for hardening, burning, or drying anything.

Kiln scum: See whitewash.

Knee vents: The middle row of vents in a charcoal kiln, at knee height.

Launder: A box conduit (sluice; trough) conveying particulate ore material suspended in water; a refractory trough conveying molten metal. See riffle.

Lime: Product of a lime kiln, made by burning limestone at high temperature without melting it.

Lime kiln: Round or square stone/brick structures for calcining limestone.

Lime mortar: Mixture of slaked lime and sand.

Lime water: An alkaline water solution of calcium hydroxide.

Lining: The refractory material of uniform and ample thickness built up within the furnace or kiln shell to form the container of the charge for melting or calcining.

Long ton: The usual unit of weight for iron: 2,240 pounds.

Loop: A mass of semimolten iron in a pasty condition, gathered into a ball from a bloomery forge or puddling furnace for the tilt (trip-) hammer or rolling mill. Also known as loupe. See bloom.

Loupe: See loop.

Machinability: The property of permitting tooling or finishing by machining.

Machine-cast: Pig iron made by running the blast furnace pig iron directly into open molds.

Malleable: Capable of being hammered or rolled without breaking; ductile.

Malleable cast iron: Originally, a white cast iron of proper composition subsequently rendered malleable by annealing without remelting.

Malms: The best-made bricks for finest quality brickwork.

Marl: Sand, silt, or clay soil that contains a substantial amount of calcium carbonate; sometimes burned in kilns for fertilizer.

Marls: Bricks made from natural clay and lime.

Meiler: A circular mound of cordwood covered with earth and wet leaves, for making charcoal.

Melting loss: The reduction in weight on the part of the metal charged incident to the melting operation.

Melting rate: The hourly tonnage of iron melted in a furnace.

Melting ratio: The proportion of metal weight charged to the fuel weight that is melting in the furnace.

Metallurgy: The art of extracting metals from their ores and refining them, up to the point required by the metal industry.

Minehead: The top of a mining pit or shaft, including the immediately adjacent ground or buildings.

Mold: A body of sand or other heat-resistant material containing a cavity, which when filled with molten metal yields a casting of the desired shape. Also spelled mould.

Mold clamps: Devices used to hold or lock the cope and drag together.

Molding sand: Sand containing sufficient refractory clay substance to bond strongly without destroying the permeability to air and gases when rammed to the degree required.

Mold weights: Weights placed on top of molds while pouring, to offset internal pressure or "floating."

Mortar: Mixture of lime and cement with sand and water. See lime mortar; cement mortar.

Mould: See mold.

Muck bar: Iron bars made at the puddling furnace.

Natural steel: See German steel.

Nowel: See drag.

Ochre (ocher): Earthy, impure iron ore, usually yellow or red, used in the manufacture of paint.

Opencast stope: See overhand stope.

Open-pit mining: The system of extracting ore from the ground by digging deep open holes or pits.

Ore: Metal-containing earthen material in its natural state.

Ore dressing: Treatment of the ore involving physical, not chemical, change such as washing, crushing, concentrating, sampling.

Oven: A stove, or an arrangement of pipes at the tunnel head, for preheating blast; a stove for roasting ore to remove gases. See recuperator.

Overhand stope: Ore mined underground from the roof of the gallery. The excavation is sometimes pyramid-shaped, but it may be any shape as determined by the outline of the ore body. Also called opencast stope, rill stope, shrinkage stope. See stope.

Over iron: The iron melted in excess of the amount estimated to cover a day's molding requirement.

Overshot wheel: A waterwheel driven by water passing over the top and in front (downstream side) of the wheel. See breast wheel; undershot wheel.

Parched: A burnt or scorched surface, as the inside stone walls of a kiln or furnace.

Parlor-cook stove: A 19th-century cast-iron parlor stove modified for cooking or baking.

Parting line: The dividing plane between the two pair of dies used in forging metal.

Paviours: Excellent-quality bricks.

Pecking bricks: See place bricks.

Picked stock: The best bricks of the lot.

Pickling: A solution or bath for treating metal (e.g., passivating).

Pig bed: Small, open, sand molds, made in the floor of the foundry near the furnace, to hold the over iron and other waste metal.

Piggin: A one-handled vessel or pail, usually of wood.

Pig iron: A cast iron that has been run into pigs direct from the blast furnace, so-called because as run from the blast furnace, the iron in the sand molds resembles a sow with suckling pigs.

Pithead: See minehead.

Place bricks: Bricks made on or near the outside of the baking kiln and not sufficiently burned; intermediate in condition between shuffs and grissels.

Pot kiln: An early-19th-century lime kiln, distinctive by its primitive, potbelly appearance.

Pot metal: Scrap iron (from old iron pots).

Press forging: A forging produced by a mechanical or hydraulic press.

Prills: Hardened droplets of metal trapped inside cooled slag, usually retrieved by picking through broken or crushed slag.

Prop: The iron post used to rigidly support hinged bottom doors of a furnace.

Puddle: To work metal, while molten, into a desired shape with a long iron tool. See loop.

Puddler: One who puddles iron. See puddle.

Puddling: The process patented in 1784 (England) in which melted cast iron is converted into wrought iron. It ultimately superseded the refining method associated with the charcoal furnace as a cheaper and faster method of making wrought iron. See loop.

Puddling furnace: A small reverberatory furnace in which cast iron is converted into wrought iron; an air furnace. See bloomery; forge.

Pug mill: An early machine for preparing clay for brick making;

also called mud mill.

Puzzolana: Lime mixed with volcanic rock; named from where first found, at Pozzuoli, near Vesuvius.

Quarter: A quarter of a cwt; 25 pounds (or 28 pounds in long tons).

Quenching: Rapid cooling by immersing in air, gas, or liquids.

Quicklime: Pure lime, after burning in the kiln, composed of calcium oxide.

Race: A natural or constructed watercourse that conveys water to power waterwheels or turbines. See headrace; tailrace; flume.

Ram: The moving part of a drop hammer; a press to which one of the dies is fastened.

Rammer: A wooden tool with a round mallet-shaped head at one end and a wedge-shaped head at the other, used in packing sand around the pattern.

Ram off: A casting defect caused by improper ramming.

Recuperator: A refractory checkerwork or other installation, heated by the exhaust gases of a furnace, and through sections or tubes of which air is drawn to provide preheated air for more efficient combustion of the furnace fuel.

Red-short: Metal that is brittle when red-hot.

Refinery: A furnace with a shallow hearth for converting (refining) pig iron to wrought iron. See puddling furnace.

Refractory: Material capable of enduring high temperature without fusing, corroding, or deforming.

Reverberatory furnace: A hearth furnace where the flame is drawn over the firebridge and sweeps through the chamber to the chimney. Burning gases heat the stock, roof, and side walls of the furnace, and the radiated heat melts and superheats the metal. See air furnace; puddling furnace.

Riddle: A sieve used to sift sand during molding to eliminate large particles of sand or foreign material.

Riddling: Waste material rejected after screening.

Riffle: Various contrivances, such as blocks and rails, laid on the bottom of the sluice to make a series of grooves to catch and retain grains of ore. See launder.

Rill stope: See overhand stope.

Riser: A reservoir of molten metal provided to compensate for the internal contraction of the casting as it solidifies; an outlet over a high part of the mold to indicate the level of the molten metal in the mold.

Rock wool: A mineral wool made by blowing a jet of steam through molten limestone or through slag, and used chiefly for heat and sound insulation.

Rolling and slitting mill: A foundry in which wrought-iron bars were rolled into plate iron, then passed through opposing disc cutters that sheared the plate into long thin rods used primarily by nail makers.

Rough stock: Irregular bricks in both color and shape.

Round furnace: A round, brick-constructed charcoal kiln.

Rubble: Rough stone as it comes from the quarry.

Rubble ashlar: Ashlar with a rubble backing.

Runner: An enlarged pouring basin or deep channel connecting with gates to bring metal to them.

Salamander: A piece of iron that solidified prematurely and formed an obstruction within the furnace, so called because of its general similarity in shape to a salamander, although usually much larger. Larger pieces were called bears.

Sand-cast pig iron: Pig iron made by running blast-furnace metal into open molds in the sand.

Scab: Imperfection on the surface of a casting due to the breaking away of a portion of the mold sand by the action of the stream of molten iron pouring into the mold.

Scaffold: An accumulation of adherent, partly fused material forming a shelf, or a dome-shaped obstruction, above the tuyeres in a blast furnace, cupola, or the like.

Scaffolding: Formation of scaffold.

Schöfer kiln: See Aalborg kiln.

Scove kiln: A temporary-type brick kiln; also called clamp.

Sea coal: A mineral coal distinguished by the English because it was first found in seacoast veins; also, pulverized bituminous coal used in sand molds. See foundry facing.

Seconds: Bricks sorted from best-quality malms but still used for building fronts.

Shell: A round iron/steel tower, 5 to 8 feet in diameter and 20 to 40 feet high, lined inside with firebrick, and rising above the base of the lime kiln to increase its draft and charge capacity.

Shellmarl: Ancient silt containing substantial amounts of shellfish remains; often burned for fertilizer. See marl.

Shingle: To subject a mass of iron from a bloomery or puddling furnace to the process of expelling cinder and impurities by hammering and squeezing.

Shingler: An ironworker who shingles by hammer, or by machine.

Shippers: Bricks of higher quality than stock bricks, burned and sound, but not perfect in form.

Short: Refuse and clippings discarded during production of castings.

Shot ore: Ore that crumbles easily (friable) into small fragments, from the size of small shot to that of a large pea.

Shrinkage stope: See overhand stope.

Shuffs: Bricks full of cracks due to wind, rain, or frost while they were hot from the kiln. See place bricks.

Siliceous: Containing silica (e.g., limestone).

Sinter: Ore that has been burned, not melted, so as to separate its elements.

Skim gate: An overhead gate so arranged that it skims dirt from the molten iron passing through it and keeps the dirt out of the casting.

Skimmer: A tool used for removing slag from the molten metal.

Skip car: A small car that carries ore, fuel, and flux from storage bins to the top of a modern blast furnace.

Skip hoist: The inclined track on which the skip car is hoisted to the top of the blast furnace.

Slack: Finest screenings of coal produced at the mine; unusable as fuel unless cleaned.

Slag: A low-melting, nonmetallic covering that forms on the surface of molten iron as a result of combining impurities contained in the original charge, including some ash from the fuel and any silica and clay eroded from the refractory lining of the furnace. It is skimmed off prior to tapping the heat. Slag occurs in virtually every iron-making and iron-working process that involves molten iron.

Slag hole: An aperture in the furnace slightly above the top level of the molten iron, through which the slag is drawn off.

Slag out: Adding flux (limestone) into the furnace.

Slag spout: The channel casting bolted to the furnace serving for the convenient removal of slag coming through the slag hole.

Slake: The process of decomposing through heat and moisture, as in slaking limestone.

Slaked lime: See hydrated lime.

Slaker: A worker who makes hydrated lime.

Slake trough: A water tank for cooling forgings or tools.

Sleepers: Timbers laid in a mine to support ore car tracks.

Slice: An iron bar flattened at one end for use as a fire shovel.

Slice bar: A steel bar with a broad flat blade for chipping or scraping (in breaking up) clinkers.

Slice up: To work a forge fire with a slicing motion.

Slitting mill: A foundry where iron plates and sheets are cut into long narrow rods, suitable for making nails or spikes. See rolling and slitting mill.

Sluice: A constructed waterway fitted with a valve or gate to regulate the flow of water to a turbine or waterwheel.

Sluice gate: A gate or valve. See sluice.

Smith forging: Forgings made by hand on an anvil or under some power hammer without dies, containing an exact finishing impression of the part. Used where the quality does not warrant expenditure for special dies. Also called hand forging or flat die forging.

Smith hammer: Any power hammer where impression dies are not used for the reproduction of commercially exact forgings.

Soft steel: A term sometimes used to designate low-carbon steel.

Sow block: A block of heat-treated iron placed between the hammer anvil and the forging die, to prevent undue wear to the anvil. Also called an anvil cap.

Spall: The cracking off or flaking of small particles of surface metal.

Spout: A channel casting bolted to the furnace that when lined with refractory material forms a continuation of the bottom of the furnace and carries the molten metal from the taphole to the ladles or molds.

Sprue: Part of the die machined out to permit a connection between multiple impressions or between the impression and the forging bar; the metal settled in the gates, risers, runners, and pouring basins of a mold and forming the scrap of a foundry, other than defective castings and over iron.

Sprue cutter: A metal tool used to cut the pouring aperture.

Steel: Iron cast from a molten state containing at least 0.30 percent carbon.

Stock brick: Bricks molded on a stock, a ½-inch-thick board nailed to the molding table. The mold fitted around it and held it in place.

Stope: Horizontal underground mining excavation forming one of a series of "steps," from which ore has been removed from the vein. See overhand stope; underhand stope.

Stove black: Blacking (graphite) used for polishing cast-iron stoves. Also called stove polish.

Stuckofen: An early German blast furnace (stack-oven).

Stull: A round timber used to support sides and back walls of a mine working; one of a series of supports wedged between the walls of a stope to hold up a platform; a platform laid on stulls to support miners, ore, or tailings.

Stuller: A miner who works at stulls.

Swage: A tool used to shape metal by holding it directly on the piece and striking the tool with a hammer.

Swage block: A perforated iron or steel block with grooved sides, used to head bolts, and for swaging bars by hand.

Taconite: A dense, low-grade (30 percent) iron ore.

Tailings: Refuse material separated from the ore as residue during the ore-dressing process.

Tailrace: Part of a race that conveys water away from the waterwheel. See headrace; flume.

Taphole: Opening in the furnace breast through which molten metal is allowed to run to the spout.

Taphole plug stick: See bod.

Tap-out bar: A bar that opens the taphole in the furnace.

Tapping: Opening the aperture at the spout to permit the molten metal to run from the furnace.

Teeming: Pouring steel from a ladle into ingot molds.

Temper: Reheating iron after the quenching operation to some temperature below critical range, to produce desired physical properties. Also called draw.

Tilt hammer: A heavy drop hammer operated by means of waterwheel and cams, or a small engine. Also called trip-hammer.

Timp: See tymph.

Tipple: A bridge-like structure on which railroad cars are tipped over to dump their contents (ore, coal, sand) into hoppers or ships below.

Tonghold: A small forging projection used to manipulate a casting with tongs during the forging operation.

Tongs: Metal holders for handling hot pieces of metal.

Tool steel: A superior grade of steel made primarily for use in the manufacture of tools and dies.

Tote box: Metal container used to convey forgings to the various foundry-processing operations.

Tremie: An apparatus located immediately above the tunnel head of a blast furnace, consisting of a hopper and cone, evenly distributing large and small particles of charge when released into the stack. The tremie also serves to block stack gases from the charging area through its double-door arrangement.

Trimmer: The dies used to remove the flash or excess stock from the forging.

Trip-hammer: See tilt hammer.

Trompe: A device that traps air in water falling through a pipe. Air is sucked through sloping holes in the sides of the pipe and collected in a box at the bottom. The slight pressure of collected air supplies a weak furnace draft.

Trunnel head: See tunnel head.

Tubs: See blowing tubs.

Tumbling: A process for removing scale from forgings in a rotating barrel containing castings and abrasives.

Tunnel head: The top of the furnace shaft at its smallest inside diameter. Sometimes called trunnel head.

Turbine: An iron wheel-type device that is rotated by impulse of the water on cups or vanes surrounding a central shaft, and connected to machinery.

Turn-bat: A piece of wood 2 to 6 inches long by 1½ inches wide, used in the bloomery to jam the handles of a bloom tong open so that the jaws of the tongs keep a firm grip on the bloom.

Turn-table: In an underground mine, a simple platform hinged to a hanging wall, raised or lowered by means of a windlass, to enable ore cars to pass to upper or lower galleries.

Tuyere: A nozzle, usually made of iron, through which the blast is supplied into the furnace.

Tymph: An overhanging stone or water-cooled iron casting inside the hearth that holds stack gases and slag from running out the taphole along with molten iron. Also spelled timp; tymp.

Underhand stope: Ore mined from the floor of the gallery in which the stope is usually shaped like an inverted pyramid, or sometimes like a rude staircase. Also called a bottom stope. See stope.

Undershot wheel: A waterwheel driven by water passing under it and rotating the wheel in reverse from an overshot wheel. See breast wheel.

Upset forge: A forging formed by pressure on hot or cold metal between dies operated in a horizontal plane.

Waist vents: The upper row of vents in a charcoal kiln, at waist height.

Warm blast: Preheated furnace blast less than 400° F.

Waterwheel: A wood or iron wheel made to rotate by direct action of water passing over, behind, or under it, and connected by shafts and linkages to drive mill machinery. See breast wheel; overshot wheel; undershot wheel; turbine.

Wheel pit: A stone- or concrete-lined channel or enclosure inside which the waterwheel is mounted.

Whim: A machine for hoisting ore from a mine, having a large vertical drum on which the hoisting rope is wound, with one or two radiating arms or beams to which a horse(s) may be yoked. Also called a horse whim, whimsey, or jinker.

Whitesmith: A smith who finishes and polishes the work, as distinguished from the blacksmith, who forges it.

Whitewash: A permanent efflorescence that forms on the inside wall of a lime kiln, caused by too rapid an application of heat; also known as kiln scum. A composition of lime and water for whiting plaster, masonry, or wood surfaces.

Windbox (equalizer): A chamber surrounding the furnace at the tuyere level, to equalize the volume and pressure of the air delivered to the tuyeres.

Wringer: A 7-foot-long iron bar used to pry the bloom free inside the forge through a side hole.

Wrought iron: A malleable iron, aggregated from pasty particles without subsequent fusion. It contains so little carbon that it does not harden usefully when cooled rapidly. Iron made by the puddling process containing iron in fibrous form intermixed with slag.

Bibliography

Abbott, Collamer M., Jan. 1965, "Early Copper Smelting in Vermont" *Vermont History* Vermont Historical Society, vol. 33, no. 1, pp. 233–242.
––––––––––––, 1973 *Green Mountain Copper* Randolph, Herald Printing.
Acts and Laws Passed by the Legislature of . . . Vermont 1810, Danville, Ebenezer Eaton, State Printer.
Acts and Laws Passed by the Legislature of . . . Vermont 1825, Simeon Ide.
Acts and Laws Passed by the Legislature of . . . Vermont 1826.
Acts and Laws Passed by the Legislature of . . . Vermont 1827, Woodstock, D. Watson.
Acts and Laws Passed by the Legislature of . . . Vermont 1835, Montpelier, E. P. Walton & Son.
Acts and Resolves Passed by the General Assembly of . . . Vermont 1862, Montpelier, Freeman Printing Establishment.
Adams, Andrew N., 1870 *History of the Town of Fair Haven, Vermont* Fair Haven, Leonard and Phelps.
Adams, Charles B., 1845 *First Annual Report on the Geology of the State of Vermont* Burlington, Chauncey Goodrich.
––––––––––––, 1846 *Second Annual Report on the Geology of the State of Vermont* Burlington, Chauncey Goodrich.
"Africa's Ancient Steelmakers," Sept. 25, 1978 *Time* p. 80.
Aldrich, Lewis C., 1889 *History of Bennington County, Vermont* Syracuse, N.Y., D. Mason.
––––––––––––, 1891 *History of Franklin and Grand Isle Counties, Vermont* Syracuse, N.Y., D. Mason.
––––––––––––, and Frank R. Holmes, 1891 *History of Windsor County, Vermont* Syracuse, N.Y., D. Mason.
Allen, Richard S., 1967, "Separation and Inspiration" *Penfield Foundation Historical Publication No. 1* Ironville, N.Y., Penfield Foundation.
––––––––––––, ms, 1980, "Skene's Ore Beds and the Cheever Mine."
––––––––––––, ms, 1982, "Vulcan's Workshops at Ticonderoga."
––––––––––––, June 1983, "The Iron Industry of Northern New York" *CIM Bulletin* Canadian Institute of Mining, vol. 76, no. 854, pp. 85–89.
American Malleable Iron 1944, Cleveland, Ohio, Malleable Founder's Society.
Anderson, George Baker, 1897 *Landmarks of Rensselaer County, New York* Syracuse, D. Mason and Co.
Anderson, George Pomeroy, Sept. 1939, "Highgate as Seen from an Old Account Book" *Proceedings of the Vermont Historical Society* Brattleboro, new series, vol. 7, no. 3, pp. 121–160.
Andrews, Ambrose, 1859 *Sutherland Falls* oil on canvas, Vermont Historical Society Archives, catalog no. A–105.
Annual Report of the Secretary of Internal Affairs of the Commonwealth of Pennsylvania 1894, Harrisburg, Clarence M. Busch, Official Document no. 10, pt. 3, Industrial Statistics: vol. 22 ("The Manufacture of Pig Iron in Pennsylvania," by John Birkinbine).
Ashton, Dorothy Hemenway, 1979 *Sheldon, Vermont: The People Who Lived and Worked There* St. Albans, Regal Art Press.
Asselin, E. Donald, M.D., Jan. 1963, "An Early Vermont Industry: Paddock's Iron Furnace, St. Johnsbury, Vt." *News and Notes* Vermont Historical Society, vol. 14, no. 5, pp. 34–35.
Austin, Aleine, 1981 *Matthew Lyon: "New Man" of the Democratic Revolution, 1749–1822* University Park and London, Pennsylvania State University Press.
Barker, Elmer E., Oct. 1942, "The Story of Crown Point Iron" *New York History* Cooperstown, New York State Historical Association, pp. 419–437.
Batchelder, Ira K., 1891 *Historical Sketch of Peru, Vermont* Brattleboro, Phoenix Job Print, E. E. Hildreth and Co.
Bearse, Ray, ed., 1968 *Vermont: A Guide to the Green Mountain State* Boston, Mass., Houghton Mifflin, 3d ed.
Beattie, Evelyn H., ed., 1977 *Peru Historical Album: Vermont Bicentennial 1977* Bennington, Hadwen, Inc.

"Beehive Coke Ovens to Fire Up One Last Time," Scottdale, Pa., Sept. 11 (AP), Sept. 12, 1982 *New York Times* sec. 1, p. 73.
Beers, [F. W.], 1869 *Atlas of Bennington County, Vermont* New York, F. W. Beers, A. D. Ellis, and G. G. Soule.
––––––––––––, 1869 *Atlas of Chittenden County, Vermont* New York, F. W. Beers, A. D. Ellis, and G. G. Soule.
––––––––––––, 1869 *Atlas of Rutland County, Vermont* New York, F. W. Beers, A. D. Ellis, and G. G. Soule.
––––––––––––, 1869 *Atlas of Windham County, Vermont* New York, F. W. Beers, A. D. Ellis, and G. G. Soule.
––––––––––––, 1869 *Atlas of Windsor County, Vermont* New York, F. W. Beers, A. D. Ellis, and G. G. Soule.
––––––––––––, 1871 *Atlas of Addison County, Vermont* New York, F. W. Beers and Co.
––––––––––––, 1871 *Atlas of Franklin and Grand Isle Counties, Vermont* New York, F. W. Beers and Co.
––––––––––––, 1873 *Atlas of Washington County, Vermont* New York, F. W. Beers and Co.
––––––––––––, 1875 *Atlas of Caledonia County, Vermont* New York, F. W. Beers and Co.
––––––––––––, 1878 *Atlas of Lamoille and Orleans Counties, Vermont* New York, F. W. Beers and Co.
Benton, Guy P., 1917 *Memorial of Vermonters* Boston, American Historical Society, Inc.
Bigelow, Edwin L., and Nancy H. Otis, 1961 *Manchester, Vermont* Town of Manchester.
Bining, Arthur Cecil, 1973 *Pennsylvania Iron Manufacture in the Eighteenth Century* Harrisburg, Pennsylvania Historical and Museum Commission.
Bishop, J. Leander, 1868 *History of American Manufactures from 1608 to 1860* Philadelphia, Edward Young.
Bixby Memorial Library, Vergennes (Monkton Iron Company misc. files; courtesy Lois C. Noonan).
Blanchard, Fessenden S., 1960 *Ghost Towns of New England* New York, Dodd, Mead and Company.
Blanchard, Harry, Jan. 1956, "The Abel Stevens Migration to Canada" *Vermont History* Vermont Historical Society, vol. 24, no. 1, pp. 63–64.
Bliss, Lou Whitney, Oct. 1954, "A Glimpse of Calais" *Vermont History* Vermont Historical Society, vol. 22, no. 4, pp. 264–272.
Boltum, R., 1881 *History of the Town of Orwell, Vermont from 1763–1851* Rutland, Tuttle and Company.
Bowie, John R., Architect, 1978 *Adirondack Iron and Steel Company: "New Furnace" 1849–1854* line drawing, Historic American Engineering Record, National Park Service, dwg. no. NY–123, sheet 8–3.
Bradder, Wilbur, ms, (n.d.), "Tinmouth Article, October 1937" (courtesy Nelson Jaquay).
Brainerd, Alfred F., 1884/1885, "Hematite of Franklin County, Vt." *Transactions of the American Institute of Mining Engineers* vol. 13, pp. 689–691.
Brandon, Vermont 1961, The Town of Brandon.
Burnell, George R., 1870 *Rudimentary Treatise on Limes, Cements, Mortars, Concretes, Mastics, Plastering, Etc.* London, England, Virtue and Co.
Butterfield, Anne Huckins, 1977 *Memories of the Early Days in the Town of Troy, Vermont* (n.p.).
The Caledonian March 2, 1841, St. Johnsbury, vol. 4, no. 3, whole no. 183.
Calendar of Ira Allen Papers in the Wilbur Library, University of Vermont 1939, Montpelier, Historical Records Survey.
Campbell, Harry Huse, 1907 *The Manufacture and Properties of Iron and Steel* New York and London, Hill Publishing.
Cantwell, B., July 1989, "In and Around Lime Rock Park—Iron Empire" *Lime Rock Park* Lime Rock, Conn., vol. 3, no. 4.
Carey, Henry C., Feb. 1851, "The Prospect: Agricultural, Manufacturing, Commercial and Financial, at the Opening of the Year 1851—On Charring Wood" *The Plough, the*

Loom, and the Anvil (n.p.), vol. 3, no. 7, pp. 513-517 (courtesy Phil Elwert).

Carlisle, Lilian Baker, ed., 1975 *Look Around Colchester and Milton, Vermont* Burlington, Chittenden County Historical Society.

Catalogus Senatus Academici . . . Collegio Yalensi 1886, New Haven, Conn., Tuttle, Morehouse and Taylor.

Caverly, [Abiel Moore], 1872 *History of the Town of Pittsford, Vermont* Rutland, Tuttle and Company.

Chambers, Capt. William, 1984 *Atlas of Lake Champlain 1779-1780* Vermont Heritage Press and Vermont Historical Society.

Chapin, J. R., July 1860, "Among the Nailmakers" *Harper's New Monthly Magazine* vol. 21, pp. 145-164.

------------, April 1885, "The Charcoal Burners of the Green Mountains" *Outing* pp. 4-18.

Chapman, Asa, 1845-1848 *Teaming Book* East Middlebury (Sheldon Museum Library, Middlebury).

Chessman, Samuel, 1898 *Leach Family Records* Albany, N.Y., Joel Munsell's Sons.

Child, H., 1880 *Gazetteer and Business Directory of Bennington County, Vt. for 1880-81* Syracuse, N.Y., Journal Office.

------------, 1881 *Gazetteer and Business Directory of Rutland County, Vermont for 1881-82* Syracuse, N.Y., Journal Office.

------------, 1882 *Gazetteer and Business Directory of Chittenden County, Vermont for 1882-83* Syracuse, N.Y., Journal Office.

------------, 1883 *Gazetteer and Business Directory of Lamoille and Orleans Counties, Vt. for 1883-84* Syracuse, N.Y., Syracuse Journal.

------------, 1883 *Gazetteer of Franklin and Grand Isle Counties, Vermont for 1882-83* Syracuse, N.Y., Syracuse Journal.

------------, 1884 *Gazetteer of Windsor County, Vermont 1883-1884* Syracuse, N.Y., Syracuse Journal.

------------, 1887 *Gazetteer of Caledonia and Essex Counties, Vt. 1764-1887* Syracuse, N.Y., Journal Company.

Chipman, Daniel, 1846 *The Life of Hon. Nathaniel Chipman, LL.D.* Boston, Charles C. Little and James Brown.

Clarke, Mary Stetson, 1968 *Pioneer Iron Works* Philadelphia, Chilton Book.

Cohn, Arthur B., June 1984, "The Eagle" *A Report on the Nautical Archeology of Lake Champlain* Burlington, Champlain Maritime Society, pp. 54-59.

Collier, Peter, 1872 *First Annual Report of the Vermont State Board of Agriculture, Manufactures and Mining for the Year 1872* State of Vermont.

Cooley, John C., 1898 *Rathbone Genealogy* Syracuse, N.Y., Press of the Courier Job Print.

Crosby, Suzanne F., Helen N. Nichols, and Margaret R. Vernon, eds., 1976 *Danby: Two Centuries* Bennington, Hadwen, Inc.

Curtis, Will, and Jane Curtis, 1974 *Antique Woodstoves: Artistry in Iron* Ashville, Maine, Cobblesmith.

Dale, T. Nelson, 1915 *The Calcite Marble and Dolomite of Eastern Vermont* Washington, Government Printing Office, USGS Bulletin 589.

Daley, Yvonne, Winter 1986, "Silas Griffith's Legacy" *Vermont Life* vol. 41, no. 2, pp. 8-13.

Dana, Henry S., 1887 *The History of Woodstock, Vermont: 1761-1886* Taftsville, Countryman Press for Woodstock Foundation.

Davis, Catherine S., and Dawn D. Hance, 1976 *A Glimpse of the Past: Pittsfield, Vermont* Town of Pittsfield.

Description of Property [of the] Brandon Iron and Car Wheel Co., with Agent's Report of 1852 and 1853 1854, Rutland, Tuttle and Co. Steam Printing Est.

Diderot, Denis, 1959 *A Diderot Pictorial Encyclopedia of Trades and Industry* New York, Dover Publications, Inc. (orig. pub. 1763).

Dimmick, Myron, (n.d.) *Tyson Furnace* oil on canvas, Vermont

Historical Society Archives, catalog no. A-80.

Directory of the Iron and Steel Works of the United States 1882, Philadelphia, American Iron and Steel Association.

Doll, Charles G., 1961 *Centennial Geologic Map of Vermont* State of Vermont.

Doomsday Book 1870 (Massachusetts, New York, and Vermont properties owned or leased by Richmond Iron Company, Mass.; on file at Berkshire County Courthouse, Pittsfield, Mass.)

Doten, Hosea, 1855 *Map of Windsor County* Pomfret.

Douglas, Bob, 1988, "Swanton Limestone" *History of Swanton, Vermont* ed. Rodney R. Ledoux, Swanton Historical Society.

Drake Family Papers [ca. 1802], Weybridge (Sheldon Museum Library, Middlebury).

Duffy, John, 1985 *Vermont: An Illustrated History* Northridge, Cal., Windsor Publications, Inc.

Eckel, Edwin C., 1922 *Cements, Limes, and Plasters* New York, John Wiley and Sons, 2d ed.

Egleston, Thomas, May 1879, "The Manufacture of Charcoal in Kilns" *Transactions of the American Institute of Mining Engineers* vol. 6, pp. 373-397.

------------, Sept. 1879, "The American Bloomery Process for Making Iron Direct from the Ore" *Transactions of the American Institute of Mining Engineers* vol. 8, pp. 515-550.

Ellis, Franklin, 1878 *History of Columbia County, New York* Philadelphia, Everts and Ensign.

Encyclopedia of American Biography 1938, New York, American Historical Society, Inc., new series, vol. 9.

Fairbanks, Edward T., 1914 *The Town of St. Johnsbury, Vermont* St. Johnsbury, Cowles Press.

Fairbanks Standard, 150 Years 1980, St. Johnsbury, Fairbanks Weighing Division, Colt Industries.

Fant, H. B., Jan. 1966, "Levi Woodbury's Week in Vermont" *Vermont History* Vermont Historical Society, vol. 34, no. 1, pp. 36-62.

Farnsworth, Harold, 1984 *New Haven in Vermont 1761-1983* Town of New Haven.

Fenn, J. T., (n.d.), "In and Around East Middlebury" *Green Mountain Whittlin's* Burlington, Green Mountain Folklore Society, vol. 13, pp. 28-32.

Fisher, Dorothy Canfield, 1953 *Vermont Tradition: The Biography of an Outlook on Life* Boston, Little, Brown & Co.

Fisher, Douglas Alan, 1949 *Steel Making in America* New York, U.S. Steel Corp.

------------, 1963 *The Epic of Steel* New York, Harper and Row.

Fleming, Stuart, July/Aug. 1983, "Where Did All the Wood Go?" *Archaeology* Boston, Archaeological Institute of America, vol. 36, no. 4, pp. 66-67, 79.

------------, Sept./Oct. 1985, "19th-Century Pennsylvanian Iron-Making" *Archaeology* Boston, Archaeological Institute of America, vol. 38, no. 5, pp. 70-71, 77.

Foyles, E. J., 1924, "The Geology of Shoreham, Bridport and Fort Cassin, Vermont" *Report of the State Geologist on the Mineral Industries and Geology of Vermont: 1923-1924* ed. George H. Perkins, Burlington, Free Press Printing, pp. 204-217.

Gale, David C., 1922 *Proctor: The Story of a Marble Town* Brattleboro, Vermont Printing.

Gazetteer of Vermont Heritage 1976, Chester, The National Survey.

Geological Surveys and Reports on the Property of the Tyson Iron Company, Plymouth, Vermont 1864, Boston, Geo. C. Rand and Avery.

Gillmore, [Q. A.], 1874 *Practical Treatise on Limes, Hydraulic Cements, and Mortars* New York, D. Van Nostrand, 5th ed.

Goodhue, Rev. Josiah F., 1861 *History of the Town of Shoreham* Middlebury, A. H. Copeland.

Gordon, George A., and Silas R. Coburn, 1913 *Genealogy of the Coburn-Colburn Families* Lowell, Mass., Walter Coburn.

Gordon, Robert B., and Michael S. Raber, 1984, "An Early

American Integrated Steelworks" *IA* vol. 10, no. 1, pp. 17-34.

------------, and Terry S. Reynolds, Jan. 1986, "Conference Reports: Medieval Iron in Society—Norberg, Sweden, May 6-10, 1985" *Technology and Culture* Society for the History of Technology, University of Chicago Press, vol. 27, no. 1, pp. 110-117.

Graffagnino, J. Kevin, 1983 *The Shaping of Vermont* Rutland, Vermont Heritage Press and Bennington Museum.

Graham, [John Andrew], 1797 *A Descriptive Sketch of the Present State of Vermont* London, England, J. A. Graham.

Groft, Tammis K., 1984 *Cast With Style: Nineteenth Century Cast-Iron Stoves from the Albany Area* Albany, N.Y., Albany Institute of History and Art.

Grout, Aaron H., Sec. of State, 1927 *Journal and Proceedings of the State of Vermont 1784-1787* Bellows Falls, P. H. Gobie Press, vol. 3.

Hammond, Frederick Stam, 1900 *History and Genealogy of the Hammond Families* Oneida, N.Y., Ryan and Burkhart.

Harte, Charles Rufus, Feb. 20, 1935, "The Connecticut Blast Furnaces and Furnace Practice" *The Early Iron Industry of Connecticut* New Haven, Connecticut Society of Civil Engineers, 51st Annual Meeting, pp. 31-69.

Hartley, E. Neal, 1957 *Ironworks on the Saugus* Norman, University of Oklahoma Press.

Harvey, [Carolyn Louise], and [Clara Mercey] Kellogg, 1941 *History of Bristol, Vermont* Outing Club of Bristol.

Haun, Charles, March 30, 1966, "West Hill, Near Stamford, Once Center of Industry" *The Transcript* North Adams, Mass.

Haviland, William A., 1973, "Mounds in Vermont: Prehistoric or Historic?" *Vermont Archaeological Society Monograph Series: Number 2* Burlington, University of Vermont.

------------, and Marjory W. Power, 1981 *The Original Vermonters* Hanover, N.H. and London, England, University Press of New England.

Hawthorne, Nathaniel, 1974, "Ethan Brand" *Anthology of American Literature* New York, Macmillan Publishing Company, vol. 1, pp. 897-910.

------------, Dec. 1983, "American Notebooks" (1896) *The Chronicle* Early American Industries Association (courtesy Richard S. Allen).

Heite, E. F., Autumn 1974, "The Delmarva Bog Iron Industry" *Early American Iron Making* Journal of the Council for Northeast Historical Archeology, vol. 3, no. 2, pp. 18-34.

Hemenway, Abby Maria, 1867 *Vermont Historical Gazetteer* vol. 1, Burlington, by the author.

------------, 1871 *Vermont Historical Gazetteer* vol. 2, Burlington, by the author.

------------, 1877 *Vermont Historical Gazetteer* vol. 3, Claremont, N.H., Claremont Manufacturing.

------------, 1882 *Vermont Historical Gazetteer* vol. 4, Montpelier, Watchman and State Journal Press.

------------, 1891 *Vermont Historical Gazetteer* vol. 5, Brandon, Miss Carrie E. H. Page.

Herald and News Aug. 9, 1917 [White River Junction?] (Vermont Historical Society misc. file no. 58).

Hinsdill, Joseph N., 1835 *Map, Survey and History in Brief of the Town of Bennington*.

Hitchcock, Edward, Edward Hitchcock, Jr., Charles Hitchcock, and Albert Hager, 1861 *Report on the Geology of Vermont* ed. Albert D. Hager, Proctorsville, vols. 1 and 2.

Hodge, James T., May 12, 1849, "Iron Ores and the Iron Manufacture of the United States: Vermont" *American Railroad Journal* ed. Henry V. Poor, New York, vol. 5, no. 19, pp. 290-291 (courtesy Richard S. Allen).

------------, May 19, 1849, "Iron Ores and the Iron Manufacture of the United States: Vermont" *American Railroad Journal* ed. Henry V. Poor, New York, vol. 5, no. 20, pp. 305-306 (courtesy Richard S. Allen).

------------, June 9, 1849, "Iron Ores and the Iron Manu-

facture of the United States: Massachusetts" *American Railroad Journal* ed. Henry V. Poor, New York, vol. 5, no. 23, pp. 353-354 (courtesy Richard S. Allen).

Holbrook, Jay Mack, 1982 *Vermont 1771 Census* Oxford, Mass., Holbrook Research Institute.

Honerkamp, N., 1987, "Innovation and Change in the Antebellum Southern Iron Industry" *IA* vol. 13, no. 1, pp. 55-68.

Hopewell Furnace 1983, Washington, D.C., Division of Publications, National Park Service, Handbook 124.

Horne, Lee, Fall 1982, "Fuel For the Metal Worker: The Role of Charcoal Production in Ancient Metallurgy" *Expedition* University Museum Magazine of Archaeology/Anthropology, University of Pennsylvania, vol. 25, no. 1, pp. 6-13.

Hough, Franklin B., 1853 *History of St. Lawrence and Franklin Counties* Albany, N.Y., Little and Co.

Hubbard, George D., 1924, "Geology of a Small Tract in South Central Vermont" *Report of the State Geologist on the Mineral Industries and Geology of Vermont 1923-1924* ed. George H. Perkins, Burlington, Free Press Printing, pp. 260-343.

Hubbard, Guy, 1922 *Industrial History of Windsor, Vt.* Windsor, Town School District.

Huden, John C., comp., 1971 *Archeology of Vermont* Rutland, Charles E. Tuttle.

Hume, Ivor Noel, 1969 *Historical Archeology* New York, Alfred A. Knopf.

Humphrey, Zephine, 1924 *The Story of Dorset* Rutland, Tuttle.

Hunt, Dr. T. Sterry, 1870, "Report of Dr. T. Sterry Hunt" *Geological Report of Canada: Report of Progress from 1866 to 1869* Montreal, Québec, Dawson Bros., pp. 260-283.

Hunter, Edith F., Nov. 30, 1984, "District 8—the Upper Falls in Earlier Times" *Weathersfield Vermont Weekly* Perkinsville, Hunter Press, vol. 55, no. 8.

Huntington, Rev. E. B., 1884 *A Genealogical Memoir of the Lo-Lathrop Family* Ridgefield, Conn., Mrs. Julia M. Huntington.

Hurd, Duane H., 1880 *History of Clinton and Franklin Counties, New York* Philadelphia, J. W. Lewis and Co.

Hurd, John L., 1978 *Weathersfield, Century Two* Canaan, N.H., Phoenix Publishing.

Hyzer, Muriel, April 1954, "Iron Mining in Pittsfield in 1880" *Vermont History* Vermont Historical Society, vol. 22, no. 2, pp. 132-133.

Ingham, Adella, ms, [1932], "In the Days of the Monkton Iron Company in Vergennes, Vermont 1807-30" (Bixby Memorial Library, Vergennes).

Ingstad, Anne Stine, 1977 *The Discovery of a Norse Settlement in America* Oslo-Bergen-Tromso, Norwegian Research Council for Science and the Humanities.

Inventory of the Town . . . of Mount Tabor 1941, Montpelier, National Historical Records Survey.

Jackson, Charles T., 1844 *Final Report on the Geology and Mineralogy of the State of New Hampshire* Concord, N.H., Carroll & Baker.

Jacobs, Elbridge C., [1918], "The Lime Industry in Vermont" *Report of the State Geologist on the Mineral Industries and Geology of Vermont: 1917-1918* ed. George H. Perkins, Bellows Falls, pp. 158-164.

------------, 1927, "Clay Deposits and Clay Industries of Vermont" *Report of the State Geologist on the Mineral Industries and Geology of Vermont: 1925-1926* ed. George H. Perkins, Burlington, Free Press Printing, pp. 191-211.

------------, [1937], "Vermont Mineral Industries" *Report of the State Geologist on the Mineral Industries and Geology of Vermont: 1935-1936* Burlington, Free Press Printing, pp. 1-24.

------------, 1944, "Vermont Mineral Industries" *Report of the State Geologist on the Mineral Industries and Geology of Vermont: 1943-1944* Burlington, Free Press Printing, pp. 38-41.

------------, April 1953, "Iron in Vermont—a Glance at Its Story" *Vermont Quarterly* Vermont Historical Society, vol.

21, no. 2, pp. 128-131.

Jillson, Mary, 1894 *Green Leaves from Whitingham, Vermont: A History of the Town* Worcester, Mass., by the author.

Johnson, Crisfield, 1878 *History of Washington County, New York* Philadelphia, Everts and Ensign.

Jones, Alvin B., (n.d.) *Cash Book of Alvin B. Jones for Drawing Flux to Royal Blake, 1835-1845* Vermont Historical Society MSS21 #85 (courtesy Phil Elwert).

Jones, Matt Bushnell, 1909 *History of the Town of Waitsfield, Vermont: 1782-1908* Boston, George E. Littlefield.

Kauffman, Henry J., 1966 *Early American Ironware: Cast and Wrought* New York, Weathervane Books.

————————, 1972 *The American Fireplace* New York, Galahad Books.

Keith Furnace Lot Aug. 3, 1791, deed, Joseph Hitchcock (Pittsford) to Israel Keith, vol. 2, Massachusetts Historical Society files (courtesy David Ingram).

Keller Photograph Collection Washington, D.C., American Iron and Steel Institute (ca.-1935 A. J. Keller photos of ironworks sites in Northeast).

Kelley, Augustus M., 1969 *Documents Relative to the Manufacture in the United States* New York.

Kellogg, Augusta W., Nov. 1897, "The Town of Brandon, Vermont" *New England Magazine* new series no. 17, old series no. 23, pp. 293-303.

Kirk, Raymond E., and Donald F. Othmer, eds., 1952 *Encyclopedia of Chemical Technology* New York, Interscience Encyclopedia, vol. 8.

Klock, Julian, ed., 1976 *A History of Wallingford, Vermont* Rutland, Gilbert Hart Library, Academy Books.

Kull, Nell M., 1961 *History of Dover, Vermont* Brattleboro, Book Cellar.

Lamson, Genevieve, 1943, "Geographic Influences in the Early History of Vermont," master's thesis, Ogden Graduate School, Chicago, Sept. 1922; rpt. Vermont Historical Society Collections, vol. 5, pp. 75-138.

Laws of Vermont 1816, Windsor, Jesse Cochran, State Printer.

Leader, Andrew, Feb. 7, 1973, "Highgate Farm Yields Surprises" *Burlington Free Press* p. 2.

Ledoux, Rodney R., 1988, "Early Swanton Families" *History of Swanton, Vermont* Swanton Historical Society.

Lefebvre, Charlotte, Oct. 18, 1984, "Old Readsboro and Whitingham" (7th-grade composition paper; courtesy Robert Dion).

Lenik, Edward J., Autumn 1974, "Peter Hasenclever and the American Iron Company" *Early American Iron Making* Journal of the Council for Northeast Historical Archeology, vol. 3, no. 2, pp. 9-17.

Leonard, Capen, 1848 *A Table Showing the Number of Cords of Wood in Any Round Body* Chittenden (courtesy Bert Muzzy).

Lesley, James P., [1858] *Bulletin of the American Iron Association 1856-1858* (n.p.).

————————, 1859 *The Iron Manufacturer's Guide to the Furnaces, Forges and Rolling Mills of the United States* New York, John Wiley.

Levin, Ruth, 1978 *Ordinary Heroes: The Story of Shaftsbury* Shaftsbury Historical Society, Inc.

Lewis, James F., 1876-1877, "Hematite Ore Mines and Blast Furnaces East of the Hudson River" *Transactions of the American Institute of Mining Engineers* vol. 5, pp. 216-235.

Lewis, W. David, 1976 *Iron and Steel in America* Greenville, Del., Hagley Museum.

Long, Jr., Amos, 1972 *The Pennsylvania German Family Farm* Breinigsville, Pa., Pennsylvania German Society, vol. 6 (courtesy Giovanna Peebles).

The Marble Border of Western New England 1885, Middlebury, Middlebury Historical Society, vol. 1, pt. 2.

Masten, Arthur H., 1923 *The Story of Adirondac* by the author; new ed., Syracuse, N.Y., The Adirondack Museum/Syracuse University Press, 1968.

McClellan's Map of Windham County, Vermont 1856, Philadelphia, C. McClellan and Co.

McWhorter, Betty, Oct. 2, 1953, "Mooney, 86, Turns Back Years: Reviews Era of Smelting" *Rutland Herald* p. 68.

Meeks, Harold, 1986 *Vermont's Land and Resources* Shelburne, New England Press.

Middlebrook, Lewis F., 1935 *Salisbury Connecticut Cannon* Salem, Mass., Newcomb and Gauss.

Middlebury Galaxy Aug. 7, 1849, Middlebury.

Middlebury Mercury May 30, 1810, Middlebury.

Middlebury People's Press Dec. 14, 1841, Middlebury.

Middlebury Register Sept. 7, 1877, May 20, 1881, June 17 and Aug. 5, 1881, Middlebury.

Miles, Henry, 1876, "Fertilization: Is Shell Marl a Fertilizer?" *Third Biennial Report of the Vermont State Board of Agriculture* ed. Henry M. Seely, Rutland, Tuttle and Co., pp. 271-277.

Miller, Harry, April 1980, "Potash from Wood Ashes: Frontier Technology in Canada and the United States" *Technology and Culture* Society for the History of Technology, University of Chicago Press, vol. 21, no. 2, pp. 187-208.

Moldenke, Richard, 1930 *Principles of Iron Founding* New York, McGraw-Hill Book Company.

Monkton Iron Works Letterbook, [ca. 1808], Vergennes (Bixby Memorial Library, Vergennes).

Morrill, Philip, and Robert G. Chaffee, 1964 *Vermont Mines and Mineral Localities* Hanover, N.H., Dartmouth College Museum.

Mower, Anna L., 1935 *History of Morristown, Vt.* Morrisville, Messenger-Sentinel.

Munsill, Harvey, [1979] *The Early History of Bristol, Vermont* Book Committee, Bristol Historical Commission.

Murphy, William, ms, 1975, "Preliminary Report on Archaeological Excavation Conducted at the Site of the Blacksmith Shop in Frog Hollow" (Sheldon Museum Library, Middlebury).

National Standard Oct. 15, 1817, Sept. 8, 1819, Oct. 2, 1821, July 28, 1824, Sept. 11, 1827, Middlebury.

Naujoks, Waldemar, and Donald C. Fabel, 1939 *Forging Handbook* Cleveland, Ohio, American Society for Metals.

Neilson, William G., [1866] *Charcoal Blast Furnaces, Rolling Mills, Forges and Steel Works of New England in 1866* American Iron and Steel Association.

Neudorfer, Giovanna, 1980 *Vermont's Stone Chambers* Montpelier, Vermont Historical Society.

New York State Agricultural Society, Transactions of 1850, Albany, N.Y., Weed, Parsons & Co.

Niles, Grace Greylock, 1912 *The Hoosac Valley* New York, G. P. Putnam's Sons.

Nordell, Philip G., Jan. 1967, "Vermont's Early Lotteries" *Vermont History* Vermont Historical Society, vol. 35, no. 1, pp. 35-71.

Northern Galaxy Feb. 7, 1844, June 15, 1847, Middlebury.

O'Hara, John E., 1984, "Erie's Junior Partner: The Economic and Social Effects of the Champlain Canal upon the Champlain Valley," Ph.D. diss., Columbia University, 1951 (facsimile copy University Microfilms Int., Ann Arbor, Mich.).

"Original Owners of Iron Ore Bed. First Worked in the Champlain Valley," April 11, 1885 *Plattsburgh Republican* Plattsburgh, N.Y. (courtesy Richard S. Allen).

Orr, J. W., April 1860, "Artist Life in the Highlands" *Harper's New Monthly Magazine* vol. 20, no. 119, pp. 577-598.

Overman, Frederick, 1850 *The Manufacture of Iron* Philadelphia, Henry C. Baird.

Parks, Joseph, 1977 *Pownal: A Vermont Town's 200 Years and More* Pownal Bicentennial Committee.

Patch, Fred R., 1918, "Old Time Iron Making" *The Vermonter* ed. Charles R. Cummings, White River Junction, vol. 23, no. 6, p. 158.

Paynter, Henry M., Fall 1990, "The First U.S. Patent" *American Heritage of Invention and Technology* New York, vol. 6, no. 2, pp. 18-22.

Pearse, John B., 1876 *A Concise History of the Iron Manufacture of the American Colonies up to the Revolution and of Pennsylvania until the Present Time* New York, Burt Franklin, rpt. 1970.

Peleszak, Christine M., 1984, "The Abandonment of Leicester Hollow," bachelor's thesis, University of Vermont, Burlington (courtesy Christine M. Peleszak).

Perkins, George H., 1898, "Marble Industry" *Report of the State Geologist on the Mineral Industries and Geology of Vermont* Burlington, Free Press Printing, pp. 10–43.

-----------, 1900, "Limestone" *Report of the State Geologist on the Mineral Industries of Vermont 1931–1932* Burlington, pp. 30–38.

-----------, 1910, "Mineral Resources" *Report of the State Geologist on the Mineral Industries and Geology of Vermont* Bellows Falls, P. H. Gobie Press.

-----------, 1930, "Mineral Resources" *Report of the State Geologist on the Mineral Industries and Geology of Vermont* Burlington, Free Press Printing.

-----------, [1933], "The Marble Industry of Vermont" *Report of the State Geologist on the Mineral Industries and Geology of Vermont 1931–1932* Burlington, Free Press Printing, pp. 1–15, 141, 145.

Peters, Richard, 1921 *Two Centuries of Iron Smelting in Pennsylvania* Chester, Pa., (n.p.).

Petersen, Max P., 1976 *Salisbury: From Birth to Bicentennial* Salisbury, Offset House.

"Phizer Completes a Major Face Lift," May 4, 1991 *Berkshire Eagle* Pittsfield, Mass., sec. D, p. 2.

Pittsford Now and Then 1980, Pittsford Historical Society.

Porter, Marjorie L., Sept. 1941, "The Pride of the Saranac" *Proceedings of the Vermont Historical Society* new series, vol. 9, no. 3, pp. 207–216.

Potter, David E., 1982, "An Informal History of Chippenhook and Vicinity" *Clarendon, Vermont: 1761–1976* Rutland, Academy Books, pp. 100–116.

Putnam, Ralph W., Dec. 1940, "Vermont's Part in Industry" *Proceedings of the Vermont Historical Society* vol. 8, no. 4, pp. 357–373.

Rann, William S., 1886 *History of Chittenden County, Vermont* Syracuse, N.Y., D. Mason and Company.

Rathbun, Robert, ms, (n.d.), "Rathbone Family History," Bowling Green, Ky. (courtesy Nelson Jaquay).

Renner, Irma E., 1961 *The Story of Sandgate, Vermont 1761–1961* Shaftsbury, Farnham and Farnham.

Revised Statutes of the State of Vermont, Passed November 19, 1839 1840, Burlington, Chauncey Goodrich.

Rice, E., and C. E. Harwood, 1856 *Map of Bennington County, Vermont* New York, C. B. Peckham.

Richards, Barry A., and John R. Bowie, Architects, 1978 *Adirondack Iron and Steel Company: "New Furnace" 1849–1854* line drawings, Historic American Engineering Record, National Park Service, dwg. no. NY-123, sheets 4–13 and 13–13.

Rider, Sidney S., 1904 *Lands of Rhode Island* Providence, by the author.

Robertson, Ross M., 1955 *History of the American Economy* New York, Harcourt, Brace and World.

Robinson, Rowland E., 1934, "Along Three Rivers" *Uncle Lisha's Outing and Along Three Rivers* Rutland, Tuttle Co., pp. 221–258.

Rolando, Victor R., ms, July 7, 1984, "Sheldon Museum Paper."

Ross, Frank Seth, 1936 *Down Through the Years at Readsboro, Vermont: 1786–1936* Towns of Readsboro, Vt. and Williamstown, Mass., McClelland Press.

Rucker, Nancy, Aug. 1981, "Henry's Collection" *Sheldon Museum Newsletter* Middlebury, vol. 3, no. 1, p. 3.

Russell Collection (Dr. George Russell coll. at the Martha Canfield Library, Arlington).

Rutland Herald Nov. 2, 1805, Oct. 2, 1815, Dec. 20, 1807, Rutland.

Salisbury Iron 1878, Salisbury, Conn., Barnum Richardson.

Sanborn, 1884-1957 *Fire Insurance Maps* Pelham, N.Y., Sanborn Map Company (University of Vermont).

Sand Cast Moulding at Hopewell Furnace 1981, Hopewell Village National Historic Site, Pa., U.S. Department of Interior, National Park Service.

Sanders, Willard K., April 1953, "Iron Mining in Elmore" *Vermont Quarterly* Vermont Historical Society, vol. 21, no. 2, pp. 240–242.

Saxe, John G., 1930 *Saxe Family Genealogy*.

Schallenberg, Richard H., July 1975, "Evolution, Adaption and Survival: The Very Slow Death of the American Charcoal Iron Industry" *Annals of Science* vol. 32, pp. 341–358.

Schuhmann, George, April 1906, "Iron and Steel" *The Pilot* Reading, Pa. and Reading Railroad Dept. YMCA; rpt. SIA Data Sheet No. 4, Oct. 1984.

Scott, Charles A., John W. Stickney, and Julian A. Pollard, 1859 *Map of the Town of Plymouth*.

Scott's Map of Rutland County, Vermont 1854, Philadelphia, C. Chase Jr., James D. Scott, Isaac W. Moore, and Owen McLeray.

Seaburg, Carl, and Stanley Paterson, 1971 *Merchant Prince of Boston: Colonel T. H. Perkins, 1764–1854* Cambridge, Mass., Harvard University Press.

Seavor, J. Montgomery, 1930 *Keith Family Records* Philadelphia.

Seely, Bruce E., 1981, "Blast Furnace Technology in the Mid-19th Century" *IA* vol. 7, no. 1, pp. 27–54.

Serafini, Enzo, Winter 1952, "Franconia's Forgotten Iron Industry" *White Mountain Echoes* Littleton, N.H., Courier Printing, vol. 1, no. 3, pp. 15–17.

Shaughnessy, Jim, 1964 *The Rutland Road* San Diego, Cal., Howell-North Books; 2d ed., 1981.

Shaw, Donald E., May 1952, "Bennington and Glastenbury Railroad—Bennington and Woodford Electric Railway" *Transportation* Warehouse Point, Conn. Valley Chapter, National Railway Historical Society; Conn. Valley Div. Electric Railroaders' Association, vol. 6, pt. 2, pp. 19–27.

Sheldon, Henry *Book #178, Middlebury Fires* (Sheldon Museum Library, Middlebury).

Shipton, Clifford K., 1975 *Sibley's Harvard Graduates, Vol. 17: 1768–1771* Boston, Massachusetts Historical Society, vol. 5.

Simmons, Fred C., April–May 1960, "Revival in the Charcoal Industry" *Conservationist* State of New York, pp. 10–12.

Skelan, James W., 1961, "The Green Mountain Anticlinorium in the Vicinity of Wilmington and Woodford, Vermont" *Bulletin No. 17* Montpelier, Vermont Development Department.

Smith, Chard P., 1946 *The Housatonic* New York, Reinholt and Co.

Smith, Harold L., 1916, "Description of the New Lime Plant of the Vermont Marble Company at West Rutland" *Report of the State Geologist on the Mineral Industries and Geology of Vermont: 1915–1916* ed. George H. Perkins, Burlington, Free Press Printing, pp. 101–110.

Smith, Henry P., 1886 *History of Addison County, Vermont* Syracuse, N.Y., D. Mason.

-----------, and William S. Rann, 1886 *History of Rutland County, Vermont* Syracuse, N.Y., D. Mason.

Smith, Lowell, 1937 *150 Years of Progress: 1937* St. Johnsbury, Cowles Press.

Soule, Allen, ed., 1962 *General Petitions 1797–1799* vol. 11, Lunenburg, Steinhour Press.

Spargo, John, 1938 *Iron Mining and Smelting in Bennington, Vermont 1786–1842* Bennington Museum Publication No. 2.

Stockton, Frank T., 1921 *The International Molders Union of North America* Baltimore, Md., Johns Hopkins University Press.

Stratton, Allen L., 1984 *History: Town of Isle La Motte* Barre, Northlight Studio Press.

Swank, James M., 1892 *History of the Manufacture of Iron in All Ages* Philadelphia, American Iron and Steel Association.

Swift, Esther M., 1977 *Vermont Place-Names* Brattleboro,

Stephen Greene Press.

Swift, Samuel, 1859 *History of the Town of Middlebury* Middlebury, A. H. Copeland; rpt. Charles E. Tuttle, 1971.

Temin, Peter, 1964 *Iron and Steel in Nineteenth-Century America: An Economic Inquiry* Cambridge, Mass., MIT Press.

Tenny, Jonathan, ed., 1886, "Manufacturing Interests of Albany" *History of the City of Albany* Albany, N.Y., Joel Munsell; rpt. *Old Albany* Morris Gerber, 1971, pp. 140-149.

Tercentenary Celebration of the Discovery of Lake Champlain and Vermont 1910, Montpelier, The Lake Champlain Tercentenary Commission of Vermont, Capital City Press.

Thomas, Peter A., 1981 *North Springfield Lake, CRM Study, Report #38, Doc 12814* (for U.S. Corps of Engineers).

Thompson, Alexander, 1884 *Pennsylvania Magazine of History and Biography* vol. 8 (footnote in Long 1972:469).

Thompson, Zadock, 1824 *A Gazetteer of the State of Vermont: Natural, Civil and Statistical* Montpelier, E. P. Watson.

------------, 1842 *History of Vermont* Burlington, Chauncey Goodrich.

Ure, Andrew, 1854 *A Dictionary of Arts, Manufactures and Mines* New York, H. Appleton & Co.

U.S. Census 1790, First (1790) "Population," Washington, D.C.

U.S. Census 1800, Second (1800) "Population," Washington, D.C.

U.S. Census 1814, Third (1810) "Arts and Manufactures," Washington, D.C.

U.S. Census 1841, Sixth (1840) "Statistics," Washington, D.C.

Van Santvoord, George, ms, 1958, "Furnace Grove: 1858-1958" (Bennington Museum Library).

Vermont: A Guide to the Green Mountain State 1937, Boston, Houghton Mifflin Company.

Vermont Aurora July 15, 1824, Sept. 22, 1825, Jan. 6, 1826, June 18, 1829, Vergennes.

Vermont Castings Owners' News Spring 1980, Randclph, Vermont Castings Inc., vol. 1, no. 2.

Vermont Centinel Jan. 6, 1808, Burlington.

Vermont Division for Historic Preservation files, Montpelier (courtesy Giovanna Peebles, State Archeologist).

Vermont Gazette June 26, 1786, Oct. 6, 1788, Feb. 1, 1793, May 9, 1794, Oct. 17, 1826, April 30, 1827, Bennington.

Vermont Insurance Company of Middlebury, Survey Nos. 502 and 504, April 9, 1844—Book 2 (Sheldon Museum Library, Middlebury).

"Vermont Limestone Quarry Is 147 Years Old," Oct. 1947 *New England Construction* Boston, Mass., vol. 12, no. 5, p. 41.

Vital Records of Mansfield, Massachusetts to 1849 1933, Salem, Mass., Essex Institute.

von Sotzman, D. F., 1796 *Vermont Entworfen* Hamburg, Germany, Eng. P. Schmidt, Carl Ernst Bohn; rpt. Compass Publications, Hardwick.

Waite, John G., and Diana S. Waite, Jan. 1977, "Stove Manufacturers, Troy, New York" *Antiques Magazine* New York, Straight Enterprises.

Walker, Joseph E., 1966 *Hopewell Village: The Dynamics of a Nineteenth Century Iron-Making Village* Philadelphia, University of Pennsylvania Press.

Wall and Forrest, 1853 *Map of Vergennes*; rpt. Vergennes Archaeological Society, 1953.

Walling, H. F., 1857 *Map of Addison County, Vermont* New York, Wm. E. Baker and Co.

------------, 1857 *Map of Chittenden County, Vermont* Boston and New York, Baker, Tilden and Company.

------------, 1857 *Map of the Counties of Franklin and Grand Isle, Vermont* Boston and New York, Baker, Tilden and Co.

------------, 1859 *Map of the Counties of Orleans, Lamoille and Essex, Vermont* New York, Loomis and Way.

Walton, Eliakim P., 1877 *Records of the Governor and Council of the State of Vermont, Vol. 5: 1810-1812* Montpelier, J. and J. M. Poland.

Walton's Vermont Register (various issues, 1844 through 1920).

Ward, Eliza, Barbara Mahon, and Barbara Chiolino, 1983 *A*

Plymouth Album: Plymouth, Vermont Randolph Center, Greenhills Books.

Watson, Pearl G., ed., 1967 *Taftsville Tales* Happy Valley Homemakers Club, Woodstock, Frank Teagle.

Watson, Winslow C., 1869 *Military and Civil History of the County of Essex, New York* Albany, N.Y., J. Munsell.

White, John R., 1980, "Historic Blast Furnace Slags: Archeological and Metallurgical Analysis" *Journal of the Historical Metallurgical Society* vol. 14, no. 2, pp. 55-64.

Whitelaw, James, 1796 *A Correct Map of the State of Vermont* Ryegate, Eng. Amos Doolittle.

------------, 1810 *A Correct Map of the State of Vermont* Ryegate, Eng. James Wilson.

------------, 1821 *Vermont from Actual Survey* Hartford, Eng. M. M. Peabody, Ebeneezer Hutchinson.

------------, 1824 *Vermont from Actual Survey* Hartford, Eng. M. M. Peabody, Ebeneezer Hutchinson.

------------, 1838 *Vermont from Actual Survey* Hartford, Eng. M. M. Peabody, Ebeneezer Hutchinson.

Wilbur, James Benjamin, 1928 *Ira Allen* Boston and New York, Houghton Mifflin, 2 vols.

Wiley's American Iron Trade Manual of the Leading Iron Industries of the United States 1874, ed. Thomas Dunlap, New York, John Wiley and Son.

Wilkinson, J. Gardner, 1883 *The Manners and Customs of the Ancient Egyptians* Boston, S. E. Cassino and Company, rev. ed., ed. Samuel Birch, vol. 2.

Willard, Joseph, 1858 *Willard Memoir; or, Life and Times of Major Simon Willard* Boston, Phillips, Sampson and Co.

Williams, David G., 1952, "Lime Kilns in the Lower Jordan Valley" *Leigh County Historical Society Proceedings* Allentown, Pa., vol. 19, pp. 77-78.

Williams, John A., ed., 1966 *Laws of Vermont 1785-1791* vol. 14.

------------, 1967 *Laws of Vermont 1791-1795* vol. 15.

Williams, Samuel, 1794 *History of Vermont* Walpole, Mass., Isaiah Thomas and David Carlisle Jun., Printer.

Williamson, Chilton, 1949 *Vermont in Quandary: 1763-1825* Montpelier, Vermont Historical Society.

Wood, David H., 1969 *Lenox: Massachusetts Shire Town* Town of Lenox.

Woolmington, Rob, July 7, 1977, "The Charcoal Era" *Bennington Banner, Vermont Summer Magazine* pp. 17-20.

------------, Dec. 1979, "Coking Charcoal Down in Rattlesnake Gutter" *Yankee* Dublin, N.H., Yankee Publications, pp. 80-85, 132-134.

Zeier, Charles D., 1987, "Historic Charcoal Production Near Eureka, Nevada: An Archaeological Perspective" *Historical Archaeology* vol. 21, no. 1, pp. 81-101.

Index